P9-DJA-485

Your
Baby's First Year™
week by week

Also by Glade B. Curtis, M.D., M.P.H, and Judith Schuler, M.S.

Your Pregnancy Week by Week

Your Pregnancy Questions and Answers

Your Pregnancy After 35

Your Pregnancy for the Father-to-Be

Your Pregnancy Journal Week by Week

Bouncing Back After Your Pregnancy

Your Pregnancy: Every Woman's Guide

Your Pregnancy Quick Guide: Fitness and Exercise

Your Pregnancy Quick Guide: Nutrition and Weight Management

Your Pregnancy Quick Guide: Tests and Procedures

Your Pregnancy Quick Guide: Labor and Delivery

Your Pregnancy Quick Guide: Feeding Your Newborn

Su Embaraza Semana a Semana

*Y*our
Baby's First *Y*ear™

week by week

Glade B. Curtis, M.D., M.P.H.

Judith Schuler, M.S.

Lori Eining, R.N., technical assistant

Da Capo Lifelong
A Member of the Perseus Books Group

Many of the designations used by manufacturers and sellers to distinguish their products are claimed as trademarks. Where those designations appear in this book and Da Capo Press was aware of a trademark claim, those designations have been printed with initial capital letters.

Copyright 2005 © by Glade B. Curtis and Judith Schuler

All rights reserved. No part of this publication may be reproduced, stored in a retrieval system, or transmitted, in any form or by any means, electronic, mechanical, photocopying, recording, or otherwise, without the prior written permission of the publisher. Printed in the United States of America.

Design by Jane Raese
Set in 10.5-point Berthold Garamond

Cataloging-in-Publication data for this book is available from the Library of Congress.

ISBN-13 978-0-7382-0974-6 (hc) ISBN-13 978-0-3782-0975-3 (pbk.)
ISBN-10 0-7382-0974-0 (hc) − ISBN-10 0-7382-0975-9 (pbk.)

First Da Capo Press printing December 2004

Published by Da Capo Press
A Member of the Perseus Books Group
http://www.dacapopress.com

Note: The information in this book is true and complete to the best of our knowledge. The book is intended only as an informative guide for those wishing to know more about their baby's first year of life. In no way is this book intended to replace, countermand or conflict with the advice given to you by baby's pediatrician. The ultimate decision concerning your baby's care should be made between you and baby's doctor. We strongly recommend that you follow his or her advice. The information in this book is general and is offered with no guarantees on the part of the authors or Da Capo Press. The authors and publisher disclaim all liability in connection with the use of this book. The names and identifying details of people associated with events described in this book have been changed. Any similarity to actual persons is coincidental.

Da Capo Press books are available at special discounts for bulk purchases in the U.S. by corporations, institutions, and other organizations. For more information, please contact the Special Markets Department at the Perseus Books Group, 11 Cambridge Center, Cambridge, MA 02142, or call (800) 255-1514 or (617) 252-5298, or email special.markets@perseusbooks.com.

9   10 ⌐ 09   08

Contents

Acknowledgments ix

About the Authors xi

A Letter to Readers xiii

Before Baby's Birth 1

Baby's 1st 48 Hours 13

First Month

Week 1 37

Week 2 49

Week 3 68

Week 4 84

Second Month

Week 5 98

Week 6 106

Week 7 119

Week 8 131

Third Month

Week 9 142

Week 10 151

Week 11 160

Week 12 169

Fourth Month

Week 13 178

Week 14 190

Week 15   201
Week 16   210

Fifth Month

Week 17   218
Week 18   228
Week 19   236
Week 20   244

Sixth Month

Week 21   255
Week 22   264
Week 23   271
Week 24   279
Week 25   288

Seventh Month

Week 26   295
Week 27   301
Week 28   310
Week 29   318
Week 30   326

Eighth Month

Week 31   333
Week 32   342
Week 33   350
Week 34   358
Week 35   366

Ninth Month

Week 36   374
Week 37   382
Week 38   390
Week 39   397

Tenth Month

Week 40   403

Week 41   410

Week 42   419

Week 43   428

Eleventh Month

Week 44   437

Week 45   446

Week 46   454

Week 47   462

Week 48   470

Twelfth Month

Week 49   479

Week 50   488

Week 51   496

Week 52   504

Emergency Situations   513

Glossary   521

Resources   527

Index   539

Acknowledgments

This book, as with others I have written, is a result of my interactions with many pregnant women and their partners. Their excitement and inquiring minds produce many questions about the miracle of birth and the development of the resulting infant. It is my privilege to participate in this wondrous process on a daily (and often nightly!) basis. Those who speak the words following the birth—"It's finally over!"—learn rather quickly that it has just begun! My thanks are sincere to these couples and families for allowing me to share some of this joy.

Lori Eining, R.N., continues to provide an important ingredient in the success of this Second Edition. Patients in my office over the years have been touched by her caring and compassionate nursing skills and genuine dedication to their care.

My five children and five grandchildren have given me "on-the-job-training" with babies week by week during their first year (and beyond), and I thank them for this opportunity. My wife, Debbie, and family offer support and understanding in professions (doctoring and writing) that require many sacrifices on a daily basis. My parents continue as shining examples to me and give me unconditional love and support.

My special thanks go to Megan and Hailey Harbertson for their dedication. Also, the always-available assistance of David Stevens has been invaluable to me. Without their help, this project would not be completed.

Glade B. Curtis

I wish to thank my parents, Bob and Kay Gordon, for their love and continued support. And to my son, Ian, whose interest, friendship and love are very important to me. Special thanks to Bob Rucinski, who checked *every* website in the Resource section to be sure they still existed and were what they said they were.

Judi Schuler

About the Authors

GLADE B. CURTIS, M.D., M.P.H., F.A.C.O.G., is board certified by the American College of Obstetricians and Gynecologists. He practices in Salt Lake City, Utah, and is a Medical Consultant for the State of Utah Department of Health. He is Co-Director of the Health Clinics of Utah. Dr. Curtis is a graduate of the University of Utah (B.S. and Master of Public Health) and the University of Rochester School of Medicine and Dentistry in New York. He was an intern, resident and chief resident in Obstetrics and Gynecology at the University of Rochester Strong Memorial Hospital.

JUDITH SCHULER, M.S., has worked with Dr. Glade Curtis for over 20 years, as his co-author and editor. They have collaborated together on 14 books dealing with pregnancy, women's health and children's health. Ms. Schuler earned a Master of Science degree and a Bachelor of Science degree in Family Studies from the University of Arizona, in Tucson, Arizona. Before becoming an editor for HPBooks, where she met Dr. Curtis, Ms. Schuler taught at the university level in California and Arizona. She has one son. She divides her time between Tucson, Arizona, and Laramie, Wyoming.

cA Letter to Readers

Dear Readers,

Your baby's birth may be one of the most exciting moments of your life. As you hold this new life you have created, you may be thinking about the future. What will baby be like? Will she be smart? Will he be athletic? How quickly will she grow? When will he walk and talk?

Every parent looks to the future with hope and maybe a little uncertainty. All parents want their baby to excel and be the best she can possibly be. When we are around others with babies who are close in age, we often compare our baby with theirs. It's not unusual—it's something we all do. But our advice is to try to avoid these comparisons.

Your baby is unique and like no other. Just like you, she will function on her own schedule. She'll eat or sleep when it's right for her. Her development is geared to her personality and focus. It'll make you crazy if you let yourself get caught up in comparing your baby to another. (We know—as parents, we've both been there!) The best thing you can do as a family is to get to know your baby. Learn what's normal for her, and you won't be as concerned about how your baby compares to others.

In this book, we've included information in each weekly discussion about a baby's mental, physical and social development. However, *when* these developmental changes occur (the weeks we put them in) are merely *estimates* of where your baby may be at any given time. Each developmental step represents an average; a baby could be anywhere from 6 to 10 weeks on *either side of the week* in which the discussion occurs and still be perfectly normal! Don't be worried if your baby doesn't do something exactly at the time it's discussed in the book. Every baby develops in her own way, at her own pace.

The important point of the developmental discussions is that baby progresses in her development in a sequential way. By this we mean that baby follows a continuous development, building upon skills she has already developed. It's important to understand that as your baby develops, she may focus on one task at a time. If she's learning to walk and concentrating her efforts on her balance and movement, her language development may slow down. When she becomes adept at walking, you may discover her babbling more and making new sounds.

❧ *Baby's Personality and Temperament*

Your baby's personality and temperament can also influence how he develops. Researchers once believed that the environment and parental child-rearing practices influenced a baby's personality more than anything else. Now they believe babies are born with definite personality characteristics shaped by many factors, including genetics and experiences in the womb and during birth.

Researchers study many areas in their assessment of personality, including activity levels, eating and sleeping patterns, and how a baby interacts with his environment. Some babies move around a lot; others are very quiet and move little. Babies who move around a lot may reach muscle control more quickly than a baby who is not as active.

Some babies are more adaptable than others. An adaptable baby often has few problems when his environment changes, even drastically. A baby who does not adjust as easily may be cautious in his approach to a new situation. This might influence his ability to learn things quickly, which really isn't a problem if he learns them well.

Another area researchers look at is baby's digestive system. Some babies have no problems in this area from birth. For other babies, it can take months for their digestion to settle down. If a baby isn't bothered by digestive upsets, physical, mental and social development may progress more smoothly because energy is not diverted to dealing with stomach distress.

If you understand your baby's personality, you will be more comfortable with the way he develops. If your baby is easy to get along with, not fussing or crying a great deal, he will probably adjust easily to various situations. Babies with this type of personality usually are fairly average in their achievement of developmental milestones. By this we mean these babies reach various points at about the time we discuss in each week, give or take a few weeks on either side, as discussed earlier.

A more-active infant may be more easily overstimulated, which can make it difficult for him to focus on various developmental tasks. But don't worry; many babies with this personality type learn to settle themselves in a short time, which allows them to progress more quickly. However, development may not be evenly paced, with gains in one area and slower progress in others.

A third type of personality type may be evident in your baby. Some babies are more withdrawn than others. They may reject new experiences and stimulation. These babies require more attention than other babies in the first few months of life. New situations must be introduced carefully to enhance the baby's ability to deal with them. As time passes and you get to know your baby better, if you believe your baby is more inclined to this personality type, you may want to ask the advice of your pediatrician about ways to help your child progress.

﹡ What Can You Do to Help Your Baby?

Parents are the key to a baby's development. You furnish stimulation in many areas, give her an environment that promotes growth, and provide the love and encouragement she needs to motivate her. Provide your baby with activities, games and play that help her develop. Provide stimulating experiences. In each weekly discussion of this book, we give you games to play and things to do with baby that help you both grow into your new environment.

﹡ A Note to Parents of a Premature Infant

You may be the parents of a "preemie," a baby born before he was fully developed in the womb. It's not an uncommon occurrence—about 10% of all babies are born before 37 weeks of gestation. Their growth is measured a little differently from a full-term baby's. However, they should develop in the same sequence as a baby born at full term; it's just the timing that will be different.

If your baby is premature, subtract the number of weeks he was premature from his actual birth age. For example, if your son was born 8 weeks before his due date, subtract 8 weeks from his chronological age. If he is now 12 weeks old (from his date of birth), his developmental age is about 4 weeks. He has used the time from his birthdate to his expected date of birth to finish developing. After he reaches his full-term due date, he will begin to grow as if he were full term. Your doctor will chart his growth to make sure he is healthy. The most important thing your physician will watch for is *steady growth* of the baby. Research has shown that by the time a premature infant reaches 2 years old, his weight is average, and by the time he reaches 3½ years old, his height will also be average.

Don't be alarmed if your premature baby seems to be slower developing and progressing than other babies his age. If they are full-term infants, they got a head start on development, but within a short time, he'll be making similar strides. Studies have shown that babies born as early as 32 weeks have often caught up completely with their peers by age 2 (if they were spared serious complications of prematurity).

If your child is consistently achieving developmental milestones, even at a slower pace than full-term babies, relax and enjoy him. Try not to compare his progress with other babies'—however, if you do, compare his progress to babies born when he was due!

Also see the discussions on premature babies that we have included in the book. They can be found in *Baby's 1ˢᵗ 48 Hours* and *Weeks 6, 9, 15, 22, 24, 36* and *49.*

﹡ A Well-Baby Book

This is a well-baby book. We do not cover problems or situations that occur when a baby is born very ill or with a major health problem.

In planning the topics that we would cover in our book, we realized we could not address a serious health situation in enough depth or provide enough information to furnish readers with the knowledge they sought. If parents are faced with a grave health problem with their baby, their pediatrician and other healthcare providers will help them find the information and solutions they seek.

We chose not to cover topics in such a brief fashion that you, the readers, would feel we were not serious about them. However, in the *Resources* section, we do provide suggestions about where to find answers about serious health issues. We hope we have not offended any reader with our decision.

✴ When You Adopt a Baby

Adopting a baby can happen after you have been informed about the upcoming event months before baby's birth. Or you may be waiting to adopt a child, and the arrival of your little one happens almost overnight!

We hope this book will provide you with the confidence most new parents need with a baby. If you have not had a great deal of time to prepare for the arrival of your baby, read the chapters that deal with preparing for baby's birth *(Before Baby's Birth),* what occurs while baby is in the hospital *(Baby's 1ˢᵗ 48 Hours)* and the first few days of baby's life *(Week 1).* They will provide you with insights into many aspects of baby's development.

Your baby may not have grown under your heart, but he or she will quickly grow in your heart. Enjoy this wonderful new addition to your lives!

✴ Enjoy the Book!

We hope the information we provide in this book is helpful to you as you watch your little one grow. This first year will be one of remarkable growth and change for your baby and will also bring great joy to you. You will be amazed, as almost all parents are, at how quickly your child becomes a person in his or her own right.

Sincerely,
  Glade B. Curtis, M.D., and Judith Schuler, M.S.

Postscript—In the book, we have alternated the use of "he" and "she" each week when referring to the baby. In the even-numbered weeks, all references to the baby will be "he." In odd-numbered weeks, references will be "she."

Although this book is designed to take you through your baby's first year by examining one week at a time, you may seek specific information. Because the book cannot include *everything* you need *before* you know you're looking for it, check the Index, beginning on page 539, for a particular topic. For example, if you're searching for information on ear infections, check the index for various page references. We may not cover the subject until a later week.

Before Baby's Birth

P *reparing for your baby's birth is exciting.* You'll need many new items to make your life and your baby's more comfortable and enjoyable.

It can be a bit stressful having to decide what you'll need to buy. Then you need to shop for it all. Comparing prices can be a tedious task, but prices can vary a great deal from product to product and store to store, so it's probably worth it to comparison shop.

There are ways to find the best deals for various baby items. Compare prices of an item at different stores, such as a discount store, a specialty store, an outlet store, a warehouse store and a secondhand store. You may be surprised how much you can save buying from the least-expensive place. Check out the Internet, if you have a computer. (See the *Resources* section, page 527, for many references.) You may want to try some items before you buy them for comfort of use. For example, if you're thinking of getting a backpack or front carrier, your size can make a difference in how comfortable one carrier is over another.

You may not think you'll save a great deal of money shopping around; however you can easily spend over $7500 the first year on baby's necessities and other basics (this includes setting up the nursery with crib, changing table and other items)! So take your time and look around. It could be very much worth your time and effort—you could save a great deal of money.

In this chapter, we discuss many items you may need for baby. We've included information on your baby's layette, swings, cribs and bassinets, and other items you'll need for the nursery. We cover infant car seats so you'll be able to choose the one that best fits your needs; you'll need it for baby's first car ride—home from the hospital. We have also provided a section on finding a pediatrician. This may be one of the most important decisions you make as a parent, so we discuss this first.

Finding a Pediatrician

It's a good idea to select the doctor who will care for your baby *before* your baby's birth. This gives you the opportunity to interview various doctors and visit their practices before you make a final decision. It's wise to make an appointment for an interview 3 to 4 weeks before your baby's due date. You never know—he or she could come early!

The reason to meet, then select, who will care for your baby before the birth is to get to know the doctor before you see him or her in the hospital. You can discuss many things at this first meeting, such as care in the hospital, whether you are planning to breastfeed or if you wish to have your son circumcised.

Choices include a pediatrician, a family physician or a general practitioner. A family physician or general practitioner may be the only type of medical practice available in some areas.

There are many ways to get a referral for a pediatrician. Ask your OB/GYN for a reference. Ask family members, friends and co-workers the names of doctors they know and trust. Or call your local or county medical society. Check with your insurance provider to see if they have a list of preapproved physicians you must use. If you are a member of a health-maintenance organization, contact the patient advocate for information on which pediatricians are accepting new patients in the HMO.

Once you've chosen someone to interview, call for an appointment. Tell the person you speak with that you are interviewing pediatricians for your soon-to-be-born baby. Some practices hold individual meetings; others have group sessions with several couples. Ask about the cost of this meeting. Some doctors meet with you for free; others charge a fee for their time.

Keep in mind that if problems arise in dealing with this physician after your baby is born, you can always choose another healthcare provider. The choice you make at this time is *not* permanent.

We have provided some questions you might want to ask the physician and some points to consider after you leave the interview. Choosing baby's doctor is a decision *both* parents should make together, so it's a good idea to make this visit as a couple.

✄ *Questions to Ask*
Below is a list of questions you may want to think about. Some may be important to you. Others you may not care about. You can call the physician's office and ask many of these questions of someone there. Others you may want to ask when you interview the doctor. They will help you create a dialogue about your child's care.

* What are your qualifications and training?
* What is your availability?
* Are your office hours compatible with our schedules?
* Do you have weekend or evening office hours for well-baby care?
* If we only need medical advice, is there someone we can call and talk with in your office?
* Can a sick child be seen the same day?
* How can we reach you in case of an emergency or after office hours?

* Who responds if you are not available?
* Do you have a website or e-mail address?
* Do you or your nurse return phone calls the same day?
* Do you have X-ray facilities and a laboratory at your office? If not, where would we need to go to have tests done?
* Are you interested in preventive, developmental and behavioral issues?
* How does your practice operate?
* Does it comply with our insurance?
* Do you have a staff person to file our insurance claims for us?
* What is the nearest (to our home) emergency room or urgent-care center we would use?
* What happens in special medical situations? To whom do you make referrals?

ﾟ *What to Consider When Selecting a Pediatrician*

Some issues can't be resolved until you analyze your feelings after your visit. You may need to examine and to consider how you felt about certain topics you discussed. Below is a list of questions you and your partner might want to discuss after your initial visit.

* Are the doctor's philosophies and attitudes acceptable to us, such as use of antibiotics and other medications, child-rearing practices or medically related religious beliefs?
* Was he or she genuinely interested in our concerns?
* Is the doctor going to be available as much as we think we will need him or her?
* Did the physician appear interested in developing a rapport with us and our expected child?
* Is this a person we feel comfortable with and with whom our child will be comfortable?
* Did the doctor listen to us and our concerns?
* Is the doctor's age, professional training, gender, availability, marital status or any other factor about him or her important to us?
* Did the office staff seem cordial, open and easy to talk to?

Preparing the Nursery

You may be surprised to discover all the things baby needs. After all, the baby doesn't do much, except eat and sleep, so why all the pieces of equipment, the clothes, the furniture? You'll find that most of what you buy or receive as gifts will be helpful, and you'll wonder how you could have gotten along without it.

Your baby's nursery may be a separate bedroom, an alcove or an area in your bedroom. The most essential pieces of equipment you'll need when you bring baby home are a place for her to sleep and a designated changing area. The other items we discuss are not essential, but they might make your life easier.

While she's still small, baby can sleep just about anywhere—in a cradle, a bassinet or a crib. If the nursery isn't ready when your baby's born, even a basket or drawer will do for a short time, until she grows too big. Your baby won't need a crib until she can sit up. Crib design and safety are discussed below.

Items to consider for the nursery include some sort of bed (crib, bassinet), a changing table (see the discussion of the *Changing Table Setup,* page 7), a rocking chair, chest of drawers, diaper pail, baby monitor, small lamp, mobile, vaporizer or humidifier, and a smoke detector.

A *rocking chair* is a wonderful place to nurse your baby and to comfort her. New designs of *diaper pails* actually keep diaper smells inside!

Monitors make it easy for you to keep tabs on baby without going into her room and waking her up. You can listen to her and also talk to her, with some models. With other models, you can actually see her!

Choose a small *lamp* with a low-watt bulb to light the room softly. A colorful *mobile* will delight and entertain baby for a long time; keep it out of baby's reach by suspending it from the ceiling. A *vaporizer* or *humidifier* will keep the air in baby's room moist and can help make breathing easier, especially when she has a cold.

Another item to consider is the paint in baby's room. Be sure the room is painted in nontoxic paint; if you're unsure, repaint the walls. Other items you might want to consider, to keep baby entertained and occupied, include a swing and a bouncer chair. Both are great when you need to put baby in a safe place that will keep her happy.

> **A Word of Caution:** Be careful about buying secondhand nursery equipment or borrowing someone else's. Some items might not meet current safety standards. See safety features described below for various pieces of equipment.

✷ Cribs, Cradles and Bassinets

Your baby needs a comfortable, safe place to sleep. Some parents decide they want their baby to sleep in a bassinet in their room for a while. Others put baby in her crib, in her own room, from the first day home. Other parents have a "family bed," in which parents and baby sleep together in one large bed. (See the discussion on *family beds* in *Week 5.*)

A *bassinet* is a small, portable bed for baby. She can sleep in it until she gets too big, then she can be moved to a crib. The mattress should fit snugly, and sheets must not pull up. A wide base is suggested so it does not easily tip.

A *crib* is a more permanent piece of equipment. Some cribs are designed to grow with your child and can be converted to a juvenile bed. Before you make a purchase, check out various safety features as established by the Juvenile Product Manufacturers' Association (JPMA), the Consumer Product Safety Commission (CPSC) and the American Academy of Pediatrics (AAP), which all help assure baby's safety. Various safety features include the following.

- Bars no farther apart than 2⅜ inches. If you can pass a soft-drink can through the bars, they're too far apart.
- Mattress should fit snugly—you shouldn't be able to fit more than two fingers between the side of the crib and the mattress.
- The mattress should be firm and supportive.
- Railings should be 26 inches higher than the lowest level of mattress support and at least 4 inches above the mattress at its highest level.
- Corner posts should not be higher than end panels, to prevent catching clothing when baby tries to climb out (when she's older).
- Finish on the crib should be nontoxic. If you're using a secondhand crib, be sure paint is lead free.
- There should be no cutouts on the headboard or footboard so baby's head can't get caught in them.
- The foot release/latching mechanism should be childproof.
- Be sure the teething rail (around the crib) and all hardware are sturdy and securely fastened to the crib.
- Never use cleaning bags or garbage bags as a waterproof cover for the mattress.

Follow safety guidelines when choosing your baby's crib.

Crib Sheets. In addition to the crib, you'll need three or four fitted sheets. It may be hard to imagine, but about 900 infant deaths occur each year related to suffocation by a baby getting tangled in the crib sheet. Crib sheets that do not come loose and wrap around baby (causing suffocation) can reduce that number.

SOME PRECAUTIONS WITH CRIBS AND SHEETS

* Never use a top sheet or waterproof pads on top of the fitted sheet.
* Many believe the crib should be free of *all* items except a fitted sheet and baby—no bumper pads, pillows, comforters or blankets while baby is sleeping to reduce the risk of SIDS, Sudden Infant Death Syndrome. (See the discussion in *Week 8*.) Keep baby's crib free of all unnecessary soft, fluffy items.
* If baby is chilly, put her in a zip-up sleeper to keep her warm and safe.

Fitted sheets should wrap at least 2 inches under the mattress on all sides. Discard sheets if they shrink after washing. With any sheet, straps that hold the sheet in place that fit under the mattress can be used; one type is a 6-point harness with heavy clips that prevent sheets from coming loose. Or consider sheets that cover the entire mattress—top and bottom. These sheets zip shut so sheets cannot come loose.

Placement of the Crib. Crib placement is also important. Don't put a crib against an outside wall. Keep it away from radiators and air ducts (hot or cold). Keep the crib away from window-blind cords or drapery cords. Don't attach mobiles or anything else to the crib that baby could get tangled in.

⚘ Baby Clothes

Buying baby clothes is something parents and grandparents enjoy. It's fun to dress baby in the cutest (boy's) or the sweetest (girl's) outfits possible. But let's be practical. Most babies don't need many clothes; they can get by just fine with some basic styles for the first year. A few cute outfits are fine, but don't spend your money on them if you don't need to. (You may receive many different clothing items as shower and baby gifts.)

A baby's needs are quite easy to meet. Diapers, T-shirts, gowns that open at the bottom, footed sleepers, socks, bibs, a hat, a warm cover-up, one-piece short- or long-legged "onesies," blankets and towels are the most basic items you'll need to stock up on. How many of each you need depends on your personal situation, but it is recommended that you have about 8 dozen diapers on hand (order 100 a week for a newborn if you have a diaper service). This can be a combination of cloth and disposable diapers, if you choose.

Both types are good in various situations. As for clothing, the list below should get you started:

- 6 to 8 T-shirts
- 4 or 5 gowns
- 4 lightweight footed sleepers
- 2 blanket-weight footed sleepers
- 6 pairs of socks
- 6 bibs
- 1 or 2 hats
- 1 warm cover-up for going outside in chilly weather
- 6 one-piece short- or long-legged "onesies"
- 6 cotton receiving blankets (look for ones that are square—it's easier to swaddle baby)
- 3 hooded baby towels and 3 washcloths

Baby Toiletries

In addition to clothes, you'll need some toiletries for baby. A brush and comb, nail clippers or scissors, nasal bulb syringe, a thermometer, baby shampoo, diaper-rash ointment, baby oil, baby powder, baby wipes, cotton balls and petroleum jelly all come in handy when you need them. Keep them together so you'll be able to put your hands on them quickly.

Changing Table Setup

You can set up the changing table in baby's room or some other part of the house. If you have a two- or three-story house, you might want to have a place to change baby on each floor! Wherever you change her, the surface must be sturdy. A safety strap is also advisable. Be sure you can store all the items you'll need safely out of baby's way. Before long, she'll be curious and active, and reaching and grabbing. *Caution:* **Never leave baby unattended on a changing table.**

Your changing table should be the right height for you to change diapers comfortably—no higher than your sternum, no lower than your hips. A pad with a raised edge is a good choice. Place the changing table away from windows to keep baby safe and warm. Put it in an area away from the crib so baby can't get items off it while she's in her crib. Don't place it near anything that hangs down, like blinds cords, to keep baby from entangling herself. To help keep her occupied while you're changing her, a bright-colored poster on the wall or a mobile hanging above her head that she can look at is fun.

Have at hand clean diapers, diaper-rash cream, baby wipes, powder (use cornstarch powder because talc can cause problems if it's inhaled), lotions (fragrance free), cotton balls, petroleum jelly, some clean clothes and clean blankets. Add anything else you think you might need for your situation. Keep items close at hand in a basket or on a shelf (out of baby's reach).

You'll also want to pack some items in a bag so you can have changing-table items on hand when you're on the go. A rubber-lined bag serves as a good diaper bag. Fill it with four to six diapers, a changing pad, waterless antibacterial gel for cleaning your hands, a bib, a spare outfit, a pacifier, formula, a couple of bottles, wipes and a toy or two.

✳ *What Kind of Diapers?*
Parents want to know which is best—disposable diapers or cloth diapers. It all depends on you and your situation.

Disposable diapers are convenient to use. They save on utilities because you don't have to wash or dry them. You can take them when you go out, and you don't have to worry about disposal. You don't have to use rubber pants or diaper pins. However, when your baby has wet pants, you may not know it because the outer lining makes it hard to know when she's wet.

> You may be eligible for a one-time free gift of diapers if you have more than one baby. Many diaper companies send parents of multiples free diapers to celebrate babies' births. Contact the company, and ask what proof they need—usually a copy of the babies' crib cards or their birth certificates are enough. To find the contact information for various companies, check the diaper package, the Internet or a mothers' group.

Cloth diapers need to be washed—by you or by a diaper service. This can be an inconvenience or an expense that you don't want. You may have to rinse diapers twice to get out all the detergent, if you wash them at home. Baby will also have to wear rubber pants, so you'll need to wash those, too. A diaper service is great but it can be a little costly.

Many parents use a combination of both cloth and disposable diapers and find it works well for them. If your baby is going to go to day-care, you may be asked to bring only disposable diapers. Whatever you choose, you'll change thousands of diapers this first year!

✳ *Thermometers*
One item you might want to have on hand is a thermometer. There are various types to choose from, including a rectal thermometer, an ear thermometer, forehead scanners and other devices. The most accurate recording of baby's temperature will be accomplished using a rectal thermometer. To learn how to use one, see *Week 4*.

You may believe an ear thermometer would be easier to use because the thermometer measures body temperature in the ear in a matter of seconds. It does record temperature quickly; however, this type of thermometer is not accurate enough for newborns and young babies. Their ear canals are small and soft, and the canal can collapse when the ear probe is inserted in baby's ear. This can cause a falsely low reading. (With older children, the reading may be falsely high!)

If you have questions about taking a rectal temperature or want a professional opinion on ear thermometers, talk to your baby's doctor.

Car Seats

The most important piece of baby equipment you can buy is a *car seat,* so choose one before baby is born. Your baby needs to ride in a car seat *every* time she rides in a car—it's the law in all 50 states. The safest place for her is the middle of the back seat.

Does every child need a car seat? Yes! It's the best protection your baby has in case of an accident. Some parents mistakenly believe they can safely hold their baby in a crash. It can't be done. Crash tests have proved that a 10-pound baby would be ripped from an adult's arms with a force of over 200 pounds in an accident at 30 miles per hour! We also caution you not to take your baby out of her car seat to feed her, change her or comfort her while the car is moving.

A car seat is a necessity. Every baby needs to be properly secured in a car seat, starting with their very first ride.

From the time your baby goes home from the hospital, she should be placed in a car seat. Until 1 year of age *and* 20 pounds, the car seat should face the rear. See the discussion in *Week 52.* After that, the seat can be turned forward, but keep it in the back seat.

When choosing a car seat for your baby, be certain it meets the safety standards of the JPMA, the CPSC and the American Academy of Pediatrics. You may choose from an infant-only seat, good until your baby reaches 20 pounds, or a convertible seat, which can be used until your child reaches 40 pounds. The infant-only seat is more comfortable for a young baby because of its semireclining position.

✧ *If Your Baby Is Low Birth Weight or Preemie*
If a baby is very small when born, parents often hesitate to put her in a car seat designed for larger babies. Nearly all car seats are designed for average-sized

babies. A small baby may be uncomfortable in one. Another concern is a small baby may have trouble breathing in a semireclined infant seat. One study showed a small baby may have decreased oxygen levels and episodes of apnea (baby briefly stops breathing) in a larger car seat.

So what is the solution? If baby experiences any breathing problems, an *infant car bed* that meets federal safety standards may be a good choice. Baby can lie flat, allowing easier breathing. And she'll be protected in case of an accident. In fact, if your baby is born before 36 weeks gestation, a flat car bed is recommended.

If she has no breathing problems, an infant-only car seat is a good choice. To ensure her comfort, use a rolled headrest pillow made especially for car seats to cradle her head. If you can't find one, a tightly rolled blanket will do the trick. (Stitch the towel together into a roll so it won't come undone.) To help keep her from slumping, you can also place a receiving blanket on either side of her and between the crotch and crotch strap.

✃ Common Car-Seat Mistakes

Did you know that statistics show that 80% of all car seats are being used improperly? Even though parents use infant car seats, many use them incorrectly. Some of the more common mistakes include:

* the car-seat harness is attached incorrectly, too loosely or not at all
* a rear-facing car seat is reclined improperly
* the seat-belt system is improperly locked or not locked at all
* car seat is not fastened tightly in the seat
* car seat is too big for baby
* baby's harness, which keeps her securely in the seat, doesn't fit correctly
* the harness straps do not go over her shoulders and lie flat against her chest

There are some things you can do to ensure your baby's car seat is properly installed. We recommend you install the seat a few weeks before baby's due date, then head for your local police or fire station to have a professional check it out. If the seat is installed improperly, ask the person helping you to teach you the correct way to install the seat. Then practice a few times with the professional standing by to offer assistance and guidance. *Both* parents should be involved in this learning experience.

Other important tips include the following.

* Never place the car seat on a rear-facing seat, such as found in some station wagons.
* Never place the car seat on a side-facing seat, such as found in some SUVs and mobile homes.
* Never place the car seat on a pull-down seat or a swivel seat.

Caution: Never put a car seat in the front passenger seat, especially if it has an air bag! If your car has side-impact air bags in the back seat, which some models have, be sure baby's car seat is placed in the middle of the back seat or ask your dealer to disable those air bags.

* If you have bucket seats, put a rolled towel or blanket under the car seat to make it more level because 80% of the car seat's surface should touch the seat of the vehicle.
* When baby is safely in her car seat, check the fit between her collarbone and the harness. You should be able to fit only *one* finger into the space.

✢ *A Car Seat with Multiple Uses*

We are often asked if a baby's parents don't have a car, such as some people who live in large cities, is a car-safety seat really necessary? The answer is an emphatic *Yes!* Even if you always ride in a taxi, baby should be placed in a safety-restraint system. A choice made by many parents in this situation is a convertible "travel system." It's really three products in one—a car seat, an infant carrier and a stroller. You can use it from birth until baby is a toddler. And it's convenient for you—one product can fulfill many needs.

BUY A NEW CAR SEAT

When choosing a car seat for baby, purchase a new one. This is one piece of equipment that you don't want to borrow or to buy secondhand. The car seat could be damaged by previous wear and use, or it might be missing important parts. Many older car seats have been recalled. In addition, technological advances may make an older car seat obsolete. So buy a new car seat for your baby—you'll feel confident you're providing her the best protection possible.

✢ *Can't Afford a Car Seat?*

If you can't afford a car seat, many organizations provide reduced-cost or free car seats to a family. Some hospitals let you borrow a car seat until you can get one of your own. Ask at your local hospital, or call your local police department for information. You might also want to check with your car insurance company—some offer discounts on car seats.

✻ *Keep Baby Safe*

The final word is: Keep your baby safe; never let her ride in any vehicle without being buckled up and belted in. One report found that an average of 35 babies a year die in auto accidents on the way home from the hospital. Don't let your baby become a statistic.

DO YOU DRIVE A PICKUP TRUCK?

In some parts of the country, many people own pickup trucks—as first or second family vehicles. Because many of these trucks do not have a back seat, where can you put baby's car seat?

There is a solution! One company, XSCI, has developed a rear-facing car seat that can withstand contact with a dashboard or front air bag in a collision. It can also be used in a regular back seat. The car seat is kind of pricey (about $250), but it may be worth it if it allows you to keep using a vehicle. The seat is for babies from 5 to 22 pounds. See the *Resources* section, page 527, for further information.

Baby's 1st 48 Hours

*Y*our baby has just been through one of the hardest battles he will ever face. It's a tough job to be pushed down the birth canal and out into the world. Often baby needs help and must be delivered with a vacuum extractor or forceps, or by Cesarean section. No matter how your baby arrives, it is wonderful to meet him.

Your newborn is amazing. When he enters the world, all his major organs are functioning. He can see, hear, smell, taste and feel. He may look like he has no awareness of what's going on, but he is very sensitive to events taking place around him. (We discuss this in depth in *Week 1*.)

Baby's Birth Weight

"How much does he weigh?" is one of the first questions new parents ask. What a baby weighs at birth is influenced by many factors, including your health during pregnancy, medications, smoking, nutrition, diet, length of the pregnancy (early or late) and the size of your partner.

The average weight at term is 7 pounds, 2 ounces, but this can vary widely. In addition to weight, other measurements are taken, including length (average is between 18 and 22 inches), head circumference and abdomen circumference.

Your baby's weight may fall a little in the days following delivery. Most babies lose a few ounces after birth because they are born with extra body fluid that they lose during the first 5 days. They generally regain the weight in the next week, so before 2 weeks of age, they are back to their original birth weight. From birth to 1 month old, most babies gain ⅔ to 1 ounce of weight *every* day! By the end of 3 months, baby will have gained an average of 1½ to 2 pounds each month! On average, babies double their weight by 6 months and triple their weight by a year. You'll really see changes in him over the next few months.

When baby is born, he is measured for length. Many babies lose a little length measurement in the days following birth if the birth was vaginal and his head was pointed. Over the next 3 months, baby will grow about 1 to 1½ inches a month. By age 1 year, your baby will have grown from 9 to 11 inches, compared with his length at birth.

What Does Baby Look Like?

If you're like most new parents, the first thing you do when you meet your baby is to examine him from head to foot. What does he look like? Does he have hair? Does he have 10 fingers and 10 toes? Is he normal? These concerns are universal—we felt the same way when our children were born.

If your baby is average size, he'll weigh between 7 and 8 pounds, and be between 18 and 22 inches long.

⨍ *His Head and His Face*
As you check him out, you may notice that his face is puffy and his head is slightly misshapen and has a "mashed" or "conehead" look. It's common for a baby's head to look like this because the skull, which is actually made up of several bones, changes shape (molds) to move through the birth canal. You may think his head looks enormous—it is! At this time, his head is ¼ of his body, which is one reason it's hard for his skull to fit through the birth canal.

Your baby's face might look a little askew, as if he'd been in a fight or slid down a slippery slide on his face. His nose may be flat and his chin a little out of place. He may have some bruises on his face. The skin over his brow may be wrinkled and loose, and his eyes may be swollen and bloodshot. As with his misshapen head, this is due to the exertion of birth. His eyes will appear blue or be dark; however his true eye color won't be evident until he's about 6 months old.

The two soft spots on the top of his head are called *fontanelles*. One is close to the crown; you'll be able to see and to feel his pulse there. The other is above his brow on his forehead. These spots decrease in size as his bones grow together. It's OK to touch them gently; they're covered with a thick, protective membrane.

You may also notice the crown of baby's head is lumpy, swollen and discolored. This is called a *caput* and results from his head pushing against the mother's cervix and the birth canal. The caput quickly disappears; it will look better every hour and often appears normal by the time you go home in a few days. It may take as long as 10 days for a misshapen head to look normal.

A pea-sized bump on the back of baby's head is probably a lymph node. Don't worry about it. If baby has a bump near the top of his head, it might be caused by overlapping bones in baby's skull. Bumps will disappear as baby's bones fuse together.

If he has hair, you may be surprised by the color. However, this hair is usually temporary, so don't worry if you don't like it. His real hair (the permanent kind) will begin to grow soon, although some babies don't get permanent hair until they're close to a year old (or older!).

You may notice a few blisters in your baby's mouth. Check his thumbs and fingers for any thickened or callused areas. Most babies suck their thumbs or fingers in the uterus; your baby may have. He may have a *nursing tubercle* on his upper lip, which stiffens the lip and makes grasping your nipple or a bottle nipple easier for him.

If his chin quivers and/or his legs and arms seem shaky, it just means that more electrical impulses are being sent to muscles than are necessary, which results in these movements. This is normal, and they will decrease over the next few months.

✿ *Baby's Skin*

Next you may look at the skin on his body. Most babies are covered with a thick, white, waxy coating when they're born, called *vernix;* it protected his skin while he was in the uterus. When he's cleaned up, you may be able to see the veins through his skin, which is still thin. His hands and feet may peel. He may have birthmarks. See the discussion of birthmarks below.

A Caucasian baby's skin color can range from purplish to pinkish gray. The pigmentation of babies of color may not be evident for hours or even a few days after birth. Many are born with light skin that darkens. If baby's a little blue in color, it may be caused by mucus in his air passages. Most is suctioned out, and he coughs out the rest.

His skin may appear yellow or orange-tinged by the second or third day—about half of all newborns experience *jaundice.* The color is caused by the inability of baby's liver to remove breakdown products of blood cells, and the buildup causes the skin to look yellow or orange. A mild case of jaundice resolves in about a week or 10 days; it may last slightly longer if your baby breastfeeds. See the discussion in *Week 1.*

It's interesting to note as you examine him that your baby's skin is the most developed sensory organ he has right now. He'll love it when you gently rub and stroke him.

Delivery Marks. Delivery marks occur in almost every delivery. They can occur while the baby is in the uterus, during the descent through the birth canal and during delivery. The use of forceps or a vacuum extractor to assist with delivery may increase the chance of delivery marks. Marks can vary from a misshapen head (it's nothing to worry about and will change rapidly after birth) or a flattened ear or nose, to bumps and bruises.

Forceps may leave marks on the side of the head, in front of the ears. A vacuum extractor may leave a mark on the back or crown of the head. These marks fade and go away within a few hours to a few days. Lotion may be helpful in some situations.

Call the doctor if any of the marks get bigger or if they don't fade after the first few days. If they become warm to the touch or hard, let your doctor know.

✳ *Birthmarks*

Many different types of marks may be seen on a baby after birth. These include salmon patches or stork bites, hemangiomas or strawberry marks, Mongolian spots, café au lait spots, port-wine stains, spider veins (nevi) and pigmented nevi (beauty marks). All are discolorations or marks on the skin.

Salmon patches, also called *stork bites,* are pinkish areas usually found on the back of the neck, the forehead, the face or eyelids. They are caused by blood vessels in the skin. Some are temporary and should disappear within a year. Some are permanent.

Hemangiomas, also called *strawberry marks,* are fairly common birthmarks. About one in 10 babies has them. They are caused by an overabundance of blood-vessel cells. They are often red or pinkish, as well as being raised and spongy. They may not appear until a few weeks after birth and may continue to grow somewhat during the next 6 to 12 months. Most disappear by age 10 and leave no scar.

Mongolian spots are flat, blue- or gray-colored marks, which look like bruises, found on the back and buttocks. They are seen most often in dark-skinned and Asian babies. They are caused by a high concentration of pigment cells in the skin. These spots are *not* a sign of disease and should fade during childhood, but they may never disappear completely.

Café au lait spots are flat spots, usually tan to light brown in color. They can be found anywhere on the body and are usually permanent. There is no treatment for these spots, but if baby has more than six spots that are larger than 1/5 inch in diameter, have them checked out by the doctor. Café au lait spots are sometimes found in conjunction with a rare neurological disorder.

Port-wine stains are pink to purple to red in color and usually flat. They are usually permanent. They may fade somewhat, and/or they may be removed by laser surgery when baby is older. If port-wine stains appear on any part of the face, they should be checked regularly.

Spider nevi are dilated blood vessels that look like the legs of a spider; they usually fade by 1 or 2 years of age. *Moles* or *pigmented nevi* come in several colors from light brown to black. They are caused by an increase in the number of pigment cells in the skin. Moles present at birth should be watched for any change in size and color. Large moles (over 3 inches wide) may be removed to avoid risk of melanoma.

Keep an eye on any birthmarks your child has. Call the doctor if a birthmark grows or changes color. If a mark is close to the eye or on baby's face, your pediatrician will check it. In most instances, birthmarks are checked to see if they fade or go away on their own. Laser surgery is being used in many instances to remove birthmarks and moles. Other treatments may be possible in specific cases.

✦ *Examining Other Parts of His Body*

Baby's hands and feet are so small they may amaze you. He'll probably hold his hands in tight fists. His fingernails may be paper thin; don't be surprised if they already need trimming!

A newborn's legs are bowed, and his feet turn in. Often his legs are drawn up against his tummy—this is called the *fetal position*. If you gently pull them out, his legs may appear short. And when you let them go, it's almost as if they were on rubber bands—they pull right up against his body! His feet have only a heel bone at this time. The cartilage that makes up the rest of his foot will become bone later. His peanut-shaped feet may turn inward.

Your baby's heel is usually pricked for a blood sample, so it may look sore or inflamed. His hips may seem loose-jointed and crack when they move. This is normal and caused by hormone's from his mother. Your pediatrician will examine your baby for signs of a dislocated hip, which can be treated.

His tummy may be prominent; this isn't fat, it's caused by a lack of muscle tone. This disappears as he becomes more mobile in the next few months.

Your baby's genitals may appear swollen and enlarged; this can happen with either sex. A girl may have a vaginal discharge. See the discussion in *Week 1*. Don't worry—this is normal and will clear up in a few days. These symptoms are caused by the mother's hormones crossing the placenta.

In a few cases, a baby may experience a bone break or fracture or a dislocation during delivery. These conditions heal well with no lasting result and are usually treated by bandaging them. You must use great care when lifting your baby. Dressing must be done carefully; bathing may have to wait awhile.

If you notice a hard lump between baby's ribs, it's a bone called the *xiphoid process*. Soon it will be covered with muscle and fat as baby develops, so don't be concerned about it. Your baby may also have a hollow vertical area running down his tummy. This is caused by the two muscle bundles on either side of the abdomen—they haven't grown together yet but will as baby grows older.

✦ *Baby's Bowels*

Even though you probably never imagined it, now that baby is here, you'll probably find yourself concerned about his bowels. It doesn't only mean changing diapers; your baby's stools can be an indication of his health.

Your baby's first bowel movement is called *meconium*. It consists of cellular material and other substances from his digestive tract as he developed in the womb; it looks yellow-green, brown or like black tar. Your baby must get rid of this material in the 48 hours after birth before normal digestion can begin. If he doesn't, your doctor may be concerned about intestinal obstruction.

Once your baby passes the meconium, his stools will be yellow-green and look like small seeds. If you breastfeed your baby, his stools will look different than a baby's who is fed formula.

Baby's Senses

It may seem incredible, but soon after birth, a baby can recognize his mother's voice *and* her scent. Before your baby is born, he is already sensitive to sounds, light and temperature. His senses develop quickly once outside the womb. As we've already mentioned, he can hear, see, feel and taste when he is born. Let's examine what his senses are like at this time.

℈ *Taste*
Your baby is born with a desire for sweet things, which is suited to the flavor of formula or breast milk. His taste for bitter, salty and sour develop later. At this time, he can distinguish bitter and sour tastes.

℈ *Hearing*
Baby's hearing is not fully developed at birth. Parts of the ear are immature, so your baby can't hear the range of sounds you can. Low-frequency sounds can be heard by baby at birth; this includes the human voice. Baby knows your voice because he heard it inside the womb!

Studies have shown that babies prefer the sound of the human voice to any other sound. To help baby develop his hearing, speak to him often in a slow, exaggerated voice. You'll both enjoy the interaction, and you'll help him develop his hearing.

℈ *Sense of Smell*
Researchers believe that your baby's sense of smell is well developed at birth. It's been found that within hours of birth, a breastfeeding baby will use his nose to find his mother's nipple. Amazingly, it has been demonstrated that your baby's sense of smell may be developed in the uterus—certain food flavors and odors, such as garlic, cross the placenta to the baby. If you love garlic and onion, baby may already be familiar with them! If you breastfeed, this continues because flavors pass into your breast milk.

Your baby will learn about some smells as he grows. He will learn which smells are "good," such as those associated with foods, and which smells are unpleasant.

✣ *Touch*

From birth, a baby is sensitive to touch; as we've already said, his skin is the largest organ of his body. It doesn't take long for him to become familiar with the touch of those close to him. Your touch will soothe him or stimulate him.

It's important to know how to touch your baby. A baby likes a firm touch. It makes him feel secure. He also likes to be stroked and massaged—that's why we include different massage techniques in the first 6 weeks of discussions. Massaging your baby has benefits for him and for you. Studies show that babies who are massaged for 10 to 15 minutes before bedtime or napping may sleep better and be less irritable.

✣ *Sight*

Eyes may be quite developed by birth and capable of seeing many things. However, the baby's brain isn't as fully developed, so he doesn't see as well as an adult. That's one reason you'll have to hold an object very close to baby for him to see it, about 8 to 12 inches away. He can distinguish light from dark and prefers black-and-white patterns. If you move an object farther away from him, his eyes may cross; he can't focus both eyes on the same thing just yet.

✣ *Vision and Hearing Tests*

Today, many hospitals and physicians are testing a baby's hearing and vision *before* he leaves the hospital. A baby's eyes are usually tested shortly after birth for eye disease and proper function, especially if there is a family history of problems. Some doctors recommend babies be examined for many types of eye abnormalities, including congenital cataracts. When found early and treated, a baby may avoid long-term problems. If a problem is discovered, your baby may need to see an ear, nose and throat specialist (ENT) or an ophthalmologist.

About half of all states now test baby for hearing problems in the hospital. Without tests, problems may not be detected until a child is 2 or 3 years old. Hearing is tested by recording electrical brain activity in response to various sounds or by listening for an echo in the inner ear. If your baby has a hearing loss, it could affect the way his speech develops. Today, hearing aids can be fitted in a baby as young as 6 months old!

Tests on Your Baby

Immediately and shortly after birth, your baby will be subjected to a variety of tests to assess his health and to provide his physician with information about any potential problems. Below is a discussion of some of the tests he may be given.

✣ *Apgar Score*
This test was developed by Virginia Apgar, M.D., and is used to assess your newborn's overall condition immediately after birth. The baby is evaluated at 1 minute and 5 minutes after birth; a score of 0, 1 or 2 is possible in five areas—heart rate, color, muscle tone, respiratory effort and reflex irritability. Scores from the five criteria are added together, for a maximum total of 10.

An average score for most babies is 7 to 9 (pediatricians' babies are the only ones to score a perfect 10!). The Apgar score is used to determine the baby's health following delivery but is not used to predict future health.

✣ *Comprehensive Newborn Screening*
The comprehensive newborn screening test can detect more than 30 metabolic disorders in a newborn, including sickle-cell anemia and phenylketonuria. Amazingly, the test can be performed with one drop of baby's blood! This is an important test because the sooner a metabolic problem is discovered, the sooner it can be treated. Many of these conditions are treatable if found early.

✣ *PKU—Phenylketonuria*
In all 50 states, newborns are tested for PKU. If a baby is born with the disorder, he can't process phenylalanine, which is present in nearly all foods. Left untreated, phenylalanine causes brain damage and mental retardation. If found early, the problem can be prevented by feeding baby a special formula. A special diet will be necessary as the child grows older; it may need to be followed for life.

✣ *Coombs Test*
Blood is taken from the umbilical cord for testing if the mother's blood is Rh-negative or Type O, or if she has not been tested for antibodies. It detects whether Rh-antibodies have been formed in the baby.

✣ *Reflex Assessment*
This assessment tests for several specific reflexes in baby, including the rooting and grasp reflexes. If a particular reflex is not observed, further evaluation will be done.

✴ Neonatal Maturity Assessment

Various characteristics of baby are assessed to evaluate his neuromuscular and physical maturity. Like the Apgar test, each characteristic is assigned a score, and the sum indicates baby's maturity.

✴ Brazelton Neonatal Behavioral Assessment Scale

The test covers a broad range of newborn behavior and provides information about how a newborn responds to his environment. It is usually used when a problem is suspected, but some hospitals test all babies.

✴ Blood Tests for Particular Problems

Blood is taken from baby's heel for a blood screen. Tests are done on the blood to look for anemia, congenital hypothyroidism, galactosemia, congenital adrenal hyperplasia (CAH), biotinidase deficiency, maple-syrup urine disease, homocystinuria, medium chain acyl-CoA dehydrogenase deficiency (MCAD) and blood-glucose levels. Results often indicate whether baby needs further evaluation or special treatment.

Baby Functioning after Birth

Baby's functioning after birth includes his first attempts at breathing, coughing fluid from the lungs, sneezing, movement of legs and arms, and often passage of urine or a bowel movement.

With those first breaths, your baby goes from being totally dependent on blood flow from the placenta to using his own lungs and airways to breathe. The blood flow in the heart changes—blood that was diverted from the lungs directly to the body before birth now flows through the chambers of the heart into the lungs then into the body.

New parents are often concerned about baby's color. "Are they always so blue?" they ask. The answer is, "Yes," but the baby soon turns pink. Hands and feet are the last areas to turn pink.

Following delivery, the baby is often quiet but is soon crying and moving. The nurses weigh, measure and evaluate your baby in the moments after birth. During this time, baby becomes more alert.

Your baby exhibits several reflexes. They are discussed below.

- When you touch or rub his cheek, his mouth will open and he will make a sucking motion; this is the *rooting reflex*. Baby outgrows this by about 4 months.
- With the *sucking reflex*, baby sucks vigorously when you put something into his mouth—your finger, nipple or a pacifier. Baby outgrows this by about 4 months.

* The baby will throw his arms and legs out, then quickly draw them in when his position is changed suddenly. This is called the *Moro reflex.* Baby outgrows this at about 3 months.
* The *grasping reflex* (also called *palmar grasp*) causes baby's hand to become a fist when his fingers or palm are touched. Baby outgrows this at 5 to 6 months.
* The *startle reflex* becomes evident as the Moro reflex fades. When startled by a loud noise, baby may look frightened and flex his arms and legs. This appears around 3 or 4 months of age and lasts until about age 1.
* With the *tonic neck reflex,* baby will extend his arm and leg outward when you turn his head to one side while he is lying on his back. Baby outgrows this by about 5 months.
* The *stepping reflex* occurs when baby is held upright. He places one foot in front of the other, as if taking a step. Baby outgrows this by about 2 months.
* When you put your baby on his tummy, he'll move as if he were crawling. This is called the *crawling reflex.* Baby outgrows this by about 3 months.
* With the *swimming reflex,* baby will hold his breath and move as if swimming if you put him underwater. Baby outgrows this around 6 months.
* The *parachute reflex* occurs if baby feels as if he is falling; he'll try to grab on to something overhead. This appears around 3 months of age and lasts until about age 1.

Baby's Care in the Hospital

Visit by the Pediatrician

Your baby will be visited in the hospital by the pediatrician you have already chosen, if you chose one. If you did not select someone, a pediatrician on call for the hospital will examine baby.

The pediatrician will examine the baby, perform a circumcision if you request it and meet with you and your partner. He or she will lay out a schedule of follow-up visits in his or her office. Be sure you know how to contact the pediatrician or the pediatrician's office if you have any questions or problems.

If you have questions, ask your pediatrician or obstetrician. No question is "dumb," so ask! You may want to make sure your partner is present when you ask a question. It's always good to have two sets of ears at such an exciting and stressful time as this is.

✻ *Circumcision*

As parents, you may decide to have your son circumcised, which means the foreskin of his penis is removed by a surgical technique. This is usually performed at the hospital as a surgical procedure, or a clamping device may be used to remove the foreskin. However, if you are Jewish or Muslim, it may be done as part of a religious ceremony, outside of the hospital.

Today, about 65% of all male babies are circumcised—in the 1970s, that number was as high as 80%. It is not unusual today for a couple to decide *not* to have their son circumcised.

Other than for religious purposes, infant boys are circumcised for two reasons. First, many couples don't want their son to look different from his father or other boys his age at school. The second reason is health related, including reducing urinary-tract infections (UTIs) in the first year of baby's life and reducing a man's chances of developing cancer or contracting syphilis or HIV in later life. The reduction in UTIs falls from 1 in a 100 for an uncircumcised male to 1 in 1000 for a circumcised infant during baby's first year.

The American Academy of Pediatrics (AAP) has taken a neutral stand on circumcision. They have concluded there is no right or wrong answer to the question. The association believes the decision is up to the parents and is based on medical reasons and cultural and religious beliefs. However, the AAP does state that pain relief is essential when a newborn is circumcised. Various techniques are available and recommended, including dorsal penile nerve block, the subcutaneous ring block or a topical anesthetic cream.

Risks with the procedure are minor and include some bleeding and local infection. The wound usually heals in about 10 days.

If you decide to have your son circumcised, performing the surgery at this early age will have little effect on him. (Postponing it until later years can be significantly more painful and can carry higher risks.) If your son was born prematurely, you may be able to have him circumcised before he leaves the hospital. However, some doctors prefer to wait until he is a few weeks older to perform this procedure. The doctor in the neonatal intensive-care unit (NICU) will advise you.

If you decide not to have the procedure performed, your child will not be the only child who is uncircumcised as he grows up. Statistically, about ⅓ of his male friends and acquaintances will also be uncircumcised. Circumcision requires surgical permission from you and your partner; it won't be done without your consent.

When you meet with your pediatrician before baby's birth, circumcision may be a subject you want to cover. If you don't have that opportunity, you can always discuss it before baby leaves the hospital.

✣ *Dislocated Hips*

Dislocation of a baby's hip(s) occurs more often in baby girls and in babies delivered in the breech position. About 1 in 60 newborns are affected; 85% of these are girls.

When your baby is examined by the pediatrician in the hospital, his hips are checked to see that the upper leg bone (femur) fits in the hip socket (pelvic bone). A "hip click" (a clicking sound) may be heard when the legs are pulled apart. Skin folds on the buttocks may not be symmetrical or one leg may appear shorter than the other. If left uncorrected, he may limp when he begins to walk.

Today, surgery is rarely required to correct the problem. Splints are usually used for a few months, sometimes called *pillow* or *diaper* splints; they keep the hips widely separated. It's like wearing three or four diapers at one time. In some cases, plaster splints (like a cast) or braces are used. In most cases, the problem is corrected before the end of the first year.

> Being a new parent can be overwhelming—there's a lot to do and to learn! Make an effort to read about the next week of your baby's development at a preset time, such as on Sunday night after baby goes to bed. In that way, you may be a little more prepared for what lies ahead in the week that follows.

If Your Baby Is Premature

Over 475,000 babies are born prematurely in the United States every year. *Premature birth* is defined as birth before 37 weeks of gestation (pregnancy). However, we see babies born very early; some come into the world as early as 23 or 24 weeks of gestation. And the incredible thing is that they often survive! At this time, a baby born at 28 weeks has a 90% chance of living–45 years ago, he wouldn't have had a 50% chance of surviving.

Premature birth occurs for a number of reasons that we can determine, including multiple babies, placental problems or pre-eclampsia in the mother, early labor that cannot be stopped and illness in the baby. However, for nearly 50% of all premature births, the cause is unknown.

If your baby is born prematurely, you may not be prepared for the event. You may feel sad if you go home without your baby. You may be angry that everything didn't turn out perfectly. Don't be too hard on yourself or your partner. Be thankful you are able to take care of your baby so he will get a good start in life.

✣ *Baby's Care*

When a baby is born prematurely, often called a *preemie,* the type of care he receives depends on how early he was born. Some babies are not extremely early, and they won't require the extensive care other babies will. Babies born closer to term may need some stabilization before they are moved to the infant nursery, but they are often soon on their way to going home.

Other babies need extensive care and will not be able to go home for weeks or months. The rule of thumb is that the earlier a baby is born, the longer he will need care.

All premature babies are individuals. Your baby will be evaluated and tended to based on his unique needs.

Immediate Care for Your Newborn.   When your baby is born prematurely, many things can happen very quickly. A preemie needs more care than a full-term baby; much of the care is necessary because his body cannot take over and perform some of his normal body functions. If baby is having difficulty breathing, the nursing staff will help him with his breathing, which can be done in many ways. Immediately after delivery, your baby may be helped in any of the following ways.

* A hood (a large translucent plastic box) may be placed over baby's head to provide additional oxygen if he needs it.
* A bag and mask may be used if baby is not breathing on his own.
* A continuous positive airway pressure (CPAP; pronounced *CEE-pap*) device may be used. It is a two-pronged tube that fits in baby's nose to provide uninterrupted pressure to baby's lungs.
* A dose of surfactant may be administered to help his lungs work more effectively.
* A UAC (umbilical artery catheter) may be inserted in an artery in the umbilicus (umbilical-cord site) to measure blood pressure, to take blood samples and to give medications.
* An I.V. may be inserted into a vein for administration of medication.
* An endo-tracheal (ET) tube may be placed if baby needs to be on a ventilator.

After baby is tended to in the delivery room, he will be moved to the infant care nursery or to a special neonatal care unit for further treatment, evaluation and care. See the discussion that follows.

✎ *Your Baby's First "Home"*
If your baby needs wide-ranging, in-depth care, he will be moved to the neonatal intensive-care unit, also called the NICU (pronounced *NICK-U*). If your hospital does not have this special unit, your baby may be transferred to another hospital that has a NICU and services to care for him.

The nurses and physicians who work in these units have received specialized education and training so they may care for preemies. A *neonatologist* is a pediatrician who specializes in diagnosis and treatment of problems in newborns. *Neonatal nurses* are registered nurses who have received additional, special training in caring for premature and high-risk newborns. You will meet these professionals in the NICU. In addition, you may also meet and work with pediatric nutrition specialists, lactation consultants, neonatal respiratory therapists and social workers. All are there to help you and your baby.

If you cannot be at the hospital all the time due to other responsibilities or distance or some other factor, call the NICU to check on baby. Most NICU staffs welcome it. You may hesitate because you believe you are bothering them. In most cases, they encourage parents to be involved and to contact them. Ask about it at one of your visits to baby.

Seeing Baby for the First Time. The first time you see your baby for any length of time may be after he has been moved to the NICU. You may be overwhelmed when you see him. All the monitors and equipment can be scary and intimidating. However, be assured that they are all being used to help give your baby what he needs to grow and to continue to develop.

You may be amazed by the size of your baby. The earlier he was born, the smaller he will be. Most preemies don't have much fat on their bodies—a baby usually gains fat during the last few weeks of your pregnancy. When baby comes early, he hasn't had a chance to gain this extra weight. Without the fat, he will need help staying warm. Your baby may be in a warmer or isolette to help him maintain his body temperature. He may be unclothed, without blankets, so the nurses can watch his breathing and body movements more closely.

Baby may have a lot more body hair than you expected. This is called *lanugo*. His skin may look thin and fragile, and it may be wrinkled. Wrinkling is due to the fact he has not gained much fat; he's not as plump and round as a full-term baby.

Become Involved with Baby. As soon as you are able to visit the NICU and spend time with baby, personnel will encourage you to become physically involved with him. In the early days, you may not be able to hold your baby, but you may be able to touch him or to stroke him gently.

As time passes and baby matures, you will probably be able to hold him. You will also be encouraged to care for him, such as changing him and feeding him. Information on feeding can be found on page 28.

When you are with baby, talk softly to him. You may be surprised how quickly he will recognize your voice and respond to you. Your love and attention are important to baby's physical development and to his psychological growth. Lots of contact with your baby helps him grow and thrive.

Massage for Preemies. In various cultures, vigorous massage is common for a newborn. Some researchers believe these babies develop certain abilities at an earlier age than usual because massage is a part of their daily routine. Massage stimulates respiration, circulation, digestion and elimination, and it helps babies sleep more soundly. Experts believe massage relieves gas and colic, and it also helps the healing process by easing congestion and pain.

For a premature baby, medical experts believe massage therapy can help in many ways. In fact, studies show nearly 75% of preemies who were massaged gained more weight and performed better with developmental tasks. One study showed that massaged infants gained nearly 50% more weight than those who were not massaged.

Babies who were massaged were also awake and active for longer periods. They scored better on various scales and left the hospital 6 days sooner than babies who were not massaged!

If you find this technique interesting and want to try it with your baby, talk to the nurses in the NICU. They will know various techniques to use and can suggest what might work best for your baby.

Kangaroo Care. When you are able to hold baby, nurses may encourage you to offer kangaroo care. *Kangaroo care* is skin-to-skin contact that is good for baby in many ways. This technique is very effective in keeping baby's body temperature normal. In fact, studies have shown that a mother's body temperature adjusts to keep baby's temperature at the right degree. Baby's breathing also becomes more even, and his heart rate and blood oxygen levels remain steady when held in the kangaroo position.

You are encouraged to hold your unclothed baby (he'll have a diaper on) against your bare chest. The personnel in the NICU can offer you some sort of privacy in which to do this.

Both mom and dad can offer this care. This type of contact helps you both bond with baby. It has also been shown to improve parenting abilities because parents become more attuned to their baby's cues.

Kangaroo care is also very important for your baby. Studies show that premature babies who are held this way for an hour or more every day were more alert and maintained eye contact better as they matured.

↣ Inside the NICU

You'll see many pieces of equipment and various machines in the unit. All are there to help provide the best care possible for your baby. Monitors record various information, ventilators help baby breathe, lights warm baby or help treat jaundice. Even baby's bed may be unique.

Equipment in the NICU is made specially for premature babies to take care of their special needs. For example, ventilators provide a smaller volume of air with each breath. Beds may contain radiant warmers to help maintain a baby's body temperature.

NICUs provide constant monitoring and round-the-clock care. They are the best chance a preemie has to develop and to grow so that he can be released from the hospital and go home.

The neonatologist and NICU nurses will determine what kind of care and treatment baby needs, including the type of equipment that will best help him. Various pieces of NICU equipment and what each is used for include:

* **ventilator**—machine that helps baby breathe through a tube inserted into his throat
* **blood-pressure monitors**—small inflatable cuffs attached to baby's arm to record blood pressure
* **cardiorespiratory monitors**—sensors that keep track of baby's breathing and heart rate
* **oxygen saturation monitor or pulse oximeters**—sensor that monitors amount of oxygen in baby's blood; attached to the foot or hand
* **feeding tube**—plastic tube passed through the nose or mouth to help baby feed
* **overhead warmer**—lights mounted overhead or on stands that can be moved; used to keep baby warm
* **temperature monitor**—sensor attached to baby to measure body temperature
* **bilirubin lights**—lights for phototherapy; used to treat jaundice
* **I.V. lines and/or pumps**—intravenous lines placed in baby's veins to deliver medication, nutrients or liquids
* **snugglies**—device used to maintain fetal position and make infant comfortable
* **umbilical-artery catheter**—catheter inserted in an artery in the umbilicus to measure blood pressure, to take blood samples and to give medications

Feeding Your Preemie

Feeding is very important for a premature baby. In fact, a baby being able to feed on his own for all of his feedings may be one of the milestones the baby's doctor looks for when considering when to release a baby.

Premature babies often have digestive problems. They need to be fed small amounts at a feeding, so they must be fed often. Special preemie bottles and nipples must be used. Babies tire easily, and they need to learn to suck or to practice sucking. Feeding your preemie may be a time-consuming task, but it's worth it when you see him begin to grow.

For the first few days or weeks after birth, a premature baby is most often fed intravenously for two reasons. The first is that when a baby is premature, he often does not have the ability to suck and to swallow, so he cannot breastfeed or bottlefeed. Second, his gastrointestinal system is too immature to absorb nutrients. Feeding him by I.V. gives him the nutrition he needs in a form he can digest.

Tube Feeding.   When baby matures somewhat, the I.V. feedings will cease, and he will have a feeding tube inserted. It is used until he gains enough strength and maturity to nurse or to take a bottle. Tube feeding is often called *gavage feeding.*

Tubes are made of soft, pliable plastic. Different tubes have been designed to deliver food by various pathways directly to baby's tummy or upper intestine. Each tube has its own name, which indicates the route and the destination, and include:

* OG tube—this tube goes through the mouth, down the esophagus, into baby's tummy
* NG tube—tube goes through the nose to the stomach
* OD tube—this tube goes through the mouth to the duodenum, the part of the small intestine into which baby's stomach empties
* OJ tube—tube goes through the mouth to the jejunum, which is farther past the duodenum

When baby is tube fed, he will receive fortified breast milk or high-calorie preemie formula through the tube. Once baby's gastrointestinal system demonstrates it can absorb nutrients, the amount will be increased, and he may also be offered a bottle or given the opportunity to breastfeed.

The end goal is to have baby breastfeeding or bottlefeeding for every feeding. This accomplishment is a major one.

How quickly your baby moves from one form of feeding to another depends on his strength, maturity and growth. Even though he may be able to take some feedings from the breast or a bottle, he may be given supplemental feedings because he tires quickly and can't get all the nourishment he needs from the breast or a bottle. That's why you may see a baby who is feeding from a bottle also has a feeding tube.

Baby may be offered a preemie-sized nipple or pacifier. These encourage development of his sucking and swallowing reflexes. They can also help soothe baby when he is fussy.

Breast Milk Is Best for Premature Babies.   Babies in NICU feed as often as every hour, although time between feedings may range from 1 to 3 hours. If you are going to breastfeed baby, you will need to supply breast milk for that purpose. Pumping may be the answer. Studies have shown that any amount of breast milk is beneficial for a preemie, so seriously consider this important task.

Two nutrients present in breast milk are extremely beneficial to preemies. DHA and ARA are two fatty acids important in baby's brain development and eye development. However, premature infants miss out on these important nutrients in the womb because they are born early. If you cannot breastfeed, ask the NICU nurses if your baby will be fed a special preemie formula that contains these nutrients.

The composition of your breast milk when your baby is born prematurely is different from the milk when baby is full term. Because of this difference, baby may also be supplemented with formula that contains extra protein, carbohydrates, sodium, folic acid, calcium, iron, phosphorous and vitamins A, D and E. In addition, these nutrients may be in a form that is easily digested and absorbed by baby. You may be advised to use similar formula when you take baby home.

Most preemies need about 55 calories per pound of body weight. If they cannot get all the nutrition they need from breast milk, they may be supplemented with formula developed especially for preemies.

✎ Problems Some Preemies May Have

When a baby is born prematurely, he hasn't had time to finish growing and developing inside the womb. Being born too early can impact on baby's health in many ways. Many of the problems a premature baby encounters pass quickly; some take longer to correct. Some are lifelong. In addition, some problems appear rapidly; others develop weeks or months after birth. In some cases, they are not evident until a child starts school. Today, with all the medical and technological advances medicine has made in the care of premature babies, we are fortunate that many children have few, or no, long-term difficulties.

Research has shown that the earlier a baby is born, the greater the chance of him having problems. It's not uncommon for extremely premature infants to have more problems than infants who were born later. Risks for the very premature infant are still very high. However, researchers continue to explore new ways of treating premature babies and increasing their quality of life.

After baby is discharged from the hospital and you take him home, you may be advised to keep him away from germs as much as possible. His immune system is immature and needs time to develop. That may mean staying away from crowds, keeping baby inside and not allowing too many people to hold him. You may also be asked to take your baby to the pediatrician weekly for weight checks.

Your baby may have diverse problems after birth and in the course of his life. He may experience anemia, hearing or vision problems, feeding and growth problems, and problems breathing. He may have developmental delays and/or learning disabilities that do not become evident for quite a while.

Some problems are discussed below. Some are short term; others may need to be dealt with for the rest of the child's life.

Jaundice. Jaundice is a condition in which the liver cannot get rid of bilirubin, the product of used red blood cells. It is more common in premature babies than in full-term babies. A premature baby's liver is less mature than a full-term baby's, so often it cannot process bilirubin effectively. Thus it builds up in baby's body, turning skin and sclera (the whites of the eyes) a yellow color.

If your baby has jaundice, he may be given phototherapy. He may be placed under a bilirubin light in the NICU. If he is treated with phototherapy, he may have to wear special goggles or eye patches to protect his eyes. Phototherapy may be administered for 7 to 10 days.

Apnea. Apnea is defined as a pause in breathing. Preemies typically have irregular breathing rhythms. They often breathe in spurts—a period of deep breathing followed by a shorter period of 5- to 10-second pauses. This is called *periodic breathing.*

If the period of pauses lasts longer than 10 or 15 seconds, baby is said to be having an *A/B spell. A* is for apnea (a pause in breathing); *B* is for bradycardia (slow heartbeat). This apneic episode may trigger alarms on baby's monitoring devices. After an A/B spell, baby's breathing and heart rate often return to normal spontaneously.

If baby experiences frequent A/B spells, the neonatologist may prescribe medication to help regulate breathing. He or she may also suggest an apnea monitor for baby to wear or to sleep on when he goes home, if he continues to suffer from the problem.

Important note: A baby that is at risk for apnea should always sleep in his own bed. Do not allow him to sleep with you or to sleep in a family bed!

Respiratory Distress Syndrome (RDS). RDS is a breathing problem caused by immature lungs in a premature baby. In the past, this condition was called *hyaline-membrane disease.* Lungs lack surfactant, which gives them the elastic qualities needed for easy breathing.

Doctors are able to diagnose RDS shortly after birth. Diagnosis is based on how much breathing trouble baby is having and a chest X-ray.

Treatment includes supplemental breaths. A baby with RDS is often put on a ventilator, also called a *respirator,* that gives him these extra breaths.

Some babies also need CPAP; a plastic tube fitted into the nostrils provides pressure to keep tiny air sacs in the lungs inflated.

If your baby has RDS, he will be monitored very closely. He will probably wear an oximeter or saturation monitor to indicate the level of oxygen in his blood. He may also have frequent blood tests to measure carbon dioxide, oxygen and pH levels in his blood to determine how well he is breathing. These tests will indicate whether any changes are necessary.

Broncho-Pulmonary Dysplasia (BPD).   If your baby requires a ventilator or supplemental oxygen a month after birth, he is considered to have BPD. Medication may be used to help with his breathing. He may also need supplemental oxygen for a prolonged time.

If your baby has BPD, take care to keep him from getting exposed to germs. If he develops a bad cold or pneumonia, he may need a ventilator.

A baby with BPD may need supplemental oxygen when he goes home, especially if you live at a high altitude. As he grows and matures, his breathing should become easier. However, children who experience BPD early in life may be more prone to asthma and episodes of wheezing.

Undescended Testicles.   The incidence of undescended testicles is higher in premature baby boys than it is in full-term baby boys. Testicles normally descend about 2 months before birth. If a baby is born before that time (before 32 weeks of gestation), his testicles may not have descended. Sometimes hormones are used to bring the testicle into place. If it has not descended by the time baby is 15 months old, surgery may be required. Left untreated, the condition can cause infertility.

Patent Ductus Arteriosus (PDA).   Before birth, baby doesn't use his lungs in the womb, so a blood vessel, called the *ductus arteriosus,* reroutes blood away from the lungs. In addition, the fetus manufactures a chemical called *prostaglandin E,* which helps keep the ductus arteriosus open. At birth, levels of prostaglandin E drop, the ductus arteriosus closes and blood is sent to the lungs.

In a premature baby, prostaglandin E levels may not drop, and the baby continues to produce it. This keeps the ductus arteriosus open, which can cause breathing difficulties.

Your doctor may treat baby with medication to stop the production of prostaglandin E. If medication does not work, surgery may be required.

Intracranial Hemorrhage (ICH).   When a baby is born earlier than 34 weeks of gestation, he is at greater risk for bleeding into his brain. This is called *intracranial hemorrhage* (ICH) or *intraventricular hemorrhage* (IVH). The earlier a baby is born, the higher the risk. If a baby has ICH or IVH, he is at risk for developing problems later in life, such as cerebral palsy, spasticity and mental retardation.

Bleeding most often occurs within the first 72 hours after baby's birth. Ultrasound is used to examine the baby's head to determine if bleeding has occurred.

If an episode of ICH or IVH is mild, no treatment is necessary. Your baby will be observed closely by those in the NICU. For more severe cases, treatment will be ordered. The type of treatment will be determined by your physician.

Retinopathy of Prematurity (ROP). Fifty years ago, some very premature babies who survived had severe vision impairment; some were even blind. The problem was called *retrolental fibroplasia.* It was believed to be caused by the use of oxygen. Today, we have a better understanding of the problem and now call it *retinopathy of prematurity.* The problem is most common in very premature babies. It's uncommon for babies born after 33 or 34 weeks of gestation to have it.

When a baby is born early, retinal development of the eye is incomplete. ROP occurs when the delicate retina development is disturbed because baby is born too early.

If personnel in the NICU believe your baby may be at risk for ROP, an ophthalmologist who specializes in premature babies can examine your baby after he is 6 weeks old. Most cases of ROP are mild and resolve on their own. If the problem is more severe, treatment with cryotherapy may be necessary.

We are fortunate that retinal detachment and blindness are uncommon today. ROP mainly affects only the very smallest, unstable preemies.

Respiratory Syncytial Virus (RSV). RSV often begins as a cold; it can develop into pneumonia or bronchiolitis. See *Week 12* for a complete discussion of RSV. The problem can arise quickly, so call your pediatrician immediately if baby develops wheezing and/or rapid breathing with a cold, once he is home.

Because there is no medication available to treat the problem, prevention is key. Keep baby away from crowds, and wash hands frequently during the cold season (winter and early spring). In addition, talk with your pediatrician about protective immunizations.

✻ Taking Baby Home

At some point, you will be able to take your baby home. If you have more than one baby, you may take them home separately, when each gains sufficient weight and is feeding well enough to leave the hospital. It's hard not to be able to take them home together, at the same time. Some babies need more time in the hospital because of complications. However, you can look forward to the day you'll all be together.

Your baby will be ready to go home when he:

* has no medical problems that require him to be in the hospital
* can maintain a stable body temperature
* can take all of his feedings on his own (no tube feeding)
* is gaining weight

This can be a wonderful experience, but it may also cause you some concern. Will you be able to meet his needs? Will you be able to care for him?

The people in the NICU will help you prepare for this important event. Many NICUs let you room in with baby just before you take him home. It's a great opportunity to take care of baby on your own while you have the nursing staff at hand. The personnel in the NICU can help you plan any special care needs before you take your baby home. Once home, most preemies do well.

When you are home, ask your partner to help you and to share the responsibility of parenting. Ask for help—or accept it—from others who offer it, including family, friends and neighbors. You'll be glad you did.

Preemie Equipment You May Want to Consider.   Your lives will be different when you take your preemie home. It's not the same as bringing a full-term baby home. You may need different equipment or not need some equipment yet. Your schedule may be very hectic because you have to feed baby more often. You may have your hands full tending to your baby and any other children you have.

For baby's first trip home and for future trips in the car, you may want to consider a car bed. This device allows baby to lie flat. This position is often better for preemies because they may have trouble breathing in a normal-size car seat. Or you may want to consider Cosco's Ultra Dream Ride; it's a car bed for preemies as small as 5 pounds. It converts to a rear-facing car seat that you can use until baby is 20 pounds. See the *Resources* section, page 527, for further information.

If you didn't get one in the hospital, consider buying a couple of preemie pacifiers. There are many on the market. This type of pacifier fits baby's tiny mouth more comfortably.

You're going to need preemie diapers. They are designed for premature babies weighing between 1 and 6 pounds. Disposable preemie diapers are adjustable (they have an expandable back panel) and have the narrowest crotch of any diaper available to allow for proper leg positioning. They are also absorbent and can absorb up to 2½ ounces or 5 tablespoons of liquid. If you want to use cloth diapers, ask at the hospital about where you can purchase them. If you are planning to use a diaper service, call the company and ask if they supply preemie diapers.

As for clothing, you may want to wait to buy a lot of clothes for baby, other than essentials, such as gowns that are open at the bottom, T-shirts or one-piece sleepers. As baby starts to grow, he'll probably grow quickly and will soon be out of these very small clothes.

✂ *Mental and Physical Development of Your Baby*
Your baby will go through many developmental stages. There are many things you can do as parents to help your baby reach important milestones. See the discussion of *Development of Your Premature Baby* in *Week 6.*

36

BABY'S IMMUNIZATION SCHEDULE

❋ *Birth*   *Date*
Hepatitis B–first shot _____
Vitamin K–only one shot _____

❋ *2 months*   *Date*
DTaP: diphtheria, tetanus and pertussis–first shot _____
Polio–first shot _____
Hib: influenza, type b–first shot _____
Hepatitis B–second shot _____

❋ *4 months*   *Date*
DTaP: diphtheria, tetanus and pertussis–second shot _____
Polio–second shot _____
Hib: influenza, type b–second shot _____

❋ *6 months*   *Date*
DTaP: diphtheria, tetanus and pertussis–third shot_____
Polio–third shot _____
Hib: influenza, type b–third shot _____

❋ *12 months*   *Date*
Varicella: chicken pox–first shot_____
MMR: measles, mumps, rubella–first shot_____
Hib–fourth shot _____

❋ *15 months*   *Date*
Hepatitis B–third shot _____
DTaP: diphtheria, tetanus and pertussis–fourth shot_____

❋ *4 years*   *Date*
MMR: measles, mumps, rubella–second shot_____
Polio–fourth shot _____

❋ *5 years*   *Date*
DTaP: diphtheria, tetanus and pertussis–fifth shot _____

Week 1

The information we provide in this section each week is based on *average* expected growth for a baby. Your baby may grow a little more or a little less in a given week. If your baby is born small, growth may be less than what we indicate. The same holds true if your baby is large; her growth may be faster or she may gain more weight. There's also a difference in size (and sometimes the rate of growth) between boys and girls.

The point of providing this information is to help you determine if your baby is growing and putting on weight at a steady pace. It's important to remember that if your baby is born prematurely, her weight gain and growth may be delayed but she will usually catch up by age 2.

Growth changes we cite here are based on a full-term baby weighing 7 pounds who is 20 inches long.

Baby Care and Equipment

✻ *Umbilical-Cord Care*

Almost every baby goes home from the hospital with a stump of umbilical cord still attached to her body. It takes from 7 to 10 days for it to heal and fall off. Until then, keep the area clean and dry to promote healing.

You don't have to do much in the way of care. When you change baby's diaper, wipe the cord with a cotton ball dipped in alcohol. Fold the diaper top down to make sure it doesn't rub against the stump. Change baby as soon as she is wet to further reduce irritation.

✻ *Penis Care for Circumcised and Uncircumcised Boys*

After the circumcision, you may notice your son's penis is a little red, and there may be a yellow secretion. Both are signs the incision is healing. Keep the area clean. Put a little petroleum jelly on the tip of the penis each time you change his diaper.

It should heal within a week; however, if you notice any swelling or sores, call your doctor. He or she may suggest using mild antibiotic gels or advise you to clean the area more often. Sometimes ice or a cold pack is used, but do this *only* when directed to do so by your doctor.

If your son is not circumcised, gently pull back the foreskin of his penis each time you change his diapers. Using warm water and a mild baby soap, wash the area thoroughly.

✄ *Feeding Your Baby*

Feeding your baby is one of the most important things you do for her. You'll know when she's hungry; she'll exhibit definite signs of hunger, including fussing, putting her hands in her mouth and turning her head and opening her mouth when her cheek is touched.

Most newborns eat every 3 to 4 hours, although some feed as often as every 2 hours. You may feed at regular intervals to help your baby get on a schedule. Or you may decide to let your baby set her own schedule—some babies need to eat more often than others. At times, a baby needs to feed more often than usual, such as during periods of growth.

A baby is usually the best judge of how much she needs at each feeding. She'll usually turn away from the nipple (mother or bottle) when she's full.

It's a good idea to burp your baby after each feeding. Some babies need to be burped during a feeding. See the discussion of *Burping* in *Week 2*.

Babies frequently spit up some breast milk or formula after a feeding. It's common in the early months because the muscle at the top of the stomach is not fully developed. When a baby spits up enough to propel the stomach contents several inches, it is called *vomiting*. If your baby vomits after a feeding, don't feed her again immediately. Her tummy may be upset; wait until the next feeding.

Many believe that breastfeeding is the best way to feed baby. Breast milk contains every nutrient a baby needs, and it's easily digested. Research has found that breastfed babies have lower rates of infection because of the immunological content of breast milk. Breastfeeding provides the baby a sense of security and the mother a sense of self-esteem. See the discussion of *Breastfeeding* in *Week 2*.

If there are reasons you cannot or choose not to breastfeed your baby, be assured she will do well on formula. It won't harm her if you don't breastfeed. No mother should feel guilty if she doesn't breastfeed her baby. An infant can still get all the love, attention and nutrition she needs if breastfeeding is not possible. See the discussion of *Bottlefeeding* in *Week 3*.

✣ *Picking Up and Handling Baby*

If you're like most first-time parents, the thought of handling your baby fills you with trepidation. She's such a tiny, delicate being. You want to be sure you pick her up correctly, and you don't want to drop her. Rest easy—she's not as fragile as you think. There are ways to handle her so you'll both feel confident. *Always* support her head with your hand or arm, and keep an arm or hand under her back. You may hold her close or a little more loosely. Use smooth motions when moving her, and always protect her head with your arm or hand.

When you hold her or if you wear her in a sling or front carrier, do so *only* when you are doing something that could not harm her. *Never* cook over a hot stove or handle hot or caustic liquids while holding baby. Don't smoke when you hold baby, and don't let others smoke when they hold her.

Never shake your baby—shaking can result in "shaken baby syndrome." This causes bleeding and bruising of the brain, injury to the eyes and damage to the spinal cord. See the discussion of *Shaken Baby Syndrome* in *Week 17.*

✣ *Diapering Baby*

Changing your baby's diapers is a necessary task; once you get the hang of it, you'll be able to do it quickly and efficiently. Many men are even capable of learning this skill!

Change baby's diapers whenever she's wet or soiled to prevent irritation and diaper rash. A newborn wets between 6 and 10 times a day. Bowel movements are more variable; some babies poop two or three times a day, others only every few days. Whether your baby is breastfed or bottlefed may also make a difference in her bowel movements.

A Quick Method to Change Baby. Try this method for changing baby; it's quick and easy. Lay baby on the changing table; strap her in or keep your hand on her tummy. Undo pins or diaper tabs, and gently lift her ankles. (You can do this with one hand.) With your other hand, wipe any feces into the dirty diaper and put it to the side. Using baby wipes or wet cotton balls, clean the genitals; with a girl, wipe from front to back to avoid contaminating the vaginal area, which could cause a urinary-tract infection. Let her air dry for a bit, or dry her with a soft washcloth. Slide a clean diaper under her as you again lift her ankles. Fasten diaper with pins or tabs, and adjust leg openings so there are no gaps.

You don't need to clean baby with baby wipes if she has only a wet diaper. Urine is germ free; using a baby wipe every time you change her could be irritating. If possible, let her "air out" (go without a diaper for a while) between diaper changings. It helps reduce the risk of diaper rash.

Folding a diaper then positioning it
under baby's bottom.

❧ Dressing Your Baby

One of the most challenging tasks for a new parent is dressing baby. It's not like dressing a baby doll—baby dolls don't wiggle and squirm! But there are a few tricks we can pass along to help make your first attempts a little easier. Our best advice is to take it slow, and don't get frustrated. With practice, you'll soon be an expert!

After you've diapered baby, put on her undershirt. Hold the shirt neck open with your fingers, and slip it over her head. Reach into the end of one sleeve, grasp her hand and gently pull it through. Adjust the body of the shirt once you've got both arms in. When you put her pants on, first reach through the bottom leg opening and grasp one foot. Slide it through the opening, then do the same for her other foot. Once both feet are through the leg openings, pull pants up to her waist.

If you're putting on overalls, we've found sliding them on from the bottom works best. Adjust them, snap the legs, then hook the straps. With a sleeper or one-piece outfit that opens down the front, lay it down on the changing table, then lay baby on top of it. Slide baby's arms, one at a time, through the sleeves, adjust, then slip baby's feet through the openings. When everything's in place, snap the snaps or zip up.

A word of advice: When changing your newborn, keep the room warm. A small baby can get cold quite quickly when undressed.

✴ *Swaddling Your Infant*

Before her birth, your baby was in a pretty tight environment, with little room to move. When she's born, the lack of confinement may make her feel a little insecure. *Swaddling,* wrapping her snugly in a soft blanket, can help if she seems discontented. It can help make her feel secure and comfort her. In fact, research shows that swaddled babies (under 3 months of age) are less restless and don't startle as easily as babies who are not swaddled. Swaddling also helps a baby sleep well on her back. She may wake up less often and sleep longer when she is swaddled.

Wrap baby snugly in a blanket to comfort her; arms may be wrapped or left free.

Lay a blanket (a square receiving blanket works well) on a flat surface in a diamond shape. You can fold the top down inside or leave it up, if it's cold and you want to protect baby's head. You may want to use a "swaddling blanket," a special blanket designed to swaddle baby. Many different types are available. Check local stores if you are interested.

Place baby on the blanket, with her head at the top of the diamond, and place her arms by her face or her side. Some babies are comforted when their hands are left by their faces—this is often the case with a premature baby.

Fold the top-left edge of the blanket across her body, pulling it taut. Tuck excess material under her back. Bring the bottom corner of the blanket up over her body. Some babies like their legs tucked into a fetal position; others don't. Fold the top-right edge of the blanket across her body, and tuck excess material under her back. She can be laid in her crib in this manner, or you can hold her. Be sure her chest and arms can't move easily, but don't swaddle her so tightly that it affects her breathing.

Changes You May See this 1ˢᵗ Week

During the first year of life, your baby grows and changes according to stages of development. The four most important developmental categories include the following.

* Motor Development—Your baby's large and small muscle groups develop dramatically this first year. At this time she moves very little, yet by the end of 12 months, she will be walking or ready to walk!
* Language Development—Development of language includes her speech and her attempts to listen to and to understand language around her.
* Intellectual Development—As your baby's brain grows, her thinking skills develop.
* Social Development—Social skills she learns help your baby relate to the world around her.

As the weeks and months pass, your baby will move from one learning task to another, and her focus will shift when this happens. Don't worry if she seems to be slow in one area for a while; it's her overall development you are concerned with.

At birth, your baby's brain is not fully developed, and a great deal of growth must still occur. A baby's brain grows most rapidly from the last trimester of pregnancy through the first 3 months of life.

✻ *Baby's Sight*

From the moment your newborn opens her eyes after birth, she can see her world, although it is a bit fuzzy. She is nearsighted; her best field of vision is about 8 to 12 inches away from her. She will stare at objects placed in this range of her vision. She can also tell the difference between a human face and other objects—she prefers faces. (If the baby is smiling at you at this point, it's probably gas.)

✻ *A Newborn's Hearing*

Your baby hears most noises in the first few weeks as echoes, not distinct sounds. However, she hears voices; she recognizes her mother's voice at or shortly after birth and will soon recognize the voices of other people around her. Speak to her often, about everything, to help develop her hearing and help her begin to relate to language. A baby can't learn to talk or begin to understand the subtle nuances of language if she doesn't hear a lot of conversation.

✻ *Other Newborn Development*

Many babies are quiet and alert for a few days after birth, then they start crying. This is normal—crying is the only way baby can communicate with you!

Soothing a crying or fussy baby takes experimentation on your part. After all, you don't know each other very well yet, so you may need to try different tactics to help baby settle. You may find your baby calms when she is swaddled. (See the discussion on page 44.) Rocking and patting her or offering her a pacifier are other options. Some babies calm down when they listen to monotonous "white" sounds. Try different things when baby needs to be comforted.

When you snuggle and/or feed your baby, your skin-to-skin contact makes her feel secure and safe. It also provides gentle stimulation. Offer her this contact as much as possible.

When your baby is sleeping or drowsy, you may notice her smiling. She's in a dream state—her eyes may be moving at the same time. Enjoy watching her. It's a beautiful sight.

Note: See also the box *Milestones this 1ˢᵗ Week*.

What's Happening this 1ˢᵗ Week?

✻ *Some Changes You May See in Baby*

Incredible as it may seem, infants often go through a growth spurt very soon after birth. At 7 to 10 days after birth, your baby may grow in length; when you take her to the pediatrician for her first checkup, she may have grown more than you realized.

Your baby's heart rate is faster than yours; her heart beats between 100 and 150 beats a minute. When she yawns, hiccups or has a bowel movement, her heart rate may decrease. She also breathes quite rapidly—up to 50 breaths a minute. This is normal.

MILESTONES THIS 1st WEEK

Changes You May See this Week as Baby Develops Physically
- responds to sudden changes with entire body
- when startled, arches her back, kicks her legs and flails her arms
- can lift head
- moves head from side to side
- controls arm, leg and hand movements by reflex
- when baby's palms are pressed, she will open her mouth and lift head slightly up
- sleeps and wakes on a continuum
- head flops forward or backward when in sitting position
- controls swallowing and rooting by reflex
- stroking bottom of baby's foot from heel to toes causes toes to flare up and out
- sleeps between 19 and 20 hours/day
- moves bowels often and sporadically
- feeds 7 to 8 times/day

Changes You May See this Week in Baby's Developing Senses and Reflexes
- blinks at bright lights
- focuses between 8 and 12 inches away
- eyes tend to turn outward
- is sensitive to direction of sound
- hands remain fisted much of time
- distinguishes volume and pitch of sounds; prefers high-toned voices
- lifts head when on stomach or at someone's shoulder
- moves head from side to side
- distinguishes tastes—likes sweet already
- will grasp and grip something if hand accidentally strikes it

Changes You May See this Week as Baby's Mind Develops
- quiets when picked up or in response to any firm, steady pressure
- stops sucking to look at something
- shuts out disturbing stimuli by going to sleep
- makes animal-like sounds
- learns to expect food at certain times
- looks at person briefly

Changes You May See this Week in Baby's Social Development
- shows excitement and distress
- seems to respond positively to soft human voice
- becomes alert to and tries to focus on human face or voice

Every baby is an individual, and your baby may do some of these things more quickly or more slowly than another baby. If you are concerned about your baby's progress, discuss it with your healthcare provider. Also see page xiii.

Some babies don't like to cuddle; it's normal. If she stiffens and arches her back when you hold her close, hold her with her back against your chest. This may be better for her.

When she cries, you may not see tears. Her tear ducts are not yet mature enough to produce tears. Tears normally flow out of tiny openings—tear ducts—located on the inner part of the lower lid. Occasionally, a tear duct is blocked by a thin membrane, which usually opens after birth. Sometimes it doesn't, so tears don't drain. They back up in the eye. This causes mucus to form on the eyes, lashes and lids.

Most tear ducts open by the time baby is 9 months old. Until this happens, gently massage the ducts with a clean index finger. Move in a circular motion toward the nose; do this throughout the day. The gentle pressure will help open the duct.

✴ Baby and Sleep

You'll notice your baby sleeps about 16½ hours a day in these first weeks. She'll slip between waking and sleeping with little regard for day or night and will eat every 2 to 4 hours. In another 6 to 8 weeks, she'll sleep longer at night and will be awake more during the day. Exposing her to daylight during the day and putting her in a dark room at night to sleep help establish this pattern.

You may be given the advice by a relative, friend or someone else to put baby on her tummy so she'll sleep better. We now know that *"back is better."* **Put your baby to sleep on her back *every* time you put her down.** Why? Research has shown that with a healthy, full-term baby, sleeping on her back lowers the chance she will have problems, especially with SIDS. See the discussion of *SIDS* in *Week 8.* Studies also show that a normal baby doesn't usually have problems choking or aspirating vomit if she spits up while lying on her back because she has a well-developed gag reflex. Some babies may sleep better on their stomachs, but don't be tempted to put your baby to bed on her tummy.

Exceptions to the rule include premature babies who have breathing problems, babies with certain upper-airway problems, babies with birth defects of the nose, throat or mouth, and babies with swallowing or vomiting problems. If your baby experiences any of these, discuss the situation with her doctor.

✴ What Baby's Crying Can Mean

Crying is one of the ways your baby has to communicate with you. It's her way of telling you she's uncomfortable, hungry or needs some attention. As you get to know your baby better, you'll be able to understand what her crying means.

Don't worry about picking her up when she cries—you won't spoil her. You'll actually be building a stronger bond with her. You are teaching her that you will take care of her, and she will feel secure with you.

It may seem like baby cries a lot, but on average, she cries only about 4 hours out of every day this first week. And that is usually only 5 minutes here and 10 minutes there. By the second week, she'll only be crying about 2½ hours a day. For ways to comfort a fussy baby, see the discussion in *Week 4*.

However, if baby cries nonstop for more than 30 minutes, call her doctor. Be sure to call if her crying is accompanied by fever, vomiting, a lack of appetite or a change in her bowel movements. It could mean she is having a problem that needs to be taken care of by her doctor.

✴ Cradle Cap

Your baby may have chunks of yellow or brown waxy material on her head— this could be *cradle cap*. Also called *seborrheic dermatitis of the scalp*, it is common in newborns and infants. It usually occurs from 1 week to 12 weeks following birth but can continue until she is 6 months old. It's very common—50% of all infants get it. If your baby has cradle cap, you'll notice patches of thick scaly skin on the scalp; these may also appear in other areas of the face or at the hairline. It's not painful or itchy, but it looks cruddy.

What You Can Do at Home.   You can treat the symptoms at home with mineral oil or olive oil. Apply the oil to your baby's scalp to loosen the material enough so you can shampoo it off the scalp. Dampen your baby's scalp with water before applying the mineral oil.

It's OK to use a soft brush to remove skin patches after rubbing with lotion. Keep the area clean and dry. Don't pick at the patches because you might irritate them or infect them.

When to Call the Doctor.   There should be no signs of infection on the scalp; contact the doctor if the area seems to be infected. Call the doctor if the problem lasts longer than 8 weeks. Call if the area shows signs of oozing or pus, if the cradle cap fails to respond to the measures listed above, if the skin becomes red or scaly, or if the area becomes inflamed.

If there are signs of inflammation or redness on other parts of the body, it could indicate another problem, so be sure to call your pediatrician. This form of dermatitis may be treated by your physician with a corticosteroid lotion.

✴ Jaundice

Your baby may show signs of jaundice, also called *hyperbilirubinemia,* about 2 to 5 days after birth; it is most obvious by day 4. It's important for you to be

TROUBLE SIGNS

As a new parent, you may be unsure what is normal and what is not with your baby; you may not know when to call the doctor. Be alert to the following signs and symptoms, and call your baby's doctor if she:

❀ has difficulty breathing—if she sucks her ribs in when she breathes or if her lips look blue

❀ vomits after most feedings, especially if it is brown or green, or is ejected with force (projectile vomiting)

❀ has a fever of 100.6F or higher, measured rectally

❀ appears yellow; it could be jaundice

❀ looks and/or acts differently, such as extreme lethargy or sleepiness, is highly irritable or is very pale

Don't worry about calling the doctor—your pediatrician and his or her staff are there to help you. Your questions won't sound silly. They've probably heard any question you can think to ask many times before!

able to identify the problem. Many newborns are discharged from the hospital 36 to 48 hours after birth, so you need to be able to recognize jaundice if it is not identified before you take baby home.

In the hospital, determining the level of bilirubin in your baby's blood may involve a blood test. This can be very uncomfortable for baby (and her parents) because it must be done repeatedly. However, another test can be done—it doesn't involve pricking baby with a needle. Called the *Colormate TLc BiliTest*, a hand-held device is used to measure the yellow tinge of baby's skin. The test is 95% accurate, and results are available in minutes. If your baby must be tested for jaundice, ask if this test is available.

Symptoms of the problem include yellow appearance of the skin (caused by excessive amounts of bilirubin, a breakdown product of blood cells), which is often first seen in the face. The whites of the eyes (the sclera) may also appear yellow. The yellowness of the skin spreads to the rest of the body. Even the nail beds may appear yellow; pinch the fingernail gently and release to check for yellow discoloration.

What You Can Do at Home.   You can test baby at home, if you believe she might have jaundice. With your finger, press on her forehead or nose. The imprint should be pale in color for *every* baby, no matter what ethnic background. If it's not, let your pediatrician know. He or she can do a blood test for definitive results.

When to Call the Doctor.   Mild jaundice is not serious; follow your doctor's advice. Bili lights, also called *phototherapy,* may be used. These ultraviolet lights break down bilirubin, making it possible for it to pass from your baby's bloodstream. It also helps improve the condition if baby is feeding well because bilirubin is excreted in her bowel movements.

Call your doctor if your baby appears to be getting more yellow, or if she is not feeding well. Your pediatrician wants to know if your baby experiences any problems.

༝ *Vaginal Discharge in Girls*

After birth, your baby girl may have a vaginal discharge that is clear or white. This is caused by the excessive hormones in her body from her mother. It is rarely a problem. To take care of it, gently clean the vaginal area. The discharge should soon disappear. Call your baby's doctor if the discharge seems excessive or if the color is yellow or green.

Toys and Play this 1ˢᵗ Week

This first week of life is the beginning of a wonderful time of games and play you will share with your child for years to come. You'll find that as you get to know your baby better, games and fun will begin to present themselves. You'll make a game out of something very ordinary, and it will be a special time for you both.

༝ *Help Stimulate Her Vision*

To stimulate her vision, hold bold-patterned objects within 8 to 12 inches of her, and let her look at them. At this time, she prefers bold patterns and the contrast of black and white because she can't see the nuances of color yet.

Baby will also enjoy looking at pictures of people's faces. Cut some large pictures out of a magazine to hold in front of her. Let her gaze at them as long as she is interested. When she begins to squirm or look away, it's time to end the game.

> Throughout this book, we encourage you to talk to your baby. It's very important to do so. One study showed that a baby needs to hear 30 *million* words by the time she is 3 years old to be prepared for maximum learning when she goes to school. So talk to her as often as you can.

༝ *Talk to Her!*

Begin your journey of play and interaction with words and music. Talk to baby as often as you can; hearing your voice is what matters. Sing to her— even if you can't carry a tune! Tell her what you're doing and what's going on. Play soothing music for her when she's fussy; it may help settle her.

Week 2

Baby weighs 7¾ pounds and is 20½ inches long this week.

Baby Care and Equipment

✤ *Breastfeeding Your Baby*

A lot of women breastfeed their babies. It's the healthiest way to feed baby, and it can help create a close bond between the two of you. For many women, it's a wonderful, loving time and often completes the birth experience.

A woman's breast milk provides benefits for the baby, including nutritional development and immunological aspects that can't be duplicated by formula feeding. Breast milk provides species-specific and age-specific nutrition for your baby.

Successful breastfeeding begins at birth. Often baby is awake, alert and ready to learn to suck properly. You can usually begin breastfeeding your baby within an hour (or sooner) after birth. This provides your baby with *colostrum,* the first milk your breasts produce. Colostrum helps boost baby's immune system. Breast milk comes in 12 to 48 hours after birth.

Whether a woman breastfeeds often depends on what her partner thinks about it. Research has shown that if a woman's partner doesn't want her to breastfeed, she usually doesn't. If this is important to you but not to your partner, explain to him the health benefits for baby. Assure him he'll be able to feed baby expressed breast milk. Often a father will be supportive once he understands how positive it is for the entire family.

It's not uncommon for a woman to have some difficulties when she begins breastfeeding. Don't be discouraged if it happens to you. It takes some time to discover what works for you and your baby.

It's interesting to note that many states and the federal government have passed laws regarding breastfeeding. These laws exist to support breastfeeding mothers. See the discussion of laws regarding breastfeeding in *Week 6.*

Benefits of Breastfeeding. There are many reasons to breastfeed your baby, including getting close to him, giving him the best nutritional start you can and feeling good about how you are taking care of him.

All babies receive from their mother some protection against disease before they are born. During pregnancy, antibodies are passed from the mother to the fetus through the placenta. These antibodies circulate through the baby's blood for a few months after the baby is born. Breastfed babies continue to receive protection in the breast milk they receive. Colostrum, the first milk that comes from your breasts, is produced and secreted immediately after birth; it gives a high level of immune protection.

The American Academy of Pediatrics recommends breastfeeding exclusively for the first 6 months of baby's life. Nursing the first 4 weeks of your baby's life provides the most protection for your baby and the most beneficial hormone release to help you recover after the birth. Nursing for the first 6 months provides baby excellent nutrition and protection from illness. After 6 months, the nutrition and protection aspects are not as critical for your baby.

If you can breastfeed only a short period of time, that's OK. Try to stick with it for the first 6 months or at least for the first 4 weeks.

Preventing Infections and Other Health Advantages.   In the first 4 to 7 days after birth, protein and mineral concentrations in breast milk decrease, and water, fat and lactose increase. The composition of breast milk continues to change to match baby's nutritional needs. This includes the right balance of immune factors and nutrients. Other factors act as biologic signals for promoting growth of cells.

Breast milk contains many substances that have antimicrobial properties, which help prevent infection. Researchers believe the protein in breast milk helps jumpstart baby's immune system. Breastfed babies get fewer infections because breast milk is bacteria free and helps a newborn avoid disease. This can mean fewer visits to the doctor and hospital, which can mean you and your partner won't have to miss work to care for a sick baby.

The incidence of ear infections is significantly reduced (by almost 50%) in babies who breastfeed longer than 4 months. Nursing may help prevent diarrhea in infants, and it may inhibit the growth of bacteria that cause urinary-tract infections.

Breastfed babies are less likely to develop allergies and asthma. Studies show that babies fed only breast milk for 6 months had fewer instances of asthma, food allergies and eczema into their teen-age years.

It's nearly impossible for a baby to become allergic to his mother's breast milk, so breastfeeding may prevent milk allergies. This is important if there is a history of allergies in your family or your partner's family. The longer a baby breastfeeds, the less likely he will be exposed to substances that could cause allergy problems.

Another benefit to breastfeeding is the presence of DHA and ARA in breast milk. DHA (decosahexaenoic acid) is the primary structural fatty

DO YOU SMOKE?

If you smoke while you breastfeed, be aware that nicotine and its by-product, coti-
nine, may be found in your breast milk and in your baby's urine. Although researchers are not sure how these substances can affect your baby, it's a good
reason to stop smoking. If you can't stop smoking, keep breastfeeding. Breast
milk may help protect your baby from some of the unfavorable side effects of secondhand smoke.

acid that makes up the retina of the eye and the gray matter of the brain. ARA (arachidonic acid) is also important in baby's brain development. DHA and ARA are provided through the placenta before birth and in breast milk after birth. They are important for baby because studies have shown that a baby who has them in his diet may have a higher IQ and greater visual development.

Other breastfeeding benefits include lowering the risk of a baby develop-ing juvenile diabetes, lymphoma and Crohn's disease later in life. Baby's permanent teeth may also come in straighter.

Other Good Reasons to Breastfeed. In addition to giving your baby a great start in life, breastfeeding offers many other great benefits. These include the following.

* Breast milk is easily digested—for a preemie, it is often the best nourishment.
* When you nurse, breast milk can't get contaminated, be mixed incorrectly or be served at the wrong temperature.
* Breastfeeding can save your family money (you don't have to buy formula), and it can help society because your child's health may be better.
* It's even good for the environment! You don't have to be concerned about ecological problems, such as disposal of formula cans, bottles and bottle liners.
* Breastfeeding is an excellent way to bond with your baby. Closeness between mother and child can be established during the feeding process.

Disadvantages to Breastfeeding. Let's be honest—there are some disadvan-tages to breastfeeding. One is that breastfeeding ties you completely to the baby. Because a woman must be available when her baby is hungry, other family members may feel left out.

A mother who breastfeeds must pay careful attention to her diet—what she eats and what she avoids are important. Most substances you eat or drink (or take orally, as medication) can pass to baby in your breast milk and may cause problems. Spicy foods, cabbage, broccoli, chocolate and caffeine are some things your baby may react to when you eat them. It's a good idea to be careful about what you eat and drink while you're breastfeeding.

In addition, you may want to avoid other activities. Don't pump your own gas, avoid nail polish, don't expose yourself to paint fumes, wait until baby is weaned to get new carpeting and use cleaning products that are safe for the environment. All of these substances contain chemicals that could pass into your breast milk.

Breastfeeding should never feel like a chore—if it does, your baby will be able to sense it. If it's not enjoyable to you, you'll be less likely to bond with your baby.

DO YOU NEED HELP WITH BREASTFEEDING?

Breastfeeding can be a challenge—to start and to continue. If you need help with breastfeeding your baby, get it immediately. Ask friends and family members for their advice. Call your doctor's office or pediatrician's office; they may be able to refer you to someone knowledgeable, such as a lactation consultant. You can also look in the telephone book for the La Leche League, an organization that promotes breastfeeding. Someone from a local affiliate can give you advice and encouragement. Join a support group; other breastfeeding moms can offer advice and support.

Breastfeed with Confidence—Tips to Get Started. It's not uncommon for a woman to experience difficulty when she begins breastfeeding. Don't be discouraged if it happens to you. It takes some time to discover what works for you and your baby. There are things you can do to help make breastfeeding a success for you both. Below are some things to keep in mind as you begin nursing.

- It takes practice! Although breastfeeding is a natural way to feed baby, it takes time and practice to get the hang of it.
- Wear the right clothes. Clothes made for nursing help you feel more comfortable—buy nursing bras and tops that let you feed baby without baring all.
- Baby must be comfortable, so change him before you start. Make sure he's warm.

Three different breastfeeding positions include
tummy to tummy, the side position and the football hold.

- Hold him so he can easily reach your breast while nursing. Hold him across your chest, or lie in bed. His tummy should touch you; tuck his lower arm between your arm and your side.
- Help him latch on to your breast. Brush your nipple across his lips. When he opens his mouth, place your nipple and as much of the areola as possible in his mouth. You should feel him pull the breast while sucking, but it shouldn't hurt.
- If you experience pain, disengage baby by slipping your finger into the corner of his mouth. Gently pull down to break the suction.
- Nurse baby 5 to 10 minutes on each breast; he gets most of his milk at the beginning of the feeding. Don't rush him—it can take as long as 30 minutes for him to finish.
- Add some cover. A receiving blanket helps add privacy to your nursing experience.
- Feed your newborn on demand—this could be as many as 8 to 10 times a day or more! A baby usually cuts back to 4 to 6 times a day by the age of 4 months.
- A breastfed baby may not need burping. As you begin, burp between feedings at each breast and when baby finishes. If he doesn't burp, don't force it. He may not need to burp.
- If you see a blister on baby's lip, it is probably from sucking. It isn't painful, and you don't have to do anything for it. It'll disappear on its own.
- Between 6 weeks and 6 months, baby grows quickly. He will probably take in about 3 to 4 ounces of breast milk for each pound of weight during this time.
- Work around baby's feeding schedule. As he gets older, you'll be in tune with his schedule and you can plan outings more easily.

Breastfeeding More than One Baby. One of the greatest challenges for parents of multiples is deciding how to feed them. If you have more than one baby, you should be able to breastfeed them. You may find it a little more challenging, but many mothers have done it. You may have to be creative in your approach, but with time, you'll probably work it out quite well.

Some mothers want to breastfeed exclusively. It's an added bonus for multiples because they are usually smaller than single-birth babies, and breast milk is extremely beneficial for them. Other moms say bottlefeeding is the only way to go. Many mothers try to combine the two, and breastfeed *and* bottlefeed their babies.

Breastfeeding your babies, even if it's only for one or two feedings a day, gives them the protection from infection that breast milk provides. Research has shown that even the smallest dose of breast milk gives baby an advantage over babies only fed formula.

One of the best things you can do is to consult a lactation specialist—you're going to need some sound advice. You might want to do this *before* babies are born so you can make a plan.

If babies are early, and you can't nurse them, begin pumping! Pump from day one, and store your breast milk for the time babies are able to receive it. In addition, pumping tells the body to produce breast milk—pump and the milk will come. It just takes some time.

Breastfeeding multiples is a challenge. If you decide to try it, experiment with various situations and positions to find what works best for you. Some mothers nurse both babies at the same time. There are special cushions on the market designed to help you hold and nurse two babies at once.

Switch babies from one breast to the other at different feedings. This ensures each baby gets visual stimulation on both sides. It also helps prevent problems for you, such as engorgement in one breast if one baby isn't feeding as well as the other. By switching breasts, the demand for milk remains about the same for each breast, so breasts tend to remain equal in size.

Supplementing with formula allows your partner and others to help you feed the babies. You can breastfeed one while someone else bottlefeeds the other. Or you can nurse each one for a time, then finish the feeding with formula. In either case, someone else can help you feed the babies.

Be sure to take good care of yourself. Your attempts at breastfeeding may make you feel like a 24-hour fast-food restaurant, but you'll be giving your babies the best start in life.

Try to Get Them on the Same Schedule. One goal to work toward is getting both babies on the same schedule. One baby may be more interested in feeding than the other, but try to feed them both at the same time, when possible. Getting your babies to sleep at night at the same time allows you some rest or free time.

Medications You May Take while Breastfeeding. Be very careful with any medications you take. Although there are many situations in which medication
is beneficial for you, sometimes it can have a negative effect on baby. Take a
medication *only* when you really need it, and take it *only* as prescribed. Ask
your physician for the smallest dose possible.

Check with your pharmacist, your OB/GYN and your pediatrician to see
if it's OK to use a particular medication while breastfeeding. Ask about possible effects on the baby, so you can be alert for them. Postpone treatment,
if possible. Consider taking a medication immediately after nursing; it may
have less of an effect on the baby.

If a medication could have serious effects on your baby, you may decide
to bottlefeed for the time you must take the medication. You can maintain
your milk supply by pumping (then throwing away) your expressed milk.

Some safe medications to use during breastfeeding include the following:
* pseudoephedrine (Sudafed, Actifed)
* dextromethorphan (Benylin, Robitussin DM)
* acetaminophen (Tylenol)
* ibuprofen (Advil)
* attapulgite (Kaopectate)
* topical hydrocortisone (Cortaid)
* calamine lotion
* certirizine (Zyrtec)
* loratadine (Claritin)
* intranasal steroid spray (Flonase)
* calcium carbonate (Tums, Maalox)
* codeine
* tetracycline
* amoxicillin
* insulin
* thyroid medication
* prednisone
* most antihistamines

Avoid radioactive drugs, anticancer drugs, ergotamine (for migraines), aspirin and lithium. Be careful with herbs when you nurse. Avoid comfrey,
fennel, sage, ginseng and fenugreek. Fennel and sage used as herbs in cooking are acceptable, if they are used in small quantities.

As we've already said, most substances you eat or drink can pass to your
baby in your breast milk. Keep this in mind when you take prescription *and*
over-the-counter medication!

Is Baby Getting Enough Milk? You may be concerned about how much
breast milk your baby gets at a feeding. There are clues to look for. Watch

DO YOU TAKE ANTIDEPRESSANTS?

If you take antidepressants, your doctor may have advised you not to breastfeed. However, research has shown that some antidepressants are OK to use while nursing. If you take tricyclic antidepressants, such as *Elavil,* no ill effects have been reported on breastfeeding babies. These drugs have been in use in the United States for over 40 years. There is less information available on newer drugs, such as selective serotonin reuptake inhibitors (SSRIs), which include *Prozac.* However, studies have shown no harm to babies who nursed while their mothers took the drug. Many medical authorities believe that breastfeeding benefits outweigh the possible risks of taking antidepressants. Discuss the situation with your doctor if you have questions.

his jaws and ears while he eats—is he actively sucking? At the end of a feeding, does he fall asleep or settle down easily? Can he go 1½ hours between feedings? You'll know your baby is getting enough to eat if he:

* nurses frequently, such as every 2 to 3 hours or 8 to 12 times in 24 hours
* has 6 to 8 wet diapers and 2 to 5 bowel movements a day
* gains 4 to 7 ounces a week or at least 1 pound a month
* appears healthy, has good muscle tone and is alert and active

Some warning signs to be alert for include:

* your breasts show little or no change during pregnancy
* no engorgement after baby's birth
* no breast milk by the 5th postpartum day
* you can't hear baby gulping while he breastfeeds
* your baby loses more than 10% of his birth weight
* baby wets fewer than 6 diapers and has fewer than 2 stools a day
* baby never seems satisfied

A baby may get extra hungry at times if he is breastfed exclusively. You may notice periods of extreme hunger in your baby around 10 days, 3 weeks, 6 weeks and 3 months of age. If you need to boost your supply of breast milk, try the following.

* Nurse more often.
* Don't use bottles or pacifiers.
* Express breast milk *after* a feeding; this tells your body to produce more milk.
* Drink lots of water, and eat small meals and protein snacks throughout the day.
* If you have any concerns, discuss them with your baby's doctor or your OB/GYN.

Insufficient Milk Syndrome.   Insufficient milk syndrome is rare. In this situation, the baby becomes dehydrated because of breastfeeding problems, such as the mother's low milk supply or the baby's failure to drink enough milk. It sometimes happens when a mother has the idea that breastfeeding is the only "right" method of feeding and takes it to extremes. This woman views using a bottle as a personal failure, even when breastfeeding complications occur.

It can also happen when a mother is unable to produce enough breast milk, due to genetic defect, injury or breast surgery. However, this problem is rare.

A concern you may have is whether baby is getting enough to eat. There are clues to look for—read the list on the opposite page. They are all indications that the process is working. If you have any concerns, discuss them with your baby's doctor.

✷ *Burping Baby*

Some breastfed babies don't need to be burped. Some do. Bottlefed babies do need to be burped. But how do you do it? There are three techniques to use when burping a baby. Try them all, and use what works best for your baby. Whichever way you hold him, rub or gently pat his lower back (*not* between his shoulder blades) until he burps.

* Hold baby seated in your lap, with his head in one of your hands.
* Hold him facing you in your arms, against your chest.
* Lay him face down on your lap, supporting his head with your hand.

In addition, be sure the angle at which you hold him is correct; he should be upright. Burp baby when he needs it—you'll soon learn his cues that it's time to burp him. However, realize that burping in the middle of a feeding upsets a few babies, so don't do it if it stresses yours unless it is necessary.

If baby doesn't burp, don't try to force it. Try for a couple of minutes, then quit. He may not need to burp.

However you hold baby, rub or gently pat his back until he burps.

✴ *Sponge Bathing Baby*

Baby's umbilical stump may not have fallen off yet and may still be a little swollen. Continue to clean it by wiping it with alcohol at every diaper change. At this time, baby needs only an occasional bath. His body isn't dirty; the only area that needs consistent cleaning is his genital area, which you clean after bowel movements. In fact, bathing too often between birth and age 3 may cause a child to develop eczema or asthma! A little dirt may actually help protect baby.

A daily sponge bath for a newborn is OK. However, as your child gets older, a regular bath every other day may be best. On nonbath days, you can wash his hands, feet and face if they are grimy.

Plan to wash baby in a warm area free from drafts. Gather together your supplies before you begin. You'll need a large bath towel, a baby towel, a basin of warm water, cotton balls, baby soap and a washcloth.

Lay baby on the towel, undressed, keeping your hand on him at all times. Wash his face first; wipe each eye outward with a damp cotton ball. Use a soft washcloth to wash his face and head, then pat dry with the towel. Put a little soap on a damp washcloth, and clean his neck, torso, legs and arms. Don't overlook his fingers and toes. Wash his genital area; if your son was circumcised, use only plain water until the circumcision has healed completely. You probably don't need to shampoo his hair; cleaning with a washcloth is fine. Rinse him, then dry with a towel. Diaper and dress him.

✴ *Taking Baby Out*

You may want to take your newborn out on errands or for short visits. If you feel up to it, go ahead. Dress him for the weather—usually only one layer more than you in cold weather, the same number of layers in warm weather. Keep outings short. You'll be surprised how quickly both of you will tire or how soon he'll get hungry.

✴ *Pacifiers and Thumbs*

Your baby may need to soothe himself at times. He may choose his thumb or a pacifier. Pacifiers are OK to use with your baby; however, he may not need one. When your baby fusses, offer him a feeding and comfort him before you give him a pacifier. If your baby needs to suck, a pacifier can help.

You'll find pacifiers in a wide variety of shapes and sizes. Your baby might prefer one kind over another. Be sure the mouth guard has ventilation holes and is wider than baby's mouth. Keep it clean; wash it when it falls on the floor. Don't tie it around baby's neck or his wrist, and don't attach it to his clothes or crib. When the pacifier gets cracked, torn, sticky or shows other signs of wear, replace it—usually after 3 or 4 months.

Most parents learn by experience that it's a good idea to have more than one pacifier. They tend to get lost or dropped at the most inconvenient times!

If your baby needs a pacifier to help him settle down, have one handy. When he's crying, it helps to have one near at hand so he doesn't get too distressed.

Your baby may choose his thumb to suck on. If so, you need to be sure his hands are clean so you don't have to worry about germs. A drawback of thumb sucking is that when you believe it's time to stop, you can't take it away from him.

For a pacifier user and a thumb sucker, it's best to stop the activity by age 2. If you don't, either action can interfere with his tooth and jaw alignment, which could result in braces as your child gets older.

✴ Baby and House Pets

If this is your first baby, you may be faced with the problem of introducing your new baby to your "old baby," that is, a dog or cat who shares your life. Sometimes a family pet will react to a new baby the same way a sibling might–with jealousy.

Keep your pet out of the baby's room. A dog or cat can carry allergens and/or infections. A dog may be jealous and resent the baby. It might do something you might not expect, so take steps to protect your baby. You'll also be protecting your pet. See a more thorough discussion of pets and a new baby in *Week 12.*

✴ Day-Night Mixup

Your baby may have his days and nights mixed up, which can be stressful for you. There are some things you can do to help him learn day is the time to be active and night is time for sleep. Try the following suggestions.

- You may notice your baby sleeps for one long period in 24 hours. Encourage him to sleep longer during the night by not letting him sleep more than 4 hours between feedings during the day.
- Let regular daytime household noises occur, such as a vacuum cleaner running, the radio or stereo playing, the doorbell ringing. This accustoms him to normal noises, and he will adjust to them.
- When he's up, expose him to family activities. Keep him near you so you can talk to him and interact with him.
- When you put him to bed at night, keep it low key. Speak quietly, keep lights low and don't stimulate him with play activities.
- When changing him and feeding him in the middle of the night, do it quietly and quickly.

❋ Don't wake him to feed him during the night, unless you are told to do so by your baby's doctor. Feed him when he wakes, unless it's been longer than 6 hours since his last feeding

Milestones this 2ⁿᵈ Week

✻ *Baby's Brain Growth*

You have an incredible effect on how your baby's brain grows. Research has shown that babies who are not touched often have smaller-than-normal brains for their age. Stimulation from you and others who interact with baby helps make his nerves stronger and more efficient. Interacting with his environment develops connections in his brain, so be sure he receives many different types of stimulation. Just be careful you don't over-stimulate him.

✻ *Your Baby Can See Clearly only a Short Distance*

It's incredible but a baby must learn to do many things that might seem simple to you. This even includes seeing objects! At birth, your baby sees clearly for only about 12 inches—this is close to the distance from his eyes to yours during breastfeeding. Looking at him while you feed him gives him a chance to practice focusing. Move your head slowly from side to side to encourage his eyes to follow you. This helps build his eye muscles.

✻ *Sounds Are Important to a Baby*

Your baby can hear, and sounds can be very important to him. Use his name often, and he will soon recognize it. Speak softly, hum, sing and make other soothing sounds when baby is restless. If those don't work, try "white sounds." Run the vacuum, turn on the radio to static, run water, play nature sounds, run the washing machine or dishwasher. Devices are also available that mimic the sounds baby heard in utero.

✻ *Communicate with Baby*

There will be times when baby is quietly alert. He'll focus his attention on you when you talk to him. He'll follow you with his eyes for a bit. To communicate with him when he is in this state, hold him close and look into his eyes. Or lean over his crib, and talk softly to him. Stroke him as you sing to him. Rock him while you pat his back. These actions help to establish communication between you.

His personality may soon begin to appear. He may be quiet and happy, or he may be noisy and active. The coming weeks will reveal his personality even more.

Note: See also the box *Milestones this 2ⁿᵈ Week*.

MILESTONES THIS 2ND WEEK

Changes You May See this Week as Baby Develops Physically
* arm, leg and hand movements still reflexive
* startles spontaneously (Moro reflex)
* hands usually fisted or only slightly open

Changes You May See this Week in Baby's Developing Senses and Reflexes
* stares at objects 8 to 12 inches away
* roots for breast, even if not breastfeeding
* is soothed more easily by higher, female voice than by a male voice

Changes You May See this Week as Baby's Mind Develops
* alert about 1 in every 10 hours
* cries for assistance
* quiets when held or when he sees faces

Changes You May See this Week in Baby's Social Development
* eyes fix on mother's face in response to her smile
* stares at faces
* responds to human voice

Every baby is an individual, and your baby may do some of these things more quickly or more slowly than another baby. If you are concerned about your baby's progress, discuss it with your healthcare provider. Also see page xiii.

What's Happening this 2nd Week?

✳ *Baby's First Checkup*

Your pediatrician will probably want to see your baby this week for his first checkup. When you go to this appointment, be sure to bring your insurance card and be ready to fill out various forms. Your baby is a "new patient."

You will be asked for all sorts of information, such as date, time, place and the name of the doctor for your delivery. You will need to supply the doctor's office with information on problems during pregnancy or delivery, and baby's weight and length at birth. If you have other children, leave them at home for this visit. You have a lot to discuss.

Because this may be new to you, you may be unsure how to prepare for the office visit. Observe your baby closely and think about things you want to discuss, such as feeding concerns, his sleep habits, health matters and anything else that is important to you. Write them down. Add any other concerns to your list that you may have. Consider some of the following areas that you may want to discuss—your physician may bring some of them up:

* umbilical-cord healing
* sleep needs (baby's, not yours)
* baby's weight and growth since birth
* eating habits, including breastfeeding concerns
* colic
* immunization schedule
* circumcision or foreskin concerns
* baby's bowel habits
* developmental landmarks, such as how well the baby is sucking

> When your baby lies on his side, you may notice that the side he was lying on is red while the other side is sort of pale. This is caused by his immature blood vessels and will soon disappear.

Immunizations for Full-Term and Premature Babies.   Your physician will advise you of developmental milestones to watch for. He or she will also probably give you a schedule of times for subsequent well-baby appointments, including an immunization schedule. See page 36.

If your baby was premature, you will probably want to discuss his immunizations. The American Academy of Pediatrics advises that premature infants be vaccinated on a schedule with their actual birth date, not their due date. Research has shown that by age 3 and 4 years, premature infants who were vaccinated on schedule had the same level of antibodies as children of the same age who were full-term infants.

✤ Milia and Baby Acne

Most parents expect their baby to be born with perfect skin. After all, haven't we heard that someone has "skin as beautiful as a baby's"? However, the truth is many babies have rashes and other skin problems when they are born, which can last from birth through the first few weeks.

Symptoms of *milia* include pinhead-size whiteheads (like very small pimples) on baby's face, particularly the nose, cheeks or forehead. They may also occur on baby's torso. Bumps are caused by a blockage of baby's oil (sebaceous) glands. *Baby acne* is similar to milia in that oil glands are blocked; hair follicles may also be involved. Baby may have a rash of bumps.

What You Can Do at Home.   There isn't much you can do to treat either of these problems. Time is the best remedy; a baby soon outgrows the rashes.

Within a few weeks, he will have beautiful baby skin. Until then, gently clean the affected areas with warm water and mild soap. Be sure baby doesn't scratch the area; it may cause more inflammation. You may have to trim his nails or put mittens or socks on his hands to prevent scratching.

Don't use strong soaps or alcohol on the areas without first checking with your doctor. Avoid squeezing, pinching, scratching or picking the pimples. It won't make them go away any faster. It may cause them to become infected.

Don't use any ointments, medicated pads or medications without your doctor's advice. Avoid adult acne creams—they are dangerous for baby. Harsh chemicals may be absorbed into his skin.

When to Call the Doctor. If the pimples or rash spread or appear red and inflamed, contact baby's doctor.

✄ When Baby Spits Up

Spitting up is very common in babies. It takes awhile for a baby's digestive tract to begin working efficiently after birth. It's not unusual nor a cause for concern when baby vomits a little or expels some of his stomach contents after feeding. It's not uncommon for this to happen, especially for a newborn.

When baby spits up, he's getting rid of excess breast milk or formula. As he spends more time sitting up, he'll outgrow this. Keep a cloth handy to wipe up any baby spitup.

What You Can Do at Home. Some babies spit up because they eat too much. The stomach can't hold all the breast milk or formula baby ate. If your baby spits up a large amount, feed him less at the next feeding. You may need to burp him more often. Try a gentle burping during and after feedings. Keeping baby upright after feeding for 20 to 30 minutes may also help.

Vomiting occurs when a baby forcibly ejects stomach contents, usually in large amounts. Nearly every baby vomits occasionally, and for many different reasons. If your baby vomits more often, contact your doctor.

When to Call the Doctor. Call the doctor if spitting up persists or becomes projectile. See the discussion of *Projectile Vomiting* in *Week 3*. If baby is bottle-feeding and continues to have problems, you may need to change formulas. Your doctor will advise you.

✄ Sleep Apnea

Some babies suffer from sleep apnea. It is not a very common occurrence. However, it is good to know the symptoms so you will be aware if baby has a problem.

Apnea refers to a temporary cessation of breathing. With sleep apnea, breathing stops briefly while the individual is asleep. It isn't unusual for healthy babies to hold their breath occasionally for 10 to 15 seconds. Most often a gentle nudge or touch causes baby to "grunt" or snort, and breathing resumes.

You probably won't need to worry about this situation with your baby. The problem occurs more often in premature or low-birth-weight infants; these babies usually outgrow the condition.

What You Can Do at Home.   If you believe your baby is experiencing sleep apnea, make note of the frequency and duration of the episodes. Discuss the situation with your doctor.

When to Call the Doctor.   Call your pediatrician if you believe your baby has sleep apnea. If your doctor believes there is a problem, he or she will suggest a solution. Some parents use intercom systems or sleep (apnea) monitors to alert them to problems.

◟ *Bonding with Baby*

Like many parents, you may have heard the term "bonding" but aren't sure what it means. *Bonding* refers to the emotional attachment formed between a baby and its parents or someone else. It is a growing process—it doesn't happen immediately—and it deepens over time.

> You're becoming more relaxed with baby as you get to know him better, so trust your instincts. If you feel something may be wrong, call your doctor.

Some women are afraid that if they don't bond with their baby in the delivery room, it will never happen. That's a fallacy. The quality of the relationship between you and your baby isn't governed by what happens immediately after birth. Bonding is a process that happens over a period of time. In fact, you will bond with your child, in one way or another, throughout his entire life.

Bonding in the delivery room is wonderful and helps both parents connect with baby, but don't worry if delivery complications delay this experience for you. The process can begin hours, or even days, after birth, and it will continue for a long time. The daily care you give your baby as parents strengthens the bond between you.

Bonding goes beyond emotional attachment. Researchers have redefined it to include physical bonding as well. It's good for you because it stimulates the production of prolactin and oxytocin, two hormones that help you feel "motherly" toward your baby. The process also helps keep your baby's hormones in balance.

A baby bonds with others besides his parents. Siblings, care givers, other relatives–baby will also bond with them. Love and care create the bond.

Ways You'll Bond with Baby. You have the opportunity to bond with baby whenever you take care of him. Spending time with him, meeting his needs and responding to him all strengthen your bond. Hold him close, talk to him, cuddle and coo, look into his eyes, make skin-to-skin contact as often as possible to continue your bonding. Encourage the baby's father to do the same.

If you breastfeed, your bond continues to develop through the feeding process. If you bottlefeed, let your partner feed baby to strengthen their bond. Other family members, such as siblings, can also bond with baby by feeding him. Below are some suggestions to help family members bond with baby.

- Lie on your side on the bed, with baby facing you. Pull him close so he can feel your breath on his face. Sing or talk to him as you stroke or massage his body.
- Hold your baby so his head snuggles under your chin. Sway together or rock him.
- Lay baby on his stomach along your forearm. Support his head and chin with your hand. Let his legs dangle down on either side of your arm. Protect his head if you carry him like this.
- Lie on the floor or bed with baby on your chest, bare skin to bare skin. Turn his head to the side so he can hear your heartbeat. Enjoy the closeness.

What if You Don't Feel an Immediate Attachment? Some parents don't feel immediately connected with their baby. They fear something may be wrong with them or with baby. Don't worry if this happens to you. Many parents feel the same way.

You may feel overwhelmed after a long and/or difficult pregnancy, labor or delivery. You may be exhausted. You may experience postpartum distress. Any of these can contribute to your feelings. Take it easy and relax. Within a very short time, you will feel close to your baby.

✵ Massaging Baby
Baby soon learns that a gentle touch expresses your love and affection. He'll feel secure when you touch him. Your soothing hands can calm and comfort him. *Baby massage* is a wonderful way to connect with your baby.

Find a quiet, warm spot to massage baby. A thin towel on your bed is a good place to start. Keep lights low. Place baby on the towel, and rub oil on your hands so they'll glide smoothly over baby's skin. With the flattened palm of your hand, rub his feet firmly yet gently, moving up his legs. Continue up his torso, then rub his hands and arms. Make strokes long and smooth. You'll find you both enjoy the interaction.

With the flattened palm of your hand, rub baby's feet firmly yet gently. Move up his legs with long, smooth strokes.

✱ *Your Newborn Will Cry*

It's inevitable—your baby is going to cry. He'll cry when he's hungry, when he's wet and when he's tired. He'll cry when he's bored, and he'll cry when he's overstimulated. It's his only way of communicating with you right now.

At about this time, your baby may fuss and cry for a few hours every day, often in the evenings. Take care of him when he cries, but realize there may be times that you won't be able to settle him. If his needs have been met, and you've cuddled him for a while, you may have to let him cry. Don't feel guilty when this happens. Do burp him after he cries for a time; a crying baby swallows air.

Toys and Play this 2ⁿᵈ Week

Play is interrelated with your baby's social, mental and physical development. There are many ways to play with him. The best "toy" at this time is you and the other people around him. The interaction between baby and others is the most stimulating experience for him.

✱ *Look into His Eyes*

One game that helps develop baby's eye muscles also promotes bonding. Hold baby close, and look into his eyes. He will look at you for a bit, then look away. Keep looking at him, and he will soon look back at you. Continue this until he tires.

✒ *Stimulate His Grasping Reflex*

Stimulate his grasp by touching his palm with your finger. He'll grasp your finger by reflex, but it helps strengthen finger muscles. Talk and sing to him as you play this game.

✒ *Toys to Entertain Baby*

Things baby might enjoy this week include a hanging mobile above his crib or bassinet, a music box or a CD or tape of soft lullabies to play in his room. Some mobiles are a combination of sight and sound. Colorful figures move slowly as music plays.

Week 3

Baby weighs 8½ pounds and is 20¾ inches long this week.

Baby Care and Equipment

✎ Bottlefeeding Your Baby

Many women choose to bottlefeed baby—studies show that more women bottlefeed than breastfeed. You're not in the minority if you make this choice. Don't scold yourself or feel guilty if you bottlefeed—it's a personal decision that you are entitled to make. You will not be considered a "terrible mother" because you choose not to or cannot breastfeed.

Baby will be OK if you bottlefeed her. Sometimes a woman cannot breastfeed because of a physical condition or problem. You may be extremely underweight or have some medical condition, such as a prolactin deficiency, heart disease, kidney disease, tuberculosis or HIV. Some infants have problems breastfeeding, or they are unable to breastfeed due to a physical problem, such as a cleft palate or cleft lip. Lactose intolerance can also cause breastfeeding problems.

Some women want to breastfeed and try to, but it doesn't work out. Sometimes you choose not to breastfeed because of other demands on your time, such as a job or other children to care for. Your baby can still get all the love and attention and nutrition she needs if breastfeeding is not possible for you. If breastfeeding doesn't work for you, please don't worry about it. It's OK!

It's an Individual Choice. We know that through the use of iron-fortified formula, your baby can receive good nutrition if you bottlefeed. Some women enjoy the freedom bottlefeeding provides. It can make it easier for someone else to help care for the baby. You can determine exactly how much formula your baby is taking in at each feeding. There are also other advantages to bottlefeeding.

* Bottlefeeding is easy to learn; it never causes you discomfort if it's done incorrectly.
* Fathers can be more involved in caring for baby.

* Bottlefed babies may go longer between feedings because formula is usually digested more slowly than breast milk.
* A day's supply of formula can be mixed at one time, saving time and effort.
* You don't have to be concerned about feeding your baby in front of other people.
* It may be easier to bottlefeed if you plan to return to work soon after your baby is born.
* If you feed your baby iron-fortified formula, she won't need iron supplementation.
* If you use fluoridated tap water to mix formula, you may not have to give your baby fluoride supplements.

With bottlefeeding, other family members can help care for baby.

Bottlefeeding is not cheap–you'll spend $1500 to $2000 to feed your baby formula for the first year.

Bonding with a Bottlefed Baby.   Most parents want to establish a strong bond with their baby. However, some parents fear bottlefeeding will not encourage closeness with their child. They fear that bonding will not occur between parent and baby. It's not true that a woman must breastfeed her baby to bond with her.

There are many ways you can bond with your baby, even if you bottlefeed. Studies show that carrying your baby close to your body in a slinglike carrier helps the bonding process. It's great because dads can also bond this way with baby. There are other ways you can bottlefeed a baby that can help develop a closer bond between parent and child. Try the following ideas.

* If you feed her warm formula, heat it to body temperature by running a filled bottle under warm water or let the bottle stand in heated water for a short time. If you bottlefeed her expressed breast milk, letting it stand in heated water is the best way to warm it. Never microwave expressed breast milk. It changes its composition.
* Find a comfortable place to feed, such as a rocking chair.
* Snuggle your baby close to you during feeding.
* Make lots of eye contact, caress her, cuddle her, coo, sing and talk to her.
* Rock gently.
* When she's finished, remove the bottle but continue to hold her close.

* Formula takes longer to digest than breast milk, so you may not have to feed baby as often. However, feeding smaller amounts more frequently helps you bond. It's also easier on baby's immature digestive system.

What's the Best Way to Bottlefeed Baby? Hold baby in a semiupright position, with her head higher than her body. Place the bottle's nipple right side up, ready to feed; don't touch the tip of the nipple. Brush the nipple lightly over the baby's lips, and guide it into her mouth. Don't force it.

Tilt the bottle so the neck is always filled, keeping the baby from sucking in too much air. Remove the bottle during feeding to let baby rest. It usually takes 10 to 15 minutes to finish feeding a bottle.

Don't leave the baby alone with the bottle. Never prop up a bottle and leave her alone to suck on it. Never put a baby down to bed with a bottle.

There's no evidence that feeding refrigerated formula without warming it will harm your baby. If you usually warm it, your baby will probably prefer it that way. If your baby is usually breastfed, she will probably prefer a warmed bottle. Be careful formula is not too hot.

Formulas to Consider. When choosing a formula to feed your baby, there isn't much difference among the brands of regular formula available. Most babies do well on milk-based formula.

Formulas are packaged in powder form, concentrated liquid and ready-to-feed. The end product is the same. All formulas sold in the United States must meet the same minimum health standards set by the FDA, so they are all nutritionally complete.

Ask your pediatrician about the type of formula you should feed your baby. Some formulas are iron fortified. A baby needs iron for normal growth; a recent study showed that too little iron can lead to mild developmental delays.

The American Academy of Pediatrics recommends that a baby be fed iron-fortified formula for the first year of her life. Feeding for this length of time helps maintain adequate iron intake.

There are several types of formula on the market today besides regular milk-based formula. They include the following:

* milk-based, lactose-free formula for babies with feeding problems, such as fussiness, gas and diarrhea, that are caused by lactose intolerance
* hypoallergenic protein formula (easier to digest and lactose-free) for babies with colic or symptoms of milk-protein allergy
* soy-based formula, milk-free and lactose-free for babies with cow's milk allergies or sensitivity to cow's milk

Some researchers caution parents about using soy-based formula. Recent studies suggest it offers no benefits over cow's-milk formula. They also warn that some of the natural compounds found in soybeans may depress an infant's immune system. The AAP recommends soy-based formula only for newborns who are severely allergic to the proteins found in cow's milk (about 3% of all babies).

If your baby must have a special formula—a prescription or a highly processed commercial brand—check with your insurance company. All or part of the cost may be covered.

Some parents are interested in giving their child organic formulas. The milk used in organic formula comes from cows that are not given growth hormones or antibiotics. The food fed to the cows is also free of pesticides. Organic formula is more expensive, but many parents are willing to pay the extra price.

New formulas on the market now include two nutrients found in breast milk—DHA and ARA. DHA (docosahexaenoic acid) contributes to baby's eye development. ARA (arachidonic acid) is important in baby's brain development. DHA and ARA are provided through the placenta before birth and in breast milk after birth. These two nutrients are especially good for preemies who missed out on them in the third trimester. Ask your doctor about this type of formula for your baby, especially if she was premature. Formulas with DHA and ARA are about 20% more expensive than regular formula. The benefit of adding these to formula will take 5 or 10 years to determine.

Some parents ask about goat's milk in an infant's diet—it was once used with fussy babies because we believed it was easier to digest. We now advise parents not to give their baby goat's milk. It has a high concentration of protein, which may make it harder for baby to digest.

> If you have two or more babies, you may be eligible for a one-time gift of formula! Many formula companies send parents of multiples free cans of formula to celebrate babies' births. Contact the company, and ask what proof they need—usually a copy of the babies' crib cards or their birth certificates are enough. To find the contact information for various companies, check a can of formula, the Internet or a mothers' group.

Feeding Equipment to Use. When you feed baby her bottle, use one that is slanted. Research has shown this design keeps the nipple full of milk, which means she takes in less air. A slanted bottle also helps ensure baby is sitting up to drink. When a baby drinks lying down, milk can pool in the eustachian tube, where it can cause ear infections.

A new type of nipple allows formula or pumped breast milk to be released at the same rate as breast milk flows during nursing. A twist adjusts the nipple to a flow that is slow, medium or fast. In this way, you can find the flow that works best for your baby. The nipple fits on most bottles. Check your local stores if you are interested.

Bottlefeeding Tips.   When you bottlefeed, there are some things you can do to help make the experience healthy and happy for you and your baby.

* Wipe off the top of the formula can (liquid or dry) before you open it.
* Follow manufacturer's instructions exactly when making up the formula.
* Wash your hands before you prepare formula.
* Thoroughly clean feeding equipment before use.
* Be sure formula use-by dates have not expired.
* If you prepare formula or bottles ahead of time, you can refrigerate them for up to 24 hours.
* A bottle can be warm or cold, but choose one method and stick to it. A baby likes consistency.
* Don't heat formula if it is at room temperature; heat only refrigerated formula.
* Before you heat a bottle, remove the nipple and cap.
* Never microwave glass bottles; they might crack or explode.
* Never microwave breast milk—it changes its nutritional content.
* Heat 4-ounce bottles no longer than 30 seconds in a microwave on high. Heat 8-ounce bottles for no longer than 45 seconds.
* After heating, replace the cap and nipple, and invert the bottle 8 to 10 times. Don't shake it.
* Test the temperature of a heated bottle by dripping a bit on the top or inside of your wrist.
* Throw away all leftover formula.
* Get rid of bottle nipples that are hard or stiff, or those that are extremely soft and gummy feeling.
* Once you find a formula baby likes, use it exclusively.
* When you bottlefeed, sterilize the water you use until your baby is at least 4 months old or when she starts solids. Do this by boiling it for 1 minute.
* Do not rely on bottled water being safer than tap water. One study showed that nearly 35% of over 100 brands of bottled water were contaminated with chemicals or bacteria. If you use bottled water, boil it!

* There is no need to sterilize bottles on a regular basis unless you use well water. In that case, boil bottles and nipples for 5 minutes.
* Always sterilize new bottles, nipples, caps and rings for 5 minutes before using them for the first time.

Other Bottlefeeding Pointers.   Bottlefed babies take from 2 to 5 ounces of formula at a feeding. They feed about every 3 to 4 hours for the first month (6 to 8 times a day). If baby fusses when her bottle is empty, it's OK to give her a little more. When baby is older, the number of feedings decreases, but the amount of formula you feed at each feeding increases.

You know baby's getting enough formula if she has 6 to 8 wet diapers a day. She may also have 1 or 2 bowel movements. Stools of a bottlefed baby are greener in color than a breastfed baby's and more solid.

If your baby poops after a feeding, it's caused by the gastrocolic reflex. This reflex causes squeezing of the intestines when the stomach is stretched, as with feeding. It is very pronounced in newborns and usually decreases after 2 or 3 months of age.

If you notice any blood or mucus in baby's stools during these first few weeks, it may be an indication of a milk-protein sensitivity. Usually a little blood in the stools and occasional fussiness are the only symptoms. These symptoms disappear when baby is put on a hypoallergenic formula. Discuss the problem with your baby's doctor if she has these symptoms.

Burp baby after every feeding to help her get rid of excess air. If baby doesn't want a feeding, don't force it. Try again in a couple of hours. However, if she refuses two feedings in a row, contact your pediatrician. Baby may be ill.

Soon after birth, your bottlefed baby was able to discriminate between sugar water and milk. Later, she will be able to express her distaste for what she is drinking. If she doesn't like what she's drinking, she will turn her head away from the bottle and may refuse to drink.

If Baby Chokes on Formula or Breast Milk
Occasionally a baby chokes on formula, breast milk or mucus. It's a common occurrence and one you can handle easily. When it happens, turn baby's head to the side and put her head a little lower than her body. Use a cloth, your clean finger or a bulb syringe to help clear any fluid from her mouth.

Bathing Your Baby
By this week, the umbilical cord has probably fallen off, and it's time to give baby her first real bath. You may be feeling a little apprehensive about it—

it's kind of scary holding a slippery little body. With practice, you'll be a pro, and this may become a favorite time with baby!

You may hear conflicting advice about how often to bathe baby. Some experts suggest 2 or 3 times a week is enough. Others say a daily bath helps keep sensitive skin from drying out. Some suggest once a week! If you have questions about your baby's bathing schedule, discuss them with your pediatrician.

To begin the bathtime ritual, gather together everything you'll need. Once you put baby in the water, you can't be distracted even for a second! Keep towels, baby shampoo, soap and a washcloth near at hand. To help keep baby from slipping, put a large terry towel or foam insert in the tub. Fill the tub (a baby tub or the kitchen sink) with a few inches of warm water. Be sure it's not too hot. Test it with your elbow or the back of your hand.

Undress baby. Slip your left hand under her shoulder. Place your thumb over her left shoulder and your fingers under her left armpit. Support her bottom with your right hand. Lower her into the water. Begin by washing her face; work down her little body.

Clean her genital area from front to back to avoid infections. Keep wiping warm water over your baby's body as you wash her to keep her warm.

> When baby is cold, small veins show through her skin, and her feet and hands may look blue. Add some clothes or a blanket for warmth.

Once you've washed her, it's time to shampoo. You only need to do this once or twice a week, not every time you bathe her. Wash her hair with a small amount of baby shampoo to make rinsing it out easier. Using a small plastic cup or your hand, rinse her head. Pour water from the forehead back to avoid getting it on her face or in her eyes.

As soon as you've finished, lift her out and wrap her in a towel. Pat her body and her head with the towel to dry her. Patting dry is gentler on her skin than rubbing it. Follow with a moisturizer if her skin is dry or if you live in a very dry climate. Diaper and dress her quickly to avoid a chill.

❧ Cleaning Baby's Ears

Your baby's ears will produce ear wax, just as yours do. It's important to realize this is a normal bodily process, and you don't need to do much about it. Ear wax is a mixture of dead skin cells and glandular secretions. It helps protect baby's ear drum and ear canal from foreign substances.

You don't have to remove ear wax from your baby's ears. It usually falls out on its own. Do not stick any type of swab into your baby's ear canal to remove wax buildup. You can clean the outer opening of the ear with a washcloth, but don't try to clean inside the ear.

⚕ *Dressing Baby for Going Out*

You'll be taking your baby out and about more now. Dressing her for the climate might cause you some concern. It's best to judge what she needs by how you feel.

Usually in cold weather, add one more layer than you are wearing. In warm or hot weather, she can wear the same number of layers you are. Be aware: When you live in hot climates, you may need to keep a blanket near for colder, indoor air-conditioned temperatures!

> Keep baby from getting your cold by washing your hands (and making sure other family members do the same) before touching her.

⚕ *"Baby Wearing"*

"Baby wearing" is the act of carrying your baby in some type of carrier on your front, close to your body. It's a wonderful way to bond with baby because of the physical closeness. Studies show it may also encourage brain growth!

A baby can learn a great deal being carried this way. She can see what you see (partially). She can hear conversations. She can feel rhythmic movements when you walk. She can feel your heartbeat, which may calm and settle her. It's a wonderful way to expose her safely to the world around her. See also the discussion in *Week 4* of *Front Carriers*.

⚕ *Baby Massage*

Your baby will enjoy a relaxing massage—it's tough to be a newborn! Research has shown that massaging your baby every day can improve her digestion and sleep. It can also help muscle development.

Choose a warm spot so baby won't be cold. With baby dressed only in a diaper, place her on a towel or in your lap. Begin by making eye contact; smile and coo at baby. Using firm, gentle strokes, make little circles around her head. Don't use oil on her face or head. Smooth her forehead by placing both hands at the center and gently stroking outward. Make little circles around her jaw.

Warm some oil in your hands, then stroke her chest. Massage her hands (you'll need to open them), then roll each arm gently between your two hands. Stroke her tummy. Move down to her legs and feet; massage each between your two hands. Turn her onto her stomach, and massage her back. Use long strokes from her shoulders to her buttocks.

Keep your massage to 15 minutes or less. Longer may be too much for a young infant.

Milestones this 3rd Week

✴ *Baby Is Accomplishing Many Things*
Baby is adapting to her place in the family, just as you are adapting to her in your lives. She is accomplishing many things by this third week. She can focus her attention on one quiet activity and shut out other stimuli. She lifts her head for a few seconds, and she turns her head from side to side when she's on her tummy. She adjusts her body posture to cuddle into someone holding her. She may be settling into a regular feeding schedule.

✴ *Your Baby Needs to Suck*
Sucking is very satisfying to baby. Many babies require more sucking than feeding time allows. Sucking is also comforting to her. Because she may not be able to find her mouth easily to suck on a finger or thumb, offer her a pacifier, if you haven't already done so.

✴ *Soothe Your Baby*
You may find you can help soothe your baby by providing her with your personal scent. Let her smell something that you have worn or had near you that has your fragrance (it doesn't have to be perfume) on it. Studies have shown that having something close to her with a familiar scent can help calm a fussy baby.

✴ *Baby's Eyes Do More than "See"*
Your baby may be making more eye contact with you. When you hold her in your arms and talk or sing to her, you are inviting her to focus on you. You'll find she'll make eye contact for up to 10 seconds, and she'll quiet to stare at a face. She'll gaze at her mother's face longer than anyone else's. In addition to faces, you might introduce new, bold-patterned objects to look at, such as a bull's eye, bold stripes or a checkerboard.

You'll notice that baby is turning her head more from side to side to track a moving object. However, her eyes may cross when she's focusing on something due to lack of good muscle control. Soon this will disappear.

Note: See also the box *Milestones this 3rd Week.*

What's Happening this 3rd Week?

Your baby continues to adjust to her new life outside the womb. She sleeps about 16 to 18 hours a day, but her schedule is probably erratic. She probably sleeps only 3 to 4 hours before she wakens again.

Her periods of sleep and wakefulness follow no pattern, so you can't depend on any time of day when she'll be sleeping. A reason for this is your

MILESTONES THIS 3ᴿᴰ WEEK

Changes You May See this Week as Baby Develops Physically
* thrusts out arms and legs in play
* can lift head briefly when lying on stomach
* may dig heels into mattress then thrust with legs (this moves her body a little)

Changes You May See this Week in Baby's Developing Senses and Reflexes
* coordinates eyes sideways when looking at a light or an object

Changes You May See this Week as Baby's Mind Develops
* has vague and impassive expression during waking hours
* prefers patterns
* may calm when you speak gently to her and hold her upright against your shoulder

Changes You May See this Week in Baby's Social Development
* makes eye contact
* adjusts posture to body of person holding her

Every baby is an individual, and your baby may do some of these things more quickly or more slowly than another baby. If you are concerned about your baby's progress, discuss it with your healthcare provider. Also see page xiii.

baby's need to eat. Her stomach is small and can't hold a lot of food. Her tummy's like an alarm clock—she wakes up when she's hungry and sleeps when she's full.

✐ *It's an Exciting Time for Dad*

For a man, attachment to his newborn can be strong and deep. The experience of becoming a father can be very emotional for him. It can be just as exciting to be a new father as it is to be a new mother. Studies show that when a father is involved with his child's care from birth, he will continue to be involved in the child's life as she grows up.

A father should be encouraged to care for his baby. Bathing, diapering, feeding, holding, comforting—all are tasks a father can perform. Divide tasks as logically as you can, and work together in caring for your child. Trust in each other's abilities as a parent.

> A baby's chubbiness is due to the fact that she gains weight faster than she grows in length. This changes as she gets older.

Research has shown that a woman can help her partner become more involved in parenting by sharing her feelings with him and asking for his help. This is a time of great change for the family. A father's involvement means sharing the responsibility and easing a mother's burden.

✦ *Dealing with Colic*

Colic is a condition in which a baby has lengthy episodes of sudden, loud crying and fussiness. About 20% of all infants experience colic, which usually appears about 2 weeks after birth and can last until baby is 3 or 4 months old.

A colic attack often occurs at night and can last up to 4 hours. Baby may draw her knees up to her chest, pass gas and flail her arms about. Her tummy muscles may feel hard. An attack stops as suddenly as it starts. It may help you to know colic is not harmful to your baby.

Although a great deal of research has been conducted on the cause of colic, there is little evidence as to why it occurs. Theories include:

* immaturity of the baby's digestive system, also called gastroesophageal reflux disease (GERD)
* sensitivity to, or intolerance of, to cow's-milk protein in formula or breast milk
* fatigue in the infant
* some foods a mother eats, if she breastfeeds

What You Can Do at Home.   At this time, we can't offer one effective treatment. However, we do advise you not to give baby any type of medication to try to relieve pain or to stop cramping. They could cause additional problems. Discuss the situation with your pediatrician.

One study found that colicky babies may be highly sensitive to the environment and have trouble transitioning from the soothing environment of the womb to the outside world. They suggest one way to deal with this is find out how your baby responds to sound, touch, light and movement. Keep trying different things to see how she reacts to them, then avoid them if baby begins to get fussy.

Elevating the head of baby's crib may help. Or you might try the Tucker sling; it fits over the crib mattress and holds the baby in a partially upright position. This may help, especially with reflux. Infant massage works with some babies.

An old remedy that some people try is to give baby a little sugar in water. Sugar causes a baby's brain to produce natural painkillers that help reduce pain. Give a few drops of water with about 15% sugar dissolved in it, once a minute for 5 minutes. To make a 15% solution, mix together 1 tablespoon and 1 teaspoon of sugar and 8 ounces of water. A syringe works well for giving baby the sugar water.

The "colic curl" works for some babies. Hold your baby facing out by cradling her in your arms with her back against your chest. Slide her down so her knees are higher than her waist. You can carry your baby around like this—she might even like the opportunity to look around.

There are some other things you can try at home to help ease baby's discomfort during an attack.

* Offer baby the breast or bottle.
* If you bottlefeed, try noncow's-milk formula. Talk to your pediatrician before making any changes.
* Carry baby in a front sling during an attack. The closeness and motion often help.
* Offer a pacifier to baby.
* Place baby across your knees on her stomach, and rub her back.
* Swaddle baby.
* Massage baby's tummy.

A baby's incessant crying can cause parents a great deal of stress, so take care of yourselves. Take turns staying with baby during an attack. Ask a family member or friend to baby-sit for an evening. Take heart—colic will disappear soon.

When to Call the Doctor.   If your baby shows signs of colic, call your pediatrician. Researchers believe Zantac may help; Zantac reduces acids in the stomach. However, some babies benefit from Reglan, which improves gastrointestinal functioning. Your doctor will assess the situation and advise you.

Studies also suggest another option—using different formulas if you bottlefeed. Nestle's Good Start empties out of the stomach more quickly, which might help. Predigested formula, such as Alimentum or Nutramigen, are already partially broken down, which may cause less of a reaction in the baby. Discuss these options with your baby's doctor.

✻ Penis Inflammation (Balanitis)

If your son was circumcised, you may notice redness, swelling, pus or bleeding from the circumcision site. This usually occurs during the first week following circumcision. It indicates the area may be slightly infected, so you may need to take steps to deal with the infection.

What You Can Do at Home.   Gently clean the red or inflamed area with a mild soap and warm water. Don't use alcohol because it could sting. Try to keep the area clean and dry. Change baby as soon as he is wet.

When to Call the Doctor.   You need to contact baby's doctor if bleeding is constant or heavy, or if there is pus or discharge. Your baby's doctor will determine a course of treatment. Antibiotic gels or creams may be prescribed to deal with any infection. Follow the doctor's instructions closely. Clean the area as directed by your doctor.

✗ *Projectile Vomiting*

Babies often spit up or vomit a little. It takes time for their digestive tracts to function normally. See the discussion in *Week 2* of *Spitting Up*. However, some babies experience recurrent or forceful vomiting, called *projectile vomiting.*

The main symptom of the problem is forceful ejection of milk, formula, food, medications, water or anything baby swallows. The problem may have several different causes, including illness (flu) or ingestion of a food or medication.

What You Can Do at Home.   If your baby experiences forceful vomiting, make sure she doesn't choke on the vomit. Discontinue giving her food or any medication.

When to Call the Doctor.   Call your baby's doctor if she is vomiting a great deal. Any treatment of the problem will be centered around the symptoms she displays, such as gastroenteritis or an allergy to food or medication.

Advisory for parents: Your baby does not have this problem if she spits up a little or vomits once in awhile. She must vomit forcefully, projecting stomach contents a fair distance, such as a couple of feet.

Toys and Play this 3rd Week

You'll find that as baby stays awake longer, you may have more time for fun and games. She's beginning to respond a little more. It's enjoyable for you to see her alertness grow and her interaction with you and others become more active.

Note: Watch baby closely when you interact with her. You'll be able to tell she's had enough when she looks away, squirms, gets fussy, kicks, yawns or seems unhappy in some other way.

✗ *Talk to Baby in "Parentese" and Call Her by Name*

When you play with baby, vary your tone of voice. Talk in "parentese," the high-pitched, singsong tone of voice many parents use automatically; she'll love it. Research shows it also serves a purpose. It helps speed an infant's ability to recognize connections between objects and words.

This week, physical contact continues to be very important. Hold baby in your arms, or sit on the floor and hold her in your lap. Look into her eyes and say her name. Vary the tone you use. Make up rhymes using her name. Use her name in the place of another name while you softly sing a funny song. Say her name often so she'll recognize it.

✎ *Play Some Vision Games*

It's never too early to start playing vision games. In a dimly lit room, turn on a flashlight, and move its beam back and forth so baby can see a reflection in front of her. Never shine the light into her eyes! Watch her eyes to see if she tracks the light. This exercise helps her develop muscles needed to follow moving objects.

From magazines or other sources, cut out bright, simple pictures with bold, contrasting colors, like a picture of the sun or a human face. Prop a picture against the side of the crib for a bit. Move it slowly to the other side so she moves her head to see it. (Don't leave the picture in the crib when you leave the room.) Special infant safety mirrors, which can be permanently attached to the side of the crib, can also add excitement when she catches sight of herself.

✎ *Help Her Tone Muscles*

While baby is lying on her back, grasp her feet and gently move her legs in a circular motion, like riding a bike. This exercise encourages toning of muscles and exposes her to rhythm. A couple of minutes is long enough for this interaction.

✎ *Make Her Part of the Family*

Although you might not think of it as a game, it's beneficial and fun for baby to be part of the family's interaction every day. Carry her in a front sling as you move around the house, or let her sit in her infant chair as the family eats together. Everyone will enjoy it, including baby!

WHAT YOUR PEDIATRICIAN WOULD LIKE YOU TO KNOW

Your pediatrician is concerned about your baby's health and welfare. Your doctor realizes and understands you may be concerned about your ability to know what is normal and what is not with a newborn.

Below is a discussion of some common issues that concern parents. These discussions may help you decide what is normal for your baby and help you relax a little. If you are concerned about something in particular, most doctors prefer you err on the side of caution and call the office for advice about taking care of baby.

Trust Your Instincts. You may be a first-time parent who has never been around newborns before. Lots of people will probably give you advice. However, you deal with your baby every day. You know her best. So after you've listened to everyone else, listen to yourself. Trust your instincts!

Babies Cry. Your baby is going to cry—it's natural and expected. A newborn may cry as much as 3 hours a day, or more. It's your baby's main way of communicating with you. Your baby will cry to tell you she's hungry, wet, tired, bored or upset.

As you get to know her better, you'll know what baby's crying means because each of her cries is different. You'll also be able to tell when something's wrong, such as if she's in pain or ill. Her crying will be different in some way. It may be piercing or uncontrollable or prolonged.

It takes a little while for you to connect with baby in this way, but you soon will. As we stated above, trust your instincts. Call your pediatrician if you are concerned.

Your Baby Will Lose Some Weight. A baby may lose as much as 10% of her body weight by the third day following birth. You may be concerned about the loss of weight and wonder if baby is OK. She probably is.

Babies are born with extra fluid to get them through the first 3 to 5 days, even if they feed well. Your little one will be losing some of the fluids she was born with. And after the trauma of birth, she may not be too interested in eating. These two situations contribute to baby's weight loss. If you breastfeed your baby, her weight loss might be a little more because it takes awhile for your breast milk to come in. Within a week after birth, your baby should start gaining weight.

If baby hasn't regained her birth weight by her 2-week checkup or if she loses more than 10% of her body weight in the first 3 days after birth, your doctor may suggest you also offer her formula, if you are breastfeeding.

Spitting Up Is Normal. Don't be surprised or worried if baby spits up. In a newborn, the muscle that closes the opening to the stomach may be underdeveloped. This allows breast milk or formula to come back up. Baby really isn't spitting up a lot, no matter how it looks.

If you're bottlefeeding, be sure baby is sitting semiupright when you feed her. You might want to use a slanted bottle to reduce the amount of air she takes in.

With bottlefeeding and breastfeeding, burp her during a feeding. Hold her or sit her upright after a feeding for a little bit. This helps keep the food down.

Do call your pediatrician if baby vomits a lot. See the discussion of *Spitting Up* in *Week 2,* and the discussions of *Vomiting* in *Weeks 3* and *24.*

WHAT YOUR PEDIATRICIAN WOULD LIKE YOU TO KNOW

Baby Will Have Some Rashes. Most babies have a rash or rashes during their first few weeks of life. Baby acne, milia, cradle cap, bumps and pimples are common. These rashes occur because the mother's estrogen is still circulating through baby's body. Rashes soon disappear, so you don't need to do anything about them. See the discussions of the various Skin Conditions in Weeks 1 and 2.

If baby has any rash that oozes, call your pediatrician. Call if a rash worsens with simple treatment. These are not common and should be treated by your baby's doctor.

When Baby Coughs and Sneezes. Your baby will cough and sneeze to clear her nasal passages of mucus, dust and other irritants. When she coughs and sneezes, it's probably not a sign of illness. It's the only way she has to clear her airways. Don't be concerned unless she also has a fever or is congested and these interfere with her eating and/or sleeping. If this occurs, call your pediatrician.

Her Belly Button Looks Like It Hurts. When you bring baby home from the hospital, her belly button probably has a black stump that looks kind of shriveled up. You may be leery of cleaning it because you believe it will hurt baby. However, the stump of the umbilical cord has no nerve endings. It won't hurt baby if you clean it.

Wipe the belly-button area with alcohol after each diaper change. Give baby a sponge bath until it falls off, within 2 to 4 weeks. If the cord stump doesn't fall off after 4 weeks, contact your pediatrician. He or she will want to know about it.

Baby's Bowel Movements. You may wonder what a normal bowel movement looks like for your baby. What's normal for one baby may not be normal for another baby. It all depends on what your baby eats and how her body processes food.

If you bottlefeed your baby, she may move her bowels two or three times a day. Her stools may have the consistency of soft ice cream and be brownish in color. As the weeks pass, she may have fewer bowel movements as her system matures.

If you breastfeed baby, she may have loose, yellow, mustardlike stools. She may have a bowel movement after every feeding. Some breastfed babies pass stools much less often. It's not unusual for them to go a day or 2, or as long as 4 days, without a bowel movement, then have a huge one.

When baby's normal bowel routine changes, it could be a sign that she has a problem. Call your doctor if you are concerned. Always contact your pediatrician if baby's stools are more watery than normal for more than a couple of bowel movements or if you notice any blood in the stool.

Week 4

Baby weighs 9 pounds and is 21 inches long this week.

Baby Care and Equipment

↝ *Baby Slings and Front Carriers*

Baby slings and front carriers offer parents and others a wonderful way to carry baby closely. It's a piece of baby equipment that can help you in many ways. You can keep baby close as you go about your daily routine. You can comfort baby when necessary. And when baby's in a front carrier, you continue bonding.

Because your baby grows so quickly these first months, you will probably use a front carrier only for 3 or 4 months. Although you'd probably like to use it longer, your back will say "No!"

There are many advantages to carrying baby "kangaroo-style" during the first few months. One study showed babies carried this way cry less. You are close to baby yet have your arms free. The swaying motion and the wrapped-close feeling may remind baby of the womb, which may help settle him. Slings are also great for nursing privately in a public area.

There are actually two pieces of equipment to consider. A sling is just what it sounds like. Baby is placed on his back in the sling and carried as if he were in a hammock, close to your body. A front carrier is like a backpack, only it's worn on your chest. Baby is placed in the carrier part, facing inward when he's very small and facing outward as he gets older (3 months).

Comfort and safety are the most important factors to search for with either type carrier. Check for the following when shopping for a sling or front carrier.

- Straps and snaps are secure so they can't work loose.
- Belts and buckles have some form of backup security, such as double loops or plastic stops.
- Check manufacturer's weight and age recommendations.
- Fabric is sturdy and washable. Is it soft enough for baby's skin?
- Seams are reinforced with double stitching at points of stress.
- Shoulder straps and neck straps are cushioned.

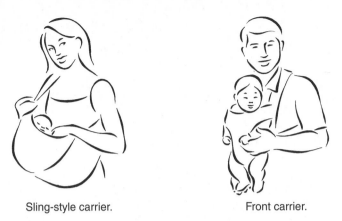

Sling-style carrier.   Front carrier.

* Padded belts make the carrier comfortable for you.
* Check to see if it meets the Juvenile Product Manufacturers' Association (JPMA) safety standards.

Do not put baby in a front carrier until he is at least 8 pounds. You can carry him in this type of carrier until he is about 30 pounds. At that time, he will probably be in a carrier you wear on your back–you won't be able to carry 30 pounds on your front without major discomfort to you.

When you use a front carrier, be sure you keep the neck support in place for the first 3 months. After 3 months, you can turn baby around and let him look out.

Nail Care

You may be surprised how quickly baby's nails grow. Sometimes a baby's nails have to be cut soon after birth! You may a feel a little leery about cutting nails that are so tiny, but once you've done it a few times, you'll be a pro.

A baby's nails are thin and very flexible, but they can soon become long enough and sharp enough to scratch him and you. Trimming them prevents injuries.

Nail scissors or clippers made for a small child are a good choice. When baby is asleep or relaxed, take one finger in your hand, hold it fingertip-down, away from you. Snip or cut the nail straight across. Don't cut into the quick (the flesh under the nail). If this seems too difficult, you can always file baby's nails down with an emery board. Some parents even nibble them off!

You'll probably need to trim his nails about every 2 weeks. There's a "rule of thumb"–the bigger the finger, the faster the nail grows, so you may have to trim the thumbs more often. (No pun intended.) As baby starts to use his hands more frequently, he'll start wearing some of the nail down. Be sure to check his nails often. Any ragged nail can scratch him or you.

Toenails must not be overlooked. They are worn down more consistently because of contact with socks, booties and footed sleepers. Check baby's toes every few weeks, but he probably won't need toenails trimmed more often than once a month, if that. Once he begins walking, you'll need to check his toenails more often. Long toenails may make walking difficult and uncomfortable.

✴ Baby Massage

Your baby is doing a lot of sucking now. That could cause tension around his mouth and jaw. To help relieve some of this tension, massage around his jaw. Make small circles on and around his jawbone with your fingertips. His mouth may open in contentment.

Make gentle little circles
with your fingertips
around baby's jaw.

✴ Keeping Baby Warm

A newborn may have a bit of trouble regulating his body temperature. It can take awhile for his body thermostat to begin working. If your baby seems chilled or you live in a cold climate, we have some tips to help keep him warm.

- ✴ Cuddle baby close to you when you hold him. This warms him.
- ✴ Swaddle him tightly in a receiving or swaddling blanket.
- ✴ Lay him down with a hot-water bottle wrapped in a soft blanket next to him or under him.
- ✴ Before he goes to sleep or takes a nap, prewarm his sheets with a heating pad or a hot-water bottle. Be sure sheets are not hot when you put him down. Remove the heat source before you put him down.
- ✴ Dress him in a blanket sleeper—you won't need blankets.

✴ Giving Baby Water

Some parents believe their baby needs more fluid than he takes in at his feedings. Unless advised to do so by your pediatrician, do not give baby water or sugar water between feedings. It will fill his tummy, and he'll eat less at his next feeding.

✴ Supplemental Feedings

If you must provide your baby with supplemental feedings while you breast-feed, wait until you've been breastfeeding for at least 4 weeks, if possible. This gives your body a chance to adjust and ensures a good milk supply. It also keeps your baby from taking a liking to a bottle (it's much easier to feed). Some babies refuse to breastfeed after they become used to a bottle. Occasional supplemental feedings shouldn't be a problem after 4 weeks.

⁎ Choosing Child Care for Baby

If you and your partner work, child care may be one of the most important decisions you must make for baby. You might find it challenging as you begin your search for child care. Where do you start? There are many things you can do as you begin your quest to find the best situation for your child.

Ask friends, family members and co-workers for referrals to people or places they know about. Talk to people in your area. Ask at your church or other churches in the area if they sponsor any programs. Contact Child Care Aware (800-424-2246) or a local referral agency about local resources. If you're interested in hiring a nanny for care in your home, contact a referral agency. See the *Resources* section, page 527, for some contacts.

Whomever you choose to provide care for your child, be sure to check references before you make a final decision! This applies to centers as well as in-home care givers (your home or theirs).

Finding the best situation for your baby can take time. Begin the process several weeks (maybe several months in special situations like twins) before you need it. Often this means finding child care before your baby is born. Some situations may require a waiting list.

There is a shortage of quality child care for children under age 2. If you find a care provider you are comfortable with, but it's not time to leave your baby, ask to put down a deposit and set a date for child care to begin. Keep in touch with the care provider, and plan to meet before you place your child in daily care.

Many decisions must be made when selecting someone to care for your baby. You want the best setting and the best care giver for your child. The way to do that is to know what your options are before you begin. There are many choices when it comes to child care. Any of a variety of situations could be right for you. Examine your needs and the needs of your child before you decide which one to pursue.

In-Home Child Care. With in-home care, the care giver can be a relative or nonrelative. When you have someone come to your home to take care of your child, it makes things easier for you. You don't have to get the baby ready before you go in the morning. You never have to take your child out in bad weather. If he's sick, you don't have to take time off from work or try to find someone to stay with him. It takes less time in the morning and evening if you don't have to drop off your baby or pick him up.

In-home care is an excellent choice for a baby or small child because it provides one-on-one attention (if you only have one child at home). The environment is also familiar to the child.

When the care giver is a relative, such as a grandparent, a sister or someone else in the family, you may find it more challenging than you anticipated. It may be more difficult to maintain your relationship with your care giver while asking or telling him or her to do things the way you want them done.

When the care giver is a nonrelative, it may be very expensive to have this person come to your home. You are also hiring someone you do not know to come into your home and take care of your child. You must be diligent in asking for references and checking them thoroughly.

One drawback to having in-home care is the isolation your child may feel as he grows older. Children have a need to interact with others, to learn to share and to play. While in-home care can be an excellent choice for your baby, as the child gets older, you may have to arrange opportunities for your child to be with other children.

Care in a Care-Giver's Home.   Taking your child to someone else's home is an option many parents choose. Often these homes have small group sizes and offer more flexibility for parents, such as keeping the child longer on a day you have a late meeting. They may offer a homelike setting, and your child may receive lots of attention.

However, homes are not regulated in every state, so you must check out each situation very carefully. Contact your state's Department of Social Services, and ask about requirements. In some places, local agencies oversee care givers who are members of their organization. Those who provide care must abide by certain standards, such as the maximum number of children allowed in the home (including their own), and the maximum fees they may charge. They may have to attain certain standards, such as CPR and first-aid certification.

Steps for Finding an In-Home Care Giver.   Whether you choose to have someone come to your home or take your child to another person's home, there are some steps you can use to find a care provider. Following the suggestions listed below can help you find the best care giver for your child.

Advertise in local newspapers and church bulletins to find someone to interview. State how many children are to be cared for and their ages. Include information on the days and hours care is needed, experience you are seeking and any other particulars. State that references are required and that you will check them. Then be sure to check all references for anyone you are considering!

Talk to people on the telephone first to determine whether you want to interview them. Ask about their experience, qualifications, child-care philosophy and what they are seeking in a position. Then decide if you want to pursue the contact with an in-person interview. Make a list of all your concerns, including days and hours someone is needed, duties to be performed and need for a driver's license. Discuss these with the potential care giver.

Check all references. Have the potential care giver provide you with the names and phone numbers of people he or she has worked for in the past. Call each family, let them know you are considering this person as a care giver and discuss it with them.

Check it out. After you hire someone, drop by occasionally unannounced. See how everything is when you do this. Pay attention to how your child reacts each time you leave or arrive. This can give you a clue as to how your child feels about the care giver. Do this for any type of child care you choose.

Child-Care Centers. At a child-care center, many children are cared for in a larger setting. Centers vary widely in the facilities and activities they provide, the amount of attention they give each child, group sizes and child-care philosophy.

Inquire about training required for each child-care provider or teacher. Some facilities expect more from a care provider than others. In some cases, a facility hires only trained, qualified personnel, or they train them and provide additional training.

You may find some child-care centers do not accept infants. Often centers focus more on older children; infants take a great deal of time and attention. If the center accepts infants, the ratio of care givers to children should be about one adult to every three or four children (up to age 2).

Don't be fooled by appearances. Even the cleanest, brightest place is useless without the right kind of care provider. Check out the center thoroughly. Visit it by appointment, then stop in unannounced a few times. Meet the person in charge and the people who will care for your child. Ask for references of parents whose children are currently being cared for there. Call and talk to these parents before making a final decision.

Care for an Infant. Be sure the place you choose for your infant can meet his needs. A baby must be changed and fed, but he also needs to be held and interacted with. He needs to be comforted when he is afraid. He needs to rest at certain times each day.

When searching for a place, keep in mind what will be required for your child. Evaluate every situation as to how it can respond to the needs of your baby.

The Cost of Child Care.   Paying for child care can be a big-budget item in household expenses. For some families, it can cost as much as 25% of their household budget. Public funding is available for some families. Title EE is a program paid for with federal funds. Call your local Department of Social Services to see if you are eligible.

Other programs that can help with child-care costs include a federal tax-credit program, the dependent-care-assistance program and earned-income tax credit. These programs are regulated by the federal government. Contact the Internal Revenue Service at 800-829-1040 for further information.

Special-Care Needs.   In some situations, your child may have special needs. If your baby is born with a problem and needs one-on-one care, you may have a harder time finding child care. In these special cases, you may have to spend extra time seeking a qualified care provider.

Contact the hospital where your child has been cared for. Ask for references, or contact your pediatrician. They may be in contact with someone who can help you. It may be better for a child with special needs for the care provider to come to your home.

Caring for a Sick Child.   All children come down with colds, the flu or diarrhea at some time and can't go to day-care. Today, there are ways to handle an illness if you can't take time off from work to stay home.

In many places, "sick-child" day-care centers are available. They are usually attached to a regular day-care facility, although some are connected with hospitals. A center provides a comfortable place where an ill child can rest or participate in quiet activities, such as story time. Often a registered nurse heads the facility. This person can administer medication when necessary. Fees for this type of service run from $45 to $75 or more a day.

Some cities have "on-call" in-home care providers who come to your home when your child is too sick to be taken anywhere. The program is usually run by an agency that deals with child care, and care givers charge by the hour. Getting a person to come to your home is usually on a first-come, first-served basis, so you may have to wait a day for a provider. However, this can be an excellent way to care for a child who is too ill to be taken away from home.

Milestones this 4th Week

✴ *Sleep and Your Baby*

By this time, baby is beginning to adapt to the cycle of day and night, and hopefully, to your schedule. He is developing regular sleep patterns. He may sleep for as long as 6 hours at a time.

Your baby's brain affects how he rests. His sleep is different from yours. A baby spends longer time in REM sleep, in which the heart rate and breathing increase, brain waves intensify and the eyes move under the lids. Dreams occur at this time. REM sleep is lighter than non-REM sleep.

REM sleep is essential for brain growth. A great deal of learning and development are occurring. Research has shown that facial expressions associated with the release of hormones and chemicals important in brain development happen in REM sleep.

While your baby is in this state, you may see him sucking, moving his legs and arms, and hear him making sounds. He wakens easily. He won't begin to experience non-REM sleep until he's about 4 months old. During the deepest phase of non-REM sleep, growth hormone is released in baby's body and he actually "grows in his sleep."

> Baby is still sleeping about 15½ hours a day.

Going to sleep and waking up helps baby bond with his parents. When he falls asleep, he is separating from you. When he wakens and needs to be comforted and you are there, it reinforces the security of your presence.

ᴊⵜ *Baby's Vision*

Your baby's color vision is not fully developed at this time. However, don't avoid colorful objects because you've heard baby sees black and white the best. Bold colors in simple shapes can be stimulating. Toys that include music, movement and color are also enjoyable.

The distance at which things are clear to baby has increased to about 18 inches by this fourth week. His eyes are coordinated most of the time, and he'll follow an object with his eyes. His favorite object to look at is still the human face. He may focus on one or two features, often toward the edge of the face, such as the chin or an ear. He loves to watch your expressions change.

You probably won't have to worry about your baby's eyesight because only 1 in 25 infants has problems with his vision. However, the American Academy of Ophthalmology recommends having baby's eyes checked at 3 months if:

* he was born more than 2 months prematurely
* he doesn't seem to pay attention to what's going on around him as he gets older
* he doesn't seem to focus well
* one or both eyes seem to turn in or out
* if either you or your partner was extremely nearsighted or farsighted as a child; a child's chance of nearsightedness is about 25% if either parent is nearsighted

✤ *Other Changes You May Notice*

Baby's grasp reflex is developing. He may briefly hold onto something you put in his hand before he lets it go. He turns his head from side to side to follow an object with his eyes. He may lift his head high enough to clear the area beneath him, but it takes awhile (as long as 30 seconds) to do it. He can hold his head up briefly while he's lying on his stomach.

When your baby kicks his legs in the air, he's starting to move. You'll notice he begins to move more as he gets older. That's why it's so important never to leave him alone, even for a second, on a changing table or some other surface he could fall from.

> When you change your baby's diaper, bend and straighten his legs in a bicycling motion. It helps strengthen leg muscles.

He may cry loudly if he finds an activity uncomfortable or painful, and he may fuss during a bath. By this time, you may be able to hear a difference in his crying. You may begin to discern whether baby's cry means he's hungry, wet, tired or bored. He may also start making noncrying sounds.

Your baby can distinguish his mother's voice from a stranger's. Some sounds cause him to quiet down and listen, such as singing, talking or music.

Note: See also the box *Milestones this 4th Week.*

What's Happening this 4th Week?

✤ *Comforting a Fussy Baby*

There will be times you need to comfort your fussing baby. Listed below are things parents have learned and shared.

- Use repetitive, rocking motions, such as swaying, rocking in a chair or just sitting down and rocking back and forth.
- Let him suck—whether on a pacifier, his fist, your finger, the breast.
- Stroke and massage him.
- Carry him in a sling or front carrier.
- Bathe him in warm water.
- Hold him close against your chest so he can hear your heartbeat.
- Take him for a ride in his stroller or the car.
- Sing to him.
- Swaddle him snugly.
- Experiment with ways to calm him, such as rubbing his tummy, blowing on his toes, humming softly in his ear.
- Massage may help. One technique to try is to hold baby's foot with one hand. Use the thumb pad of the other hand to press gently and firmly on the sole of baby's foot for a couple of seconds, then release.

If this helps calm baby, continue pressing and releasing his foot for a little longer, then repeat with his other foot.

✒ *Vitamin Supplements*

If your baby was full term, he probably won't need vitamin supplements, whether you breastfeed or bottlefeed. A recent study showed giving a baby vitamins too early may increase the risk of his developing asthma and food allergies later in life. Talk to baby's doctor if you have questions.

In some special situations, vitamins may be recommended. Premature infants may need additional iron because they didn't store it up before birth. Discuss it with your pediatrician if you are concerned.

Make your baby's 1-month well-baby checkup now. See page 36 for any immunizations he may receive at this next visit.

✒ *Regularity of Bowel Movements*

About this time, baby's bowel movements begin to fall into a regular pattern. Your baby may have one or two movements a day that look like a mustard puddle or thick green soup.

✒ *Crossed Eyes*

Many babies have crossed eyes, also called *strabismus* or *lazy eye,* at this early age. It is normal for baby's eyes not to move in unison because his eye-muscle control has not fully developed. You don't need to worry that baby has a problem if you notice this condition at this time.

When this problem does occur, it usually appears in an older baby, around 3 or 4 months of age. If you notice your baby's eyes are crossed at that age, consult your baby's doctor. Many treatments are available, including an eye patch to cover one eye, glasses, exercises for the eye, medication or surgery.

✒ *Failure to Thrive*

If your baby has not gained back enough weight to reach his birth weight by this time, his doctor may be concerned about failure to thrive. The problem may also be suspected if baby was gaining weight then suddenly stops for no apparent reason.

What You Can Do at Home.   Increase the frequency of the feedings you give baby. Feed him longer. Try to get him to take more at each feeding–don't

---

MILESTONES THIS 4ᵀᴴ WEEK

Changes You May See this Week as Baby Develops Physically
* rolls partway to side from back
* when pulled to sitting position, may hold head in line with back

Changes You May See this Week in Baby's Developing Senses and Reflexes
* can grasp object when fingers are pried open but quickly drops it

Changes You May See this Week as Baby's Mind Develops
* remembers object when it reappears within a couple of seconds
* may make an "ah" sound when he sees parents or hears parents' voices

Changes You May See this Week in Baby's Social Development
* may clutch at person holding him
* may make throaty sounds

Every baby is an individual, and your baby may do some of these things more quickly or more slowly than another baby. If you are concerned about your baby's progress, discuss it with your healthcare provider. Also see page xiii.

---

rush him to eat. Setting up a schedule of feedings may help increase his caloric intake. Consultation with a dietician or breastfeeding (lactation) specialist may offer you additional strategies to try. If your baby is not getting enough breast milk from nursing, you may be advised to supplement with formula or pumped breast milk.

When to Call the Doctor.   Contact your pediatrician if this situation occurs. He or she will want to know about it because weight gain is extremely important to baby at this time. In addition to extra or supplemental feedings, baby's doctor may advise you to give baby vitamin or nutritional supplements.

When the above measures don't solve the problem, baby may need to be admitted to the hospital for further evaluation. I.V. therapy may be needed. More serious causes of failure to thrive may also be considered.

⭑ How to Take Baby's Temperature

In some situations, you may be advised by your doctor to take baby's temperature. This can be a little unnerving if you've never done it before. There are several ways to take a baby's temperature. You can take it rectally, axillary (under the armpit) and with an ear thermometer, although experts agree that an ear temperature may not be the best way to take baby's temperature. See the discussion in *Before Baby's Birth*.

Using a Rectal Thermometer. This is probably the most common, accurate way of taking a baby's temperature. Rectal thermometers are inexpensive to purchase and easy to use. Follow the suggestions below to make the task easier.
  * Apply a lubricant, such as petroleum jelly, to the tip of the thermometer.
  * Lay baby on his stomach, across your lap or on a firm surface.
  * Hold him steady to prevent sudden movements. Spread his buttocks so you can easily see the anal opening. Gently insert the tip of the thermometer about ½ inch into the rectum. Hold it in place with your hand to get an accurate reading and to prevent injury.
  * After 2 to 3 minutes, carefully slide out the thermometer and read it.

To take a rectal temperature lay baby on his stomach, across your lap or on a firm surface.

Using an Axillary Thermometer. When you take baby's temperature under his arm, use a rectal thermometer.
  * Make sure your baby's underarm is clean and dry, then place the thermometer in the armpit.
  * Press baby's arm tightly against his side, or hold it across his chest to keep the thermometer in position.
  * After 4 to 5 minutes, remove and read.

Using an Ear Thermometer. This type of thermometer is a fairly new addition to a parent's medicine cabinet.
  * Lay your baby on his back on a safe surface, and turn his head away from you.
  * Gently pull back on his ear to straighten the ear canal. Point the thermometer straight into the ear canal.

Using an ear thermometer.

* Activate the thermometer while holding the ear canal open.
* Wait for a beep, and repeat in the other ear. Use the higher number.
* Because of the difficulty with correct placement in young infant's ears, accuracy may be affected.

What the Temperatures Mean.   If this is all new to you, you may need some interpretation of what various thermometer readings mean. Below is a list of the normal ranges:
* rectal temperature—98.2 to 100.4F
* axillary temperature—95 to 99F
* ear temperature—97.8 to 99.7F

Toys and Play this 4ᵗʰ Week

Choosing Appropriate Toys
When you choose toys for baby, think about his development. Choose ones that are safe and appropriate for his age. It's smart to select toys that he'll be able to play with in many different ways as he begins to mature.

Make Funny Faces
By this time, your baby may be playing with you. A 4-week-old can use his facial expressions to engage your attention. This is his form of play! You can play with him by holding your face about 12 inches away from his and making funny faces. Or stick out your tongue. He'll enjoy it, and it's a wonderful way to communicate.

Bring your face close to baby's, and slowly move your head from side to side. Make mouth noises. Open and close your eyes in an exaggerated movement. Hold his hands near your eyelashes so he feels the movement. Blow gently on his neck. These silly games help him focus and direct his attention.

Keep Talking to Baby
Your baby can pick up your mood from your voice, so talk to him a lot. You can talk in parentese (see *Week 3*) and regular speech. This helps him begin to understand that communication can express emotion.

Read aloud to him; read books, the paper or anything else you read. Material doesn't matter—it's the sound of your voice he'll enjoy. Talk to him while you stand behind the head of his crib, out of his range of vision. Move into his field of vision as you speak to him, so he makes the connection between your voice and your presence.

Sing nursery rhymes to baby, while you gently clap his hands together. Clap in time with the song you sing. Play music to him when he's awake, but don't leave it on as background noise. You want baby to listen to some sounds, not learn to ignore them.

⅍ *Expose Him to Different Textures*
Babies like texture; you can let your baby experience many different textures by lightly stroking his skin with different types of fabric. Velvet, silk, terry cloth, light wool, corduroy—use any at hand, but try not to tickle him.

⅍ *Shake a Rattle*
Lay baby on the floor on his back. Kneeling behind him, gently shake a rattle about 12 inches above his head until his eyes find it. Move it slowly from side to side while his eyes follow it.

Week 5

Baby Care and Equipment

✻ Bathing Baby in a Family Tub

In *Week 3*, we discussed bathing your baby. Some parents enjoy sharing their time in the bathtub with their baby—you might also.

If you bring your baby into the tub with you, there are some precautions to take to keep her secure. Follow the suggestions below to make family bathtime happy, fun and safe.

* Put a rubber mat in the bottom of the tub so you won't slip while you're getting in or out of the tub with baby.
* Have supplies close at hand, such as baby soap and baby shampoo.
* Cotton gloves provide a good grip on her.
* Be sure the bathroom is warm but not hot (about 75F).
* When placing baby in the water, slide her feet into the water first. If she objects to being in the tub (it may seem too big and insecure to her at this time), remove her immediately.
* Hold baby's head in your arm while you wash her.
* Don't stay in the water too long.
* Keep temperature of your water heater below 120F to prevent accidental scalding.
* Lift baby out of the water first. Wrap her in a towel and lay her on the floor, or give her to your partner before you get out.

✻ Baby Swings

A baby swing can be a wonderful piece of equipment when baby is fussy and you need a rest or a free hand. Some people don't like them because they believe baby is too easily neglected when placed in one. Some refer to swings as "neglect-o-matics." However, there are many others who believe swings are heaven sent.

There are various features you might want to consider if you purchase a swing. Be sure any swing you choose has a stable, wide base. With some swings, you place baby in it from the front; other swings are open on the top for ease in getting baby in and out. All swings move in a front-to-back swinging motion; a few also rock from side to side, in a cradle motion.

To make the swinging mechanism work, you must wind or crank it in some swings. In other swings, the mechanism is battery operated. Some swings have only one speed, but speed options range from one to six speeds!

In some swings, the seat that baby sits in reclines in various positions. Some swings are a combination of cradle, swing and infant carrier. These are convenient if you don't want to buy a lot of products or if you don't have a lot of space in your home. Other features include a timer, a toy bar, music and a washable seat pad.

৬ *Baby's Feeding Routine*
By this time, your baby is settling into a routine in her feeding schedule. She's feeding about 6 to 8 times a day and taking in about 2 to 5 ounces at each feeding. She's probably nursing 5 to 10 minutes on each breast; your milk supply is well-established by now. In the next few weeks, you may notice she drops a feeding but increases the amount she takes in at each feeding by about an ounce.

Ways to determine she's doing well include how many wet diapers she has a day—six is a good sign—and how much she is growing and gaining weight. If your doctor is concerned about her development, he or she will discuss it with you at your next well-baby check.

Milestones this 5ᵗʰ Week

৬ *Baby Enjoys Various Sounds*
At about this time, your baby begins recognizing your face and voice. When you talk to her, she may open and close her mouth and bob her head. She is beginning to connect what she hears with what she sees.

She is very sensitive to the sound of the human voice. She listens to voices and may respond to the higher-pitched female voice with her own sounds. She may also move her arms and legs. Whenever someone speaks to her, many impulses go through her nerve cells. Repetition of these kinds of interactions help build existing brain connections and make new ones. Baby also enjoys many other sounds, such as soft music.

Just recently, your baby would stop sucking to listen to a new sound. She still does, briefly, but pays little attention to it unless it's a human voice. She also stops sucking and becomes quiet when studying a person's face. She still doesn't have much of a memory for objects and people, but that is slowly changing.

✴ *Your Baby Continues Her Physical Development*

When she's in a supported sitting position, your baby can hold her head up briefly. She can also raise her head for a brief moment when she's lying on her tummy. To help her develop and strengthen neck muscles, place her in many different positions throughout the day, such as on her back, on her tummy, in an infant seat, in a stroller, in a front carrier or sling, or in your arms.

> By this week, you are probably seeing definite signs of baby's personality! She may be quiet and intense, or she may be active and verbal.

As you play with baby, you'll notice she thrusts her legs and arms out and grasps your finger when you put it in her hand. She relaxes her fist to open her hands and fingers. If her hand finds it's way to her mouth, she may begin sucking and mouthing her fingers or her fist. It's a way to soothe herself.

You may notice her body is uncurling from the fetal position. Her legs are beginning to stretch out a little more. She may arch her back and throw out her arms and legs. She may also stretch her fingers and toes, and twist from side to side. She's gaining more control of her body.

✴ *Her Vision Continues to Improve*

She can now see clearly up to 18 inches. She doesn't have much control over her muscles, so the best she can do is wave her hand and arm in the direction of what she sees. She may try to push at a hanging toy. She'll even hold a toy in her hand a little longer than she did a week ago.

Note: See also the box *Milestones this 5th Week*.

What's Happening this 5th Week?

✴ *Baby Cries to Communicate*

Crying is baby's main form of verbal communication with you for quite a while. By this time, you are probably beginning to recognize her various cries. She may be overwhelmed by her needs and sensory experiences, so answer her cries as soon as you can. Take the following steps to respond to your crying baby.

- ✴ Make sure she isn't hungry, wet, cold, hot or hurt.
- ✴ Take her in your arms as you sit in a comfortable chair. Look at her face. If her eyes are open, look into them. Hold her calmly; don't bounce her.
- ✴ Talk to baby in a quiet voice. Tell her she's safe with you.
- ✴ Gently touch her arms and legs to reassure her.
- ✴ Hold her until her crying ebbs.

MILESTONES THIS 5ᵗᴴ WEEK

Changes You May See this Week as Baby Develops Physically
* actions become more voluntary; reflexes begin to disappear

Changes You May See this Week in Baby's Developing Senses and Reflexes
* may bat at objects
* more easily calmed by a female voice

Changes You May See this Week as Baby's Mind Develops
* memory for objects continues to grow in length

Changes You May See this Week in Baby's Social Development
* can quiet self by sucking on fingers or a pacifier
* quiets when held or when she sees faces or hears voices
* prefers to watch a person as compared to an object

Every baby is an individual, and your baby may do some of these things more quickly or more slowly than another baby. If you are concerned about your baby's progress, discuss it with your healthcare provider. Also see page xiii.

If these measures don't work, you may have to try some other things. The list below offers many suggestions.

* Take baby for a ride in the car—the movement of a car ride often settles a fussy baby.
* Take a shower, and place baby in a safe spot in the bathroom with you. The sound of running water may soothe her.
* Put her in the baby swing, crank her up and let her go. Be aware that when the swing stops, you may wake her up if you have to rewind it.
* A walk might also do the trick, whether in an infant sling or her stroller.
* Massaging can work wonders; we've included a variety of different massage exercises in discussions these first 6 weeks. See the massage technique described on the following page to help relieve gas.
* If you cannot console or calm baby, schedule a visit with her pediatrician to rule out a medical problem, such as an ear infection or strep throat.

Responding to her cries immediately during the first 6 months of life does not spoil her. It does teach her that you will be there when she needs you. Even at this early age, you are teaching her to trust you. This helps her develop confidence, which in turn makes her more able to learn. She will also be more independent as she grows older.

✳ *Stimulate Baby's Gums*

It's never too early to help baby develop strong, healthy gums for the teeth that will soon be breaking through. You can do this by wiping her gums with a clean damp washcloth or a piece of gauze several times during the day and before bedtime at night. This cleaning stimulates the gums, which keeps them healthy and free of bacteria.

This routine also helps her later. She'll be used to having her mouth cleaned, so when it comes time to start brushing her teeth, she won't object!

✳ *Baby Massage*

Place your hands on one of baby's arms; put one hand above the other. Straighten her arm, and gently rotate your hands back and forth, in opposite directions, as you move down baby's arm. Squeeze lightly as you work toward the wrist. (This is not like the "Indian burn" your brother gave you when you were little!) Do this with each of baby's arms before moving on to the next move.

Next, firmly stroke her back, moving from her neck down to her bottom. Firmly pat her back twice and her bottom once in an alternating rhythm. Make a game out of it, and sing her a song in rhythm to your pats.

Massaging baby's arms.

If she has gas, massage her tummy in circles, in a clockwise motion. Press knees into the abdomen to push the gas out. Repeat the massage and leg presses to relieve gas.

✳ *Should Baby Sleep Alone?*

Some parents put baby to bed in her own room from the first day she comes home from the hospital. Some parents want to keep baby close, such as in a bassinet in their room. Other parents want baby in bed with them—a "family bed" situation.

William Sears, M.D., is a pediatrician in favor of the family bed. In a family bed, parents share their bed with their baby. Sears believes sharing a bed develops closeness between the parents and child, and bonding is stronger. There are positive aspects to it—a breastfeeding mother doesn't have to get up to feed baby. She can roll over and let baby feed whenever she wants.

This situation may work only if baby won't disturb you and you can fall asleep quickly. You must be able to sleep in any part of the bed, snuggled closely with another person. And you should have at least a queen-size bed.

A Warning about Family Beds.   There is a downside to the family bed. The number of infants who have died while sleeping in a family bed has increased greatly in the past 10 years. In fact, your baby is 40 times more likely to suffocate if she sleeps in a family bed rather than a crib.

The American Academy of Pediatrics states that bed sharing with family members in an adult bed can be dangerous for baby. Soft sleep surfaces, such as blankets and comforters, can also cause problems. The baby may be more likely to roll onto her stomach. If you or your partner smoke, the risk of SIDS associated with co-sleeping is greater.

Recent research shows that infants who sleep with their parents are at risk of injury from others in the bed. Evidence suggests that a parent can inadvertently roll on top of or next to the baby and smother her. A baby can also get buried in the bedding or caught between the mattress and the wall.

> Baby may be sleeping for as long as 7 hours a night by this time, if she weighs at least 11 pounds and has no digestive problems.

Some studies have shown that babies wake more often in a family bed, and they have less slow-wave sleep. There is no evidence that bed sharing protects against SIDS.

With baby in bed with you, you may not get a restful sleep. It's hard to sleep with a baby in the bed. You may not be able to relax for fear you'll roll on her. Experts believe the only safe place for a baby is in a crib that meets current federal safety standards.

Manufacturers have recently introduced some new items that might help solve some of the problems discussed above. One item is a soft minibed that is placed on top of an adult mattress. One side folds down for access to baby and for easy nursing. Another product rests next to the bed and is for parents who want baby close but not necessarily in bed with them. The unit is placed next to the adult bed, allowing baby her own space right next to mom and dad. Baby can easily connect to parents in the adult bed for cuddling and nursing.

✺ Dehydration

Dehydration results when baby doesn't take in enough fluids or loses too much fluid from her body. It can occur if your baby is not breastfeeding properly or if you are not producing enough milk. It may also arise in cases of vomiting and diarrhea. Dehydration occasionally occurs when a baby becomes overheated then does not receive enough fluid to compensate for her overheating. When this occurs, it usually happens in hot summer months.

Dehydration should be a concern if baby's coloring becomes grayish, her mucous membranes are dry, urination has decreased, there is an absence of tearing, her fontanel (the soft spot on the top of her head) has sunken in and she has a rapid pulse and respiration. (You should be changing six to eight wet diapers a day, and your baby should have three or more stools each day.) Your baby may also be very lethargic.

What You Can Do at Home.   If you notice these symptoms, and you are breastfeeding, carefully monitor your baby's feeding patterns. Make sure you can see or hear her gulping milk when she feeds. Does she seem satisfied after a nursing session? A full baby will be content.

To avoid dehydration, keep baby out of the sun so she doesn't get sunburned or overheated. In hot weather, make sure she has plenty of fluids. Give her water only when advised to do so by your pediatrician. Dress baby appropriately.

When to Call the Doctor.   Call your pediatrician immediately if your baby:
- hasn't had a wet diaper in 6 to 8 eight hours
- has been vomiting for more than 12 hours
- has passed more than 8 diarrheal stools in 8 hours
- has a dry mouth and cries without tears (newborns may not show tears with crying)
- is inconsolable
- seems unusually drowsy or sleepy, or doesn't respond to you
- has a sunken fontanel

Your baby's doctor may recommend oral rehydration in mild to moderate cases. In this situation, baby is given a prepared solution with electrolytes to drink. Frequent, small amounts are fed to her over a period of time.

If the situation is severe, a pediatrician may admit the baby to the hospital. I.V. fluids are given to replace lost fluids. Accurate measurements of fluid intake and output are also recorded.

Hiccups

A hiccup is a contraction of baby's diaphragm; the diaphragm separates the chest and abdominal cavities. It's not uncommon for a baby to have hiccups. Your baby may have had them in the womb. After birth, most babies have frequent episodes of hiccups.

It is unknown why babies hiccup so frequently. We really don't have any way to prevent or to stop hiccups. They commonly occur after feeding, particularly after burping. They aren't harmful but may cause baby to fuss or to cry. You won't need to do anything when baby has the hiccups unless they keep her from eating and/or sleeping. If that happens, call the doctor.

Toys and Play this 5th Week

✿ *Play Songs for Her*

If you have a recording of nursery rhymes to play for baby, she may enjoy the rhythmic cadence. Or you can recite some to her from a book. She'll enjoy the interaction.

✿ *Rattles and Rings*

Because she's beginning to develop her grasp, you might choose some safe rattles or rings. They come in many shapes and sizes. Make a hand puppet out of an old sock, and use it to talk to baby in a high, singsong voice. You may offer her rubber or cloth animals or dolls that have squeaks or bells securely fastened inside. Be sure toys don't have any small parts, such as eyes, that could come loose.

✿ *Rolling the Ball*

Choose a brightly colored ball for baby that is big enough for her to see easily. Sit on the floor while she lies next to you, or place her in your lap. Roll the ball on the floor near her. Let her watch it. She may try to reach for it, or she may just enjoy watching it.

✿ *Tour the House*

Take baby on a tour of the house while you're holding her. Watch her to see what objects she's attracted to. Point them out, and talk about them as you see them.

When you do routine tasks and chores around the house, keep baby close. Talk about what you're doing, and describe your activity. For example, if you're washing the clothes, tell her, "This is the washing machine where we wash our clothes." Let her watch you as you put the clothes in and start the machine. Let her see the water flow in. Describing your activities exposes her to household activities, and your conversation stimulates her.

Week 6

HOW BIG IS BABY THIS 6ᵀᴴ WEEK?

Baby weighs 9½ pounds and is 21¼ inches long this week.

Baby Care and Equipment

✻ *Nursing in Public*

In many countries, breastfeeding in public is a natural part of life. However, some women in the United States feel uncomfortable breastfeeding their baby in public.

If you're like most women, you believe nursing your baby is a private time for the two of you. However, you may find yourself out and about, with baby screaming at the top of his lungs to be fed now! Below is a list of some of the places where you can breastfeed baby with some privacy.

- ✻ The women's lounge–This offers some privacy; if someone walks in on you, it's another woman who is probably not offended if you breastfeed your baby.
- ✻ A women's restroom–A lounge may not be available, but a restroom usually is. Go into a stall, close the door and nurse your baby.
- ✻ A fitting room–If baby's crying is getting on everyone's nerves, including your own, dash into a fitting room for a quick feeding.
- ✻ Your car–Park your car in a place that's away from high-traffic areas, and feed baby there.
- ✻ A local park–Your park may have picnic tables and benches that are somewhat removed from the main area. Using your ever-handy baby blanket, drape it over your shoulder and baby's head for added privacy.
- ✻ Carry baby in a sling–When you carry baby in a front sling designed for breastfeeding, it only takes a minute to undo your nursing top and nursing bra. You can feed baby on the go!

To date, more than half of the states in the U.S. have passed laws dealing with breastfeeding. Seventeen states have passed laws making it explicitly legal to breastfeed in public. These laws exist to support breastfeeding mothers. In six states, laws have been passed that require employers to give breastfeeding mothers break periods to express milk and a private place in which to do it. In 1999, a federal law was passed that allows women to breastfeed on federal property, including federal office buildings, national parks and museums.

✎ *Keep Baby's Head Covered*

A small infant loses a great deal of heat through his head, hands and feet. Before you go out in cool or cold weather, cover baby's head with a cap or warm bonnet. Add a blanket over your carrier for extra warmth, if necessary. When you go into a building that is warm, or when the car gets warm, remove the extra cover from baby. He can be just as uncomfortable overheated as when he is cold.

✎ *Some Additional Facts about Breastfeeding*

By this point in baby's life, your breast-milk supply has balanced out with your baby's demands. You've established a basic routine, and you've discovered what works for you and your baby. You're still feeding him 8 to 10 times in 24 hours, which will continue for the next month or so.

You may notice that around this time (6 weeks), your baby wants to feed more often. At about 6 weeks, many babies go through a growth spurt. Your baby may need to feed more often because he's growing right now. Feed him when he is hungry.

A recent study of more than a thousand children showed that children who were breastfed as babies scored higher on intelligence tests than children who were bottlefed. It also revealed that the longer a woman breastfed, the smarter the child was! Why? Breast milk contains over 400 nutrients that infant formula does not. Omega-3 fatty acids, like DHA, found in breast milk may play an important role in how different parts of the brain develop and communicate with each other.

Your baby may begin to show a preference for one breast over the other about this time. He may even refuse to suck on the other breast. Researchers believe this is an additional effect of the tonic neck reflex, in which turning the baby's head to the side causes him to extend his arm and/or leg on that side.

✎ *Baby's Bowels*

A breastfed baby's bowel movements may become more infrequent. He may poop only once every few days.

Pay attention to baby's bowel movements. A change can alert you to a problem. If the amount of baby's stool—too much, too little—changes, or the stool differs from your child's normal pattern, you may want to call baby's doctor. If any change in baby's stool is associated with a decrease in appetite or fussiness, contact your pediatrician.

If you notice any blood in the stool, call your doctor or take baby to the emergency room. The most common cause of blood in the stool is an anal fissure (see the discussion in *Week 11*), which is a tiny cut or tear in the anal opening.

✶ *Accidentproof Your Baby Carrier*

Nearly 13,000 babies a year are hurt in carrier-seat accidents. Whether you use a car seat or an infant carrier to cart baby around, there are some precautions you should take to make it safer. Choose a carrier with a handle that locks securely in place. It should have a seat belt with a crotch-strap restraint. The base must be wide, for stability, and it should have rubber tips or other nonskid material to keep it from sliding.

Precautions you can take when using an infant carrier include the following safety measures.

- Always use the safety restraint. Be sure it holds baby securely in the carrier.
- Keep baby's hands out of the way when you adjust the handles— you don't want to pinch his fingers.
- Never place the carrier on a counter, table or piece of furniture unless you are holding it. Place it on the floor, away from sharp edges and corners.
- When you carry it, keep one hand on the carrier handle and the other hand under the base.
- Don't leave baby alone in a carrier, even if it is placed safely on the floor.
- Be careful when carrying baby in a carrier—avoid making sharp turns and bumping baby.
- Don't use the carrier when baby is too big or when he begins to squirm and wiggle. He could cause it to fall over.
- If the seat is also a car safety seat, be sure it is correctly installed every time you put it in the car.

✶ *Baby Massage*

Place baby on his stomach on a towel on the floor. He should be wearing only a diaper. Gently turn his head to his right side. Place your left hand on his bottom; with your right hand move your hand down, in one sweeping motion, from the top of his back to your left hand. Repeat as you cover his entire back.

To massage baby's back, move your left hand downward in a sweeping motion from the top of baby's back to your right hand.

✴ *If Baby Is Colicky*

Good news—if your baby has been colicky, it often peaks at about 6 weeks. It may continue until 10 weeks, but it will gradually fade and will be over soon.

Milestones this 6ᵗʰ Week

✴ *Greater Neck and Muscle Control*

Baby is gaining more control over his neck muscles. You may notice he shifts his head more often now for a new view of what's around him. He can hold his head up for a few seconds and may extend his legs when he holds his head up.

✴ *Is He Smiling?*

Baby may be smiling on his own by now. His first smiles were probably not ones of joy or recognition, but by now they are more social in nature. He has been making facial expressions that look like a smile since birth. When you started responding by smiling back at him, you were teaching him one way to interact.

Researchers believe one reason that many of baby's facial expressions are smiles is to encourage attachment between parent and child. Baby makes a grimace that looks like a smile. A parent reacts by smiling and cooing at baby. This reinforces in baby that his actions caused a reaction, and he will continue. Soon his smiles will be social, and he'll smile at you (or anyone else) because of the wonderful interaction it brings.

It is interesting to note that all babies smile, even those who cannot see to interact. Blind babies smile, even though they do not see someone smiling at them. Smiling may be one of nature's ways to ensure a baby can connect socially and emotionally with those around him.

✲ Baby Needs Time on the Floor

Remember to keep putting baby down to sleep on his back. However, he also needs some "tummy time" to develop muscles needed for upcoming developmental tasks.

When you can spend some time with baby without interruption, place him on his tummy on the floor on a blanket. This allows him the chance to lift his head up and eventually to push up with his arms, strengthening neck, shoulder and chest muscles. Baby needs to develop these muscles to push up off the floor, then later to roll over from his front to his back.

✲ He Expresses Excitement

You may notice that baby becomes excited in anticipation of regular activities, such as bathtime or playtime. He may demonstrate this by chortling, cooing or making other noises, while he kicks out his legs.

> You're becoming more relaxed with baby as you get to know him better, so trust your instincts. If you feel something may be wrong, call your doctor.

✲ Vision and Hearing Changes

Baby is more visually alert now when he is in a sitting position. He's beginning to associate lying down with sleeping. Keep him upright, in a semisitting position, for part of his waking hours. He'll enjoy seeing what's going on around him.

Loud noises may startle him. He may also look surprised when he hears a sudden loud noise.

Note: See also the box *Milestones this 6th Week.*

What's Happening this 6th Week?

✲ Introducing the Bottle to a Breastfed Baby

If you find it necessary to feed your breastfed baby from a bottle, there are some things to keep in mind as you help him learn this new skill. It may take some time and repeated effort on your part, but you can help baby by using the techniques described below.

* Don't offer a bottle until breastfeeding is well established. Wait as long as you can, at least until 4 weeks, before offering baby a bottle. Introducing one too soon can interfere with your milk supply.
* Let someone else give the baby a bottle. He associates breastfeeding and breast milk with you.
* Offer the first bottle when he's not hungry. If you wait until he's starving, he may be too distressed to eat. If you feed him a bottle when he's only a little hungry, he'll be able to deal with it better.

MILESTONES THIS 6ᵀᴴ WEEK

Changes You May See this Week as Baby Develops Physically
* can hold head up at 45-degree angle for a few seconds while lying on stomach
* muscle tone improves

Changes You May See this Week in Baby's Developing Senses and Reflexes
* stares vaguely at surroundings

Changes You May See this Week as Baby's Mind Develops
* studies movement of his own hands
* may become excited in anticipation of objects

Changes You May See this Week in Baby's Social Development
* may smile when you smile
* will stay awake longer if interacting with someone

Every baby is an individual, and your baby may do some of these things more quickly or more slowly than another baby. If you are concerned about your baby's progress, discuss it with your healthcare provider. Also see page xi.

* Introduce the bottle slowly. Drop a little milk on his lips from the bottle, then wait until he opens his mouth before you put the bottle in.
* Your baby may take to the bottle better if you hold him in a different position than when you nurse him. When bottlefeeding, sit baby in a more upright position.
* Don't lose your cool—be patient. You may need to try this more than once before baby takes to it. If he gets frustrated, angry or upset, you may need to take a break and try again later.

☙ *Some Baby Hair Facts*

If your baby was born with blond or red hair, he probably had very little of it. With blonde and redheaded babies, hair goes into a resting phase and is shed before birth. Your little one may have been bald or had little hair when he was born. If he had any hair, he'll probably lose it very quickly, and most of it may be gone by this week.

If your baby was born with dark hair, this shedding phase happens later. Your baby will probably have his hair for a while longer, but be aware that he'll probably shed it before long.

✧ *Use What Works to Calm Baby*
Experts recommend that for the first 8 weeks of his life, do whatever helps calm and lull your child to encourage good sleep habits in him. Walk him, rock him, sing to him or play "white noise" in the background. Try many different things, and use what works best with your baby.

✧ *Babywearing May Result in Smarter Babies*
Babies who are carried in front slings or carriers appear to cry less. (For more information, see the discussion of *Front Slings* in *Week 4.*) Instead of fussing and crying, researchers believe the babies spend more time in a state of quiet alertness. During this state, an infant is content and receptive to his environment. He may be more ready to learn during these times.

✧ *Dermatitis*
Dermatitis is a term used to describe several skin conditions. Symptoms of dermatitis include irritation of the skin with itching, mild swelling, redness, oozing with crusting, scaling or thickening of the skin with a shiny surface.

What You Can Do at Home. If your baby has any of these symptoms, try the following measures. Lubricate the affected area with dye-free, perfume-free creams or lotion. Apply cool, wet dressings to relieve itching.

> Your kitchen sink may be just right for baby's bath. It's small enough to make him feel secure, and it's the right height so your back won't be strained!

   Avoid irritants to baby's skin. Don't use soaps or harsh shampoos. Use lukewarm water, not hot water, for bathing. Keep baths short to avoid removing natural oils from skin. Dress baby in light, smooth, soft, loose clothing. Over-the-counter medications may be used to relieve symptoms; check with your pediatrician before using them.

When to Call the Doctor. Call your pediatrician if the rash is persistent and/or causes discomfort to your baby. Call the doctor immediately if signs of infection appear, such as redness, swelling, the area becomes hot to the touch or if the baby acts ill.

   Your doctor may prescribe a topical steroid preparation and other medications to reduce itching. If a secondary infection develops, antibiotics may also be given. In stubborn or severe cases, baby may be referred to a dermatologist.

✧ *When Baby Has a Fever*
A fever may be a sign that the immune system is at work. When your baby has a fever, he may be fighting an infection. Fever is defined as a rectal temperature greater that 101F. See also the discussion of *Fevers and Febrile*

Seizures in *Week 34* and the discussion of *How to Take Baby's Temperature* in *Week 4.*

What You Can Do at Home.   You can try some treatments at home to help reduce baby's fever. The following measures are often used with babies.
- Encourage baby's fluid intake.
- Provide him with plenty of rest.
- Don't dress him too warmly.
- Give him acetaminophen for babies, if he seems uncomfortable. Be very careful not to exceed the recommended dosage. Follow directions and measurements carefully.
- Pay special attention to other symptoms your baby may have.

> Keep baby safe from germs by avoiding crowded areas. Ask people to look but not touch. If family members or friends have a cold, ask them to wash their hands before they hold baby.

When to Call the Doctor.   It's hard not to panic a little when baby has a fever. You are probably very concerned as to what's causing it. If your baby is only 1 or 2 weeks old, call your pediatrician immediately. He or she will probably want to see baby. Call your doctor if the following situations occur.
- Baby is less than 3 months old, and his temperature is higher than 101F.
- Fever is 104F or higher.
- Baby is crying inconsolably and cannot be settled.
- He is lethargic or difficult to wake.
- He has breathing difficulties.
- He seems to be suffering from abdominal pain.
- He has a sore throat and/or difficulty swallowing.
- He looks or acts very ill.
- He shows no signs of improvement after you give him acetaminophen.
- He's had a fever for more than 72 hours.
- He was better, but the fever returned.
- He seems to be having ear pain.
- He has difficulty or pain when urinating.
- He has a febrile seizure.

Your doctor may prescribe various treatments to deal with a fever. Below are some things he or she may recommend:
- alternate ibuprofen with acetaminophen
- antibiotics for an infection causing fever, if it is easily identified
- hospitalization for further testing, fluid hydration and I.V. antibiotics

Toys and Play this 6ᵗʰ Week

✴ *Play Many Sounds*

Some toys that baby may enjoy are those that play or make various sounds. You may be playing CDs or cassettes of lullabies. Baby will also enjoy other sounds, such as water sounds or the sound of waves. There are many CDs and tapes of these sounds.

Some toy manufacturers now make toys that play many different sounds, such as white noise, rain, ocean waves, wind chimes and the tick-tock of a clock. Some toys that play music or sounds have timers that turn off automatically after a certain period.

✴ *The Reaching Game*

Play this game with baby to encourage him to begin using his arms. When you hold a toy near him, he may arch his neck and crane his head to see it in his field of vision. Move it a little closer to him, and place it near his hands. Does he reach for it? If not, place one of his hands on the toy. See if he will hold it for a second or two. If he doesn't hold it, try again, but don't force it.

✴ *Gentle Pulling Can Be Fun*

While baby is lying on his back, grasp his hands and gently pull forward just a little. He will probably flex his neck and lift his head slightly. This encourages him to lift his head and to hold it steady. Make a game of it by singing some rhythmic song as you pull him forward. Be sure you don't pull him up too hard or too fast.

DEVELOPMENT OF YOUR PREMATURE BABY

In some ways, a premature baby is a smaller version of a full-term baby. But in other ways, a preemie is very different. Premature infants live in a world that is different from the womb and also different from the life of a full-term infant at home. Preemies are unique—they require special attention and treatment. And your preemie is unique in his own right!

Never compare your baby to another child, even another premature baby (this may happen when multiples are born). He will grow and develop at his own pace. It's helpful to consider his due date as the point from which his development actually begins. Think of the time between his actual birthdate and his predicted due date as "catch-up time." This period of time allows your baby to finish growing and maturing as if he had still been in your womb. His due date is the point from which to gauge his growth and progress.

Note—When we speak of a "young preemie" in this section, we are talking about a baby born earlier in pregnancy. Although we cannot give an exact time frame, a young preemie refers to a child born between 24 and 31 weeks of gestation.

Your Baby's Overall Development. A premature baby doesn't act like a full-term baby. To help you understand why there is such a difference, it's helpful to know how babies develop. Each baby has five important areas of development—they are all controlled by the brain and develop together. The five developmental areas are:

* physiological—bodily functions that happen automatically, such as heart rate, breathing, digestion, elimination
* motor—body movements, muscle tone
* states of consciousness—sleeping and wakefulness, and the change from one to another
* attention—being able to focus
* self-regulation—keeping the other four areas in balance

The nervous system of a premature baby is not as mature or as developed as that of a full-term baby. This can affect a preemie in many different ways. Below is a list of some of the things you may see with immature development:

* immature physiological development—baby gags easily, has an uneven heart rate, breathing is uneven, he changes color often
* immature motor development—baby twitches, tenses or trembles, is limp or doesn't stay curled up
* immature control of states of consciousness—baby doesn't stay alert for long, fusses a lot
* immature development of attention—baby can't focus on you, tires easily when trying to respond
* immature self-regulation—baby has difficulty calming down, cannot deal with many things going on at the same time

(continues)

DEVELOPMENT OF YOUR PREMATURE BABY (*continued*)

A baby's hearing is fairly well developed by 20 weeks of gestation. He can hear inside the womb, so even when he is born early he will be able to hear. Sight takes longer to develop. Preemies take longer to focus on an object than full-term babies. Vision is not as clear for a preemie either.

The Sleep/Wake States of Preemies. Sleep states for a baby are different from those of an adult. Babies have two distinct sleep patterns, three wake states and an in-between sleep-and-wake state. All babies go to sleep in light sleep, and if they aren't disturbed, wake from a light sleep. The various sleep and wake states are discussed below.

* *Deep sleep* (non-REM sleep)—In this state, baby is motionless. Occasionally he will sigh or twitch. Breathing is even. This type of sleep is important for baby's growth. A full-term baby spends about 15 to 20 minutes in deep sleep and 65 to 70 minutes in light sleep. Young preemies have very little deep sleep; they may move more, and breathing may be uneven. A young preemie may spend only a few minutes in deep sleep before moving back into light sleep.

* *Light sleep* (REM sleep)—During this state, baby may move a lot and make noises. Breathing is uneven, and eyelids may open and close. This is called *rapid eye movements.* Young preemies spend most of their time in light sleep.

* *Wake states*—Babies have several levels of wakefulness, including drowsy, actively awake and alert. When baby is drowsy, he has trouble staying awake or waking up; he doesn't move much. When he is actively awake, he's awake but not looking at anything; he may be quite active. When he is alert, his eyes are wide open, and he looks around. Preemies may try to focus but their eyes are not wide open, and they do not seem fully alert.

* *Sleep-wake transition*—It's hard to determine if your baby is in this state. A baby may actually wake a little then go back into light sleep several times before finally waking up. Young preemies may be in this state quite often.

If a baby is born before 26 or 27 weeks, it may be difficult to determine if a preemie is awake. There is no alert state. When birth is between 27 and 30 weeks, a preemie may be alert for a short time only. When he is awake, he may be drowsy or actively awake.

As baby grows, the amount of time he spends in an alert state increases. The alert state is important because baby must be alert to focus on, and pay attention to, what he sees. This is an important function of learning.

Reaching Milestones. When a baby is born early, it may take him longer to reach an event marking a significant new development or stage. These are called milestones and help you determine how your baby is progressing. In each weekly discussion, we include social, mental and physical milestones to look for as baby grows. Use them to track how your baby is growing and developing. And keep in mind, it really doesn't matter when your child reaches a milestone as long as he eventually reaches it!

DEVELOPMENT OF YOUR PREMATURE BABY (*continued*)

When you evaluate how your child is developing, correct his age for the weeks of prematurity. Consider his development from his due date, not his actual date of birth! For example, if baby was born on April 18th but his due date was actually June 6th, begin measuring his development from June 6th. Consider this his "developmental birthday."

You Can Help Your Baby's Development.   We know preemies may face many challenges in their lives as they grow. However, research shows that many children who were born prematurely may be on a par with their peers as they get older if their home environment is stimulating and they are offered a great deal of interaction. These are within your control—you can make a difference in your child's life in many ways!

As parents, you are your baby's most important social partner, whether baby is a preemie or a full-term infant. There are many ways you can help your baby in his development. It takes patience and attention on your part, but if you make the effort to do the things listed below, you'll help your baby and yourself.

* Learn how to assess your baby's behavior. Become familiar with his different moods, and determine what he needs from you.
* Determine what kind of interaction baby wants and how you should respond.
* Create a comfortable environment for baby by keeping noise levels low, allowing him to sleep when he needs it and providing chances for him to interact when he is alert.
* Acknowledge that your preemie is like no other—allow him the time to progress at his own rate.
* Trust your instincts. As we say throughout this book in various discussions, you know your baby better than anyone else. If something doesn't feel right to you, check it out!

Things to Do When Baby Goes Home.   There are many activities you can do with baby when he goes home that will help him grow and develop. In this section, we will give you some things to do together that will help foster normal development in your baby. Remember to use baby's age as determined from his due date, not his birth date. From his due date until about 8 weeks, try the following.

* Hold baby high enough when holding him at your shoulder so he can look around.
* Let baby raise his head but offer some support in case he needs it.
* Walk around the house with baby so he can see new things.
* Have someone stand behind you and talk to baby.
* Let baby look at himself in the mirror.
* Let baby have some tummy time, but only when he is alert. Never leave him alone on his tummy!

(continues)

DEVELOPMENT OF YOUR PREMATURE BABY (*continued*)

By Age 4 Weeks.   Your baby will continue to grow and to develop when you bring him home. His progress will now be measured in new ways. Look for the following.

* Baby responds to sounds by blinking, crying or startling.
* He cries a lot.
* He follows an object with his eyes.
* He can be comforted.
* He will lift his head for a bit when he's on his tummy.
* He moves his arms and legs.

Follow the suggestions we give each week for toys and play activities to do with baby. Your interaction and attention may be the best gifts you can give him during this first year of life.

When to Be Concerned.   Most of the time, babies who are born early catch up with their peers, and by the time they are in school, no one would ever know your baby was born prematurely. However, sometimes reaching a milestone late can signal a problem for the child. Be concerned when the following occur.

* Your child is delayed in more than one area. Often a child will slow up in development in one area if he's concentrating on another. However, if your child is not developing in quite a few areas, it's time to be concerned. If you use the developmental milestones we present in this book to measure how your child is progressing, and you notice he's fallen behind in many areas, discuss it with your pediatrician.
* Delay is far from the norm. If baby is delayed 3 or 4 months beyond the point at which he should be doing something, it's time for concern.
* Your child doesn't respond when you speak to him or he doesn't seem to understand. Your baby should be able to follow simple directions at various ages. By 1 year, baby should be able to point to a favorite toy if you ask him where it is. By 15 months, he should follow simple requests, such as bringing you his sock if you ask him to. If he doesn't, talk with your pediatrician about it.

If you have questions or concerns about delays your child is experiencing, it may be time to explore the situation with your pediatrician. Discuss your concerns with your baby's doctor; he or she will advise you and recommend specialists if they might provide further medical assessment or treatment.

Note—In various weekly discussions throughout the book, we will include a box of suggestions for activities to do with your preemie. Remember always to consider your baby's "due-date age" as your point of reference for all developmental discussions.

Week 7

Baby weighs 9¾ pounds and is 21½ inches long this week.

Baby Care and Equipment

☙ *Avoiding Burns*

One of the worst feelings you can experience as a parent is accidentally to harm or to allow your child to be harmed, whether sticking her with a diaper pin or tugging her hair too hard when combing it. More seriously, burning or scalding your child can be avoided if you think ahead.

- Never carry baby and a hot beverage at the same time. If baby jerks or squirms, you might accidentally spill some of the hot beverage on her.
- Never cook with baby in your arms. Reaching for back burners or frying foods exposes her to unnecessary risks.
- Place her crib well away from a radiator or heater.

As baby gets older, you'll have to take other measures to avoid burns.

- Block off unused outlets with covers so she can't stick anything in them.
- Keep cords from appliances out of her reach to keep her from pulling them down on top of her.
- Handles on pots and pans on the range need to be turned in, away from the edge, so curious fingers can't grab them and pull them off.

By using a little forethought and planning, you can reduce and/or eliminate some of the hazards that are common around every house. Then you'll be confident that baby is safe.

☙ *Your First-Aid Kit*

It's a good idea to have a first-aid kit at home, in your diaper bag and maybe in your car to deal with small emergencies. You can put one together from items you already have around the house. A small plastic container or a large plastic zip bag work well to keep everything together. Items you might consider include the following:

- a few adhesive bandages (include various sizes, from small to large)
- a tube of triple antibiotic cream

119

* antiseptic spray
* sterile wipes in individual packets
* liquid fever reducer/pain medicine (acetaminophen or ibuprofen for children)
* a bottle of electrolyte solution
* a small pair of scissors
* a pair of tweezers
* a container of waterless antiseptic gel or lotion

> To ensure the good health of your child, you should have five basic first-aid skills. You should know how to:
> * administer CPR
> * give the Heimlich maneuver
> * deal with poisoning
> * control bleeding
> * treat burns
>
> Contact your local hospital or the Red Cross for information on first-aid classes.

Your Diaper Bag—Taking It with You

It's always best to be prepared when you take baby out, even if you're just running to the store for a bottle of milk. Take your diaper bag along; you'll probably need it if you leave it behind. You'll quickly discover this piece of equipment is one of the most valuable you'll have in your collection! Some families even keep an extra diaper bag in the car so they don't get caught without one.

There are many types of diaper bags to consider when choosing one. Some are small and compact. Others are large and roomy. Most bags have long handles that you can sling over your shoulder. Some parents (especially dads) prefer the backpack type that you wear; designs vary and a bag may include a center handle and/or shoulder strap so you can carry it many different ways. This allows both hands to be free for holding baby, setting up the stroller or other tasks. When you choose a bag, pack it with the essentials you'll need to see if it all fits.

No matter what type of bag you choose, opt for a heavy-duty fabric on the outside. While a quilted cotton bag with cute designs is sweet, it may not last as long as a nylon bag with canvas webbing. It probably won't clean up as easily, either.

A zipper on the top of the bag keeps things from falling out. It may also keep baby from getting into the bag as she gets older.

The inside of the bag is also important; easy-to-see-through mesh pouches and dividers make it easy to find things. It's nice to have an assortment of pockets in various sizes to store pacifiers, clean nipples and bottle bags, plastic bags for dirty diapers and other paraphernalia you'll accrue.

Make sure it's well stocked. You may want to include the following:

* clean diapers
* baby wipes
* diaper-rash ointment
* a tube of petroleum jelly
* a changing pad
* a burp cloth
* extra clothes
* a light blanket
* a couple of pacifiers, if baby uses one

If you bottlefeed, include formula and bottles for longer outings. You don't have to worry about these if you breastfeed, but you may want to include some extra breast pads for you.

‿ *When Baby Is Restless*

By this time, your baby is crying less and interacting more. She probably cries about 1¾ hours a day. However, she'll still have periods of fussiness. Because she's a little older, you might want to try some new things to help calm her.

* Let her look around her environment to help calm her. Put her someplace where she can gaze about, such as near a window so she can see outside.

> When baby fusses, take her outside, give her a ride or put her in a carrier. Turn on some music and dance around the room! Keep trying different things.

* While holding her, do vertical knee bends to provide a rhythmic motion. (If you do them correctly, they're also good for you.)
* Have an older sibling or your partner distract her with songs, stories or just talking to her. Sometimes a change with whom she interacts can distract her.
* Massage her using the techniques described in previous weeks and those listed on the following pages.
* Skin-to-skin contact has been shown to stabilize baby's heart rate, regulate her breathing and calm her. Lie down, open your blouse or shirt, and press her naked body against your chest. This is called the *kangaroo carry*.
* "Shush" her; a loud "shhhh" sound is similar to what she heard in the womb. It may help settle her.

* Some devices can offer distraction, such as a battery-operated swing, a vibrating infant seat or a crib-rocking device.
* Hold her as much as she is willing to be held. Research has found that a parent's nurturing may influence genes that affects a baby's response to stress.

As you get to know your baby better, you'll discover what helps calm her. Some babies prefer something that another baby will not like!

✎ *Baby Massage*

Place baby on her back on the floor or the bed. Put your right hand around baby's ankle and your left hand around her thigh. Slide your left hand down to her ankle as you gently squeeze her leg. Then move your right hand up to the thigh. Repeat. When you finish, push the bottom of baby's foot gently with your thumb. Trace a line from the heel to the toe.

If your baby's tummy seems upset, here's a massage technique to try. Gently stroke her tummy from top to bottom; use the outer edges of one hand, then use the other hand. Push her knees gently to her tummy, and hold for a count of 8. Massage her tummy in clockwise circles, one hand following the other. Walk your fingers across her tummy from one side to the other. Repeat as needed.

Gently massage baby's tummy from top to bottom using the outer edge of one hand, then the other.

Milestones this 7ᵗʰ Week

✎ *Her Senses Are Developing*

Your baby's senses are becoming more coordinated around this time. You may notice that she looks toward an interesting sound—she's coordinating sight and sound! She may begin to suck vigorously when she sees a bottle or your breast.

Baby's eyes can easily track a moving object now, beginning from side to side and progressing to up and down. Her focus is also adjusting. She prefers moving objects. She may be distracted when she's feeding as she stops to watch what is going on around her.

She may let you know what she likes to look at, such as bright colors instead of drab ones. She also prefers 3-dimensional objects to 2-dimensional ones. She's becoming more sophisticated in what she likes to look at.

> It's normal for your baby to have flat feet at this time. It takes a few years for the arch to become prominent.

✻ Baby Is Beginning to Use Her Hands

Her hands are becoming more of a focal point for her. She may open and close them, bring them together, wave them around and move her fingers. She may hold a toy for a short time if you put it in her hand. She'll reach toward a toy held in front of her with both hands. She'll even bat at something hanging near her. Soon she will begin staring at her fingers with fascination.

✻ She Uses Her Mouth to Explore

You may notice that your baby is using her mouth to explore her environment each day. She'll put many things in her mouth, including hands (hers and yours), toys, her blanket and anything else she can get there. She doesn't want to eat the things she puts in her mouth; it's her way of exploring. She's using her senses—touch, smell and taste—to get information about her world.

✻ Her Strength Is Increasing

She's raising herself onto her forearms and is holding her head more steadily. She can lift her chest off the surface she's lying on and turn her head from side to side. This gives her a much better view of what's going on around her.

✻ She May Need to Suck

Sucking is still very satisfying to her, especially now that she can find her mouth a little more easily. Some babies have an extremely strong desire to suck; don't worry if your baby has this need. It may be months before it passes.

There is controversy about the thumb versus the pacifier for sucking. Some say a pacifier looks like the parent has "put a plug" in their baby; the thumb is better. Others say the pacifier has the advantage of being permanently removable after a certain age and it's better for baby's teeth when they come in. Whatever your philosophy, realize your baby may need something to suck on!

✢ *She Likes Many Sounds*

Baby may be more vocal; she listens to many sounds. She may quiet and stop sucking to listen very closely to a sound. She still prefers the human voice, and she may be vocalizing more in response to what she hears. Around this time, she is probably cooing. It's her way of connecting with you.

✢ *When She's Tired*

When baby's tired or bored interacting with you, she may turn away from eye-to-eye contact. Or she may arch her back or cry. Some babies become hyperactive.

Learn your baby's signals. She may suck her thumb when she's ready for some quiet time. Quiet time can range from baby lying in her crib to sitting in her infant carrier watching you make dinner to being carried in a front carrier as you work around the house. By being alert to her cues, you'll help her feel she has some control over her situation, which can in turn help boost her self-confidence.

Note: See also the box *Milestones this 7th Week.*

> If you think baby has a diaper rash but the redness appears in the skin creases and has lasted more than 3 days, with no improvement, it may be a yeast infection. Call your pediatrician—he or she may prescribe an antifungal cream to treat the problem.

What's Happening this 7th Week?

✢ *Diaper Rash*

Nearly every baby experiences some form of diaper rash. The most common cause of diaper rash in babies over 6 months old is ammonia, trapped in a diaper against baby's delicate skin. The ammonia forms when bacteria from feces reacts with baby's urine. You'll actually be able to smell an ammonia smell.

Fortunately, diaper rash is not a serious problem, but that doesn't make it any less irritating. When it occurs, skin in the diaper area is irritated and bright red. It often resembles a sunburn when it begins.

What You Can Do at Home.   A diaper rash occurs because skin is irritated from contact with urine and feces. To treat baby's diaper rash, thoroughly clean the irritated area with mild soap and warm water when you change her. Do this with as little rubbing as possible. Avoid baby wipes because they might contain alcohol. Then let her "air dry" for a while. Exposing her skin to air helps. Apply a soothing ointment, such as petroleum jelly or zinc oxide, to the area to protect skin from further irritation. Change her as soon as she is wet again. To help prevent diaper rash, change your baby's diapers frequently to prevent irritation.

The type of diaper you choose when baby has diaper rash may help her. (The diapers discussed here are all disposable diapers.) Some diapers contain aloe to soothe and to protect baby's skin. Some contain baking soda to deal with the ammonia odor. Some diapers contain an antibacterial application. Others are superabsorbent to keep urine away from baby's skin. Another type has a hypoallergenic solution that protects baby's skin from irritants.

When to Call the Doctor. Diaper rash needs medical attention if the above measures don't deal with the problem in a few days. Baby's doctor may prescribe a mild hydrocortisone cream. If the rash persists, your baby may be referred to a dermatologist.

✲ *Hernias in Babies*
Some babies develop a hernia; it is more common in baby boys. The main symptom of a hernia is a bulging on either side of the groin. This may include pain or bloating of the abdomen.

There is nothing you can do to treat the problem. If you believe your baby has a hernia, contact your pediatrician. Surgery is usually recommended to correct it.

Umbilical Hernia. Some babies have an umbilical hernia. This is a weakness or small opening in the abdominal wall around the belly button where a bit of intestinal tissue protrudes when baby coughs or cries. It is more common in low-birth-weight babies, girls and African-American babies.

This type of hernia is often present when baby is born; however, it may not be evident until baby is older. When she strains in some way, it may stick out more.

Most cases of umbilical hernia that appear before baby is 6 months old heal on their own by the time baby is about 18 months old. No special care is needed. In some cases, surgery will be needed to correct the condition. Your pediatrician will advise you.

✲ *Baby's Sweat Glands*
Your baby's sweat glands aren't very active this early in her life. That's why you may notice she doesn't sweat, even when it's hot! A baby doesn't usually

MILESTONES THIS 7TH WEEK

Changes You May See this Week as Baby Develops Physically
* stays awake for longer periods during the day

Changes You May See this Week in Baby's Developing Senses and Reflexes
* visually tracks from outer corner of eye past midline of body

Changes You May See this Week as Baby's Mind Develops
* is interested in sounds
* may glance at hand

Changes You May See this Week in Baby's Social Development
* responds with excitement to a person's presence

Every baby is an individual, and your baby may do some of these things more quickly or more slowly than another baby. If you are concerned about your baby's progress, discuss it with your healthcare provider. Also see page xiii.

begin perspiring until after she is 2 months old. You'll also note that the oil glands in her skin don't produce as much oil as an adult's skin.

Establishing Bedtime Routines

About this time, your baby's physical development stabilizes somewhat, and she'll begin sleeping better. This allows you to introduce a bedtime routine or ritual. She'll learn it's time to settle down and go to sleep when you begin your routine each night.

A routine can include bathing her, dressing her for sleep, feeding her, singing to her or saying her prayers. Place her in her crib while she's still awake. Offer her something to help her settle, such as a pacifier or her thumb. It's probably better if you don't give her a blanket or a stuffed toy so you can keep the crib free of anything that isn't necessary. See the discussion of *SIDS* in *Week 8*.

Should I Give My Baby Water?

Often parents ask about giving baby water as she gets older. Your baby still doesn't need this extra fluid. Breast milk and formula contain enough water for her at this age. Too much water can dilute a baby's blood, which could cause sodium levels and electrolytes to fall, sometimes dangerously. In severe cases, overhydrating with water has caused seizures and coma in an infant.

Until baby begins solids, don't give her extra water. Be sure you mix formula exactly as directed. After she begins eating solids, 1 or 2 ounces of water each day is OK.

Toys and Play this 7th Week

Continue with the play you've been engaging in with baby. She'll still enjoy many of the games you play.

⚹ *Help Her Language Development*

You can encourage her language development by talking to her as often as possible. Describe what you're doing as you feed her, bathe her, change her or put her to bed. Show her different items, and tell her what they are. Take her on a walk outside, and describe the flowers, plants and trees. Go to a park and point out the play equipment there. You may think this is silly, but it actually helps baby in learning to speak later.

⚹ *Dancing Bear (or Other Toy)*

Entertain baby by making one of her stuffed animals dance and sing for her. She'll enjoy watching the movement and listening to the sounds. Sing a song she likes, or make one up as you go. Be creative—she'll love it!

FEEDING YOUR BABY

Feeding your baby is one of the most important things you do as a parent. With your newborn, you must decide whether to breastfeed or to bottlefeed her. See the discussion in *Week 2* on *Breastfeeding* and the discussion in *Week 3* on *Bottlefeeding.* As baby gets older, you will begin adding solid food to her diet.

Baby's Feeding Routine in Her First Few Months of Life.   In the first few months of your baby's life, baby settles into a feeding schedule. She feeds about 6 to 8 times a day and takes in about 2 to 5 ounces at each feeding. If she's nursing, she spends about 5 to 10 minutes on each breast. As she gets older, she may drop a feeding but increase the amount she takes in at each feeding by about an ounce.

By the time your baby is 4 months old, she's taking in between 25 and 40 ounces a day of formula or breast milk. Around this time, she may be ready to start solid foods. Before you make any changes, discuss with your pediatrician when and how to introduce solid foods to her. In this discussion, you will also cover the amounts and kinds of solid foods to offer your baby.

What Is Solid Food?   You may be confused about solid foods. When baby starts solids, is she ready for hot dogs and bran cereal? Does it mean she'll be eating "people" food?

When applied to baby's diet, the term "solids" or "solid foods" means any food that is not breast milk or formula. Even though you will introduce her to many different types of solid food during this 1st year, they do not supply her with the nutrients and calories she needs. She will continue to get that from the breast milk or formula you give her. You offer her solid food to help her learn how to move food around in her mouth with her tongue and to learn how to swallow it. You also expose her to different food textures.

Solids for Baby's 1st Year.   Solid food for baby's 1st year is actually a progression from very watered-down cereal to actual table food you eat. Very thin cereal is considered a "solid food." On page 130, you'll find a guide to the kinds of foods baby will be eating at various times during her first year. Baby will continue to receive most of her calories and nutrition from breast milk or formula until she is 1 year old.

- 4 to 5 months—infant's rice cereal, very thin, made with breast milk or formula
- 4 to 6 months—infant's rice cereal, thicker, made with breast milk or formula
- 5 to 6 months—in addition to infant's rice cereal or barley cereal made with breast milk or formula, pureéd foods, such as meat, fruit and vegetables
- 7 to 8 months—in addition to oatmeal or infant's rice, barley or wheat cereal made with breast milk or formula, strained foods, such as meat, fruit and vegetables

❀ 9 to 10 months—infant cereal and lumpy or mashed foods, such as meat, fruit and vegetables

❀ 10 to 11 months—infant's cereal and junior commercial baby foods

❀ 12 months—bite-sized table ("people") food

Is She Ready for Solid Food?   Some babies are ready to start solids before other babies of the same age. Before a baby can begin eating solids, she must be able to control her neck muscles, sit with support, show when she is full and indicate her wants by reaching or leaning toward something. She also needs to be able to move her tongue back and forth. Most babies can't do these things until they are between 4 and 6 months old. In addition, baby should also have nearly doubled her birth weight.

Beginning solid foods is a big step in baby's life. Below is a checklist to help determine if your baby is ready for this important step. Your baby should be able to do most, if not all, of the following:

✓ control her neck

✓ sit up with support

✓ show when she is full (turns her head or refuses to open her mouth)

✓ show interest in food when you eat

✓ mimic you when you eat, such as opening her mouth when you open yours to take a bite

✓ indicate her wants by reaching or leaning toward something

✓ seem hungry for more food

FEEDING YOUR BABY

The amount of food your baby eats changes during her first year. You will probably begin with two feedings each day of thin cereal made with breast milk or formula. Each feeding may be as small as 2 teaspoons or as large as 2 tablespoons. As she grows older, you will add more variety to her diet. Below is an overview of baby's first year of feeding.

Newborn to 1 month
6 to 8 feedings/day of breast milk or formula,
2 to 5 ounces at each feeding

1 to 2 months
5 to 7 feedings/day of breast milk or formula,
3 to 6 ounces at each feeding

2 to 3 months
4 to 7 feedings/day of breast milk or formula,
4 to 7 ounces at each feeding

3 to 4 months
4 to 6 feedings/day of breast milk or formula,
6 to 8 ounces at each feeding

4 to 6 months
4 to 6 feedings/day of breast milk or formula,
6 to 8 ounces at each feeding
2 feedings of infant's rice cereal,
1 to 2 tablespoons at each feeding

6 to 8 months
3 to 5 feedings/day of breast milk or formula,
6 to 8 ounces at each feeding
2 feedings of infant's rice or barley cereal,
2 to 4 tablespoons at each feeding
2 feedings of fruit,
2 to 3 tablespoons at each feeding
1 feeding of fruit juice,
3 ounces juice; 3 ounces water
2 feedings of vegetables,
2 to 3 tablespoons at each feeding

8 to 12 months
3 to 4 feedings/day of breast milk or formula,
6 to 8 ounces at each feeding
2 to 3 feedings of infant's rice, barley or wheat cereal,
2 to 4 tablespoons at each feeding
2 to 3 feedings of bread or crackers,
1/2 slice; 2 crackers
2 feedings of fruit,
3 to 4 tablespoons at each feeding
1 feeding of fruit juice,
3 ounces juice; 3 ounces water
2 to 3 feedings of vegetables,
3 to 4 tablespoons at each feeding
2 feedings of meat, egg yolk or cooked, dried beans,
3 to 4 tablespoons at each feeding

Week 8

Baby weighs 10¼ pounds and is 21¾ inches long this week.

Baby Care and Equipment

↞ *Are Plastic Nipples and Pacifiers Safe?*

Some concern has been raised in the past about the plastic used in bottle nipples and pacifiers; some parents wonder if they contain DINP (phthalate), a toxic chemical. Rest assured—a spokesman for the Consumer Product Safety Commission stated that no products on the market today contain phthalate. Nipples and pacifiers are all made of silicone or latex. Those that contained phthalate were removed from the shelves in 1998.

For further information on DINP, see also the discussion in *Week 34*.

↞ *The Safety of Plastic Baby Bottles*

News stories have suggested that clear plastic baby bottles might be unsafe because they contain BPA (bisphenol-A). It was implied that heating a baby bottle could cause BPA to leach into formula or breast milk. The Food and Drug Administration (FDA) has studied the situation and maintains these bottles are safe. Their ongoing research has found no problems with baby-bottle usage and no risk from other food containers that contain BPA.

If you want to make sure your bottles are OK to use, don't heat formula in them in the microwave. Instead, heat formula on the range, then put it in a bottle. Using soft plastic liners made of opaque, colored plastic is also safe.

↞ *Baby Massage*

This massage technique helps baby relax, and it can also help relieve any gas he may have. You might even feel the gas bubbles releasing under your fingers as you massage baby's chest and tummy.

Place baby on his back on the floor or on the bed. Use your fingertips to walk across his tummy lightly from right to left. Next, massage baby's chest by placing your hands in the center of his chest. Moving your hands in a heart-shaped motion, move hands out to the side at the same time, down the side of his chest. Move down the rib cage, then back to the starting position. Repeat 8 to 10 times.

✢ *The Facts about SIDS*

In the U.S., Sudden Infant Death Syndrome (SIDS) strikes about 3000 babies a year; it most often occurs in children under 1 year of age. In fact, 90% of all SIDS deaths occur within the first 6 months of life. More boys are affected than girls, and there is a higher rate of SIDS among Native-American and African-American infants. Premature infants, low-birth-weight babies and babies exposed to secondhand smoke suffer more often from SIDS. In addition, a higher-than-ordinary number of SIDS deaths occur in infants who suffered from a recent infection, such as a respiratory illness or intestinal problem. There are few warning signs, and the cause is still not completely understood.

A few years ago, the American Academy of Pediatrics began advising parents to place a baby on his back or his side to sleep. This advisory was based on foreign studies that showed babies who slept on their stomachs were at higher risk of SIDS. Since this sleep position has been adopted, some researchers claim a 50% reduction in the rate of SIDS. Be aware that when a baby sleeps on his side or back consistently, his head may become flattened as a result. It's not a serious problem, but discuss it with your pediatrician if you notice it.

There are other factors believed to contribute to the occurrence of SIDS. Recently, parents have been advised to remove everything from baby's crib

Lay baby on his back when you put him to bed. Remember— "back" to sleep is best.

except a fitted crib sheet and baby himself. Keep baby's crib free of bumper pads, toys, blankets, sheepskin pads, pillows and comforters. Make sure his mattress is firm and flat—don't use a waterbed mattress and avoid buying a used crib mattress! If baby needs added warmth, dress him in warm sleep clothes, such as a blanket sleeper. Researchers believe these practices could reduce the rate of SIDS by an additional 30%!

Further recommendations to reduce the risk of SIDS include the following.

- ✢ Don't smoke around baby! We know that secondhand smoke contributes to the problem.
- ✢ Keep baby off soft surfaces, such as couches, waterbeds, bean-bag chairs,

adult beds, quilts and comforters. Some of these surfaces may trap carbon dioxide.

* Breastfeed baby. We aren't sure why this protects him, but it appears breastfeeding does offer added protection.
* Don't keep your house or baby's room too warm. Keep the temperature at a point that is comfortable for you. It has been shown that babies who become overheated are at higher risk of SIDS.
* If your baby sleeps with you, keep him near but not too close to reduce the possibility of suffocation. Many experts suggest baby sleep alone.
* If you are concerned, discuss the situation with baby's doctor. With certain medical conditions, such as symptomatic gastroesophageal reflux, it may be better for baby to sleep on his tummy.

Babies who are used to sleeping on their backs are at particular risk of SIDS when they are put on their tummies to sleep. People who care for your baby may not know about back to sleep, so be sure to tell them always to put baby down on his back. Your mother or mother-in-law may fall into this category—20 years ago, we were all told the opposite of what you are advised today!

> Remember— "back" to sleep is best!

Alternative Sleep Position. If baby has a difficult time sleeping on his back, place him on his side with his lower arm brought forward. This keeps him from rolling onto his stomach.

If your baby sleeps on his side, be aware that he might develop a flattening of the side of his head. It's not a serious problem, but it's not attractive either. Place him on his other side if the problem occurs, or turn his crib around so he turns his head to the other side to see what's going on around him.

If your baby is premature, discuss this situation with your pediatrician. He or she may have particular advice for you.

Milestones this 8ᵗʰ Week

⅃ *Baby's Memory Is Growing*

At birth, baby had recognition memory. He would behave differently when shown objects, sounds or smells he had seen before than with new things. He had not developed much of a short-term or long-term memory. But as he is growing older, he can now remember how to perform certain tasks.

His short-term memory is beginning to develop. Baby's expanding memory allows him to associate certain events with particular consequences. He begins to anticipate certain events when given a particular clue, such as getting excited about feeding when he sees a bottle.

✎ *He's Smiling and Making Noise Now*

By this week, he's smiling when you smile at him. He may even smile on his own! He's making many different noises now, such as gurgling, grunting and humming to express his feelings. He may try to imitate your exaggerated facial expressions, and he'll probably enjoy looking at himself in the mirror.

✎ *His Physical Control Increases*

His physical abilities are also increasing. He can lift his head up 45 degrees when he's hungry. When you hold him in a sitting position, he can keep his head up most of the time. His eyes can focus up to 10 feet away, and they will follow you when you move away from him. Bright colors are still favorites. He may turn his head and look toward a sound that interests him.

His increased physical control spurs him to constant activity. When he's on his back, he may make bicycling motions with his legs. In a sitting position, he may circle his arms above his head. When he's on his tummy, he may rock back and forth with his arms and legs stretched out and his back arched.

✎ *He's Fascinated with His hands*

Now that he has discovered his hands, he may examine them closely. He'll bring them to his face and touch his nose, eyes and mouth. If he puts something in his mouth, such as a toy, he'll suck on it and his fingers! He experiences the double sensation in his fingers and his mouth. Sucking helps him realize that his fingers are a part of him, and the toy isn't. He's beginning to distinguish between what is part of his body and what is separate.

Note: See also the box *Milestones this 8th Week.*

What's Happening this 8th Week?

✎ *Traveling with Baby*

Because baby is getting a little older, you may be planning to take him out of town to meet his grandparents or other relatives. This discussion deals with some general advice when getting ready to go; we cover travel by car and by plane in later weeks.

As we've discovered, along with almost every other parent we know, when you travel with baby, you're going to need a lot more stuff than you normally would. It might seem like a lot to cart around (and it is!), but we know from experience that if you don't have it, you'll undoubtedly need it!

As you pack, think about what you'll need in the short term (have at hand in your diaper bag) and the long term (in the suitcase). For the diaper bag, consider the following:

* two changes of baby clothes, including extra socks
* plenty of disposable diapers, at least 8 or 10

MILESTONES THIS 8ᵀᴴ WEEK

Changes You May See this Week as Baby Develops Physically
❧ head remains fairly erect when baby is in the sitting position, but it is still wobbly

Changes You May See this Week in Baby's Developing Senses and Reflexes
❧ cycles arms and legs smoothly

Changes You May See this Week as Baby's Mind Develops
❧ can discriminate among voices, people, tastes and size of objects
❧ picks out mother's voice from a group of others
❧ repeats actions for own sake

Changes You May See this Week in Baby's Social Development
❧ watches a person alertly and directly

Every baby is an individual, and your baby may do some of these things more quickly or more slowly than another baby. If you are concerned about your baby's progress, discuss it with your healthcare provider. Also see page xiii.

❧ a few cloth diapers to use as bibs and burp cloths (they can also be used as diapers in an emergency!)
❧ one resealable plastic bag containing a damp washcloth
❧ baby wipes
❧ something for baby to eat, already prepared, such as premixed formula
❧ a couple of large plastic bags for soiled things
❧ 4 or 5 medium-sized resealable bags
❧ 2 or 3 bottles
❧ some toys for baby—include his favorites
❧ several pacifiers—you want more than a couple, in case you lose one or two
❧ some object that comforts baby, such as a blanket or stuffed toy
❧ your first-aid kit, including infant pain reliever, bulb syringe, diaper cream, decongestant and/or antihistamine, a thermometer, bandages, antibiotic cream, ear drops and any prescription medicines your baby uses
❧ your pediatrician's contact information

For summertime outings, dress baby in the same number of layers you are wearing.

In addition to the clothes you pack for baby, you may want to include other things in your suitcase that may make traveling a little easier for all of you. Select those items you believe you'll need from the list below:

* familiar toys for baby to play with
* clothes for various climates—if you're going to a warm place, don't forget to pack a couple of sweaters because air-conditioned buildings can be quite chilly
* a copy of baby's medical history and important numbers for reference, if needed
* prescriptions to be filled, if baby will need any medications
* extra formula, bottles, nipples and liners, if you use them
* extra diapers

Malabsorption Syndrome

Some babies suffer from malabsorption syndrome. They do not absorb enough nutrients from the food they eat. When a baby has malabsorption, he loses weight, displays physical weakness and has gas and diarrhea, often with foul-smelling bowel movements. The problem can arise from, or be associated with, infections, lactase deficiency or antibiotic treatment.

What You Can Do at Home.   If you believe your baby may be experiencing this problem, observe his bowel movements. Make note of their amount and regularity. Indicate whether they are particularly foul smelling. Increase the number of times you feed him each day, and offer him more at each feeding.

When to Call the Doctor.   Call your doctor for advice. He or she may want to see the baby, especially if there is no obvious reason for problems, such as baby has been taking antibiotics. Your physician may change baby's diet and/or prescribe vitamins. Further testing may also be necessary.

Diarrhea

When your baby gets diarrhea, it's not an illness. It's a symptom of a medical problem, usually one involving the gastrointestinal area. It's more common in older infants, although babies of almost any age can have diarrhea.

If your baby has more than five loose, liquid or watery bowel movements in one day, and he is otherwise healthy, he has diarrhea. Loose stools may be accompanied by irritation and/or diaper rash around the anus. Baby may be fussy and/or have cramplike pains in his lower abdomen. In some cases, he may run a fever.

What You Can Do at Home. When baby has diarrhea, the most important thing you can do is increase his fluid intake. Don't give him any medications, unless your pediatrician tells you to do so. If baby is eating solids, decrease the amount you feed him.

When to Call the Doctor. Contact your pediatrician if you notice any of the following.

* Diarrhea lasts longer than 36 hours.
* There is blood in the stool.
* His temperature is higher than 102F.
* He isn't feeding well or refuses to eat.
* He appears dehydrated—his mouth is dry or urination decreases.
* You see worms or other parasites in the stool.

Your doctor probably won't prescribe medication to treat the diarrhea if baby is less than a year old. Your pediatrician may recommend you stop feeding him his regular diet of formula or breast milk and solids. You may be advised to give him an electrolyte solution to replace those he has lost. In some cases, you will be advised on how often to feed baby and the amounts to give him.

Make your baby's 2-month well-baby checkup now.
See page 36 for any immunizations
he may receive at this next visit.

WELL-BABY CHECKUPS

During this first year of baby's life, you'll probably see your pediatrician quite a lot. It's not uncommon for a baby to have ear infections, colds, diarrhea and other ailments that require medical care. In addition to seeing baby's doctor for illnesses, you'll also need to visit the office for well-baby checkups.

According to the American Academy of Pediatrics, your pediatrician should see your baby about eight times during his first year. Checkups are done within 24 hours after birth in the hospital, a few days after discharge if you were in the hospital less than 24 hours, at 2 weeks, 4 weeks (1 month), 8 weeks (2 months), 16 weeks (4 months), 26 weeks (6 months), 36 weeks (9 months) and 52 weeks (1 year).

What Happens at Well-Baby Checkups?
When you take baby in for his well-baby checkups, he will receive his scheduled immunizations. See the chart on page 36. His weight, height and head circumference will be measured at each visit. His progress will be noted on a weight-and-height chart. Your baby's doctor will also check him out from head to toe. At each appointment, your pediatrician will check the following.

* Head check. Your pediatrician will examine the fontanel to see how it is closing. He will measure baby's head and record it on his growth chart.
* Eye check. Baby's eyes are examined to see how his pupils dilate. The doctor will look for any vision problems and check his vision and eye movement by moving a light in his visual field.
* Mouth check. An examination of his mouth will reveal any problems, such as infections. Signs of teething will also be noted.
* Nose check. Looking into his nostrils will reveal signs of infections. The doctor also examines nasal passages for signs of abnormal development that could interfere with breathing.
* Ear check. Your pediatrician may do some things to test baby's hearing. He or she will also look for signs of ear infection. If there's any wax buildup, your doctor will note it, as well as fluid behind the eardrum.
* Abdomen check. Feeling baby's abdominal area reveals any abnormal growths or enlarged organs. You may also be asked questions about your baby's feeding routine and any problems he may be experiencing. His bowel habits will also be discussed.
* Chest check. Examining baby's heart and lungs is important. The heart will be evaluated for abnormal sounds or rhythms. His lungs will be listened to and examined for signs of infection or breathing difficulties.
* Legs, hips and feet check. A dislocated hip is checked for when the doctor rotates baby's legs. Legs and feet are examined for proper growth and development. When he starts walking, your doctor will check for proper leg-and-feet alignment and for any walking difficulties.

WELL-BABY CHECKUPS (*continued*)

❧ Genital check. Your pediatrician will check baby's genitals to make sure there are no unusual symptoms or signs of infections. With a baby boy, the doctor will check that a circumcised penis has healed properly. If a boy is uncircumcised, the doctor will make sure the penis is being cleaned properly. He will also check the testicles.

❧ Baby's development check. You will be asked questions about your baby's development. These questions will cover physical, mental and emotional development. Your observations of baby's development are important in this assessment.

❧ Diet and sleep check. Your pediatrician will ask you questions about how your baby is eating and sleeping. As baby gets older, his diet will change as you offer him solid foods. Sleep problems may appear then disappear throughout this first year.

❧ Parent check. Baby's doctor will answer your questions and will be interested to hear your concerns about various aspects of your baby's development. He or she will offer you advice and resources to help you be the best parent you can be.

What the Doctor Looks for at Particular Times

During the year, your pediatrician will look for baby to achieve certain milestones at well-baby checkups. Some of the things he or she will take note of are listed below.

2-Week checkup. Your doctor will use this visit to ask about baby's family medical history. You will also be asked questions about your pregnancy and the baby's birth. Your doctor may discuss baby's feeding (bottle or breast). His height and weight will be compared to his birth height and weight. The PKU test may be repeated.

2-Month checkup. Milestones the pediatrician will look for include smiling, cooing, following a moving object with his eyes and whether baby grasps an object momentarily when it is placed in his hands.

4-Month checkup. Your pediatrician will determine if baby tries to grab an object hanging above him. He should also be able to hold his head up without support.

6-Month checkup. Your doctor will observe whether baby reaches for an object he wants. He should also repeat some spoken sounds. Has he doubled his birth weight?

9-Month checkup. Baby's doctor will note his many accomplishments—sitting unsupported, crawling, cruising. His pincer grasp should be well developed. His legs and feet will be examined. A test for anemia may be done.

(continues)

WELL-BABY CHECKUPS (*continued*)

1-Year checkup. Baby's legs and joints will be examined for any problems. Milestones the doctor will look for include cruising or walking on his own and climbing. Any words he is speaking and his understanding of other words are also noted. He may be tested for tuberculosis at this visit.

What You Can Do During Visits

It's hard for a baby to be poked and handled during an examination. It may be especially hard for him to have an injection—and it can be hard on you, too! To calm him when you go to the doctor, you might want to try a few tricks parents have learned over the years.

* Schedule the appointment when baby is at his best.
* Hold your baby during the exam and any procedures. It keeps him calm and helps the doctor.
* Distract him when possible with a favorite toy or a pacifier. Sing, if you think that may help.
* Breastfeed him. When he receives injections, this can help a great deal.
* If you're not breastfeeding, hold him close. Skin-to-skin contact helps soothe him.
* Don't get uptight yourself; baby can sense it. If you just can't stand watching baby have an injection, leave the room.

Toys and Play this 8ᵗʰ Week

By this time, when baby is tired of playing, he may begin sucking, wrinkling his face, staring vacantly, yawning, squirming or crying. Be aware of these various clues that he wants some quiet time.

Your baby continues to learn from toys that appeal to his developing senses. Bright colors, bold patterns, interesting textures and fun sounds will make him smile as they help him learn. Around this time, or in the near future, he'll begin to enjoy colors more—red, green and blue are the best! He likes bold color, not muted colors or pastels. In a short while, baby will even begin to see different shades of color.

✸ *Encourage His "Pushups"*

Because his neck muscles are getting stronger, your baby may start doing "minipushups," which raise his head and chest off the floor. As he has the opportunity to lift his head, he learns to coordinate his head and eye movements. This allows him to see more of his surroundings.

Put him down on his tummy on the floor several times a day to practice. If you place an unbreakable mirror or a dangling mobile (be sure it's completely out of reach) a little off the floor in front of him, it encourages him to practice this activity, which helps strengthen his neck muscles. Be sure to turn him over occasionally so he can lie on his back and see what's going on.

✎ *Tell Him Stories*
Storytelling may be one of your earliest interactions with baby. Make up stories about what you're doing with any activity. You might want to show him some simple pictures in a magazine or book, and make up a story about them. They don't have to make sense. It's fun to be silly together.

✎ *The Bell Game*
Find a tiny bell to use with baby; if you don't have a bell, use a rattle. Tinkle it on one side of his head, then move it slowly to the other side while ringing or shaking it. Bring it into his line of sight, and let him reach for it. This helps him develop eye–hand coordination. It also strengthens his ability to locate a sound while it's moving.

✎ *Act Like Baby's Mirror*
Act like a mirror with baby. When you're interacting, such as changing his diaper or giving him a bath, imitate his facial expressions. When he smiles, smile back at him. When he grimaces, you grimace. Exaggerate your expressions. When he sees his face reflected in yours, it reinforces his self-awareness.

> Playing helps strengthen family bonds, while it helps your baby develop physically and mentally.

Week 9

HOW BIG IS BABY THIS 9ᵀᴴ WEEK?

Baby weighs 10½ pounds and is 22 inches long this week.

Baby Care and Equipment

✎ *Vaccinations Are Important for Your Baby*

Today, by the time a child is 2 years old, she may have had as many as 20 immunizations. These immunizations protect your baby against many serious diseases. The American Academy of Pediatrics recommends vaccinating your baby against the diseases we can protect her from. However, some people believe having their baby immunized could be harmful to the child. The truth is that vaccinations strengthen a baby's immunity. By giving your baby small, harmless amounts of a germ in a vaccine, the body is stimulated to produce an immune response.

Vaccines available today protect against whooping cough, tetanus, diphtheria, hepatitis B, polio, measles, mumps, rubella, influenza and chicken pox. Immunizations are given at various intervals throughout a child's life, although the majority of them are given by the time a child reaches the age of 5.

Super-Combination Vaccines. The first combination vaccine was the DPT shot—we received the series as children. It protects against diphtheria, pertussis (whooping cough) and tetanus. Then the MMR vaccine was developed; it protects against measles, mumps and rubella. Today we have other combinations to help make getting all these injections easier on your baby.

Pediarix is a combination of the diphtheria, tetanus, whooping cough, hepatitis B and polio vaccines. A child receives one injection at 2, 4 and 6 months of age. This combo eliminates 6 of the 20 immunizations babies get in their first 2 years.

In the future, you may see the *MMRV vaccine,* to protect against measles, mumps, rubella and varicella (chicken pox). In addition, researchers are working on vaccines to protect against RSV (a life-threatening respiratory infection in babies and small children) and rotavirus (a diarrheal disease). Some of the vaccines may even be delivered as a nasal spray—*FluMist* is a flu vaccine that is given as a nasal spray.

Some Recommendations. All children should be vaccinated for their safety and the safety of others. When a child is not vaccinated, she puts others at risk, especially those children who cannot be vaccinated because of allergies or poor health. Have your baby vaccinated against childhood diseases, and always follow her immunization schedule!

If a child is immunized too early or too late, the effectiveness of a vaccine may be affected. Be sure to follow your pediatrician's recommendations. A child can receive an immunization when she is sick, as long as she is not running a high fever or is severely ill.

The Centers for Disease Control (CDC) recommends that all children over the age of 6 months receive the pediatric influenza vaccine. Infants who get the flu can become very ill, often ending up in the hospital. It also helps lower the rate of transmission.

The CDC also recommends Prevnar be given to children under age 2—it protects against bacterial meningitis and ear infections. It is especially recommended for children with tubes (cochlear implants) or compromised immune systems. However, the vaccine is very expensive ($250 for a four-dose series) and often is not covered by insurance.

> You may have heard rumors linking the MMR vaccine to autism. Numerous studies have shown that the vaccine does not increase the risk of this occurring. So go ahead and have your baby vaccinated!

✎ Front Carriers

A front carrier is a soft carrier that you wear on your chest. When you wear it, you can comfort and/or entertain baby. If she's fussy or needs calming, face her toward your chest. She'll feel secure, and it helps calm her. When she's alert and active, face her out so she can see the world. She'll enjoy seeing what you see.

Some carriers serve more than one purpose. Some can be worn on the back. Others can be used as infant seats. These carriers can be used until baby weighs a little over 20 pounds, although some models support higher weights. Check weight specifications when you are comparison shopping.

An added plus—because these carriers look so much like a backpack, men usually don't mind wearing them. It's a great way for Dad to interact with baby.

✎ Should You Pierce Baby's Ears?

Many mothers want to have baby's ears pierced at an early age. Some doctors advise against the procedure, stating that during the first few months, baby's immune system is not fully developed. Others believe that if a sterile technique is used to pierce the ears and other precautions are followed, it's OK.

Some physicians advise against piercing the ears until at least two immunizations against diphtheria, whooping cough and tetanus (DPT) have been given to your baby. This is usually done by the time your baby is 4 months old.

Be sure the person who is piercing baby's ears has experience piercing the ears of very young children. Use 14k gold posts to avoid allergic reactions. Some babies develop an allergy to the nickel in sterling silver or stainless-steel posts.

Keep the area very clean after piercing (follow the technician's instructions) to avoid infections. Strep or staph bacteria can get into an open wound, causing the earlobe to become red, swollen and sore. This type of infection is treated with antibiotics.

Once the ears are healed, your greatest concern will be the earrings themselves. It might be best to choose earrings that have a screw-on or tension back so they have less chance of coming off. When baby starts playing with her ears, you don't want her to put an earring in her mouth and choke on it.

✴ *Radiators and Forced-Air Heat*

When placing baby's crib in a room, keep it away from heaters or radiators, and out of the line of air flow from hot or cold air ducts. If a baby touches a hot radiator, she can get a bad burn. Her chances of getting a cold or other respiratory infection increase when she is exposed to heated air from air ducts. It dries out her nose and throat, which may increase her chances of infection.

✴ *Car Essentials*

When you travel with baby in the car, it's a good idea to have various items at hand—not for baby but for you, in case of a roadside emergency. Keep the following with you, if possible:

- cell phone or CB radio
- first-aid kit
- jumper cables
- flares and/or reflectors
- flashlight and batteries
- reflective clothing
- blankets and towels (a lightweight solar blanket is a good addition)
- water and basic foodstuff
- fire extinguisher
- basic tool kit
- flat-tire aerosol repair kit

> Always carry extra baby basics when you go out, like pacifiers and burp cloths.

You may never need these things, but having them available gives you an added sense of security.

Milestones this 9th Week

A child's early experiences in life actually help her brain grow. That's why it's so important to interact with baby as often as possible. It takes effort on your part, but the payoff is a happier, healthier baby.

✒ *Patterns Become More Established*
Baby is settling into sleeping and feeding patterns now. She is more alert and responsive at certain times during the day. She may be sleeping as long as 7 hours at night.

✒ *She's Attracted to Sounds*
Your baby is becoming more attentive to various sounds, and she can locate a sound source with her eyes. She can pick out her mother's voice from a group conversation. She listens intently and watches your eyes and mouth when you speak to her. She may enjoy listening to some sounds and may stop feeding to listen more closely.

Even though baby cannot speak, she is listening to the sounds around her. The more words she hears before she speaks, the larger her vocabulary will be when she does start to speak. She is now cooing and gurgling. She makes vowel sounds, such as "ah" and "oh," in response to what she sees and hears.

✒ *She's Responding More Actively*
Baby is also more responsive. She smiles in reaction to someone smiling at her. She smiles for pleasure. There is more recognition in her eyes now. You'll notice how she anticipates a feeding and starts sucking when she sees the breast or a bottle.

She discovers new objects every day. She likes more-complex patterns now, with curved lines and shapes. She will study the interior pattern as well as the outer edge. She enjoys looking at hanging objects; one safe object is a hanging green plant. Baby still enjoys the human face. She's especially interested in the area between the tip of the nose and the hairline.

✒ *Some Reflexes Begin to Fade*
Her reflexive actions are beginning to fade now, as they are replaced by voluntary movement. Her arm and leg motions are becoming less jerky and more rhythmical. She may be making creeping movements on her tummy. You may find that she scoots forward in her crib until her head touches the

end. She may even roll from her back to her side or accidentally push from her tummy to her back.

> Even young babies can wiggle and roll off the changing table, the bed or the sofa. Always keep one hand on the baby if you place her on a high surface!

⊁ *Dad's an Important Stimulant*

Baby's father represents a different kind of stimulation. Playing together is important for both because it helps establish a good relationship between them. Sometimes a father must be encouraged to play and interact with baby. Often a man doesn't feel comfortable handling a small baby, but with patience and practice, he'll soon be a pro!

Note: See also the box *Milestones this 9th Week.*

What's Happening this 9th Week?

⊁ *Baby's Crying Can Mean Many Things*

A baby is born with very little patience; this is essential to her survival. A human baby is one of the most helpless creatures born. Everything she needs to survive—food, shelter, warmth—must be provided for her. Crying is one of the only ways she can communicate. Often when she cries, she is telling you she needs something. You must take care of her needs. Sometimes, she's crying because she's bored or tired. At other times, you have no idea why she's crying.

Most of the time you'll be able to discover what she needs when she cries. But sometimes, you'll be at a loss to know what she needs. When that happens, try some of the following coping strategies.

- Check for signs of an illness, such as a fever, swollen gums or warm, red ears. Call baby's doctor if you see any signs of illness.
- Put baby in a front carrier and hold her close to your body. If you speak to her softly and calmly, she may settle down.
- If you are breastfeeding, evaluate your diet. Avoid foods that could cause her problems, such as onions, garlic, broccoli and cauliflower.
- Massage baby using the techniques we have described in previous weekly discussions.
- If you are bottlefeeding, you may want to discuss the possibility of allergies to formula with baby's doctor.

MILESTONES THIS 9ᵗʰ WEEK

Changes You May See this Week as Baby Develops Physically
* may sleep through the night
* can hold object for a few seconds
* body tone improves

Changes You May See this Week in Baby's Developing Senses and Reflexes
* walking reflex disappears
* coordinates eye movements in a circle when watching light or an object

Changes You May See this Week as Baby's Mind Develops
* sucks at sight of breast
* recognizes breast or bottle, and squirms in anticipation

Changes You May See this Week in Baby's Social Development
* smiles easily and spontaneously
* begins to enjoy taking a bath
* may laugh and chuckle

Every baby is an individual, and your baby may do some of these things more quickly or more slowly than another baby. If you are concerned about your baby's progress, discuss it with your healthcare provider. Also see page xiii.

✴ Baby's Sleep Schedule

By now, your baby is probably settling into a regular sleep schedule. At this time, she's still probably sleeping a little over 15 hours in a 24-hour period. She gets most of her sleep at night (probably about 10 hours) and has a regular nap routine–probably several 1- to 1½-hour naps a day. Typically, she'll have her first nap about 2 hours after she gets up in the morning. Her midday nap may occur shortly after lunch and her afternoon nap between 3 and 4pm.

When baby's sleep schedule becomes more regular, it makes things easier on you in some ways. You have an idea of when she'll need to nap so you can make plans when to go out or take a nap of your own! It's harder in other ways, though, because when baby needs her sleep, she may get very fussy if she's not put down for her nap.

Holding, rocking and stroking baby can affect her in two ways. It helps calm her when she's upset, and it makes her more alert when she's tired.

✒ *Conjunctivitis*

Acute conjunctivitis, also called *pink eye,* occurs for a variety of reasons. The causes are typically age-related. In a newborn, conjunctivitis can occur from infection during birth, most often from chlamydia trachomatis. In infants, recurrent conjunctivitis may be a sign of tear-duct obstruction. In older infants and children, the cause is usually a bacterial infection or a viral infection, if it is accompanied by a cold. Not all irritation is caused by infection. Irritation may be allergy related or possibly caused by a foreign object.

Symptoms of conjunctivitis include redness and swelling of the eyelids and inflammation of the white part of the infant's eyes, giving it a blood-shot appearance. With bacterial, viral and allergic conjunctivitis, both eyes are usually infected. Mucus or matter may also be present; it can range from thick yellow-green, to thin and watery. Eyelids may stick together upon awakening and may need to be washed to get them open. Your baby may also experience sensitivity to bright light. If only one eye is affected and accompanied by pain, a foreign body may be involved.

What You Can Do at Home.   Wash the outside of the baby's eyelid with plain warm water and cotton balls. Clean the eyes by wiping from the inner part of the eye to the outside part to prevent spreading infection. Use a clean cotton ball for each eye.

Conjunctivitis is highly contagious. Wash hands carefully to prevent spreading the infection to other family members. Don't use baby's towels, washcloths, blankets or pillows with other family members. Use them once, then wash them in hot water.

When to Call the Doctor.   Call the doctor if your baby develops any of the following symptoms:
   * a red, swollen eyelid with a lot of discharge
   * a fever
   * she starts acting ill
   * the symptoms of an ear infection are present (see the discussion in *Week 28*)
   * she doesn't seem to improve after you begin using drops or ointment

Your doctor may treat your baby with antibiotic eye drops or ointment. Symptoms should start to clear up within the first few days, although redness may persist a little longer.

Note: Within the first hour of birth, all newborns are treated with a silver nitrate solution or an antibiotic ointment to prevent conjunctivitis for a period of time.

YOUR PREEMIE'S DEVELOPMENT

Your premature baby should be able to do many things now. Remember always to use baby's "due-date age" as your point of reference for the following accomplishments. In the next few weeks, she should be doing many things, including:

* cooing and making other noises
* smiling in response to someone smiling at her or speaking to her
* keeping her hands open most of the time
* controlling her head more when held in an upright position
* being interested in different sights and sounds
* taking three naps a day
* sleeping 5 to 6 hours during the night

To help her accomplish these tasks, there are many activities you can do with your baby. Try the following:

* let her feel different fabric textures
* offer her musical toys
* repeat sounds she makes
* make faces at her (not scary ones—funny ones)
* give her tummy time on the floor when you can spend time with her

⋊ *Hives*

Hives is an allergic reaction that produces a splotchy, red, raised rash that is irregular in shape. The affected area also itches. Hives can appear anywhere on the body, or they may be localized in one specific area. Hives may also come and go over a period of several days.

In infants, viral infections are the most likely cause of hives. Hives may also occur as an allergic reaction to food, soaps or medications.

What You Can Do at Home.   If your baby develops hives while taking a medication, don't give her any more doses until you check with your pediatrician. Keep a journal of possible causes to avoid future reactions. Dress baby in cool, loose-fitting clothing to minimize discomfort and itching. Bathe your baby in lukewarm water to reduce itching.

When to Call the Doctor.   Call the doctor if your baby has any of the following problems.

* She develops hives while taking a medication.
* She experiences any difficulty breathing or swallowing.
* Her joints appear to be sore.
* Her symptoms last longer than 1 week.

Your pediatrician may recommend giving your baby an antihistamine, such as Benadryl, to reduce allergic reaction. In severe cases, epinephrine may be used.

Toys and Play this 9th Week

You don't have to buy a lot of toys to play with baby. You can use many things you have at hand to engage her in play. Help her develop her grasp by wearing patterned scarves and ties while you're interacting with her. Let baby reach and grab for the patterned piece as you play with her. Measuring spoons securely fastened on a ring make a good rattle. Pictures cut from magazines can be fun to look at.

Choose Easy-to-Hold Toys
Toys that are easy for baby to hold are good choices at this age. Blocks made of wood or plastic can be easily grasped. Balls of various sizes are also good choices—just be sure they aren't too small. They should not be able to fit through a toilet-paper tube. A small cloth doll can be easily held and may be comforting.

Encourage Her Muscle Development
Help baby's muscle development with a beach ball. Inflate it until it is almost full, then hold baby on her tummy on top of the ball. Hold her securely as you gently rock her from side to side, and back and forth. Sing or play music as you roll her around on the ball.

Begin very slowly, and gradually increase the speed as she gets used to it. You'll help her use her muscles (thereby helping to develop them) as she uses her body to help maintain her balance.

Week 10

HOW BIG IS BABY THIS 10TH WEEK?

Baby weighs 11 pounds and is 22½ inches long this week.

Baby Care and Equipment

✿ Strollers

One of the most important pieces of equipment you buy for your baby is a *stroller*. It makes taking baby out a more enjoyable experience for everyone. It's a piece of equipment you may use for years—some strollers are designed to carry children as old as 5 years. If this is your first baby, the type of stroller you choose is important if you think you may need it for future use with other children.

There are many different types of strollers on the market, so it's important to decide how, where and when you'll use the stroller and which features you need most before you begin looking for one. Some of these characteristics include size, weight, portability, convenience of opening and closing, appearance and special features. How much you spend is a big consideration—prices for strollers range from under $100 to over $400 for a top-of-the line model.

If you feel overwhelmed by all the choices you have, do some research. Read magazine articles and consumer reviews. Talk to other parents; they can tell you what they like or don't like about the strollers they have. Go to different stores and check out the strollers they carry. Get hands-on experience in a store by closing and opening the stroller to check ease of use.

Types of Strollers.   One of your biggest decisions when choosing a stroller is the type that will best meet your needs. The different types available include *carriage, carriage/stroller combination, umbrella stroller, two-seater stroller, jogger stroller* and *stroller/car-seat combination.*

The *carriage* type has a flat surface, which is useful for a newborn. You may have heard it referred to as a "pram." When we were kids, they called them "baby carriages." It should be used only as long as your baby is lying down; once he begins sitting up, he could fall out.

151

A carriage/stroller combination comes in handy for all kinds of
activities. A jogger stroller is great for heavy-duty use.

The *carriage/stroller combination* does not have a flat surface for your baby
to lie on. Its flattest position is one that reclines, which is OK for newborns.
As baby gets older, you can raise the back of the seat to convert it into a
stroller. This type of stroller is usually very comfortable for baby because it
contains a well-padded seat and backrest.

An *umbrella stroller* is lightweight and easy to fold, to carry and to pack in
the car or carry onto a bus or plane. It's great if you take your baby with you
a lot. However, this type of stroller is less comfortable for baby because de-
signers sacrificed most of the padding to make it lightweight and convenient
to use. If baby will be in a stroller for a long period with each use, this might
not be a good choice.

A *two-seater stroller* is great if you have twins or two babies of different
ages who can be transported together. Some have special features, discussed
below, that make it easier to push two in one stroller.

The *jogger stroller* is built for heavy-duty use. This type often has a heavier
frame, special shock absorbers and oversize and/or all-terrain tires that make
it sturdy on any type of surface. You may find some of these strollers have a
unique design, with one tire in front and two in the rear, which makes it
more aerodynamic.

The *combination stroller/car seat* connects the stroller to the car seat when it
is removed from the car. This is convenient if baby is sleeping or if you're
moving from vehicle to vehicle (less stuff to take with you).

Features to Consider.   There are a variety of features to investigate before you
make your decision. It's important to determine if the stroller meets the Juve-

nile Products Manufacturers' Association (JPMA) standards. To be certified by this organization, a stroller must meet specific safety guidelines.

Be sure the stroller's seat or safety belt is securely fastened to the stroller, easy to fasten and unfasten by you, and designed so it does not allow baby to slide out the bottom. The "T-strap" that comes between the baby's legs and fastens at the waist is the best design. Always use the safety strap when your baby is in the stroller.

If it is foldable, the stroller system should lock securely when in use, and the brake should be easy to set. Some strollers have a brake on one wheel; others have brakes on two wheels. The two-wheeled brake system is more secure. Always set the brake when you stop for any length of time.

Storage space is important. The stroller should have room for your purse, the diaper bag and anything else you need to carry for baby. It may have a shopping basket or bag for carrying gear. This basket/bag should be located at the back of the stroller, preferably over the back wheels. Never hang packages on the handles or place them on the top of the stroller (if it has a canopy).

Removable padding that can be washed is a good choice, especially if you plan to keep the stroller for a long time or use it a great deal. Accidents do happen! It's nice to be able to clean everything up if you plan to use the stroller for other children or to lend it to someone. A canopy is great if you take your baby outside a lot because you must be careful with baby's sun exposure for the first year. (See *Week 48* for more about sun exposure.)

Check out the stroller handles. Are they adjustable? This could be important if different-sized people will be pushing baby.

Some strollers have special features that might interest you. Some have a safety mesh so your baby can't slide out. A clear plastic curtain that attaches to the stroller on three sides to protect baby from inclement weather is an added bonus. One-touch reclining and one-hand steering make moving and handling the stroller easier for you. Double tires on the front and/or rear wheels add durability and stability. Canopies with plastic windows offer baby the opportunity to see what's going on around him.

A Few Words of Caution.   Most accidents related to strollers occur when a child falls out of the stroller. This can happen when the child leans out too far or stands on the seat. You must take precautions when you are out and about with your child in his stroller. The following suggestions will help you prevent an accident when you use your stroller with baby.

- Never leave your baby alone in a stroller; too many mishaps can occur.
- Watch baby, even when he is buckled in.
- Don't let your child stand on the seat.

* When you're opening or closing the stroller, make sure baby's hands are out of the way. His little fingers could get pinched in the process.
* Never leave a stroller at the top of the stairs.
* Lock wheels when you aren't moving.

↻ *Feed Baby Solids to Help Him Sleep Through the Night?*

Some people mistakenly believe that a baby needs solids to help him sleep through the night. A friend or relative may mistakenly have given you this advice. Don't believe it!

According to the American Academy of Pediatrics, until your baby is at least 4 or 5 months old, he should not be given *anything* except breast milk or formula. Solid food offers no nutritional advantage, and it does not help baby sleep longer. In fact, feeding your baby cereal or other solids before the fourth or fifth month could actually cause him stomach distress. That could defeat the purpose of helping him sleep through the night by keeping him awake with a tummy ache! (See the discussion of *Readiness for Solids* in *Week 17.*)

Milestones this 10ᵗʰ Week

↻ *Baby Develops from Head to Toe*

Development in your baby usually progresses from his head to his feet. This means you will see your baby develop strength and skills in his head and arms before he develops them in his legs or feet. In addition, development moves from the center of the body outward. He will be able to control his torso before he can control his hands or feet.

By this time, baby's head is less wobbly because his neck muscles are developing. He can probably sit with your help, although he won't be sitting erect. When he's on his tummy, he can push up off his chest a little. You may notice his arm movements are more controlled. You may see him moving his arms and legs symmetrically while he's on his back. Or he may move them in a bicycling motion.

He may swing his arms and reach for objects that are hanging near him. He likes to feel different textures, and he may explore his face with his hands.

↻ *His Developing Language Skills*

Baby's brain begins to process language very early—long before he ever begins saying words. At this point, your baby's language development is moving right along.

Your baby may coo and gurgle while eating. He may babble when someone talks to him. When he coos or gurgles at you, and you respond in kind to him, you're playing a game. When you do this, you're also helping him discover sounds that eventually become language. You may hear him growl, squeal, screech, coo, gurgle or chortle. He can hear the emotional changes in your voice. He will even begin responding to his name.

Research has found that language development is slower in twins and bilingual babies. Twins receive only half as much individual attention, even when parents talk with them a lot. Bilingual babies are in the process of learning two different languages, which can take more time. However, the research has found that all these babies catch up and usually have no lasting problems.

✴ Interaction Is Important for Baby
By this time, your baby may be smiling at you (and everyone else he sees). He is beginning to recognize family members. He may widen his eyes, smile and wiggle his body when someone familiar approaches.

Even if your baby seems content to stay in his crib, get him up and interact with him. He needs it, and it's good for him. Make him part of family activities going on around him. Put him in his infant seat, a carry sling or his stroller. Let him be near you as you work or relax. He enjoys interacting with you and other people.

✴ Colors Excite Him
Your baby can see color, and it is becoming exciting to him. He likes vivid colors because pastels are harder for him to see. Bright primary colors (red, green, blue, yellow) and bold patterns are interesting and give him a lot to look at. Find pictures in magazines of simple shapes and bold colors to show him. Some books for babies contain these pictures; your baby may enjoy looking at them.

Note: See also the box *Milestones this 10ᵗʰ Week.*

What's Happening this 10ᵗʰ Week?

✴ Baby Is Changing and Growing
A big accomplishment occurs around this time—baby may be sleeping through the night. If he isn't, don't despair. He soon will be.

Baby can hold his head up without support. His neck muscles grow stronger every day.

You may be concerned about how your baby is growing. The best indicator of how well he's doing is how much he grows. If his growth is progressing normally, he is gaining weight steadily, growing in length, starting to imitate your behavior and gaining control of his muscles, he is doing well.

You'll also discover how much baby enjoys interacting with others. He likes meeting new people. But beware of overstimulating baby; it's easy to

MILESTONES THIS 10ᵀᴴ WEEK

Changes You May See this Week as Baby Develops Physically
* holds chest and head up for a short time while lying on stomach
* may move arms together or legs together at same time
* brings body up compactly when picked up

Changes You May See this Week in Baby's Developing Senses and Reflexes
* grasping reflex disappears
* may bring hands together
* follows slowly moving object with eyes and head, from one side of body to the other

Changes You May See this Week as Baby's Mind Develops
* explores own face, eyes and mouth with hand
* stops sucking to listen

Changes You May See this Week in Baby's Social Development
* gurgles and coos in response to sounds
* crying decreases

Every baby is an individual, and your baby may do some of these things more quickly or more slowly than another baby. If you are concerned about your baby's progress, discuss it with your healthcare provider. Also see page xiii.

do. Watch for signals from your baby that he wants to be left alone for a while—we all need that sometimes, even babies! Signals he's headed on a downward curve include whimpering, looking away or closing his eyes. Quiet time, either alone by himself or with you rocking him or speaking softly to him, can help calm him.

⚘ *Smoking Around Baby*

If anyone in your household smokes, now's the time to think about quitting. Studies have shown that smoking around a baby can have many harmful effects on him. Secondary smoke contains over 200 poisonous substances, which your baby breathes in every time you or someone else lights up a cigarette near him.

When your baby inhales secondary smoke, it increases his risk of developing many problems, including respiratory infections, middle-ear infections, asthma, breathing problems after being given general anesthesia, bronchitis and pneumonia. Secondhand smoke may also be a factor in

SIDS (Sudden Infant Death Syndrome); see the discussion in *Week 8*. In addition, anyone smoking around the baby could accidentally burn him with a lit cigarette.

There are measures you can take to protect your little one. Be sure no one smokes around him—not anywhere in the house. Smoking should be done outside. Never allow anyone to smoke in an enclosed space, such as a car, when baby is with you. Avoid smoke-filled areas when possible, such as restaurants or places in public areas where smokers gather. Make sure that no one smokes around baby when he's in child care.

> If you've got a cold or cough, it's no cause for alarm. Nursing baby or cuddling with your baby won't pass your cold on to him.

⁂ *Baby's Cold*

The common cold is an upper-respiratory-tract infection (URI) that can be caused by one of many viruses. A cold generally lasts a few days to a week but can occasionally persist longer. Colds are more often transmitted by touch, not by someone coughing or sneezing on your baby. Babies can get as many as six colds a year, due to their immature immune systems.

What You Can Do at Home.   When your baby gets a cold, give him plenty of liquid to drink. Because it may be difficult for your baby to nurse or bottlefeed because he is congested, encourage frequent feedings. Drain his nose with a bulb syringe as needed, especially before eating. If he can't breathe well, he can't eat well. By nature, babies are nose breathers and don't breathe through their mouths. Nonprescription saline nose drops can be used to thin nasal secretions, which makes it easier for you to suction mucus.

Use a cool-mist humidifier to keep air moist. Run the humidifier in the room where your baby spends most of his time. Don't let the mist spray directly over your infant or his crib. Bedding can become damp and chill your baby.

Babies younger than 6 months of age are rarely given over-the-counter (OTC) medications, with the exception of child-strength acetaminophen or ibuprofen. However, don't use them unless your doctor tells you to do so. Ask *before* you give them! If you are advised to use them, follow package instructions very carefully. Infants under 2 months of age should *not* be given any medication unless specifically ordered by your pediatrician.

Do not give baby echinacea—it may be OK for you, but it's *not* OK for your child! It is ineffective in children, and its use could lead to a rash in your child. Avoid all cold medicines—they are too powerful for baby. (Some contain as much as 25% alcohol!)

A word to the wise—if baby seems fairly OK and not too troubled by his cold, wait to give him any medication. If he's miserable, coughing and/or congested, use an OTC *child's* decongestant or cough suppressant, as instructed by your physician.

You can do several things to help prevent your baby from getting lots of colds. First of all, breastfeeding is the number-one way to prevent colds and flu in babies under 1 year of age, so keep breastfeeding! Wash your hands frequently, and have others wash their hands before touching or holding baby. Avoid taking your infant out in crowded places where he might be exposed to people with colds. If possible, try to keep your older baby from putting his mouth on objects that have been handled by others. Ask your pediatrician about a flu shot after baby reaches 6 months of age.

When to Call the Doctor.   Call the doctor if baby:
* has difficulty breathing or is breathing rapidly
* flares his nostrils with each breath
* wheezes
* has bad color, such as pale, ashen, gray or bluish-tinted skin
* is not eating well
* cries uncontrollably
* is listless
* has a fever that rises above 101F and lasts for 2 days or longer
* tugs on his ears
* is not having wet diapers

If your baby has some of the above symptoms, your pediatrician may want to see him to rule out anything more serious. Your baby may be treated with antibiotics if a secondary infection has occurred, like an ear infection. Antibiotics don't work on viruses, so don't ask your pediatrician to prescribe one. Unnecessary antibiotics may be more harmful to your baby than the cold itself.

Doctors are now writing fewer prescriptions for antibiotics for young children. This is good news because too-frequent use of antibiotics has led to growth of antibiotic-resistant bacteria. That has made many infections harder to treat. So if your pediatrician doesn't prescribe an antibiotic, the doctor is doing it for baby's own good!

✶ *Fluoride Supplementation*

Fluoride helps the development of baby's healthy teeth. Discuss with your pediatrician your baby's need for a fluoride supplement. Most pediatricians begin the supplement when a baby is about 6 months old. Correct dosage is based on the amount of fluoride in your water supply and whether your baby is receiving any of that water.

Your use of powdered formula, made with local water, compared to ready-to-use formula or breast milk, may determine if your baby needs supplementation. Too much fluoride can result in discolored or mottled teeth, so follow your pediatrician's recommendation.

Toys and Play this 10th Week

✶ *Be Careful with His Toys*

It's important to become aware of potential toy hazards now that baby is getting a little older. Avoid toys that have small parts, such as eyes or noses that could be pulled off a stuffed toy.

Don't let your baby have toys that are too small or that have small pieces to them. Here's an easy way to determine if a toy or part of a toy that can be removed is too small for baby to play with. Save an empty roll from toilet tissue, and use this as a guide. If a toy or part of a toy fits through the center of the roll, keep it away from baby. He could choke on it. This includes rattles, rubber toys or toys that can be compressed. In their most-compressed form, they should be too large to fit through the roll.

✶ *He Wants Your Attention*

One game you can play with your baby is to sit him on your lap. Look into each other's eyes; your baby may look away. Then you glance away. When baby looks back and sees you aren't looking at him, he may make noise to get your attention again. This is a fun game.

✶ *Encourage Him to Reach*

Another game to play with baby involves holding a string of bright, colorful objects above baby's head. He will reach out to grab for it. Hold it just a little out of his grasp, to encourage him to stretch and to reach. You're also helping him develop eye–hand coordination. *Caution:* Don't tie anything like this onto his crib or leave it where baby could become tangled in it.

Week 11

HOW BIG IS BABY THIS 11ᵀᴴ WEEK?

Baby weighs 11½ pounds and is 22¾ inches long this week.

Baby Care and Equipment

❧ *Ways to Relieve Baby's Gas*

A baby often swallows air when she eats, so it's not unusual for her to have some gas. Burping often takes care of the problem, but when it doesn't, you may need to try some other things. The following may help.

* Use a different burping position. Lay her face down on your lap, and pat her back. Or sit her on your lap while you rub her back.
* Stop in the middle of her feeding, and burp her. Burp her again when she finishes.
* Don't let her cry for long periods. When she cries, she gulps in air, which can cause gas.
* When you feed her, keep her upright, at least at a 30-degree angle. This helps her food go down more easily, and she'll swallow less air.
* If you normally lie down when breastfeeding, sit up to feed her.
* When using a bottle, be sure the nipple is the right size for her. Too much milk going through too fast or sucking too hard on a nipple with an opening that is too small can both cause her to swallow air.
* Go modern—use an angled bottle, a dial-the-flow nipple and disposable plastic liners that collapse as baby sucks. In all cases, she'll take in less air.

In a very few cases, gas may be caused by a digestive problem. If baby has diarrhea, vomits, cries inconsolably and suffers from bloating, call your doctor. She may have lactose intolerance, be allergic to her formula or suffer from some other problem.

❧ *Feeding Tips for Trips*

Later in this weekly discussion we cover traveling with baby in greater depth. In this section, we provide you with some tips for bottlefeeding and breastfeeding baby when you're on the road.

If you feed baby formula, refrigerate any prepared formula, if directions call for it. If this isn't possible, premeasure water into a clean baby bottle. When she's hungry, just add powdered formula to the water. When possible, bring water from home to mix with formula so it tastes the same. You can buy premixed, ready-to-feed formula in cans or bottles. Pour canned formula into a bottle when she's hungry. Discard any leftovers.

It's easy if you breastfeed, as long as you can find a place to feed her where you feel comfortable. Feed baby when she's hungry. If you have to be away from her for a time, pump extra breast milk, then refrigerate or freeze it. Breast milk doesn't have to be refrigerated immediately. It will stay fresh up to 4 hours at temperatures as high as 77F and for 24 hours at 60F. You can refrigerate breast milk for up to 72 hours. It can be frozen for up to 6 months in a refrigerator freezer and up to 12 months in a deep freezer.

You can combine fresh breast milk with frozen breast milk. Cool the expressed milk before adding the thawed breast milk. Use more thawed breast milk than fresh breast milk. Once milk is thawed, use immediately or store in the refrigerator up to 24 hours.

✤ Some Safety Tips for Sleep

To help baby get a good night's rest, keep in mind her comfort and safety. As we've already advised, *always* place baby on her back to go to sleep. When she's old enough to turn over, she can choose her own sleeping position. The room temperature should be about 70F for her comfort and yours. Keep her away from any soft surface that can mold to her face and interfere with her breathing. Use only approved mattress covers for her crib or bassinet. Avoid plastic bags or wrapping material that could come loose and suffocate her. Never leave baby alone on a sofa or bed. Even if she's not rolling over yet, she could wiggle around and fall off.

If you have a family bed, and share it with baby, avoid using soft materials that could cause problems. Don't use a feather-bed pillow. The mattress should be firm. Don't place quilts, pillows or comforters under the baby. Don't use any substances (medications, alcohol or drugs) that could interfere with your ability to wake up! If you're a very sound sleeper, a family bed is probably not a good choice for you and baby.

✤ Baby Bouncers

When baby wants to move and to wiggle, you may want to consider buying a bouncer, if you haven't already. A bouncer is an angled, wire-framed, fabric chair that bounces or an infant-carrier seat type that rocks, with a harness to hold baby. Its semireclining seat is designed to allow her to see the world and to move her gently when it is put in motion. It can be used until she's about 25 pounds or until she can sit up on her own. When she can sit by herself, she's no longer safe in it. Most bouncers are well padded and comfortable for baby to sit in.

Sitting in a bouncer allows your baby the opportunity to see you and to see what's going on around her. At the same time, she can be soothed by the rhythmic rocking motion, if you choose to "start her bouncing."

Many bouncers have removable cushions and covers so you can wash them. Some even have a toy bar across the front so baby can look at, and eventually play with, brightly colored toys.

CAUTIONS FOR USING BOUNCERS

* Never place the baby bouncer (with baby in it) on a chair, counter or other place where it could fall off.
* Don't place a bouncer on a bed or upholstered furniture. If it falls over, it could suffocate baby.
* Never try to move a bouncer when baby is in it. It's *not* a carrier.
* As baby gets larger, her weight and movement could cause it to become very unstable.
* *Never* use a bouncer as a car seat for baby when she's riding in a car!

Milestones this 11ᵗʰ Week

✴ *She Uses Her Senses to Explore*
By this time, baby recognizes familiar sights and sounds. She uses all of her senses to explore her world. She's also learning self-control. You'll be amused how she may stop crying and start smiling when you make silly noises or funny faces.

✴ *Understanding Her Cry*
By this time, baby is probably crying only about 1 hour each day. Your continuing experiences with her help you understand many things about your baby. By this time, you probably recognize her "crying language." You probably know when she cries if she's hungry, in pain, tired, bored or wants attention. Her crying is decreasing because she's more involved in interacting with her environment.

✴ *Playing with Baby*
You've also probably come to understand when is the best time to play with baby. Some days she'll want to play more than others. If she's sleep-

ing and eating a lot, due to a growth spurt, she may be a little less interested in playtime. Other times, when she's learning a new task, she'll want to continue to play long after her usual limit. Be flexible. Let her help set the playtime.

When she's awake, baby may no longer want just to cuddle. She wants to play and to interact. She doesn't like being left alone for long. She has many facial expressions now, such as frowns, smiles and grimaces. She may stop nursing to smile at you, then return to sucking.

✴ *She's Getting Stronger*

Her strength is increasing. By now, she may be able to sit up quite well, if she's securely propped against something. When she's on her stomach, with her weight on her elbows and forearms, she can push her chest up.

✴ *Baby's Hands Help Her Learn*

She's using her hands a lot more. She no longer holds her hands in fists; they are now loosely clenched. Sometimes they are open. She has discovered her hands are more than mere fists—now they are fingers and a thumb. They are very interesting to her.

The reflexive grasp she was born with is disappearing. Now she must learn to use her hands to hold onto something. Your baby will bring her hands together at the center of her body. She's beginning to coordinate the look/grasp/suck system. She's putting everything into her mouth. Be careful with what she puts in her mouth. Unclean objects may expose her to germs. She could choke on small objects. Other than that, don't worry too much.

She likes to touch or to handle just about anything. She's not content to just look any longer—she also wants to touch! She'll study a plastic rattle placed in her hand, then wave it around. She likes to make noise.

Different textures are interesting to her—a hard rattle, a soft doll, a fluffy stuffed toy. She'll repeat an action many times as she plays with something. Does the rattle always make noise when she shakes it? Does the foam toy always pop back into shape when she lets go of it? By repetition, she's learning the basic laws of physics.

✴ *Baby Likes to Look at Patterns*

The contrast of light and dark still pleases her, but she also likes bold, contrasting colors. Pastels don't excite her much. She pays attention to details, patterns and the play of light on an object. And when she drops something, she will stare in puzzlement at the place it disappeared from!

Note: See also the box *Milestones this 11th Week*.

MILESTONES THIS 11ᵀᴴ WEEK

Changes You May See this Week as Baby Develops Physically
* leans on elbows while on stomach

Changes You May See this Week in Baby's Developing Senses and Reflexes
* turns head and neck to find source of sound
* may hold and wave a toy

Changes You May See this Week as Baby's Mind Develops
* begins to show memory

Changes You May See this Week in Baby's Social Development
* reacts differently to parents' presence

Every baby is an individual, and your baby may do some of these things more quickly or more slowly than another baby. If you are concerned about your baby's progress, discuss it with your healthcare provider. Also see page xiii.

What's Happening this 11ᵗʰ Week?

Is Baby Sleeping All Night?

Around this time, your baby should be sleeping all night. However, "all night" is defined by pediatricians as not waking up between midnight and 5am. Most people don't consider this an entire night, but if you've been sleep deprived since baby's birth, even this amount of time can be a cause for celebration!

You can help the process by feeding your baby more frequently during the day. If she naps longer than 3 hours, wake her up. Establish a bedtime routine, as we've previously discussed. This helps her realize it's time to go to sleep. If you get up at night to feed her, keep lights low and interaction to a minimum. Change her, feed her and put her to bed with as little stimulation as possible.

Taking Baby on the Road

When you think about traveling with baby, a family car trip is often the way to go. You can go on the spur of the moment and take along as much stuff as you need. You can stop whenever you want. It's OK when baby fusses. You probably won't set any speed records. What used to take you 3½ hours will now take at least 5, but it's a great way for a family to travel.

Be prepared so the trip is enjoyable for everyone. Build in some extra time for unplanned stops. Below are ideas for making your next trip a happy experience.

* Feed baby just before you leave, so you won't have to make a feeding stop too soon. *Never* take baby out of her car seat to nurse or to bottlefeed her while the car is moving!
* Leave just before nap time, if possible, or when she's awake but close to her nap time.
* Know baby's tolerance for being confined. When she's little, this usually isn't a problem. But as she gets older, it could become one. Many parents drive while baby is napping or sleeping.
* Be prepared to stop often. It's hard for her to be stuck in a car seat for a long time. You'll need to stop more often to give baby a break (you, too!).
* Factor in extra time for *everything.* You need to feed and to change baby, sometimes not at the same stop. You may need to comfort baby if she's fussy. Some babies have a hard time sleeping in their car seat, so you may need to stop to let her lie down for a while.
* Keep cassette tapes and CDs handy that she likes. Include lullabies and funny songs. Even stories can entertain her.
* Have her favorite toys near at hand. Keep close something that comforts her.
* Make sure you have enough supplies—disposable diapers, baby wipes, extra pacifiers, formula, bottles, nipples, burp cloths, clean clothes, blankets—before you hit the road.
* Take your food with you—picnic whenever you can. Sometimes it's a lot easier to eat when and where you want than to go into a restaurant with a young child.
* Neck supports or a rolled soft blanket help provide baby a comfortable sleeping position.

> By this time, your baby has probably settled into her sleeping pattern and eating pattern.

Think before you pack the car. Plan on what you want to take with you, then pack the things you'll need during the trip last. That way, they're on top in the trunk and readily available. Keep essentials up front with you.

Carry a small cooler for snacks and formula or expressed breast milk. If baby wants warmed formula, put the correct amount of powdered formula in a bottle. Add warm water from an insulated container when it's time to feed her.

Keep as close to your routine as possible, such as the time you put her to bed. Put her down about the time you normally do, and follow your bedtime ritual. This helps her fall asleep, even when she's not in her own bed. If you travel to a different time zone, let her adjust gradually, just as you do.

> Plan to make part of your trip when your baby is asleep.

Reserve a crib and bedding if you're staying at a hotel or motel. If you're visiting relatives, ask them to borrow or to rent a crib. Be sure to check the crib for its safety. Bring baby's favorite blanket or toy to comfort her. Take along a crib monitor if you're staying at a suites-hotel (with separate bedrooms) or at someone's home. It provides you with some freedom.

You may have to make some adjustments in *your* routine. You may have to go to bed when baby does, or wait until she falls asleep before turning the TV or radio on softly. Often, you get up when she gets up!

If baby is curious and crawling, it may be a good idea to have childproofing supplies with you. Most hotels and motels don't supply these. Family members and friends may not have these devices any longer if their children are older. See the discussion in *Week 21* on *Childproofing Away from Home.*

Anal Fissure

An *anal fissure* is a small tear in or around the opening to the anus (rectum) that can occur at any time. You may notice a little bit of blood in baby's stool or on her diaper. There may also be a red rash around the rectum that may itch and cause baby discomfort. She may cry with a bowel movement or be constipated.

What You Can Do at Home. To treat the problem, begin by increasing baby's fluid intake. As previously advised, do *not* give her water if she is not eating solids. Increase the amount of breast milk or formula you give her. If she is eating solids, give her foods that soften bowel movements. Ask your pediatrician for advice. If you give her vitamins or formula that contain iron, stop for a while. Discuss this with baby's doctor before making any changes.

When to Call the Doctor. Call your baby's doctor if you notice any of the following symptoms.

* You see blood on the diaper or in the stool.
* She's crying or fussing with bowel movements.
* She suffers from severe or prolonged constipation.

Baby's doctor will prescribe treatment for the problem. You may be advised to use a small rectal suppository or a lubricated, gloved little finger to dilate the rectum gently. You may need to give her medications to soften the stool. Sometimes mineral oil is used. The problem usually heals fairly quickly.

✴ *Gassiness*

Problems with gassiness or flatulence can occur at any age. It is more common once baby starts eating solid foods. Symptoms include:

* abdominal pain
* bloated or distended abdomen
* fussiness
* frequent passing of gas

What You Can Do at Home. There are some things you can try to help ease baby's discomfort. If you are breastfeeding, make note of foods you have eaten. Some of them could cause her to be gassy. Avoid these foods in the future. If she's eating solids, keep track of the foods your baby is eating that might cause her to be uncomfortable.

Lay her on her tummy on top of a hot-water bottle or a warm (not hot!) heating pad for a short time. Massage her tummy. See the discussion in *Week 7* for *Tips on Relieving Gas*. Burp her again. If she's crying, try to soothe her. Crying causes her to swallow more air, which could cause more gas.

When to Call the Doctor. Most of the time you won't have to call your doctor about this problem. It usually resolves on its own. However, call the doctor if you notice any of the following symptoms:

* severe abdominal pain that is not relieved by passing gas
* baby is still uncomfortable after using the above treatments
* she has a fever
* you notice any blood in her stools

If the problem is severe, baby's doctor may suggest changing formulas if you are bottlefeeding. Your pediatrician may also prescribe medications to help eliminate gas in the intestines. Do *not* give her any medication on your own, before consulting the doctor. If the problem becomes chronic or severe, further testing may be done to find the cause of the problem.

Toys and Play this 11th Week

✴ *Capture Baby's Attention*

When you talk to baby, capture her attention before you begin. You'll hold her attention longer, and you're more likely to get a response. Keep using her name. She may not associate her name with herself yet, but if she hears it frequently, she'll eventually realize it is a special sound.

Use short sentences of four or five words when you talk with her. Choose

one- or two-syllable words that can be drawn out when you speak them, such as "liiitttle prinncesss." When possible, show her what you mean. When you say, "Wave bye-bye to grandma," wave as you say it. It's easier for her to recall a word associated with an animated gesture.

Ask her questions. She can't answer you, but just the change in the way a question sounds (raising the tone at the end of the question) exposes her to different language sounds.

At 11 weeks old, your baby may interact with you.

Read to her when you can. She'll love nursery rhymes and poems with a singsong cadence. Sing, too; she'll love to hear familiar songs over and over again. You may find she wiggles with anticipation when you begin a favorite of hers.

✻ Finding Her Playmate

Your baby is fascinated by noise and movement. Entertain her by slowly moving around her while you talk so she can practice finding one of her favorite playmates—you. You may find baby cooing at you with pleasure when you play this game.

See if baby can focus on your voice from the direction of the sound. In a singsong voice say, "Baby, baby, baby" while you stand in front of her. Then move behind her, and sing out again. Move to her side. Change the rhythm of the chant, or chant faster or slower. Chant loudly, then chant softly. Is she listening alertly? Does she follow your sound?

✻ Bells on Her Wrists!

Use her fascination with sound to play a fun game. Tie a ribbon around her wrist that has one or two small bells attached to it. Lift her arm, and gently shake the bells. If she notices the sound, she may start moving her arm to make the sound again. Then put bells on her other wrist, then her ankles. Be sure bells are securely attached to the ribbon. *Never* leave her alone with the ribbon tied to her, and remove the ribbon when you are finished playing.

Week 12

HOW BIG IS BABY THIS 12TH WEEK?
Baby weighs 12 pounds this week and is 23¼ inches long.

Baby Care and Equipment

✑ Pets and Baby

You may have a pet that has been your "baby" until your child was born. When you bring your new baby home from the hospital, it also means a lifestyle change for your pet.

An animal is sensitive to a routine, so making changes before baby is born may be easier on your pet. During your pregnancy, try the following.

* Decrease the time you spend with your pet–you'll have a lot less time to spend with it after baby's birth.
* Change and adapt your pet's feeding, exercise or play schedule in the weeks before baby's birth.
* Make any changes in where your pet will be kept. If baby will be in your room and your pet has slept there, move your pet's sleeping site to another location so it will be familiar.
* Evaluate your dog's obedience training. He should react to basic commands.
* Expose your pet to other children when possible. It can be a shock to an animal to be confronted with a small baby. A baby's crying and other reactions can startle or frighten an animal.
* Put out baby's things, such as the bassinet or crib and the changing table. Let your pet smell everything.
* Keep pets off baby furniture and out of baby's room.
* Give your pet an area that is all its own and off-limits to baby.

---

*AUTHORS' NOTE: About this time in baby's life, you may stop referring to his age in weeks and begin to refer to it in months. For that reason, we will also provide baby's age as a monthly reference for each week that follows.

Introducing Your Dog to Baby.   After your baby is born, before you bring him home, have someone bring home a piece of baby's clothing. Let your dog sniff it. This allows the animal to become familiar with baby's scent.

When you bring baby home, go into the house alone to greet your pet. Put your dog on a leash before you bring your baby in, then sit in a chair with baby in your lap. Cover the baby's head with your hand to show your pet you are protective of this new addition to the household.

Don't put your baby on the floor. Don't hold baby over your dog's head. It might encourage your dog to jump up. Talk to your dog in a normal voice, and pat him for reassurance. If your dog displays any aggression, such as growling, putting his ears back or his tail down, remove baby immediately. If your dog seems OK with baby, let it sniff him.

Never leave baby unsupervised around your pet, even if everything seems all right. You don't want to create an unsafe situation in which baby could be harmed.

Don't let your dog lick your baby—it's not healthy. A dog's mouth has germs that you don't want to expose baby to at this time.

If your dog shows unacceptable behavior, say "No!" If he backs off on his own, praise him. If he doesn't, remove the dog from the room. To be on the safe side, keep your dog on a leash for the first few weeks around baby.

After 3 or 4 weeks, if all seems to be going well, you can begin to include your pet in your daily routine. Let him follow you around as you care for baby. Give your pet attention when baby is present, not when baby is asleep or in another room. In this way, your pet will accept baby's presence and not see it as a threat. If your dog walks well on a leash, take him with you when you take baby out in the stroller.

Introducing Your Cat to Baby.   If you have a cat, you know how unpredictable it can be. It's best to keep a cat away from baby when possible. Let the cat watch from a distance. If it shows any signs of aggression, such as biting, nipping, growling, raising its hair, spraying, putting its ears back or pointing its tail down, remove the cat from the area. If the cat slinks toward baby, it is a sign of aggression, so do not let it near the baby. Reward your cat for any positive actions, such as staying off furniture or away from baby.

If Your Pet Is Young or Old.   If you have a puppy or kitten, it may have a lot of energy. It could be a challenge handling it, especially now that you have a baby to care for. You may have to spend extra time with a young pet.

If your animal is fairly old, understand that this change in routine could cause other problems. If your pet has had the run of the house, it may take some time to train it to stay out of certain areas. An older pet may be less flexible about adding baby to the household. It may sulk, ignore you or beg for your attention. Your pet may also be jealous of the time and attention you give the baby. You may have to set aside some time alone with an older pet.

☙ *Dealing with Unwanted Advice from Others*

Your mother may tell you you're starving your child. Your mother-in-law may advise you to let baby cry for "his own good—you'll spoil him if you pick him up all the time." If you're like most new parents, you may wonder if what they're saying is true. You may doubt your own instincts.

Everyone means well. They're not saying you're a bad parent. They just want to be sure baby is being well taken care of. Much of the advice they share with you was acceptable when they were parents. We know today that some of their well-intentioned advice could put baby at risk.

If you are given unwanted counsel, don't get upset or angry. Follow your own plan for raising your baby, and trust your instincts. Thank your helpers for their advice. Use what you think is acceptable, and ignore the rest.

☙ *Does Music Make Baby Smarter?*

Should you play classical music for your baby? Some people believe that a child who listens to classical music may grow up to be smarter and to do better in math.

However, recent studies have debunked this idea. Researchers state there is no correlation between listening to classical music and a baby's brain development. However, the soothing sounds of classical music might help calm and settle a restless baby. Listening to classical music could be enjoyable for both you and baby!

☙ *Be Prepared with this "Parents' Kit"*

If you're a new parent, you may have little idea what items you need to provide baby the best care you can give him. Below is a list of some things to help you deal with almost any minor medical situation. Keep the following items together in a handy location:

- a thermometer—the ear kind or a rectal one
- rubbing alcohol
- cotton balls and cotton swabs
- premoistened baby wipes
- diaper-rash cream
- a medication to reduce pain and relieve fever (ask your pediatrician for suggestions)
- a cool-mist humidifier (don't use a steam humidifier with a baby)

* something to measure accurately any liquid medication you must give baby–a dropper or an oral syringe are good choices (avoid a kitchen teaspoon because it is *not* an accurate measurement)
* electrolyte solution, to use if baby has diarrhea (ask your pediatrician for suggestions)
* nasal syringe for clearing nasal congestion

If you keep these items together and readily available, you'll be prepared to deal with many of the common small medical problems you may face with your baby.

Milestones this 12ᵗʰ Week

Baby Can Lift His Head

Your baby's strength and control continue to increase. He can easily lift his head now. When you hold him, he may push away and look over your shoulder. He turns his head when lying on his stomach.

Some babies can kick themselves from front to back as early as 3 months of age, but most babies do not accomplish this task by that age. And to roll the other way–from back to front–most need the strong neck and arm muscles they will have developed by about 5 or 6 months.

His Vision Sharpens

By this time, baby's vision is becoming sharper. Now when you hold him, he can see details of your face, such as your eyebrows and lips. He's becoming familiar with your facial features and those of others in the family. He's beginning to distinguish between family members. You'll notice that his face lights up when he recognizes you.

He's also better able to track objects and can follow them as they move through his field of vision. Move a brightly colored object in a circle in front of him, and watch his eyes track the movement.

His Sleep Needs

Your baby should be sleeping between 14 and 15 hours a day–10 hours at night and two or three naps during the day. However, research has shown that infants age 3 to 11 months often get only about 12¾ hours of sleep daily. Try to ensure that your baby gets enough sleep; it's important for his growth and development.

When baby awakens in the morning may depend on the time of his last feeding the night before. Some babies wake up about the same time every morning, no matter when they last ate.

Note: See also the box *Milestones this 12ᵗʰ Week.*

MILESTONES THIS 12ᵀᴴ WEEK

Changes You May See this Week as Baby Develops Physically
* holds head at 90-degree angle when on stomach
* facial expressions increase
* vocalization increases

Changes You May See this Week in Baby's Developing Senses and Reflexes
* hands usually held open
* likes to gum objects
* may gaze at hands for 5 to 10 minutes

Changes You May See this Week as Baby's Mind Develops
* distinguishes speech from other sounds

Changes You May See this Week in Baby's Social Development
* begins to recognize and to differentiate between family members

Every baby is an individual, and your baby may do some of these things more quickly or more slowly than another baby. If you are concerned about your baby's progress, discuss it with your healthcare provider. Also see page xiii.

What's Happening this 12ᵗʰ Week?

Baby's Sleep Cycles

By this time, your baby's sleep cycles begin to resemble those of an adult. He passes through cycles of deep sleep and active sleep (REM). Both of these stages are critical to his development.

Researchers have discovered that human growth hormone is released when a child is in deep sleep. This sleep stage is required for growth. They also believe that REM sleep is necessary for the development of learning and memory.

Baby's Soft Spots

The soft spots on your baby's head allow his head to grow. The spot behind the head should be closing about this time. The large one at the top of his head takes longer to close. He'll be about 18 months old before this spot hardens completely.

It's OK to touch these soft spots, just be gentle when you do it. If a soft spot sinks in or bulges, or becomes hard before it should, call your pediatrician. He or she may want to see baby.

✻ Begin Thinking about Babyproofing Your Home

It won't be long before baby is moving around. It makes sense to think now about how you will babyproof your home. In the following weeks, we go into detail about particular things to do to make your home safe for your baby. This discussion revolves around *what* you should do and *how* you should do it.

There are two schools of thought about what parents should do around the house. One group believes that nothing should be moved or put away. In this way, baby learns what he can and cannot touch. Another group believes that anything reachable should be moved so you never have to say "No" to baby.

You might want to consider the middle ground. You don't need to put away *everything* that baby could touch. That's no fun for you, and it's boring for baby. You may want to put away some of your valuable, breakable or dangerous items, or at least place them out of reach for a while.

Baby will explore as he becomes mobile, so put things within his reach that are safe for him to touch. Sooner or later, your baby will have to learn the meaning of "No." Let him learn on objects that won't hurt him that are expendable to you. In that way, baby expands his horizons without destroying things that are valuable to you.

✻ Bronchiolitis/Respiratory Syncytial Virus (RSV)

Bronchiolitis, also referred to as *respiratory syncytial virus* or *RSV*, is an infection in the lungs that occurs primarily in the winter and spring months. Each year more than 125,000 babies are hospitalized with RSV. It is rare in children over 2 years of age.

It begins as a cold, with a nasal discharge and mild fever. Most children easily fight off the virus. However, some infants get more seriously ill because their lungs aren't fully developed, and their bodies cannot fight infection as well. These babies gradually develop increasing respiratory distress, with rapid breathing, coughing, irritability and possible wheezing. They may also have episodes of apnea. See the general discussion of *Apnea* in *Week 2*.

Research has found that some children are more at risk than others. These children include babies:

* born prematurely (earlier than 36 weeks gestation)
* with lung disease
* with heart disease
* who are in day-care
* with school-age siblings
* exposed to secondhand tobacco smoke

What You Can Do.   Keep sick people away from your baby, especially from fall through spring. Don't allow anyone to smoke around your baby. Frequently wash your hands with soap and water to prevent passing germs to baby.

Use a cool-mist humidifier in his room; see *Week 13* for information on *Humidifiers.* Give him lots of fluids. Keep him quiet. Depending on baby's age, acetaminophen may be given to ease discomfort and to reduce fever.

When to Call the Doctor.   Call your pediatrician if baby's coughing increases, he wheezes, breathes more than 50 breaths a minute or if the skin between and underneath his ribs is pulled taut with breathing. Notify the doctor if baby's skin becomes blue or gray, he is extremely irritable, he has apnea spells or is very listless.

In some cases, baby will be hospitalized and given mist therapy combined with oxygen. He may be given an I.V. if he is unable to eat. X-rays may be taken to check for pneumonia. In severe cases, a ventilator may be used to assist and to control breathing. An antiviral agent may be given to your baby, but its use is controversial and expensive.

If your baby was premature, ask your doctor about medication that prevents RSV. He or she will be able to give you further information.

✸ Clubfoot

Clubfoot, also called *talipes,* is any of a number of deformities of the foot. Most are present at birth, although one type of clubfoot may occur after someone is infected with polio. When present at birth, it is either an inherited condition or is caused by the positioning of the fetus in the uterus. The problem is more common in boys than girls. Symptoms of a clubfoot can vary, depending on the part of the foot involved, and include:

* heel and foot turn outward
* heel turns inward
* foot is extended
* arch is exaggerated
* foot points down, turns inward and curls under

Your pediatrician should recognize the disorder when the physical exam is done after birth. Medical treatment is necessary to correct the deformity. Your doctor may advise stretching exercises, massage, physical therapy, splints for day or night, or casts. A positive attitude on your part during physical therapy is very important.

The goal of treatment is to correct the problem. If left uncorrected, it prevents normal walking. The deformity is not painful, but it may be uncomfortable when treatment begins. Your doctor may recommend surgery if treatment methods described above are unsuccessful.

Toys and Play this 12ᵗʰ Week

Your baby loves to reach for and to swat at objects. He's beginning to grab at things. Around this time, you can introduce your baby to a gym toy. This toy has objects firmly attached to a bar that hangs above his head. Your baby will enjoy looking at the colorful objects and may try to grab or swipe at them.

As his muscle control improves, these bright objects help him develop his eye–hand coordination. However, he'll quickly lose interest in them if they are beyond his reach.

> During the first few months of life, respond to baby's cues immediately as he adapts and changes to this new world he's in. As he gets older, you probably know him pretty well, so you can begin to react in ways that feel right to you.

✻ *It's Pushup Time*
Help baby increase his upper-body strength by placing him on the floor on his stomach, with his arms out in front of him. Shake a rattle above his head to encourage him to look up. Then shake the rattle down low so he looks down. Do this a few times so he is moving up and down.

✻ *Baby's Kick Toy*
Baby is using more than his hands as he becomes more active. Kick toys are favorites. Some toys can be activated to make noise or to flash lights when he kicks them. You can make your own kick toy. Attach a rattle or bell to baby's ankle with self-adhesive cloth tape. When he kicks, he'll delight himself with the noise he makes! Don't leave baby alone with these toys.

✻ *Little Piggies Go to Market*
It's time to introduce your baby to some of the fun interactive games you remember from your childhood. "This Little Piggy Went to Market" is a game babies love. Sit baby on your lap, or lay him on his back on the floor. Say one line of verse as you gently wiggle each toe on his foot. As you say or sing the last verse, run your fingers up baby's body, lightly tickling him.

> *This little piggy went to market.*
> *This little piggy stayed home.*
> *This little piggy had roast beef.*
> *This little piggy had none.*
> *And this little piggy cried "Mama!* (or baby's name)*"*
> *All the way home!*

✳ *Hand-Puppet Playtime*

Hand puppets are fun toys. Your baby will enjoy exploring one with his eyes and his hands. You can buy simple hand puppets, or make one out of an old clean white sock or a couple of washcloths sewn together on three sides. Draw on features with a permanent marker. When you engage in puppet play, you encourage baby's visual, verbal and motor development.

Week 13

Baby's Age as a Monthly Reference—3 months

HOW BIG IS BABY THIS 13ᵀᴴ WEEK?

Baby weighs 12½ pounds and is 23½ inches long this week.

Baby Care and Equipment

✢ *Humidifiers*

When baby suffers from a cold or other respiratory problem, your pediatrician may recommend a humidifier to increase the level of moisture in the air. There are two types to choose from. A *cool-mist* humidifier forces cool mist into the air. A *warm-mist* humidifier heats water before sending the warm mist into the air.

Lack of moisture in the air dries out baby's nasal passages and causes dehydration. When the delicate layers of the mucous membranes dry out and become thicker, mucus stops functioning the way it should. This can weaken the respiratory-defense system. Moisture also helps in other ways. It can prevent mucus from crusting inside and outside the nose, and it relieves itchy skin and dry throats.

A humidifier is used most often when it is dry outside and when your home heating system is running. This is usually during the winter months.

Caution: Because a humidifier is an electrical device that also contains water, exercise extreme caution when using it to prevent a hazardous situation.

It's a good idea to clean and thoroughly disinfect a humidifier on a regular basis. This prevents mold and bacteria from growing inside the appliance. Use fresh water each time you fill the humidifier. Empty the humidifier when it's not being used. Always check the device to be sure there is enough water in it before you turn it on.

When it's running, don't place the humidifier too close to baby's crib or bed because it might chill her. Run it *only* when you need to. When baby gets older and is more mobile, place the humidifier completely out of her reach, on a high, stable surface.

✢ *When to Call the Doctor*

You may be unsure when to call the doctor or when to seek medical treatment for your baby. Knowing what to watch for may help you relax a little.

Below is a list of symptoms; if you notice any of these signs or symptoms, call your pediatrician immediately.

* Skin around her mouth or on her body looks blue.
* She is struggling to breathe, or she breathes more than 50 breaths a minute.
* Skin or whites of her eyes look yellow.
* Soft spot on her head sinks or bulges.
* She is very lethargic.
* She cries and is inconsolable, or her crying is high-pitched and frequent.
* Baby has fewer than six wet diapers a day.
* She is shaking and extremely irritable.
* She has a convulsion.
* She vomits forcefully (vomit travels several inches—not the usual spitting up or dribbling), or she vomits repeatedly.
* She refuses two feedings in a row.
* She has a rash that causes her discomfort.
* Her temperature is higher than 100F or lower than 96F.
* She has persistent diarrhea.
* There is blood in her urine or her stool.
* You notice any unusual discharge from her eyes, navel or genitals.
* She has white patches in her mouth (it could be thrush, which isn't serious but it can make her very uncomfortable).

> If you notice bumps on baby's gums and the roof of her mouth and she seems OK, don't worry. The bumps are immature oil glands that should disappear very soon.

◌ *When Baby Gets Excited*

Sometimes baby will become overstimulated. When it's time to go to sleep, she has a hard time settling down. There are some things you can do to help her calm down so she can get the rest she needs. Offer her a pacifier or her thumb. Hold her close, and rock her fairly quickly—about one rock per second. Or walk her around, but don't bounce.

As you get to know your baby better, you'll know what works for her. You may need to make some changes in these techniques as she gets older. What may have worked with her when she was very small may not work now that she is growing up.

❧ *Things Babies Don't Like*

There are some things that most babies *don't* like. Keep them in mind as you interact with your little one.

Bitter or very sour tastes are unpleasant to your baby. If you give her anything bitter or sour, she'll probably scrunch her face and turn her head away from it.

Movements and sounds that are irregular can cause distress. A baby prefers regularity in sound and motion. Unusual patterns can be upsetting to her.

Faces that do not move may disturb her. She studies people's faces so she can learn about them; when they don't move, it may frighten her. This does not hold true for pictures she looks at, only for real people.

Sudden changes in the environment may unsettle your baby. If something unexpected happens, it can upset her. Let her know what you're going to do before you do it.

Don't overstimulate her when possible. She'll react to stress in many of the same ways as you do.

Abrupt volume changes can disturb your baby. She likes gradual change, so keep this in mind as you deal with her.

Loud, deep noises may be unpleasant. Your baby likes higher-pitched sounds, such as a woman's voice.

Bright lights may hurt baby's eyes. Bright lights include the sun and high-wattage light bulbs.

Milestones this 13th Week

❧ *Tonic Neck Reflex Disappears*

The tonic neck reflex, which kept baby's head turned to one side most of the time, has just about disappeared by now. She can now turn her head to either side, which makes it easier for her to turn toward a sound.

❧ *Her Visual World*

Baby may be able to follow a moving object with her eyes. She can follow something as it moves vertically and/or in a circular pattern. She can

> Ask relatives and family members to kiss baby's hands, not her face. The skin on her face is very sensitive and easily irritated.

also see things as far away as 15 to 20 feet. Her view of the world is vastly different from yours. As an experiment, get down on the floor for a view of what she sees. Her sight of table legs and furniture feet under the coffee table gives a different perspective to the world. Seeing things through her eyes may help you understand her environment.

↳ *She Can Sit When Supported*
She can sit erect when supported at her hips and enjoys sitting in a semi-upright position. This position is best for learning and play.

↳ *She Uses Her Hands*
Her hands are now open most of the time. She holds and shakes a rattle. She may grab at your hair, your jewelry or your clothes. She may swipe at a toy with her closed fist. Be alert for her quick movements!

↳ *When She Vocalizes*
It's a thrill to hear your baby laugh and chuckle, which she may be doing now as her verbal skills improve. She is also vocalizing more, such as cooing, squealing, whimpering and gurgling. As you talk to her, she is beginning to understand your message is made of syllables. She soon starts making vowel sounds, such as "ooh" and "aah."

↳ *When Should You Be Concerned?*
If your baby has trouble reaching certain developmental milestones, it could signal various problems. If your baby exhibits any of the following at this time, discuss the situation with your pediatrician.
- She can't support her head.
- She doesn't turn her head toward the sound of your voice or other noises.
- Her movements still seem to be reflexes; they are not deliberate.

Note: See also the box *Milestones this 13ᵗʰ Week*.

What's Happening this 13ᵗʰ Week?

↳ *If Baby Has Difficulty Getting to Sleep*
Baby is sleeping about 10 hours at night, although she may wake for short periods during the night. If you find your baby has trouble going to sleep when you put her down, she may not have been awake long enough during the day. To help solve this problem, don't leave her in her crib too long when she wakes up. She needs to associate being in her crib with sleeping. Avoid overstimulation of your baby, especially just before bedtime. This could contribute to her sleep problems.

↳ *Baby's Skull Measurement*
During the first 4 months of her life, baby's skull grows faster than at any other time during her lifetime. Your baby's doctor will measure her head at her well-baby checkups to see that her brain is developing normally. During

MILESTONES THIS 13TH WEEK

Changes You May See this Week as Baby Develops Physically
❧ she is able to sit with support

Changes You May See this Week in Baby's Developing Senses and Reflexes
❧ may bat at object with closed fist

Changes You May See this Week as Baby's Mind Develops
❧ waits for expected reward, such as feeding

Changes You May See this Week in Baby's Social Development
❧ tries to attract attention when a parent or sibling is nearby
❧ may be attentive for up to 45 minutes

Every baby is an individual, and your baby may do some of these things more quickly or more slowly than another baby. If you are concerned about your baby's progress, discuss it with your healthcare provider. Also see page xiii.

the first month, baby's head may have grown as much as 1 inch. For the remainder of her first year, average head growth is about ½ inch per month.

☙ More than One Baby

Having one baby is a wonderful experience–having two or more is incredible! You'll need more of everything–equipment, assistance, time, patience. You'll probably get less sleep, but your rewards will be great as your babies grow up.

With the wide availability of prenatal testing, most parents know if they are expecting more than one baby during a pregnancy. Ultrasound has made the prediction of multiple births easier. However, the birth of more than one baby is a surprise to some parents and catches them unaware.

Family Adjustments.   If you are the lucky parents of multiples, you will be making many adjustments as a family. It may be necessary to ask others for help. It's in everyone's best interest, including your babies'. Don't try to do everything yourself, or you'll be overwhelmed and exhausted. Take good care of yourself and your partner so you can both tend to babies' needs. Below is a list of some things you can do to lighten your load.

❧ Keep diapers and supplies close at hand, in various places around the house. It saves energy and provides you more time with your babies.

* Use an answering machine to take phone calls when you're resting, feeding or spending time with the babies. Return calls when you have time.
* Use a monitor when babies are napping. You can keep an ear open anywhere in the house without having to check on them repeatedly.
* Take care of yourself. Get out of the house when you can. Ask others in to help. They'll love the opportunity to interact with your babies.
* Eat well, and rest when babies rest. You need to keep your energy and strength levels up.
* When you want to go out when babies are older, and you wonder if a sitter can handle more than one baby, hire a sitter for each baby.
* Hire a mother's helper for part of each day. A teenager may be a good choice to help out around the house. Even if you can't leave a helper alone with the babies, he or she can tend them and entertain them, while you relax or do things you've been putting off.
* Don't do anything you don't have to. Let some chores go for a while, if they can be ignored.
* Alternate tasks with your babies. For example, bathe one baby one day and the other the next day. As long as faces, hands and diaper areas are clean, babies don't need a bath every day.
* Be as efficient as you can. Plan ahead to save time. If you bottlefeed, make bottles up 24 hours in advance and store in the refrigerator. Don't change babies' clothes if they're not dirty; you'll save time and energy.

Equipment You'll Need.   You're going to need more items on hand with multiples, but you don't need two of everything. Some things can do double duty. You will need a crib for each baby, although a drawer or basket will work while a baby is small. You *must* have an approved car seat for each baby. Individual infant seats and high chairs are necessary, as are diapers and clothes for each baby. A stroller with a seat for each baby is a good investment.

With some equipment, one item is enough. You probably need only one swing, playpen, rocking chair, diaper bag, changing table and infant tub. Use these items as they are needed.

Feeding Your Babies.   One of the greatest challenges for parents of multiples is deciding how to feed them. Some mothers want to breastfeed exclusively. (It's an added bonus for multiples because many are born earlier than single-birth babies, and breast milk is extremely beneficial for preemies.) Some moms say bottlefeeding is the only way to go. Others try to combine the two, and breastfeed *and* bottlefeed their babies.

Breastfeeding your babies, even if it's only for one or two feedings a day, gives them the protection from infection that breast milk provides. Research has shown that even the smallest dose of breast milk gives baby an advantage over babies fed only formula.

> If you have more than one baby, feeding them at the same time (or one right after the other) helps get them on the same schedule.

One of the best things you can do is to consult a lactation specialist— you're going to need some sound advice. This expert can help you by providing advice on many aspects of feeding multiples, from positions for holding two babies to helping a preemie latch onto your breast.

If babies are early, and you can't nurse them, begin pumping! Pump from day one, and store your breast milk for the time babies are able to receive it. You may also be asked to bring your pumped breast milk to the hospital so that it can be fed to your babies there. Pumping tells the body to produce breast milk—pump and the milk will come. It just takes some time.

Breastfeeding multiples is a challenge. This is one area in which the advice of a lactation consultant can be very valuable to you. Some moms pump their breast milk and divide it between the babies; this allows accurate measurement of how much breast milk each baby is receiving. They then finish with formula, if babies are still hungry. This method also works well for triplets.

If you decide to try to breastfeed your babies, experiment with various situations and positions to learn what works best for you. Some mothers nurse both babies at the same time. There are special cushions on the market designed to help you hold and nurse two babies at once.

Switch babies from one breast to the other at different feedings. This ensures each baby gets visual stimulation on both sides. It also helps prevent problems for you, such as engorgement in one breast if one baby isn't feeding as well as the other. By switching breasts, the demand for milk remains about the same for each breast, so breasts tend to remain equal in size.

Supplementing with formula allows your partner and others to help you feed the babies. You can breastfeed one while someone else bottlefeeds the other. Or you can nurse each one for a time, then finish the feeding with formula. In either case, others can help you feed the babies.

Be sure to take good care of yourself. You need rest and good nutrition so your milk supply will be adequate. You want to remain healthy so you can continue to perform this important task.

Your attempts at breastfeeding may make you feel like a 24-hour fast-food restaurant, but keep at it as long as you can. You'll be giving your babies the best start in life.

Try to Get Them on the Same Schedule.   One goal to work toward is getting both babies on the same schedule. One baby may be more interested in feeding than the other, but try to feed them both at the same time, when possible. Getting your babies to sleep at night at the same time also allows you some rest or free time.

Feeding Premature Babies.   Many multiple pregnancies are delivered early, which results in babies being premature. Breast milk is the best nutrition for a premature baby. It is rich in antibodies and nutrients essential for baby's well-being. However, human milk alone may not provide adequate iron for some premature infants. Talk to your pediatrician if you have questions.

Many preemies are not strong enough to breastfeed, so they are fed electrolyte solutions intravenously (through an I.V.), or they may be fed formula or breast milk through a tube in the nose. Intravenous solutions contain water, protein, fat, minerals, such as calcium, carbohydrates and electrolytes, such as sodium, potassium and chloride. A premature baby's intestinal system may be too immature to absorb nutrients from milk. Feeding through a tube gives your baby the nutrients she needs until she is mature enough to suck and to swallow.

Baby is fed a small amount at first, but this gradually increases as she is better able to handle it. As baby grows and matures, she will learn to suck and to swallow–things that a full-term baby does automatically.

If a mom can't breastfeed her premature baby, there are specialty formulas available. One preemie formula by Enfamil contains DHA and ARA. See *Week 3* for further information on *DHA* and *ARA*. Similac has introduced a formula to use when baby comes home from the hospital. Ask your baby's doctor if fortified preemie formula is right for your baby.

Playing and Interacting with Babies.   You'll find you may not have as much time to spend playing and interacting with your babies as you'd like. Set aside solitary time with each baby because it's an important part of the bonding process.

Choose a time when the baby is quiet and alert. Play with him or her and interact as we've already described in previous weekly discussions. It's important to talk and interact with each baby separately, to help develop language skills and to connect with their personalities.

Are You Fighting Favoritism?   It may come as a shock to you if you find yourself feeling closer to one baby than another. There are many reasons for these feelings. One baby's temperament may be easier to deal with. Maybe you prefer the sex of one baby over another. Some parents harbor a little resentment toward a second, unplanned-for baby. Whatever the reason, try to overcome it.

The first step is to admit your feelings. They are not abnormal, so be kind to yourself. Admit you have the feelings, and go from there. If one baby is more demanding than another, focus on his or her positive traits. If you feel a little resentful, give each of your babies time and attention. Get to know them. The feeling will soon pass.

No two babies are alike, in personality or development. Accept each as an individual and treat them fairly. Soon you will feel loving affection for each baby.

Find Moral Support.   Contact clubs and groups in your area for parents of multiples. Being able to talk about your stresses and distresses with others who have been there can be a great help. These organizations are usually listed in the telephone book. Also see the *Resources* section, page 527, for a list of national organizations and contacts.

> If you think baby has a diaper rash but the redness appears in the skin creases and has lasted more than 3 days, with no improvement, it may be a yeast infection. Call your pediatrician—he or she may prescribe an antifungal cream to treat the problem.

✻ *Acid Reflux (GERD)*

Acid reflux, also called *gastroesophageal reflux disease* or *GERD,* occurs when baby's stomach contents bubble up into the esophagus. This can irritate baby's throat and cause her to pull away from the bottle or breast while she's feeding. She may refuse to feed for a bit but then want to feed again immediately.

Acid reflux can occur at any age; everyone experiences it at some time. Only the frequency and persistence of the problem make it abnormal. Acid reflux is usually a mild problem that improves by about 1 year of age. Symptoms indicating baby may have acid reflux include the following:

- spitting up
- vomiting (can be forceful)
- inconsolable crying
- weight loss
- failure to gain weight
- gagging or choking at the end of a feeding
- fussiness after eating
- respiratory problems
- irritability

* restless sleep
* hiccups
* wheezing
* coughing
* apnea

What You Can Do at Home. For a mild case, consider breastfeeding exclusively. Your baby doesn't swallow as much air when she breastfeeds, and breast milks empties from the stomach faster than formula. That means there's less time for stomach contents to flow back into the esophagus.

Feed baby half as much as usual, twice as often. A smaller volume of food empties faster, so she doesn't spit up as much. You can also burp baby, then hold her upright for about 30 minutes after she eats. Burp her more frequently during a feeding. Change the position of her infant seat or the head of her crib so she is more upright.

Comfort her and soothe her when she's fussy. When she cries a lot, she can swallow air, which increases the pressure inside her abdomen. Increased pressure can trigger GERD.

Sometimes adding rice cereal to formula can help, but *do not do this* unless your pediatrician says it's OK. If the problem is severe, discuss it with baby's doctor. He or she may want to treat baby with medication.

If baby has a bad case of GERD, she may spit up, arch away from the bottle and cry. If this happens, it's time to call the doctor.

When to Call the Doctor. Contact your pediatrician if baby vomits excessively, loses weight or has respiratory problems. If you see any blood in the vomit or she has apnea spells, contact your pediatrician.

Medication may be prescribed to decrease the amount of acid in the stomach contents or to promote gastric emptying. The first medications prescribed are generally acid reducers, such as Zantac, that keep acid from reaching the esophagus. If acid reducers do not work, proton pump inhibitors (PPIs), which include Prilosec and Prevacid, may be prescribed. These medicines stop completely the production of stomach acid. However, these stronger medications cause many side effects, and a baby must be under the supervision of a physician while they are being taken.

A word of warning: Never give your baby over-the-counter acid reducers or PPIs without specific instructions from your pediatrician!

If the problem is serious, nasogastric feedings (putting a tube through the nose into the stomach) may be necessary for a baby who has severe GERD. Surgery may be needed if there are severe complications, such as recurring aspiration pneumonia, apnea or severe irritation or inflammation of the esophagus, or if medication doesn't work.

⊰ *Chapped Skin*

During the winter months, your baby's skin may become chapped. It will appear dry and flaky. It may itch. Often it is slightly reddened. To ease baby's discomfort, try the following measures.

* Bathe baby less frequently.
* Use warm water, not hot water, in her baths.
* Use soap sparingly.
* Pat her skin dry, rather than rubbing it.
* Apply lubricants to dry skin before chapped areas become inflamed; petroleum jelly is fragrance free and lubricates skin very well.
* Use a cool-mist humidifier in rooms with very dry air.
* If you live in a very dry climate, add a humidifier to your heating system or put humidifiers in various rooms of the house.

What You Can Do at Home.   For minor discomfort, use nonprescription skin lubricants, such as petroleum jelly, mineral oil or alcohol-free, fragrance-free lotions. For serious discomfort, you doctor may prescribe topical cortisone creams or lotions.

When to Call the Doctor.   Call the doctor if your baby has severely chapped skin and home care doesn't relieve symptoms in 1 week. If her chapped skin becomes inflamed, call your pediatrician.

Toys and Play this 13ᵗʰ Week

A baby likes to explore textures. Touching different objects gives her much pleasure. It also helps her learn what the world is like. Offer her a variety of safe things to touch and to feel, such as soft cloth, sheepskin, a shiny leaf, a smooth plastic spoon. Remain alert and vigilant when you give her various objects. She'll probably try to put everything in her mouth!

⊰ *Reach for the Rattle*

Help baby develop her eye–hand coordination with a brightly colored rattle or toy. Hold it at different distances in front of her. Encourage her to reach for it. Be sure you give it to her often, or she may become frustrated.

⊰ *Pat-a-Cake, Pat-a-Cake*

Finger games stimulate your baby to hold, stare at and clench her hands. One game that encourages this development is "Pat-a-Cake, Pat-a-Cake."

Clasp one of baby's hands in each of yours. As you sing, clap baby's hands together in time to song.

Pat-a-cake, pat-a-cake
Baker's man.
Bake me a cake
As fast as you can.
Pat it, and roll it
And mark it with a B.
Put it in the oven
For baby and me!

✤ *Object in Motion*

Because baby's eyes can now move in a circular pattern, hold a shiny object tied securely on a string above her head. Be sure to keep it out of her reach. Move it slowly in a circle, and let her watch it. Then hold it at her eye level. Move it around her head. She will follow it with her eyes. After a couple of times, she may also anticipate it as it moves around her head, then comes back into view. This game exposes her to the concept of objects in motion.

> If she hasn't already learned this new trick, she soon will. It may surprise you, but she can blow bubbles with her saliva!

Week 14

Baby's Age as a Monthly Reference—4 months

HOW BIG IS BABY THIS 14TH WEEK?
Baby weighs 12¾ pounds and is 23¾ inches long this week.

Baby Care and Equipment

✣ *Does Baby Need a Social Security Number?*
Although most parents don't think about it, it's important for your baby to have a Social Security number. You need this number to claim him as a dependent on your income tax. It's also important for future benefits your child may be eligible for. You'll need a Social Security number (SSN) to open a bank account, buy him a savings bond or apply for many government services. However, getting a Social Security number is voluntary—you won't get one unless you ask for it.

The government has made it easy for you. You don't need to fill out special forms to apply for a number. Advise your hospital representative or doctor to have your state's vital statistics office share information from baby's birth certificate with the Social Security Administration. This information is confidential and is not given to anyone else. After the information is forwarded to the Social Security Administration, a card with baby's number on it will be mailed to you.

If you apply for a number when baby is born, you save yourself time and effort. You won't have to visit the Social Security office in person, fill out any forms or submit a birth certificate.

If you have any questions or concerns, call the Social Security Administration at 800-772-1213. You can also contact them on the Internet. See the *Resources* section, page 527, for their web address.

Protect Social Security Numbers. A Social Security number should not be given to everyone who asks for it. You may have been asked in the past, and you will probably be asked in the future, to supply your SSN or your baby's SSN for various reasons, such as when you fill out forms, apply for services or for other reasons.

We suggest you *not* give a SSN to anyone who doesn't need it. Your employer and your bank need it—there are few reasons for others to have it. For baby, it is necessary to have it when you fill out tax forms or open a savings account. Otherwise, do not give it out.

Why do we give you such a warning? Because when someone has your SSN, it's much easier to steal your identity. We speak from experience. Safeguard your number, your spouse's number and your child's number.

✤ *Follow Your Instincts for Dressing Baby*

Has someone older than you said baby is cold, even though you dressed him in one more layer than you have on? Don't be disturbed. The older generation overdressed babies and overheated their homes when their children were little.

It isn't healthy to keep baby too warm. As we've previously stated, dress baby depending on what *you're* comfortable in. Add one more layer than you if it's cold, the same number of layers if it's warm. In cold weather, keep his hands, feet and head covered to preserve body heat.

Don't overheat your home—72F is fine for when baby is sleeping. Research has shown that overheating a room may be linked with SIDS.

> Baby should be sleeping about 10 hours a night, napping about 4½ hours and awake for interacting and play time about 9 hours *each day.*

✤ *A Few More Minutes with Your Doctor*

In this first year, you'll see your baby's doctor at least five times (for well-baby checkups) and probably more. Most doctors have very busy schedules, and you may find your office-visit time limited. You may feel as though you never have enough time to discuss *all* your concerns.

There are ways you can get the most from your next doctor's appointment. In *Week 15,* we discuss some specific ways to get the most out of a well-baby checkup. Below are some ideas for every office visit. Consider the following suggestions.

* Ask if it's possible to schedule more time when you make your appointment. It may mean coming into the office early or late, but if it's important to you, make the time.
* Prepare before you go. Think about your concerns, and write them down. You'll save time, and you'll be able to cover what you want. Keep questions limited to these topics.
* Before you leave, be sure you understand the answers to your questions. Ask for clarification if you don't understand something.
* If some of your questions can be answered by a nurse practitioner or someone else in the office, ask to speak with him or her. Get to know *everyone* on the office staff. They are also available to answer your questions.

- Don't bring any other children with you when you go to the appointment.
- It can be helpful to have another person with you. Consider asking your partner or your mother or mother-in-law to come to visits. That way there will be two sets of ears to hear advice and instructions.
- If you are satisfied with the care your baby is receiving, express your appreciation to your pediatrician and his or her staff. When you are dissatisfied, let them know that, too.

Milestones this 14th Week

Baby Visually Tracks Objects
Your baby easily tracks objects with his eyes by this time. Earlier in infancy, he had trouble fixing both eyes on an image. Now he can lock his gaze onto an object moving several feet away from him. He watches people moving around him, and he gazes across the room. He sees in full color, and prefers red and blue.

His Strength Improves
His arm and leg movements are more controlled. He holds his head erect when sitting. His grasping ability is much better, and he makes greater efforts to use it. It's time to store the infant mobiles and bring out toys he can grab and hold. A crib gym encourages him to reach for, and to hold, an object.

Baby Drooling
You may notice your baby begins drooling around this time. Some babies drool so much they are constantly wet around their neck and face. Some attribute drooling to teething, but this isn't always the case. Some babies cut their first tooth this early, but most don't start teething until they're at least 6 months old. If your baby drools profusely, put a bib on him. Also see the discussion below on the rash that can develop with excessive drooling.

Routine Is Important
It's important to provide your baby with a predictable routine. When you do this, you help him anticipate events that occur regularly in his life. This helps him develop attention and memory.

When Baby Is Tired
By now, you can probably tell when baby's tired. He probably sends some definite signals that indicate he's done in. Obvious signs are yawning, rubbing his face and eyes, avoiding interaction with others, crying or fussiness.

A very tired baby may regress in behavior to earlier kinds of reflexes and actions. He may suck his thumb, roll his head, cry or act unhappy and be hard to soothe or calm. When you become aware of what these actions mean, you can remove him from a stimulating environment and allow him to rest or to go to sleep.

Note: See also the box *Milestones this 14th Week.*

What's Happening this 14th Week?

✂ *Is Baby Drooling a Lot?*
As mentioned above, some babies drool a lot beginning around this time. Drooling begins shortly after birth and peaks between 3 and 6 months. Baby drools because he doesn't have as much control over his lips and tongue as you do, and he is unable to swallow his saliva the way an adult does. Drooling can actually be good for baby. It helps by:

* cooling his gums
* reducing teething pain
* keeping his lips and gums moist
* softening food so it's easier to digest

Drooling is usually *not* a sign of anything serious. However, it can be. Drooling may accompany croup and epiglottitis, which is an infection of the throat.

If baby seems happy and content, even though he's drooling quite a bit, don't worry. If drooling is accompanied by other, serious symptoms, call your doctor.

Some Problems You May See with Drooling. The neck and face area get very wet and stay that way when baby drools a lot. This can cause a rash from the constant dampness and the irritation of wet skin against clothing. Sometimes putting a bib on him helps soak up some of the drool.

When baby drools, protect his face with some petroleum jelly. Dry his face, and apply the protective barrier. Placing cornstarch on his neck can help protect that area. If the rash becomes severe or seems to cause baby major discomfort, call your pediatrician for advice.

✂ *Plane Travel with Baby*
You may have decided to make a plane trip with your new baby to visit relatives or friends. Plane travel is one of the best ways to make a long journey with a baby. To make your trip enjoyable for everyone, it takes planning and preparation on your part. It may seem like a lot to think about, but you'll be glad you took care of everything once you begin your journey.

MILESTONES THIS 14ᵀᴴ WEEK

Changes You May See this Week as Baby Develops Physically
* can focus eyes at different distances
* holds head steady and erect for short periods

Changes You May See this Week in Baby's Developing Senses and Reflexes
* clasps fingers and hands in play

Changes You May See this Week as Baby's Mind Develops
* smiles and vocalizes more to an actual face than to an image

Changes You May See this Week in Baby's Social Development
* attempts to soothe himself
* may prefer a particular toy
* can be quieted with music

Every baby is an individual, and your baby may do some of these things more quickly or more slowly than another baby. If you are concerned about your baby's progress, discuss it with your healthcare provider. Also see page xiii.

Making Plans

* Keep your travel short when possible. Book a nonstop flight. The faster the trip, the better it is.
* Allow extra time for everything. Time your arrival at the airport at least 30 minutes earlier than when you travel alone. You may need the extra time for checking baby's car seat, changing diapers or feeding him.
* When you make your reservation, get your seat assignments so you can sit together.
* Check your baggage at the curb to save time and effort for you.
* When possible, schedule your trip for baby's naptime or bedtime. Hopefully, he'll sleep through at least part of the trip. A morning flight might be good, if baby is more alert and happier at the beginning of the day.
* If you can travel during quieter times of the day, such as late at night, you may find an empty seat next to you, allowing you to spread out a little. And baby may sleep through the flight.
* Dress baby comfortably, in layers. Bring an extra blanket or two because planes can be very cool.

* Change baby just before you board the plane. If your trip is short, you may not have to change him again until after you land.
* If you have an umbrella stroller, take it with you. It's easy to stow in the plane, and it's helpful when you have to walk long distances in the airport. If you can't take it on board, you can check it at the gate as you board the plane. (You can also do this with a regular stroller.)
* If your baby is under 3 months old, a front carrier lets you keep hands free. With an older baby, a backpack carrier is a good choice.
* Most airlines offer preboarding if you have a small child. Use it! It gives you more time to get settled and to stow all your gear.
* Although most airlines let a baby fly free and sit in an adult's lap until age 2, consider buying a ticket for him and putting him in the plane's seat in his car seat. See the discussion below.
* Offer baby a pacifier or a feeding during take off and landing. Sucking can reduce the effects of changing air pressure; it helps equalize pressure in his ears. See the discussion below.
* Always carry extra of *everything* you normally have in your diaper bag! If you're delayed anywhere, you'll have the supplies you need.

Your Carry-on Bag.   With most airlines, you are limited to two pieces of carry-on baggage. If you carry a purse, your other piece of luggage has to carry everything you'll need for baby during your trip. Include disposable diapers and baby wipes, diaper-rash ointment, a small changing pad for your lap or other surface, a few pacifiers, a couple of changes of baby clothes, formula, bottles and nipples, baby food (if baby's eating it), burp cloths, a favorite comfort toy, a blanket and at least half a dozen resealable plastic bags. If your baby is teething, a frozen washcloth in a plastic bag can come in very handy.

Some moms carry a couple of diaper bags. They put their wallet, tickets and a few necessary things for themselves in a pocket of one bag. They pack their empty purse in their luggage to use when they get to their destination.

> When flying with baby, be prepared for any situation.
> Don't assume the airline will provide anything to
> make your trip easier or more comfortable.

Where to Sit?   When you make your airline reservations, tell them you are traveling with a baby. You may be advised by some to request the seat behind the bulkhead, which provides more leg room. However, there are drawbacks with bulkhead seats. The armrests are fixed in place, so you can't raise them to increase your space if no one else sits in your row. You also lose underseat storage.

A window seat is a good choice because no one will have to climb over you and baby to get in and out. If you have a seat for baby, place yourself between your baby and another passenger.

Ear-Popping Advice.   When there is a change in air pressure during takeoff and landing, your eustachian tube temporarily closes, causing fluid to build up. This makes your ears feel stuffy and may cause discomfort or pain. You may also have a temporary hearing loss. You can take care of this by chewing gum, swallowing or sucking on something.

Your baby experiences the same feelings in his ears. You need to help him clear his ears to relieve his discomfort. To keep his tubes open, feed him during takeoff and landing. Or offer him a pacifier so he sucks during this time. If baby is asleep when you're preparing to land, wake him up and try to feed him.

Can Baby Fly with a Cold?   It's usually OK for a baby to fly if he has a cold, but the change in air pressure can cause fluid buildup, increasing his risk for an ear infection. If baby is congested, ask your pediatrician about giving him a decongestant the night before your trip. With an ear infection, antibiotics should be given at least 48 hours in advance of the trip. This should keep symptoms from getting worse during the flight. Acetaminophen for children can relieve any discomfort. Ask your doctor about it. Discuss your plans to fly with your pediatrician, if your baby has a cold or an ear infection.

Keep Baby (and You) Hydrated.   The cabin air in a plane is usually very dry. Humidity can be as low as 10%. Offer baby lots of fluids to prevent dehydration. It's a good idea for you to drink extra fluids, too. You can use saline nose drops or nasal spray with baby to help with the lack of humidity. Spray a little into each of his nostrils about once an hour. Or let baby breathe through a damp washcloth held in front of his nose. *Note:* Never place the washcloth over baby's nostrils.

Changing Baby in Flight.   Most airplane bathrooms don't have a changing table for baby, and they're too small to change a baby. You won't have many options about where you change diapers. You may have to do it on an empty seat or on your lap. If your baby is quite small, you might get by with using the closed lid of the toilet seat.

Carry some plastic bags with you. The airlines require you to use them for disposable diapers. If you use cloth diapers, flush the feces down the toilet and put the soiled diaper in one of the plastic bags you brought along until you can rinse it out after you land.

Getting Baby to Sleep during the Flight.   Some parents plan a trip so baby naps during the flight. Others want to travel after baby wakes up, so he'll be rested. Don't change baby's schedule to fit your flight time. Try to make baby comfortable during the flight so he can relax and sleep. If he doesn't sleep, be prepared to entertain him.

Feeding Baby during Your Trip.   If you bottlefeed, bring enough formula for an entire day. Using powdered formula and bottled tap water from home avoids spoilage. Mix a bottle as you need it. With an older baby, take prepared baby food in addition to formula. Some airlines provide baby food. Request it at least 24 hours in advance.

If you need to breastfeed baby, you'll have to take him out of his seat to do it. It may be better to offer him a pacifier or his thumb during take off and landing so baby is safe and secure during this time.

Using Baby's Car Seat.   The Federal Aviation Administration (FAA) strongly recommends a baby be placed in an FAA-approved car seat, strapped into an airplane seat, when flying. It's impossible for an adult to hold onto an unrestrained child in severe turbulence or during an accident. In fact, research shows that some young children who died when a plane hit violent turbulence or in plane crashes would have survived if they had been strapped in to an approved seat.

If you choose to have your baby ride in his car seat while flying, you'll be required to pay for his seat. Ask the airline about discount seats for infants. Many airlines now offer half-price seats for children under 2 if they are placed in a child-restraint system. The safety seat must be an FAA-approved car seat and marked with the label "certified for use in an aircraft." When you book the tickets for you and your baby, ask for adjoining seats in a row that is not an exit row. Some airlines require the car seat be placed in a window seat.

If you can't afford to buy an extra ticket, ask your travel agent or the airline reservation clerk which flights are likely to have empty seats. It may be possible to book this type of flight and use an empty seat for free. Unfortunately, you can't *count* on an empty seat unless you purchase a ticket for it.

The rules governing whether a child should be in an approved seat may be changing in the future. It has been reported that the FAA is now considering legislation to require all children be secured in an FAA-approved safety seat when flying, which means parents will no longer be able to hold babies and small children in their laps. *All* children will be required to have their own seat, and parents will have to purchase tickets for them, although hopefully at a reduced cost.

When Things Don't Go Smoothly.   Some trips won't go according to your plans. If this happens, do what you can to deal with the situation, then ask the airline for help. You are entitled to food vouchers if you are delayed beyond a certain length of time. You may be entitled to hotel accommodations if your delay is very long.

Ask if the airline has a family area where you can take baby and rest a little yourself. If you belong to an airline club, there may be a lounge available for your use.

✴ Constipation

When a baby is constipated, he has difficulty having bowel movements, infrequent bowel movements or sluggish bowel action. It occurs more often in older infants, when baby begins eating solids or with other dietary changes.

The main symptom of the problem is baby's difficulty passing dry, hard stools. This may be accompanied by abdominal pain, which decreases after a large bowel movement. Baby may go several days between bowel movements. You may notice stool is blood streaked. *Be aware*—If your baby is breastfeeding and goes a few days between bowel movements, this is *not* considered constipation.

What You Can Do at Home.   If your younger baby seems constipated, use a rectal thermometer lubricated with petroleum jelly to stimulate the passage of stools. Gently place the thermometer in the rectum, then remove it.

If your baby is older and eating solids, offer him lots of fluid and diluted juice. Be careful with apple juice—it often has a laxative effect. Increase the fiber content of baby's diet. Most cases resolve with time if they are caused by a change in diet.

When to Call the Doctor.   Call your pediatrician if the above measures don't work. Call the office if baby's constipation is accompanied by severe abdominal pain or vomiting. Do *not* use any medication to relieve constipation without first consulting the doctor.

Your doctor may suggest an enema or a mild laxative for baby. If constipation becomes chronic or serious, testing may be ordered to determine the cause.

✦ *Measles*

Measles, also called *rubeola,* is a highly contagious virus that can occur at any age. Symptoms of the measles include:

* a cough
* runny nose
* fever
* fussiness
* a rash of small red bumps that begins on the face and spreads downward to his trunk, arms and legs

The rash is more severe at the beginning of the breakout then becomes less intense as it spreads.

A vaccination (MMR—measles, mumps, rubella) to prevent measles was developed years ago in the United States, so now the occurrence of measles is not very common. However, if baby has not been vaccinated and he develops the symptoms described above, measles must be considered.

What You Can Do at Home. Isolate him during the early stages of the disease. Give him plenty of fluids and acetaminophen for fever and discomfort. Keep his skin clean. Give him warm, tepid baths to reduce the itching.

When to Call the Doctor. Call your pediatrician if you believe your baby has the measles. He or she will probably want to see baby to confirm the diagnosis. Once measles has been confirmed, call baby's doctor if he develops a high fever, becomes extremely irritable or if the rash becomes infected.

Prevent measles by vaccinating your baby!

> Your baby's hair may be changing in color and texture now. His baby hair is being replaced with new hair. This process will continue for the next few weeks.

Toys and Play this 14ᵗʰ Week

Your baby probably needs some practice grasping different objects with his hands. Offer him toys that make noise, such as rattles, and toys that feel good to his gums, such as rubber or plastic teething rings. When he's lying on his stomach on the floor, place several different toys within his reach. Let him choose the ones he wants to reach for and to hold.

✦ *Family Pictures*

Make a display of family photos for baby to look at. He likes to gaze at people's faces, or pictures of them, especially people he knows. Put enlarged photos on the wall or on a table where he can see them. Point to and name the people in the pictures as he looks at them. He may reach for the photos. Let him touch them. It helps him recognize those around him.

✴ *Shake that Rattle*

Help baby develop his visual acuity and motor skills at the same time. Put a toy in his grasp that is easy to hold and makes noise. Out of his line of vision, shake his hand so the toy makes noise. Does he lift the toy into his line of vision to see what's making the sound? If he doesn't, raise his arm, and shake the toy again. Tell him what's happening. Do this with both hands.

✴ *Ride the Horse*

If you're like most parents, you'll soon become your baby's "horsie" and will be for quite a long time. These games help your baby bond with you and improve his ability to create and maintain social relationships. It also helps develop his muscle coordination and balance.

While singing the song "Ride a Cock Horse," cross one knee over the other and place baby on your free foot. Holding his hands firmly, gently swing your foot up and down, bouncing him while singing:

> *Ride a cock horse to Millbury Cross*
> *To see a fine lady upon her white horse.*
> *With rings on her fingers and bells on her toes*
> *She shall hear music wherever she goes.*

> When baby laughs,
> laugh back at him!
> He'll love the interaction.

Week 15

Baby's Age as a Monthly Reference—4 months

Baby weighs 13 pounds and is 24 inches long this week.

Baby Care and Equipment

✣ *Does Baby Need Vitamin D?*

Yes, according to the American Academy of Pediatrics. The AAP now recommends that *all* babies from the age of 2 months (continuing until baby is drinking 17 ounces a day of vitamin-D-fortified milk) receive 200IU of vitamin D every day to prevent rickets.

In the past, parents were advised to put a baby outside in the sunshine because she needed vitamin D. The baby got vitamin D from the sun's ultraviolet rays. Dr. Benjamin Spock's baby book actually included a schedule for "sunbathing baby." Parents were also advised that baby needed lots of fresh air. Many babies spent as long as 2 or more hours a day outside, but thankfully only a short time in direct sunlight!

Today, we advise you to protect your baby from harmful UV rays by keeping her completely out of the sun. Sunscreens and sunblocks can protect her delicate skin, but nothing protects better than *no* exposure at all! (Sunscreens and sunblocks should not be used on babies younger than 6 months of age. See the discussion in *Week 20*.)

Vitamin-D supplements alone are very concentrated and unsafe to use for children. The AAP recommends using a multivitamin containing 200IU of vitamin D, which is available over the counter in tablets or liquid form. Talk to your baby's doctor if you have questions or are confused about vitamin-D supplementation.

✣ *Medication Guidelines*

You must be very careful when giving your baby any type of medicine. You don't want to give her too much, and you want to be sure you give her the right kind! Below are some guidelines to keep in mind when giving medications to your baby.

- ✹ When you give your baby liquid medication, use a measuring spoon, a plastic medicine spoon or an oral syringe. Don't use tableware—they don't hold the correct amount of liquid!

* Be sure the measurement unit on the device you use is the unit of measurement you need.
* Make sure you give the correct amount–don't confuse tablespoon (T. or tbsp) with teaspoon (t. or tsp.).
* Store medication for each family member on a separate shelf in a safe place, out of a child's reach.
* Don't keep medicine in a bathroom cabinet. Steam and moisture can affect medication.
* Tape a note on each prescription stating the dosage schedule.
* Be sure you have the correct medication. Double-check the name on the label.
* Never guess at the amount of medicine to give. Double-check the dosage amount.
* Don't make conversions. If directions call for 2 teaspoons, don't try to convert it to ounces.
* If your baby is prescribed more than one medication, be sure they are OK to take together. Check with your physician and pharmacist.
* Don't keep old medications; get rid of them.
* Use clean droppers and spoons. Rinse between use, then air dry. After you give a medication, wash these utensils in warm, soapy water. Store in an airtight plastic container or sealed plastic bag. Don't wash them in the dishwasher. Openings are too small to be cleaned properly; soap residue might remain.
* Don't give medicine to anyone other than the person it was prescribed for, and give baby the complete course of treatment.

Your Well-Baby Checkups

There are some things you can do when you take baby in for her well-baby checkups to ensure you get the best care possible. Follow the suggestions in *Week 14,* and add these specific points to your list.

* Ask the doctor to describe the procedures he or she performs, the reasons for them and what the results may indicate. This helps you better understand your child's development. It also lets you ask questions while the procedure is going on. You may forget questions if you wait until the end of the appointment.
* If any tests are performed, ask about the results. When will they be available? Do you have to call the office for them? What do results mean? When would other tests be indicated? When would further treatment be indicated?
* Ask questions about nonmedical issues, such as emotional

development, discipline, learning and socialization of your baby. Ask about resources available to help you find answers.

* Request any printed material that might be useful to you. Doctors' offices have many pamphlets, booklets and other handouts available for you to take home. They can help a lot, especially when you've discussed a lot of different things with your physician at one appointment.

* Ask if there is a nurse, nurse practitioner or physician's assistant who can help you with questions and problems. Often these professionals are more readily available to help you.

* See if your pediatrician has a recommended reading list or a library of books that you can borrow. He or she has probably seen many of the books on the market and may have suggestions for a book that will help you with a particular situation. Lists and libraries often contain books on child care, child development, discipline, potty training and other topics of interest to you.

Helping Baby Relax

Studies have shown that when a baby feels relaxed, she falls asleep more quickly. You may not know what to do to help your baby relax. Below are some methods parents have used to help settle their babies.

* A warm bath may help your baby relax. Some babies like to be in the water. Others like the sound of running water and the steam hot water produces. Try bathing your baby when she's fussy. If that doesn't work, she may settle if you put her in a safe place in the bathroom while you shower.

* Noise can be soothing. White noise is often helpful for calming baby. Run the clothes dryer or the vacuum cleaner. Be careful with very loud sounds. They could startle baby and cause her distress.

* Music can soothe a fussy baby. Try different types of music with your baby. Some babies like lullabies. Others prefer classical music. Some are calmed by music with more of a beat.

* Motion may help distract a baby and calm her. Riding in a car, swinging in her swing, walking, bouncing, rocking—they can all work.

* Put your baby to bed at the first signs of fatigue. This helps her relax more easily.

Infant Carriers

Many parents use their baby's car seat as an infant carrier. It's convenient, and it saves money not to have to buy another piece of baby equipment. Other parents choose to use a separate infant carrier in the house or on errands. It's easier than hooking up and unhooking the baby's car seat every time they leave the car.

If you choose to use an infant carrier, there are some things you should know about their safety. The three greatest safety concerns are:

* a baby becoming entangled in restraining straps
* a carrier falling over on a soft surface, resulting in suffocation
* an unrestrained baby falling out of a carrier

The Consumer Product Safety Commission (CPSC) has made some recommendations for parents to follow to ensure baby's safety. By practicing these measures, you will help prevent injury to your baby.

* Make sure the carrier you select has a wide, sturdy base.
* Never leave baby alone in an infant carrier when it is not placed on the floor. In fact, you should never be farther away than arm's reach when baby is in one.
* Place an infant seat *only* on a hard surface. Stay away from upholstered furniture and beds.
* Use safety straps and belts when baby is in the carrier.
* Keep an eye on your baby when she's in her infant carrier. Keep her away from pets, out of drafts and away from areas where she can be hurt.
* Be careful when carrying baby in an infant carrier—avoid bumping the carrier into walls and other objects.
* *Never* use an infant carrier as a car seat, unless it was also designed for this purpose!

When you put your baby in an infant carrier, maintain your vigilance. You may believe she's out of harm's way and is protected. However, it's your care that will keep her safe.

Milestones this 15ᵗʰ Week

☆ *When Baby Is Happy*

Your baby is learning many new things. When she's excited about something, she may jerk her arms and legs crazily to demonstrate her joy. She's not in total control of her body yet, so her actions appear spastic and jerky.

When baby is unhappy, you can soothe her by holding her and talking to her. Sometimes your presence is all she needs to calm down. This is a sign of her increasing trust in you. In the next few weeks, she may become attached to something soft or cuddly as a security object.

☆ *Her Legs and Feet Strengthen*

She loves to kick her legs and feet. You may notice her holding up her legs, flexing her feet and making bicycling motions in the air. She may be able to touch her knees with her hands. She delights in splashing in the bathtub. These practices help develop the strength she needs to support her weight in the coming months.

Evidence she's preparing to begin the rudiments of creeping and crawling can be seen in her swimming motions. She may lie on her tummy, hold her head up, and kick and move her legs and arms at the same time.

✣ She May Partially Roll Over
A big accomplishment around this time is baby's ability to roll herself over partially. She'll probably master rolling in one direction in the next few weeks—usually from tummy to back. It's easier to roll this way first. Rolling from her back to her tummy requires a degree of physical strength and control that she won't have for a while yet.

Once she's mastered rolling from tummy to back, she'll concentrate on rolling the other way. At this time, she probably can't make it *all* the way over onto her back, but she'll soon accomplish that feat.

✣ Baby Pleasures
Your baby may enjoy being rocked and bounced. The receptors in her brain make this activity pleasurable to her. Whirl her in your arms. She may enjoy her swing or bouncer now more than ever because of their back-and-forth or up-and-down motion.

Baby likes to look at bright colors and is less interested in black and white. She recognizes family members and may become more attached to individuals, especially her mother.

✣ She Makes Many Noises
Baby may spend a lot of her time making noises. You may hear her pant, grunt, groan, coo, babble and shriek. She listens to herself talk. You may hear her making "ba, da, ga, pa" sounds. These various sounds let her express her wants and needs with less crying. She vocalizes more to an actual person than a picture of a person. She loves to laugh and to play with people.

Note: See also the box *Milestones this 15ᵗʰ Week.*

What's Happening this 15ᵗʰ Week?

✣ Sitting Pretty
By this time, your baby may be sitting very well when she's propped up. To help her practice, sit cross-legged on the floor. Place her in your lap facing outward. Your stomach and legs provide support for her back. She'll enjoy being close to you while she increases strength in the muscles she'll use to sit up on her own.

MILESTONES THIS 15ᵀᴴ WEEK

Changes You May See this Week as Baby Develops Physically
❋ can turn head in all directions

Changes You May See this Week in Baby's Developing Senses and Reflexes
❋ splashes and plays in bath

Changes You May See this Week as Baby's Mind Develops
❋ has memory span of up to 7 seconds

Changes You May See this Week in Baby's Social Development
❋ interested in mirror image; may smile at it
❋ adjusts responses to different people

Every baby is an individual, and your baby may do some of these things more quickly or more slowly than another baby. If you are concerned about your baby's progress, discuss it with your healthcare provider. Also see page xiii.

✐ Eyes Changing Color

By this time, your baby's eyes may have changed color, if they are going to. Blue eyes may start to darken. If they're still blue by age 6 months, they'll remain that color. Babies of color are usually born with brown or dark-colored eyes. If eyes are light-brown, they may gradually darken.

✐ Make Her Car-Seat Experience More Interesting

Your baby is still facing the rear when she's riding in her car seat and will be until she turns 1. But it's boring for her. She can't complain about it; however, she'll be happier if you add some interesting things for her to look at and to do while she's in the car.

Dangle a toy at a safe distance in front of her car seat. This encourages her to reach forward and to bring her hands together. An activity bar on the car seat can also engage her. As she gets older, rattles, other toys and books will keep her entertained.

For your peace of mind, a mirror that attaches to the rear window can provide you with a view of her while you're driving. You can check on her quickly without having to stop the car.

✐ Cat Scratch Disease and Cat Scratch Fever

Cat scratch disease is an infection transmitted by the bite or scratch from a cat. An abscess forms at the site, followed by swelling in the lymph nodes within 2 weeks. The lymph nodes may feel hard or soft, and are usually very tender. Fatigue and fever may be other symptoms of the problem. Cat scratch disease is benign and subsides spontaneously.

Cat scratch fever is also believed to be transmitted by cats. A few days after a minor scratch, a pustule develops at the site. Fever, a general feeling of ill health and headache are seen with this problem.

What You Can Do at Home.   The best way to avoid the problem is to keep baby away from cats. If she does get scratched, clean the area thoroughly with soap and water. Apply a topical antibiotic to the scratch to deal with any infection. You can give acetaminophen for fever and discomfort, if baby's doctor says it's OK.

When to Call the Doctor.   Call the doctor if your baby develops a high fever or experiences severe pain or extreme irritability. If lymph nodes get larger or if there is redness of skin above and around the lymph nodes, contact your pediatrician.

YOUR PREEMIE'S DEVELOPMENT

Your premature baby should be able to do many things now. Remember always to use baby's "due-date age" as your point of reference for the following accomplishments.

By this week, she should be able to bring her hands together near her face and chest—this helps prepare her for reaching and exploring with her hands. To help her accomplish this task, try the following:

* place baby with her arms forward when she's in her infant seat or when you hold her
* play "Pat-a-cake", see *Week 13*
* use a toy to help baby learn to bring her hands together in front of her
* lay baby on her side with her hands together

Baby should also be able to grasp toys and other objects—this is a more purposeful grasp than her reflexive grasp, which is now disappearing. To help her accomplish this task, try the following:

* give her things to hold, such as rattles, toys, small stuffed animals, teethers
* if she has trouble letting go of an object, you can help her by gently stroking the back of her hand

Learning to roll from her tummy to her back is another important accomplishment for baby. Help her in her efforts by placing her on her tummy, then holding a favorite stuffed animal or toy in front of her so she can see it. Move the object toward the side and back; as she stretches to see it, she may start to roll over. If she doesn't completely roll over, give her a gentle push so she is lying on her back.

In severe cases, lymph nodes may be aspirated to relieve the pain. Antibiotics may also be prescribed.

✴ *Kidney Problems*

The general heading *kidney problems* can include many things, such as a kidney infection (pyelonephritis), kidney stones, polycystic kidneys or kidney injury. These are significant medical problems. Fortunately, they are unusual in newborns and young infants. The most common problem you may see is a kidney infection. Symptoms of a kidney infection include:

* blood in urine
* decrease in, or very low, amount of urine
* bruising of the body
* seizures
* irritability
* itching
* nausea
* vomiting
* lethargy or stupor

When to Call the Doctor.   There is nothing you can do at home. If you think your baby has a kidney problem, contact your pediatrician. Abnormalities of the kidneys can be a clue to other problems. Treatment is determined by the underlying cause.

> If you use a spoon out of your silverware drawer to give baby medication, your dose will probably be incorrect. If your "teaspoon" is off by even 1ml (0.0338 fluid ounce), you could be giving her 20% more or less of the medication than she needs! Always use proper measuring devices when giving your baby medicine.

✴ *Pyloric Stenosis*

Pyloric stenosis occurs when baby's pyloric muscle (the muscle that pushes the food from baby's stomach into her small intestine) begins to swell and to grow. The increased size of the muscle results in food being vomited because it cannot pass into the intestine to be digested. This vomit is different from spitup because the entire contents of baby's stomach is emptied in one intense motion.

When to Call the Doctor.   Call your baby's doctor if you believe she has this problem. Your pediatrician will probably want to see baby. Tests are usually done to determine the cause of the problem. Pyloric stenosis is fairly common and occurs more often in boys. The condition is easy to correct with minor surgery. If left uncorrected, a baby can become malnourished and dehydrated. She may even suffer developmental delay.

Toys and Play this 15th Week

As baby gets older, it's tempting to start buying her all sorts of different toys to delight her. But play it safe. Choose toys that are appropriate for her age. Don't buy her a toy if the box describes it "for 12–18 months." She won't get much enjoyment out of it.

Don't give her toys that have small, detachable parts, long strings or sharp edges. Check her toys periodically to make sure they're still safe to play with.

✿ *Here Comes the Bumblebee*

A surprise tickle game is lots of fun for baby. "Here Comes the Bumblebee" is a game babies usually love. Once she's played the game a few times, she'll begin to anticipate the tickle at the end, which is part of the fun.

Lift one hand high above baby. While slowly spiraling your hand downward toward baby, sing:

> *Here comes the bumblebee, the bumblebee, the bumblebee.*
> *Here comes the bumblebee, and he's going to get (baby's name).*

When you sing baby's name, tickle her lightly in the ribs or tummy. As she gets older, this game demonstrates her memory and anticipation of events to come. She'll start giggling and/or wiggling when you start singing because she knows the bumblebee is going to "get her."

Babies love to look at faces, especially other babies' faces. Don't be surprised if your baby stares at another baby then reaches out to push or to poke her.

Week 16

Baby's Age as a Monthly Reference—4 months

HOW BIG IS BABY THIS 16ᵀᴴ WEEK?
Baby weighs 13¼ pounds and is 24¼ inches long this week.

Baby Care and Equipment

✎ Stray Strands of Yarn and Fabric

As you dress or bathe your baby, you may notice his toe or finger is swollen. Did he get an insect sting? Did he pick up a splinter? Many scenarios may run through your mind, but you might overlook the obvious. Check the area very closely. A thread or hair may have wound around the finger or toe, and cut off the circulation. It's as if baby has a tourniquet!

A baby is at greatest risk during his first year because he cannot respond to these kinds of problems. He can't tell you his finger hurts. He has to wait until you notice it. It may be difficult for you to see what's causing the problem. Sometimes the thread or hair is so fine, even a physician may have difficulty spotting the cause.

To help avoid the problem, check your baby's toes, fingers and penis (cases have been reported) for swelling when dressing or changing him. If you notice any swelling, examine the area for a strand of hair or thread wrapped tightly around it. If possible, clip it with small manicure scissors to release the pressure.

If you can't clip the hair or thread, see your pediatrician. Always contact your doctor if you notice *any* unusual swelling anywhere on your baby's body.

✎ Prevent Choking

Your baby continues to put objects in his mouth and will for a long time. He's exploring and learning about his environment when he does. Unfortunately, a baby doesn't have any idea about what's safe to put in his mouth. It's up to you to be vigilant about these objects.

When you find him putting things in his mouth that aren't safe, such as a button, a small toy or one of your earrings, substitute a safe toy. You should know how to perform CPR and the Heimlich maneuver, in case of an emergency. See *Emergency Situations,* page 513, for further information.

✤ *Front and Back Baby-Carrier Safety Tips*

A carrier you wear on your front or back is still a convenient way to carry baby around with you. It keeps him safe and happy while freeing your hands for various tasks. It gives baby a different view of the world and may increase his learning experience. However, there are some safety tips to keep in mind before you place baby in an infant carrier.

* Read the directions, and follow them as to weight limits.
* Position baby in the carrier correctly to avoid falls and other hazards. Always use belts and straps to keep him secure.
* *Never* bend over while carrying baby; he could fall out.
* Don't use a front carrier while drinking a hot beverage or working over the stove.
* Don't use any type of carrier while riding a bike.
* Never leave baby alone in a carrier, even if it has a stand; it could tip over.
* If you have a secondhand carrier, contact the Consumer Product Safety Commission for recalls. See the *Resources* section, page 527.

✤ *What Is Baby Eating?*

Your baby's nutrition still comes from formula or breast milk. He's taking in from 25 to 40 ounces a day. He may be ready to start on solids very soon. See the discussion in *Week 17.*

If you believe your baby is ready to begin solids, discuss it with your pediatrician *before* you do anything! He or she will help you determine whether your baby is ready to take this important step. Your baby's doctor will also recommend the type of cereal to offer (probably iron-fortified), when to offer it and how to introduce it to baby.

> Make your baby's 4-month well-baby checkup now.
> See page 36 for any immunizations
> he may receive at this next visit.

✤ *Back Sleeping and Baby's Development*

As we discussed in *Week 8,* back sleeping is the safest position for baby to decrease the risk of SIDS. Placing him in this position reduces the risks of SIDS by 50%. However, research has shown that back sleeping may delay slightly some developmental milestones. Studies show babies who slept on their backs rolled over, sat up, crawled and pulled themselves to a standing position 2 to 4 weeks later than babies who slept on their tummies.

Is this anything to be concerned about? Most doctors say "No" because the delay was not significant. Keep putting baby down to sleep on his back. It's worth it.

Milestones this 16th Week

☀ *Eye–Hand Coordination*

Baby's eye–hand coordination is improving. When he sees an object, he moves his hand toward it. His fingers open to its approximate size. Both of his hands grasp at the object to manipulate it, and he often grasps with either hand. Whatever he finally gets his hands on eventually ends up in his mouth.

His desire to grasp is stronger, and he is now able to manipulate an object more easily. He likes to explore his body with his hands. He is also more deliberate in reaching for an object. He'll grab at something that captures his attention, such as a woman's necklace or a man's mustache.

☀ *Baby's Emotions*

Your baby enjoys the stimulating interaction he shares with you and other family members. He's beginning to express an array of emotions, including joy, unhappiness, contentment, displeasure. His crying diminishes as he uses his newfound emotions to express his feelings. When he's tired, he lets you know by yawning, rubbing his eyes or face, refusing to play or becoming restless and cranky.

☀ *Ways Baby Interacts*

Your baby's temperament and interest determine how much he will focus on an activity. His personality is developing and is determined in part by his daily routine. You are learning how active he is, how he responds to various activities, how patient or impatient he is and what his frustration levels are.

If your baby is left alone for long periods, the lack of stimulation may cause him to become drowsy or fussy. He may be responsive to interaction for as long as an hour at a time. He will often let you know he wants to play by vocalizing to you.

His smiles now indicate true recognition. When he smiles at you it's because he knows you. While he'll smile at different faces, he still prefers yours.

☀ *When He "Talks" to You*

You may be surprised to hear him putting together a series of syllables when he "talks" to you. These are the basic sounds of language development. Your continuing conversations with him help him in this development. So keep talking together!

ᴥ *He's Getting Stronger*

His strength is also increasing. When he lies on his stomach, baby can support his head and chest with one arm. He may be rolling over easily from his tummy to his back.

ᴥ *His Focus Increases*

Your baby focuses at different distances, but he prefers to look at things that are close to him, within 3 feet. In a few weeks, he'll be able to focus on near or distant objects as well as you do. His eye movement is less jerky.

Note: See also the box *Milestones this 16ᵗʰ Week.*

What's Happening this 16ᵗʰ Week?

ᴥ *His Bedtime Routine*

Your baby is definitely growing up. He's becoming more of an individual and is able to be a little more independent. Now may be a good time to start thinking about easing him away from some dependencies, such as rocking him to sleep every night. In this way, you encourage more independence in his sleep habits.

Instead of waiting until your baby is falling asleep in your arms, put him to bed when he's still awake. A bedtime routine helps him understand it's time to go to bed. See the discussion in *Week 7.* The routine helps him understand he goes to bed to go to sleep. If you haven't established a bedtime routine, it's time to begin. Both you and your baby will benefit from it.

View a bedtime routine as a parent–child interaction that is special to you. This lets baby know his bedtime is different from other times during the day, such as playtime, feeding time and naptime. It also becomes a reliable occurrence. It signals to him that the day is over.

Each family develops different rituals for bedtime—a bath, stories, rocking, prayers, soft lullabies. Try different things, and use what works best for you all. Using the routine every time you put baby to bed, even when you're away from home, offers him security that this day is over and a new one begins tomorrow.

ᴥ *Common Misconceptions about Babies*

Parents may have preconceived notions about babies—often they are wrong! A recent survey of over 800 parents revealed many had misconceptions about a baby's emotional development. Below are some of the more common misconceptions cited and what the truth really is.

Misconception #1—The greater number of care givers a child has before age 3, the better he will be able to cope with change.

MILESTONES THIS 16TH WEEK

Changes You May See this Week as Baby Develops Physically
* may roll over from back to stomach or stomach to back
* sits, with assistance and support

Changes You May See this Week in Baby's Developing Senses and Reflexes
* pulls dangling object toward himself and brings it to his mouth
* stares at the place from where object dropped
* displays interest in smells

Changes You May See this Week as Baby's Mind Develops
* initiates several tonal sounds

Changes You May See this Week in Baby's Social Development
* can play alone for longer periods
* vocalizes to initiate socializing
* laughs when tickled

Every baby is an individual, and your baby may do some of these things more quickly or more slowly than another baby. If you are concerned about your baby's progress, discuss it with your healthcare provider. Also see page xiii.

Fact—Too many changes can actually cause him to be reluctant to form new relationships.

Misconception #2—Young children do not get depressed.

Fact—Studies have shown that babies can show signs of depression as early as 6 months of age. When these symptoms appear, every effort is made to work with the entire family to treat the problem.

Misconception #3—The more stimulation the baby receives, the more he'll learn.

Fact—We know that too much stimulation can irritate a baby and actually interfere with his learning.

As you are getting to know your baby better, you may be aware of what is true with your little one. Trust your instincts!

✹ Read and Sing to Your Baby

Reading to your baby enhances his language skills as it promotes emotional development. When you read to your baby, you make him feel loved. He'll also feel special because you're holding him on your lap, interacting only with him. Later, he'll associate those wonderful feelings with reading!

When you read to your baby, read slowly. Change your voice for different characters. Pause often to watch his reactions. You may discover he loves rhythm—most babies do. The nursery rhymes of Mother Goose are fun to share. You'll probably enjoy them as much as he does!

Baby will also enjoy hearing songs and music. Sing to him, even if you can't carry a tune. Play fun songs, written especially for young children. There are many cassettes and CDs available on the market and at your local library. Lullabies are good choices for soothing baby. Play classical music, jazz and pop tunes. Expose him to everything you have in your musical library!

It's never to early to start reading to your baby. Check out www.rif.org for some ideas to use with your little one.

⚘ *Bowed Legs*

Your baby may have legs that bend outward in the lower part of the limb. It can occur from infancy through 2 years of age.

Symptoms of the condition include bowing of the legs when the baby stands. The space between the knees is greater than 2 inches. After they begin to walk, toddlers are usually bowlegged until their lower-back and leg muscles are well developed.

Don't be concerned about bowed legs at this early age. You don't really need to worry about the problem unless baby has bowed legs beyond 2 to 3 years of age.

Your pediatrician will monitor baby until he begins walking. If he has persistent bowing after age 2, if bowing is increasing instead of decreasing or if there is bowing of only one leg, you may be referred to an orthopedic specialist for further evaluation. Applying a brace may be appropriate. In rare cases, surgery is performed to correct the problem.

> Your baby's knees and elbows may "crack" often. As his muscles become stronger, this will disappear.

⚘ *Wandering Eye or Lazy Eye*

When a baby has a wandering eye or a lazy eye, also called *strabismus,* he can't focus both of his eyes on one object at the same time. It is common in the first 3 months of life because his eye muscles are not yet fully developed. By the age of 3 to 4 months, baby is usually able to fix both eyes on an object. The most common symptom is baby's eyes look crossed or appear to be wandering.

What You Can Do at Home.   Play vision games with baby to help develop his eye muscles. Help him track a moving object. Using a bright, colorful object, move it slowly from side to side and up and down. Also read the *Toys and Play* sections of each week. In many, we include vision games.

When to Call the Doctor.   If you notice your baby has any difficulty tracking objects after 3 or 4 months of age, bring it to the attention of your pediatrician. He or she will assess the situation and suggest a course of treatment. Treatment ranges from glasses, an eye patch, eye exercises and medication to surgery, in extreme cases.

✲ *Ichthyosis*

Ichthyosis is a skin disease. With this condition, skin is dry and scaly, and looks like fish skin. Some forms of ichthyosis are inherited; others are not. Ichthyosis may be present at birth, or it may not appear until later. Symptoms include:

* scales of varying thickness on the skin
* scales may be yellow or dark in color
* skin thickens on palms of hands and soles of feet

What You Can Do at Home.   If your baby has ichthyosis, you will probably be advised to apply lotion or ointment to soften and to soothe his skin. Use soaps sparingly. Baths may have to be limited.

When to Call the Doctor.   Call your pediatrician if symptoms worsen or do not get better after home treatment. If medication is necessary, your physician will prescribe it.

> When baby cries, to help determine *why* he's crying, ask yourself the following questions.
> * Is he thirsty?
> * Is he hungry?
> * Does he need to be changed?
> * Is he too hot?
> * Is he too cold?
> * Is he wrapped in his blanket and his circulation is cut off?
> * Is he sick? What's his temperature?

Toys and Play this 16ᵗʰ Week

It's a good time to think about replacing some of baby's toys in the next few weeks. If your baby has a mobile or other toys fastened to his crib, they should be removed when he's 5 months old or when he can push up on his hands and knees. Because he puts everything in his mouth, and will for quite a while, these toys can be dangerous if he gets hold of them. They are often made with string, cord or wire, and may have small parts.

When selecting toys for baby, choose those that serve more than one purpose. It may be less expensive to buy these toys in the long run, and they may keep baby entertained for a much longer time. For example, some toys can be used as a rattle and other things, such as a stackable toy. When making selections, look for toys that have versatility.

Your baby will enjoy looking at interesting things every day. To help him develop his coordination, place him on the floor on his tummy. Place an array of brightly colored toys in front of him, near his hands. He'll reach out to touch each one as he enjoys looking at them.

✎ *Soapy Bubbles*
Because your baby's eyesight is so good now, you might entertain him with soap bubbles. Buy some soap bubbles or make your own mixture. Blow bubbles away from baby. The soap from a bubble can sting his eyes. He'll enjoy watching the bubbles drift slowly around the room. The exercise also helps him practice tracking a moving object.

✎ *Roll Baby Over!*
Help baby develop his upper-body strength. Lay him on the floor, and gently roll him from side to side or from his stomach to his back. Using a large beach ball, hold baby with both of your hands as you rock him on his tummy on the ball.

To help baby perfect the task of rolling over on his own, you can play another game. Lay him on his back on the floor. Place a bright toy to one side of him. If he turns toward it, give him a gentle push to help him go all the way over. He'll enjoy the game, and it will help him develop the coordination to roll over on his own.

✎ *Yarn Strips*
To encourage finger dexterity, let baby play with some strips of yarn. Braid together several strands so each strand isn't too thin. While you're interacting with him, let him have the yarn pieces. Watch him closely, and *never* leave him alone with the yarn pieces.

Week 17

Baby's Age as a Monthly Reference—4 months

HOW BIG IS BABY THIS 17TH WEEK?

Baby weighs 13½ pounds and is 24½ inches long this week.

Baby Care and Equipment

⚜ *Is Baby Ready for Solid Food?*

You may be wondering if your baby is ready to start eating solid food. Every baby is different. Some babies may be ready to start eating solids before other babies of the same age. Discuss it with your pediatrician before you make *any* changes in your baby's diet.

When you begin feeding her solids, it may be one of the most exciting, and sometimes frustrating, times during your baby's first year. Together you will move from baby cereal to vegetables and fruit to finger foods. You'll begin by feeding her, and by the end of her first year, she'll be trying (and often succeeding!) to feed herself.

Eating solid foods—anything beyond breast milk or formula—is an important step forward for your baby. She must be ready for the task. You don't want to start too early, and you don't want to wait too long. Together with your pediatrician, you will decide when to begin and how.

Check the Checklist.   Beginning solid foods is a big step in a baby's life. Below is a checklist to help determine if your baby is ready for this important step. Most, if not all, of the following should apply to baby:
- ✓ controls her neck
- ✓ sits up with support
- ✓ has doubled her birth weight
- ✓ shows when she is full (turns her head or refuses to open her mouth)
- ✓ shows interest in food when you eat
- ✓ mimics you when you eat, such as opening her mouth when you open yours to take a bite
- ✓ indicates her wants by reaching or leaning toward something
- ✓ seems hungry for more food

Before she can begin eating solid foods, your baby needs to be able to control her head and neck muscles. She also needs to be able to move her tongue back and forth. These two skills help her avoid choking. Most babies do not achieve these skills until they are between 4 and 6 months old. Before this age, your baby's *tongue-thrust reflex* is still very strong. This reflex helps baby draw a nipple into her mouth but pushes out solid food. The reflex begins to diminish around 4 months, when baby will be better able to take food from a spoon and swallow it.

What to Feed Baby.   Most pediatricians recommend you start baby on rice or oat cereal made especially for babies. Dry cereals in a box have more iron than jarred baby cereal. You can mix the dry cereal with breast milk or formula. Make cereal very thin, then thicken it as baby gets used to it.

If you breastfeed baby, another food you can begin with is mashed bananas. They are sweet, like breast milk, and are less likely to cause food allergies. If you bottlefeed baby, she is used to blander tasting formula, so mix formula with dry cereal.

Keep giving your baby breast milk or formula. At this time, cereal is only a small portion of her diet—2 or 3 *teaspoons* to begin with. Discuss with your pediatrician the amount of formula or breast milk and the amount of solids to feed baby.

When she is eating well, and you begin to add more variety to her diet, do *not* reduce the amount of fat she consumes. Some parents believe that reducing fat will keep baby from gaining too much weight. However, studies show that fat and protein are crucial for tissue growth and brain development in the first 2 years of life. Your baby *needs* fat in her diet.

How to Begin Feeding Solids to Baby.   You may be wondering how to start the process of feeding baby her first solid food. You might want to use your finger as her first spoon. Wash your hands well, then dip your finger into prepared cereal. When she opens her mouth to eat, place a few drops on her lips. Let her suck on your finger. Next, place some cereal on the tip of baby's tongue. When she swallows this bit of cereal, place some in the middle of her tongue. If she makes faces, it's only her reaction to this new experience.

For now, you'll use a baby spoon, but baby may also want to use her hands.

Watch her closely to see how your baby responds to eating solids. She may open her mouth wide for more. If the food comes back out, it doesn't mean she doesn't like it. She may need to learn to keep her mouth closed to keep the food inside.

If baby rejects the food, her tongue-thrust reflex is still strong. Let her practice. If she still has trouble, you may need to wait 1 or 2 weeks before trying again.

As baby becomes more adept at eating cereal, gradually increase the amount she takes in. About ¼ cup should be sufficient for a meal. Feed her solids once a day. Within a month or so, they'll become a regular part of her meals.

> Baby will soon be eating solids. To prevent accidents and choking problems, *never* leave her alone while she is eating.

Once you begin, offer her only *one new item* at a time. In your first efforts, feed her one food for a while. It gives her the chance to become familiar with eating solid food. It also lets her become familiar with many different tastes. If she has an allergic reaction to any of the foods she eats, it's easier to identify the problem food.

The Logistics of Feeding Baby Solid Food   When you feed your baby solids, she must be in a sitting position. Place her in your lap or her infant seat. As she gets older and sits more confidently, you can place her in a high chair. Use a baby spoon or some other small spoon. Her mouth isn't very large, so she won't eat comfortably from a larger spoon. There are products available now that even tell you if baby's food is too hot. One spoon turns a different color to indicate the temperature of the food.

> Solid food will *not* make baby sleep through the night, so don't make the decision to feed her solids because you want her to sleep longer. If you begin feeding her solids before she's ready, you can actually cause her more problems. A baby's digestive system isn't ready for solid food when she's very young. In fact, she'll be about 9 months old before she develops certain digestive enzymes, which help her get the most nutritive value from the foods she eats. At this point, solid food is offered for two reasons—to help her become familiar with the taste and texture of these new foods and to help her learn to move food around in her mouth with her tongue.

Be Patient.   Your baby will take her own time to settle into an eating routine. She may eat a couple of tablespoons one day, then not eat well for the next day or two. She may like a food one day, then not eat the same food the next.

Remain calm and reassuring as you begin this new adventure. Never try to force her to eat something she doesn't like. Wait for a while, then try again. She may like a food the next time.

Be careful of your own reactions. If you don't like a particular food, baby may sense it and refuse to eat it.

Will Baby Stop Formula or Breast Milk?   As your baby begins solids, she'll be exposed to a variety of new tastes. As she settles into eating solids as a part of her daily diet, she may want to nurse less or drink less formula. However, during the first year, breast milk and formula should be the main source of her nutrition.

Encourage her to keep nursing or taking formula. These are the most complete sources of the nutrition, vitamins, minerals and other important substances your baby needs this first year.

A Word of Caution.   You may have heard from someone, such as your mother or mother-in-law, that putting cereal in a baby's bottle is a good way to start solids. Don't do it! When your baby begins solids, it's a new learning experience for her. She needs to develop the techniques for eating solid foods, so don't undermine your efforts by putting her food in her bottle.

Milestones this 17th Week

✵ *How Baby Develops*
Babies usually develop "from head to toe." As she grows, your baby is gaining strength and muscle control from her head down to her toes. She can control her head quite well. When she's on her tummy, she can hold her head at a 90-degree angle. She turns her head in all directions.

A big accomplishment is her developing ability to raise her head when she's lying on her back. She can look at her toes. She is also able to move her head far back to see what is above her.

✵ *Sitting Pretty*
Your baby enjoys sitting up. Her back still needs some support, such as pillows or an infant seat, but she can easily be propped in a sitting position. She can sit for longer periods. Her neck is stronger now, and she holds her head erect. She is getting strong enough to lift her head and almost pull herself up to a sitting position when you hold her hands without pulling her.

In the next few weeks, her strength will increase to the point she'll be able to sit in your lap with very little help from you. She once molded her body to yours when you cuddled. Now she sits a little straighter and farther away from you. She's becoming more independent.

✒ Exercise Her Legs

When you lift her to a standing position, baby's legs straighten as her feet press against the hard surface. She likes to stand briefly. This exercise is good for her.

✒ Baby's Socialization

Baby is socializing more each day. She likes to listen to speech and music. Her brain can respond to every sound produced in every language of the world. She makes many noises, entertaining herself and others. She may cough at will (there's nothing wrong with her) and loves to mimic the expressions and movements of others. When you tickle her, she laughs out loud. This response is a sign of social development.

✒ The Beginning of Speech

Baby repeats sounds many times. These sounds will become words in the months to come. When she "talks," her speech may have the inflections and intonations of actual speech. You may hear some of her speech ending in a high note, as if she were asking a question.

✒ Her Behavior

Your baby is beginning to react to your tone of voice and to your expressions. She can sense when her behavior is unacceptable. She may demand attention by fussing and may cry when her play is disrupted.

Note: See also the box *Milestones this 17th Week.*

What's Happening this 17th Week?

✒ Teething May Begin Soon

Some babies begin to teethe around this time. If your baby pulls at her jaw or ear, drools or acts fussy for no reason, teething may begin soon. Because symptoms are often the same, it may be difficult to decide whether she has an earache or is teething. If in doubt, rub her gums. If she's teething, she'll probably yell because gums will be tender and sore. Also see the discussion of *Teething* in *Week 27.*

✒ Should You Discipline Baby?

Parents often ask at what point in baby's life should they begin to discipline her. A lot depends on your child, but as a rule of thumb, it's too early to start discipline.

Repetition is still very important in baby's life. You may want to teach her something, but to her, her actions are a game. For example, if she drops food from her high chair, you may want her to stop so you don't have to

MILESTONES THIS 17ᵀᴴ WEEK

Changes You May See this Week as Baby Develops Physically
* may make swimming motions, resulting in moving around in her crib

Changes You May See this Week in Baby's Developing Senses and Reflexes
* may be ready to start solid food
* can distinguish between smells
* may hold object between index and second fingers

Changes You May See this Week as Baby's Mind Develops
* has responsive periods of 1 hour or more
* is interested in making new sounds

Changes You May See this Week in Baby's Social Development
* laughs when playing
* may cry if playing is disrupted
* may interrupt feedings with play

Every baby is an individual, and your baby may do some of these things more quickly or more slowly than another baby. If you are concerned about your baby's progress, discuss it with your healthcare provider. Also see page xiii.

keep cleaning it up. To baby, it's a game, and she enjoys it very much. It'll be quite awhile before she'll begin to understand what she is doing.

ᴬ *Baby's Developing Motor Skills*

Baby is probably warming up for the crawling she will be doing in the coming months. When she's lying on her tummy, she lifts her head, arches her back and kicks her legs. She may also make swimming motions with her arms. Her kicking and bouncing strengthen her leg muscles. Her arm motions also help develop arm and shoulder muscles.

She'll probably begin with a little creeping. This moves in quick succession to crawling, pulling up, cruising, then walking. However, don't be concerned if she skips one step entirely or seems stuck on another. She's making progress at her own pace—she'll be moving soon enough.

ᴬ *When Baby's Activities Affect Her Sleep Habits*

This is a time of great change and accomplishment for your baby. She's beginning to move more, and her activities can affect her sleeping. She may be moving around her crib, getting herself into situations that she can't get out of, such as jamming her head against the rails. When she begins standing, she may find herself up, with no way to get down. She'll need your help when this happens, especially during the night.

When she begins crawling and walking, her muscles might be sore from her exertions. You may discover she can't sleep because of the soreness or because she's excited about her accomplishments. On the other hand, she may sleep more soundly because she's so exhausted.

The key is to be tuned in to what's happening in baby's life that could affect her in ways you might never imagine. Be patient and offer her the help she needs, if she needs it.

◦* *Celiac Disease*

Celiac disease is an allergic condition that is triggered by gluten, a protein found in many grains and cereals. The disease affects the small intestine, so it cannot absorb some nutrients. The body is unable to break down the gluten protein found in some grains, including wheat, barley and rye. About 1 in 100 people suffer from the problem; it is 30 times more common than once believed.

The problem can occur any time from infancy through early childhood. It usually occurs when a baby begins eating cereal and bread. Symptoms of celiac disease include:

* weight loss or slow weight gain after adding cereal to her diet
* poor appetite
* diarrhea
* foul-smelling stools
* frequent gas
* swollen abdomen
* abdominal pain
* mouth ulcers
* baby's skin is pale in color
* tendency to bleed easily

It was once believed that babies outgrow celiac disease. We now know this is not true. Some symptoms may subside, such as cramping, gas and diarrhea, but if celiac disease is left untreated, it can be harmful to your child. In addition, your child's growth may suffer and neurological problems may arise.

What You Can Do at Home.   If you suspect your baby may have celiac disease, carefully monitor her diet. Document any changes you see as you introduce or withhold foods. One study showed the risk of celiac disease was reduced by nearly 40% if a baby continued breastfeeding while beginning solid foods that contained gluten, such as bread and cereal.

When to Call the Doctor. If your baby has many of the above symptoms, and there is a family history of the problem (most forms are inherited), call your pediatrician. If symptoms don't decrease within 3 weeks of changing baby's diet, your pediatrician will probably want to see her. It's also serious if your baby doesn't regain lost weight or if she fails to grow and to develop as expected. Call if a fever develops.

Your doctor will assess the situation and offer a course of treatment. He or she may prescribe oral cortisone drugs to reduce baby's inflammatory response during a severe attack.

✢ Shaken Baby Syndrome

When a baby suffers from shaken baby syndrome, it can cause serious physical and mental harm. The statistics are alarming—over 40% of babies who are shaken are under age 1; 25% of that total number die. Nearly 50% of all adults do not know shaking a baby can cause brain damage or death! People who would never think of hitting or hurting a baby might give her a "good shake" to quiet her or to discipline her. They do not realize how dangerous it is.

The problem usually occurs when a baby cries persistently. Out of frustration, the parent or care giver shakes baby in an attempt to make her stop crying. Most occurrences of shaken baby syndrome last less than 20 seconds. In that time, a baby may be shaken 40 to 50 times, which can seriously harm or even kill a child!

Shaken baby syndrome is particularly serious in young babies because their neurological systems are still developing. Although there may be few outward signs, symptoms a baby has been violently shaken include:

* unexplained lethargy
* decreased muscle tone
* decreased appetite
* vomiting
* poor sucking or swallowing
* difficulty breathing
* extreme irritability
* inability to lift head (after being able to do this)
* inability to focus eyes or to track movement
* pupils of unequal size
* seizures
* blindness
* problems with speech
* bruising
* change in behavior after being cared for by someone else
* any signs of abuse

The best advice we can give you about shaken baby syndrome is *never* shake a child or baby for *any* reason. Make sure anyone who cares for your baby knows that one shake can seriously harm or kill a child.

What You Can Do at Home.   Prepare for times when baby can't be comforted with a strategy to deal with your own frustration. All babies cry, some more than others. If you don't think you can deal with a situation, ask for help from family members or friends. Don't let your emotions take control of you.

Caution: It's OK to play with baby, just don't play too roughly. Be careful when you toss her into the air, swing her or spin her around. Even bouncing may be done with too much vigor.

When to Call the Doctor.   If you believe your baby has been shaken, contact your pediatrician immediately. He or she can treat specific problems.

SAFETY PRECAUTIONS FOR YOUR BABY

* Never leave baby alone in the car or the house.
* Be near baby when she's eating.
* Always stay with your baby when she is in the bathtub.
* Keep crib side rails up when baby's in bed.
* Pick up baby by grasping her chest; don't pull her up by the arms.
* Attend baby when she's on the changing table, bed or sofa.
* Never use a plastic bag as a cover.
* Keep a watchful eye for small objects she could choke on.

Toys and Play this 17ᵗʰ Week

Your baby delights in discovering her actions can make something happen. She enjoys shaking toys that make a sound. Offer her toys that reinforce the cause-and-effect relationship. Because she can sit up well when propped up, she may be interested in toys that are more easily played with in a sitting position. When she's in her infant seat or high chair, attach an activity bar within close proximity. She'll enjoy playing with the different toys attached to it.

Reading Helps Development
Continue to read to her. Sharing picture books with her develops intimacy between you. The words you read help her development of language skills.

Because she sees color quite well now, she'll enjoy a book with brightly colored, simple illustrations or pictures. She also sees small objects more easily, so a book with lots of things to look at is fun to share with her.

⋆ *Give Her a Gentle Push*

Help your baby feel what it's like to crawl. When you see her making pushing or swimming motions on her tummy, press your hands firmly against the soles of her feet. She may inch forward as she pushes. If she doesn't move, wait and try again later.

Week 18

Baby's Age as a Monthly Reference—5 months

HOW BIG IS BABY THIS 18TH WEEK?

Baby weighs 14 pounds and is 24¾ inches long this week.

Baby Care and Equipment

♪ *What Changes Do You Need to Make as Baby Begins Solids?*

Once your baby begins eating solids on a regular basis, he may be less interested in breast milk or formula. However, breast milk or formula continue to be his primary source of protein and calories for his first year. Even when he is 1 year old, about half of baby's caloric needs are provided by breast milk or formula.

Before baby begins eating solids, he drinks between 35 and 40 ounces each day. Over the next few months, his interest in food increases and his interest in nursing or bottlefeeding decreases. However, he should still be drinking a little over 20 ounces of breast milk or formula at age 1.

♪ *The Scoop on Baby Cereals*

You'll have a lot of products to choose from when you buy baby cereal. You'll have to examine many cereals before you make your decision. Below are some points to keep in mind as you begin feeding cereal to baby.

* Begin with rice cereal. This type of cereal causes the fewest food-allergy problems.
* Buy only iron-fortified cereal. Baby needs iron in his diet.
* In the beginning, buy single-ingredient cereal, such as rice, barley or oatmeal. As baby gets used to eating different foods, and has no reactions to them, you can add foods to his cereal or choose cereals that include other foods.
* Begin with a thin mixture—mix 1 teaspoon of cereal with 4 teaspoons of breast milk or formula.
* Don't make more than a small amount because it can go to waste.
* If your baby has any problems eating the cereal, call your pediatrician before offering it to him again.

* After baby learns how to move food to the back of his throat and swallow it, you can make the cereal thicker.
* Offer baby cereal once a day, either at breakfast or dinner.
* As he becomes more adept at eating, offer him two "meals" a day, one at breakfast and one at dinner.
* If baby refuses to eat the cereal, don't push it. Wait a few days before trying again.
* Feed your baby only one new food a week. In the beginning, this will be one cereal each week. As he gets older, you can add different types of baby food, such as fruits and vegetables. Discuss it with your pediatrician.

> If baby refuses to eat the cereal you offer him, don't despair. Try again in a few days.

✳ Precautions to Take to Protect Baby from the Sun

The best advice your pediatrician will give you about exposing baby to the sun is "Don't, when possible." Keep baby out of the sun whenever you can. The worst times of exposure for a baby are between 11:00am and 3:00pm in spring and summer months. At other times of the year, avoid the sun between 10:00am and 2:00pm. If you live in a very hot climate, such as the Southwest, just about any time of the day during the summer can be hazardous.

Keep baby well covered and preferably out of the direct sun.

Keep your baby under an umbrella or completely dressed to avoid sun exposure. Don't use sunscreen or sunblock on baby until he's at least 6 months old.

Using Sunblocks and Sunscreens When He's Older. When you use sunscreen or sunblock, always choose an SPF (sun-protection factor) of at least 15. There are many products on the market available for babies with much higher SPFs. Apply the lotion to every part of his exposed skin; be careful not to get it in his eyes. If you put it on his fingers, he'll probably put them in his mouth, so avoid his hands when possible. Reapply every 2 hours, and always reapply if he's been in the water.

Some sunscreens have stronger ingredients than others. You may find your baby gets a rash with one product. Try another. A product made especially for babies may not contain some of the more irritating ingredients.

Sunscreen and sunblock should be used year-round. Sun damage can occur at any time of the year. And it's cumulative, which means it builds up as time passes. Avoiding sun damage now may decrease your child's risk of developing skin cancer later in life.

✒ *Don't Forget to Buckle Up Your Baby*

All 50 states have laws requiring infants and young children be restrained in car seats or safety-restraint systems when riding in a vehicle. However, many parents don't take this precaution. According to a recent study, more than half of all the children killed in car accidents were not in safety restraints. If you don't use a car seat, you cannot protect your baby.

In addition, infant car seats *must* be installed properly to reduce the risk of injury in an accident. One study showed that 85% of parents who use car seats installed them incorrectly!

Make periodic checks of your baby's car seat to ensure installation is correct. It's easy to make a mistake when you move a car seat from one vehicle to another. But it's a mistake you want to avoid. Also keep in mind the following tips.

* If baby is under 20 pounds and/or less than 1 year old, use a rear-facing car seat. Some researchers now believe that a baby should be in the rear-facing position until at least 18 months of age.
* Harness straps should be secure. You should be able to place only one finger between the car-seat straps and your baby.
* Keep the car seat in the middle of the back seat—it's the safest position.
* Don't place a car seat in a front seat; if that is an impossibility, be sure the front-seat position doesn't have an air bag or the air bag has been disabled.
* Don't use a car seat if it has been in an accident; it might have structural damage that is not easily detected.
* Carefully check a car seat if it has been used before. Often there are recalls on older seats. In addition, used car seats may have broken or missing parts.

Milestones this 18th Week

✒ *Anticipating Results*

Your baby is learning to anticipate results. You can see this when he reaches for his bottle or shakes his rattle to make noise. He looks for an object when it drops. He knows where his hands are when they disappear, but he can't find a hidden object yet, even when he watches you hide it.

✴ *Baby Play*

Baby can play alone with toys for up to 15 minutes. Think about rotating his toys every so often. Put some away when you take others out. He doesn't need an overwhelming number of toys—a few at a time are the most enjoyable for him. If you put some away for a while, it'll be like having new toys when you bring them back out!

✴ *Baby's Eyesight Improves*

Your baby's eyesight is sharp. He now sees things at various distances and follows moving objects easily. His depth perception is improving. He may look where you look. He likes the colors blue, green and orange. He will watch your face closely and may imitate your expressions. If he can't imitate them exactly, he's making an effort to do so!

✴ *Baby Vocalizes*

He continues to practice talking, while listening to everything around him. He may make sounds to draw your attention to him if you're talking or interacting with someone else.

✴ *Eating Solid Food*

> The ability to taste salt develops around this age.

Feeding baby solid food may be a challenge at times. He may want to play between bites. Maybe he'll let the food ooze back out of his mouth. He may even blow the food out of his mouth. These actions are baby's way of exploring his environment. Food is new to him. He's trying many different things to learn about it.

✴ *He's Rolling Over and Sitting Up*

Your baby is probably rolling over from front to back fairly easily by now. He starts by pushing himself onto his side with his arms, then drawing up his top leg. Its weight helps pull him over the rest of the way onto his back. The more-difficult back-to-front roll occurs a few weeks later.

Now that baby is sitting up more comfortably, it's fun to take him out in the stroller. Being out and about exposes him to things he doesn't usually see in his restricted world view.

Note: See also the box *Milestones this 18ᵗʰ Week*.

> Because baby can roll over now and reach for objects, you need to be extra vigilant. Pick up *every* small object off the floor that you can see. If you don't, baby may get it and put it in his mouth.

Milestones this 18ᵀᴴ Week

Changes You May See this Week as Baby Develops Physically
* balances head steadily in different positions
* brings feet to mouth; may suck on toes

Changes You May See this Week in Baby's Developing Senses and Reflexes
* grasp is steadier
* plays with rattle, if placed in his hands

Changes You May See this Week as Baby's Mind Develops
* can squeal, grunt and make a "raspberry" sound

Changes You May See this Week in Baby's Social Development
* smiles and vocalizes to gain attention and to make social contact

Every baby is an individual, and your baby may do some of these things more quickly or more slowly than another baby. If you are concerned about your baby's progress, discuss it with your healthcare provider. Also see page xiii.

What's Happening this 18ᵗʰ Week?

✴ Can Baby Learn a Foreign Language?

Many parents want their child to grow up speaking more than one language. If this is a desire of yours, it's never too early to begin. Studies show there is a developmental window between birth and age 10, when the ability to learn another language is greatest. In fact, it doesn't matter how many different languages you expose your child to; the ability does not decrease.

A baby's brain can learn a foreign language as easily as he can learn his native language. If a baby's parents each speak a different language, he will be able to learn both languages if they are spoken to him. If grandparents have a different native tongue and speak to baby in that language, he will be multilingual. It's a matter of exposure.

Some parents who do not speak other languages want their baby to speak more than English. There are products available to help accomplish this task. Some are audiocassette packages that the parent uses with the child. Other products offer videos along with audiocassettes; some even use an interactive CD-ROM. If you are interested, check the media stores near you to find out what types of products they carry.

Be aware that if your family is bilingual or multilingual, it may take baby longer to begin speaking. Researchers believe this occurs because it takes more time for a baby to sort out the vocabulary and grammar of different languages. However, these babies do catch up!

✒ *Building Self-Esteem*

We all know how helpless a baby is when he is born. He depends on others for everything. By responding to his needs and caring for him, he learns he can count on you for your help. He learns to trust you.

When your baby trusts you, it is a crucial point in his development. Trust in others is one of the main building blocks of self-esteem. If a child cannot trust his environment, he will be hesitant to try things in the future. So by meeting your baby's needs, you are contributing to his well-being now and in the future.

✒ *Convulsions*

A convulsion occurs when a baby has an episode that includes strong involuntary muscle contractions and relaxations. It is sometimes called a *seizure*. Nearly 10% of all children have at least one, usually between the ages of 6 months and 6 years. Boys are more susceptible than girls to these types of seizures. Most of these convulsions are febrile seizures.

Febrile Seizures or Convulsions.   Most convulsions are triggered by a high fever (101F or higher) and last less than half a minute. When triggered by a rapid rise in body temperature, it is called a *febrile convulsion.* This is the most common type of convulsion babies experience. Convulsions can also be caused by a number of other things, including meningitis, epilepsy, tetanus, blood poisoning and other types of poisoning.

An infection accompanied by a fever often precedes a febrile convulsion. Occasionally, a febrile convulsion may be the first sign of fever. Symptoms that a baby has had a convulsion include:

- baby's body stiffens
- his body twitches
- he rolls his eyes
- he is irritable after convulsion stops

What You Can Do at Home.   During a convulsion, lay the baby on the floor or in an area that is safe. Move any dangerous objects away from him. If baby has had a febrile convulsion in the past, take immediate measures to reduce a fever when he develops one.

When to Call the Doctor.   Call your doctor immediately if your baby has a seizure. He or she can treat the underlying cause. Despite its frightening appearance, a convulsion caused by fever in a baby is rarely serious. Convulsions caused by infection or disease can be dealt with individually.

Is It Epilepsy?   A febrile seizure is *not* a sign of epilepsy! Symptoms of epilepsy include loss of consciousness, body jerking and twitching that can last as long as 3 minutes. These symptoms occur without the presence of a fever. Discuss the situation with your pediatrician if you are concerned.

✼ *Hair Loss*

It's very common for a baby to lose his hair in the first few weeks or first few months of life. This is *not* an indication of any medical problem. It's a natural part of his development. When his hair falls out, it will be replaced by hair that is more permanent. However, it might take some time before his new hair grows in.

Infant hair usually grows very slowly. When it does appear, it may be very different from the hair your baby had when he was born. It can differ in texture, color and thickness.

Hair loss in certain spots on your infant's head may indicate he is lying in the same position too much. This type of hair loss is due to friction. Hair will grow back once he begins to move around.

Toys and Play this 18ᵗʰ Week

Toys for baby at this time include the noise-making toys he's been playing with. If you want to add some toys to his toy box, choose brightly colored balls he can roll and watch. Toys with handles or loops that are easy to grasp are fun. Be sure loops are small enough so he can't get tangled in them. He'll even enjoy playing with your plastic measuring cups and measuring spoons.

✼ *Mirror, Mirror on the Crib*

If baby doesn't already have a mirror to look at himself, now's the time to get one. Choose a mirror made of unbreakable material for babies. It should be about 6 inches across and not distorted, so baby can clearly see himself in it.

Attach the mirror to the outside of his crib where he can look through the bars at it. Or put it near his changing table so he can look into it when you change him. You may find he spends quite a long time (for him) studying the other baby. If you have a full-length mirror in the hall or a bedroom, let him gaze into that. He'll delight in seeing you in the mirror *and* holding him or sitting next to him!

✼ *Telling Him Stories and Reading Them, Too*

Stories continue to be important. You can read them to him or make them up as you go along. If you tell him a story, it can be as simple as describing what you plan to do. For example, "First we'll take a bath, then we'll eat lunch" or "We're going to take our nap, then go to the store" can be considered stories for your baby.

If you read him a story from a book, point out pictures and describe them to him. If you have a book on trucks, point out the trucks and identify each one for him. He may not understand what you're saying, but you're helping him understand that trucks are a category.

✋ *So TALL*

To increase his strength and help him practice his balance, play this game. Place baby on his back. Gently grasp his forearms, and slowly pull him into a sitting position. He'll help you by using his muscles to help pull himself up. Then gently pull him into a standing position so he can practice balancing on his feet.

When you do this exercise, make it a game. Recite in a singsong voice what you're doing. "We're helping baby to sit up, sit up, sit up." When you pull him to a standing position, recite in a singsong voice, "We're helping baby to stand up, stand up, stand up." When he's standing, sing "Baby's standing, he's standing, he's standing *SO TALL!*"

> Keep playing tickle games with baby—he loves them! They stimulate his senses and help him learn to anticipate your words and corresponding actions.

Week 19

Baby's Age as a Monthly Reference—5 months

HOW BIG IS BABY THIS 19ᵀᴴ WEEK?

Baby weighs 14¼ pounds and is 25 inches long this week.

Baby Care and Equipment

✴ *Should You Wait to Introduce Solids?*

There are advantages to starting baby on solid food between 4 and 6 months, so don't postpone it beyond 6 months of age. During this time, a baby learns to develop a taste for the *texture* of food. Once your baby reaches 9 months, she might have difficulty accepting solids if she hasn't already experienced them. Some children gag and have trouble swallowing if they are not offered food until they are older. When this happens, it may be hard to overcome the problem.

Offering baby solid food between 4 and 6 months exposes her to the tastes and textures of a variety of foods. She needs experience eating different foods to become proficient at it. It may take her awhile to get the knack, but she soon will.

Your baby will enjoy the new foods once she's used to them. She'll also be more satisfied because solids fill her up more than formula or breast milk.

> Wait to introduce a new food if baby has a cold or isn't feeling well. Her appetite may be affected, and she may not want to eat much of any food.

✴ *Feeding Tips for Baby*

Embarking on this new experience with baby can be fun *and* frustrating. It's exciting to see her growing up and beginning to eat food. Soon she may be part of the family during mealtimes. It can also be frustrating to feed her because this new activity can take some time to master. Keep your cool when you feed her, and keep in mind the following suggestions.

* ✴ When she can sit up well, put her in a high chair to feed her. It's more convenient for you and more fun for her.

236

* When you warm her food, don't make it too hot. Always stir her food well and taste it before you feed it to her. Her mouth is sensitive, and she could easily burn her tongue if food is too hot.
* Don't add anything to baby's food, such as salt, sugar, pepper or any other flavoring. Avoid honey at all costs! See the discussion in *Week 29*.
* Use a small spoon to feed her. She has a small mouth, so a regular-sized spoon is too big and could cause problems, such as too much food or difficulty getting the spoon in and out of her mouth.
* Don't put food in her bottle. She needs to learn to eat it, not drink it!
* Keep trying. It can take some time for baby to learn all she needs to know to eat solids. She may reject food one day, then eat hungrily the next. It'll be awhile before she settles into eating solid foods.

⁂ *Baby-Care Mistakes*

Being a parent may be one of the hardest jobs you'll ever do; you're bound to make some mistakes. We all do. You can take steps now to help prevent "baby-care mistakes." Try the following.

* Don't dress baby too warmly. Many people believe a baby has to be bundled up to protect her. Resist the temptation, and you'll avoid a situation in which baby becomes overheated.
* Don't give baby your keys as a chew toy. Some contain lead, and research has shown that even low levels of lead can contribute to problems with intellectual development.
* Don't deny comfort to your baby when she's under 6 months old. During these first months, you can't hold her too much. In fact, you're building a stronger bond with her when you do pick her up and comfort her. You're teaching her that you'll be there when she needs you.
* Don't freak out when baby's stools change a little; it's normal. *Do* be concerned and call your doctor if baby has any blood in her stools or if a change in stools is accompanied by other symptoms, such as fever, extreme fussiness, lethargy or refusal to feed.
* Don't ignore instructions for giving baby medications. Follow your doctor's advice to the letter, including the amount to give, when to give it and how long to give it. Use the correct measuring device, and follow directions on how to store it, such as keeping it refrigerated.
* Don't wait too long to childproof your home. Be sure to look everywhere baby might explore for small objects you might not see. Look behind and under furniture. And keep your eyes peeled for objects that aren't there now but could appear later, such as dropped food particles or other items.

✴ Using Superabsorbent Diapers

As baby gets older, a good type of diaper to have on hand is the superabsorbent type. They keep baby's bottom drier because of special liners. Some also contain aloe to protect her skin. Their stretchy sides and gathered leg openings help stop leaking when baby's on the move, crawling or walking.

Considered "premium diapers," they cost a little more, but these diapers may be well worth the extra cost. You don't need to use them at every diaper change, but they can make baby more comfortable during the night. It's no fun to wake up in soaked pajamas and a sodden diaper. Use of these diapers may keep baby drier and happier.

Milestones this 19th Week

✴ When Baby Is Active

Baby is a lot more active now. She reaches out and grabs things on her own. You need to be careful of her attempts to grab your hair, jewelry, glasses or scarf—it's a game to her. She's also practicing her leg and arm motions, getting ready to creep and crawl.

Because she is so active, it may be time to put her infant carrier away. A bouncer or play chair may be a good choice. You might want to use the infant seat for feedings, if she can't sit well in a high chair, but never leave her alone in it!

✴ She May Need to Suck More

You may be surprised if your baby displays the need to suck more. This may occur as baby sucks less on the breast or bottle because she is now eating solid food. She may also be frustrated by her attempts at locomotion and be trying to soothe herself. She may need a pacifier to satisfy her desire to suck. You may find she sucks on her hands *and* her feet!

She'll put anything into her mouth that she can grab.

✴ Exploring with Her Mouth

She still puts everything she grasps into her mouth to learn more about it. She explores its texture and shape thoroughly with her lips and tongue. She'll put anything into her mouth that she can grab on to, such as daddy's tie or mommy's necklace. You need to keep a close eye on her when she puts things in her mouth.

✴ Quiet Periods

Your baby may have quiet periods during the day. She may spend an hour or more by herself playing. She may play longer with you. She still enjoys looking at your face and may focus on your eyes, if you return her gaze. In addition to your face, she'll now study your body and your clothes!

If she wants to skip a nap, encourage her to rest in her crib. Even if she doesn't fall asleep, the quiet time is good for her.

> Don't attach rattles, pacifiers or other toys to baby's crib or stroller with string, ribbon or elastic bands. Baby could get tangled up in them.

✿ Putting Sounds Together

Putting together consonants and vowels happens more often now. She may even double some consonants, such as "da" into "da-da." Your positive response reinforces her behavior, and she may repeat "da-da" more often. She has no idea what it means at this point, but she will soon make the connection.

✿ Label Things for Baby

When you interact with baby, label various objects. When you read to her, point to the baby's eyes, nose and mouth in the book. Then point out her eyes, nose and mouth. Label the actions in the books. Tell her the baby in the book is jumping, running or swimming.

✿ When She Discovers Her Genitals

You may notice baby has discovered her genitals. Don't be alarmed—she's exploring this part of her body just like she explores her hands and feet. Because the area is usually covered, she may be more interested in exploring it when she's undressed or in the bathtub. This type of exploration is normal. Don't act as if it is unacceptable. When baby touches her genitals, use the correct names for her body parts.

Note: See also the box *Milestones this 19ᵗʰ Week.*

What's Happening this 19ᵗʰ Week?

✿ How Much Is Baby Sleeping Now?

By this time, your baby needs only two naps a day. She's sleeping longer during the night—up to 12 hours! She probably naps in midmorning and again soon after lunch.

Her naps should last no longer than a couple of hours. She should be up at least 4 hours between waking from her afternoon nap and going down to sleep at bedtime. If she sleeps a lot in the afternoon, she may have trouble falling asleep at night.

MILESTONES THIS 19TH WEEK

Changes You May See this Week as Baby Develops Physically
* lifts both arms and feet while lying on stomach

Changes You May See this Week in Baby's Developing Senses and Reflexes
* raises hand near object
* will grasp onto an object
* brings object to mouth

Changes You May See this Week as Baby's Mind Develops
* utters vowel sounds and a few consonants

Changes You May See this Week in Baby's Social Development
* likes to play at mealtime

Every baby is an individual, and your baby may do some of these things more quickly or more slowly than another baby. If you are concerned about your baby's progress, discuss it with your healthcare provider. Also see page xiii.

At times, she'll want to sleep more. She may be going through a growth spurt. The extra sleep helps her catch up with the changes her body is going through.

✴ *Is Baby Still Waking Up at Night?*

Some parents find baby is still waking up at night, sometimes three or four times during her longest sleep period. Studies have shown that *all* babies wake up at night! However, many babies do not fuss or cry when they waken. They soothe themselves and fall back asleep.

Babies who cry out during the night, awakening their parents, are the ones parents are usually most concerned about. They are often described as "problem sleepers." Experts believe these babies don't have a problem *sleeping;* they have a problem *soothing themselves back to sleep.*

Parents of these babies are advised to give baby a chance to fall asleep on her own. If you continue to take her out of bed and feed her or comfort her, you encourage baby to keep waking up. She expects to be taken care of in the middle of the night.

As difficult as it may be for you, if baby wakes up regularly at night, give her a chance to go back to sleep on her own. Wait 5 minutes before you go in to her. Gradually lengthen the time each night until she learns to soothe herself. However, if baby has been sleeping through the night regularly (at least not waking you up) and wakens during the night and fusses, tend to her. She may be having some problem and needs you to take care of it.

> By this age, baby is crying an average of about
> 2¹/2 hours a day. Crying may increase a little for a
> while, then drop quite a bit in the months to come.

✶ *Impetigo*

Impetigo is an inflammatory bacterial infection that affects the skin, most often around the mouth and nose. It is very contagious; children are especially susceptible to it. Symptoms of the problem include:

* ✶ a red rash, with lots of small blisters
* ✶ some blisters contain pus
* ✶ yellow crusts form when pus-filled blisters break
* ✶ blisters aren't painful but may be itchy
* ✶ a low-grade fever

What You Can Do at Home.   There are some measures you can take at home, but do call the doctor if you believe baby has impetigo. Treatment is often necessary.

* ✶ Keep baby's fingernails short.
* ✶ If there is an outbreak in your family, have everyone wash with antibacterial soap.
* ✶ Use separate towels for each family member.
* ✶ Wash bed and bath linens in hot water daily.

When to Call the Doctor.   If you think your baby might have impetigo, call your doctor. Impetigo is highly contagious, so your pediatrician will probably prescribe treatment. Call the doctor if baby has a fever or the sores spread or don't begin to heal in 3 days, even with treatment. Treatments your doctor may prescribe include the following.

* ✶ Gently scrub lesions with disposable gauze and antibacterial soap. Break pustules, remove crusts and clean lesions. If crusts are hard to remove, soak them in warm, soapy water then scrub gently.
* ✶ Cover cleaned sores with gauze and tape.
* ✶ Your doctor may prescribe oral antibiotics or an antibiotic ointment.

✶ *Coughing*

Coughing can occur at any time, and it may sound frightening to you. However, there's usually little reason to be overly concerned. Coughing actually is beneficial–it helps the body get rid of germs and keeps airways clear.

There are different kinds of coughs. Baby may have a dry, hacking cough or a wet one that produces mucus. Or she may bark like a seal. Each type of cough may indicate a different cause, and each is treated differently.

A *wet cough* often accompanies a cold or viral infection. It is treated with an expectorant. A *dry cough* can accompany a cold but may also indicate asthma or allergies. A *barking cough* is often a sign of croup; using a humidifier can help relieve it. Each of these ailments is discussed in a separate week.

What You Can Do at Home.   There are some other things you can do to help relieve baby's cough. *Caution:* Don't give baby any cough-suppressing medication without your doctor's advice. Increase the amount of fluids you offer her to help thin secretions. Decrease her activity level because being active can cause her to cough more.

If baby's cough is more than just an occasional one, use a cool-mist humidifier to help relieve the dryness often associated with coughing. Put the humidifier in her room when she's sleeping; direct mist so it doesn't hit her directly or dampen her bedding. Keep the humidifier out of her reach. Also see the discussion of *Humidifiers* in *Week 13*.

If you don't have a humidifier, take the baby with you into the bathroom. Close the door, and turn on the hot water in the shower. Let it run. Expose baby to the steam for at least 10 minutes.

Some coughs, such as that with croup, respond better to cold air for about 10 minutes. In winter, some pediatricians recommend bundling baby up and taking her for a short walk outside when she has a croup-related cough. If she's warm enough, a jaunt even at night is OK if it's not too cold outside.

When to Call the Doctor.   It's important to call her pediatrician if your baby experiences any of the following:
* difficulty breathing
* shortness of breath
* fever
* irritability
* a marked decrease in appetite
* difficulty eating
* wheezing
* coughing persists

If coughing is caused by a viral infection, you can only treat the symptoms. If it's caused by a bacterial infection, an antibiotic may be prescribed. If a cough is severe or persistent, X-rays may be taken to rule out pneumonia. In very severe cases, a baby may need to be hospitalized for oxygen therapy and fluids by I.V. to treat dehydration.

Toys and Play this 19ᵗʰ Week

⚘ *Tickle Me!*

Tickle games are lots of fun. One tickle game you can play with your baby involves identifying different parts of her body. Begin by touching parts of her body, according to the rhyme. Trace circles on her tummy at the end.

> *Where are baby's fingers?*
> *Where are baby's toes?*
> *Where, oh where, oh where?*
> *Is the baby's nose?*

You can change the parts of her body that you identify in the song–point out her ears, chin, forehead, hands, feet, tummy. The words don't have to rhyme. Name anything that comes to mind. Repeat a few times, if baby is enjoying this tickle game.

⚘ *Imitate Her Sounds*

To help encourage your baby's vocalization, imitate the sounds she makes when she babbles. Hold her facing you in your lap. Let her babble. Wait until she pauses, then repeat one groups of syllables, such as "da-da-da." She'll probably listen closely. She may try to repeat the sound, or she may babble something else. Smile and hug her when she tries to repeat your sounds. Keep playing the game with her, even when she doesn't repeat sounds. You are helping her learn through imitation, which is one way she'll master her language.

Infant clues that indicate baby is "ready for interaction" include the following:
* she smiles
* she listens closely to sounds and sights
* her eyes are wide open
* her arms and legs are relaxed
* she's making cooing sounds
* her mouth moves as if she's talking

Week 20

Baby's Age as a Monthly Reference—5 months

HOW BIG IS BABY THIS 20ᵀᴴ WEEK?

Baby weighs 14¾ pounds and is 25¼ inches long this week.

Baby Care and Equipment

✦ *Feeding Your Baby*

Your baby is making progress in learning to eat solids. By this time, he is probably eating two meals each day of cereal made with breast milk or formula. He may be taking in as much as 2 tablespoons at each feeding. He is still drinking lots of breast milk or formula—it's his main source of nutrition. It's normal for him to drink four to six servings a day, of 6 to 8 ounces at each serving.

Packing Your Diaper Bag.   Now that solids are a part of his daily diet, you may need to make some adjustments and/or additions in what to pack when you go out. Below are some ideas we've gathered for you.

*   Carry premeasured amounts of dry cereal in a zipping plastic bag. Or buy dry cereal in premeasured packets.
*   Before you leave the house, put a premeasured amount of dry cereal in a plastic bowl with a lid. When you want to feed baby, just add breast milk or formula.
*   To make it even simpler, if you bottlefeed, add dry formula (in the correct amount) to the dry cereal. You only need to add water when you want to mix it up.
*   Keep an extra baby spoon and bib in your diaper bag.
*   Always pack more dry cereal in your bag than you believe you might need. Baby may be hungrier than you thought he would be, or you might get stuck someplace with a hungry baby. This way, you'll be prepared!

Mealtime for Baby.   Some parents are concerned about when baby should be fed. Does he need one large meal and one small meal? Should meals be of equal size? Is one time of day better to feed him than another?

It doesn't make any difference, nutritionally. However, you might want to offer new foods in the morning. If he has any problem with the food, tummy upset should wear off before he goes to bed that night. Your baby is probably the hungriest in the morning and in a good mood, so offering him a new food then might also work best for you.

If you breastfeed baby, offer food nearer to the end of the day. At this time, your milk supply is probably at its lowest, and baby may be more keen to eat. Offer him solids *between* breastfeedings. Solids may interfere with the absorption of some nutrients in breast milk.

If you bottlefeed, it may be a good idea to give him his larger feeding of cereal in the middle of the day to help him get through the day. You don't have to feed him at dinnertime if you feed him in the morning and at lunch. At night, he can join you in his high chair. Give him a cracker to play with (he probably won't eat it) while the family eats.

When he begins eating a more varied diet, you may decide to feed him his main meal at night. Offer him solids when he seems the hungriest. In this early exposure to solids, allow lots of time to feed baby. He'll want to play with his food, smear it, drop it and examine it closely. It's all part of the learning process!

✌ *Assessing Baby's Temperament*

What kind of temperament does your baby have? It may take a few days of close observation, but cluing in to the following categories can help you assess your baby's disposition. Evaluate each of these nine categories to help put together the puzzle of who your baby is. Your baby will range from high to low in each one; when you've finished your assessment, you may have a clearer picture of this little person you are living with.

What Is His Initial Reaction in Situations? How does your baby respond to something new and unusual, such as new faces, different food, atypical situations? Does he smile and seem to accept what's going on, or does he turn away and get fussy? His initial reaction to a situation can give you some clues as to his overall personality.

Is Baby Predictable in His Actions? Does your baby react similarly to everyday activities? Are his bodily functions fairly predictable? With some babies, you can be fairly certain he or she will wake up, nap, go to bed, eat and go to the bathroom at just about the same time every day. With other babies, there is no schedule or even a hint of one.

What Kind of Mood Does He Generally Display? Some babies always seem to be fussy or very serious. Other babies smile all the time. Most babies fall somewhere in between these two extremes.

Is He Active?   This assessment involves determining how active your baby is during the day *and* night. Baby may be very active, kicking and waving vigorously. He may also be very vocal. Or he may be quiet and make smaller movements.

How Intense Are His Emotions and Responses?   Some babies put a lot of energy into responding to the world around them. Crying may be one way to gauge emotional responses. Does baby cry heartily or seem more to fuss?

Is He Adaptable?   How baby adjusts to new situations or changes in routine help clue you in to how adaptable he is. Some babies are flexible; others are rigid. Most babies fall somewhere between these two extremes.

> Don't push baby too hard in your efforts to help him learn. Your love and nurturing are the secrets to aiding in his development, not toys, gadgets or programs.

How Long Is His Attention Span?   Does baby pay attention to something for a long while or a short while? Does he get easily frustrated? Being attentive to a task—playing, concentrating or having fun—can give you an idea about his personality.

Can You Distract Him Easily?   Some babies are very good at tuning out interruptions; they can focus on something quite easily. Other babies seem to be drawn away quite easily from the task at hand. Another way to measure this quality is to determine how easily a baby can be soothed. If he is soothed easily, you can probably distract him without too great an effort.

Is He Sensitive?   Some babies seem to be extremely sensitive—they are aroused quite quickly. With other babies, it seems to involve a major effort to get them to respond. There are many stimuli that can excite a baby. Some babies are set off by the slightest change. With other babies, even something major fails to arouse them.

✴ Do You Have a High-Maintenance Baby?

Now that you've grown to know your baby so well, you may realize he's more difficult than your sister's baby or a friend's baby. A high-maintenance baby displays some, if not all, of the following characteristics.

* He's easily startled and acts jumpy or cries when he hears various sounds.

* He's extremely sensitive and is uncomfortable with bright lights, lots of activity, some clothes.
* He protests about everything, from bathing to sleeping.
* He is restless and refuses to take a nap.
* He may be upset by new people, places or experiences.
* He may rarely smile, instead crying, whimpering, wailing or screaming.

Within a few weeks of birth, most babies show some sign of their temperament. It can be frustrating to parents when they realize baby is not going to be "easy."

Most of baby's traits are set in place at birth. High-maintenance babies have many of their characteristics *before* birth. Don't feel guilty if your baby is fussy or difficult. There's nothing wrong with you or your baby—it's just the way he is.

You can't change your baby's temperament, but you can clue in to what may upset him. Try to avoid those situations. Respond to his needs in any way you can. This will take experimentation and work on your part, but it'll pay off in the end. Keep in mind the following situations.

Look for Patterns in His Mood Swings. This may help you discover what sets off his fussiness. If he's hungry when he gets up from his nap, feed him then. Establish a routine; it may help him if he knows what to expect and when to expect it.

Reduce Stimulation. By stimulation, we mean lights, noise, color, activity. Reduce the amount of stimulation baby is exposed to. Set up a routine that helps calm him before bedtime, such as a bath then rocking or cuddling. If he's sensitive to the clothing he wears, dress him in natural fabrics. Keep him comfortably layered.

Be Consistent. It's important for you to be consistent in your dealings and interactions with baby. Respond to him in the same way, as often as possible, when he fusses. Set up a routine baby can depend on. Keep your cool; don't get overwhelmed and frustrated. Baby may sense your feelings, which could agitate him more.

Ask for Help When You Need It. Get a sitter when you need to get out, or ask family members to keep baby. Encourage your partner to take care of baby to bond with him and to provide you with some free time for yourself.

Stay Focused on the Positive. As baby gets older and becomes more mobile, you may see a change in him. Take comfort in the fact that you have done your best for him.

✳ *Babyproofing Your House*

It's time to start making your home safer. Baby may be crawling soon, so you'll need to make some changes to protect him. Below is a list of safety precautions to take in the weeks to come, before baby becomes more mobile.

* Buy and install electrical outlet covers. Little hands love to poke things into open sockets.
* Put appliance cords up so they can't be pulled down by an exploring baby.
* Push heavy appliances to the back of your kitchen counters.
* Store knives, glasses and other kitchen hazards, such as toothpicks and twist ties, where your child can't get them.
* Keep matches and lighters out of reach.
* Put your tablecloths away. A baby can easily pull a tablecloth, and everything on the table, down onto himself.
* Keep refrigerator magnets high and out of baby's reach. He could choke on them if he grabs one or if one falls off.
* If you have radiators for heating, place guards around them so baby can't touch them.
* Store collections of small items, such as coins, shells and rocks, in a safe place.
* Move furniture away from any window baby could fall out of.
* Clear bedside tables and end tables of small items baby could choke on, especially medications.
* Keep sewing supplies out of reach.
* Store office supplies in a cabinet out of baby's reach.
* Keep jewelry, hairpins and other small objects in a safe place.
* Put corner guards on tables.
* Unplug appliances in the bathroom, such as hair dryers and electric toothbrushes, and put them away after using them.
* Buy a toilet lock for every toilet.
* Be sure safety razors and razor blades are safely put away, especially when you dispose of them.
* Check floors and baseboards for loose nails and splinters.
* Be sure curtain and blind cords are out of baby's reach.
* Plan where you'll put gates and other barriers, such as at stairs and doorways without doors. Be sure to have them on hand when baby starts to move!

Check out areas that baby uses *from the floor*—that may provide you a view of hazards you can't see when you're standing up. A baby's curiosity can lead him to explore things you didn't even know were there! Also see the box on the opposite page about poison prevention.

POISON PROTECTION

Baby will soon be mobile, so it's time to take precautions at home to protect him. The following suggestions help you make your home *poison-safe* for baby.

* Store household products, such as cleaners, bleach and other toxic substances that could harm baby, in a locked cabinet.
* Install latches on cabinet doors and drawers.
* Lock up all alcoholic beverages.
* Check out your garage. Store products you keep there, such as antifreeze, gasoline, kerosene, turpentine, weed killer, plant food, charcoal lighter fluid, batteries and insecticides in locked containers. Always keep them in their original containers.
* Keep toiletries, perfumes, aftershave and cosmetics out of reach.
* Lock medicines and vitamins in a cabinet. Dispose of all that you no longer need or that are out of date.
* Use child-resistant caps for medicines, and keep them in the locked position.
* Use door-handle safety covers to keep some rooms off limits.
* Pick up and dispose of any cigarette or cigar butts that smokers might leave in your yard.
* Choose plants carefully—some are highly toxic if a baby eats them.
* Keep telephone numbers of the poison control center or local hospital near the phone.

In the past, we used to advise parents to keep syrup of ipecac available for accidental poisonings. Researchers now believe it is ineffective for this purpose. If you have some on hand, throw it away!

Sunblock versus Sunburn

In the discussion of sun protection for baby in *Week 18*, we advised you not to apply sunblock to a baby's skin until he is at least 6 months old. If you read most product labels, they contain the advisory, "Consult a physician before using on a child under 6 months of age." However, if the alternative to using a sunscreen or sunblock is baby getting a sunburn, most pediatricians would recommend you use the sun-protection product!

If you find yourself in a unique situation in which baby could be sunburned, then it's better to protect him rather than let him get sunburned. Doctors prefer you keep your baby completely out of the sun as long as you possibly can. But *occasional* use of sunscreen or sunblock is OK before he reaches 6 months. Even after that age, it's best not to expose him to the sun when possible.

Milestones this 20th Week

✴ *How Much Does He Weigh?*

In the next few weeks, baby will probably have doubled his birth weight. He'll start slowing down in his weight gain, and during the second 6 months of his first year may only gain at half the rate he did during the first 6 months. He may go through some growth spurts and gain weight at irregular intervals.

✴ *Baby's Hearing Affects His Life*

When you read baby stories, you expose your baby to more than just your interaction together. Reading exposes him to speech sounds and patterns of intonation. Listening to words helps him put together the sounds he babbles into actual speech. He is developing a type of rhythmic dialogue that he will soon use in his "conversations."

He also likes to listen to other sounds. He can pick out each of several different voices of people talking around him. If he hears his name, he may turn his head toward the speaker. He can distinguish between tones of voice, such as displeasure, approval or acceptance. Don't be surprised if he frowns or cries when he hears an angry voice.

Baby likes music; he may swing his body when he hears a tune. He may also hum to himself. He loves it when you sing and clap.

Hearing is a very important part of baby's life. Even if his hearing was tested at birth, if you are concerned he might have a hearing problem, have it checked again now. If testing reveals a moderate hearing loss, steps can be taken to deal with it.

✴ *Using His Hands*

Baby continues to use his hands. He "reaches" with his eyes first; his eyes direct his hands. He can grab an object fairly easily. He reaches for a toy with one hand, and his hands adjust to an object's shape.

His grasp is stronger. He likes the feeling of different textures, so touch-and-feel books are very exciting to him.

He may transfer objects from hand to hand or grasp one object with both hands. He wants to touch everything near him. He still likes to put things in his mouth and may chew on them.

✴ *His Personality*

Baby begins to demonstrate other emotions and is starting to reveal his personality around this time. Your baby may be quiet and contemplative, or active and babbling. He may be physical and concentrate his energies on

---

MILESTONES THIS 20TH WEEK

Changes You May See this Week as Baby Develops Physically
* may move by rocking, twisting or rolling

Changes You May See this Week in Baby's Developing Senses and Reflexes
* aims well when reaching
* may be able to hold bottle with both hands

Changes You May See this Week as Baby's Mind Develops
* wants to touch, hold, turn, shake and mouth objects
* deliberately imitates sounds and movements

Changes You May See this Week in Baby's Social Development
* imitates facial expressions
* waves arms to be picked up

Every baby is an individual, and your baby may do some of these things more quickly or more slowly than another baby. If you are concerned about your baby's progress, discuss it with your healthcare provider. Also see page xiii.

---

constant movement. Or he may focus on one task, excluding most other stimuli. He may be "easy" or "high-maintenance." See the discussions earlier in this week. Whatever his personality, it is unique to him.

Note: See also the box *Milestones this 20th Week.*

What's Happening this 20th Week?

✳ *Baby's Body Language*

Your baby is beginning to express himself in many different ways. His body language can tell you a lot about what he's feeling at a particular time. When he's *fearful* or *afraid* of something, he may express his fear by raising his eyebrows or furrowing his brow, pursing his lips then opening his eyes wide. He may also draw back from you or tense his body. He may express *anger* or *frustration* by lowering his eyebrows, staring and pressing his lips together.

When baby is *bored,* he may show it with glassy or glazed eyes that don't blink much, and a display of sleepiness or dullness. He may hold his body very still. If he is *repulsed* or *disgusted,* wrinkling his nose, pursing his lips and lowering his eyebrows might indicate his displeasure.

It's easy to see when he's *happy* and *satisfied*. Smiling and laughing out loud are typical indicators of happiness. He may wrinkle the corners of his eyes while he relaxes his eyebrows. When baby becomes *engaged in an activity,* he usually indicates his involvement by opening his mouth and raising his eyebrows. He may also relax his shoulders and open his hands.

Sometimes baby becomes upset when he is *startled* or *surprised* by something. It's not unusual for him to cry when this happens. If he is not unduly startled, you may see him furrow his brow, drop his jaw and raise his eyebrows. He may also form his hands into fists.

As he grows older, there will be more situations when baby is *unhappy* or *sad*. When he feels this way, he may turn down the corner of his lips, tremble his lower lip and open his mouth. He may also raise his eyebrows and make circles in the air with his arms.

✴ How Babies Express Pain

You may have wondered how your baby will let you know when he's in pain. You'll be on the front line—the first to recognize it—so trust your intuition about whether baby is in pain.

Unfortunately, with an infant, there's no single sign or symptom that indicates he's hurting. Instead, different babies express pain in different ways. The following indicate a baby might be in pain:

* crying for long periods
* pulling away if you touch a part of his body
* after a long bout of crying, baby becomes very still and may even cease crying
* changes in sleeping
* changes in eating
* changes in the way he moves or how much he moves
* changes in other normal behavior

If your baby displays any of the above signs, or if you believe your baby is in pain for any reason, contact your pediatrician. He or she will advise you.

✴ Intestinal Blockage

A blockage in the intestines can occur at any age. Intestinal blockage may be a complete blockage or partial blockage. Symptoms of the problem include the following:

* abdominal pain and swelling
* nausea
* vomiting
* weakness
* decrease in, or absence of, bowel sounds

* in partial obstruction, diarrhea
* in complete obstruction, no stools

When to Call the Doctor. There is no treatment you can try at home. When an obstruction occurs, it usually becomes an emergency fairly quickly. Call the doctor if there is a change in baby's bowel pattern, accompanied by abdominal pain and vomiting. Hospitalization is necessary to diagnose the problem by X-ray. Surgery is done to remove the obstruction. Also see the discussion of *Intussusception* in *Week 34.*

✷ *Allergies*
An allergy is defined as an acquired sensitivity to some substance that doesn't usually cause a reaction. When we speak of "allergies" in this weekly discussion, we include hay fever (allergic rhinitis), contact dermatitis, atopic dermatitis or any other types of dermatitis. Some of these have been covered in other weeks, so you may want to check the index for further references. See *Week 31* for a complete discussion of *Food Allergies.*

An allergy can occur at any time in life. Symptoms of an allergy include:
* itching
* rash
* dry skin
* redness of skin
* difficulty breathing
* congestion
* runny nose
* shortness of breath
* watering or tearing of eyes
* sneezing

What You Can Do at Home. If you believe your baby is suffering from an allergy (you've ruled out a cold or other illness), attempt to identify the cause. Is it a soap or lotion? Is it a food, a plant or something in the air?

If you think you know what it is, keep baby away from it. If it's hay fever, consult your pediatrician about treatment for the problem.

When to Call the Doctor. Call your pediatrician if baby has symptoms of an allergy. Any occurrence of difficulty breathing needs immediate attention. Call about a rash that doesn't improve or one that gets worse.

There are skin tests that can be done to identify the cause in some cases. Medications, such as Benadryl or lotions, may be suggested, but don't use them without asking your pediatrician first.

Toys and Play this 20ᵗʰ Week

Just about any safe object you have around the house can be used as a toy. Be sure baby can't damage an object. Most plastic kitchen utensils are fun to wave around and shake. They're pretty indestructible, so baby probably can't hurt them. Plastic measuring cups and plastic spoons on a ring are good for little fingers to manipulate. Even a pan lid and a large spoon can entertain him for a while.

✳ *Encourage Him to Move*

You can begin encouraging baby to practice his crawling skills. Place him on the floor with a few toys he likes just out of reach. Let him choose which toys he wants to play with, then let him try to move to get it. In addition to stimulating him to move, it gives him the opportunity to begin making some decisions about choices. However, be careful not to let him get too frustrated with this activity. Give him the chosen toy within a minute or so if he can't reach it.

✳ *Baby, Do What I Do*

Encourage baby to imitate you to stimulate his visual sense. With baby facing you, open your eyes wide. Stick out your tongue. Wiggle your nose. Puff your cheeks. Baby may try to imitate you. When he does, imitate him back. Games like this can delight baby. He can also play this game with his siblings; they'll all enjoy the interaction.

✳ *Roll Over for the Toy*

If baby hasn't quite mastered rolling over yet, help him get the hang of it with a toy. Lay him on his back, and get his attention with a toy. Move the toy slowly above him in an arc so he turns his head and shoulders to keep it in view. He should also have to arch his back and neck to see the toy.

His effort to keep the toy in sight may help him complete his roll-over. If he's close but not quite there, a gentle push on his bottom may help. This game helps baby develop the muscles he needs to complete the task, even if he doesn't roll over completely on his own.

Week 21

Baby's Age as a Monthly Reference—5 months

HOW BIG IS BABY THIS 21ST WEEK?
Baby weighs 15 pounds and is 25¼ inches long this week.

Baby Care and Equipment

✴ *Baby High Chairs*

Once baby is eating solids, it's time to think about a high chair. It may be one of the most-used baby products you'll buy. You can feed baby in the high chair. She can sit in her high chair while the family eats. You may use it as an activity center when you're busy preparing a meal. When she's in her high chair, you know she's off the floor and out of harm's way.

Many high chairs are adaptable to baby's age and developmental abilities. Some can even be made into a youth chair. Other types attach to the table; they save space, and they're portable and less expensive than a regular high chair. See the discussion in *Week 44.*

Choosing a High Chair to Suit Your Tastes. There is a wide variety of high chairs available on the market, so you should be able to find what you want. Whatever one you choose, it may be used by baby for 2 to 3 years. If you have other children, they may also use it. Choose something sturdy that you can live with for a long time.

You can choose from high chairs made of wood, plastic or metal. Some styles serve only one purpose—holding baby so she can eat. Others have a variety of uses.

A wood high chair may be appealing, but it has some drawbacks. The seat may be too deep and the footrest too low for a small baby. If the tray is wood, it may be harder to clean and keep clean than plastic or metal. A wood chair may not fold up, so storing it and transporting it can be difficult.

If you're looking for a simple high chair to serve baby's feeding needs, a basic metal-framed or plastic-framed model is fairly inexpensive. These are usually lightweight and collapsible, and they're portable.

Full-featured high chairs are often convenient to use and very comfortable for baby. Seats are well padded. Trays are easy to detach, and the entire chair cleans up easily. Some have reclining seatbacks. Some adjust to baby's growth. Many have wheels for ease of moving. Prices can range from $50 for a basic high chair into the hundreds of dollars for a top-of-the-line, full-featured model.

Features to Consider in a High Chair.   Below is a list of features you may want to think about before you buy a high chair.
- A wide base keeps it from tipping over easily.
- The seat should be well padded and covered with sturdy plastic.
- No sharp edges are evident.
- It is easy to clean.
- The tray is easy to attach and to remove—with one hand, if possible.
- The restraint system securely fastens baby across hips and between legs. Straps should be adjustable.
- Wheels lock to keep the chair from rolling while baby's in it.
- Chair adjusts so baby will be able to use it for a long time.
- It folds up compactly so it can be stored between uses or easily transported when eating away from home.

Use a Drop Cloth.   Whether baby is eating a meal or just a snack, a drop cloth under her high chair may be a good investment. Putting a large, heavy-duty piece of plastic under her keeps your floor neat and makes cleanup easier. As baby is learning to eat, she is also experimenting with her food. She's sloppy, and a lot of what she "eats" actually ends up on the floor!

✸ Childproofing When You're Away from Home
Your family may travel a lot, or you may spend extended periods of time with relatives or friends. Even when you're away from home for only a short time, you need to think about childproofing your baby's environment.

In your own home, you are aware of various hazards to baby. At someone else's home, there may be dangers you haven't even thought about. In addition to safety measures to take at home, discussed in *Week 20,* add some of the following suggestions to your list for when you're away. Also see the box on the opposite page for additional suggestions. Below are some precautions to take when you travel with a baby or small child.
- If you borrow or rent a crib, be sure it meets safety standards. Crib slats should be no farther apart than 2⅜ inches, and the crib should have a snug-fitting mattress, no high posts, no decorative cutouts.
- When possible, push crib and other furniture away from windows so baby can't fall out and she can't get tangled in drapery and blind cords.
- Check floors for choking hazards, such as plastic bags, coins or other small objects.

* If the people you are visiting have a pet, ask if you can move the pet's water and food dishes to somewhere baby can't get to them.
* Remove small items from tables that baby could choke on, such as candies or nuts.
* If anyone smokes, empty ashtrays often.
* Take steps to protect baby from hazards she is unfamiliar with, such as a fireplace, wood-burning stove or a pool.
* Take along your safety gate(s) if family and friends have stairs that cannot be easily closed off.
* Close doors to rooms so baby can't get in them.
* Be vigilant about watching your baby. It's up to you to keep her safe!

When you travel, pack these safety devices; they help childproof wherever you stay when you're away from home. Take along plenty of:
* outlet plugs
* corner guards
* portable locks for cabinets and toilets
* a gate to block stairs

❧ *Foods to Avoid with Baby*

Some foods should not be given to a baby under the age of 1 year. Below is a list of various foods to avoid and an explanation of why each could be harmful to your baby. Although baby is not eating anything like this now, it's a good idea to be aware of what *not* to give her this first year.

* Any food that is a choking hazard, including candy, gum, cut-up hot dogs, peanut butter, ice cubes, marshmallows, grapes, popcorn, nuts, potato chips or tortilla chips, raisins and raw carrots.
* Cow's milk because the proteins are too hard for baby to digest.
* Spinach, beets, carrots and turnips prepared at home. Each contains large amounts of nitrates and could cause anemia. Prepared baby food is OK because manufacturers remove harmful substances.

Studies have shown that babies have favorite foods, including:
* bananas
* applesauce
* pears
* sweet potatoes or yams
* carrots

* Egg whites because the protein is too hard to digest. They may also cause allergic reactions. It's OK to feed baby egg yolks.

* Fruit juices, such as pear and apple juice. Between 4 and 6 months of age, fruit juice can make baby gassy, irritable and fussy. Don't offer fruit juice until baby is at least 6 months old. When you do offer juices, always dilute them with as much water as juice, such as ¼ cup of juice diluted with ¼ cup water.

Milestones this 21st Week

✦ *Your Baby's Vision*

Your baby's world is becoming more 3-dimensional now. Both of her eyes are working together, and her depth perception has improved. She may study her hands or feet with fascination; she sees them differently now. Her color perception has also improved. She can distinguish between several shades of one color, but she still prefers primary colors.

To evaluate baby's vision, hold a toy some distance away in front of her. Move it closer. See where she begins to notice it. Watch her hands—are they beginning to grasp for it? Don't move it away. Let her focus on the toy. Her eyes are directing her hands more now. Keep your face out of the way so she doesn't focus on you. Let her practice without interrupting her.

Her eye-hand coordination is also improving. She can reach out and grab objects easily. She can also find her toes, grab them and put them in her mouth. Baby delights in this new trick.

✦ *Baby Can Show Her Emotions*

Baby's emotions are fairly evident—she can show disgust, fear, anger, happiness and boredom. She expresses her emotions with facial expressions and sounds. Her moods may change quickly. She gives you behavioral cues, such as holding her hands up when she wants to be picked up. She squirms, looks at the floor and fusses when she wants to be put down. She stares blankly when she's bored and is cranky when she's tired.

> If baby is playing by herself and seems content, leave her alone. This encourages her independence.

Your baby smiles easily, but she may no longer smile at everyone she sees. She may be more sociable with strangers if she has a chance to watch and to study them first. She needs to size them up before she makes any overtures.

✦ *She Likes to Listen to the Human Voice*

She listens very intently to many sounds, but a person's voice is always the most interesting to her. She can easily pick out your voice from other voices. She likes rhythm, especially verses and songs. Her "passive vocabulary" is increasing, which means she understands the meaning of more words. She may soon look at an object when you name it.

✼ *Food Is not Just for Eating*
Eating may be more enjoyable now for baby because she can manipulate a few food items. She likes to feed herself a cracker or small piece of bread. She wants to taste food, but she also wants to play with it, squeeze it, smell it, crumble it, mash it and smear it. Being messy is part of her learning process.

✼ *She's Moving More Now*
Baby likes to change her body position and to move. When you grasp her arms, she helps pull herself to a sitting position by lifting her head and flexing her elbows. She may be able to lift her arms and her legs when she's on her tummy. Soon she may be able to get one leg up under her when she's lying on her tummy.

If she's very active, she may slowly propel herself across an area by kicking with both legs. Prop her up with pillows so she can sit up and watch the world. Never leave her alone when she's propped up.

Note: See also the box *Milestones this 21ˢᵗ Week.*

What's Happening this 21ˢᵗ Week?

✼ *Solo Time for Baby*
Even at this age, baby may need quiet time by herself. She may want to be alone sometimes. If she seems irritable or fussy, turns her head away, cries or closes her eyes, she may be signaling she wants some quiet time.

If you notice baby acting this way, put her down on the floor on a blanket or in her playpen. Don't put her in her crib—that's for naps and bedtime. She may enjoy playing with a toy or she may be content just to sit and look around her.

Right before a nap may be a good time for baby to be by herself. The time alone can serve as a transitional time between being awake and going to sleep. Sometimes after a nap is also a good time to let baby play quietly by herself. This allows her to nurture her self-play skills. She needs to learn she can entertain herself, so let her practice.

✼ *Is Baby Ready for a Cup?*
About this time, your baby may show an interest in drinking from a cup. Help her hold a cup, and see how she responds. If she seems interested and willing to drink from it, use it as a *supplement* to bottlefeeding or breastfeeding. Don't use it as a replacement.

MILESTONES THIS 21ST WEEK

Changes You May See this Week as Baby Develops Physically
* alert at least half of her waking hours

Changes You May See this Week in Baby's Developing Senses and Reflexes
* can grasp a large ring

Changes You May See this Week as Baby's Mind Develops
* looks around in new situations
* holds one block, looks at second; drops first to take second

Changes You May See this Week in Baby's Social Development
* will protest and resist someone who tries to take toy away

Every baby is an individual, and your baby may do some of these things more quickly or more slowly than another baby. If you are concerned about your baby's progress, discuss it with your healthcare provider. Also see page xiii.

Spillproof cups, made especially for a baby, are available in many stores. They usually have two handles for baby to grip and a cover, with a spout. It's even better if the cup has a weighted bottom. Using one of these cups helps keep baby from spilling liquid all over herself.

When she takes her first sip, she should be sitting in her high chair or infant seat. Show her how you drink from one of her cups. Then help her drink from hers. After she gets the hang of it, let her experiment with it. Put a few sips of water in the cup while she's learning. It's not as messy or as wasteful as using breast milk or formula. A small amount is also easier for her to handle.

It may not take long for baby to become adept at drinking from a cup. She'll master it quickly if she has your help. However, don't get frustrated if it takes her awhile to catch on. For some babies, it's months before they master drinking from a cup. If she doesn't seem interested or ready, wait for a while, then try again. Some babies are not ready to drink from a cup until they're 8 or 9 months old.

This is an important transition for baby. Smile and praise her when she's practicing. You'll be glad she can drink from a cup when she's thirsty and a cup is the only thing available!

✲ *Itching*

Itching is a symptom of a problem, not an illness. You'll notice baby rubbing or scratching her skin. Itching can occur for many different reasons, including reaction to a drug, food, lotion or soap, from a fungal infection or from an insect bite.

What You Can Do at Home.   If your baby appears to have a problem with itching, try to identify the cause. Determine whether she has been exposed to anything that could cause the irritation. Has she eaten or taken anything unusual or not normally part of her diet? Have you started using a new lotion or detergent? Often you can find the source of the problem. Eliminating it stops the itching.

When to Call the Doctor.   Call the doctor if baby's skin is yellow (jaundiced) or if baby has difficulty breathing. Call if the itching doesn't improve in 24 hours or if she has scratched enough to cause the skin to bleed or get infected. Call if she develops a fever.

Treatments for the problem include identification of a cause for the itching and avoidance in the future of possible causes. Don't give your baby any medication to help relieve itching. Don't use lotions or gels unless directed to do so by your doctor.

Ointments containing zinc oxide or Benadryl might be prescribed. It may be necessary to put socks or mittens on baby's hands to keep her from scratching herself.

✴ *Thrush*

Thrush is a yeast infection of the mouth, also called *candida albicans.* It is a common infection and isn't serious, although the initial appearance may be startling. It often looks like curdled milk in baby's mouth or on her lips. Thrush occurs most often in newborns and infants. It may be passed from mother to baby as baby passes through the birth canal, if the delivering mother has a yeast infection. It has been seen as early as a few hours following birth. It may also be passed from baby to mother's nipples during breastfeeding. See the discussion below.

The most common symptom is white patches or "plaques" in baby's mouth. They may be found on gums, tongue, cheeks, lips or the soft palate. Patches appear white or cream-colored and may be raised. They are not usually painful. Baby's mouth may also be dry.

If you have a yeast infection on your breasts, you can pass it to your baby in the form of thrush. Be sure to take care of any infection as soon as possible. Signs of a breast yeast infection include dry, itchy nipples that are also painful.

If you are breastfeeding, you may contract thrush from your baby. Your nipples may suddenly be sore, red, itching, and burning. Deep shooting pain around your nipples after feeding is another warning sign.

What You Can Do at Home.   If you are bottlefeeding, sterilize nipples and bottles by boiling them. Sterilize pacifiers by boiling them for a few minutes. Wash any toys baby chews on—use soap and water or put them in the washing machine or dishwasher, if it is safe to do so. If these various items are not sterilized, baby can become reinfected.

When to Call the Doctor.   Call the baby's doctor if she is feeding poorly, is dehydrated or if she loses weight. If she develops a fever or has signs of a secondary bacterial infection, with redness or bleeding, contact your pediatrician.

Antibiotics can trigger the infection. However, if your baby is taking antibiotics, don't stop giving them to her without consulting your doctor.

Your doctor may prescribe an oral antifungal medication. Keep up baby's fluid intake. If you have the infection on your nipples, you will need to be treated while baby is being treated.

Toys and Play this 21st Week

Bath toys may be some of baby's favorites, and she may love playing in the tub. You don't have to buy expensive toys. Small plastic toys that float are fun to play with in the tub. Let her watch you pour water out of a plastic cup when she's bathing. She may also want to try it.

Because babies like music, you might want to get her a musical toy. She might enjoy a toy that she can start herself by pulling a handle or pushing a button. A floor gym that she can lie under is fun if it has lots of things she can grab, pull or swing at.

She likes the colors red and blue. Find a poster with these two colors dominant in the picture, and put it up in her room for her to look at. Try putting it on the ceiling over her crib. She'll enjoy looking at it when she's having quiet time or when she wakes up.

Taking in the Outdoors
Take her outdoors so she can see outside colors. Sit with her on the porch or in the yard, and tell her what she sees. Let her examine trees with leaves and plants close up. Let her touch them, but don't let her put them in her mouth.

Shake It Up, Baby
Play a game with baby and her rattle. Shake the rattle as you sing,

> *Shake it up, shake it up,*
> *Shake it up, baby.*
> *Do it like, do it like*
> *Do it like this, baby.*

Hand her the rattle and sing the verse again to her. If she doesn't shake the rattle, help her.

You can continue the game by engaging in other activities as you sing to her, such as brushing her hair, washing her face and tying her shoes. Sing about anything baby does!

Week 22

Baby's Age as a Monthly Reference—
end of 5 months or beginning of 6 months

HOW BIG IS BABY THIS 22ND WEEK?

Baby weighs 15¼ pounds and is 25½ inches long this week.

Baby Care and Equipment

✤ *From Breast Milk to Bottlefeeding Formula*

You may decide about this time that you want to wean baby from breast-feeding and start him on formula. It's best to *ease* a breastfed baby into formula when you make the switch. Don't do it all at once, or baby may refuse to cooperate.

Many breastfed babies don't like the taste of formula. To make the change, give him a bottle that contains only ¼ formula. Express your breast milk, then mix one part formula to three parts breast milk. This allows him to become accustomed to the different taste. Every few days, replace a little more of the breast milk with formula.

If he refuses to take the bottle when you change the ratio of formula to breast milk, go back to the ratio you were using before. Offer him this for a few days, then add a little more formula while cutting down on the breast milk. Keep it less than the amount he refused. Some babies can take weeks to accept straight formula.

If your baby has difficulty drinking from a bottle, or if he refuses to drink from one, you may have to take additional measures. As we discussed in *Week 21,* it's not too early for him to begin drinking from a cup. This might be the solution if you can't get him to take his formula mix from a bottle. If you use a cup instead of a bottle, you won't have to wean him off a bottle in the near future.

✤ *Is Baby Enthusiastic about Solids?*

Many babies take to solids and eat solid food with gusto from the time they are first introduced to cereal. Other babies don't like the taste or texture of solid food and refuse to eat it. At this point, solids account for about 100 calories of baby's total calories for the day.

If your baby decides he doesn't want to eat solids, don't fight with him about it. It may be a good idea to make the decision now that you will *never* fight with your child about food—at any age!

When baby refuses solid food, continue offering him a spoonful of cereal at each meal. Your purpose in offering him solids is to introduce him to the taste and texture of food. If he won't eat, call your pediatrician for advice. He or she can give you suggestions on ways to handle the situation.

> Once baby starts eating solids on a daily basis, he'll cut down on the amount of formula or breast milk he drinks. But he should still be taking in most of his calories from formula or breast milk. By the time he reaches his first birthday, baby will probably be eating three meals a day and only nursing or taking a bottle at bedtime.

Milestones this 22nd Week

✳ *Imposing Restrictions*

As baby begins moving more, you will have to impose certain restrictions on him. You may need to block access to some areas. You may have to remove him from situations that could harm him. Don't be surprised when he resists your efforts. This is normal. He isn't defying you or acting naughty. He's just reacting in the only way he knows how.

When this happens, don't make too many demands of him. He needs stability and regularity in his life. When you provide them to him, you also offer him security. You need to be flexible. Realize his actions are normal. Don't expect more from him than he is capable of giving.

✳ *He Likes to Play to Learn*

Baby engages in play that makes noise. He loves toys that shake and rattle. He's learning that some toys make noise, and others don't. He doesn't realize it's the toy making the noise, not his hand. He compares sounds when he bangs two objects together or drops them on the floor.

When he drops the same toy over and over again, he's learning many things. He's trying to see if it falls the same way and makes the same noise each time it drops. Although this can be frustrating to you, it's fascinating to him.

✳ *He May Be More Wary of Strangers*

In a short time, baby may become wary of strangers. This is called *stranger anxiety*. You may be surprised when he suddenly hesitates to go to someone he doesn't know. He may study a stranger when he or she comes close. He may react by crying loudly when left alone with a babysitter he doesn't know. It's natural, but explain to those people baby sees only once in awhile that it's just a phase he's going through.

✴ *Creeping*

Your child may be moving around more now. He wants to investigate many things. He will begin creeping soon so he can get where he wants to go. When he *creeps,* he moves on his tummy while he pushes against the floor. He isn't crawling on his hands and knees, and won't for a while.

He may go backward instead of forward. He may also move in other ways, such as scooting or rolling. It may amaze you when you see how he gets to where he wants to go when he *really* wants to get there!

Note: See also the box *Milestones this 22ⁿᵈ Week.*

What's Happening this 22nd Week?

✴ *Teething Symptoms*

Signs of teething can appear weeks or even months before you see baby's first tooth. As baby's tooth moves through gum tissue and bone, symptoms may appear and disappear. See the complete discussion in *Week 27.*

When he starts teething, your baby may refuse to eat solids. Eating puts pressure on his gums, which increases his discomfort. You may find he wants more formula or wants to nurse more. But this also puts pressure on his gums, so he may not want to continue after he begins. If you find baby pulls away from the breast or bottle after his initial sucking effort, he may be feeling some discomfort in his mouth.

✴ *Solitude for Baby*

Continue to allow baby quiet time by himself. It's OK to leave him safely on the floor or in his playpen while you attend to tasks. Don't feel guilty when you leave baby alone; it's an important part of his development.

When he's alone, baby can process and internalize various pieces of information. He can observe his surroundings at his own pace. He can also rest physically, which he needs for his well-being.

It may be hard to determine if your baby needs something. He will tell you in the only way he can right now—with body language. Be alert for the following clues from him:
- ✲ whimpers and looks from side to side (he may want a change in his environment)
- ✲ nuzzles his hand or blanket (he may be hungry)
- ✲ whimpers and tosses about (he may need calming)

MILESTONES THIS 22ND WEEK

Changes You May See this Week as Baby Develops Physically
* on his back, baby may move by kicking against a flat surface
* turns and twists in all directions

Changes You May See this Week in Baby's Developing Senses and Reflexes
* sits supported for up to 30 minutes

Changes You May See this Week as Baby's Mind Develops
* can discriminate self from others in mirror
* leans over to look for fallen object
* can recognize object from only seeing part of it

Changes You May See this Week in Baby's Social Development
* interest in breastfeeding may lag
* vocalizes pleasure and displeasure
* smiles at self in mirror

Every baby is an individual, and your baby may do some of these things more quickly or more slowly than another baby. If you are concerned about your baby's progress, discuss it with your healthcare provider. Also see page xiii.

Being by himself allows baby a chance to practice various skills, such as soothing himself. He may also learn to fall asleep on his own without you being there to comfort him with cuddling or rocking.

✴ Anemia

Anemia is the condition in which a child doesn't have sufficient iron in his blood; the number of red cells in the blood decreases. Sometimes it is referred to as *low iron* or *iron deficiency*. It is the most common nutritional deficiency in the U.S.–about 9% of all children under the age of 3 have iron-deficiency anemia (IDA).

Anemia can occur at any time. Symptoms may include:
* pale skin
* lethargy
* feeling of ill health
* change in his sleeping habits; he sleeps too much

Most babies have enough iron to get them through the first 4 to 6 months of life. They stored the mineral while growing in the uterus. However, premature babies may be at a higher risk for IDA because they may not get enough iron before birth, and they use it up faster after birth.

After 6 months of age, a baby's iron stores may be depleted. He is also growing. Combined, these two factors can affect a baby's iron levels. However, around this time, your baby will also be starting on baby food; many are iron fortified, which can help with the problem. The iron content in these foods is one of the reasons we encourage parents to start feeding solids between 4 and 6 months of age.

What You Can Do at Home.   If you believe your baby may be iron deficient, there are some things you can do before you contact your physician. One way you can check your baby's iron levels is to examine his lower eyelid. Gently pull it down, and look at the color of the skin inside the eyelid. Is it a healthy pink? If so, baby is getting enough iron. If not, it could indicate baby has IDA.

Be sure baby's vitamins contain iron. If you are bottlefeeding your baby, use formula that contains iron. When baby starts eating solids, give him iron-fortified foods. The use of iron-fortified formula has helped reduce the problem of IDA greatly in the United States. The AAP recommends that babies should always be given iron-fortified formula, unless there are reasons not to do so. Your pediatrician will advise you.

When baby begins eating solids, be sure you offer him iron-rich foods, such as iron-fortified cereal, egg yolks, strained beef or chicken, strained carrots or strained pears. Be sure to give him these foods at the appropriate ages. About 2 tablespoons a day may be enough.

Breastfeeding mothers should continue to take their prenatal vitamin and eat foods that are iron rich. This helps ensure baby gets the iron he needs.

Be alert for any signs of bleeding by your baby, such as blood in bowel movements or on the diaper, or blood in urine. Call your doctor's office for suggestions for dietary supplements.

When to Call the Doctor.   If the above measures don't help, contact your baby's doctor. Call the office immediately if baby has any symptoms of bleeding. If your baby develops new symptoms, call the office for advice.

The most common course of treatment is vitamins and iron supplementation. If additional measures are needed, your doctor can prescribe them.

Research has found that starting a baby on cereal between 4 and 6 months of age may help reduce his risk of developing Type-1 diabetes later in life. However, starting solids before 3 months or after 6 months of age actually *increases* his risk 4 times of developing Type-1 diabetes. And beginning solids too early can cause abnormal reactions in a baby's immature immune system. So follow your baby's doctor's advice on when to begin feeding your baby solid food.

YOUR PREEMIE'S DEVELOPMENT

Your premature baby should be able to do many things now. Remember always to use baby's "due-date age" as your point of reference for the following accomplishments. By this week, he should be exploring his feet. To help him accomplish this task, try the following:

* help baby find his feet with his hands—this may take some help from you
* play with his feet, exercise or massage them, and play "This Little Piggy Went to Market," see *Week 12,* and other games with his feet
* assist him in examining his toes with his mouth, but be careful he does not overstretch his muscles

✴ *How to Give Your Baby Medication*

Medication can be given to a baby or young child by mouth, injection, as a suppository or directly, such as eye, ear or nose drops. Giving a baby or young child medication can be one of your most challenging tasks as a parent. It's not easy to get a spoonful or syringe of liquid medicine in a baby who squirms or refuses to open his mouth!

To give a baby or young child any medication, you may need some help! If someone else isn't available, try wrapping your baby gently in a blanket, with his arms down at his sides. This keeps him from batting at your hand with his.

You can buy "medication syringes" at the drug or grocery store. They are easier to use and more effective than a spoon. These syringes allow you to measure accurately how much medication to give. They may also be easier for you to control. See the discussion in *Week 47* on ways to administer medication if baby is not cooperating.

Do *not* use a spoon from your kitchen tableware set to measure medicine. It is very inaccurate. You could end up giving your baby a lot more or a lot less medicine than was prescribed!

Some medications can be given in foods, juices or formula. A good resource for help is the nurse at your pediatrician's office. Grandma may also have some good advice that will help.

Caution: Don't give your baby any medications unless directed to do so by your doctor. This includes over-the-counter medications. What may be all right for you or an older child may *not* be OK for a baby!

Toys and Play this 22ⁿᵈ Week

✴ *Prism on the Wall*

It's not too early to introduce some "science" to baby. Buy a prism at a toy store. Hang it in a window, or hold it in the light when you interact with baby. Show him the beautiful rainbows it makes on the wall. You'll enjoy his reactions when he sees the patterns glitter and sparkle on his hands or on your face. If possible, hang the prism in a window in baby's room where he can watch it when it makes patterns on the wall.

✵ *Play the Trumpet*

A fun interaction between parent and child is playing the trumpet on baby's tummy! After his bath or when you're dressing him, put your lips against his bare tummy and blow. The sound comes out like a bad trumpet player trying to blow a horn. Baby will laugh and giggle. It tickles, and it's a funny sound. It'll delight you, too.

✵ *This Is the Way the Lady Rides*

You can play a bouncing game now that baby is older. Sit him on your knees, with your legs together and feet flat on floor. Hold his arms or hands firmly so he won't fall off. Support his upper back, head and neck. Very gently bounce the baby while singing:

> *This is the way the lady rides, lady rides, lady rides.*
> *This is the way the lady rides, so early in the morning.*

With the next verse, bounce the baby a little harder while singing:

> *This is the way the gentleman rides, gentleman rides, gentleman rides.*
> *This is the way the gentleman rides, so early in the morning.*

With the last verse, bounce baby even more vigorously while singing:

> *This is the way the farmer rides, farmer rides, farmer rides.*
> *This is the way the farmer rides, so early in the morning.*

At the last "farmer rides," while firmly grasping and supporting him, straighten out both of your legs or open your knees so baby drops a little.

Week 23

Baby's Age as a Monthly Reference—6 months

HOW BIG IS BABY THIS 23ᴿᴰ WEEK?

Baby weighs 15¼ pounds and is 25¾ inches long this week.

Baby Care and Equipment

✻ *Framed Baby Carriers*

Now that baby is older and heavier, you may be thinking about a different kind of carrier than a front carrier to carry her around. A good selection is a *framed carrier*, which is similar to the type of backpacks used by hikers and campers. These carriers have a sturdy metal frame that holds baby in a cloth seat. They offer greater back support for you. They adjust to fit most adults.

Most framed carriers are for use with babies older than 6 months. Baby needs to be able to hold her head and body steady. When she's on your back, you can't see her. You need to be confident she is able to sit well so you won't worry about her.

If you decide to get a carrier, take baby with you to the store. It's a good idea for her to be placed in the carrier when you are trying it on. That way you can see how it fits you when you are carrying her, and you can check to see how the carrier fits baby.

Carriers offer different features that may make one type more comfortable for you. Many of the framed backpack carriers have a kickstand to hold the carrier steady. This makes it easier to load and unload baby, which makes it easier on you. However, *never* leave baby unattended in a carrier supported by a kickstand.

A framed carrier can be used until your child is between 40 and 45 pounds. Various models have different weight maximums. This type of carrier could be a good investment—many run around $100—because you may be able to use it with baby until she is 3 or 4 years old.

Caution: Be careful when you carry your baby in a backpack carrier. Even though you've strapped her in, *never* bend forward when carrying her. If her straps have come loose, she can fall out and could be hurt!

✻ *Furniture Hazards*

By this time, you've probably taken many steps to prevent baby hurting herself around the house. In previous weekly discussions, we've discussed

271

precautions to take at home and on the road. Baby isn't moving too much yet, but there are some other considerations for baby's safety that you should keep in mind. The furniture and equipment in your home can pose dangers you might not be aware of.

It may be important for you to keep baby from going into certain areas of the house. A good choice is a barrier of some sort to keep her out. Safety gates block areas, but avoid *accordion gates* (those that fold up) with diamond-shape openings. Many have openings large enough for baby to stick her head into; she could get stuck!

When baby starts pulling herself up, she'll practice on anything handy. You need to be alert to situations in which she can tip over furniture when pulling herself up. Bookcases and cabinets are dangerous. Block off access to them, or bolt them to the wall. Bedroom dressers can also be hazardous, especially when children start opening drawers to use as a ladder to climb up. Bolt these to the wall, too.

Be sure your TV is high enough so it's out of reach, or fasten it securely to the wall. If you own a recliner, be careful when baby's in the room. Her head, legs or arms can become trapped when it's closing. Never leave it open when you're not using it, and keep a close eye on baby when you recline in one.

Your exercise equipment can pose hazards, so be careful with it. Exercise machines can pinch fingers. Free weights can roll onto little hands and feet. If you use a jump rope, baby could get tangled in it.

It takes some forethought on your part, but being aware of these hazards can help you protect baby against unforeseen injuries.

✸ *Laundry Detergents and Skin Rashes*

When baby gets a rash, many parents wonder if it might be the laundry detergent they use. However, studies show detergents are not often the cause of skin irritations.

If your baby has normal skin, you don't need to buy hypoallergenic soap to wash her clothes. Using your regular detergent is OK. To protect her newborn skin, rinse her clothes and diapers twice for the first few months.

Fabric-softener sheets used in the dryer can occasionally cause itchy, red patches on baby's skin. Some of the softener chemical remains on clothes. A liquid fabric softener that is made to be added to the *wash cycle* leaves less residue, which may mean less chance of irritation.

If your baby does have sensitive skin, you need to take steps to protect it.

* ✸ Choose a gentle, fragrance-free soap or detergent to wash her clothes. They contain fewer additives, so she may have less of a reaction.
* ✸ Rinse clothes twice to be sure you rinse out irritants.
* ✸ Dry items in the dryer without fabric sheets.

Taking in Less Formula or Breast Milk

As baby begins to take in more nutrition from solid foods, she may begin to cut back somewhat on her intake of formula or breast milk. This is normal. If she is breastfed, she may do this on her own. If she is bottlefed, she may need some help.

Ask your pediatrician for advice on how much formula or breast milk baby should be drinking. Although you want her to eat solid foods, you don't want her to give up other important nutrition sources. Neither do you want her to take in too many calories. It's best to work this out with help from baby's doctor.

> After introducing a new food to your baby, call the doctor if any of the following occur within 24 to 48 hours:
> * wheezing
> * a skin rash
> * diarrhea
> * vomiting

Milestones this 23rd Week

Her Social Interactions

Your baby is becoming very social. She smiles and laughs, and is more able to express her feelings. She doesn't wait for you or other family members to initiate social interaction. She may smile and coo at you to let you know she wants to play or snuggle. When you reach to pick her up, she may hold out her arms. She is attached to you but willing to relate to others. Her anxiety around strangers may be more evident now.

She Studies Faces

Your face is very interesting to baby; she studies it from all angles. She wants to touch your face all the time. She sticks her fingers in your eyes and nose. She grabs onto an ear or hair, and doesn't let go.

She's doing this to learn more about you and herself. She's beginning to realize you are a separate person from her. She can pull your hair, and it doesn't hurt. When she pulls her own hair, it does!

Development Can Be Erratic

You may notice your baby focuses temporarily on a particular area of development. If she does, she may ignore other things. She may concentrate on trying to move and won't vocalize as much as she did. She may also become frustrated when she can't do something. You may hear her whine or see her get angry.

✴ *Exploration Continues*

Baby is more coordinated now. She's curious about exploring her environment and goes about it very seriously. She can reach, grab, hold and tug at various objects. One thing she may need to practice is letting go—she doesn't quite have the hang of it yet.

You may notice she transfers an item from one hand to the other. This helps her practice releasing something.

✴ *Her Understanding of Speech Increases*

Her understanding of speech is growing. She responds to you in many ways. When you say hello to her, she pays attention to the sound of your voice. When you repeat yourself, she may coo and gurgle. She may try to imitate some of the sounds you make.

✴ *She's Getting Stronger*

Baby's arm and trunk muscles are getting stronger. When she's on her tummy, she can hold herself up on her arms for longer periods. She may even twist her entire torso to look over her shoulder. She can sit erect briefly, using her hands for support and balance.

Note: See also the box *Milestones this 23rd Week.*

What's Happening this 23rd Week?

✴ *Ferber Basics—Teaching Babies to Fall Asleep on Their Own*

Many parents want baby to learn to fall asleep on her own. You may still be rocking your baby to sleep or keeping her up if she's fussy, then putting her down after she goes to sleep. You can put up with an occasional sleepless night, but you don't want baby crying every night you put her down. You may be getting very tired of having to make this extra effort.

Richard Ferber, M.D., is a Harvard-trained physician who directs a sleep-disorder clinic for children. He believes many poor sleep habits are learned, and they can be *unlearned!* He has developed a method to use with babies older than 6 months to help them accomplish this task. You may hear the term "Ferberize"; it refers to the program Dr. Ferber originated.

It may take a lot of effort on your part to practice the plan, but it's worthwhile. Baby learns to soothe herself, and it may also offer you some respite. Below is a description of each step to take to help your baby become independent.

* Put baby down in her crib while she's still awake. Tell her it's time to go to sleep. Leave the room. If she doesn't start crying, you don't need to do anything. If she does cry, let her cry for 5 minutes before going back into her room.

MILESTONES THIS 23ᴿᴰ WEEK

Changes You May See this Week as Baby Develops Physically
* sits with little support; may slump forward on hands for balance
* reaches with one arm

Changes You May See this Week in Baby's Developing Senses and Reflexes
* may bend herself almost into sitting position when rolling from back to side
* turns head freely

Changes You May See this Week as Baby's Mind Develops
* will gaze at object for a long time
* can utter several additional consonant sounds

Changes You May See this Week in Baby's Social Development
* giggles and laughs
* coos, hums and stops crying when she hears music

Every baby is an individual, and your baby may do some of these things more quickly or more slowly than another baby. If you are concerned about your baby's progress, discuss it with your healthcare provider. Also see page xiii.

* Don't turn on the lights in her room. Keep your physical contact to a minimum. Speak softly to her again. Tell her she's a big girl, and she can go to sleep on her own. Leave the room again.
* If she continues to cry, this time wait for 10 minutes before entering her room. Speak to her again. Don't stay too long; leave within a minute or so.
* If crying continues, wait 15 minutes between each visit to her room, until she falls asleep.
* On the second night, start with 10 minutes of crying before you first enter her room.

Gradually increase the length of time from there. If it's too difficult to let baby cry for 5 minutes the first night, wait 2 or 3 minutes before going in. You need to do what is comfortable for you. Many parents have reported that after only a few nights of using this system, baby fell asleep on her own.

Expect Some Setbacks. When baby is sick, she's often sleepless. While she is ailing, you may have to get up with her in the middle of the night. This might cause a setback in the progress you have made in helping her learn to fall asleep on her own.

Once she's feeling better, you may have to begin the process again. If she was successful in learning to fall asleep on her own before, she can be successful again.

✧ *Encouraging Baby's Motor Development*

You don't have to buy anything fancy to help baby develop her motor skills. The best thing you can do is give her the opportunity to explore and to practice the new skills she has learned.

Of course there will be times you need to restrict baby for her safety, but try not to do it unnecessarily. Provide her with a babyproofed area where she can practice some of the skills she's developing that help her move around.

In addition to giving her the space she needs, get down on the floor with her. Play games with her to encourage rolling or crawling. Roll a ball back and forth with her. Play tag. You'll both have fun, and you'll be helping her practice the motor skills she'll be using in the upcoming months.

✧ *Croup*

Croup, also called *laryngo-tracheo-bronchitis,* is a viral infection that can occur at any age. It is an infection or inflammation of the vocal cords (larynx) and the tissues surrounding them.

It can be a little scary when baby gets croup. Attacks happen most often quite suddenly, at night, although it may begin gradually, with cold symptoms. Croup may be associated with a viral or bacterial infection of the respiratory tract, or it may be caused by allergies. Symptoms of the problem include:

* a "barking" cough that sounds like a seal
* difficulty breathing
* hoarseness or raspiness of voice

What You Can Do at Home.   Don't panic if baby has croup. Your anxiety may add to the problem by scaring her.

One of the first things you can do is set up a cool-mist humidifier in her room. See the discussion of humidifiers in *Week 13.* You may also consider adding a humidifier to your home heating/air-conditioning system, especially if you live in a very dry climate. This can help avoid the problem and may decrease her symptoms.

If you don't have a humidifier, take baby into the bathroom and run hot water (to create steam). Exposure to cold night air (go for a walk) may help; be sure she's dressed warmly. Keep her in a semiupright position—don't lay her flat or sit her directly upright.

When to Call the Doctor.   It may be hard for you to determine if the situation is serious. If baby has a barking cough but is happy and playful, not having trouble breathing and sleeping OK, it's probably not serious. Symptoms of mild croup should improve in less than 1 hour. If they don't, call the doctor.

If baby's throat in front of her neck caves in when she takes a breath, her breathing is labored and noisy (especially when she's resting), she seems anxious and she can't get her breath, the situation is serious. Call 911 or go the hospital immediately.

Call the doctor if your baby is having trouble breathing or swallowing. You may be directed to go to the emergency room. If her respiratory rate (number of breaths in a minute) is above 50 or if her fingernails turn blue, contact your pediatrician or go to the nearest emergency-medicine facility.

Medications are given if the cause is believed to be bacterial. Most of the time antibiotics are not indicated nor are they helpful. Steroids may be given to improve breathing. Frequent, smaller feedings with liquids may help in some situations.

> Whenever you are in doubt about your baby's health, call your pediatrician's office. Talk to the nurse or physician's assistant about baby's specific symptoms. He or she will determine if the doctor needs to see baby. You may be reassured that baby is OK. If you can do anything at home to keep baby comfortable, you'll be given suggestions on what to do.

✳ *Nasal Congestion*

When baby has nasal congestion, she has trouble breathing freely through her nose. It may occur with a cold, upper-respiratory infection or with allergies. Symptoms include:

* discharge (thick or watery) from either or both nostrils
* difficulty breathing
* a fever sometimes
* agitation or fussiness
* snorting or sniffling sounds
* difficulty sleeping or feeding
* baby may rub or scratch her nose
* other symptoms of a cold, such as a cough or sore throat, may be present

What You Can Do at Home.   Use a cool-mist humidifier to help keep secretions flowing and draining. Gently clean her nose with a soft tissue or cloth. Use a bulb syringe to clear nasal passages for easier breathing. Don't give her any medications, including over-the-counter medicine, without consulting your doctor.

When to Call the Doctor.   Call the doctor if baby has a respiratory rate of 50 breaths per minute or more, difficulty breathing, shortness of breath, she appears blue or has a dark color around her mouth or nose. If the discharge from her nose is bloody, yellow or green, or if she runs a persistent temperature, contact your pediatrician.

In addition to using a humidifier, nose drops, antibiotics and decongestants may be used. However, use them *only* under the direction of your doctor.

> If baby is feeling ill during the day, call your doctor's office. Don't wait until later, in hopes she'll get better. It may be much easier to deal with the problem during the day, when appointments can be made or prescriptions easily called in to the pharmacy.

Toys and Play this 23rd Week

✵ Play Ball!

Now's a good time to introduce your baby to playing with balls. She can sit up well, and she's becoming more mobile, so playing with a ball is fun. It allows her to practice tracking a moving object with her eyes. This type of play also helps her develop coordination.

Choose a brightly patterned ball. One that makes noise is even more fun! Roll it against the wall so it comes rolling back. Watch her watch it. Slowly bounce it up and down. These two activities help her exercise her visual skills. And you're having fun playing together.

See if she reaches for the ball. When she does, give it to her so she can feel its texture and weight. She won't be able to throw it, but show her how to roll it. She'll enjoy this fun interaction.

✵ Water Play

It's fun to play safely with water. Your baby will enjoy the novelty of playing with water. You can play in the bathtub, the sink, outdoors in a baby pool or anywhere you won't be making a big mess.

Gather together some different-sized plastic cups. Plastic or aluminum measuring cups are great because they are each a different size. Pour a little water into one cup. Let her watch you pour the water from one cup to another. Or pour the water onto the grass or into a pail.

While you share this interaction, use words such as *pour* and *splash* to describe what she sees. She may want to put her hand in the water as you pour it from one container into another. Let her feel the water, if she wants to do so. This can be kind of messy, so be sure you do it someplace where getting the area wet won't matter.

Week 24

Baby's Age as a Monthly Reference—6 months

HOW BIG IS BABY THIS 24ᵀᴴ WEEK?
Baby weighs 15½ pounds and is 26 inches long this week.

Baby Care and Equipment

✼ Baby Jumpers

Your baby may enjoy a baby jumper at this time. Viewing the world from an upright position can be very exciting for him. Baby sits in a swinglike device suspended from a free-standing frame or doorframe, and he can jump and bounce and move as much as he wants.

A jumper stays in one spot, so baby can't take off on his own. He can rock, spin, bounce and jump sitting in it. He's safe because it doesn't move like a walker. See the discussion of *Walkers* in *Week 38*. He can develop strength and coordination, and have fun doing it.

Some jumpers are basic models and hold baby in an upright sitting/standing position. Some have padded seats. Some seats adjust to various positions. Other bouncers have trays to hold baby's toys.

A baby can usually use a jumper between 4 and 12 months of age. It can be used until baby gets too heavy for it or is too mobile to be pent up in this way. Follow the manufacturer's weight-limit guidelines. Until he starts walking, your baby might have a great time observing the world from his jumper.

Caution: Be sure the jumper is secured in a safe place, away from stairs, opening doors and any other hazards to baby.

✼ Bathtub Seats

Your baby is probably ready for the big bathtub now. You only need a few inches of water to bathe him. Once your baby can sit up unsupported, you can put him in a bathtub seat when you bathe him in a big tub. You don't have to hold him up, so

When your baby is older, sitting in a bathtub seat
allows him to enjoy the big bathtub.

279

he can splash and play in the tub with more freedom. Follow the manufacturer's guidelines as to weight and age recommendations for the particular
seat you choose.

There are two types of seats. One reclines so baby can relax and enjoy the
water. (See the illustration on the previous page.) The other type is similar to
a little cage baby sits inside—a round plastic ring surrounds baby at waist
height, with three or four legs that attach to the tub bottom with suction
cups. It helps keep baby sitting upright. With this type of seat, suction cups
should stick properly to the tub bottom for safety. If you have a used bath
seat, be sure the suction cups are in good condition and clean, or they
might not stick to the tub. Before placing the seat in the tub, clean the tub
surface thoroughly. Cups won't stick to a vinyl bath mat, nonslip decals or a
film of soap scum.

Gather together all the bath products you use before you put baby in the
tub. Have them near at hand. A seat does *not* guarantee protection—never
leave baby alone in it while he's in the tub! If you have to leave the room,
take him with you.

When you remove baby from the bathtub seat, lift him out of it. Don't
lift the seat with him in it. It's too easy for him to fall out.

> *Never* assume baby is safe in a bathtub seat! Keep an eye on him
> while he's in the tub, and remain by his side until he's finished
> with his bath. In addition, to ensure baby's safety in the tub, put a
> soft, insulated cover over the bathtub faucet. Never let your baby
> stand in the tub—he can easily fall face-first into the water. Bring
> a portable phone with you into the bathroom so you won't have to
> leave the room if someone calls.

↳ *Is Baby Getting Enough Nourishment?*

Babies of this age need about 800 calories a day—from a combination of formula or breast milk *and* solid foods. You probably don't have to worry that
he isn't getting enough nourishment. As long as he takes in formula or
breast milk, and eats the various solid foods he can manage, he should get
enough calories. If you are concerned, discuss it with your pediatrician.

The best indications he is eating enough calories are his growth and well-
being. If he's growing and putting on weight, and he is energetic, he's getting enough nourishment.

Remember, feeding him solids at this time isn't for the nutrition he receives. It's more for socialization and introducing him to the taste and texture of eating "grown-up" food.

↳ *Shopping-Cart Safety*

Now that baby is sitting up more easily, you may want to place him in the grocery shopping cart so he can shop with you. Use caution when you do this—each year more than 12,000 children under the age of 5 are seen in emergency rooms all over the country because of shopping-cart accidents!

Many stores now supply customers with shopping carts with built-in infant seats. If you use this type of cart, be sure to fasten all the safety straps to keep baby safe. If straps are missing or broken, do not use the seat carrier.

If the cart has only a wire seat, sit baby upright with his feet through the holes. Fasten the safety strap around him. As he gets older, do not allow him to stand up on the seat or to ride or to stand in the basket.

> By this time, baby has his own predictable sleep pattern. He probably goes to sleep, wakes up and takes a couple of naps around the same times each day.

If you're thinking about balancing your infant car seat or infant carrier in the wire part of the cart, don't do it. It won't fit securely and will be unbalanced; you or someone else could accidentally knock it out of the cart. Put the seat inside the body of the lbasket—tow another grocery cart behind you to carry the items you want to buy.

↳ *His Taste Buds Are Developing*

Your baby has hundreds more taste buds for sweets than you do. That's one reason he loves sweet-tasting foods, such as applesauce or mashed bananas.

Don't offer him foods sweetened with sugar or any other sweetener. He doesn't need them. The fruits and vegetables he eats that taste sweet naturally will satisfy him for a long time.

Milestones this 24th Week

↳ *Baby's Growing Memory*

Your baby's memory continues to grow, especially his short-term memory. He recognizes faces, names, routines, basic words and sounds he is familiar with. He remembers favorite toys and looks for them when he can't see them.

Baby follows your direction of pointing and may point at things when you name them. Touching objects helps him learn about their texture—he wants to touch everything!

He remembers daily rituals, so establishing routines may help boost his memory. One way to do this is by greeting him with the same phrase every morning.

✢ His Moods Change

You may notice baby has abrupt mood changes. He may get mad when something doesn't suit him. But he may quickly forget his anger when distracted by a toy. In a few weeks, this tapers off as baby begins to gain some control over his feelings. Don't expect too much, though—the process of learning to control his emotions continues for years.

✢ He's Interested in Sounds

His babbling may be taking on a more definite shape. He may combine some consonants with vowel sounds. If you repeat his sounds, he may listen intently. He is learning to vary the pitch and volume of his "speech" and may be using sounds more deliberately now to get your attention.

✢ He Likes to Play

Playing is very important to baby. He plays by himself for longer periods, in part because he sits better. He can now grasp an object purposefully with one hand and manipulate it. He still enjoys dropping things. He seems to be making decisions when he chooses toys to play with. Soon he may attempt to stack one block on top of another, if he watches someone do it first.

> Games may seem silly to you, but they aren't to baby. Games that involve movement and action enhance your baby's body awareness and improve his motor skills.

✢ He's Stronger Now

Your baby's strength is increasing in many ways. He may be able to sit alone. If he still slumps forward or to the side, he's not ready yet. His arms are very strong, and he may be exercising his leg muscles. He may develop the urge to stand but probably can't do so without your help.

If he's rolling over confidently, he may use the technique to move around the room. Occasionally you'll have to help him when he rolls himself into someplace he can't get out of.

Note: See also the box *Milestones this 24th Week.*

If baby slumps forward or to the side, she isn't ready to sit alone yet.

MILESTONES THIS 24ᵀᴴ WEEK

Changes You May See this Week as Baby Develops Physically
❧ while lying on back, grabs and holds foot in play

Changes You May See this Week in Baby's Developing Senses and Reflexes
❧ may manipulate objects

Changes You May See this Week as Baby's Mind Develops
❧ shows different emotions, such as happiness, unhappiness, even a temper
❧ may have abrupt mood changes

Changes You May See this Week in Baby's Social Development
❧ coos and gurgles with pleasure
❧ turns when own name is heard

Every baby is an individual, and your baby may do some of these things more quickly or more slowly than another baby. If you are concerned about your baby's progress, discuss it with your healthcare provider. Also see page xiii.

What's Happening this 24th Week?

✄ Establishing Trust

Bonding with your baby helps establish his trust in you. It provides him with a sense of security and faith in others. It also gives him security in himself.

You have bonded with baby by responding to his basic needs–feeding, changing and caring for him. You have also done it in other ways, such as talking, singing and playing with your baby. The introduction of rituals increases his feeling of safety.

You may not realize what kind of impact your daily interaction has on baby. But you are shaping his view of his world and those in it.

✄ Reading Together

Building on the discussion above on establishing trust, reading with baby is a wonderful way to combine learning with closeness. You expose baby to language's rhythms and tones. You also create a bond between you as the two of you share this experience.

When you read to baby, you are opening a new world to him. Introducing him to books may shape his future reading habits. He may become a lifelong reader because of the interactions you share now.

To instill a love of reading in your child, choose books and stories that are age appropriate. Think about the books you liked as a child. As unbelievable as it may seem, many are *still* available today! It's fun to read a story you loved as a child to your child.

If you are unsure what books might be appropriate for your baby, visit your local library. The children's librarian can direct you to many books for your baby. Choose books that are fun to read. With young babies, colorful pictures are often the key. Singsong verses are also good because baby likes the sounds of the rhythms.

When you read a book or a story to baby, your voice conveys a great deal. Read with pleasure in your voice. Be enthusiastic. Change voices for different characters. Make it exciting for baby to listen. He will sense your enjoyment and pay closer attention to you.

Borrowing books from your local library is a great way to expose baby to all kinds of books and stories. If any become favorites, you may be able to buy them for your own at-home library!

Keep in mind that baby can get tired from this activity, just as any other. Watch for clues that he's had enough. When he's tired, stop reading. Continue another day.

✻ *Bronchitis*

Bronchitis is an upper-respiratory-tract infection (URI) that can occur at any age. If your baby has bronchitis, you may feel a "rumbling" with each breath when you place your hand on his chest. Other symptoms of the problem include:

* a cough that may produce phlegm
* fever
* difficulty breathing
* wheezing
* symptoms of a cold

What You Can Do at Home.   Use a cool-mist humidifier to help relieve congestion. See *Week 13* for a discussion of *Humidifiers*. Run the shower to create steam in the bathroom. Don't expose baby to secondhand smoke or other irritants in the air.

When to Call the Doctor.   Bronchitis is more complicated than a "cold" and may require antibiotics and/or other medications. Call your pediatrician if you suspect your baby has bronchitis. Call if baby is coughing up yellow or colored sputum, if his fever increases, if phlegm contains blood, if he experiences shortness of breath or if he vomits. If baby doesn't improve on antibiotics or other treatments, your doctor will want to know.

YOUR PREEMIE'S DEVELOPMENT

Your premature baby should be able to do many things now. Remember always to use baby's "due-date age" as your point of reference for the following accomplishments. By this week, he should be doing many things, including:

* holding his head erect and raising his body on his hands when lying on his tummy
* arching his back and rocking on his tummy
* smiling and laughing
* rolling over from his tummy to back
* bringing an object to his mouth
* reaching for and batting at objects
* recognizing his name
* passing an object from hand to hand
* standing if supported under the arms

To help him accomplish these tasks, there are many activities you can do with your baby. Try the following:

* offer him rattles and toys to hold and to shake
* play "Pat-a-Cake," see *Week 13*
* let him look in the mirror
* give him teething toys
* let him have tummy time to help strengthen back, leg and arm muscles
* take him to different places in the house to play—a change of scene is good for him

To treat bronchitis, the doctor may prescribe antibiotics or decongestants. Other medications, such as acetaminophen, may be given. Give these *only* as directed by your doctor. Follow your doctor's instructions on ways to make baby more comfortable.

✴ *Vomiting*

Vomiting is usually a symptom, not an illness. It's a *sign* that something might be making baby feel ill. Vomiting usually results from stomach or intestinal upset. It can also be a symptom of other problems, including appendicitis, pneumonia, strep throat or meningitis. It may occur after ingestion of a medication or chemical.

Vomiting is different from when baby "spits up." That usually occurs after a feeding, and he spits up only a little bit of the total amount he has taken in. See the discussion in *Week 2*. When your baby vomits, he expels the contents of his stomach. Other symptoms that may accompany vomiting include fever, listlessness, poor feeding, coughing, constipation, diarrhea or dehydration.

What You Can Do at Home.   When baby vomits, try to identify the cause. Is he getting a cold or the flu? Did he eat something he shouldn't have? Did you give him a new food? Don't force him to eat, but offer him liquids to avoid dehydration.

When to Call the Doctor.   If your baby vomits repeatedly or if vomiting lasts more than a few hours, call your physician. If your baby is under 6 months old, it's important to contact your doctor.

Treatment your doctor may prescribe depends on the cause of the vomiting. You may be advised to stop feeding him solids and offer only liquids. You may be advised to give him an electrolyte solution. Medication may be prescribed, depending on the cause.

✎ Does Baby Cling to You?

If you're like most parents, you love to cuddle your baby. But there are times you have other demands on your time and need to put him down. Does he cry and scream when you do? Some of the following suggestions may help you deal with this situation.

* You don't have to hold him, but keep him close. Put him in his infant seat, swing or stroller, and let him be near you when you can't hold him. Your closeness may do the trick.
* Play games that help him learn that you're still near, even when he can't see you. Peek-a-boo is a good game to teach him this concept.
* Help him learn to be independent. Don't be available immediately when he fusses a little. Let him know you're near by calling out to him and telling him you're coming, but don't always pick him up immediately. Assess the situation, and see what needs to be done. Let baby work things out for himself as much as he can.
* Don't ignore baby in an attempt to make him deal with a situation by himself. Observe what is happening, and use your parenting skills to help him, but don't ignore him. He needs to know he can count on you to help him when he needs it, but he needs to know he must try to do some things on his own before he calls on you for help.

> At this time, babies cry for about 2¾ hours a day.

Toys and Play this 24ᵗʰ Week

Tickle games are still favorites. Continue playing these games with your baby. You might want to buy a feather and use it to tickle him. He will enjoy the game, and you'll be providing him the opportunity to examine a new object (the feather).

✣ *Make Baby's Own Storybook*

Now that you're reading more, make a soft storybook for baby. Buy pieces of different-colored felt at a craft store or fabric store. Cut some into squares to use as "pages." Cut familiar shapes out of different colors. Mark on them with black markers to add details. Use nontoxic glue to attach pieces to the pages, or sew them on. Punch a couple of holes on the left side of each page, and tie together with yarn. Baby has a book all his own!

✣ *Look for the Toy*

You can start teaching your baby to search for things. Sit him on the floor. Using a toy he likes, hide it partway under a blanket that is close to him. Leave enough of the toy visible so he knows what it is. Ask him to find the toy. Help him lift the blanket to find it, if he has any problems.

When you find it, act surprised and happy. Continue the game by concealing the toy, then slowly pulling the blanket to reveal it. Once he catches on to the game, hide the toy under the blanket completely.

Week 25

Baby's Age as a Monthly Reference—6 months

HOW BIG IS BABY THIS 25TH WEEK?

Baby weighs 15¾ pounds and is 26¼ inches long this week.

Baby Care and Equipment

✣ *What Baby Is Eating*

Your baby is eating larger amounts of cereal now. Until this time, you've given her only formula or breast milk and cereal. Baby takes three to five servings of formula or breast milk a day; each serving is probably 6 to 8 ounces. She's also eating two servings of cereal a day; each serving is probably 2 to 4 tablespoons by now. Because her appetite is increasing, it may be time to add more variety to her diet.

If your baby has tried all the different varieties of baby cereal and seems ready for more food, you can add a few new food items. Call your pediatrician *before* you feed baby more than just cereal. He or she may have particular suggestions or advice for your baby.

It's best to begin with *strained* fruit and vegetables. Finger foods, such as toast and plain crackers, are also good to try. Suggested foods to offer baby at this time, and the amounts of each, are listed below:

> Your baby may be eating solids pretty well by now. To encourage her to try new foods, start offering a new food to her *before* you give her a bottle or nurse.

* bread or toast, unbuttered–½ slice
* crackers–2
* fruit–2 to 3 tablespoons, 2 servings a day
* fruit juice (diluted with equal amount of water)–3 ounces, 1 serving a day from a cup
* vegetables–2 to 3 tablespoons, 2 servings a day

✯ *Adding Fruits and Vegetables to Baby's Diet*

After eating baby cereal, fruits and vegetables can take some getting used to. Even strained baby food can have a strong taste after such bland fare. When making your choices at the store, buy strained fruits and vegetables. They are a little easier for baby to swallow and to digest. She doesn't have to chew any of the strained variety.

Offer baby only one new strained fruit or vegetable *each week*. You can see if she has any problems with the food, such as an allergic reaction to it or trouble digesting it. Give her 1 to 2 tablespoons of either a fruit or vegetable at two meals when you first offer it. You want to work up to 2 to 3 tablespoons at each meal.

If baby doesn't like the food you offer her, wait a couple of days before trying it again. Let her eat what she was eating before you introduced the new food.

When selecting juice for baby, buy vitamin C-fortified apple, pear or grape juice—it's OK to give her these now. Avoid orange juice or grapefruit juice at this time. They're too acidic for her. Dilute any juice you give baby. Add as much water to the juice as the amount of juice. If you want to give baby 4 ounces of fluid, mix 2 ounces of juice with 2 ounces of water. Offer her the juice in a cup.

> Let baby hold a cracker or small piece of toast while you feed her. It may keep her from grabbing the spoon when you feed her—at least with one hand!

Are Fruits Better than Vegetables?   Vegetables are more nutritious than fruits. However, offering vegetables before you offer fruits may not entice your baby to eat them. Fruit tastes better, so baby may accept them more readily in the beginning.

At this point in baby's life, you aren't trying to meet all of her nutritional needs with solids. That's one reason you continue giving her formula or breast milk. The goal at this point is to teach baby to swallow foods with different textures. You will probably have more success feeding her fruits than vegetables.

When you introduce vegetables, try the sweeter ones first. Carrots and sweet potatoes are good choices. She may not like them as well as the fruit, but keep trying. If you keep offering them to her, she'll learn to like vegetables.

Milestones this 25ᵗʰ Week

✳ *What Baby Sees*

Although baby's eyesight is pretty developed, she will continue to perfect her visual abilities for a long time. By this time, her vision is about 20/50; things she sees are only mildly fuzzy. She can see details fairly well, such as patterns on fabrics or details on a face. She sees colors and can distinguish between them quite well now.

> As your baby prepares to start crawling, it's time to start keeping an eagle eye on the floor. When she starts to crawl, she'll be very curious and will explore wherever she can. So pick up after yourself, keep an eye on pet dishes, including the cat's litter box, and try to keep ahead of your curious crawler.

✳ *She's More Physically Developed*

Baby probably likes rolling from her tummy to her back, and from her back to her tummy. She may propel herself around the room in this manner.

She isn't crawling yet, but she may raise herself into a crawling position and rock back and forth. This activity helps her get a sense of how to balance her body for when she does start crawling.

Your baby can sit well alone but may need help getting into the sitting position. She has a different view of the world when she's sitting up!

✳ *Baby Uses Her Hands for Many Things*

Baby is using her hands to do many things. She uses them to feed herself. She can clap. She manipulates objects more easily as she passes them from hand to hand. She grabs anything within reach, including her body parts and your body parts. She sucks on her fingers and hands to learn about her

environment. She sucks on her toes, too! Don't worry; it's not unsanitary. Her toes are about as clean as her hands because she's not getting them dirty by walking on her feet.

Baby will suck on anything, including her toes!

✣ Baby Wants Her Own Way

Her glances, facial expressions and gestures invite you to play with her. She becomes very interested in studying an object. She may protest loudly when you take something, such as a toy, away from her. Or she may get angry.

✣ Teething May Begin Soon

Teething symptoms may begin to appear. She may play with her ears or suck her lower lip. See the complete discussion of *Teething* in *Week 27.*

Some babies suffer more than others while teething. Teething can cause a low-grade fever and a change in bowel movements. If baby displays these and other symptoms, check with your pediatrician to rule out anything more serious.

Note: See also the box *Milestones this 25th Week.*

What's Happening this 25th Week?

✣ Allow Baby the Opportunity to Make Mistakes

Your baby is beginning to attempt many new skills. She's moving around a lot, working on her gross (large) motor skills. She's also developing her fine motor skills. You can see evidence of this when she tries to hold a spoon. Give her a helping hand to get started, then back off a little. Let her make mistakes. It's how she learns.

This may mean she gets a few bruises from falls, but it's also letting her grow and expand her horizons. Provide her the freedom to explore her environment. She has many new concepts to learn. Praise her when she does something correctly, like putting the spoon in her mouth.

> By this time, baby is sleeping close to 11 hours at night, and her naps total about 3$\frac{1}{2}$ hours. She's awake and active about 9$\frac{1}{2}$ hours each day.

✣ Your Baby Is an Individual

Don't expect your baby to be like any other baby, even if you have multiples. No two babies are alike. Different personality types will approach the same situation differently. If you try to push her to do something, and it just isn't in her personality to do it that soon or in that way, more harm than good could result. Allow her to be the way she is.

✣ Baby's Learning Capacity

It may seem impossible, but by the time your baby reaches this age, her brain has reached 50% of its weight at maturity! She is developing at an in-

MILESTONES THIS 25TH WEEK

Changes You May See this Week as Baby Develops Physically
* tries to move by propelling herself on stomach with legs and steering with arms
* rotates wrist to turn and to manipulate objects

Changes You May See this Week in Baby's Developing Senses and Reflexes
* likes to play with food
* passes object from hand to hand

Changes You May See this Week as Baby's Mind Develops
* enjoys looking at objects upside down
* likes a change in perspective

Changes You May See this Week in Baby's Social Development
* may cry when parent leaves the room

Every baby is an individual, and your baby may do some of these things more quickly or more slowly than another baby. If you are concerned about your baby's progress, discuss it with your healthcare provider. Also see page xiii.

credible rate. Consider what she's accomplished by this time. She's grown from a newborn, unable to do much at all, to an active baby who rolls over, probably sits up, plays actively and tries to feed herself.

Your baby is also learning at an incredible rate. She is prepared to learn certain skills at certain ages. Her *visual development* begins at birth and continues for many years. From even before birth, her *understanding of speech* and *syntax* has been developing. This will also continue for many years. Her *emotional attachments* and *social attachments* develop the most during her first 18 months. Her *motor development* begins at birth and develops in stages for years.

As we mentioned in *Week 18,* now is the time to begin exposing her to a foreign language. She's like a little sponge—it all soaks in! She's also ready to learn other new skills and accomplish new tasks, so allow her the freedom to experiment *safely* within her environment.

☀ Allergies to Medications
An allergic reaction to a medication, also called a *drug allergy* or *drug hypersensitivity,* can occur anytime following administration of a drug. Symptoms that your baby is experiencing an allergic reaction include:
* itching
* red or flushed skin
* rash
* hives

* restlessness or anxiety
* fever
* lethargy or hyperactivity
* anaphylaxis—severe difficulty in breathing (only in rare instances)

What You Can Do at Home.   If your baby experiences a mild reaction, with itching, she may not need to be treated. But it can be very helpful to identify the cause.

When to Call the Doctor.   Nausea and vomiting following a medication dosage is *not* usually due to a medication allergy. However, with this reaction, contact your doctor. He or she may want to consider other things, such as a medication used to treat the same problem that is different from the one causing the reaction.

More severe reactions, including anaphylaxis, are serious and require immediate medical help. Call the doctor if you think your baby is having a reaction to a medication.

In addition to the measures listed above, your doctor may use medication, including antihistamines or cortisone, to treat the problem. Some adults choose to wear a bracelet identifying the allergy in case of an accident. However, this isn't usually done with a baby.

✻ Moles

Moles, also called *pigmented nevi,* can occur anytime. A mole is a flat or raised area on the skin. Some moles have hairs growing out of them. The colors of moles can range from dark or black to blue, yellow, red or brown. Moles can vary greatly in size, from a small skin tag the size of a grain of wheat to one that is a few centimeters in diameter.

What You Can Do at Home.   Most moles require no treatment. However, stay alert for any changes in the mole, such as a change in size, color or shape. Show any mole to your baby's doctor at regular visits.

When to Call the Doctor.   Call the doctor if the mole bleeds, gets darker (changes color), grows larger or changes shape in any way. A biopsy of the mole may be taken, or the mole may be removed by surgery.

Toys and Play this 25th Week

✻ Peek-a-Boo Time

The peek-a-boo game is fun to play with baby. She'll giggle with pleasure as you hide your face, then reappear. Then hide her face with your hands. This game helps her learn about her environment. It teaches her that you can go away and come back. This is an important concept for her to learn.

Baby loves to play peek-a-boo.

✻ *Upside Down!*

Baby enjoys looking at things from a different perspective, such as upside down. To give her practice in looking at things from a different angle, turn a toy upside down in front of her. See if she turns it right side up. If she doesn't, show her how to do it. Repeat a few times.

✻ *Itsy-Bitsy Spider*

As baby begins to use her hands more, hand-movement games are fun to play together. As you "walk" the fingers of one hand up the fingers of the other hand, sing the "Itsy-Bitsy Spider" song. You may remember it from your days as a baby and young child! Your baby will probably enjoy it very much.

> *The itsy-bitsy spider climbed up the water spout.*
> *Down came the rain and washed the spider out.*
> *Out came the sun and dried up all the rain,*
> *And the itsy-bitsy spider went up the spout again!*

✻ *Listen to the Sounds*

It's good for baby to hear a wide variety of pleasant sounds. You can help her do this by introducing her to sounds all around her. Give her some tissue paper, and let her crumple it. Watch her so she doesn't eat the paper! If you have fall leaves on the ground, take her outside so she can hear you walk through them. If she has a toy piano or xylophone, tap the keys or bars. Help her make some of the sounds so she begins to realize she can create sounds herself.

Week 26

Baby's Age as a Monthly Reference—6 months

HOW BIG IS BABY THIS 26ᵀᴴ WEEK?
Baby weighs 16 pounds and is 26½ inches long this week.

Baby Care and Equipment

✻ *Some Tips for Feeding Baby*
When you feed jarred baby food, take out only enough for one feeding. Put the rest back in the refrigerator; don't feed baby out of the jar. Once opened, refrigerate unused baby food to prevent bacterial growth for up to 3 days. Buy small jars of baby food when you're traveling. If you can't refrigerate leftovers, throw them away. Or buy dried baby food, and mix up the amount for one meal.

To help baby learn to drink from a cup, give him his juice in a cup. He enjoys the taste of the juice and may be more willing to drink juice, rather than formula or breast milk, from a cup.

Buy the spillproof kind of infant cup; it holds from 6 to 10 ounces. Some have handles for baby to grasp. The top doesn't come off easily, so when baby drops it, it stays sealed. Choose a cup that has a self-sealing valve. Juice stays in the cup, even when it's turned upside down!

Now that your baby is closer to teething, a baby spoon with a rubber or heavy plastic coating over the bowl area may be easier and more comfortable for him. They are inexpensive to buy, so you may want to add a few to your utensil drawer.

> It's not unusual for a baby to have doubled his birth weight by this time.

✻ *Baby Wants to Feed Himself*
Your baby may enjoy feeding himself foods he can easily hold in his hand. He may try to thwart your efforts to feed him because he wants to do it himself. Unfortunately, he doesn't have the coordination. He can't guide the spoon to his mouth on a consistent basis, so it's too soon to let him try to feed himself. Keep giving him finger foods to help him develop the skills he needs so he can feed himself in the not-too-distant future.

✣ *He May Be Bored with His Bottle*
About this age, a baby may become bored with the bottle. If he drinks well from a cup, he may be ready to give up a few bottles a day, but don't push it. Even at this age, a baby needs to suck and may not be ready for weaning. Total weaning from the bottle can wait another 6 months.

> By this time, baby should be waking up less during the night. When he does wake up, he should fall back asleep fairly quickly.

Milestones this 26ᵗʰ Week

Your baby has reached half a year! He may be in a good mood most of the time, when he's not frustrated with trying to become mobile. Enjoy him.

✣ *Baby's Depth Perception*
His pictorial depth perception has improved. This change helps him see the world more realistically. When he looks across his bedroom and sees a toy lying in front of his dresser, he realizes the toy blocks part of the dresser. The toy is in front, and the dresser is in back. This is important in his understanding of his environment.

✣ *Use of His Hands*
Baby's ability to grasp objects is more developed now. He can hold his own bottle. He may be using his fingers to pick up something. He passes items from hand to hand and lifts, shakes, pushes, pulls, squeezes and tosses things close to him.

✣ *Baby Is Vocalizing More Sounds*
Vocalizing is an important part of baby's activities. He indicates pleasure with many different sounds. He may try to imitate sounds you make to him.

He may be putting together sounds and repeating them, such as "ma-ma" or "da-da," but he doesn't know they have meaning. But it won't be long before he knows who "mama" is.

Watch baby when you use his name in conversation. Does he pick it out? If he does, he knows his name!

✣ *He's Chewing and Biting Objects*
In addition to putting things in his mouth, baby may be chewing or biting them. When he does this, he's learning about the world around him. Just be sure that the things he puts in his mouth are safe for him to chew on.

✴ *His Ability to Sit*

Baby's strength is increasing, which allows him to sit briefly without support. When he starts to tip over, he may place one hand on the floor to keep himself erect for a short time.

> When baby can sit up in his crib, remove all objects that hang above or near his crib, such as mobiles. This avoids his getting tangled in them. Also lower the mattress so he can't pull himself up and fall out of the crib.

He may grab at an object with one hand, while he supports himself with the other. This action displays how his strength and balance have developed. He couldn't have done this a few weeks ago.

Note: See also the box *Milestones this 26ᵗʰ Week.*

What's Happening this 26ᵗʰ Week?

✴ *Baby's Fear of Strangers and/or Fear of Separation*

You may have noticed your baby is becoming less willing to go to strangers. In certain situations, he may be afraid to part from you. To help baby through this difficult time, be more alert to conditions that intensify his fears.

Baby may respond differently when he's tired or hungry. When you have to leave him, try to do so after he's been fed and is rested.

Illness can cause stress to baby, and he may not want to be apart from you when he's not feeling well. If possible, stay home when he's sick.

When you're on the move, a change in routine can upset baby. Stick to his schedule, when possible. Put him down for his nap and feed him just as if you were at home. This helps him feel more secure.

If you've been away from baby for a while, spend some time alone with him. He may cling to you more, or he may ignore you. Extra time together will help ease his fear of separation.

Leaving him with a new sitter or at a new infant-care center can make him feel unsettled. It takes time for him to accept this new situation, whether it's a new person or a new place, so be patient.

The way your baby expresses his fears is tied to his personality and previous separations. If your baby tends to be clingy and needs security, these situations may cause him stress. If he's more independent, he may display less fear, but he may still be unhappy. It's a natural part of his development.

✴ *Baby Starts to Creep*

If your baby is starting to creep, he's progressing in a normal pattern. Many babies creep before they crawl. When he creeps, your baby uses his arms to pull himself forward while keeping his legs flat on the floor. A baby often creeps first because he has better control of his arms than his legs. When he starts to crawl, he will use his legs a lot more.

MILESTONES THIS 26ᵀᴴ WEEK

Changes You May See this Week as Baby Develops Physically
* may be able to sit alone
* stands with support

Changes You May See this Week in Baby's Developing Senses and Reflexes
* holds own bottle
* may hold cup handle
* displays some interest in feeding self with fingers
* has strong taste preferences

Changes You May See this Week as Baby's Mind Develops
* may compare two objects

Changes You May See this Week in Baby's Social Development
* may be disturbed by strangers

Every baby is an individual, and your baby may do some of these things more quickly or more slowly than another baby. If you are concerned about your baby's progress, discuss it with your healthcare provider. Also see page xiii.

When Baby Stands

When your baby stands, a new world opens up for him. Of course, he can't stand alone yet, but he may be able to with your help. Standing allows him to see more of his surroundings.

When you lift him to a standing position and hold him there, he may support his own weight. He may even bounce up and down as he flexes his legs.

This is very exciting to baby, and he may become very stimulated at this new accomplishment. Enjoy it with him.

Bruises

Now that baby is becoming more active, you may notice he bruises more. Bruises can occur at any age. A bruise results when tissue is injured but skin is not broken (as it is with a cut). Symptoms of a bruise include:
* discoloration of the skin—may appear red, blue, purple or any shade in between
* pain, at times
* tenderness
* swelling

What You Can Do at Home.   When baby gets a bruise, in the first 24 hours apply ice, a cold cloth or an ice pack. Be careful when putting extreme cold on baby's skin. Cold treatments can be extremely painful. Wrap the ice or ice pack in a towel; never lay anything cold directly on the skin. After 24 hours, apply heat, such as a warm, damp towel. This may help with discomfort if the bruise is painful.

Keep an eye on bruises. Note any changes in size and color. It can also be helpful to be aware of the cause of the bruise.

When to Call the Doctor.   Bruising on the shins from falling or bumping them is normal. However, large bruises that seem to appear for no reason are not. Neither are scattered red dots that look like tiny blood spots; these are called *petechiae.* Either can signal a serious blood problem or infection. Report them immediately to your doctor, especially if either is accompanied by a fever.

Call the doctor if a bruise starts to bleed, such as from the mouth, if the bruise seems to take a long time to go away, if baby has a fever that increases or if pain is severe or doesn't go away. Your doctor will advise you.

✻ *Tapeworms*

A tapeworm is a parasite that can live in a person's intestines. A person can get a tapeworm from eating raw or undercooked meat that contains the tapeworm larvae. It is not contagious from one person to another. Symptoms of a tapeworm include:

- ✻ diarrhea
- ✻ tenderness of the upper abdomen
- ✻ failure to thrive
- ✻ weight loss
- ✻ listlessness
- ✻ poor feeding
- ✻ irritability
- ✻ worms or eggs in the stool

What You Can Do at Home.   To avoid the problem, do *not* eat or feed other family members raw or undercooked meat. Always cook meat thoroughly.

> You may be tempted to compare your baby with others. Don't. Your baby is an individual and will do things according to his own schedule. Enjoy each of his accomplishments.

When to Call the Doctor.   Call the doctor if you notice an increase in diarrhea or blood in the stools. Tests may be done, and antiparasitic medication may be prescribed.

> Make an appointment for your baby's 6-month well-baby checkup now. See page 36 for any immunizations he may receive at this visit.

Toys and Play this 26ᵗʰ Week

A Little Roughhousing Is OK

Now is the time baby may enjoy roughhousing with you. He may yelp with pleasure as you roll around on the floor together. Be careful when you roughhouse. He's still a baby and can be more easily hurt than you might imagine.

Baby may also enjoy being swooped up into the air. If he giggles and laughs while you swing him, it's fun. However, some babies don't like being swung into the air. If he protests, stop doing it. It's not a good idea to throw a baby into the air because it can injure his neck. Don't swing him by his arms, either—you could hurt his arms and shoulders.

More Peek-a-Boo

Many games you play with baby promote eye development and intellectual development. When you play peek-a-boo, you teach him that you're still there, even if he can't see you. When you play hide the toy under a blanket, you reinforce his understanding of object permanence (an object is permanent, even if you can't see it for a while). Continue these games to aid in your child's development.

Mist Him with Water

Water play is always fun. When baby is in the tub or outside on a warm day, spray his arms and legs with a water mister. Tell him how soft the spray feels. Let him see how the water falls lightly through the air. Spray some mist above his head, and let it drift down on him. Help him spray the mister. He'll enjoy experiencing the different ways water feels as mist and as a body of water in the bathtub.

Week 27

Baby's Age as a Monthly Reference—7 months

HOW BIG IS BABY THIS 27TH WEEK?

Baby weighs 16¼ pounds and is 26½ inches long this week.

Baby Care and Equipment

✤ *First Aid for Baby's Cold*

A cold is a common ailment, but it's no fun for anyone when baby suffers with one. (See the discussion of *Colds* in *Week 10*.) There are some things you can have on hand and other things you can do for baby to help her deal with her discomfort. The following measures can help her feel better.

* Her lips and nose may get chapped if her nose is runny. (It also happens to adults.) A bit of petroleum jelly or lip protector dabbed on the nose and around the lips helps ease dryness and protects the area.
* Saline nose drops can help thin mucus congestion in the nose and remove it, when used with a bulb syringe.
* A nasal bulb syringe is a necessity for a little one who cannot blow her nose. It removes mucus from the nose. Use it after the saline drops. First squeeze the bulb, then gently insert it into the nostril. Release the bulb to suck out mucus.
* If you use tissues to wipe baby's runny nose, be sure they are soft and thick. One with aloe may help prevent further irritation.
* A cool-mist humidifier can be a great relief because dry air irritates breathing passages. See the discussion of *Humidifiers* in *Week 13*.

The way you dress her can also help when she has a cold. If it's very cold when you take baby out, don't expose her to the elements for more than 15 minutes. Be sure you cover her face with a light blanket or a cover on her infant carrier.

For clothing choices when baby has a cold, consider what you're wearing. Add one extra layer to keep her warm but not hot. When you go outside, bundle her up, but use appropriate types of clothing. Keep her head covered, even if it's not extremely cold. Heat escapes through the head, so always put a hat on her. Keep fingers and toes covered, too; heat is quickly lost through them.

A blanket wrapped around your dressed baby helps keep hands and feet warm. A pair of socks under a snowsuit with feet should also do the trick. Use the same rule of thumb when it's warm. If you need to take off your sweater or coat when you go indoors, you should also take baby's off.

✤ *Stroller/Backpack Combinations*
If you and your family love to be outdoors, there's a piece of baby equipment you might want to purchase to save some money. You may be thinking about purchasing a backpack carrier. See the discussion of these *Backpack Carriers* in *Week 23*. If you are, consider the stroller/backpack carrier, which quickly goes from the stroller mode to the backpack mode.

It's perfect for strolling around a park or forest area that's paved or firmly packed. When you want to "pack" your little one with you, the stroller quickly converts to a carrier for your back! Check out these combo carriers at your local baby store or a sporting goods store.

✤ *Getting Baby to Eat*
Offer new foods and urge baby to try them, but don't get into a battle with her if she doesn't eat them. She doesn't need to eat everything she's given. She can get filled up quite quickly—she has a tiny tummy!

Remember, she continues to get most of the nutrition she needs at this time from the breast milk or the formula you give her. Try to make meal times enjoyable for her and you. When she loses interest or gets fussy, she's finished.

> When you feed baby, take into account her mood. If she's happy when it's time to eat, feed her solid foods first, then give her a bottle or breastfeed her. If she's fussy, give her a bottle or breastfeed first to help her settle down, then feed her solids.

Milestones this 27th Week

✤ *She Sits Well*
Between 6 and 8 months of age, your baby will probably be sitting up on her own. It usually occurs after she begins rolling over. She uses the same muscles to achieve both goals. Sitting up takes longer because baby has to figure out where to put her legs and how to balance her upper body. When she's in a sitting position and waving her arms around, she's practicing her balancing act!

When she can sit up well, you may want to introduce her to a high chair. She'll enjoy being part of the family and interacting at the table.

Once she is able to sit unsupported, it leaves her hands free for other activities. You may see her trying many new things.

✴ *Her Play Is Expanding*
When she's sitting, you may notice baby uses her hands more to play with toys. This is because her hands are free; she doesn't need them for support. She may reach for an object, grab it, examine it, put it in her mouth, then drop it to move on to the next exciting item. You may find she plays quite vigorously with her toys now. She'll shake her rattle or plastic keys and listen to the noises she makes. She even enjoys splashing with toys in the bathtub.

Tumbling on the floor, having fun with mom, dad or a sibling, is also great fun. Playing this way helps socialize your baby. Just be careful about stimulating play close to bedtime. When some babies get excited, they have a hard time settling down.

✴ *She Has Some Control Over Her Environment*
Your little one is beginning to understand that she can control her environment to some extent and make things happen. You may see her use something to help her achieve a goal, such as pulling her blanket toward her to get a toy on it that is beyond her reach.

Another way she explores her environment is the game of deliberately dropping objects—toys, food or anything else she can grab. She may do this quickly, dropping as many things as she can in quick succession. She's testing the effect of her actions. You may be amused by the way she focuses on what happens when she drops an object.

Dumping toys or items out of a box or pan is also great fun. The filling and emptying of a container helps baby begin to understand the concept of full and empty. Even though all the above activities may seem pointless to you, they are big achievements for baby.

Baby's exploring may make it difficult for her to sit still for long. If you want to read books at this time, she may be a little restless. Some babies are ready for quiet listening. Others are not. If you show her an activity book for very young children, she may be fascinated by the book's contents. If she wants to touch a book, pull it, chew on it or just hold it, that's OK. She's exploring it in her own way.

✴ *Is She Scooting or Rolling?*
Your baby may be propelling herself across the floor in some manner. Some babies scoot backward; others move by rolling on their sides. Soon she'll be crawling, although it may not be the right hand/left knee propulsion you expect. Some babies leapfrog (both hands followed by both knees) or crab-walk (not on knees but on feet).

✤ *Baby's Eyesight Is Improving*
By this time, your baby has close to 20/20 vision. She can see details about as well as you can (if you don't have eye problems!). She can also differentiate among subtle shadings of color. Bright toys, mobiles and other objects that have some detail will entertain her.

✤ *Her Leg Strength Increases*
You may notice baby's legs are getting stronger. She may be helping more when you hold her in a standing position. It won't be long before the strength in her legs develops even more. She'll soon be pulling herself to a standing position.

✤ *Her Sleep Needs*
Baby may be exhausted after a hard day of play and activities. She may sleep very well, or you may notice that she gets overly tired. This could lead to sleep problems. If she wakes in the middle of the night, let her settle herself back to sleep when possible. It's important for her to learn to comfort herself.

Note: See also the box *Milestones this 27th Week.*

What's Happening this 27th Week?

✤ *Teething*
It's not too early to begin to see signs of teething. Drooling, chewing on everything, fussiness, wakefulness and swollen gums are signs teething has begun. Not all babies have a problem with teething, but some do.

Baby teeth often come in twos—typically the lower teeth appear before the upper ones. The two bottom-center teeth emerge first, followed by the two upper-middle teeth. Next come the teeth on either side of the front teeth. Following those teeth, baby will cut her molars. It can take 15 to 28 months from the arrival of the first tooth until all 20 of her first set of teeth are in.

Some doctors believe the very first teeth may cause the most distress because your baby has never experienced teething before. After the first teeth appear, teething may not be much of a problem.

What You Can Do at Home.   If you're fairly certain baby is teething, there are some things you can do to help her deal with teething discomfort. "Cold" seems to offer some relief. Let baby chew on something cold, like a chilled plastic teething ring or a cold washcloth. Don't offer frozen foods, such as a piece of frozen banana. Small pieces could lead to choking.

MILESTONES THIS 27ᵀᴴ WEEK

Changes You May See this Week as Baby Develops Physically
* balances head well
* may begin teething

Changes You May See this Week in Baby's Developing Senses and Reflexes
* likes to explore body with mouth and hands
* may like to suck on toes

Changes You May See this Week as Baby's Mind Develops
* plays vigorously with noisemaking toys, such as bells or rattles

Changes You May See this Week in Baby's Social Development
* may chew fingers and suck thumb
* recognizes family members

Every baby is an individual, and your baby may do some of these things more quickly or more slowly than another baby. If you are concerned about your baby's progress, discuss it with your healthcare provider. Also see page xiii.

Massage baby's gums with a clean finger (yours). Rub on gum-numbing medication. It can be purchased over the counter. Don't overuse it! Cold drinks or chilled food may also help. Let her chew on other foods that are fairly hard, such as baby teething biscuits or crackers.

If teething pain is keeping her up, use pain medication, such as acetaminophen or ibuprofen, to help her sleep. Consult your doctor about the correct dose and how long it can be used. ***Caution:*** Never rub liquor, such as brandy, on baby's gums to help relieve pain!

When to Call the Doctor. Your biggest challenge may be discerning between teething and illness. Even with common teething symptoms, if she also has a high fever and vomiting, it's probably not teething. Don't ignore these symptoms. Discuss them with your pediatrician if they last longer than 24 hours.

Some Old Wives' Tales about Teething. You may have heard some horror stories from well-meaning people about baby's teething. Teething can cause baby some discomfort, but it is not a serious situation. On the next page are some myths followed by the correct information.

Baby will always get a fever when she teethes. The truth is there is no physiological reason for this to occur. It may happen, but it does not always occur.

Nighttime is the worst part of the day. The truth is that no particular part of the day is any better or worse than another. However, because nighttime is usually the end of a very busy day for your baby, she is probably tired and may be cranky. She may be more sensitive to the discomfort and let you know it more vocally.

Teething babies should be treated more gently, as if they are sick. The truth is that a teething baby is not sick; she is just experiencing a situation that causes discomfort. Comfort and cuddle her, but don't go overboard. Distraction may be one of your best tools.

It hurts a lot when the tooth breaks through the skin. The truth is that when the tooth erupts (breaks through the skin), the peak of discomfort has probably passed. The real cause of pain is the pressure the erupting tooth generates against the gum.

Taking Care of Her Teeth.   The American Academy of Pediatric Dentistry recommends you take baby to the dentist when she cuts her first tooth. If your baby is one of the few born with teeth, take her to the dentist as soon as possible.

Once six or seven of her teeth are in, brush them at least once a day with water and a soft baby toothbrush. By the end of her second year, she should be brushing after breakfast and at bedtime. Use fluoride-free toothpaste until she's 3 years old. Swallowing too much fluoride can lead to tooth staining.

✴ Saying Good-bye

Baby may not want you to leave her now. She may cry and fuss when you depart. This is natural. Your reactions can do a lot to reassure her. When she starts fussing, keep your emotions in check. If you are anxious, she'll sense it.

When you treat leaving as *not* something special, you're helping her learn to cope with your absences, which is part of life. Below are some things you can do to help make separation a little easier for both of you.

Develop a "Parting" Ritual.   Routines and rituals give baby a sense of security. She may not be happy when you leave, but knowing what's happening can help make things better.

Give Her a Special Toy or Object to Cuddle.   A special object to hold onto when you leave can help comfort her when you're not there. You might want to use a stuffed toy or a favorite blanket.

When It's Time to Leave, Go Quickly. Waiting for baby to stop crying or to calm down might take forever. Give her a quick hug and a kiss, and soothing words, then depart. She's more easily distracted if you're not there.

Give Baby Time to Check Out Anyone New. Ask people to approach quietly and to wait for a while before they interact with her. She needs time to check them out. Be prepared to have baby view you as someone "new" if you make a dramatic change in your appearance, such as cutting your hair or shaving off your beard. When you look drastically different, you're a new person for a few seconds, until she hears your voice and recognizes you!

✂ Chicken Pox
Chicken pox, also called *varicella,* is not common among infants. It's more common in school-age children. However, your baby may be exposed if she's around other children. Chicken pox is highly contagious and usually appears 13 to 17 days after exposure. Symptoms of chicken pox, which occur in the first 24 hours and may last 3 or 4 days, include:
* a slight fever
* fatigue
* loss of appetite
* runny nose
* coughing
* rash on the trunk and face, consisting of small red blisters that can cover ears, eyes, nose, mouth, throat and genitals
* first crop of blisters becomes crusty and begins to dry after 1 or 2 days
* new spots continue to appear for 4 or 5 days
* rash is extremely itchy

What You Can Do at Home. There is no cure for chicken pox, so try to keep baby comfortable. Dress her in loose-fitting clothing to prevent irritation. A cool bath every 3 to 4 hours helps with itching. Add baking soda to bath water to soothe skin. Apply witch hazel, calamine lotion or hydrocortisone cream to reduce itching. Keep her fingernails short and clean. Put mittens on hands to prevent scratching.

    Caution: Do *not* give your baby aspirin! It increases the chance of *Reye's syndrome:* see the discussion in *Week 37.*

When to Call the Doctor. Call the doctor if your baby starts acting very ill, has difficulty breathing or has a high fever that lasts longer than 4 days. Contact your pediatrician if she has difficulty eating or drinking, has redness or tenderness around blisters or if blisters drain pus.

Have your baby vaccinated between 12 and 15 months of age to prevent chicken pox. If you know a child has chicken pox and your baby has not been immunized, keep baby away from the child.

❧ *Hearing Problems*

You spend a lot of time with baby, so you would probably recognize or question hearing problems before your healthcare provider. Notify your pediatrician as soon as you think there might be a hearing problem. If you identify a hearing problem early, the chance of baby having a normal vocabulary is greatly increased. The first 6 months of baby's life are critical to her language development.

Your baby may be at risk for hearing problems if she:

* was born prematurely
* was oxygen-deprived at birth
* has severe ear infections
* has cleft palate, ear deformities or birth defects of the head, neck or spine
* has a family history of hearing loss
* had bacterial meningitis

Observe your baby's development and her interactions with you. Notify your pediatrician if you have any concerns regarding your baby's hearing. New technology uses electrodes and ear probes to detect hearing problems quickly.

Signs your baby may have a hearing problem include:

* doesn't blink or startle at loud sounds
* doesn't turn toward voice when someone speaks to her
* hasn't progressed from cooing to babbling
* doesn't look for the source of a sound
* doesn't recognize her name
* doesn't listen to simple songs or stories

Note: In many hospitals and birthing centers, newborns are tested for hearing problems within a few hours of birth.

Changes in baby's environment may surprise her or make her uneasy. For example, if you rearrange furniture in a room, she will notice. Her depth perception is fairly acute now, and she is able to distinguish near and far objects, so she can easily see these changes.

Toys and Play this 27ᵗʰ Week

Toys to choose for her now include those that cause her to react, such as rattles or squeaky toys. She'll probably love looking in the mirror, so do some activities while she's watching herself, such as combing her hair. Bathtub play is always exciting, especially now. Let her pour water (with your help) from plastic cup to plastic cup. Or pour water into a small colander, and let it run out the bottom. She'll enjoy almost any water activity.

✐ *Identifying Sounds*
Baby loves toys that make noise–rattles, bells, squeaky toys. Part of her enjoyment arises from her interest in tracking sounds. When you hear various sounds in your environment, turn her toward the source of the sound and identify it. A cat's meow, a car's revving engine, a jet flying overhead–all are sources of interesting sounds. After you identify the sound, imitate it and name it again. This helps her understand where sounds come from.

✐ *Encourage Dexterity*
It's important to help your baby practice picking up things that are different shapes and sizes. It helps increase her dexterity. Games you can play to achieve this goal include placing floating toys of various shapes and sizes in the tub or giving her different types of food to play with in her high chair.

Caution: Don't give her small pieces of food that she could choke on. She'll probably put everything in her mouth!

Week 28

Baby's Age as a Monthly Reference—7 months

HOW BIG IS BABY THIS 28ᵀᴴ WEEK?

Baby weighs 16½ pounds and is 26¾ inches long this week.

Baby Care and Equipment

✣ *The Ear-Check Monitor*

When baby rubs his ear and acts cranky, is he teething or does he have an ear infection? Before you rush him to the doctor, you can now check for yourself. One device you may want to check out is the *ear-check monitor* or the *home otoscope*. This device aids you in many ways. It can:

* help determine if baby has an ear infection
* monitor symptoms
* monitor progress after treatment
* allow you to examine eyes, ears, nose, throat and teeth

Using sonar technology, the monitor measures the presence of fluid in the middle ear. It interprets the results in easy-to-understand language. If baby suffers from frequent ear infections, this might be a device you want to add to your medicine cabinet.

Also see the discussions of *Teething* in *Week 27* and *Ear Infections* later in this weekly discussion.

You're adding new foods to baby's diet. It's probably a good idea to feed him solids at *three* meals now, so he doesn't get too much food at one feeding. Below is a suggested feeding schedule for baby.

cereal	breakfast and lunch	at least 2 tablespoons
fruit	breakfast and dinner	1 to 2 tablespoons
vegetables	lunch and dinner	1 to 2 tablespoons

✣ *When Baby Refuses Food*

Don't be surprised or frustrated when baby spits out a new food you offer him. All babies do this at one time or another. It's the newness of the food that causes baby to spit it out. It doesn't taste bad or smell bad.

If baby repeats his actions more than a few times, wait for a while before offering the food again. It may take awhile for him to get used to it.

> When you add new green vegetables to baby's food choices, offer them slowly. Offer only one at a time, every week or so.

✳ *Playpens and Portacribs*

Playpens lost popularity among parents awhile ago when psychologists said putting a child in one was akin to caging him. However, times have changed. Researchers now believe they aren't so bad. Playpens allow a parent a bit of free time to do something, such as shower or get dressed, while keeping baby out of harm's way. Putting baby in a playpen ensures his safety.

Many of these devices now serve two purposes—as a playpen *and* a portacrib (portable crib). A dual-use pen/crib can keep baby safe and can serve as a crib when you're on the go.

Some issues have been raised about safety. The greatest risks to baby are suffocation or strangulation. If a mesh drop side is left down, it may create a pocket that can suffocate a baby. If the drop side is not properly locked, it may collapse and strangle baby. If mesh is too wide, baby could get his head caught in it and strangle.

To ensure safety when choosing a playpen/portacrib, consider the following.

* A model with mesh should have automatically locking top rails.
* Mesh netting openings should be less than ¼ inch wide.
* Slats in a wood model should be no wider than 2⅜ inches apart (the same standard as for baby's crib.)

If you have any questions about a playpen or portacrib you are considering, contact the U.S. Consumer Product Safety Commission; see the *Resources* section, page 527. Ask them about the latest news on safety for playpens and portacribs.

Milestones this 28th Week

✳ *Curiosity and Fear*

Your baby is very curious. His curiosity struggles with his fear. Curiosity motivates him to leave your side to explore, but he returns often for reassurance. Each trip away from you may last a little longer. He may be desolate if you disappear while he's gone. If you're busy in different parts of the house, let him know where you are every few minutes. It makes him feel secure.

✳ *Baby Uses His Hand and Arms*

Baby uses his hands to imitate actions. He may clap when you clap or imitate you when you wipe the counter. He enjoys feeding himself finger foods and likes to drink from a cup. He's becoming more independent in his actions.

He matches the feel of an object with its appearance when he examines it. He is learning how to release something voluntarily to put it where he wants it to go, in a specific place.

He will soon begin creeping forward or backward by pulling himself along with his arms. He may not be using his legs, but as they get stronger, he will. Before he can crawl, baby needs to learn to coordinate digging in with his knees and pushing off with his hands. When he does, he'll really be crawling!

✒ *Baby in the Mirror*

If you show him his image in a mirror, baby will reach out to pat it and smile at himself. He may touch a part of his clothing while he watches the baby in the mirror. He may not realize he's looking at himself; if he doesn't, he'll soon make this discovery.

Note: See also the box *Milestones this 28th Week.*

What's Happening this 28th Week?

✒ *When Baby Wants Only Mom*

You've probably experienced stranger anxiety with baby by now. It's natural, and most parents expect it. However, it can be unsettling when baby wants only mom and rejects dad. (It can also be the other way around.)

Preferring one parent over the other is normal. A baby often turns to one parent for comfort. He may turn to the other parent for play and interaction.

If you are rejected by baby, it's best to back off a bit. Evaluate the situation. What does he need right now? When you determine this, approach him quietly. Speak gently to him. Cuddle him, if he wants it.

If he still wants only the other parent, keep it in perspective. Don't take it personally. Your baby isn't rejecting *you.* He is showing that he gets something different from his other parent. Allow him the freedom to express his preferences. He'll soon be more confident, and this will pass.

✒ *Signs Baby May Have a Vision Problem*

You want your baby to have excellent vision because it's such an important part of his development. Some babies do have problems seeing the world around them. Today, we are fortunate that we often can correct vision problems once they are diagnosed.

How can you determine if baby has problems seeing? Signs he might have a vision problem include the following:

MILESTONES THIS 28ᵀᴴ WEEK

Changes You May See this Week as Baby Develops Physically
* turns over easily

Changes You May See this Week in Baby's Developing Senses and Reflexes
* sips from two-handled cup with assistance

Changes You May See this Week as Baby's Mind Develops
* can concentrate attention
* shows greater interest in details

Changes You May See this Week in Baby's Social Development
* shows humor
* likes to tease
* pats at mirror image

Every baby is an individual, and your baby may do some of these things more quickly or more slowly than another baby. If you are concerned about your baby's progress, discuss it with your healthcare provider. Also see page xiii.

---

* pupils that don't focus
* a white pupil
* a fluttering eye
* when you offer him an object, he gropes for it
* he doesn't seem to notice you
* he tilts his head at an unusual angle to see an object
* one eye strays
* eyes move abnormally

If you notice any of these signs, contact baby's doctor. There are tests your pediatrician can do to determine if baby needs corrective lenses or some other treatment.

⚕ Ear Infections

Most new parents hear stories about babies getting an ear infection. Many wonder if they'll know if *their* baby is suffering from one. There are various types of ear infections. It's important to know about the different types so you'll be aware of the signs and symptoms of each one.

Ear infections are very common in babies and young children—by age 2, nearly 90% of all babies have had an ear infection. The incidence of ear infections decreases after age 3.

A *middle-ear infection,* also called *otitis media,* occurs inside the ear, where nerves and small bones are located, past the eardrum. An *outer-ear infection* occurs on the outside of the ear canal, away from the eardrum. It is also called *otitis externa* or *swimmer's ear.*

Otitis media is the most common ear infection in infants and young children. The problem may also be more common in children with cleft palates and Down syndrome because they have various anatomical differences that make them more susceptible to ear infections.

Middle-ear infections often occur because baby's eustachian tube, which connects the middle ear and throat, is slanted less in children than in adults. This allows mucus and other fluids to move from the throat to the ear when baby has a cold. It also makes it more difficult for fluid to drain from the middle ear.

Infections often occur with a cold or the flu. Symptoms of middle-ear infections and outer-ear infections are similar, except baby usually has a higher fever and more pain (is "sicker") with a middle-ear infection. Symptoms of an ear infection include:

* ear pain
* cold symptoms that worsen
* baby pulls or rubs the ear
* fever
* sleeplessness
* discharge or liquid coming out of the ear (pus)
* difficulty feeding or not eating well
* flulike symptoms
* increase in fussiness
* touching or pulling baby's ear causes him pain

What You Can Do at Home.   Prevention may be the key. You can help prevent ear infections in your baby. Stop smoking; smoking around a baby increases the child's risk of getting an ear infection by 50%. Breastfeeding has been shown to help reduce the incidence of colds and ear infections in babies, so keep breastfeeding.

Don't give your baby a bottle or pacifier when he's lying down. Sucking and swallowing while lying down make it easier for fluid, along with germs in the throat, to reach the middle ear. Consider having your child vaccinated; the pneumococcal vaccine helps reduce the risks for ear infections. Studies show the vaccine can help in many ways.

If you believe your baby has an ear infection, give him ibuprofen or acetaminophen for pain or fever, as directed by your doctor. Apply a warm towel to the ear that hurts to help soothe baby. Use ear drops and other medications, including over-the-counter medications, *only* under the direction of your baby's doctor.

When to Call the Doctor.   Call the doctor if you believe your baby has an ear infection. It's important to take care of it as soon as possible. If you notice any of the following signs, tell the nurse when you call. They are more serious signs that your doctor will want to know about:

* high fever (102F or higher)
* worsening of other symptoms
* swelling of the ear
* muscles of baby's face twitch or jump

Your physician may suggest a variety of treatments, such as ear drops containing both antibiotics and pain medication, oral antibiotics and/or decongestants.

Studies have shown that antibiotics are *not* always necessary. Pediatricians today do not prescribe antibiotics for ear infections the way they did in the past. Many are now waiting for a few days while giving the child pain-relief medication; if the child doesn't get better in that time, then antibiotics are prescribed. Antibiotics only treat ear infections caused by bacteria. Infections caused by a virus will not be cured with antibiotics.

If the problem recurs often, your pediatrician may recommend further measures, such as tubes that are placed in the ears with a minor surgical procedure. Your baby's doctor will discuss the situation with you.

> Your baby will let you know in various ways that he is soothing himself. Watch for the following signs. He may:
> * suck on his fingers or his hands
> * clasp hands together
> * hold onto his foot or feet
> * snuggle against the side of his crib or carrier
> * begin to close his eyes

✱ *Medication Poisoning*

Fortunately, medication poisoning is a rare occurrence. Medications and drugs are not often given to babies. Most often, this type of poisoning results from a mistake by the person giving the medication—the wrong medication or the wrong amount is given. It can also happen as baby becomes more mobile. A curious baby may ingest a medication if he gets his hands on it.

Symptoms of medication poisoning depend on the medication. Some symptoms to be aware of include:

* listlessness
* hyperactivity
* nausea
* vomiting
* diarrhea
* difficulty breathing
* unexplained bleeding or bruising
* rash
* hives
* fever

What You Can Do at Home.   If you believe your baby has ingested any medication, get medical help immediately! This is an emergency. Keep the telephone numbers for the poison-control center and your physician's office by the phone at all times. If you are too distraught to call either of them, call 911.

When to Call the Doctor.   Call the doctor immediately if you believe your baby has been given the wrong medication or the wrong amount of a medication. Call if it appears your baby has had a reaction to a drug. See the discussion in *Week 25* on *Medication Allergies*.

Treatment may include care in an emergency facility. The doctor will ask which medication and how much of it was given to or taken by baby. Bring any bottles or containers with you so they'll know the substance, the dosage and any other information medical personnel need to help them make treatment decisions.

Toys and Play this 28th Week

When choosing books to share, select ones that baby will be interested in. Books with pictures of other babies, animals, a ball or doll, a blanket and crib, or baby in the bathtub are fun to read together. Choose sturdy books made of cardboard, plastic or cloth that he can handle.

ﻌ *Roll the Baby Over!*
If you have a bolster or large ball, help baby develop his leg muscles. Place a toy just out of baby's reach. While holding him, drape baby over the bolster or ball. Encourage him to get the toy. You may be surprised to see how he digs his feet in to push and roll himself forward to get the toy!

✤ *Find the Sound*

A squeaky toy can help baby learn to use sound to locate things he can't see. Show him the squeaky toy, and squeeze it to make some sound. Squeeze it, then hide it under his blan-

> Periodically check baby's toys for damage and loose parts.

ket or a cloth. Squeeze it again. Ask him where the noise came from. If he doesn't find it, help him. Repeat the game, and praise him when he finds the toy.

✤ *Learning to Take Turns*

Baby doesn't play with others yet, but he will as he grows older. Now may be a good time to begin teaching him about taking turns. Give him the end of a piece of cloth, such as a scarf. Hold the other end. Gently pull on your end, then release it. Does baby take a turn pulling on his end? If he doesn't, put your hand over his and show him how to pull.

Week 29

Baby's Age as a Monthly Reference—7 months

HOW BIG IS BABY THIS 29ᵀᴴ WEEK?

Baby weighs 16¾ pounds and is 27 inches long this week.

Baby Care and Equipment

✻ *Some Fruits and Vegetables Baby Might Like*

Most of the fruits and vegetables you offer baby are normal ones you probably think of when you think about baby foods, such as applesauce and pears. Both are great for baby. Applesauce has a great texture, and it's low in citric acid. Pears are easily digested and a good source of potassium.

Research has shown that offering your baby some fruit every day may help protect your child against cancer as an adult. One study found that the younger a child starts eating fruit on a regular basis, the greater the protective benefits are against cancer in later life. The vitamins, minerals, nutrients and antioxidants in fruit help lower the risk of cancer developing in the bowel, lungs and breasts.

These researchers advise feeding a child between 6 and 8 months of age from 2 to 4 tablespoons of fruit every day. Between 8 and 12 months, 4 to 8 tablespoons of fruit a day should be offered. They further suggest offering a variety of fruit for the best protection.

What Fruits and Vegetables Do We Feed Her?   Some foods you may *not* think about giving baby are ones you may eat yourself. As far as fruit goes, offer baby any fruit you like, but be sure it is mashed and/or puréed. Our only advisory is to remove all seeds before you prepare the fruit for baby.

With vegetables, the list seems almost endless. Sweet potatoes and winter squash are often favorites with baby because of their taste, texture and color. They both contain beta-carotene. Thoroughly mash up the cooked food. Don't add butter, sugar, salt or anything else to it. It's better for her to try a food without anything extra added.

A ripe avocado is great. You can feed her a little right out of the skin! Avocados contain lots of vitamins and minerals—A, B_6, E, folic acid, niacin, magnesium, potassium and phosphorous. The texture of an avocado is unique, and the flavor is mild. She may really enjoy it.

Be careful with vegetables that are very acidic, such as tomatoes. Baby may not be ready for them yet. But do offer small pieces of cooled, cooked potato or some mashed potatoes. Don't be surprised if baby decides to use her mashed potatoes to "paint" her food tray!

Never give baby a large amount of any new food. Give her a few tastes, then wait to see if she has any reactions. See the box of food reactions on the following page; the list tells you what to be alert for.

As baby is eating more fruits and vegetables, offer her vegetables before fruit in each meal. It's better for baby to be a little hungry when you feed her vegetables. A baby likes the tastes of sweets, so even if she's eaten some food, she doesn't have to be as hungry to eat her fruit.

✢ *Giving Baby Sweets*
You may wonder about giving baby sweets. Will offering them to her cause her to develop a sweet tooth? Will it affect the foods she chooses or wants to eat? Are sweets empty calories?

It may be hard to avoid giving her *any* sweets. If you don't give them to her, someone else might, such as grandma or a sibling. There will be times that a little sweet food is acceptable, so you might want to allow her a treat. During her first year, don't give her ice cream as a sweet treat. The milk protein is too hard for her to digest.

If you give your baby sweets, you are giving her calories that have little nutritional value. However, it's not a problem if you don't do this too often and don't give her large amounts. A small taste is all she really needs. If you deny her *all* sweets, you could be setting the stage for eating problems in the future. Control what sweets she receives, how much she gets and how often she eats them.

✢ *Don't Give Baby Honey!*
Caution: Do *not* give your baby honey or foods made with honey during her first 2 years! Although honey is a natural substance, there could be a risk of baby getting botulism from it. Baby's digestive system is not ready to handle the botulism spores sometimes found in honey. See the discussion of botulism later in this weekly discussion.

✢ *Iron Sources—Is Supplementation Necessary?*
By this time, your baby needs a more balanced diet. She has nearly depleted the iron supplies she received before birth. Iron deficiency is the most com-

mon nutritional deficiency in the United States, and babies can also suffer from it! It is evidenced as anemia; see the discussion of *Anemia* in *Week 22*.

Between 7 and 12 months of age, baby should receive about 11mg of iron a day. Over 1 year of age, she needs only 7mg. If baby drinks iron-fortified formula, she's getting the iron she needs. If she's breastfeeding, she may need extra iron. Some good food sources of iron include infant cereal, egg yolks, strained beef or chicken, strained carrots and strained pears.

If you are concerned about your baby receiving enough iron, discuss it with your pediatrician at one of baby's well-baby checkups. Your doctor will advise you whether any changes are necessary, such as giving her vitamins with iron.

ℐ *Some Tips for Offering New Foods*

As you begin to expand her diet, baby may not take to a new food immediately. When that happens, try combining a small portion of the new food with one she's been eating. For example, introduce green beans to baby with her sweet potatoes. If she normally eats 3 teaspoons of sweet potatoes, put 2 teaspoons of sweet potatoes in a bowl and add 1 teaspoon of green beans. Mash them all together. The next day, add a little more of the green beans to a little less of the sweet potatoes. Keep doing this until she's eating only the green beans.

This practice allows baby to get used to a new taste gradually. It also makes it easier for you to spot any allergic reactions to a new food.

> Avoid feeding baby the following foods for her first year. They are the most common allergy-causing foods:
> * nuts and nut products, including peanut butter
> * egg whites
> * citrus fruits
> * citrus juices
> * strawberries
> * shellfish
> * chocolate

Milestones this 29th Week

ℐ *She Needs to Explore*

Your baby is probably very busy now. She wants to move, open, bang, chew, touch or empty everything she comes across. To encourage her learning, keep baby's environment safe for her, and allow her to explore. Limit the time she is confined in a playpen or a small area so she has plenty of opportunity to investigate her world.

✲ Sounds and Rhythms

Sounds and rhythms are interesting to baby, and she is picking up words. She may increasingly repeat the sounds of words you speak. She's also becoming aware of the differences in sounds. She is interested in hearing many different sounds. By this time, she has an easier time finding a sound's source.

✲ Stranger Anxiety

Stranger anxiety may be lessening now, or it may be getting worse. A baby this age has a strong attachment to family members. She may be very wary of someone she doesn't recognize.

If she doesn't know someone, let her warm up to the person at her own speed. As she recognizes more people, she will feel less threatened by a strange face.

> It may be hard to believe, but separation anxiety is a sign of a baby's healthy development.

✲ Baby's Accomplishments

Baby is becoming more coordinated. She reaches for and grasps a toy with her fingers, instead of her palm. She may point to something she wants. If you point to an object, she can probably find it.

Being able to sit on her own and shift positions at will allows her greater freedom. She can reach her toys and other objects more easily now. Turning her entire upper body to reach for something gives her access to objects that she wouldn't have been able to reach a short time ago.

Your baby may be trying to stand more often. You can't teach her to stand, but you can help her in her efforts. She needs to make her own mistakes. It's how she learns. Soon she'll find her own way to a standing position. Once she's able to stand comfortably, she'll spend several weeks practicing.

✲ Sleeping Through the Night

Your baby is probably sleeping through the night now on a consistent basis. Cuddling with her, rocking her, reading or singing to her before she goes to bed can help her relax. If she cries excessively when you put her down at night, be firm. Soothe her, then leave her room after a short time. She needs to know bedtime is for going to sleep.

Note: See also the box *Milestones this 29ᵗʰ Week*.

MILESTONES THIS 29ᵀᴴ WEEK

Changes You May See this Week as Baby Develops Physically
* may use rolling over to move around room
* may raise and lower buttocks, while lying on back, to move about

Changes You May See this Week in Baby's Developing Senses and Reflexes
* grasps, manipulates, mouths and bangs on objects

Changes You May See this Week as Baby's Mind Develops
* likes to say "ma, mu, da, di"
* may associate picture of baby with herself and make appropriate sounds

Changes You May See this Week in Baby's Social Development
* wants to be included in social interactions

Every baby is an individual, and your baby may do some of these things more quickly or more slowly than another baby. If you are concerned about your baby's progress, discuss it with your healthcare provider. Also see page xiii.

What's Happening this 29ᵗʰ Week?

✣ Creeping Means Independence

Baby may be getting around more easily now. She may be moving forward on her arms while her tummy and legs drag on the floor. She may scoot backward on her bottom or sideways. Once she begins moving, she's no longer helpless. She can get things she wants now on her own. She's becoming more independent.

Baby is starting to creep and mainly uses her arms.

✣ She's Starting to Recognize Words

Researchers believe a baby begins to recognize words at 7 to 7½ months of age. A study was done with babies of various ages. They listened to a couple of words for a short time, then heard paragraphs that included these words. Babies at 7½ months old listened to the paragraphs longer when they heard the familiar words. Younger babies didn't.

The study also demonstrated babies at 7½ months could tell the difference between like-sounding words. They could differentiate between words that sounded very much alike, such as "cat" and "hat."

✳ *Botulism*

Botulism is a severe form of food poisoning. The toxins that cause botulism are found in the soil and in improperly canned meats and vegetables. In newborns and infants, exposure to botulism most often comes from raw honey and other uncooked foods. Symptoms of botulism include:

* ✳ vomiting
* ✳ diarrhea
* ✳ nausea
* ✳ abdominal pain
* ✳ dizziness
* ✳ problems sucking, swallowing or eating
* ✳ dry mouth
* ✳ weakness
* ✳ lethargy
* ✳ weak cry
* ✳ constipation (in infants)

What You Can Do at Home.   If you believe your baby has botulism, identify others who are sick. Determine if they ate the same foods or were exposed in some other way. You may also want to find out if anyone fed baby honey or any foods containing honey.

When to Call the Doctor.   Call the doctor immediately or go to the emergency room if you believe your baby has botulism. You will be directed by your baby's doctor or an emergency-medicine physician as to treatment. It can include botulism antitoxin, which is given by injection. Bed rest and fluids may be prescribed. Baby may also be admitted to the hospital for I.V. therapy.

✳ *Vitamin and Mineral Supplementation*

Some babies need additional vitamins and/or minerals in their diet. Your pediatrician may advise you to give your baby vitamins. However, this is a decision for your doctor to make. Do *not* give your baby any supplements without discussing it first with your baby's doctor.

If you bottlefeed, many formulas contain the necessary amounts of various substances that your baby needs. Ask your doctor about adding vitamins or minerals to baby's daily routine at a well-baby checkup.

If you breastfeed, your baby may need supplementation. Your doctor will advise you. Most doctors suggest you continue taking your prenatal vitamins. Don't take extra vitamins, minerals or herbs unless your doctor tells you to do so. If you have specific concerns or questions, check with your baby's doctor.

✴ When You Leave Baby for Any Length of Time

Are you going to be going out of town with your partner and leaving baby in someone else's care for a short time? It might be a business trip you're taking together or a short vacation for just the two of you.

If you leave baby in the care of someone else, even for only a day or two, be sure you leave a *notarized* medical permission slip. With this form, a care giver can get medical treatment for baby, if it is needed.

No one expects to have to use a form such as this one. But by thinking ahead, you are protecting baby in case something happens and she needs to be treated by your pediatrician or needs treatment in an emergency facility.

s It might be a good idea to give one of these forms to the person who cares for baby, if you and your partner work very far from where baby is cared for. It could be very helpful in an emergency situation. See a sample of a permission slip in the box below.

PERMISSION SLIP

You may want to copy and use the sample permission form shown below for your little one. Be sure to have each copy notarized separately if you are giving permission to more than one person.

To Whom It May Concern:

I, (parent's name), as the mother (or father) of (baby's name), give my permission for her/his (add relation to baby, such as care giver or grandparent, and name of person), to seek any type of medical or dental treatment, as needed, while I am out of town or unavailable.

I agree to be financially responsible for all medical and/or dental costs incurred for her/his treatment.

Date _____ Parent's name _____

Toys and Play this 29ᵗʰ Week

✎ *Music Is Fun*

Baby loves music, so let her enjoy it! Record or buy different kinds of music, and play it for her. Let her listen to marches, rock and roll, lullabies, symphonies, children's songs and anything else you think she might enjoy. Play soft tunes before naptime, an upbeat march before you go out for a walk or children's songs while she's playing. Expose her to many types of music.

✎ *Games Help in Many Ways*

Play peek-a-boo and other hide-and-seek games with baby. Playing together helps her realize the pleasures of sharing a game. This interaction will help her in the future when she begins playing with other children.

Playing games also helps her begin to understand how to evaluate another person's mood. She will learn to sense when someone is interested in playing with her.

✎ *Water Play as a Teaching Tool*

Water play in the tub is fun. Find a plastic squeeze bottle or a plastic jar. Fill it with water and a little baby shampoo that won't sting eyes.

When she's in the tub, tip the bottle or jar over. Let her see how the water moves inside it. Describe how the water is sloshing. Let her see you shake it up, then together watch the bubbles inside.

If the bottle has a squeeze tip, pour some of the bubbles into and over her hands. Show her how to squeeze some of the water out of the bottle, then let her do it herself.

> When you choose toys for baby, be sure they aren't made of brittle plastic and don't have sharp edges. Avoid toys that have parts that could pinch or nip baby's fingers.

Week 30

Baby's Age as a Monthly Reference—7 months

HOW BIG IS BABY THIS 30TH WEEK?
Baby weighs 17 pounds and is 27¼ inches long this week.

Baby Care and Equipment

✻ *Forbidden Foods*

As baby becomes more proficient at eating, you'll be considering different foods to add to his diet. Once he can eat more than puréed food, you may mistakenly believe he can eat anything. He can't.

Below is a list of different foods that might be too difficult for baby to eat at this time. Be cautious with these foods until your baby has a full set of teeth and you feel certain he won't choke. It may be a good idea *not* to offer baby any of these foods until he is much older.

* Raw foods that snap into small, hard pieces. These include celery, carrots, green peppers, hard apples, hard pears, jicama.
* Hot dogs, sausages or bratwurst. Slicing this type of meat doesn't make it safer. If you want to offer your baby these foods, remove all the skin from the meat. Cut each piece into lengthwise quarters, then slice each quarter into ¼-inch segments.
* Chunks of meat.
* Peanut butter of any sort. See the discussion in *Week 37.*
* Fruit with seeds and pits. Core then remove pits and seeds. Mash the fruit before feeding baby.
* Fruit that has thick skin, such as plums. Skin, remove pits and seeds, then mash fruit before feeding baby.
* Seeds, even small ones, such as sunflower seeds.
* Olives, cherries or grapes, unless they have been cut into *very* small pieces.
* Any food that is smooth and round that baby could easily choke on.
* Meat bones or chicken bones.
* Any food that might contain bones, such as fish.

A word of advice: Teach your baby to say "aaah." If you find baby has something in his mouth that you want to see and/or remove, you can do it quickly when he says "aaah."

❧ *Check Your Stroller*

By this time, your baby's stroller may have gotten a lot of use. It's a good idea to check it on a regular basis to make sure there are no loose or broken parts. Be sure safety features work properly, such as brakes.

Check to see if anything has come loose that baby could pull off and put in his mouth. Examine wheels, straps and other parts to ensure each is in proper working condition. Look for any sharp edges that could poke or scratch him.

Clean the stroller if it needs it. Wash the parts that are washable, and wipe off others. If it has a fabric cover that has gotten dirty, wash it in the washing machine.

> Foods you might not consider dangerous are hard chunks of uncooked vegetables. Don't offer your baby these foods, or any others that present choking hazards, until he has a full set of teeth.

Milestones this 30ᵗʰ Week

Your baby is becoming quite accomplished. He may be able to do many things for himself, including standing with support, transferring an object from hand to hand, pushing up on his hands and knees, rolling around to get where he wants to go and sipping from a cup with a little help.

❧ *Standing and Sitting*

Your baby probably sits well without support for a fairly long time. He may even be able to get into a sitting position on his own, but he may not have mastered this task yet. As his leg muscles strengthen, he uses them to try to stand. But he needs more than just strong muscles. To stand by himself, he needs coordination, balance *and* strength, in addition to some planning.

❧ *Attracting Your Attention*

He knows he can attract your attention by "talking" to you or crying. He's also learning the meaning of "no" by the tone of your voice and your reactions. He may react to you by looking startled or crying or changing his facial expressions when you tell him "no." He may be reluctant to stop an activity because he's intrigued by what he's doing.

❧ *Helping Him Overcome Fear of Strangers*

Fear of strangers can be lessened somewhat if you communicate trust in someone who is a stranger to baby. Even if he allows himself to be held by someone he doesn't know, he doesn't want you far away. He probably won't make eye contact with people he doesn't know.

✣ *Sense of Permanence*

His sense of object permanence is increasing. If he drops something, he searches the floor for it. If you hide a favorite toy under his blanket, he is beginning to understand it is still there.

✣ *His Language Development*

It's amazing to note that by this time, your baby has stopped making sounds he does not hear on a daily basis. He doesn't practice what he doesn't hear! The syllables he does make imitate the language he hears around him every day. If your baby is exposed to more than one language, you may hear him practicing sounds of the various languages he is exposed to regularly.

✣ *His Hand Use Increases*

Holding two objects—one in each hand—at the same time is an accomplishment for baby. He holds objects between his fingers and his thumb. He also uses both hands for one task. It's not unusual for him to study his hands as they manipulate a toy or other object.

✣ *Sleep Needs*

His napping may have dwindled to one nap a day by this time. If he's very active, he may sleep more, or he may sleep longer during times he is "practicing" some new task.

Note: See also the box *Milestones this 30th Week.*

What's Happening this 30th Week?

✣ *When Baby Spends More Time Playing with His Food*

Your baby may spend more time playing with his food than he does eating it. You may want him to stop this and attend to the task of eating. However, as messy as he may be at this time, let him continue. Playing with his food helps baby become aware of the various textures of different foods. It's his way of exploring and learning.

Let him experiment with the various foods he's eating. You don't have to let him become destructive, but a little testing won't do any harm. He'll find his mouth when he gets hungry.

> For safety reasons, it's not a good idea to let baby walk around while he's eating. He may not concentrate on eating his food and could choke or gag on something.

MILESTONES THIS 30ᵀᴴ WEEK

Changes You May See this Week as Baby Develops Physically
* pushes up on hands and knees; rocks back and forth

Changes You May See this Week in Baby's Developing Senses and Reflexes
* holds two objects at same time, one in each hand
* uses fingers to grasp objects

Changes You May See this Week as Baby's Mind Develops
* understands that objects don't disappear when hidden
* imitates sounds and series of sounds

Changes You May See this Week in Baby's Social Development
* is learning meaning of "No" by tone of voice used

Every baby is an individual, and your baby may do some of these things more quickly or more slowly than another baby. If you are concerned about your baby's progress, discuss it with your healthcare provider. Also see page xiii.

When to Worry

By this time in baby's development, if your baby exhibits some of the signs listed below, he may have some sort of developmental or medical problem. Remember, a lag of up to 10 weeks is usually OK, but after that time, you may want to call your pediatrician's office and discuss it with one of the nurses. He or she will advise you whether the doctor will want to see your baby.

When interacting with and observing your child, be alert for the following.
* He has limited control of his neck.
* He doesn't roll over in either direction.
* His muscles seem uncommonly soft and slack or unusually tight.
* He can't bear any weight on his legs.

Amebic Dysentery

Amebic dysentery, also called *amebiasis* or *entamebiasis*, is a parasitic infection of the large bowel or colon. It is spread when food is contaminated with human feces. It occurs most commonly when food handlers don't wash their hands after using the bathroom. Flies and insects can also contaminate foods. Some raw fruits and vegetables fertilized with human feces or washed in polluted water may be contaminated.

The problem can occur at any age. Symptoms of amebic dysentery include:

* diarrhea
* bloating of the abdomen
* nausea
* vomiting
* fever
* foul-smelling stools
* gas
* cramping and pain in the abdomen
* blood or mucus in the stool
* irritability

What You Can Do at Home.   Avoid the problem by washing hands thoroughly after using the bathroom. Wash raw fruits and vegetables well before preparing or serving. Cover food to keep flies and other insects from contaminating it. Kitchen counters should be cleaned with soap and water, bleach or some disinfecting agent. Take care in preparing and storing food.

When to Call the Doctor.   Call the doctor if your baby has symptoms of amebic dysentery. It becomes more serious if baby experiences an increase in diarrhea, blood in his stools or pain becomes severe.

Occasionally, antibiotics are prescribed. Rest and fluid replacement are also good measures. If your baby gets amebic dysentery, use extra care in the future with food preparation and storage. Practice good hand washing. When you can't wash your hands with soap and water, consider using waterless antibacterial gel cleaner.

☙ *Influenza*

Nearly every winter there seems to be an influenza or flu breakout. Influenza is an acute, contagious respiratory infection caused by a virus; it usually lasts from 3 to 10 days. Flu can occur at any age, but it is unusual in infants. Symptoms of an attack of influenza include:

* fever
* cough
* sore throat
* runny nose
* listlessness
* disinterest in eating
* vomiting
* diarrhea
* chills

* headache
* aches and pains

It may be difficult to distinguish the difference between a cold and the flu in a baby. Symptoms of the two are similar, and babies are not often affected the same way as adults when they have the flu. A baby may become fussier and more irritable. His fever may stay higher for a longer period of time.

What You Can Do at Home.   If the flu strikes your family, use a cool-mist humidifier in baby's room. See the discussion in *Week 13* of *Humidifiers*. Increase baby's fluid intake. Do *not* give your baby any medication unless instructed to do so by baby's doctor. Be sure everyone practices good hand washing to help prevent the spread of germs.

When to Call the Doctor.   Call the doctor if your baby develops neck pain or neck stiffness, has diarrhea for more than 36 hours or his fever increases in spite of treatment. Contact your physician immediately if any blood comes from his mouth, new symptoms appear, such as ear discharge or pain, or he has any difficulty breathing. For minor symptoms, ibuprofen or acetaminophen, decongestants and cough medications may be suggested. If baby has additional problems or if symptoms become more serious, your pediatrician may recommend hospitalization.

You may also want to ask baby's doctor about a flu shot for baby. Immunization with the flu vaccine may be recommended.

✲ Fecal Impaction
When a baby suffers from fecal impaction, he has a large amount of stool or feces he cannot pass. His intestines are overloaded. It's a form of constipation and can be very uncomfortable. The problem can occur at any age. Symptoms of fecal impaction include:
* no bowel movements
* hard mass in the lower left abdomen
* abdominal discomfort
* irritability
* poor feeding

What You Can Do at Home.   If you believe your baby is suffering from fecal impaction, increase the amount of fluid you offer him to avoid dehydration.

When to Call the Doctor.   Contact your pediatrician. He or she may want you to bring baby into the office. You may be advised to give the baby an enema to deal with the constipation.

HOUSE-PLANT AWARENESS

Some common house plants could poison baby if he eats the leaves or other parts of the plant. If baby ingests any part of the following plants, call the poison control center:

- caladium
- castor bean seeds
- daffodil bulbs
- dieffenbachia
- elephant's ear
- holly berries
- hyacinth bulbs

- Jerusalem berries
- mistletoe berries
- narcissus bulbs
- poinsettia leaves
- rosary pea seeds
- some varieties of philodendron

Toys and Play this 30th Week

Kitchen Exploration

One of your baby's favorite play areas may be your kitchen. There are a lot of fascinating drawers and cupboards he may want to explore. He may also want to empty them.

You've probably babyproofed your home and locked the kitchen cabinets. If you have room in your kitchen, leave one lower cabinet or drawer unlocked, and put some unbreakable kitchen things in it. Let him play with measuring spoons, measuring cups, plastic containers, an old pan and some wood spoons when you're in the kitchen with him. Add anything else you think is safe and fun to experiment with.

Which Toy?

To help baby learn to release one toy to get another, play this game with him. When he is sitting on the floor and holding a toy in each hand, put another toy in front of him. Call his attention to the third toy. Ask him, "Which toy do you want?" He will probably reach for the third toy with the other toy still in his hands. Show him how to release or put down one toy so he can take the third one. He will soon learn how to drop one to pick up the other.

Clap, Clap, Clap

Baby learns by imitation. This game teaches him how to imitate gestures. As you sing a song, clasp his hands together in time to the rhythm. After doing this a few times, clap your hands as he watches you. Or put his hands on yours as you clap. Next, tell him to clap as you sing. Learning to clap on his own can take some time, so be patient. He'll soon get the hang of it.

Week 31

Baby's Age as a Monthly Reference—
end of 7 months or beginning of 8 months

HOW BIG IS BABY THIS 31ST WEEK?
Baby weighs 17½ pounds and is 27½ inches long this week.

Baby Care and Equipment

✢ *Are Baby's Gums Sore?*

Your baby may soon be cutting new teeth. When she does, it could interfere with her sleep. She may even start waking up again during the night. The cause—sore gums.

Baby may also run a low-grade fever and experience mild diarrhea. Experts believe the slight fever may be caused by gum inflammation. Swallowing excess saliva may contribute to the diarrhea. Ask your pediatrician about giving baby acetaminophen or ibuprofen to help relieve gum soreness and any fever.

Offer her a pacifier when she's cutting teeth. It may help soothe her sore gums to suck on the pacifier.

✢ *Some Safety Guidelines*

You've already begun babyproofing your home, as described in previous chapters. By now, baby has a safe environment to play in. Some safety guidelines can help protect family even more. Use all that apply to your home situation.

* Always use a mat in the tub when you bathe baby.
* Turn down your water heater so the water temperature is no higher than 120F. If temperature is set at 160F, it can cause third-degree burns in *one second!* A temperature of 120F allows you 2 to 3 seconds to respond before it causes burns.
* Put your baby in fire-resistant nightwear. Check labels to be sure clothing meets safety standards.
* Store your iron in a safe place, out of baby's reach. It's heavy and can cause injury if baby pulls it down on herself.
* Keep all plastic bags out of baby's reach.

* Use a harness or belt to secure baby in her stroller or high chair.
* Don't give baby balloons as toys; she might choke on them.
* Begin teaching baby *now* not to touch matches, safety pins, ashtrays, cigarettes or cigars, the garbage, dog or cat food, or an animal's water bowl.

> Don't be surprised if baby becomes frustrated as she tries to stand and to crawl. She's very determined!

✧ Feeding Tips

By this time, baby may be eating solids fairly well. She is becoming more adept at eating many different types of food. Below are some tips to keep in mind when feeding baby.

* When you open a jar of baby food, take out only what you need for that meal. Refrigerate the rest for up to 2 days.
* If baby has any food left in her bowl, throw it out when she's finished.
* Don't add any sweeteners to baby's food, especially honey!
* When you warm her food, check it before you serve it to her. Stir and taste before serving.
* Offer fruit juice in a cup. If you put it in a bottle, it may stay in contact with her teeth for a longer period, which could cause cavities.
* Even if you've already fed her, make baby a part of the family at mealtimes. It's good for her to be exposed to the interactions of family members during this time.

Milestones this 31ˢᵗ Week

✧ Her Grasp Is Improving

Baby has learned to use her thumb as an "opposable digit" and can grasp objects between her thumb and fingers. This accomplishment helps develop her "pincer grasp."

Because of this achievement, she can hold an object for a longer period now to examine it more closely. She can also pass it back and forth quite smoothly from hand to hand. She may shake a toy or bang it on the floor. You may see her firmly grasp an object in each hand and bang them together.

Her refined pincer grasp will soon allow baby to pick up very small objects, such as cr,umbs and pieces of lint. Be alert for small items she could pick up and put in her mouth.

> At this time, baby prefers reaching for objects that are about 8 inches away.

She has much greater control over her reach/grasp/release ability. This permits her to concentrate more on the item she holds. She doesn't have to think about what her hands are doing.

✻ *She's Very Interested in People*
Baby is still very interested in people. She likes to watch you closely and to imitate you. She may try to imitate the sounds you make. She likes to make a series of sounds and may utter many sounds in one breath.

✻ *Baby May Be Developing Her Own Patterns*
Eating and sleeping patterns are different for different babies. One baby may sleep well. Another may wake several times throughout the night. A baby may refuse to feed herself or rejects your efforts to feed her. If she's teething, she may have *no* interest in eating.

✻ *She's Moving a Lot*
Baby's been working on her crawling techniques. She may be fairly adept at getting around now. When she crawls around the house, it helps your baby in more ways than just getting from one place to another. She is learning to judge distances, and she is developing her memory skills so she can get back to where she came from.

Your baby may follow you around the house. Be cautious when opening and closing doors and cabinets. Babies love to put little fingers in the crack of an open door.

When she becomes more stable standing up, baby may lean against some form of support. This frees her hands to do other things. Once up, she may be unable to get down, which can frustrate her greatly. It will probably be awhile before she can get back down on the floor on her own (without falling over!). She'll need your help until she masters this task.

> Baby's mobility may cause her world to seem unstable. She is learning to separate from you; sometimes this upsets her. Be understanding when she gets upset.

✻ *Is There Sibling Rivalry at Your House?*
If you have any other children, you may see evidence of sibling rivalry. The novelty of having a new baby brother or sister has worn off by now. Don't be surprised by this occurrence. It's natural. Help the older sibling adjust by making time for him or her and focusing on their activities.

Note: See also the box *Milestones this 31ˢᵗ Week.*

MILESTONES THIS 31ST WEEK

Changes You May See this Week as Baby Develops Physically
* may crawl (with abdomen off floor) rather than creep

Changes You May See this Week in Baby's Developing Senses and Reflexes
* may bang objects together
* transfers objects from hand to hand
* feeds herself crackers or small pieces of food
* tastes everything

Changes You May See this Week as Baby's Mind Develops
* vocalizes several sounds in one breath
* begins to learn implication of own actions

Changes You May See this Week in Baby's Social Development
* resists doing something undesirable
* is attached to parents
* may still be wary of strangers

Every baby is an individual, and your baby may do some of these things more quickly or more slowly than another baby. If you are concerned about your baby's progress, discuss it with your healthcare provider. Also see page xiii.

What's Happening this 31st Week?

How Baby Responds When You Return

Baby may still be upset and anxious when you part. Some experts believe that the way your baby reacts when you are reunited is a better indication of her attachment to you than her reaction when you leave. If she's happy when you return, she is reconnecting with you in a healthy way.

However, if she's angry with you for 10 minutes or longer when you return, or she ignores you for more than 10 minutes, take note. You may need to spend more time with her to establish a healthy bond.

Babies Can Experience Stress

Just like an adult, a baby can experience stress. What things cause stress to your baby? A change in her routine, separation anxiety, teething, developmental advances—all can contribute to an increase in her stress levels. And when your baby is under stress, it may change her sleep habits.

Studies have shown that when a baby experiences stress, she may sleep shorter or longer periods. She may sleep more deeply or sleep very lightly. Baby's sleep system responds to her environment.

If you find your baby is not sleeping well, look for something that might be causing her stress. Eliminating or alleviating a stressful situation for baby could make for peaceful sleep for the entire family.

✶ Before Baby Starts to Crawl

You may notice baby is rocking back and forth on her hands and knees but not moving anywhere. This is normal. She may spend a few weeks rocking back and forth while she tries to figure out how to move herself forward.

Babies at this age often have well-developed arms, but their legs are not as strong. When she starts to move, she may push herself backward because her arms are stronger.

Your baby may spend a few weeks rocking on her hands and knees before she actually begins to crawl.

You can encourage her to move forward by placing one of her favorite toys a few feet in front of her. If she wants to reach it, she may crawl forward in an effort to get it. Or sit in front of her, and call her name. Your excitement at her achievement makes her want to try harder.

✶ Food Allergies

A food allergy is hypersensitivity to a particular food. About eight foods cause up to 90% of all food reactions. The most common foods that cause allergic reactions include peanuts, tree nuts (walnuts, pecans, cashews, almonds), fish, shellfish, eggs, cow's milk, soy and wheat. Other offending foods include some fruits, tomatoes and some legumes (peanuts are legumes).

Peanut allergy may be very severe in some children. Avoiding peanuts during pregnancy and breastfeeding is recommended by the AAP. One study showed that mothers who ate peanuts more than once a week were more likely to have a child who was peanut sensitized than mothers who did not eat peanuts as often. We believe a peanut allergy occurs because a baby is exposed to peanuts before his immature immune system can properly handle them. See the discussion of *Peanut Allergy* in *Week 37.*

Although a food allergy can occur at any time, the chance of your baby having one is relatively low—only about 6%. Call your pediatrician if you believe baby has a food allergy.

Allergic reactions to foods can cause hives, vomiting, abdominal pain, diarrhea and eczema. (See the complete list of symptoms below.) A milk allergy may result in blood in baby's stool. In some cases, respiratory symptoms are also present with a food allergy, ranging from a stuffy nose to anaphylactic shock.

> **Be aware**: If your baby is allergic to eggs, be sure any doctor who treats her is aware of it. Certain vaccines are egg-based. Your baby will need to avoid them or to take precautions with these vaccines.

Food allergy can occur at any age but usually does not occur until a child begins eating solid foods or when he begins drinking cow's milk. Occasionally a baby is allergic to formula made of cow's milk and must be put on a different type of formula.

As you add new foods to your baby's diet, make note of each food you offer her. If she has any reactions, you'll have a better idea of what may be causing it. Different allergies may cause different kinds of symptoms.

It's important to recognize the signs and symptoms of a food allergy. Symptoms of a food allergy include the following:
* bloating and gassiness
* nausea
* vomiting
* itching
* hives
* abdominal pain
* skin rash
* crying or fussing
* fatigue
* eczema
* feeding problems
* congested nose or a runny nose, with a thin, clear discharge
* sandpaperlike red rash on the face
* watery, itchy eyes
* upset stomach
* diarrhea or mucus in the stools
* red rash around the anus
* fussiness

What You Can Do at Home.   First of all, breastfeed your baby. This helps reduce the risk of her developing food allergies. Nurse baby for at least 6 months if there is a history of food allergies in the family. Feeding for this length of time helps some babies avoid the problem. Many children eventually outgrow food allergies.

Research has found that if a mother breastfeeds her baby, *her* diet is important. If she eats a diet higher in carbohydrates and lower in total and saturated fats, baby has a lower chance of developing allergies by age 1.

Be aware of allergy signs; know what to look for. (See the list above.) Follow your pediatrician's instructions for adding new foods to your baby's diet. If you or your partner has a food allergy, discuss the situation with your baby's doctor. It might affect the types of food you feed her.

In a notebook or journal, write down every new food you give baby and the amount you give her. Introduce new foods one at a time. Wait to see if she has any reactions before you offer her another new food. Start with rice products when beginning solids. They cause fewer allergy problems than wheat products.

If your baby displays any symptoms of a food allergy, try to identify the problem food. Eliminate foods you can identify that might be causing the problem. Don't give the food to her again without first discussing it with your pediatrician. Increase the amount of fluid you give her. Decrease solid food until she feels better.

First foods that most often cause allergies include egg whites, cow's milk and some citrus fruits and juices. Wait until baby is at least 9 months old before you offer her any citrus juice. Don't give her any peanut products before age 3.

If baby has a skin rash, bathe her with a mild, nondrying soap. Use a lubricating cream to decrease redness or itching. Avoid frequent bathing.

Treatment for a food allergy is avoidance of the food. However, it may be difficult to identify the food causing the problems. In this case, allergy testing can be done.

When to Call the Doctor.   Call the doctor if any reaction is severe. Call immediately if your baby develops any breathing difficulties! Contact your pediatrician if a rash looks infected or if the treatment you have tried is not working.

✈ *Ear-Wax Blockage*

Does your baby have ear wax? It's common in everyone, so don't be surprised if baby has it. Wax is made by the ear to protect the canal that leads from the eardrum to outside the ear. However, sometimes too much ear wax can cause a blockage. Symptoms that your baby has ear-wax blockage include:

* the ear wax itself
* ear pain

* pulling, rubbing or tugging on the ear
* decrease in hearing

What You Can Do at Home.   Clean *only* the outside of the ear. It may be very tempting to clean the ear canal with a cotton swab, but don't do it! It's dangerous and unnecessary to put anything in your baby's ear. You could actually make things worse.

Sometimes ear drops are used to soften wax. There are also soft rubber ear bulbs that can be used with warm water for irrigation. However, do this only when directed to do so by your baby's doctor.

You can usually take care of ear wax by letting it take care of itself. Just let it move out of baby's ear. Clean it up when it reaches the outside of the ear.

When to Call the Doctor.   Call the doctor if you notice your baby has symptoms of ear-wax blockage or has a fever and/or ear pain. Treatments for the problem include ear drops or irrigation of the ear canal and ibuprofen or acetaminophen for fever or pain. Your doctor will advise you what to do. Don't do *any* of these things unless directed to by a doctor.

Folliculitis

Folliculitis is a contagious bacterial or fungal infection of the hair follicles. It can affect any part of the body but most often affects the arms, legs and face. It can occur at any age. Symptoms of the *bacterial folliculitis* include:

* a few or many pimples or pustules on the skin, surrounded by red rings
* pustules may contain white or yellow fluid
* pustules may be tinged with blood
* pimple may be adjacent to hair follicle or have a hair growing through it

Symptoms of *fungal folliculitis* include:

* patches or flat areas, with clearly defined borders
* patches or flat areas have white blisters
* blisters often appear in clusters

What You Can Do at Home.   If you believe your baby has any type of folliculitis, keep her skin clean and dry. Don't scratch or pinch pustules. If necessary, cover baby's hands with mittens so she can't scratch herself.

When to Call the Doctor.   Call the doctor if baby develops a fever. If pustules spread after treatment or if pustules come back after treatment, contact your pediatrician. Treatment for the problem includes warm-water soaks, antibiotic gels or antibiotics. Antifungal drugs may be prescribed.

Toys and Play this 31ˢᵗ Week

✴ *Bang the Lids Together*

You can help baby develop the coordination she needs to bang two objects together. Take two pot lids or two spoons, and tap them gently together. Let baby watch you while you entertain her. Then hand the objects to her. Move her hands together while she's holding them to show her how it's done. She'll be delighted when she makes the same noises!

✴ *The Dumping-and-Filling Game*

Dumping things out of a container is fun for baby. Let baby play with a plastic bucket or other container filled with smaller toys that fit inside it. Fill it up, then let her dump the objects out. Keep filling the container as long as she is interested.

✴ *The Bye-Bye Game*

Separation anxiety, and the way baby displays it, can be difficult on everyone. Help her realize you always return by playing this game. Even when leaving for a short time, such as going out of the room to get the laundry, say "bye-bye." Tell her you'll be right back. Return in a few minutes. She will learn you haven't gone for good. Gradually lengthen the time you are gone, but while you're playing this game, don't be out of sight for too long.

Week 32

Baby's Age as a Monthly Reference—8 months

HOW BIG IS BABY THIS 32ND WEEK?
Baby weighs 18 pounds and is 27½ inches long this week.

Baby Care and Equipment

✎ *Preventing E. coli*

E. coli is a bacteria that is present in the alimentary canal (the digestive tube from the mouth to the anus) of humans and other animals. E. coli is responsible for infections, such as urinary-tract infections, stomachaches and diarrhea.

How can your baby be exposed to E. coli? There are various ways to expose him, including the foods you feed him and your own habits. If you take your baby into a swimming pool that is used by a lot of kids, you also risk exposure. Some kids urinate in the pool. Others swim with dirty diapers. When they do, microorganisms can wash into the water. Chlorine may not kill all these organisms, so if baby drinks the water, he can be exposed.

Food Preparation Tips. Take the following steps to protect baby from E. coli when you are preparing and serving foods.

* Wash your hands, cutting boards, utensils and any other items that come in contact with raw meat or raw poultry. Use hot water and soap.
* If you prepare beef, cook it until it is well done or at least 160F internally.
* Beverages should be pasteurized, if necessary.
* If you prepare chicken, cook it until the internal temperature reaches 180F.
* Never place cooked meat on a plate that was used for raw meat unless it has been thoroughly washed with soap and water.
* Wash all fruits and vegetables before serving raw. Manure on the outside peel could cause contamination.

When You Go Swimming.   There are some steps you can take to protect your baby when you go swimming. Follow these measures.

* If a child has diarrhea, don't let him swim in your pool. Even if his diapers are clean, germs on his skin can taint the water.
* Check your baby frequently when he's in the pool. Change him immediately when his diaper is dirty. Diapers made for swimming help somewhat, but they're not perfect.
* If a child isn't toilet trained, don't let him in the pool without a diaper.
* Change diapers in the changing room, not at poolside, to keep the area free of germs.
* Clean baby's bottom well with diaper wipes or soap and water after a bowel movement, before he goes back into the pool.

✴ When Baby Refuses Food

Around this time, your baby may begin refusing to eat baby food because he wants to feed himself. His developing pincer grasp, see *Week 31,* allows him to pick up food with his thumb and forefinger. Feeding himself foods he can pick up becomes enjoyable.

Keep in mind that eating solids during this time is not for the nutritional value of the food. Baby eats solids to help him learn to swallow different textures. He also eats solids to allow him to experiment with moving foods around in his mouth. He can't use utensils yet—he's just not coordinated enough. So eating food with his fingers is easier and a lot more fun.

If baby decides he doesn't want you to feed him or he wants to eat only what he can put in his mouth, consider some of the following foods. They allow him to feed himself, and they're not too messy. Foods that are easy for him to eat include:

* small bits of meat, such as ground meat (cook thoroughly!)
* pieces of well-cooked macaroni or spaghetti
* baby bite-size chunks of soft foods, such as mashed yams or mashed bananas

Be sure the foods you feed your baby do not cause him to choke. At this time, he may not realize how much he can put in his mouth. It's easy for him to put too much into his mouth and choke or gag himself.

✴ Organic Baby Foods

Some baby-food manufacturers offer foods that are grown without synthetic pesticides or fertilizers. Their baby food is organically produced. Baby-food producers do this because some consumers are interested in feeding baby naturally grown foods. Read the labels on the baby foods you choose, if this is important to you.

୪ *Car Safety*

One car hazard that exists even before you turn on the engine is catching small hands in car doors. It's easy to pinch baby's fingers when a door is mistakenly closed on them. Before you close your car doors, check to be sure baby's hands are out of the way.

Milestones this 32ⁿᵈ Week

୪ *Baby Has Accomplished Many Things*

By this time, your baby is quite accomplished. He can sit without support when his legs are out in front of him. His neck, hip and back muscles are getting stronger and more coordinated.

As he begins crawling, his activity level increases dramatically. He no longer just has to "sit there." He can go to whatever attracts his attention. He'll move from one toy or one activity to another quite quickly.

> When baby starts to crawl, his hands do most of the work pulling him forward.

You may see him practicing knee bends while he holds onto something for support. This will soon progress to squatting to pick up an object with one hand while he supports himself with the other.

୪ *Baby's Independence Can Also Mean Dependence*

Your baby will feel great being able to get around on his own. He is becoming increasingly independent and will have longer play periods alone. But as he moves away from you physically, he may feel the need for your love and security even more. Having you in sight is still very important.

୪ *Sleep Problems May Arise*

You may notice your baby is having trouble sleeping at night. One reason for this is that he may be waking up to practice standing and crawling in his crib. When he wakes up and needs soothing, offer him reassurance, then tell him it's time to go to sleep. This phase shouldn't last too long.

୪ *Help Baby Learn to Sit Down Safely*

Because baby is practicing standing, you may be able to show him how to sit down safely. Make it a game so it's fun. Show him how to bend forward from the waist as he begins to sit down. In this way, he'll land on his fanny, not his back or front!

୪ *Hand Usage*

Baby still uses either hand indiscriminately. Sometimes he'll use his right hand to pick up something then he'll use his left hand. He isn't making the right-hand or left-hand distinction yet.

✐ Sounds Are Important to Baby

Baby still responds mainly to a speaker's tone of voice. He doesn't fully understand the meaning of the words, but he's learning!

He may have developed favorites in the music and songs you play for him. When a favorite is played, he may giggle and coo. It's fun when he starts rocking-dancing to the tunes.

When you speak to your baby, watch him closely. Is he watching *you* closely? Often by this age, baby will study the movements of your mouth and jaw. If you repeat a string of syllables he vocalizes, he may try to imitate mouth and jaw movements.

Note: See also the box *Milestones this 32nd Week*.

MILESTONES THIS 32ND WEEK

Changes You May See this Week as Baby Develops Physically
* crawls forward or backward

Changes You May See this Week in Baby's Developing Senses and Reflexes
* claps and waves hands
* can hold and manipulate one object while watching another

Changes You May See this Week as Baby's Mind Develops
* may say "mama" or "dada" as names
* enjoys games, such as "so big" or "catch me"
* looks for dropped object

Changes You May See this Week in Baby's Social Development
* shouts for attention
* pats, smiles and tries to kiss image in mirror

Every baby is an individual, and your baby may do some of these things more quickly or more slowly than another baby. If you are concerned about your baby's progress, discuss it with your healthcare provider. Also see page xiii.

What's Happening this 32nd Week?

✐ Does Baby Have a Sleep Disorder?

Does your baby sleep during the day and stay awake at night? Sometimes a medical or biological problem can disrupt baby's sleep. The most common disorders are listed on the following page.

Asthma.   This breathing disorder inflames the small airways in the lungs, causing coughing and wheezing. See the discussion of *Asthma* in *Week 44.* The problem is often diagnosed before baby is 3.

If baby wakes up coughing, especially in the early-morning hours, asthma may be the problem. If baby coughs during the day when he's excited or running around, it could indicate asthma. Asthma can be treated with medication, which will reduce sleep interruptions.

Acid Reflux.   When the muscular valve between the esophagus and stomach doesn't work right, stomach contents back up into the esophagus. This is called *acid reflux* or *gastroesophageal reflux disease (GERD).* See the discussion of *GERD* in *Week 13.*

The problem occurs more frequently when baby is lying down. It may disappear by the time he is a year old. Medication may be used to relieve discomfort. Rarely surgery is necessary to correct the problem.

Obstructive Sleep Apnea.   With this condition, enlarged tonsils or adenoids block the upper airway during sleep. This results in loud snoring. Surgery to remove the tonsils or adenoids often corrects the problem.

✴ *Crawling Takes Practice*
It takes a lot of practice to master crawling. Baby must keep his head up and his chest off the floor. He must also coordinate moving his arms and legs. Some babies learn to crawl as early as 7 months. Others don't become adept until they are 10 months old. Give your baby lots of opportunities to practice crawling!

> It's OK to begin offering baby wheat cereal or other cereals that contain wheat about this time.

✴ *Don't Make Mealtime a Battle*
Don't get too uptight at mealtime. If you do, researchers believe it could lead to feeding problems for baby.

A baby often gets rambunctious when he's eating. Stay cool, calm and collected when he does. Within reason, follow baby's wishes. If he wants to help out with the spoon, let him give it a try. If he wants to eat with his fingers, it's probably OK. Experimenting with his food is a learning experience for him.

✴ *Baby May Be Very Curious*
All human babies and baby animals go through a stage of heightened curiosity. Your baby may be experiencing this now. The main difference is that human babies have few instincts to rely on. He must depend on his learned

knowledge. When you see baby exploring, touching, examining and experimenting, he's storing the knowledge for future use.

The dangerous aspect of his curiosity is that he has no awareness that his activities can cause him harm. That's why it's important to provide baby a safe environment in which to explore. It's how he learns!

> Baby has no awareness of danger to himself yet. You must still be diligent about keeping him safe.

⚘ Baby Eczema

Eczema is a skin disorder, also called *atopic dermatitis*. The problem can occur anytime in early childhood and affects about 10% of all children. Sixty percent of the cases occur during a baby's first year. Most cases are not severe. The problem tends to decrease as baby gets older.

In babies, the problem often occurs when baby's delicate skin comes in contact with the floor once he's crawling. It may also be triggered by a food-related allergy. Dry, scaly red patches first appear on the face. The rash then moves down to the trunk and limbs. It does *not* usually affect the diaper area. Symptoms include:

* itchy skin
* flaking or peeling of skin
* small blisters that leak a little fluid (in some cases)
* infection

What You Can Do at Home.   If your baby gets eczema, give him fewer baths. When you do bathe him, pat him dry. Lubricate skin after every bath with a mild baby lotion. Reapply lotion to baby's skin 2 or 3 times during the day. Ask your pediatrician which is the best kind to use. Dress baby in loose-fitting clothing that allows his skin to breathe. Keep layers light to help avoid perspiration, which may cause additional irritation. Avoid any foods baby is allergic to.

When to Call the Doctor.   Call the doctor if you believe your baby has eczema. It's important to call if blisters appear to be infected or get worse.

Medications to treat eczema are used only under the direction of a doctor. They may include ointments containing steroids (cortisone) or coal tar, antihistamines (for itching) or antibiotics, in case of an infection. If problems persist, you may be referred to a pediatric allergist or dermatologist.

∗ Lice

Although no parent ever wants to believe *their* child could get lice, it can happen. Head lice has nothing to do with cleanliness or hygiene. Lice thrive in crowded environments. Exposure may occur in day-care and child-care situations. Also called *crabs, head lice* or *body lice,* this infestation is caused by a small parasite that lives on the body, most often where there is hair. Symptoms include:

* itching and scratching
* redness of scalp
* eggs (nits) in the hair
* hives

To check for head lice, examine the scalp on the back of the head at the hairline. Check around the ears. Use a magnifying glass. Tiny, gray, oval-shaped specks, called *nits,* that are firmly attached to the hair may be visible. If you can't see nits, you may see evidence of intense scratching.

What You Can Do at Home.   If your child gets lice, wash all sheets, towels and clothing in hot water that contains a disinfectant. Dry everything on the hot cycle in the dryer. Also wash scarves and hats. Items that can't be washed should be dry-cleaned. Soak combs and brushes in very hot water (over 130F) for at least 10 minutes. Don't share towels, combs, brushes or other hair-care items.

When to Call the Doctor.   Call the doctor if you believe your baby has lice or if someone in your household has lice. Don't use any over-the-counter medicated shampoos without your pediatrician's recommendation.

Your baby's doctor may advise using an over-the-counter medicated shampoo to deal with the problem. It's important to keep these shampoos out of baby's eyes. After shampooing with the medication, comb the hair thoroughly while it is still wet to remove the nits. Sometimes application of a medicated shampoo must be repeated. Use shampoo *only* as recommended by your physician.

If your pediatrician recommends an over-the-counter medication that doesn't work, you may have to use a prescription shampoo. Ask for one that doesn't contain lindane. Overuse of lindane has been linked to harmful side effects in children.

> At this age, babies cry an average of about 1 3/4 hours a day.

Toys and Play this 32ⁿᵈ Week

✎ *Dropping His Spoon Can Be a Game*

When baby drops his spoon from his high chair, make a game of picking it up. Reach down and pick it up, then say something silly like, "Baby dropped the spoon. We have to pick it up!" (He'll drop it again quite quickly, no doubt.) This game reinforces to baby that an object continues to exist, even when he can't see it.

✎ *Sooo Big!*

Look at baby and ask, "How big is baby?" Stretch your arms far apart and say, "Sooo big!" Your baby will enjoy watching you do this. He may not be able to show you how big he is yet, but he soon will.

✎ *Make a Tunnel*

To help baby in his desire to crawl, make a fun tunnel. In addition to encouraging him to crawl, it gives him the chance to see the difference between "inside" and "outside."

Find a sturdy box that is larger than your child. Remove the flaps or fold them inside at both ends. Place baby on the floor near one end of the tunnel. Then sit yourself down at the other end. Talk to baby, and encourage him to come to you through the tunnel. If he doesn't quite get the hang of it, crawl into the box yourself and guide him to the other end.

Later, after he's mastered the art of going through the tunnel, enter it from one end while he is also inside. Tell him you're "inside." When you crawl out of the tunnel, tell him you're "outside."

Week 33

Baby's Age as a Monthly Reference—8 months

HOW BIG IS BABY THIS 33ʳᵈ WEEK?

Baby weighs 18¼ pounds and is 27¼ inches long this week.

Baby Care and Equipment

⁂ *Are You Interested in Making Your Own Baby Food?*

Many parents want to make their own baby food. You can do it and maintain baby's health by keeping a few things in mind. Follow the suggestions listed below.

* Thoroughly cook the foods you choose.
* Purée cooked food so it is very mushy.
* Use only fresh foods.
* Don't add salt, sugar, spices or anything extra to the food.
* Good choices to start with include sweet potatoes, peas and squash.
* Make only a little at a time, so you don't have to store it.
* If you make more than you need, store leftovers in a sealed container in the refrigerator.
* Keep leftovers no longer than 2 days.

You may also want to check the *Resources* section, page 527, for references to websites that provide different recipes for making your own baby food.

⁂ *Fighting Toxic Mold*

Nearly every house in the United States has some sort of mold growing inside it, according to a recent study. Most mold can be found on windowsills, in cabinets under the sink and on the seals of refrigerators. Some mold cannot be seen. Mold is a powerful allergen for many.

To clean up the areas in your home where mold might grow, try the following suggestions.

* Clean areas that might harbor mold with diluted bleach or cleaners that contain bleach.
* If possible, keep the humidity level below 40% in your home. There are many devices on the market today that measure humidity levels.
* Use an air conditioner during humid times of the year.

* If a floor area is exposed to water, such as in kitchens and bathrooms, don't carpet it.
* Leaving shoes by the door avoids bringing mold into the house.

Mold from Water Damage.   Do you have water damage in your home that hasn't been cleaned up? You may want to take care of it, to help keep baby healthy.

Water damage that is ignored can lead to growth of a particular type of mold that could cause an infant to develop bleeding lungs, also called *pulmonary hemorrhage*. The problem is attributed to a toxic mold that grows on wet wood and paper products. When the mold dries out, its spores can get into the air. If an infant inhales them, they can affect her rapidly growing lung cells. This is especially true if baby is under 6 months of age.

It's important to dry out wet areas as soon as possible. Throw out any items that were water-soaked if they do not dry within 24 hours. Clean walls and anything made of wood with water and bleach—one part bleach to four parts water. Take care of any leaks so water damage doesn't recur.

✕ Grain-Based Finger Foods

If baby wants to feed herself, offer her some grain-based foods. These foods become mushy in her mouth, which make chewing and swallowing them easier for her.

Baby crackers, well-cooked pasta (not al dente), bread and oat-circle cereal pieces are good choices. These foods are easy to chew and to swallow. They also offer many of the same nutrients—B vitamins and iron—that are found in infant cereals.

Now is a good time to offer baby oat-circle cereal pieces.

When you serve baby these foods, and she eats them, it also helps you out. You'll be able to eliminate one or two servings of cereal each day from her meal plan.

Milestones this 33rd Week

✕ Baby Has a Stronger Sense of Self

As your baby develops a stronger sense of herself, she is also developing likes and dislikes. She may push away or turn away from a toy she isn't interested in. She may cry for one that she wants but doesn't have.

She enjoys playing by herself for longer periods. However, she still enjoys interacting with other people.

⚘ Emotions Are Strong Now

You may be surprised at the range of emotions your baby can express. She can express the emotions of anger and frustration. They may disappear as quickly as they appeared.

She may still be somewhat anxious about separation from you. This may appear as bashfulness, nervousness, whining, crying and turning away from unfamiliar people. She still wants to be close to you.

⚘ Is She Standing on Her Own?

When baby can stand fairly steadily, you may notice she begins trying to pull herself up on anything handy. Some very active babies may try to cruise a little–by moving sideways while holding on to something solid.

Give her some help if she gets stuck standing up. It will happen frequently as she tries to master this new task. When she needs some help, release her hands from what they're holding, and gently lower her to the ground.

> Don't be upset if your baby seems to prefer one parent over the other. It's normal at this age.

⚘ She's Beginning to Understand Relationships Between Objects

You may notice your baby is beginning to apply what she has already learned to new situations. She is starting to understand there is a relationship between objects. She'll place a lid on her drinking cup or put a used paper towel in the trash can. She may place her toy gently on the table. This demonstrates her awareness of how some things fit together.

⚘ Her Hand Control Increases

You may notice your baby holding an object in one hand and banging it with something in her other hand. She may bang two objects together in front of her. These accomplishments are due to her increasing hand control. She's also using her thumb and first and second fingers to grasp larger objects.

> Baby can easily crawl to the top of the stairs. But once she gets there, she doesn't know how to crawl back down. Until you can teach her how to do it safely (it may be months before this is accomplished), put a gate or other barrier across the stairs.

⚘ Sounds Can Be Fun

Your baby is becoming more sophisticated in her appreciation of sounds. She can probably identify various household and outdoor sounds by now.

She will imitate rhythmic banging. She likes banging things together for the sounds they produce.

> Baby should be using sounds to get your attention by this age. If she isn't, bring it up at your baby's next well-baby checkup.

She may also display a sense of rhythm. When you turn on some music (no matter what kind!), she may bounce while she's standing and holding on to something. Or you may see her sitting on the floor and bouncing on her bottom. She may even move in time to a song when you sing it or play it for her.

Note: See also the box *Milestones this 33rd Week.*

What's Happening this 33rd Week?

✦ *Baby's Not Very Patient*

Two or 3 minutes can be a long time for a baby! When you expect her to be patient, 3 minutes is about as long as you can ask her to wait.

When baby's needs are not quickly met, she may cry harder. In addition, any lessons she's learned about patience are quickly forgotten.

By responding to her quickly, she learns her needs will be met. This establishes her trust in you. It also encourages her to wait a little longer next time.

✦ *Baby May Be Less Interested in Breastfeeding*

It's not unusual for baby to lose interest in breastfeeding now. But she still wants the closeness with you. Encourage her to crawl into your lap whenever she needs a little comforting. You'll both enjoy it.

✦ *Can You Avoid Stereotyping a Child?*

Most parents want their children to grow up without stereotyping. Do boys always have to play with trucks? Do girls always have to play with dolls?

Some experts believe that there are basic differences between boys and girls that cannot be eliminated. Others believe that although those differences do exist, there are some things parents can do to embrace those differences. Consider the following.

Offer Your Child Many Different Toys.   Give your baby many different options when it comes to toys. Let girls play with trucks and cars. Let boys have a doll or stuffed animal. This allows them the opportunity to play with all sorts of toys. But don't be surprised if your child chooses gender-specific toys. Girls do like dolls, and boys do like trucks!

Set an Example.   During the early years, your child is going to get most of her ideas about gender roles from observing your family. It's a good idea for

MILESTONES THIS 33RD WEEK

Changes You May See this Week as Baby Develops Physically
* stands with hands free if leaning against object

Changes You May See this Week in Baby's Developing Senses and Reflexes
* pincer grasp is developing more
* follows with eyes to what someone points to

Changes You May See this Week as Baby's Mind Develops
* begins establishing differences between one and more than one
* combines known bits of behavior into new acts

Changes You May See this Week in Baby's Social Development
* pushes away undesirable objects
* imitates people and behaviors, out of sight and earshot

Every baby is an individual, and your baby may do some of these things more quickly or more slowly than another baby. If you are concerned about your baby's progress, discuss it with your healthcare provider. Also see page xiii.

parents to share chores and responsibilities. In that way, your child will learn that dads and moms do lots of different things.

Don't Overprotect Girls.   Let girls have the same experiences as boys. Encourage them when they get frustrated. Push them a little more when they need it.

Cuddle Boys More.   It's good to comfort your son by holding him. Researchers now believe that touch is very powerful and can even lower stress-hormone levels.

✴ Parents Need to Set Good Examples
You can help your child develop social skills. Set a good example, and provide her with an opportunity to learn. Both of these activities are vital to the process.

She needs to learn that everyone is important. It can be difficult for a parent to find a balance among teaching a child others are important while meeting her needs and encouraging her self-esteem.

You can teach baby to be considerate of others. Don't give her everything she wants when she wants it. Don't let her win all the time (but she shouldn't always lose, either). Teach her to take turns and to follow the rules. Guide her in ways so she will be considerate of others.

Although many parents find it a bit difficult, you'll be doing baby a favor. When she goes to day-care or preschool, she'll have learned some social skills for interacting with others.

✳ *Eye Injury or Contusion*

When baby becomes more mobile, many things can happen when she takes an occasional fall. However, few things are as alarming as an eye injury. Injury is usually caused by trauma to the eye and can occur at any age. Symptoms of an eye injury include:

* ✳ swelling
* ✳ discoloration around the eye or in the white part of the eye–red, blue, purple or any shade of these colors
* ✳ tenderness or pain
* ✳ may be accompanied by a cut or laceration

What You Can Do at Home.   If your baby has an eye injury, gently apply cool compresses to the area. After 24 hours, you can use a warm (not hot) compress.

When to Call the Doctor.   Call the doctor if there is a cut or laceration near the eye, if swelling continues or increases, if baby is in pain. Most injuries to the eye are emergencies. The doctor may prescribe eye drops or ointments. Sometimes a patch is recommended to protect the eye from bright lights.

Now that baby may be crawling all over the house, take some precautions to protect her. Think about the following.

* ✳ Put your purse up high so baby can't get into it.
* ✳ You might want to move wastebaskets out of reach, especially in the kitchen and bathrooms.
* ✳ Be careful with coins, safety pins, pen caps, paper clips, buttons, balloons, screws and anything with tiny parts. Pick them up, and put them away.
* ✳ Make sure cosmetics are out of baby's reach.
* ✳ Empty and wash all ashtrays after they are used.
* ✳ Be careful about what you put on low tables and night stands.
* ✳ Store prescription and over-the-counter medications, vitamins, minerals, herbs and botanicals in a locked cabinet.

✹ *Splinters and Slivers*

A baby can get a splinter fairly easily. When she's crawling on the floor, she may come across objects you didn't even know were there! Some of them may have splinters. In addition to seeing the splinter, some symptoms your baby has a splinter include:

* pain in the area of the splinter
* redness or swelling in the area
* bleeding, occasionally

What You Can Do at Home.   When you notice baby has a splinter, wash the area with soap and water. Put pressure about ¼ inch from the puncture site. It can help dislodge the splinter so you can get a grasp on it. If it doesn't, carefully break the skin with a sterilized needle.

You may try to remove the splinter if it seems an easy task. Grasp the splinter with a pair of sterilized tweezers. Pull gently and slowly to remove it. It can be very difficult to get a baby to hold still long enough to allow you to remove it. You may want to try this when she's asleep or have someone else hold her.

After the splinter is out, wash the area with soap and water, then keep it clean and dry. Apply a triple antibiotic ointment to the area to avoid infection. Cover it with a bandage.

When to Call the Doctor.   If a little inflammation or redness occurs after you remove a splinter, a bit of the material may have been left behind. Contact your physician.

If you can't remove a splinter, call the doctor, especially if it is deep or it is a large one. Call the doctor if red streaks become visible, if the area appears to be getting infected or if yellow or green pus comes from the area of the splinter. These signal infection. Your pediatrician may treat the problem with antibiotics.

If your baby has a splinter of glass or metal, *don't* try to remove it unless it is tiny and hardly punctures the skin. If it is deep, a splinter of this type needs to be removed by a medical professional.

Toys and Play this 33rd Week

✹ *Catch Me!*

Baby loves to play games with everyone in the family. One of her favorites might be "catch me." When she scrambles off while you're playing together, crawl after her. Tell her, "I'm going to get you." Crawl slowly after her, so she has a chance to get away. She'll love being pursued.

✴ *"Baby, Baby Dumpling"*

While your baby's lying on her back, pretend to cook her and eat her up.
Try the following while you sing this nursery rhyme to her.

> *Baby, baby dumpling*
> *Cook her in a pan* (tickle her legs)
> *Sugar her* (lightly tap her tummy)
> *Flour her* (stroke her tummy lengthwise, then use the back
>   of your hand the other way)
> *And eat her when you can!* (make munching noises as you
>   nibble her tummy)

✴ *Teach Baby to Anticipate Actions*

This simple game can teach baby to anticipate your actions. Hold her firmly
on your lap. Gently bounce her up and down while you sing a simple song
she knows. At some point in the song, lower her between your knees a little
as you open them. Look at her and laugh. Sing the song again, lowering her
between your knees at the same point in the song each time.

Soon she'll begin to anticipate you lowering her at that point in the song.
You'll see her anticipation as she smiles or laughs when you get near to the
part of the song where you open your knees. Or she may tense her muscles
in readiness for the drop.

Week 34

Baby's Age as a Monthly Reference—8 months

Baby weighs 18½ pounds and is 27¾ inches long this week.

Baby Care and Equipment

✦ Baby's Teeth Do More than Chew Food

Your baby may have some new teeth. It's important to take care of them from the time they first appear. They are only temporary or "baby teeth," but they are important.

In addition to helping him chew his food, teeth enable him to speak clearly (when he learns to talk). Primary teeth also reserve jaw space for his permanent teeth when they come in, usually around 5 or 6 years old. Primary teeth allow the jaw bones and other facial bones to grow properly. So begin early taking care of baby teeth. You'll be glad you did.

✦ Baby's Eating Plan

By this time, your baby may be eating lots of different foods. He is still taking in 24 to 32 ounces of formula or breast milk each day. However, he's probably started tasting (and eating) some other new foods. By this point, his daily diet may consist of:

- ½ cup each of cheese, plain yogurt or plain cottage cheese
- 2 or 3 servings of 2 to 4 tablespoons of iron-fortified baby cereal
- 2 or 3 servings of ½ slice of bread or 2 crackers
- 2 servings of 3 to 4 tablespoons of fruit
- 3 ounces of diluted fruit juice from a cup
- 2 or 3 servings of 3 to 4 tablespoons of vegetables
- 2 servings of 3 to 4 tablespoons of protein, including chicken, beef, pork, cooked dry beans or egg yolks

If you offer baby any meat products, they should be strained or finely minced. Feed him only *one* new meat a week. When you offer eggs, just give him the yolks. Some babies are sensitive to egg whites until after they are 1 year old.

✣ Reptile Warning

If you have a reptile as a pet, you may want to get rid of it. The Centers for Disease Control advises keeping children younger than 5 away from all pet reptiles, including pet turtles. These animals can be a source of life-threatening salmonella infections. Symptoms of a salmonella infection include:

* fever
* vomiting
* bloody diarrhea
* abdominal pain

A child can become infected from handling the animal or by handling objects contaminated with the reptile's feces. Some cases have been reported in infants who never touched the reptiles. Researchers believe infants were infected when they were held by those who handled the reptiles!

✣ The Facts on Plastics and Vinyls

In the past, you may have read articles that stated "chemical elements in vinyl toys cause liver damage in rats." Or "plastic toys linked to a cancer agent."

Should you be worried? Should you throw out all your baby's pacifiers, teething rings, bottle nipples and plastic and/or vinyl toys?

A lot of research has been done on the hazards of various substances by many agencies. The culprit was the chemical *diisononyl phthalate*, better known as DINP or just phthalate. This chemical is often used to soften hard plastic into PVC (polyvinyl chloride).

In the past, some public-interest groups joined together to publicize test results, which did show some dangers. That's where all those reports came from. However, the U.S. Consumer Product Safety Commission (CPSC) reported that few, if any, children were at risk. They stated that the amount of DINP a child might ingest from contact with products made from phthalate doesn't reach a harmful level. They did suggest, however, that as a precaution parents not keep any single plastic or vinyl item for too long a time, especially if baby chewed on it a lot.

The CPSC didn't ban phthalate outright. However, they did ask companies to stop using the chemical voluntarily in soft rattles, teethers and toys for babies under 3 years old. Most manufacturers complied with the request. By the middle of 1999, nearly all products on the store shelves were DINP-free. Some companies have chosen to label their products as "phthalate free." You might want to check the product labels.

Your only real concern may be products that were produced *before* the middle of 1999. If you have any plastic or vinyl toys that you used with previous babies or if these items were given to you by someone else, you may want to toss them out, just to be safe.

Milestones this 34th Week

Baby's Intellectual Capacity Is Growing

Even when he cannot see a person or an object, baby now usually knows they haven't disappeared forever. This has come about from his various activities, including putting small objects into larger objects. Covering something so he can't see it, then showing him it's still there is a similar activity. Continue playing games like these to build his awareness.

He has the mental model of a human face now. He studies everyone's faces to compare them. Baby also notices objects and may point to what he wants. He is paying greater attention to details.

Baby understands "routines" now. If you put him in his high chair, he knows it's time to eat. If you get the stroller out and place him in it, he knows he's going for a ride. A change in his routine may upset him somewhat.

> Babies who can soothe themselves may not be born that way. When baby wakes up during the first few months, he'll cry out. If you comfort him when he cries, by the time he's 8 or 9 months old, he'll feel secure enough to go back to sleep on his own.

He's also exploring the concept of "cause and effect." He is beginning to understand that when he does something, it results in the same effect over and over again. That's why you may notice him repeating the same action many times. When he plays with a toy that has more than one activity, he realizes each hand movement causes a different effect.

His Muscular Development

Muscular development is finally reaching baby's legs and feet. You may notice him kicking vigorously when he's on his back. He may even propel himself across the floor on his back by squirming and kicking. Baby may also move himself around by creeping on his tummy, using his arms to pull himself along. If he isn't crawling already, it won't be long till he is.

You may also notice he's beginning to throw things. This develops as a controlled motion of his hand and arm. He likes to throw things to see what happens.

Because of his increased muscle control, he may be able to fit small objects through a hole in a larger object. He may build a tower of two blocks or gather items for sorting and building.

He may also stand up and lean against an object with his hands free. This allows him greater freedom to get into mischief. He may also divide his weight between his arms and legs when he plants his hands on an unmovable object for support.

↲ *Keep Talking and Reading*

Continue talking to your baby. Use short, simple sentences. Talk about the present, and repeatedly use the names of people and things. Avoid "it" and "them" because baby has a short memory and can't think in the abstract yet. But he's listening.

> Don't rush baby into giving up his bottle. It won't do any harm for him to continue it, even into his second year. If you don't make an issue of it and his emotional needs are being met, he'll get rid of it on his own.

When appropriate, use exaggerated hand motions. He's learning to connect words with people, objects and events.

He enjoys having you read simple books to him. When selecting books to read, choose those with clear, colorful illustrations or pictures. If pages are uncluttered and simple, he can focus his attention more easily. About three objects per page is enough.

When you read to him, point to the pictures, and read slowly. Use your finger (and his) to trace shapes. Tell him about the animals, people or objects. For added fun and excitement, sing, exaggerate and use sound effects—it makes your shared experience more interesting.

↲ *Baby's Safety*

The urge to climb is an instinct your baby will display. Once he's up, getting down can lead to calamity. He'll find all sorts of places to climb. Many of them probably are less than safe.

It will soon be simple for him to push a stool to the sink. He'll be able to climb high enough to reach the medicine cabinet. Or he may open drawers and use them to climb. You may have to take measures to protect baby, such as turning furniture so it can't be used as a ladder or bolting it to the wall so it won't topple over if he climbs on it. You may also need to remove some things that invite baby to climb.

Note: See also the box *Milestones this 34ᵗʰ Week.*

What's Happening this 34ᵗʰ Week?

↲ *Baby Is Experimenting with Standing and Balancing*

When baby starts crawling, his world perspective changes. He sees everyone around him walking, so he wants to walk. Because his arm muscles are stronger, he will use them to pull himself up to stand. He'll use whatever's handy–even you! Once he's up, he'll hold on to anything that's near him.

After he's practiced standing for a period of time, usually days or weeks, he'll begin to experiment with letting go. He'll put his arms out for balance and may stand for a few seconds before sitting down again.

> Baby will have many stumbles and false starts before he learns to crawl. When he falls, don't make a big deal out of it, and he won't either.

MILESTONES THIS 34ᵀᴴ WEEK

Changes You May See this Week as Baby Develops Physically
❋ uses furniture to pull himself to standing position

Changes You May See this Week in Baby's Developing Senses and Reflexes
❋ points with finger

Changes You May See this Week as Baby's Mind Develops
❋ can recall past events
❋ can solve simple problems, such as getting an object by pulling it

Changes You May See this Week in Baby's Social Development
❋ may try to use parents to get things
❋ mimics other people's mouth and jaw movements

Every baby is an individual, and your baby may do some of these things more quickly or more slowly than another baby. If you are concerned about your baby's progress, discuss it with your healthcare provider. Also see page xiii.

✯ Fever and Febrile Seizures

Nearly every parent worries that a fever will hurt their baby. And nearly every baby gets one–fevers account for nearly ⅓ of all visits to the pediatrician. A fever is often a sign that baby's body is doing its job of fighting against germs that invade it. It can actually help the body because as a fever rises, it impairs the growth of some viruses and bacteria.

Medical experts have deemed 100.4F as the upper limit of a normal temperature, so when baby gets a fever, he has a temperature of *at least* 100.4F rectally. However, for a baby under age 3 months, even a slight fever can be serious. If your young infant has a fever, call the doctor.

A fever usually does not cause neurological damage until it surpasses the 105F mark. In reality, everyone has a normal temperature range, and a person's temperature can vary quite a bit during the day. Your baby's actions are a good indicator of how sick he really is.

Like other medical conditions we have already discussed, fever is a *symptom* of a problem. It is often a sign the body is fighting off an infection and is often associated with other symptoms in many illnesses.

Getting an accurate temperature with a newborn or an infant can be challenging. Methods that work best include a rectal thermometer, an axillary thermometer (a rectal thermometer placed under baby's armpit) or an ear thermometer. For information on *Different Types of Thermometers* and *How to Take a Baby's Temperature* using each, see *Week 4.*

If your baby feels warm, if his skin and mucous membranes are dry, if he shows signs of not feeling well or has the symptoms of a cold or flu, you'll probably need to take his temperature. If you call the pediatrician's office to make an appointment, they often want to know if your baby has a fever. It might be a good idea to take his temperature before you call.

What You Can Do at Home. If your baby has a temperature, there are plenty of things you can do at home. You might want to try some or all of them.

* Cool him down by either sponging him with a damp cloth or giving him a cool bath.
* Increase his fluid intake.
* Don't dress him too warmly or pile lots of blankets on top of him.

You might also want to look for other symptoms to help identify a possible cause of the fever. This can be very helpful to the doctor if you take baby in to see him or her.

When to Call the Doctor. Call the doctor if your baby has a rectal temperature over 100.4F. Contact the office if your baby is irritable, won't nurse or take a bottle, and is getting dehydrated. Call if he's having problems breathing. If your baby is a newborn and running a fever, it's important to contact your pediatrician immediately.

Treatment depends on the cause of the fever. Acetaminophen and/or ibuprofen may be recommended. Medication to deal with the cause of the problem, such as an antibiotic for an infection, may be prescribed.

Call the doctor immediately if your baby has a febrile seizure—this is a seizure related to a fever. Seizures can occur when a baby's body temperature rises too fast. Although they may be frightening for you, a febrile seizure is usually not a cause for great concern. See the discussion of *Febrile Seizures* in *Week 18*.

✴ *Intussusception*

Intussusception occurs when the bowel folds into itself, causing a blockage or obstruction of the bowels. It most often involves the large intestine. The problem occurs most often in babies and children between 2 months of age and 5 years of age. It is twice as common in baby boys than in baby girls. Symptoms of intussusception include:

* sudden, acute abdominal pain
* drawing knees up to the chest
* screaming
* vomiting
* lethargy
* passage of red, jellylike stools (stools mixed with blood and mucus)
* tender, distended abdomen
* palpable, sausage-shaped mass in upper-right quadrant of abdomen

Baby appears normal and comfortable between episodes of pain.

When to Call the Doctor.   Your quick response to these symptoms is crucial. If you believe your baby has intussusception, call your pediatrician immediately! This is an emergency.

If the problem is identified early, it can sometimes be relieved without surgery. A barium enema or a water-soluble contrast may be done to try to push the inverted bowel into its original position. If this doesn't work, surgery may be necessary.

Your doctor will probably recommend restricting fluids. When you get to the hospital, I.V. therapy, nasogastric decompression and antibiotic therapy will be started before surgery is performed.

✴ *Scabies*

Scabies is a highly contagious skin disease caused by a mite. It is passed from one person to another when bed sheets, towels or clothing are shared. Symptoms of scabies usually appear on the hands, wrists, genitals, chest, inner thigh and between fingers, and include:

* intense itching
* small blisters
* scaling or flakiness of skin
* slightly discolored lines on skin, up to several inches long in some cases

What You Can Do at Home.   At home, thoroughly wash hands before and after touching anyone who is infected. If you know someone in the family has scabies, wash their bedding, towels and clothing in hot water with bleach added to the wash cycle. Don't share towels, bedding or clothing. If baby gets infected, try to keep him from scratching or rubbing the infected area.

When to Call the Doctor.   Call the doctor if you believe your baby has scabies. Contact your pediatrician if the blisters become infected or you see any redness or swelling in the area of the blisters. Medication may be prescribed by baby's doctor.

Toys and Play this 34th Week

✴ *Show Baby He Can Reach Things by Standing Up*

This game will increase baby's realization that he can get things by standing up. Place a favorite toy on the seat of a sturdy chair. With words and movements, encourage him to pull himself up by holding onto the chair.

If this is difficult or he doesn't understand, help him to his feet. Then lean him against the chair so he can get the toy.

When he does get the toy, clap and praise him. Then place him back on the floor and start over again.

> Baby may now be making sounds by putting his lips together. These include *mmm, bbb, ppp* and babbling. Listen for them.

✴ *Using One Object to Get Another*

Help baby understand he can use one object to get another. Tie a string around a favorite toy. Place the toy beyond his reach. Leave the end of the string in front of him.

Show him how he can get the toy by pulling the string. Praise him when he finally does it on his own.

Caution: Never leave the string on the toy or let baby play this game by himself. Remove the string from the toy before you leave the room.

Week 35

Baby's Age as a Monthly Reference—8 months

HOW BIG IS BABY THIS 35TH WEEK?
Baby weighs 19 pounds and is 28 inches long this week.

Baby Care and Equipment

✣ *Seasonal Safety*

If Christmas or Chanukah is approaching, you may be looking forward to sharing the holiday season with your baby. It's a time of wonder and excitement, especially this first holiday together. As you prepare your house for the celebration, be aware that there could be many hazards to baby. By being mindful of them, you can protect your little one.

Keep Candles to a Minimum.   Candles are beautiful at holiday time, but they can be dangerous. If you just can't do without the soft glow candles produce, use electric candles or light bulbs instead. If you must use candles, place them up, out of baby's reach. Keep all of these attractive nuisances out of baby's reach, including tables with tablecloths or runners that baby could pull.

Christmas-Tree Tips.   Never leave a crawling or toddling baby alone with the Christmas tree. If you have any breakable glass ornaments on your tree, place them out of her reach. Keep cords for tree lights well out of reach.

Anchor the tree firmly so it can't easily tip over. Don't place the tree near radiators or the fireplace. Keep wrapped presents out of baby's reach—baby might try to put bow and ribbons in her mouth. Don't put presents under the tree until you are ready to open them. If you do, you may discover baby has opened them long before Santa arrives!

> At holiday time, don't burn wrapping paper in the fireplace. It could cause a flash fire.

Don't let the tree get dried out—it could become a fire hazard. Check all lights on the tree (and other decorations around the house) to be sure cords are not frayed or broken. Babies have been known to chew on or bite strings of lights, so keep her away from them (and them away from her!).

Watch Her at Parties. When you visit someone else's home, they may not be aware of the things that could harm your baby. You need to be vigilant when going to holiday parties and family celebrations with your little one. Be alert for:

* open sockets
* fireplaces
* small breakables within her easy reach
* nuts and candies placed on lower tables
* food she could choke on
* alcoholic beverages left within her reach
* ashtrays with cigarettes, cigars or pipe ashes
* decorations and/or candles that she could get at
* the tree and presents, which will probably attract her attention

When you take baby to parties at other people's homes, be aware of hazards, such as unprotected electrical outlets.

Are Your Ornaments and Decorations Dangerous? Some ornaments contain small pieces baby could choke on. Keep them out of her reach. Pick up tree needles, tinsel and anything else off the floor so baby can't put something in her mouth and choke on it. Keep a sharp eye open for anything that might be hazardous, such as ornament hangers that could fall off the tree or other decorations.

Holiday plants, such as mistletoe berries, amaryllis and holly, are *poisonous* if they're eaten. Poinsettias can cause stomach upset if they're ingested. Don't let her get at any of these.

Artificial snow can be poisonous if it's ingested. Fire salts, which produce colored flames, are also poisonous if swallowed.

Always turn off holiday lights before you go to bed or leave the house.

Ribbons used to decorate packages can cause harm if baby becomes entangled in them. Plastic wrap can be a suffocation hazard.

Some parents don't want to put all the decorations and presents up or out of baby's reach. They have devised various ingenious ways to protect baby and their decorations. One particularly clever solution to the problem is to put up the tree, decorate it and put the presents out—all inside baby's playpen!

Other Holidays. Some other holidays may present some situations to be aware of. Each can pose separate issues.

On *Valentine's Day,* be careful with candy or flowers you may receive. Prevent problems by keeping these things out of baby's reach.

At *Easter,* keep baby away from egg whites (from hard-cooked eggs). She shouldn't eat them until she's 1 year old. Egg shells may also be hazardous. Chocolate should not be given to her either.

The *4ᵗʰ of July* may be dangerous if you live in an area that allows fireworks. (Some states do not.) Keep your little one away from anything that could burn her.

Halloween can be frightening to a small child when she encounters people in face paint, masks and costumes. In addition, be careful about dressing her up in any type of costume that has parts that cover her face.

✴ When Baby Eats Food Off the Floor

Does your baby drop food all over the floor, then go back later and eat it? As diligent as you may be about cleaning up after her, you may miss something. It's normal. When baby crawls around on the floor, she's sure to find something you missed.

> Keep seemingly harmless items out of baby's reach. You might not believe dry beans or peas could cause injury. But they can if they're pushed into baby's ears or up her nose. They could get stuck and/or swell and cause a great deal of discomfort.

Most parents are concerned that the oat-circle cereal pieces or the macaroni they missed when cleaning the floor may harm baby when she eats it. Most experts agree if baby occasionally eats food off the floor, it probably won't harm her. The exception is a household with pets that are not housetrained. Food off a floor contaminated with animal urine or feces could cause baby problems.

The germs on your floors aren't usually the ones that make baby sick. So don't get panicky when your baby eats food she finds on the floor.

If baby uses a pacifier and it falls on the floor, you don't normally need to sterilize it. However, do rinse it off to remove any dirt or crud.

Milestones this 35ᵗʰ Week

✴ She's Understanding More Words

Your baby understands more of what is being said to her now. Keep talking to her, telling her stories and having conversations with her. Between 8 and 12 months old, common words she can comprehend include juice, cookie, ball, baby, shoe, bottle, no, bedtime, mommy, daddy and bye-bye. In addition, she can follow simple instructions. She'll wave bye-bye when asked to do so. If you ask her to "come here," she'll probably come to you.

She continues creating dialogue and babbles quite a lot. She may expect you to answer her! You may notice she imitates various noises for her toys, like "rrrr" for a car.

⁂ *Baby Is Getting Stronger*

Baby is able to get into a sitting position quite easily now. She can sit and pivot to get a toy. This is due to the increased strength in her trunk muscles.

She raises herself up on her hands and knees. She can lift her chest and tummy off the floor and hold them parallel to the floor. If she's not moving along on all fours, she soon will be!

⁂ *She's Interested in Many Objects*

Your baby is very interested in small objects. She can use her fingers to rake a piece of cracker off the floor, then pick it up with her fist. You may notice her chasing a piece of dust around the floor.

She can visually compare large and small objects. This allows her to adjust her grasp to the size of an item.

It's amusing to see her attempt to lift an illustration off the page of a book. She can see the object clearly. However, she doesn't yet understand the difference between two dimensions and three dimensions.

⁂ *Exploring Objects*

She continues to learn and to explore many different objects. One thing she's learning is that an object remains the same (at least most do) every time she plays with it. That's why she explores the size, texture, shape, hardness, taste, smell and sound of something over and over again. It reinforces the lessons for her.

⁂ *Is It Time to Wean Her?*

You may be thinking about weaning baby from the breast. Check with your pediatrician before you do. He or she will let you know if baby is ready for it. You'll also learn how to do it.

Weaning should be baby's decision. She'll know if she's ready or not. Note: See also the box *Milestones this 35th Week.*

What's Happening this 35th Week?

⁂ *Answering the Middle-of-the-Night Call*

If you have been diligent in your efforts to teach baby to go back to sleep by herself, she should be waking up less often during the night. Keep up the good work! When she does wake up during the night, which we all do, let her try to fall back asleep on her own. If she seems to be having a lot of difficulty

MILESTONES THIS 35ᵀᴴ WEEK

Changes You May See this Week as Baby Develops Physically
* if held in standing position, puts one foot in front of the other

Changes You May See this Week in Baby's Developing Senses and Reflexes
* can rake a small object with fingers, then pick it up with fist

Changes You May See this Week as Baby's Mind Develops
* understands simple instructions
* shakes head "no"
* examines objects as external, 3-dimensional realities

Changes You May See this Week in Baby's Social Development
* doesn't like to be confined

Every baby is an individual, and your baby may do some of these things more quickly or more slowly than another baby. If you are concerned about your baby's progress, discuss it with your healthcare provider. Also see page xiii.

doing this, encourage her to go back to sleep. Don't play with her or get her up, if you can avoid it. She needs to learn to fall back to sleep on her own. With practice, she will.

⭑ *Baby's Reaction to Those She Doesn't Know Can Hurt Their Feelings*

Baby can clearly distinguish between voices and faces of people she knows and people she doesn't know. She craves familiarity—it's her security. She may still be wary of strangers.

Her reactions can dishearten grandparents, other relatives and friends she doesn't see often. To avoid hurt feelings, don't use the word "stranger." Explain to them that she has been a little shy when she encounters anything new, including people. Ask them to give her some time and space. It won't be long before she's ready to make friends.

⭑ *Insect Bites and Stings*

A baby of any age can get an insect bite or sting. As baby starts moving around more, she may be at greater risk, due to her curiosity.

If you notice any unusual swelling or redness on her skin, accompanied by itching, look for a bite or sting mark in the area. Reactions in infants are often more severe than they are in older children and adults. To prevent your baby from being bitten or stung, take the following measures.

* Dress baby appropriately when you go outside. Cover as much of her skin with clothing as you can, without overdressing her.
* Avoid areas where insects are commonly found, when possible.
* Don't use strong-scented soaps, lotions or powders on baby or yourself before you go outdoors. Their scent often attracts insects.
* Insect repellents should *not* be used on a baby under the age of 1. You don't want to expose her to DEET, a common ingredient in many repellents. However, you can use repellent on yourself to keep insects away when you're holding her.

What You Can do at Home.   If your baby has been stung or bitten, you can use calamine lotion, hydrocortisone cream or a paste of baking soda and water on the area. Check with baby's doctor before using an antihistamine to reduce swelling and discomfort.

If your baby is stung by a bee, carefully remove the stinger. Grab it with tweezers and pull it out. Apply ice to relieve pain.

When to Call the Doctor.   Call baby's doctor if she has any trouble breathing or experiences excessive swelling or redness in the area around the bite or sting. Call if she develops a fever or is more irritable than normal.

Your pediatrician may tell you to use an antihistamine to help relieve baby's discomfort. If a secondary infection develops, the doctor may prescribe an antibiotic. If baby has a severe allergic reaction, she may be hospitalized for further treatment.

> When baby wants a change of pace, she'll have ways of letting you know. Pay attention to these clues.
> * She looks away from you or some other object.
> * She grimaces.
> * She arches her back and neck while you're holding her.
> * Her eyes wander around without focusing on anything.
> * Her arms and legs thrash around.
> * She stiffens her arms and spreads her fingers open.

Yeast Infections

A yeast infection, also called *monilia,* is an inflammation and/or infection of the vaginal area. It can affect girls of any age. A yeast infection can occur at any time, and often occurs following antibiotic use. Symptoms that your baby has a yeast infection include:

* itchiness in vaginal area

* skin in vaginal area is red
* skin in area is dry
* may be burning, pain or discomfort with urination
* thick white discharge from vagina

What You Can Do at Home.   If your baby has the symptoms described above, keep the area as clean and dry as possible. Change her diapers as soon as they are wet. Wash the area with mild soap when bathing or cleaning after bowel movements. Don't use diaper wipes that contain alcohol. It could cause her discomfort.

When to Call the Doctor.   Call the doctor if you believe your baby has a yeast infection. Your pediatrician will probably prescribe topical antiyeast medications. Call the doctor's office if symptoms don't improve with treatment, if there is any bleeding from the vagina or baby experiences persistent pain.

Toys and Play this 35ᵗʰ Week

✶ *Fill It Up*

One of baby's greatest interests at this time is how a big toy relates to a smaller one. How does the smaller one fit into the larger one? Stacking and fill-and-empty games may be favorites now.

Fill a shoe box with plastic or wood blocks. Empty it out in front of baby. Watch her figure out how to put the blocks in the box.

Gather together some nesting plastic bowls. She'll have fun putting them inside one another.

When she's taking a bath, let her have a couple of plastic measuring cups that fit inside one another. She'll enjoy filling them up and emptying them with water or putting them inside one another.

✶ *Catch Me!*

This fun chasing game also helps baby learn to follow you. Then she can keep you in her sight when she wants to.

Sit on the floor with baby. Crawl a little way from her. Turn around, and tell her to come and get you. Let her catch you. Laugh, hug her and crawl away again.

She may play this for a while, then crawl away from you. If she does, tell her you're going to get her. Crawl slowly after her.

✶ *Let It Drip*

In the bathtub or in an outdoor play pool, let baby play with dripping water. Use a squeeze bottle or a baster for this game.

When baby is in the water, partially fill the bottle or baster. Squeeze a few drops of water on her arm. Say "Drip, drip, drip. The water drips on baby" as you let some drops fall on her arm or leg. Help her squeeze some of the water out so it drips on her or on you.

As you play the game, show her that squeezing a little harder makes the water squirt. Explain this to her, as you let her feel the water squirting onto her arm or leg.

Week 36

Baby's Age as a Monthly Reference—9 months

HOW BIG IS BABY THIS 36ᵀᴴ WEEK?
Baby weighs 19¼ pounds and is 28¼ inches long this week.

Baby Care and Equipment

✣ *Start Taking Care of Baby Teeth*

If baby has finally cut a tooth or two, take care of them. If you've followed our suggestions, you've been massaging his gums with a soft cloth or gauze for quite a while. With his first teeth, you can clean them with a cloth. Don't use any toothpaste at this time; it isn't necessary.

Try to clean baby's teeth every day; it's a good habit to begin. Lay baby face up in your lap. Open his mouth gently with your fingers, and rub both sides of each tooth with a cloth. A good time to do this is after his last feeding. Use a small, soft baby toothbrush when your baby has about eight teeth.

Keep massaging his gums (where there aren't any teeth) with the cloth. It helps toughen the gums where new teeth will soon be coming in.

✣ *Concerns about Poison Ivy*

Do you believe if your baby scratches his skin when it is irritated by poison ivy or poison oak it will spread the infection? Baby's scratching doesn't spread the irritation. It's just that new areas are breaking out. These areas were in less contact with the plant oils, or they were exposed later on. They break out a day or two later as the oils irritate his skin.

As long as baby's skin itches, keep using anti-itch tactics, described below. If he keeps scratching the skin, it can cause a secondary infection, which can spread the rash even further.

To relieve itching, ask your doctor about giving baby an antihistamine. Over-the-counter lotions, such as calamine lotion and those made with camphor or oatmeal, might be helpful. Check first with your pediatrician.

Itching should clear up in a few days. Sometimes it takes longer. You may need to keep mittens or socks on baby's hands so he can't scratch himself.

In rare cases, a baby will have a violent reaction when exposed to poison oak or poison ivy. If you notice your baby is having any problems beyond the rash and the itching, contact your pediatrician immediately. Some people have severe reactions to poison oak, poison ivy or even poison sumac.

✣ *Puréeing Protein Foods*

If you want to purée some tender beef or chicken for baby, go ahead. Thoroughly cook the meat with broth or water, then purée. Or mash the yolk of a boiled egg. Serve any of these foods once a day. You can move on to finely minced protein when baby eats mashed protein foods without any problems.

Baby's protein needs are still quite low. Don't worry about whether he's getting enough nutrition. His needs are still being met with formula or breast milk.

✣ *Breastfeeding Babies May Forgo Middle-of-the-Night Feedings*

By this age, a healthy breastfeeding infant can probably skip his middle-of-the-night feed. He should be able to go from late at night to early morning without too much trouble. However, he may resist your efforts.

To deal with the situation, let dad go in when baby wakes up. Baby may fuss for a few nights, but he'll soon settle down. If you have any problems, contact your pediatrician for advice.

✣ *Offering Him a Cup*

If baby has been bottlefeeding, he may show less interest in it now. Offer him some formula (not cow's milk!) in a cup. Many babies are ready to be weaned about this age. Don't be surprised, however, if he changes his mind next month. His willingness will probably reappear by the time he's 1 year old.

Milestones this 36ᵗʰ Week

✣ *Baby's Intellectual Capacity Continues to Grow*

By this age, a baby can form specific memories from his experiences. He may remember how to push a ball to make it roll or how to shake a toy so it makes sound. Some familiar words will cause a response. He clearly recognizes his name and responds to it. He also recognizes the names of familiar objects.

Baby can now more accurately judge an object's size. He is more accurate when grasping an object. His improved eye–hand coordination allows him to bang two objects together in front of him. He can also drop things into a container.

✣ *Is He Talking to an Object?*

If your baby makes certain sounds in connection with a particular object or event, he may be making an attempt at talking. For example, he may say "doh" for dog or "bah" for bottle. It's a good start. He'll probably say some real words in the next few months.

> Don't get frustrated if baby's separation anxiety gets in the way of him entertaining himself. Solo play doesn't mean he has to be alone. He can play by himself with you in the room.

✴ His Physical Accomplishments Are Many

Your baby can do many things now. He can sit steadily for up to 15 minutes. He grasps with his thumb against the side of his index finger and can pick up small items fairly easily. He leans forward while sitting to pick up a toy, and he doesn't lose his balance.

You may notice his play is different. He may play with two objects at the same time. He may sort various items. He may put small toys in a bucket or pan.

> Don't be surprised or concerned if baby seems to be slowing down in his development around this time. He's spending time perfecting his newfound skills.

He may be standing with little support. He may be able to balance well enough to play with a toy while standing.

If he hasn't already done so, he will soon begin "cruising." It often starts as a trip up and down the length of a piece of furniture, as he holds on for support. Next, he will probably flop or stumble from one piece of furniture to another while holding on or leaning against it.

Baby may also have become a little more confident getting down from a standing position. If he hasn't mastered it yet, keep working with him on it.

✴ Be Careful of Spoiling Him

By this age, it is possible to spoil baby. To prevent it, you may need to be firm with him—more firm than you have been in the past. He needs to feel your confidence and conviction. It will be hard for him to hear "No," but it is necessary. When you tell him "No" or "Don't," he also needs to be reassured that his world will be OK again. Be sure you offer him the reassurance he needs.

✴ Baby Can Interpret What He Hears

Your baby's brain is making associations. He can interpret what he hears. He knows when he hears "meow" that it's coming from the cat. Or the doorbell means someone's at the door. You can help him make these associations by pointing them out to him.

Note: See also the box *Milestones this 36th Week.*

> Mealtimes may be more pleasurable for the entire family if you let baby feed himself between spoonfuls that you feed him. He loves practicing his independence by feeding himself.

What's Happening this 36th Week?

✐ *Teaching Baby to Be Calm*

If you get upset or angry when things don't go your way, your baby may do the same thing. Don't set a bad example for him. He's like a little sponge that takes in everything you do. You may not think he's aware of what's going on around him, but he is!

Be a good model. If you do the right thing, your child will model that behavior. When he spills his juice, calmly clean it up. You'll teach him about dealing with problems in a mature way. If you yell at him, you teach him to get angry and upset when things go wrong.

✐ *Animal Bites*

Be careful when you and baby are around animals, especially ones you aren't familiar with. It's easy for baby to get bitten. It can happen at any time—a situation can develop before you even know it!

What You Can Do at Home. Animal bites in babies occur most often from household pets. If you have a pet, take extreme care to protect your baby. See the discussion of *Pets and Baby* in *Week 12.* Be aware of where your pet is, if baby is on the floor or within reach of the pet. If you're visiting a friend or when you leave your baby with someone, take care to know that baby will be safe.

Never let your child approach an unfamiliar animal. Because children are small and at eye level with many dogs, a dog may feel threatened. Even the nicest dog can react and bite when it feels threatened. Animal bites can be very serious in a baby.

Symptoms the baby has been bitten include:
* puncture wounds
* torn or ripped skin
* bruising
* bleeding from skin

MILESTONES THIS 36TH WEEK

Changes You May See this Week as Baby Develops Physically
* can stand up if he's holding on to something
* sits well in a chair

Changes You May See this Week in Baby's Developing Senses and Reflexes
* approaches large objects with both hands
* can pick up and manipulate two objects, one in each hand

Changes You May See this Week as Baby's Mind Develops
* may remember game that was played the previous day
* responds to his name

Changes You May See this Week in Baby's Social Development
* wants to play near parent
* imitates play
* objects when something is taken away from him
* feeds himself some foods

Every baby is an individual, and your baby may do some of these things more quickly or more slowly than another baby. If you are concerned about your baby's progress, discuss it with your healthcare provider. Also see page xiii.

When to Call the Doctor.   Call the doctor if you believe your baby has been bitten by an animal. A tetanus shot may be necessary. If a wound is deep or ragged, stitches may be required. Your pediatrician can clean the wound.

Animal bites often contain lots of bacteria, so follow directions about wound care. In some situations, antibiotics or antibiotic gels or ointments may be prescribed. It is very important to know if the animal that bit baby is up to date on its rabies shots and other vaccinations.

✂ *Tonsilitis*

Tonsilitis, also called *pharyngitis,* is an inflammation and infection of the tonsils. Baby's tonsils are clumps of tissue located at the back of his throat. Infection can occur at all ages but is most common in children between 5 to 10 years old. Symptoms include:
* fever
* difficulty swallowing
* tonsils are swollen
* listlessness

* poor feeding
* swollen lymph nodes on either side of the jaw
* difficulty breathing

What You Can Do at Home. If your baby develops these symptoms, use a cool-mist humidifier in his room when he's sleeping. See the discussion of *Humidifiers* in *Week 13.* Increase his fluid intake. Keep him quiet.

When to Call the Doctor. Call the doctor if your baby displays the above symptoms. Your pediatrician will probably want to see him. If symptoms worsen, such as his fever rises, he has difficulty breathing or difficulty swallowing, call your doctor.

Treatments include acetaminophen or ibuprofen for fever and general discomfort. Your doctor may prescribe antibiotics, such as amoxicillin or penicillin, to deal with the infection.

> Make your baby's 9-month well-baby checkup now. See page 36 for any immunizations he may receive at this next visit.

✲ Rubella

Rubella, also called *German measles,* is most common in children, but adults can also get it. It is caused by a virus passed from human to human in the air we breathe. Symptoms of rubella include:

* fever
* listlessness
* a fine red rash on the head and body
* swollen lymph nodes (glands) behind the ears and the back sides of the neck

What You Can Do at Home. Your baby should be immunized against rubella at about 15 months of age when he receives the MMR (measles, mumps, rubella) vaccines. See the *Immunization Schedule* on page 36.

A rubella titer, a blood test done to see if the baby's mother has antibodies to rubella, is done at the beginning of a pregnancy. If it is positive (most are), the antibodies protect baby while he is in the uterus and for a short time afterward.

When to Call the Doctor. Call your doctor if you believe your baby has rubella or has been exposed to rubella. If your baby has contracted rubella, keep him away from any pregnant women you know. Exposure to rubella is most serious in a pregnant woman who does not have antibodies to rubella during the first trimester.

Treatment for rubella includes over-the-counter medications, such as acetaminophen or ibuprofen, for fever or achiness. Do *not* give baby aspirin to avoid the possibility of *Reye's syndrome; see Week 37.*

YOUR PREEMIE'S DEVELOPMENT

Your premature baby should be able to do many things now. Remember always to use baby's "due-date age" as your point of reference for the following accomplishments. By this week, he should be doing many things, including:

* sitting up unassisted
* rolling over from back to front
* scooting or crawling
* learning to use his fingers
* "talking" a lot
* looking at and studying an object for quite a while
* learning to manipulate objects, such as making a toy make sound

To help him accomplish these tasks, there are many activities you can do with your baby. Try the following:

* allow him to explore safely—it's an important part of his learning experience
* read books together
* talk about what you do together as you do it
* give him containers for holding objects (a box or a pan), and show him how to put things into it
* play hide-and-seek with a toy and one of his blankets—don't make it too hard

---

Toys and Play this 36th Week

At this time in baby's life, he loves to play games with you. He will take the initiative more often now. He may grab your hands to play "Pat-a-cake" or try to crawl on your lap if he wants to play "This is the way the lady rides." This is important. The best times for learning occur for parent and child when the child initiates it.

✷ The Warm-Breeze Game

Baby will enjoy playing this touch-and-sing game with you. He probably has lots of fun with you when you tickle him! As you sing this song, carry out these actions.

A warm breeze (blow gently on his neck)
A warm squeeze (hug him)
Baby's got the tickles! (tickle him lightly all over)

◡ *Make Noise while You Drop Blocks Together*
This game is fun because you make lots of noise! Choose a metal pan or dish. Drop some blocks into it. The metal "clink" is a fun sound. In addition to entertaining baby, this game helps him improve his ability to release an object.

Pick up a block, show it to him, then turn your hand over. Spread your fingers wide as you drop the block. You want baby to see your actions clearly. Let him try next. He may not do it the same way you did. That's OK.

Make it fun! Respond positively even when he misses the dish or bangs the block on the side of the dish.

◡ *Stacking Can Be Fun*
Your baby may enjoy stacking toys now. A round plastic spindle with different-sized rings to stack on it is enjoyable. Wide-mouthed plastic containers that he can fill with blocks are also good choices.

◡ *Let Him Make Music*
Let baby make his own music with a pan and a wood spoon. An aluminum pie plate can become a musical instrument when you attach bells to it. Let baby play with these items when you can interact with him, not on his own alone. You want to be sure he doesn't hit himself in the head with the spoon or chew on a bell!

Week 37

Baby's Age as a Monthly Reference—9 months

HOW BIG IS BABY THIS 37ᵀᴴ WEEK?

Baby weighs 19½ pounds and is 28¼ inches long this week.

Baby Care and Equipment

✎ *The American Academy of Pediatrics and Child-Rearing Issues*

The American Academy of Pediatrics (AAP) is the medical association that directs pediatricians. They make information available to its members—medical professionals who take care of children—so they may provide the best, most up-to-date care for their patients.

The AAP has advice for parents on many child-rearing issues. To learn more about these issues, you might want to contact them for information. See their listing in the *Resources* section, page 529. Or ask your pediatrician if he or she has booklets or pamphlets the AAP publishes. Some areas they address include those discussed below.

Breastfeeding. The AAP believes human milk is best for all infants, with only a few exceptions. Advantages to breastfeeding your baby include health, psychological and economic benefits. A pediatrician will usually promote breastfeeding for the first year if baby is growing normally and it doesn't cause undue stress or problems for you.

Pacifiers. Pacifiers do *not* cause psychological or medical problems. Some babies need to suck more than others. Pacifiers help them meet this need.

Spanking. When you spank your child, it is usually ineffective in changing behavior. The AAP suggests parents find other ways to discipline a child.

Temper Tantrums. Temper tantrums are normal in children. They help a child vent frustration. Parents are advised to remain calm and to distract the child or to ignore her when she succumbs to a tantrum. Punishing a temper tantrum is not advised. Parents are also encouraged not to give in to a child when she has a tantrum.

Bed Sharing. The AAP does not encourage bed sharing. See the discussion of baby sleeping alone in *Week 5*. Adult beds are not made for babies, and safety is a concern. Parents can accidentally trap or suffocate a baby.

◡ *Peanut Allergies on the Rise*

Peanut allergies seem to be on the rise. The number of children allergic to peanuts *doubled* in the years between 1980 and 1994; about 1% of all Americans has this allergy.

Some experts believe the increase has occurred because more children are being exposed to peanut protein before age 3. A child's immature immune system may consider the protein harmful and develop antibodies to it. This triggers an allergic reaction.

Researchers advise parents to delay introducing peanut butter to children if there is any family history of peanut allergies. **Caution:** To help avoid developing the allergy in *any* child, do not offer your child peanut butter or other products made with peanuts until she's 3.

Symptoms of a Peanut Allergy. Symptoms of an allergic reaction to peanuts include hives, diarrhea, a stomachache, swelling in the throat, wheezing, vomiting and faintness or unconsciousness. Hives or swelling may also appear when the nut comes in contact with the skin. In those who are extremely sensitive to peanuts, 1/44,000th of a peanut kernel can cause a reaction!

A skin test can be done to determine if a child who has had certain reactions after eating peanut protein is allergic to peanut products. A "direct oral challenge" may also be used to determine if a child is allergic. In a hospital setting, the child eats a small amount of the nut. This kind of testing is the most reliable for detecting a nut allergy. Discuss the situation with your pediatrician if you have questions.

Hidden Sources of Peanuts. Whether your child develops an allergy to peanuts is hard to determine. However, to help avoid building antibodies to peanut protein, don't give your baby any peanut protein until she's at least 3 years old.

It isn't just peanuts and peanut butter that can cause problems. Foods made without peanut products can be contaminated. If food is mixed or stirred with utensils that were used with peanut-protein foods, they can become cross contaminated if utensils are not thoroughly cleaned. If your child has a peanut allergy, ask when you eat out if food might have come in contact with peanuts or peanut products.

It's important to read labels on the foods you buy. Many foods contain peanuts, peanut oil or other peanut products. Check labels very closely.

Peanuts may be near the end of the list. Unexpected sources of peanut protein include the following foods:

- bakery items
- potato chips
- packaged cheese and crackers
- many chocolate candies–not only the peanut varieties
- chili sauces at restaurants
- gravies at restaurants
- Asian, Thai, Chinese and African dishes often use peanut butter and other peanut proteins

Milestones this 37th Week

Baby May Enjoy It When You Read to Her

You may be surprised when you find your favorite magazine torn apart or its pages crumpled. It happens when your baby investigates the magazine. She enjoys ripping the pages out. She may also want to handle books that attract her attention. Give her picture books with hinged or spiral bindings made just for babies. She'll be fascinated by the pictures and the way the book is put together!

Want to help someone break the ice with baby? Have the adult play peek-a-boo with baby or bounce her gently on the knee when she feels comfortable with them.

Baby May Exhibit New Fears

Your baby may be getting over her fear of strangers, although with some babies, it lasts a little longer. She may now demonstrate new fears. She may begin to be afraid of things that didn't bother her before, such as visiting a strange place or taking a bath.

Don't be alarmed–this is natural. She is becoming more conscious of herself as separate. She's developing concerns for her own well-being.

One way to help her overcome some of these fears is to take her shopping or out on errands with you. She'll realize that although these situations are new, there's nothing to fear.

Sitting Is Comfortable for Baby

Your baby is becoming very adept at sitting and all it involves. She can push up into a sitting position when lying down. She can lean over, change positions and go from lying on her stomach to sitting up with ease. She may like to practice moving from one position to another.

ᏊᎡ *Crawling Is Her Main Form of Transportation*

Baby is probably crawling all over the place by now. She can turn around and change direction while she crawls. She may even crawl while holding a toy in one hand.

She may crawl stiff-legged or with her limbs straight. This is the precursor to walking.

Stairs are very attractive to her. However, she still can't get down if she crawls up, so keep an eye on her. Stay close when she's near stairs, or block them off. Going down stairs safely is usually too difficult for a baby to learn at this age.

> You may notice baby sometimes pushes up on all fours. She does this as she gets ready to walk.

ᏊᎡ *She May Be More Vocal*

Is she "talking" a lot? You may notice she is more verbal or babbling a lot. She loves it when you cough or click your tongue against your teeth. She may try to imitate you.

She may be saying more words. Sometimes she'll get it wrong, but that's OK. She may look at a picture of a cow and say "dog." She'll feel very good about naming the animal. To her, the cow does look like a dog. She's made an important connection between the picture in the book and the concept.

ᏊᎡ *Curiosity Propels Her*

Your baby is extremely curious. Nothing in her environment is off-limits—at least to her! She's inquisitive and wants to investigate everything.

Her curiosity may get her in trouble, such as when she empties a trash can, then digs through it. Keep the bathroom door closed when you're not using it. The toilet is a fun place to put things. You may find all the paper on a toilet-tissue roll or a box of tissues ends up in the toilet!

ᏊᎡ *Some Warning Signs*

By this age, baby should be babbling. If she isn't, discuss it with your pediatrician at a well-baby checkup. In addition, between now and the end of this first year, baby should look at those who talk to her. She should show an interest in communicating with those around her, and she should be making some efforts to do so. If she doesn't communicate or even try to, bring it up at her next well-baby checkup.

ᏊᎡ *Patience and Firmness*

Keep practicing patience and firmness with your baby. Added to your perseverance, patience and firmness eventually teach her many things, such as self-management. If an object or situation is dangerous to baby, you must handle it firmly. By being confidently firm and practicing patience, you teach her that certain issues are not open for discussion.

Note: See also the box *Milestones this 37th Week.*

What's Happening this 37th Week?

❧ *When Baby Is Shy*

If your baby is shy, don't despair. It's probably not a permanent condition. She may only need a little help exploring a new or different situation. Research has shown that children who are shy do not have low self-esteem. Shyness doesn't affect her ability to make friends, either.

To help her, gradually ease into new social situations. Let her take her time getting her feet wet. The most important thing you can do is *not* to force her into any interaction.

Watch for her cues. If she hangs onto you for dear life, she's not ready to interact yet. Encourage her to play or to get involved. As she gets older, she'll probably be less shy.

❧ *Your Baby Is an Explorer*

As stated above, your baby may be exploring even more by now. She can crawl and stand while holding onto something, often with one hand. This frees her other hand to reach out and to grab things that are near her. Be diligent about putting things out of baby's reach, if you don't want her to touch them.

She'll explore at every opportunity. When you are away from home, keep your eyes open to what's around her. A cigarette off the floor can be very interesting. You'll be surprised at the things she'll find when she crawls under the bed or behind a chair.

It may be a good idea to make a quick search of an area every time you place her on the floor. Things are dropped or overlooked all the time. That usually isn't a problem, but with an inquisitive baby, it might turn into one!

> Your baby may be taking one or two naps a day. She is probably sleeping about 10 1/2 hours at night. Your baby may be having trouble going from waking to sleeping. Help her relax before bedtime. Put her in her crib when she's calm, before she's asleep.

MILESTONES THIS 37ᵀᴴ WEEK

Changes You May See this Week as Baby Develops Physically
* crawls while one hand holds an object
* can turn around when crawling

Changes You May See this Week in Baby's Developing Senses and Reflexes
* bangs objects together at center of body

Changes You May See this Week as Baby's Mind Develops
* uncovers a toy that she saw hidden

Changes You May See this Week in Baby's Social Development
* deliberately chooses a toy for play
* imitates some sounds, such as cough, hisses
* manipulates and drinks from cup

Every baby is an individual, and your baby may do some of these things more quickly or more slowly than another baby. If you are concerned about your baby's progress, discuss it with your healthcare provider. Also see page xiii.

Falls

A fall occurs most often in a young child who is learning to walk. It may also occur when she is crawling and climbs up some stairs. In addition to crying, symptoms include:
* bruises
* bumps (from swelling)
* lacerations

What You Can Do at Home.   The first time baby falls hard can be traumatic for mom and dad, too! No matter how safe you make your home for baby, she'll probably fall and get some bruises.

If your baby takes a tumble, apply cold to the area for the first 24 hours, then apply something warm. Lacerations need to be repaired right away.

When to Call the Doctor.   Call the doctor if your baby has any serious lacerations. They may need to be stitched. Call if she strikes her head hard when she takes a tumble.

If a bruise gets bigger or becomes more painful, call the doctor. If she seems to get bruises without any injury, falls down a lot or bleeds very easily, contact your pediatrician.

⋆ Reye's Syndrome

Reye's syndrome is a rare disease that can occur from infancy through childhood. It usually follows a viral illness, such as chicken pox or flu, and is associated with aspirin used to treat the problems. It occurs more frequently in white babies than in babies of color. Symptoms include:

* weakness
* lethargy
* drowsiness
* seizures

What You Can Do at Home.   The best treatment is prevention. *Don't* give your baby aspirin or any other medication (including over-the-counter medications) unless directed to do so by your baby's doctor.

When to Call the Doctor.   Call the doctor immediately if your child has symptoms of Reye's syndrome. It's an emergency! Your doctor will probably prescribe rest and increased fluid intake. If your baby has seizures, she may need antiseizure medications. Antibiotics are prescribed if a bacterial infection occurs afterward.

   Caution: Don't give your baby aspirin for *any* illness with a fever, unless your baby's doctor specifically says it's OK.

> Baby is taking in between 200 and 300 calories of solid food now. She's still drinking 20 to 30 ounces of formula or breastfeeding a total of 10 to 90 minutes each day.

Toys and Play this 37ᵗʰ Week

Toys are important to baby. You may notice she deliberately chooses a toy to play with. She may even fight to keep it away from someone else!

   Check her toys frequently. By this time, some of them might have become worn. By checking them closely, you can deal with any loose parts or sharp edges, keeping them safe for her.

⋆ Mimic the Mirror

Sit baby in front of a large mirror. While she is watching you in the mirror, make different gestures with your hands. Wave at her. Blow her a kiss. Make faces; wrinkle your nose, or stick out your tongue. Nod your head, or shake it. See if she'll imitate your movements.

Ask her to point to the baby. Point to her image in the mirror and say, "There's the baby!"

✳ *"Hickory, Dickory, Dock"*
This game of tickling is fun for baby and her play partner. Lightly walk a couple of your fingers over baby, from head to foot, while you sing:

> *Hickory, dickory, dock!*
> *The mouse ran up the clock.*
> *The clock struck one, and down he came.*
> *Hickory, dickory, dock!*

Then reverse the way you tickle her—from foot to head—while you sing the song again.

✳ *Find the Toy*
This game helps baby in her concept of object permanence. While she watches you, place one of her favorite toys in a box. Cover the box with one of her blankets. Ask her to find her toy. Help her if she can't find it.

Another way to play the game is to hide a small toy in one of your hands. Ask her to pick a hand. Switch the toy back and forth between your hands. If she doesn't find it in one hand, she'll soon learn to look in the other one.

It's important to encourage baby in her search. Clap when she finds the favorite toy. Exclaim how fun it was to find it. Be enthusiastic with her.

Week 38

Baby's Age as a Monthly Reference—9 months

HOW BIG IS BABY THIS 38ᵀᴴ WEEK?

Baby weighs 19¾ pounds and is 28½ inches long this week.

Baby Care and Equipment

◦ *Baby Walkers*

In the past few years, parents have been warned not to put a baby in a baby walker. Why?

One reason is the number of injuries attributed to them. A recent study found that nearly 15,000 children under 15 months old were treated in emergency rooms for walker-related accidents in 1 year. No one knows how many children were injured who didn't seek medical attention. Another reason is that researchers believe using a baby walker can delay a baby's motor development. A third reason is that mental development may also be delayed.

Contrary to popular opinion, a baby walker *won't* help your baby learn to walk. He does use his legs to propel himself in a walker. But propelling himself forward doesn't strengthen the muscles he uses for walking.

The Safety Issue. Baby walkers give baby instant mobility. He can quickly go places in a walker that would take a lot longer to reach if he were scooting or crawling. He can be in harm's way in a moment. A baby on wheels may be exposed to other serious dangers, such as a tumble down a flight of stairs or access to an area with "dangerous" equipment or hazardous situations.

Walkers are now being manufactured that are safer for baby. The Consumer Product Safety Commission has mandated new safety standards. If you decide to buy a walker, choose one that is too wide to fit through a standard doorway. Check to be sure it has a gripping mechanism to stop the walker at the edge of a step. These two features make it a safer choice for your little one.

Developmental Delays. Research has shown that, on average, babies who *did not* use walkers walked at 11 months. By comparison, babies who *did* use walkers walked at 12 months. Babies who used walkers also scored lower on a battery of tests covering memory, language and perception.

Researchers believe that a baby needs to see his feet for optimum development. Babies who could see their feet when they were in the walker had closer-to-normal motor development.

As we've discussed each week, a baby needs to explore his environment to learn. A baby in a walker can't do this as easily or as thoroughly. This inhibits his development.

Another view is that parents pay less attention to a baby in a walker. This may mean less parental interaction for baby, which could lead to a delay in some aspects of development.

Some Guidelines.   If you do put baby in a walker, choose one that is safe for him. Be sure it meets current safety standards. Choose a walker that allows him to see his feet. Limit the amount of time he's in a walker. He needs time on the floor to develop his motor skills.

A Safer Alternative.   One product available on the market is a good alternative. It is a stationary chair that does not have wheels and cannot move. Baby sits in it in an upright position and can push up on his legs to a semistanding position. It usually has a large tray and some toys to entertain baby.

⚶ Finger Foods
If you haven't started feeding baby finger foods, now's a good time to start. "Finger foods" are small, bite-sized pieces of food. Crackers, teething crackers, pieces of toast, pieces of cheese, small bits of meat, pieces of soft tortilla and well-cooked pieces of pasta or macaroni are good finger foods to begin with.

The object of giving baby finger foods is to help him learn to feed himself. Because he can't use a spoon effectively, finger food allows him to practice.

> You may need to be diligent about putting your magazines and books away. Your baby loves to pull things apart, and books and magazines are fairly easy to destroy.

Offer him many different kinds of food. Let him touch, taste and smell them. Remember to be patient. It takes him much longer to eat when he feeds himself.

Milestones this 38ᵗʰ Week

⚶ Different Stages of Motor Development
At this time, babies of the same age may be at very different stages of motor development. Most babies are crawling by now. Many are standing but may

need help maintaining their balance. Some are cruising around the furniture. Some may take steps all by themselves. In some instances, baby is actually walking!

Development varies because babies are different. If baby is concentrating on one aspect of development, another aspect may lag behind.

The important thing to remember is that *every* baby is an individual. Don't compare your baby with any other baby—even with multiples. Your baby is progressing normally for him. He'll get there (wherever "there" is) in his own good time. As long as he is making forward progress, there is nothing to be concerned about.

> Shaking his head from side to side is easy for baby. However, nodding won't be accomplished for several more months.

✎ Things Baby Enjoys
By this time, baby enjoys many things. He likes to dance. He likes to pull things apart—probably to your dismay. He loves to play simple games, like "where's baby" or "chase the baby." He may initiate games more often. Storytime may be a favorite time for him.

✎ His Language Development
His ability to understand words is increasing. Reading to him helps his comprehension. His responses show he understands a lot. When you ask, "Show me . . ." he can correctly point to an object. When you play the game "So big!" he may smile and shoot his arms into the air to show you how big he is.

✎ When You Say "No"
Your baby may have difficulty when you tell him "No" or "Don't." He may look hurt or get angry. That's OK. You need to enforce some restrictions on him, so don't let his dismay or anger keep you from parenting him.

✎ He Better Understands His Visual World
Your baby knows quite a bit about his visual world now. His sense of perspective is more developed. He understands how objects appear larger or smaller in relation to how close they are to him.

He has an understanding of up and down. You may notice this when he is afraid to get down off a chair he climbed on top of. When he turns his sippy cup right-side up, he's showing you he knows how it should go.

৵ *His Memory Is Improving*

Your baby's memory is developing along with the rest of him, but he needs practice. If you get him a new toy, show him how to work it, then let him try it himself. In a few days, he'll probably know what to do with it and how to make it work correctly.

> Baby may be hugging you and blowing kisses to you now. If he's not doing it yet, he will be soon. This is quite an accomplishment for him!

৵ *Let Him Practice Walking*

Give baby many opportunities to practice walking. Let him hold on to both of your hands and walk in front of you. Don't strain his arms. See if he watches his feet. Allowing him to practice builds his confidence. It won't be too long before he's taking his first steps by himself!

Note: See also the box *Milestones this 38th Week.*

MILESTONES THIS 38TH WEEK

Changes You May See this Week as Baby Develops Physically
* can take a few steps if supported; walks with adult holding his hands

Changes You May See this Week in Baby's Developing Senses and Reflexes
* approaches small objects with finger and thumb

Changes You May See this Week as Baby's Mind Develops
* grows bored with repetition
* is aware of vertical space

Changes You May See this Week in Baby's Social Development
* begins to evaluate people's moods

Every baby is an individual, and your baby may do some of these things more quickly or more slowly than another baby. If you are concerned about your baby's progress, discuss it with your healthcare provider. Also see page xiii.

What's Happening this 38th Week?

৵ *Restrictions Are Necessary*

Baby loves his freedom. But as a loving parent, you will need to impose some restrictions. When necessary, block off areas you don't want him to explore. Keep cabinets and cupboards off-limits to him if you don't want him in them.

When you set parameters, you help baby understand that he can't always do what he wants, when he wants. That's a fact of life all of us must face.

Setting some restrictions is good for baby because it makes him feel secure. It's also good practice for you. It's much easier to learn to set restrictions when baby is young. He'll know you mean business when you consistently follow through. When he gets older, it's harder to make him believe you are serious if you've let him get his way all the time as a baby and toddler.

✽ *Burns*

In a baby or an infant, a burn can be very serious. A burn may be caused by contact with fire, electricity or chemicals. It usually occurs due to an accident or the carelessness of those caring for baby. Symptoms of a burn are categorized in three degrees.

- ✽ **1ˢᵗ degree burns** involve the upper layer of skin; skin may be red and swollen
- ✽ **2ⁿᵈ degree burns** involve deeper skin layers; skin may have blisters
- ✽ **3ʳᵈ degree burns** involve *all* layers of skin; skin may appear white

What You Can Do at Home.   If your baby receives a minor (1ˢᵗ degree) burn, quickly remove any clothing covering the burned skin. Run water continuously over the skin or immerse the affected area in cold water for 15 to 25 minutes, if possible. Don't use ice or butter—it makes it worse. Loosely cover the burned area with sterile gauze. Call your pediatrician for advice. If your baby gets a 2ⁿᵈ or 3ʳᵈ degree burn, go to the nearest emergency-medicine facility!

When to Call the Doctor.   Call the doctor if your baby gets any type of burn, even if it seems minor. He or she will advise you how to care for it. If a burn blisters, call your pediatrician. If a burn appears infected, with a discharge, or if it doesn't heal with recommended treatment, notify your pediatrician.

The type of burn dictates the treatment. In a serious burn, I.V. medication to relieve pain may be administered. Antianxiety medication may be used for various procedures that are painful. With a less-serious or minor burn, antibiotics, gels or salves, topical anesthetics and pain relievers may be prescribed. Once the burn begins healing, medication to deal with itchiness may be needed.

Caution: Be extremely careful with anything that might burn your baby. Keep chemicals out of reach. Never leave matches or lighters lying about. If you smoke, don't smoke around baby. Turn handles of pots and pans so they cannot be grabbed by baby. Cover all electrical outlets, and keep electric cords up out of reach when possible. Turn your water-heater temperature down. Check your entire house to keep your little one safe.

✤ *Ringworm*

Ringworm is a fungal infection that can affect many parts of the body, including the scalp, skin, nails and feet. It has different names for each body part involved. The most common ringworm infection is *athlete's foot*. A ringworm infection can occur at any age. Symptoms of ringworm include:

* itching
* scaliness
* pain
* lesions
* red rings, with a distinct border

What You Can Do at Home. If you believe your baby has ringworm, keep his skin dry. Dress him in loose cotton clothing to allow air flow. Wash clothing, bedclothes and towels in very hot water with added bleach or disinfectant. Clean the bathroom floors, tub and shower stall with a disinfectant (for athlete's foot).

When to Call the Doctor. Contact your doctor if your baby appears to have ringworm. He or she may prescribe a topical antifungal medication to deal with the problem.

✤ *Strep Throat*

Strep throat is an infection of the pharynx by the streptococcus bacteria. It can occur at any age and can be quite painful. Symptoms include:

* fever
* difficulty swallowing or eating
* swollen neck glands
* swollen tonsils
* irritability

What You Can Do at Home. If your baby has these symptoms, use a cool-mist humidifier when he's sleeping. See *Week 13* for information on *Humidifiers*. Try to increase fluids, although this may be difficult if baby's throat is extremely sore.

When to Call the Doctor. Call the doctor if baby has symptoms of strep throat. Contact your pediatrician during or following treatment if fever persists or rises, or if new symptoms appear, such as an earache or a cough.

Your doctor may prescribe medications to deal with the infection, such as antibiotics. You may also be advised to give baby acetaminophen or ibuprofen for fever or a sore throat.

Toys and Play this 38th Week

Playing together tells your baby that he is important to you, and he is worth your time. It's important to keep responding to your child through play activities. When you do, you help build his self-esteem.

It's helpful to set conditions that make it easier for baby to accomplish a task. You don't do the task for him, but you help him be successful in his efforts. In play activities, you can do this by helping baby when he gets frustrated in his play, such as when a toy doesn't work the way it should. Don't take the toy away and do it for baby. Show him how to do it so he can learn, then he'll be able to do it on his own.

> Let your baby set the pace of your playtime activities together. Baby will want to play for longer periods with you if you let him direct the play. Letting him take the lead helps build his confidence.

⚶ A Cardboard Megaphone

This is a fun game to play with baby. It lets him listen closely to your voice. Get a long cardboard tube, like those used with paper towels or wrapping paper. (If you use one from wrapping paper, cut it so it's not quite so long.) Sit across from baby, and talk to him through the tube. Make funny noises. Watch his reactions.

Then hand the tube to baby. Help him put it up to his mouth, and show him how to use it. You may be surprised at his actions.

The tube concentrates the sounds, so speak softly. Leave a small space between the end of the tube and baby's ear.

⚶ Where's Baby?

Your baby may institute a game of "find the baby." Play along with him when he does.

If he puts his blanket over his head or buries himself in it, say, "Where's baby?" Pretend to look around and keep saying you can't find him. He may pull the blanket off himself immediately. When he does reappear, exclaim, "There's the baby!"

If he stays hidden for a while, pretend to keep looking. You may discover he is having a wonderful time playing this trick on you. Enjoy it with him.

Week 39

Baby's Age as a Monthly Reference—9 months

HOW BIG IS BABY THIS 39ᵀᴴ WEEK?

Baby weighs 20 pounds this week and is 28½ inches long.

Baby Care and Equipment

✳ *Good Food Choices for Your Baby*

Some good choices to offer baby now include bananas and ripe apricots. Well-cooked vegetables, such as carrots, yams, potatoes and peas, are also tasty. If you want to offer meat, choose soft meats, such as turkey and well-cooked stew beef.

Cut food into small enough pieces so baby can gum them. Food pieces should be small enough that if baby swallows a piece whole, she won't choke. Cut pieces so they are no larger than her thumbnail.

Your baby may be even less interested in drinking her formula or breast-feeding now. Offering her 1 or 2 tablespoons of a protein food every day helps her get the nutrition she needs. In addition to meat, cheese, egg yolk and tofu (microwaved for 15 seconds, then cooled) are some interesting choices.

Offer her foods of various textures. Slippery spaghetti, sticky mashed potatoes, crunchy oat-circle cereal pieces—each one offers something different.

✳ *Citrus Juice*

If your baby hasn't had any problems with the foods you've offered her, you might want to try a citrus juice. Limit the *total amount* of all juice you give her to 4 ounces a day. Be sure you cut the juice with at least as much water— 2 ounces of juice to 2 ounces of water. Give her the juice in a cup.

Offer her orange juice, but don't give her grapefruit juice yet. It may be too hard on her stomach. Another good selection is a small amount of citrus juice mixed with another juice, such as apple juice or pear juice then dilute the mixture with an equal amount of water.

✳ *Let Her Hold the Toothbrush*

If baby has more than four teeth, you should be brushing them at least once a day. When you brush her teeth, gently massage each tooth with a soft-

397

bristled infant toothbrush. Massage in circles. Clean the rest of the gums with a cloth or gauze.

You might want to let her hold the toothbrush. Help her by holding your hand over hers. (You don't want her to stick it in her eye!) She may just want to play with it or suck on it. That's OK. It's the exposure that's important at this point. As she gets older, you want her to learn to brush her own teeth.

> If your baby is teething, give her teething biscuits. They can help make her sore gums feel better. You're becoming more relaxed with baby as you get to know her better, so trust your instincts. If you feel something may be wrong, call your doctor.

Milestones this 39ᵗʰ Week

✳ *Baby's Language Development*

Your baby is making many sounds that have the tones of language. Some babies of this age are able to speak some words, such as "hi," "bye," "mama" or "dada." She may imitate a few animals sounds. She usually responds to her name. By halting an action when you tell her to stop, she shows she understands what "No" means.

✳ *She Learns about Things that Interest Her*

Your baby is willing to cooperate and to learn about things that are interesting to her. However, you may find her quite stubborn when she's *not* interested in something. She may want to feed herself (she's interested in it) but not want to help dress herself (she's not interested).

She'll display many moods. Don't get frustrated or upset when she's unwilling to do something. She may change her mind tomorrow!

✳ *Baby Can Anticipate Events*

Your baby can now anticipate events better than she could a short while ago. For example, she puts together certain sounds and actions with getting ready for a bath. She knows when you are in the kitchen making certain noises, she'll soon eat. Learning anticipation helps her learn to wait for something. However, she won't wait long!

Another example of this is some of the games you play. When you play a tickle game, such as "Here comes the bumblebee!" she may start laughing when you begin. See *Week 15* for this game. She knows when you start to sing that particular song that tickling will follow. She enjoys these games.

✤ *She Can Be Emotional*

Even babies this age can be emotional. Your baby may object vehemently when you try to take a toy away from her. She may cry copious tears when you scold her or tell her "No." But just as quickly, she can be all sunshine and smiles if something amuses her. She may show off for an audience, especially if they appreciate it.

The moods of others may affect her. When a sibling is excited, she may be, too. If she sees another baby crying, she may burst into tears!

✤ *Is Your Baby Lagging Behind?*

As your baby develops different skills, she may concentrate on only one area right now. She may be vocalizing more or involved with studying details. She'll probably begin her motor activities soon. You may be pleasantly surprised when she does. Often babies who start later accomplish a task more quickly than babies who started early. Don't despair, and don't push her!

Note: See also the box *Milestones this 39th Week.*

MILESTONES THIS 39TH WEEK

Changes You May See this Week as Baby Develops Physically
* can climb
* crawls up stairs

Changes You May See this Week in Baby's Developing Senses and Reflexes
* clasps hands

Changes You May See this Week as Baby's Mind Develops
* can follow simple instructions
* is becoming afraid of heights

Changes You May See this Week in Baby's Social Development
* may begin to protect herself and her possessions
* performs for audiences; repeats act if applauded

Every baby is an individual, and your baby may do some of these things more quickly or more slowly than another baby. If you are concerned about your baby's progress, discuss it with your healthcare provider. Also see page xiii.

What's Happening this 39th Week?

✢ *Start to Say "No" for Her Safety*

In this book, we've suggested many ways to make your house safe for baby. The ideas are good ones that you may have used. But practically speaking, you can only do so much to make the environment safe for your baby. You don't want to feel as if you live in a dwelling devoid of all comfort or interest. You want to feel like it's home!

At this point, you may want to start telling baby "No" when she wants something she shouldn't have or can't have. She needs to learn there will always be some areas that are off-limits to her. This also helps you when you go to other people's homes. If she knows there are some things she can't have, she may not have a tantrum when you tell her "No" at someone else's house. Also see the discussion in *Week 40* of *Alternatives to Saying "No."*

✢ *Baby's Bowels May Change with New Foods*

You may notice a change in baby's bowels now that she's eating more "grown-up" food. As you change the foods she eats, there will be a change in the consistency, color and frequency of her bowels. This is normal. It's not a sign of food allergies or food intolerance.

✢ *Heat Stroke*

In extremely hot conditions, it's not uncommon for someone to suffer from heat stroke, also called *heat exhaustion, sunstroke* or *heat prostration* (similar to hyperthermia). It can occur at any age. Symptoms include:

* fever or high body temperature
* hot, dry skin
* little or no urine production (no wet diapers)
* listlessness
* irritability
* poor feeding

> A baby-sized sports bottle may be useful with your little one when she wants to hold her drink. One shaped like an hourglass with a snap-on lid is also great for travel.

What You Can Do at Home.   It's best to try to avoid the problem, when possible. When it's very hot, give baby lots of fluids. Keep her hydrated and as cool as you can. Heat stroke can be a serious problem.

When to Call the Doctor.   Call the doctor if you believe your baby is getting, or has gotten, heat stroke. It's an emergency! The baby's body temperature must be cooled down. Because it is a serious problem, this procedure should be done at the hospital or under the direction of qualified medical personnel.

✣ *Ruptured Eardrum*

A ruptured eardrum can occur at any age. It may be a cause of otitis media. See the discussion of *Ear Infections,* including otitis media, in *Week 28.* Symptoms that your baby's eardrum may be ruptured include:

* ✣ earache
* ✣ fever
* ✣ fussiness
* ✣ irritability
* ✣ pulling or rubbing the ear

What You Can Do at Home.   Your care of baby can sometimes help prevent a ruptured eardrum. *Never* put anything inside baby's ear, including cotton swabs. Clean only the outside of baby's ear. If you believe your baby's eardrum may be ruptured, keep the ears dry. Don't allow baby to put her head under the water.

When to Call the Doctor.   Call the doctor if you believe your baby has a ruptured eardrum. If her fever rises above 102F or if she shows signs of a middle-ear infection, contact your pediatrician. Your baby's doctor may prescribe ear drops or antibiotics to deal with any infection and acetaminophen or ibuprofen for fever and/or pain.

Toys and Play this 39ᵗʰ Week

✣ *Distract Your Cranky Baby*

Sometimes playing this game with a cranky baby will help distract her. She may forget why she was cranky. Instead of hiding something, like other games you've been playing, you find it!

Go on a search for various objects in the house. Make it interesting. Holding baby in your arms, ask her, "Where's the . . . ?" Look for a toy, the doggie, her blanket, a book. Choose anything that she might be interested in. Go through the house, and ask her to find whatever you're looking for. She can probably point to it quite easily by now.

✣ *Exploring Light and Dark*

This game lets baby explore the differences between light and dark. Find a large cardboard box. Cut a hole in one side. Place the box so the cutout part is on the side. Baby should be able to crawl inside the box.

Invite her to crawl inside the box. It's darker inside than outside. Tell her, "It's dark in there." Ask her if she can see her hand. Encourage her to crawl to the cut-out part of the box. Ask her if it's light outside. When she crawls out of the box, say, "Now you're crawling back outside, where it's light."

✻ Hammer, Hammer

Your baby is learning to use her fist and extended arm as a tool. This game helps her develop her gross-motor skills.

Show her how to make a hammer with her fist. Guide her arm up and down to "hammer" the hammer. While moving her arm up and down, sing:

> *(Baby's name) hammers with one hammer,*
> *One hammer, one hammer.*
> *(Baby's name) hammers with one hammer.*
> *Now she hammers with two!* (Make a hammer with her other
>   fist, and alternately move each one up and down.)

✻ Show Me

Place two familiar toys in front of baby, one at a time. Name them for her. "This is your dolly, and this is your ball." Ask her to point to the one you name. "Which one is the dolly?" Any response is OK, such as reaching, touching or just looking. Praise her for her response. If she doesn't respond, give her the toy you named. Tell her what it is. Then try again.

Week 40

Baby's Age as a Monthly Reference—10 months

HOW BIG IS BABY THIS 40TH WEEK?

Baby weighs 20¼ pounds and is 28¾ inches long this week.

Baby Care and Equipment

✧ Barefoot Cruising

When baby "cruises," he's not really walking yet, but he's getting there! It's best for him to go barefoot when he's practicing. When this isn't possible, there are other measures you can take.

When you're indoors, put booties or socks on him that have grippers on the bottom. This gives him some traction so he won't slip on linoleum or hardwood floors. If you're outside, shoes protect his feet.

✧ Don't Ignore Recalls

By now, you're becoming an old hand at the parenting game. You may feel a lot more confident now dealing with the many and varied situations parents face. That's great, but don't overlook your parental duty when it comes to recalls of baby items.

If the manufacturer or the Consumer Product Safety Commission determines a product is unsafe, it probably is. It's up to you to protect baby from hazards that you might never have thought about. When you see a recall in the paper or hear about one in a news report, pay attention to it. Return the product, or find out if there's any way to modify it. You can call the CPSC directly or visit them on the web. Ways to contact them are listed in the *Resources* section, page 527. Recall websites are also listed.

✧ Begin Adding Lumpier Foods

By this time, baby may be ready to start eating lumpier puréed foods. Some new table foods may also be offered. You're probably already giving him crackers and bits of cheese. Add cooked rice and baked potato removed from its skin. Be sure pieces are no larger than a green pea.

Offer baby a spoon, and let him feed himself. Don't give him the baby spoons you've been using to feed him. Choose a spoon with a fairly large handle so he can grasp it. Don't be concerned about the mess he creates. It'll take quite a bit of practice before he can get the spoon and its contents to his mouth.

> It's fun having baby join you at the table. He may not be ready to eat with the family, but he can interact with all of you. If you're looking for a high chair, a good selection may be one with a large tray that can be used to hold baby's toys while he visits with you.

Milestones this 40th Week

❧ *He May Be Standing on His Own*

Balancing on his two feet involves baby learning to coordinate his upper-body muscles with his lower-body muscles. He does have better control over his legs and feet now.

Baby is probably cruising around the furniture with confidence. He may be able to stand without support for a short time. He may be confident enough to squat down to pick up a toy or turn to the side to reach something. It is easier for him to go from a standing position to sitting down. If supported by someone, he may take some steps.

❧ *Baby's Developing Hand Control*

Your baby's control over his hands continues to improve. He's refining his ability to pick up small objects. His coordination is also improving. He may pound one object on the ground while he feels another with his fingers. He can grip one item while he reaches for another. Or he may hold something in one hand while leaving the other free to explore.

His pincer grasp is quite developed by now. He can pick up very small things between his thumb and index finger. Stay alert to what's on the floor around you!

Releasing an object is still a little difficult. You may notice he drops it or throws it when he loses interest.

He uses his little hands and fingers to explore everything around him. He'll stick fingers into just about any opening. Protect him from those that might cause him injury.

❧ *He Continues to Master His Language*

By this time, you may notice many things about baby's grasp of language. He may do something when he's asked to, such as wave bye-bye. He may respond to a simple request, such as "Bring me the dolly, please." He can also follow one-step instructions, like "Go to Grandma."

He may say a few simple words or make animal sounds. He can imitate you when you say "shhh" by putting his finger over his mouth.

↣ *Baby Enjoys His World*

Your baby may love to play in the water. He'll splash and kick when he takes a bath. He may be intrigued by the toilet. He can swish things in it, and it's a great receptacle.

It's a good idea to keep your bathrooms off-limits to him. You can keep the bathroom door closed to keep baby and the toilet safe. Now may be the time to invest in a toilet-seat lock. It's a simple device that locks the lid shut, keeping baby from opening it.

Baby may imitate some of the things you do, such as combing your hair or brushing your teeth. When you clean up his high-chair tray after eating, he may want a cloth so he can clean, too! This is lots of fun for him.

> If baby has any trouble sleeping, give him a massage. It will help him relax. It also helps lower stress-hormone levels.

↣ *How Much Sleep Does He Need?*

Your baby may not need as much sleep as he's needed in the past. If he's very active, he may sleep about 11 hours at night and need only a 1-hour nap in the afternoon. You'll be able to tell whether he's getting enough sleep by his actions. If he seems fussy and cranky, try putting him down to bed at night a little earlier. If he doesn't seem to need the extra sleep, it's OK if he's up a little longer.

↣ *Baby Needs His Own Space*

If it's not possible to put baby in a room of his own, you might want to set aside a place in a room for his toys. He won't spend much time there, but he'll know it's his. This is a good idea if you have other children around, especially a toddler. Baby needs to know there is someplace that's all his own.

↣ *Fearfulness May Appear*

Even if your baby has been confident about doing many things, he may be afraid to do some of them now. It's a stage he's going through, and it will soon pass.

He still needs reassurance of your presence. He may check often to see if you are near. He wants to break away, yet he needs to hold on. He enjoys his independence, but it can also make him a little fearful.

Note: See also the box *Milestones this 40th Week.*

MILESTONES THIS 40TH WEEK

Changes You May See this Week as Baby Develops Physically
❋ stands with little support
❋ may develop sleep problems caused by practicing standing in the middle
   of the night

Changes You May See this Week in Baby's Developing Senses and Reflexes
❋ voluntarily releases object in awkward manner
❋ grasps tiny objects with thumb and index finger

Changes You May See this Week as Baby's Mind Develops
❋ increasingly imitates actions of others
❋ understands and obeys some words and commands

Changes You May See this Week in Baby's Social Development
❋ enjoys playing in water
❋ prefers one of several toys
❋ repeats sounds and gestures to get attention
❋ waves bye-bye

Every baby is an individual, and your baby may do some of these things more quickly or more slowly than another baby. If you are concerned about your baby's progress, discuss it with your healthcare provider. Also see page xiii.

What's Happening this 40th Week?

✧ *Alternatives to Saying "No"*

Now that your baby is getting around more easily, you may have to tell him "No" more than you did in the past. There are going to be places that are off-limits to him. There will be objects you don't want him touching.

A stern "No" is fast and easy, but you probably want to avoid using this negative all the time. You can't strip your home completely or put everything out of reach. What are some other ways to deal with the situation?

Show Him the Way.   Show baby another way to deal with an object. He may want to tear the pages out of one of your magazines. Instead of letting him destroy it, sit down with him and show him the pictures on the pages. Point out some of the animals or people. Share it with him, then put it where he can't reach it.

Turn Your Baby's Attention.   Before you tell baby not to touch something, try to redirect him. He may be reaching for the glass object because it's pretty and attracts his attention. Instead, offer him something shiny that is also safe, such as a metal spoon or a baby-safe mirror.

Give Him "The Look." He may glance at you before he does something. When he does, and it's something you don't want him to do, look at him sternly. It may be enough to divert him.

Restrain Him When Necessary. When he does something physical, you may have to get physical yourself but not in the same way. If he's pulling the cat's tail or hitting the dog, restrain him. Hold his hands in yours, and quietly tell him "stop pulling the cat's tail" or "it hurts when you hit the dog."

When You Have to Say "No." There are times you are going to have to say "No" to baby. In reality, baby needs to have limits and safety rules; they increase his trust in you. If you keep changing the rules all the time, not saying "No" sometimes and saying "No" at other times, it's confusing for baby. This type of confusion can actually lead to his feeling insecure.

When he's in a dangerous situation, you may not have time to try to distract him or to give him a stern look. It'll be quicker and easier to say "No." But try to keep the word "No" for times you really need it. When children hear the same word over and over, after awhile they don't hear it any more.

> Although baby is learning the difference between *before* and *after,* he lives in *right now.* He still expects his demands to be met immediately.

✴ Is Your Baby Serious?

Some babies seem more serious than others. Often, when a baby is serious, it's not actually a reflection of his personality. It may reflect where he is developmentally. He may study something new very intensely.

A baby's seriousness may also reflect stranger anxiety, which we've discussed in previous weeks. He may not exhibit classical symptoms of screaming or crying when he encounters someone new. But being quiet and a little withdrawn are also signs he's anxious about this new person.

Another reason for his seriousness is that he may be trying to figure out what you think about a stranger. This is called *social referencing.* It often begins around 9 or 10 months of age. He is looking to someone who is important to him—you—to get some clues as how to react. He may be more comfortable with a stranger after he sees you interacting with him or her.

✴ *Hand-Foot-and-Mouth Disease*

When a baby gets hand-foot-and-mouth disease, it can be quite painful for him. He'll have painful sores in his mouth and sores on his hands and feet. Caused by the *coxsackie* virus, it is very infectious.

The problem can occur anytime from 2 weeks after birth through childhood. Parents can become infected when their children do. Symptoms of the problem include:

* rash of blisters involving hands, feet or mouth (throat)
* rapid onset of fever
* sore throat, with ulcers in throat
* feeds poorly
* irritability

What You Can Do at Home.   If these symptoms appear in your baby, try increasing fluids, although that may be difficult because his mouth is sore. Boil bottle nipples and any other items used to feed baby.

When to Call the Doctor.   Contact your pediatrician if your baby has any symptoms of hand-foot-and-mouth disease. Because the problem is caused by a virus, antibiotics are not prescribed. Acetaminophen or ibuprofen may be suggested for baby's fever and/or pain.

✴ *Styes*

A stye is an inflammation, with swelling, of one of the sebaceous glands of the eyelid. It is caused by a bacterial infection and can occur at any age. A stye can be spread by contact with someone who has one, if they touch the infected area then touch someone else. Symptoms include:

* swelling
* redness on the edge of either the upper or lower eyelid
* pain on the edge of either the upper or lower eyelid
* sensitivity to bright lights
* increased tearing

What You Can Do at Home.   If your baby has symptoms of a stye, apply warm-water soaks for 10 to 20 minutes at a time. Decrease light in his room. Everyone should wash their hands frequently. Don't share towels. Avoid irritants, such as cigarette smoke.

When to Call the Doctor.   Call your doctor if your baby has a stye. Treatment he or she will probably prescribe include topical antibiotics, antibiotic eye drops or oral antibiotics. It may be necessary to treat both eyes.

If baby isn't crawling by this time, you might want to discuss it with your pediatrician at your next well-baby checkup.

Toys and Play this 40ᵗʰ Week

✲ *All Gone!*

To help baby learn the difference between full and empty, play this game. Use a couple of plastic see-through boxes or two open-weave laundry baskets. Together, fill one with some objects. When you finish, tell baby, "All filled up!"

Next, encourage baby to move all the objects to the other basket or container. If he needs some help, move the objects with him. He'll love doing this.

When he's finished, turn the empty basket over. Tell baby the objects are "All gone." This fun activity helps him learn a very important concept.

✲ *Bathtime Fun*

If baby is having fun playing in the bath, add some new activities to his bathtime. Get a large plastic straw, and blow bubbles in the tub. Bring the colander or a strainer to his bath, and pour water into it. Tell him it's raining! Show him how to kick his legs and splash.

Week 41

Baby's Age as a Monthly Reference—10 months

HOW BIG IS BABY THIS 41ST WEEK?
Baby weighs 20½ pounds and is 28¾ inches long this week.

Baby Care and Equipment

✄ *Can Yogurt Help Prevent Diarrhea?*
A recent study followed babies between 10 and 18 months old. In the study, some babies were fed yogurt, while others were not. Each baby's stool was evaluated throughout the study. Researchers found that babies who ate yogurt had more "good" bacteria in their intestinal tracts.

Good bacteria in the intestine is a plus for baby. Too much "bad" bacteria can cause diarrhea. Findings suggest that if a baby has some yogurt in her diet on a regular basis, it may help keep harmful bacteria from growing, thus helping to prevent diarrhea.

A bonus to eating yogurt is its calcium content. It also contains riboflavin, potassium and magnesium. Baby needs all these minerals in her diet. Yogurt is a good transitional food for your baby.

You don't have to feed her large amounts of yogurt. A few teaspoons of *plain* (not flavored or sweetened) yogurt might be beneficial for her. Try it—you may be surprised at how much she likes it.

✄ *Dressing for Snowy Weather*
Until your baby is walking and playing in the snow, she probably won't need a one-piece snowsuit when she goes outside. A warm jacket and a blanket may be enough when you just take her in and out of the car while you're out and about.

A good jacket choice is one with a hood that fastens under her chin. Another feature you might want to look for is one with "built-in" mittens. Mittens are attached to sleeves and flip down over baby's hands.

If you live in a very cold area or you and baby spend time outdoors when it's cold, a snowsuit may be necessary. When selecting one, a suit that zips from ankle to neck is the best choice. When baby is walking, don't buy a snowsuit with permanently attached booties. This style can make it difficult for her to walk.

☀ *Don't Let Baby Have Fruit with Seeds*

Does your baby like the fruit of apples, watermelon and grapes? Even if she's not eating them much now, she may be soon. An inhaled seed from these types of fruit can be very dangerous. Under age 5, a child can easily suck a seed into her airway. An inhaled seed can block breathing and cause choking. And if a seed remains in the lung, it may cause an infection.

The best plan is to get rid of all seeds before giving a piece of fruit to baby. Don't give her edible seeds, such as sunflower or pumpkin seeds, until she's at least 5 years old.

If your child begins to cough or to wheeze after eating some fruit, she may have inhaled a seed. Call your pediatrician; he or she may want a chest X-ray taken. If a seed is found, it may need to be removed by a specialist with a tool called a *bronchoscope.*

WATER ALERT!

Water can be deadly to a baby, in more ways than one. Take the following precautions at your house to protect your baby.

- ☀ Tap water can seriously burn a baby. Keep the temperature of your water heater no higher than 120F.
- ☀ Always turn off the hot water before you turn off the cold water.
- ☀ Never leave baby alone around *any* water. It only takes *1 inch* of water for a baby to drown.
- ☀ Fasten every toilet seat closed with special locks/fasteners; a baby can drown in a toilet.
- ☀ Watch out for pet's water dishes—children love to play in them.
- ☀ If you have other children, warn them to close bathroom doors after they use them.

Milestones this 41st Week

☀ *When She "Talks" on Her Toy Telephone*

Your baby may be entertaining you with her "conversations" on a toy phone when she imitates you talking on the telephone. At this age, she is beginning "pseudo-conversation," which means her babbling may sound like a real conversation. She's varying her pitch and changing the rate and volume of what she hears every day. When she "talks" on the phone, it may sound almost like a real conversation.

☀ *Baby Expresses Her Emotions*

Your baby is capable of expressing many emotions, such as sadness, anger, happiness and enjoyment. She learns about emotions from her experiences.

In a situation, she will watch how others react when things happen to them. That's one reason not to overreact when something happens. If you do, you'll soon see baby acting the same way!

Baby may also act like a baby. She is! She may need a reassuring hug or cuddle. Give it to her whenever she asks. When she feels secure, she's ready to learn even more.

✎ *Her Physical Accomplishments Are Many*

Pulling herself to a standing position is easy now. Baby may refuse your help, if you offer it to her. She is also capable of sitting down without falling.

Her grasp is fairly firm. She can use her thumb with more precision. She is steadier in her use of her fingers, so don't be surprised when she does something that requires dexterity, such as putting a coin in a slot.

If your baby appears loose-jointed, it may be due to the fact she is less active physically than other babies. This looseness gradually disappears as her muscles get stronger. She is probably not walking yet, if she's loose-jointed. She needs the support in her hips and knees that stronger muscles offer. But don't be concerned—she'll be walking soon.

✎ *She Continues to Explore*

As baby explores her world around her very thoroughly, she learns many things. She studies various objects and notes the differences in size and shape. She realizes that small objects fit into larger ones. She's even learning that large objects won't fit into smaller ones!

She will search for an object if she sees it hidden. And if you hide it in a place that's a bit difficult to find, like under her blanket, she'll look for it for quite a while. She fully understands that a hidden object continues to exist, even if she can't see it. She is also learning that if a toy or something else is hidden in a second place, it won't be found by looking in the first hiding place.

Trying to figure out how big her body is can be fun. She may crawl into small spaces to see if she fits there. Sometimes she doesn't, which means you'll need to rescue her!

Note: See also the box *Milestones this 41st Week.*

What's Happening this 41st Week?

✎ *Repetition Is Important to Baby*

You may be surprised to discover your baby has favorite stories. She may want to hear them over and over again. It's boring for you, but your little one actually feels more secure with a story she knows.

MILESTONES THIS 41ˢᵀ WEEK

Changes You May See this Week as Baby Develops Physically
* walks while holding both of your hands

Changes You May See this Week in Baby's Developing Senses and Reflexes
* may begin to show preference for one hand and one side of the body

Changes You May See this Week as Baby's Mind Develops
* searches for an object if she saw it hidden

Changes You May See this Week in Baby's Social Development
* shows various moods, such as hurt, happy, sad, angry
* imitates facial expressions
* imitates sounds
* enjoys variations of peek-a-boo

Every baby is an individual, and your baby may do some of these things more quickly or more slowly than another baby. If you are concerned about your baby's progress, discuss it with your healthcare provider. Also see page xiii.

As baby gets older, you'll see more evidence of this type of repetition. It's not unusual for a child to want to watch the same video over and over and over. Experts believe the repetition offers security. Think about it. For a child, every day holds a great many experiences. Many of them are new. So when a child does something repetitious, like watching the same video until it wears out, it provides her a sense of security and control. She *knows* what is going to happen, and it makes her feel safe and secure.

Don't fight it. Read her the stories she loves, and add a new one occasionally. Who knows—one of the new stories may become a favorite for you both!

✴ Cold Sores (Fever Blisters)

Cold sores, also called *fever blisters,* are a common, contagious viral infection. They are caused by the herpes simplex virus Type 1. A cold sore can occur at any age. Most sufferers have their first infection by age 5. Symptoms of a cold sore include:
* eruptions of very small, painful blisters, usually around the mouth
* red ring around blisters
* blisters fill with fluid, then dry up and disappear
* pain at the cold-sore site

A cold sore can result from a fever—that's why they're also called fever blisters. If you find your baby gets these sores when she has a fever, use cold on the area as soon as one begins! It may help stop its development.

What You Can Do at Home.   You can help prevent cold sores by avoiding physical contact with others when they have active lesions. If you've got a cold sore, don't kiss baby! Don't let others with cold sores kiss her, either.

If your baby has a cold sore, there are some things you can do at home to help her feel more comfortable. Some treatments to try at home include the following suggestions.

* Offer baby cold liquids to drink, or have her suck on a frozen pop. This helps ease discomfort.
* Try to keep baby from scratching or picking at the blisters.
* To prevent flare-ups, use zinc oxide on baby's lips when you're going to spend a lot of time outdoors.
* Give her acetaminophen or ibuprofen for discomfort, after consulting with your pediatrician.
* With future outbreaks, apply cold to the area when redness appears. Viruses don't like cold, so it may help prevent an outbreak or lessen its severity.

Ask your baby's doctor about various products now available for treating cold sores. Many are OTC; however, their use may not be appropriate for a baby. Discuss it with your pediatrician.

When to Call the Doctor.   Call your baby's doctor if baby develops signs of a secondary bacterial infection, such as fever, if pus oozes from blisters instead of clear fluid or if she becomes extremely irritable. If your baby has an eruption of lesions on the genitals similar to those around the mouth, notify a doctor.

Your doctor may prescribe antiviral topical or oral medication. Antibiotic ointment may be used if lesions become infected.

> It may be time to start bathing baby every day. She's getting dirtier from trying to feed herself. She's also exploring everyplace, which adds to the dirt. Bathing her in the evening is a good practice. A nice warm bath may help her relax before she goes to bed.

Mumps

Mumps is a contagious disease that causes inflammation of the salivary glands. It can occur at any age but is most common in children between 2 and 12 years of age. Symptoms that your baby has the mumps include:

* inflammation, swelling and pain of the salivary glands
* glands feel hard
* pain increases with chewing or swallowing
* mild fever
* chills
* headache
* pain below ears
* sore throat
* saliva may be increased or diminished
* facial features may be distorted by swelling
* in males, testicles may become painful and swollen

Protect your child by having her immunized against the mumps with the MMR vaccine at the appropriate age. See the immunization schedule on page 36. Immunization offers real protection.

What You Can Do at Home.   If your child gets the mumps before she is immunized, apply heat or ice to the swollen glands. Heat and cold may be alternated. Give her acetaminophen or ibuprofen for discomfort. Don't use aspirin, to avoid *Reye's syndrome; see Week 37.* Offer her plenty of mild fluids; be careful with tart juices because they may increase the pain.

When to Call the Doctor.   Call your pediatrician if you believe your baby has the mumps. He or she will want to know this important information. Other reasons to call the doctor include:

* fever rises above 101F rectally
* vomiting
* abdominal pain
* severe headache not relieved with over-the-counter medication
* swelling or pain in a testicle
* twitching of facial muscles
* seizures
* discomfort or redness in the eyes
* lethargy or extreme irritability

Your baby's doctor may prescribe stronger pain medication to help relieve pain. Cortisone may be used if testicles are involved. Once the disease begins, it must run its natural course. There is no safe, readily available medicine or treatment.

✤ *Upper-Respiratory Infection*

The term *upper-respiratory infection* covers almost any kind of infectious disease involving nasal passages, pharynx (the passageway for air between the larynx and nasal cavity) and bronchi (the two main passageways to the lungs for air). Infections can be caused by either a virus or bacteria.

An infection can occur at any age. Infants under 3 months old have a lower infection rate. This rate soars between 3 and 6 months of age. It remains high through toddler and preschool age. By age 5, respiratory infections are much less frequent.

Infants and young children react more severely to acute respiratory-tract infections than older children. Symptoms of an upper-respiratory infection include:

* fever often appears as the first sign of infection and may reach 103 to 105F, even with mild infections
* listlessness and irritability, or euphoria and hyperactivity
* vomiting
* diarrhea—usually mild but may become severe
* nasal blockage due to swelling, which may interfere with breathing and feeding in infants
* nasal discharge, either thin and watery or very thick
* cough
* sore throat

What You Can Do at Home. If your baby has signs and symptoms of an upper-respiratory infection, use a cool-mist humidifier in your baby's room when she's sleeping. See the discussion of *Humidifiers* in *Week 13.* Warm mist from a hot shower also helps. Offer her lots of liquids so she doesn't get dehydrated.

Before you put her down to sleep in her crib, raise the top (head) end of the crib. This is the best position for easier breathing. Give her ibuprofen or acetaminophen for discomfort and/or fever. If your pediatrician says it's OK, over-the-counter cold medications may be given.

Clear baby's nasal secretions with a bulb syringe and saline nose drops. This helps baby if she's having a hard time breathing and eating at the same time.

When to Call the Doctor. It's important to call baby's doctor if she's under 3 months of age. Also call if a high fever is not relieved with medication, baby shows signs of dehydration, she has difficulty breathing or rapid, labored breathing, she turns blue or gray, or is extremely irritable and can't be comforted.

Your doctor may prescribe antibiotics, if baby has a secondary bacterial infection. Otherwise your doctor will recommend ways to treat symptoms. If baby is extremely dehydrated, she may be admitted to the hospital for hydration. A baby may also be hospitalized if she develops other respiratory problems that may need close monitoring or support.

✤ *Is It the Flu or a Cold?*

Sometimes it's difficult to determine if baby has a cold or the flu. Below is a comparison chart to help you determine which ailment your little one might be suffering from.

Cold	Flu
Baby is slightly tired	She's weak and seems exhausted
She doesn't seem too achy	She seems to feel muscle aches all over
Fever is slight, if at all	Chills, followed by fever
Nose is runny or stuffed up	Signs of respiratory congestion, like a cough
Throat is scratchy after a few days	Sore throat quickly develops
Symptoms begin slowly	Onset of symptoms is very fast

> Don't let your child run around or talk while she eats. She could choke on something. When she doesn't run around with food, it also helps keep the house cleaner.

Toys and Play this 41st Week

✤ *Ice Down the Baby*

When it's warm outside, cool off and have fun at the same time. Fill a plastic or aluminum bowl with water. Place an ice cube in the bowl. Holding baby's hand, touch it to the ice cube for a second. Tell her "The ice cube is cold!" then shiver. Holding the ice cube in your hand, lightly (and very briefly) touch it to parts of her body. Touch her leg, her hand, her arm and her face. Keep telling her that it's cold.

✤ *Hidden Under the Blankets*

Now that baby understands a hidden toy is still there, turn the learning experience into a game. Let her watch you hide a favorite toy under three or four light blankets. Tell her to find the toy. As soon as she catches on, she'll have a great time pulling off each blanket until she reaches her toy.

✤ *Making Noise*

Put uncooked popcorn or rice in a clear plastic bottle with a screw-on lid. A clean 1-liter soda-pop bottle is a good choice. After filling ⅔ full, glue the top on so it can't be removed by baby. Let her shake it. You may have to show her what to do at first, but she'll soon get the hang of it.

Show her how the popcorn or rice bounces. Talk about the loud noise the kernels make in the bottle. Roll the bottle back and forth between you. Shake it in time to some music. Play with it in the bathtub. You'll discover many ways to play with this new toy.

❧ *"Baby, Imitate Me"*
Now that baby is imitating others' behaviors, make it a game. Encourage her to copy simple, fun actions. It will help her learn.

Bang a spoon on a pan. Touch one of your feet, or open and close your mouth. Bounce up and down. Pat your stomach, then rub your head. After each action, encourage baby to try. If she doesn't quite get it, help her repeat the activity. Pretty soon she'll be responding and doing all sorts of things.

Week 42

Baby's Age as a Monthly Reference—10 months

HOW BIG IS BABY THIS 42ND WEEK?
Baby weighs 20½ pounds and is 29 inches long this week.

Baby Care and Equipment

✧ Baby's First "Real" Shoes

Until this time, your baby has probably been wearing shoes to match an outfit or to keep his feet warm. Those shoes weren't made for walking. Now that he's getting ready to walk, it's a good idea to start thinking about shoes that *are* made for walking!

Most pediatricians recommend baby practice walking in his bare feet when he's in the house. Walking barefoot helps strengthen foot muscles. Bare feet also allow baby's foot to spread, increasing ground contact. And the bare arch forms a suction that helps the foot grip. When baby's wearing shoes, his foot can't do these things.

When and How to Buy Shoes. When your little one is steady on his feet (leaning or standing on his own), it's time to buy real shoes. It's a good idea to go to a shoe store that specializes in children's shoes. Be sure the salesperson is trained in fitting shoes to babies' feet. Have your baby's feet measured while he's standing up. If one foot is bigger than the other, buy shoes to fit the *larger* foot.

The shoe you choose should have a little room in the toe to allow for growth. Don't buy shoes that are too big in hopes you'll save a little money and not have to replace them as often. When a shoe is too big, baby has to adjust his stride to keep it on. They may also cause him to stumble a lot.

If your baby is fairly active and moving around a great deal, a sturdy athletic shoe may be a good choice. There are many to choose from.

When you do need to buy his next new pair of shoes, probably in 2 to 3 months, be sure to have his foot remeasured. You can't just buy the next size.

What Kind of Shoe Is Best? Some parents believe a baby shoe must be hard soled to support the foot. However, your baby's first shoes should be light and flexible. The shoe should bend at the ball of the foot, not just the arch. This allows a shoe to conform to the foot more readily. The more a shoe bends, the better it is for baby's foot. If a shoe bends easily, it helps baby's arches develop properly.

Squeeze the sides of the shoe at the ball of the foot. The shoe should buckle slightly at the top. Check the inside of the shoe for defects, such as poorly sewn linings or little pieces that stick out. They could cause discomfort.

You don't have to buy high-top shoes. The high-top baby shoes that you might have worn don't offer any greater support to the ankle or foot than low-cut shoes. If baby likes to take his shoes off or has trouble keeping them on, high tops may be a good choice for him.

Baby's feet perspire more than yours do, so avoid shoes made of vinyl, plastic or synthetics. A natural material, such as soft leather or canvas, allows his feet to breathe. A shoe should be sturdy but not rigid. Baby should be able to flex his forefoot slightly, which helps him walk better.

A round-toed shoe is a good choice. They don't restrict movement as much. Check to be sure the soles have some tread for traction but not too much. You don't want soles to be slippery, but you don't want them to grip the floor too tightly, either. Avoid bulky or platform soles.

If you want to buy dress shoes, that's OK, but save them for special occasions. They don't usually offer enough support to wear every day. Be sure laces are not too long. Buckles or straps are good choices.

Checking the Fit.   When you buy baby shoes, check the fit very closely. There should be about one finger's width (baby's finger not yours) between the end of the toes and the end of the shoe. This space allows for some growth.

Check the fit of baby's shoes every week. Baby could have a growth spurt at any time! As long as there is adequate space between the end of his big toe and the tip of the shoe, he's OK. However, when his toe touches the tip of the shoe, it's time to buy a new pair.

If shoes seem to cause discomfort, watch how your baby walks in them. If his coordination, balance or walking pattern change, it could indicate a problem. Be careful to keep checking his feet for blisters and other problems.

Other Baby-Shoe Tips.   Choose plain socks to wear with shoes. If socks have grippers on them, it's hard to slide baby's feet in and out of shoes.

Clip baby's toenails on a regular basis. Long toenails can interfere with a comfortable shoe fit.

If someone offers you a pair of shoes from another baby, pass them up. A shoe molds to the shape of a child's foot. This could result in a poor fit or inadequate support for your baby.

✼ Scheduling Solids

By offering your baby more solid food at mealtime, you reinforce your baby's milk-feeding schedule. Even at this age, when he's eating at least two meals a day, breast milk or formula should still be supplying much of his nutrition. Offer the breast or a bottle when he's hungry, in between meals.

✼ A Sunburn with Little Sun Exposure?

How is it possible for a baby or child to get a sunburn when he's outside for only a very short time? Look to the medication he's taking!

Sometimes a medication can cause skin to become more sensitive to sunlight. Sun exposure can actually cause a rash or sunburn on exposed skin. It may not be apparent; it can take several days to appear.

At other times, when baby's not taking medication, sun exposure on skin that has touched fresh foods can cause problems. Celery and the juices and/or oils from lemon or lime rinds can cause a rash. The rash may itch, blister and turn red or dark brown.

> Some common drugs that can increase sunlight sensitivity include those listed below:
> * Advil, Nuprin, Motrin (ibuprofen)
> * Bactrim (sulfamethoxazole)
> * Benadryl (diphenhydramine hydrochloride)
> * Cipro (ciprofloxin)
> * Floxin (ofloxin)

If your child experiences any reaction, treat it like you would a normal sunburn. Cool compresses help relieve irritation, as does fragrance-free lotion. Some products are designed to reduce and/or relieve sunburn pain. Check with your pediatrician before using them. In some cases, cortisone cream helps relieve discomfort. Again, make sure it's OK with baby's doctor.

Before giving your child any medication (prescription or over-the-counter), check with the doctor and pharmacist about any possible sunlight reactions. If a reaction is indicated, keep baby out of the sun while he's taking the medication. If you have to go out in the sun, be sure he's covered by long pants, long sleeves and a hat. See the box above for some common medications that cause sunlight reactions.

Milestones this 42ⁿᵈ Week

✼ Baby May Take only One Nap

At around this age, some babies take only one 1-hour nap during the day. They may sleep longer at night to help make up for it. Many babies choose to nap in the morning. However, it may be difficult for a baby who naps in the morning to make it all the way through the afternoon in a pleasant mood.

Now may be the time to encourage an after-lunch nap. It will help your baby retain his good mood through dinnertime. You may have to make some adjustments in his routine to accomplish this. You may have to promote a later waking time. Lunch may have to be fed earlier than normal, such as 11:00am. These changes, and any others you choose to make, can make the evenings more enjoyable for everyone in the family.

✴ *Does Baby Act Helpless?*
Baby has learned a new lesson. One of the best ways to solve a problem is to have someone do it for him!

Sometimes your baby will pretend to be helpless. He will expect you to take care of him immediately. It doesn't help him learn what he is capable of doing if you always respond to his demands. As hard as it may be to do, let him try to do many things on his own. You want baby to learn to think for himself and to do things he is capable of doing.

✴ *When Baby Ignores You*
Sometimes it seems as if your baby is ignoring you. He doesn't seem to hear you when you talk to him. Don't get upset. He probably *isn't* ignoring you. He may be concentrating so much on doing something that he just doesn't respond. It may be difficult for him to switch from one task to another (from concentrating on a toy to concentrating on you!). Allow him the time he needs to make transitions.

✴ *Being Able to Move about on His Own*
At this age, your baby may dislike being confined. He may fight being put in a stroller or his car seat. When possible, allow him the freedom to move around. Instead of putting him in a stroller and taking him for a walk, let him crawl around on the grass in your yard.

A word of warning: Even if baby doesn't want to be put in his car seat, it's important for you to place him in it *every time* he rides in the car. You may have to devise ways he can't undo restraints or get out of them. He is not safe in a car unless he's in his car seat!

Note: See also the box *Milestones this 42ª Week.*

What's Happening this 42nd Week?

✴ *Make Mealtime Fun*
Is mealtime with baby a hassle? Is it messy? Make feeding easier on you and baby by trying some of the following suggestions.

- ✴ Feed yourself first. Eat in an exaggerated way. Show how much you like the food. He'll probably want to try it if he thinks *you* like it.

MILESTONES THIS 42ND WEEK

Changes You May See this Week as Baby Develops Physically
* sits down from standing position

Changes You May See this Week in Baby's Developing Senses and Reflexes
* responds to music by rocking, bouncing, swaying, humming

Changes You May See this Week as Baby's Mind Develops
* may repeat word incessantly, making it an answer to every question

Changes You May See this Week in Baby's Social Development
* grows aware of self
* imitates gestures

Every baby is an individual, and your baby may do some of these things more quickly or more slowly than another baby. If you are concerned about your baby's progress, discuss it with your healthcare provider. Also see page xiii.

* "Open the door." When baby is hungry, but not *too* hungry, open your mouth wide. Say "open the door." Once he opens his mouth, put the food in.
* Up and in. When feeding baby, put a spoonful of the food in his mouth as you lift the spoon up. His upper lip will clean the spoon, which helps food stay in his mouth!
* Don't push it. If baby doesn't want to eat a meal, he'll be OK. Sometimes he just doesn't feel like eating. He may be teething, and his mouth is a little sore. He may be getting a cold. Or maybe he doesn't like what you're offering. Skip solids for a meal or two, then offer them again.
* Occupy his hands. Some babies want to take the spoon themselves. Some like to pour their liquids on the high-chair tray. Some want to drop food on the floor. Give baby a spoon of his own when you feed him. Use plates and bowls that attach to the tray. Some high chairs have activity bars that will entertain him. Use whatever methods work best for you.

Undescended Testicle

Before birth, a baby boy's testicles travel down the pelvis and into the scrotum. This usually occurs around the 7th month of gestation. An *undescended testicle* means that the testicle did not make this journey.

About 3% of all full-term baby boys are born with one or both testicles undescended. By about 6 months after birth, most testicles descend on their own. However, about 1% of all baby boys under 1 year have a testicle that has not descended to the proper position.

Surgery to correct the problem is not usually performed until after a baby is 6 months old. However, it is often considered if a baby's testicles have not descended by then. If a testicle hasn't appeared by 6 months of age, it is unlikely to descend later. If the testicle remains in the pelvis, it begins to change microscopically around 1 year of age. These changes could affect fertility later in life.

Performing surgery to correct the problem on a baby around 6 months of age is considered safe. He's old enough to tolerate the surgical procedure and the general anesthesia. Most medical problems that could interfere with surgery have usually been discovered by then.

What Surgery Involves.   A small incision is made in the groin. The surgeon finds the testicle and frees it from the tissue that is restraining it. Next, an incision is made in the scrotum. The testicle is pulled down into the scrotum.

Surgery for an undescended testicle is often done as an outpatient procedure. Recovery takes only a couple of days.

✿ *Food Poisoning*
The term *food poisoning* is a term used to describe an illness resulting from eating a food that contains poisonous substances. True food poisoning includes poisoning from mushrooms, shellfish, insecticides and milk from cows that have eaten poisonous plants. The food-rotting process can also poison foods.

Food poisoning usually occurs in those who eat solids. It would be extremely rare in a baby that is not yet eating solid foods to be exposed to contaminated foods. Symptoms of food poisoning include:
* nausea
* vomiting
* severe abdominal cramps
* profuse diarrhea

What You Can Do at Home.   If your baby exhibits any of the above symptoms, offer him lots of fluid to help prevent dehydration. Allow him plenty of rest.

When to Call the Doctor.   Call the doctor if your baby develops a fever or signs of dehydration. Medical treatment is usually unnecessary. Symptoms usually improve within 24 hours.

✳ *Tick Bites*
A baby can get bitten by a tick at any age. This can be serious for two reasons. The first is that the tick can attach itself to the baby and must be removed by you. The second is the chance of contracting various diseases from tick bites, including Lyme disease, Rocky Mountain spotted fever, tick fever, spotted fever or tick typhus.

You may notice a tick attached to baby when you bathe him or change him. Or you may notice various symptoms of a tick bite, which include the following:

* a red rash on the skin
* fever
* lethargy
* nausea
* vomiting
* chills
* difficulty feeding
* irritability

What You Can Do at Home. Always examine your baby's body if you have been in a tick-infested area. Look over his entire body, particularly his hair (if he has any).

If you live in an area where ticks are common, take some preventive measures for baby. If he's sitting in the grass, be sure he is dressed in long sleeves and long pants. Keep socks on his feet and a hat on his head. Check him thoroughly each time you undress or bathe him to see if he has any ticks on his body or any signs of a tick bite.

When to Call the Doctor. If you think your baby has been bitten by a tick, call your doctor. He or she may prescribe antibiotics, such as tetracycline or chloramphenicol, depending on baby's age. Acetaminophen or ibuprofen may be suggested to treat pain and/or fever.

If you notice a sore with a bull's-eye appearance, it could be the sign of Lyme disease. Contact your doctor immediately!

✳ *Puncture Wounds*
A puncture wound occurs when baby's skin is pierced by a sharp, pointed object. If the object is dirty or rusty, there is concern about tetanus infection. A wound of this type can occur at any age. Symptoms of a puncture wound include:

* a hole in the skin
* bleeding from skin
* redness or swelling in the area

What You Can Do at Home.   If your baby gets a puncture wound, wash the area with soap and water. Keep the area clean and dry by covering it lightly with a bandage. Apply gentle pressure if the wound bleeds.

When to Call the Doctor.   Call the doctor if your baby gets a puncture wound. Your physician will want to know about it. If bleeding continues, if there is extreme swelling or pain, or if you are concerned about damage to underlying structures or organs, call your doctor. If the wound occurs near the eyes or any other vital structure, call your pediatrician.

Your doctor will probably suggest antibiotic gels or oral antibiotics. He or she will advise you on how to clean and dress the wound.

Toys to entertain baby that also help his development include:
* nesting cups, stacking rings, pails, balls and soft bags to encourage swatting, stacking, throwing and grasping
* stable push toys to encourage walking
* pop-up toys, reversible dolls and reversible puppets to help him learn what's out of sight hasn't disappeared forever

---

Toys and Play this 42nd Week

✶ *Play the Tickle Game*

Most babies love to be tickled. Your fingers are the best tickle tools around, but you can also use other things. If you have long hair, lightly stroke it on baby's arm. Gently move the fringe of a blanket over his face. A clean feather duster can delight him. A soft tissue or the fingers of a glove can make him laugh.

After you tickle him, encourage him to tickle you. Let him start with his fingers (he'll probably need your help). Then show him how to use the other tickle tools. You'll soon be laughing together.

✶ *Talking on the Telephone*

As we discussed previously, your baby may enjoy "talking" on his toy telephone. He will also be happy when he hears a voice he knows on a real telephone!

He's probably watched you talk on the telephone countless times. He can't hold the receiver himself yet, but he can listen. When grandma calls or daddy calls, let him listen to their voice on the phone. In addition to the fun he'll have, it helps him concentrate on speech, even when he can't see the speaker.

✎ *Making Up Songs*

To help your baby recognize parts of his body, make up a song. Sing a song or rhyme that names body parts and what they do. Bathing or changing are good times to sing them. You can sing a song about how his legs are for walking and his lips are for talking. Or his arms are for waving and his head is for shaving. Anything silly and fun can help him learn.

> Baby may be doing something new—asking for something by pointing to it.

✎ *Construct an Indoor Sandbox*

When it's rainy or cold outside, bring the fun indoors! Make an indoor "sandbox," and your little one will have lots of fun playing in it.

Gather together a large, shallow pan, cornmeal, a tarp or sheet to cover the floor and some toys. Lay the tarp or sheet on the kitchen floor or some other uncarpeted area (a bare floor is easier to clean than carpet). Place the container on top of the sheet, and put about an inch or so of cornmeal in it. Sit baby down next to the container, and give him a spoon and some other toys to "play in the sand." Plastic cups, small strainers and scoops are all fun to use.

Week 43

Baby's Age as a Monthly Reference—10 months

HOW BIG IS BABY THIS 43ᴿᴰ WEEK?

Baby weighs 20¾ pounds and is 29 inches long this week.

Baby Care and Equipment

✎ *Taking Care of Baby's Hair*

By this time, your baby may have enough hair to brush and to style. If she's had hair for a while, you've probably had to deal with it. If she doesn't have any yet, don't be too concerned. She'll be getting some soon. (Until then, just tape a bow to her head or use one of those cute little decorated bands that fits around her head!)

When you wash her hair, apply a conditioner once a week. Do that *only* if she needs it. If her hair is fairly manageable, you won't need conditioner.

The best time to style a baby's hair is after washing, while it's still wet. It should hold its shape while it dries. You can use your fingers to style it during her first 6 months. Arrange it in a style that it wants to go in. If baby has stick-straight hair, ringlets just won't hold!

As baby gets older (or if you absolutely need it), use a soft baby hairbrush to brush and to style baby's hair. Avoid using a hair dryer until baby is about 2 years old. The heat from a hair dryer can damage baby's hair shafts.

You may notice that baby has a bald spot on one side of her head. Check her while she's sleeping. Does she always turn her head to the same side? If she does, she may be rubbing the same spot against the sheets every night, resulting in a bald spot. After she goes to sleep, gently turn her head to the other side.

Baby hair is very fragile, so take care of it. Don't use barrettes or elastic bands very often. When you do use them, be gentle. Don't pull hair too tight. If you do, you can damage baby's scalp. If you notice a red rash on her scalp after pulling her hair tight in a band or barrette, her hair follicles are inflamed. If you pull the same area of hair too tightly for too long, you may cause permanent hair loss.

Your baby may not be very cooperative, either. Many babies pull out every hair accessory you or anyone else puts in her hair. Be careful of the types of accessories you choose if your baby does this. She might pull it out of her hair and put it in her mouth. She could choke on it.

✻ *When Baby Gags on Foods*
Are you still feeding your baby puréed foods because you're afraid she might choke? Some parents hesitate to add lumpier foods to baby's diet because they don't want her to gag or to choke. However, not offering these foods can interfere with baby's learning to eat properly.

One of the goals of feeding solids to a baby during the first year is to teach tongue control. Your baby needs to learn how to push food around in her mouth with her tongue. She needs to progress through the different textures of food—from strained to puréed to lumpy to small bits of "real food," such as well-cooked meats and vegetables. If she doesn't progress through these foods, she may have problems later.

You may not know exactly when to offer the next level of food. Experts suggest offering baby foods of the next level in manageable bites when she masters a level. For example, when she's eating puréed food without problems, begin introducing lumpier foods.

Don't be alarmed when baby gags on a food every once in awhile. When she's learning to swallow, she gags as a normal way to protect herself. Some babies have a more-sensitive gag reflex than others and may gag more easily. However, if baby gags consistently, contact your pediatrician. It may indicate a problem.

> Experts believe that family dinnertime is important in raising happy, well-adjusted children. Statistics show that 67% of all families eat a meal together at least 5 times every week. Make it a practice in your family.

✻ *Thirst Quenchers*
As baby is getting older, your pediatrician may recommend giving her more fluids. There are many liquids you can offer her. Some are better than others. Below is a comparison of various liquids you might be thinking about offering baby:
- water—one of the best because it doesn't contain sugar, caffeine or flavorings
- fruit pieces—contain a lot of water, often as high as 85%
- juice—often contains lots of sugar
- soda—usually high in sugar and caffeine
- ice pops—often contain flavorings and sugar
- sports drinks—contain sugar and electrolytes, which are usually unnecessary

At a well-baby checkup, discuss offering baby other fluid sources. Your pediatrician will probably have some valuable suggestions.

Milestones this 43ʳᵈ Week

✻ *Baby's on the Move*

By this time, your baby is probably moving all over the place. She may be cruising around the furniture with ease. She may crawl into corners and get stuck when she can't get out. She may pull herself up to a standing position and hold on with only one hand.

During this time, your baby will fall and have other minor accidents. It's only natural. If you don't get upset when she falls, she probably won't either.

The exception—when she really hurts herself, take care of her. But when she takes a minor spill, react with a laugh, as if it were a big joke. You may be surprised when she falls again—just to hear you laugh!

✻ *Your Baby's Relationship with You*

Your relationship with your baby is valuable to her and to you. However, she will probably have a different relationship with each of her parents. The way one parent interacts with her affects their parent–child relationship. Each parent expands baby's understanding of her world around her but in different ways. This is natural in any parent–child relationship.

Baby may be cruising around the furniture now.

She feels a very strong attachment to her parents and other care givers. She will seek the attention of these special people. On the other hand, she may be even more wary of strangers. She may look to her parents when a stranger approaches.

✻ *Baby's Vocabulary*

Your baby probably isn't talking much. But she understands quite a bit about her world. She knows the names of as many as a dozen objects (or more). She can follow simple instructions or directions.

Because she is beginning to understand a lot more, you might want to begin saying "please" and "thank you" when you make a request of her. You may be doing this already. If she hears it now, it will become part of her vocabulary.

♪ Baby Likes to Stand

By this age, many babies like to stand whenever they can. Your baby may want to stand up for baths, diaper changes and even meals. Allow her the opportunity to stand *when* it is safe, but don't let her endanger herself. You may have to be forceful with her, if she wants to stand when it is unsafe to do so.

> If baby is pulling herself to a standing position, lower the mattress in her crib to its lowest setting. You don't want her to fall out!

♪ Her Perception Sharpens

You may notice baby playing very intently with her toys. She may move them up and down. Or she may move them closer, then farther away. When she turns them upside down, she gets another view. Squinting provides a different perspective. When baby engages in these activities, she is exploring what objects look like. It's all part of her learning experience.

Note: See also the box *Milestones this 43rd Week.*

What's Happening this 43rd Week?

♪ Who Should Not Be Immunized?

Some children who have special health problems may need to avoid certain immunizations. Your pediatrician will discuss the situation with you if he or she believes your child is in a high-risk group. He or she will discuss your child's health history and the potential risks of immunizing her, including side effects. The Centers for Disease Control (CDC) publishes *Vaccine Information Statements.* Ask your doctor for copies if you are concerned.

Children who should not receive certain immunizations include those with seizure disorders, immune problems and neurological disorders. For these babies, some vaccines are safe; others are not. Your doctor will carefully evaluate your child.

If your child suffers from an allergy to a component of a vaccine, such as eggs or yeast, a vaccine may not be recommended. If your child has a food allergy or drug sensitivity, discuss every immunization with your pediatrician *before* it is given.

A word of caution: Some parents may choose not to have a child immunized for personal reasons. However, every unimmunized child puts every other child at risk, especially those who cannot receive immunizations

MILESTONES THIS 43ᴿᴰ WEEK

Changes You May See this Week as Baby Develops Physically
* may be able to raise herself to a standing position

Changes You May See this Week in Baby's Developing Senses and Reflexes
* can carry two small objects in one hand

Changes You May See this Week as Baby's Mind Develops
* reaches behind her to get a toy without seeing it
* is interested in fitting things together

Changes You May See this Week in Baby's Social Development
* seeks social approval
* seeks companionship and attention
* fears strange places
* can feed herself entire meals

Every baby is an individual, and your baby may do some of these things more quickly or more slowly than another baby. If you are concerned about your baby's progress, discuss it with your healthcare provider. Also see page xiii.

for the reasons stated above. Immunizing your child is a protective measure, and every parent should consider a decision not to immunize very carefully.

✶ *Solo Play Is Important*
Solo play teaches baby many things. She is learning how to entertain herself. When concentrating on a task, she may make developmental advances. Allow her the opportunity for solo play, but make sure she's safe.

When baby is playing by herself, always stay within hearing range of her. Make sure the area she's in has been childproofed. Below is a discussion of some safety measures you may want to take to keep your little one extra safe.

* Examine her toys for loose threads and tags. Remove them.
* Keep the playpen free of objects she could use to crawl out of it.
* Use gates or barriers to keep her in one area or out of another.
* Give her age-appropriate toys. If you give her toys that are too old for her, they aren't very much fun for her to play with. They might also contain pieces or parts that could harm her.

✶ *Blisters from New Shoes*

When your baby starts wearing shoes, she may get a blister or two. It's not unusual—nearly everyone has gotten a blister from a new pair of shoes at some time.

> When baby is concentrating on an activity, don't disturb her. Let her make her own discoveries.

A blister is caused by something rubbing on the outermost layer of skin, such as with new shoes. This top layer of skin separates from the under layer. The space between the two layers often fills with fluid. Symptoms of the problem include:

* redness of skin
* fluid-filled blister
* baby cries when shoes are put on
* baby refuses to wear shoes

What You Can Do at Home.   To help prevent the problem, put socks on baby when she wears shoes. Her socks should fit well; they shouldn't be too tight or too loose, nor too heavy. When she's moving around and walking, buy shoes that fit correctly, not ones that just look "cute."

If you notice a blister on your baby's foot after she wears new shoes, there are some measures you can take. Apply a cold compress to the area for a few minutes. Wash the area with mild soap and water. Pat dry.

Using a sterilized needle, puncture the blister at the edge. Gently squeeze out the fluid. Leave the skin in place. Cover with a light bandage. Before you put baby's shoes on again, apply moleskin to the area to protect it from rubbing.

You might want to talk to your pediatrician before you buy baby shoes to see if there is a type of shoe that would be best for your baby. Do this at one of your well-baby checkups.

When to Call the Doctor.   Call your baby's doctor if she has a blister that appears to be infected. If there is any discharge, bleeding or swelling at the site, call your pediatrician's office. If there is a problem, you may be advised to put antibiotic ointment on the area to deal with any infection.

✶ *Gastroenteritis*

Gastroenteritis is an inflammation of the stomach and intestinal tract, resulting in irritation or infection of the digestive tract. It can be contagious and can occur at any age. Symptoms of gastroenteritis include:

* vomiting
* diarrhea
* irritability
* poor appetite
* fever

What You Can Do at Home. You can try various treatments at home. Fluids are necessary, but the bowel also needs to rest. Offer a clear-liquid diet for the first day or two. In young infants, a commercial electrolyte solution, such as Pedialyte, can be used. In older infants, clear liquid is "anything you can see through."

For a child under 1 year, give ½ ounce of fluid every 20 to 30 minutes. For a child over 1 year, give 1 ounce every 30 minutes. Consult your pediatrician before using this treatment.

When a child has been free of diarrhea for 1 day, a bland diet may be offered. This includes bananas, rice, applesauce, tea and toast. This called the *BRATT diet.* (You may decide not to offer tea at this age.) If diarrhea doesn't recur within 2 hours after eating, continue feeding the bland foods for 24 hours. Gradually work back to a normal diet.

Caution: Do *not* use any nonprescription antidiarrheal drugs without first consulting your baby's doctor.

When to Call the Doctor. If your baby has symptoms of gastroenteritis, you may be able to take care of the problem at home. However, you should call the doctor if:

* rectal temperature rises to 103F or higher
* child shows signs of dehydration
* symptoms don't improve in 48 hours, despite treatment
* your baby is under 2 months old

Your physician will probably recommend treating symptoms at home. However, hospitalization may be required for I.V. hydration, if baby is dehydrated. The condition should improve in 48 hours.

✣ *Pneumonia*

Pneumonia is an inflammation of the lungs caused by bacteria, viruses or chemical irritants. There are over 50 causes of pneumonia. It can occur at any age but is most severe in infants and young children. Symptoms of pneumonia vary. Those you should be alert for include:

* fever—can range from mild to high (99 to 105F)
* cough—slight to severe
* sputum may contain blood or bloody streaks
* rapid breathing
* fatigue
* chills
* pain in the chest
* loss of appetite
* difficulty breathing

What You Can Do at Home. If your baby develops symptoms of pneumonia, use a cool-mist humidifier to increase air moisture when she's sleeping. See the discussion of *Humidifiers* in *Week 13*. Don't use cough medicine, unless advised to do so by your pediatrician. You don't want to suppress the cough with medicine if it produces sputum. Sputum helps the body get rid of lung secretions.

Offer lots of fluids. Let baby sleep when she wants to. Give ibuprofen or acetaminophen for discomfort and/or fever.

When to Call the Doctor. Call your pediatrician if you are concerned that your baby may have pneumonia. Treatments he or she will recommend include X-rays to diagnose pneumonia and a sputum culture. Antibiotics may be prescribed to fight the infection. In severe cases, a baby will be hospitalized.

> Your baby's weight at this age has nothing to do with her weight in the future. During the first few months, some babies grow very quickly. As they get older, their growth slows down. The important focus is the height-to-weight tables. If baby's height stays apace with her weight, she's doing OK.

Toys and Play this 43rd Week

To encourage your baby's independence and solo play, clear out a low shelf in the family room or another room. Put some of her toys and books on the shelf. When she can get to her things without your help, it increases her sense of independence. It also lets her play by herself when she wants to.

﹡ *The Finger-Counting Game*

This finger-counting play helps baby develop some math concepts. Touch each finger of one of her hands while you recite:

> *1, 2, 3, 4, 5*
> *I caught a bird alive!*
> *Why did I let her go?* (gently squeeze her thumb)
> *Because she bit my finger so—ouch!*

Repeat the song touching each toe on her foot. Change the last line from "finger" to "toe."

✢ *The Egg-Carton Delight*

Babies love to poke and touch things. Feeling objects helps them learn about them. Glue different items in the cups on the inside of an egg carton. Choose hard pasta or cereal pieces, fabric, paper or plastic wrap—anything that baby might like to touch and feel. Give her the egg carton, and let her explore the different objects. Be sure you stay with her while she plays with it, in case small pieces break off. You don't want her to choke on anything.

✢ *Make an Obstacle Course*

Set up a fun obstacle course in the family room. Put down a blanket, pillows and other objects for baby to climb over or crawl around. Be sure they will support her weight and do not move easily. Encourage her to traverse the obstacle course one way, then another.

Week 44

Baby's Age as a Monthly Reference —
end of 10 months or beginning of 11 months

HOW BIG IS BABY THIS 44TH WEEK?
Baby weighs 21 pounds and is 29½ inches long this week.

Baby Care and Equipment

✣ *Portable Seating for Baby*
When you take baby out to eat at a restaurant, you can usually find high chairs or baby seats. However, some places don't have them. When you go to relatives' or friends' homes who don't have children or grandchildren, you may wish you had a high chair.

A product that can help you out in these situations is a portable baby seat. This device is actually a hook-on high chair that folds up for easy transport. Its grippers attach the seat to the edge of the table, and baby is "suspended" at the table. It's very handy and can be used with most tables and many counters. It's safe for children from age 6 months to 3 years or up to 50 pounds. Before placing baby in this type of chair, check to be sure it is stable.

✣ *Keep Minor Abrasions Moist*
A study by plastic surgeons has shown that minor wounds heal faster when they are kept moist and covered. When your baby gets a cut or scrape, keep this in mind.

After gently cleaning the area with soap and water, apply a triple antibiotic ointment to the cut or scrape. Cover with a bandage. The ointment helps protect against infection and keeps the area moist so it doesn't form irritating small cracks as it heals. Keep the area covered until a scab forms.

✣ *Could Baby Have a Rubber Allergy?*
An allergy to rubber isn't too common—only about 1 person in 100 suffers from it. However, it's good to be aware of it, especially if your baby has un-explained symptoms.

Research has shown that if a baby is allergic to rubber and sucks on a rub-ber pacifier, he may have a reaction. The most common reactions include

437

itching, coughing, wheezing, sneezing and swelling. When babies with this allergy were given a silicone pacifier, symptoms disappeared!

✻ *Can a Baby Eat a Vegetarian Diet?*
Some parents choose to feed their families a vegetarian diet for religious or personal reasons. Many want to know if a baby can get the nutrients he needs from a vegetarian meal plan.

A baby can be fed a vegetarian diet if he is offered a wide variety of foods. Seek the advice of your pediatrician if you want to feed baby a vegetarian meal plan. He or she will advise you about any special concerns or needs. Different vegetarian eating plans require special considerations.

The Ovo-Lacto Vegetarian Diet.   This type of vegetarian diet includes dairy products and eggs. When baby is eating solid foods, be sure he receives adequate amounts of food that contain protein, iron and vitamin B_{12}. However, don't feed him any egg whites until he is at least a year old. This helps him avoid developing an allergy to eggs.

The Lacto-Vegetarian Diet.   Dairy foods are part of this vegetarian diet, but eggs are not. Adequate amounts of food that contain protein, iron and B_{12} are necessary in this diet plan.

The Vegan Diet.   This diet does not include any animal products, such as dairy foods or eggs. When solids are introduced to baby, they must contain adequate amounts of calcium, protein, iron and B_{12}.

You can meet these needs by giving baby iron-enriched grains and cereals. Serving them with vitamin-C foods helps with iron absorption.

Soy products are rich in protein, and many are enriched with calcium and B_{12}. Soy products baby may like include tofu, soy hot dogs, soy cheese and soy milk. By around 7 months, you can start adding puréed beans, lentils and split peas as other sources of protein to baby's diet.

If you choose to feed your baby a vegetarian diet, be sure you discuss it first with your pediatrician. It can be difficult for baby to get all the nutrients he needs. You may need assistance from a dietician in meeting his nutritional requirements.

Milestones this 44ᵗʰ Week

✻ *He's Very Curious*
Baby's curiosity leads him into many activities. He opens drawers to explore the contents. He may decide to pull everything he can out of the drawer. He

pokes his fingers into objects to see how far his finger will go. He pushes, pinches or rolls an object to see what will happen. He tries to fit objects together. You may find baby also wants to take things apart.

✣ *Baby's "Talking"*

Baby talk exists all over the world. "Baby words" help your child communicate his wishes or express his feelings. A word in baby talk is usually shorter and easier to say than the same word in adult language. For example, baby can say "mama" and "dada" long before he can say "mommy" and "daddy" or "mother" and "father."

Your baby has learned that he can say some words that carry authority. You may hear him say "No," even when he means "Yes." As he begins to be more discriminate in his use of the word, he may say "No" and shake his head at the same time.

✣ *His Love of Books*

> Be ready! Keep a one-time-use camera close at hand—in your diaper bag, glove box or purse. You'll always be prepared when baby is doing something you want to remember.

Your baby enjoys books; he likes to listen to you read to him while he looks at the pictures. You may notice him pointing to and labeling pictures in a book.

Choose books that contain words and pictures of objects he's familiar with. A simple book with a picture of a ball on one page and a shoe on the other is a good choice. These are things he knows.

Let him turn the pages, if he is able. If he wants to turn them but can't, help him out. Spend as much time as he wants on each page of a book. He may be studying a picture in relation to something else he is learning.

> You may find your baby is more cooperative now. He may help dress himself or want to dry himself after his bath.

✣ *As Baby Moves Around*

Your baby is probably walking around the edges of the furniture a lot now. When he's comfortable cruising, he'll begin to let go a little or hold on less tightly. You'll see him practicing standing on his toes or standing on one leg. He is probably comfortable bending over to pick up an object, supporting himself with only one hand.

Baby may be climbing more. He may try to climb on top of an object as high as 1 foot. You may even see him climb on and off a chair. When he gets on something, he makes an attempt to get off. He knows about how far away the floor is. He can slowly back down off an object when he wants to. He uses his feet as "feelers." Don't be surprised when he calls for your help if he gets stuck.

His feet may roll in somewhat at the edges. This condition corrects itself as he learns to balance and his foot muscles get stronger.

✻ *Baby Play*

Your baby may become bored with some of his toys. If he doesn't seem interested in some of them, put them away for a while. He'll let you know if he wants them again.

Baby wants to play games with people. But it's a good idea to encourage him in his solo play. Let him play by himself near you.

Note: See also the box *Milestones this 44th Week.*

MILESTONES THIS 44TH WEEK

Changes You May See this Week as Baby Develops Physically
✻ climbs up and down from chairs

Changes You May See this Week in Baby's Developing Senses and Reflexes
✻ may differentiate use of hands

Changes You May See this Week as Baby's Mind Develops
✻ likes to take things apart and put them back together
✻ opens drawers and cupboards to explore contents
✻ experiments with means to a goal, such as using a large-wheeled toy for a walker

Changes You May See this Week in Baby's Social Development
✻ begins to learn sexual identity
✻ helps dress himself
✻ enjoys games, such as hide-and-seek, rolling back and forth on floor
✻ drops objects for someone else to pick up

Every baby is an individual, and your baby may do some of these things more quickly or more slowly than another baby. If you are concerned about your baby's progress, discuss it with your healthcare provider. Also see page xiii.

What's Happening this 44th Week?

⚘ *Play It Safe in the Sand*

A lot of infectious organisms live and thrive in sandy areas. Some of these include staph, strep and pinworms. These organisms are more prevalent at beaches where waste water collects near the shoreline. A sandbox can also be suspect. Cats often use them for litter boxes.

Before you put baby down in the sand, make sure any cuts are bandaged. When he's finished playing in the sand, bathe him thoroughly, especially his hands. If he gets any cuts or scrapes while playing, wash the area with soap and water, apply triple antibiotic ointment and bandage.

⚘ *Making Friends*

It's a good idea for baby to start interacting with other children, if he hasn't already. If he's not in day-care and doesn't have siblings, get him together with a companion of the same age on a regular basis. Two or three times a week is fine.

The social interaction your baby has with another baby is different from his interactions with you and other family members. Adults usually direct the interaction. Babies often alternate who directs the action. Don't expect them to "play" together. At this age, they often engage in parallel play. This means they play next to each other but do not play together. Your child will benefit from this exposure.

You can get together with other parents in your neighborhood or church. Or join a play group in the area.

⚘ *If Baby Pulls His Ears*

You may notice your baby pulling at his ears. This can occur when he starts to cut his first molars. If he is teething, he may run a low-grade fever. His symptoms should respond to acetaminophen or ibuprofen.

If he runs a higher fever, has obvious pain in his ears and doesn't feel better when you give him acetaminophen or ibuprofen, he may have an ear infection. Don't ignore these symptoms. Call your pediatrician.

⚘ *When Your Baby Points at Things*

If your baby is pointing to various things, it's one way of speaking without words. When a child points, an adult usually responds! You probably label or describe what he's pointing at.

When your baby points, he may be asking you to provide verbal labels to things in his world. His pointing also shows you some of the things that attract his attention.

Parents know they shouldn't turn baby's car seat around until he's 1 year old and weighs at least 20 pounds. However, if your child reaches this weight limit well before his 1st birthday, you may be at a loss as to what to do. The best solution is to switch to a convertible seat that holds a child up to 30 pounds. Keep it in the rear-facing position. Before baby reaches 1 year, his bones and muscles are not strong enough to withstand damage in an accident if he is facing forward. So don't turn the car seat around, even if he weighs over 20 pounds.

✲ *Asthma*

Asthma is a chronic respiratory disease in which airways tend to swell and to fill with mucus when a person with asthma is exposed to "triggers"–things that cause a reaction. Some triggers include dust, mold, cigarette smoke and chlorine from an indoor swimming pool. When an attack begins, the child will usually cough, wheeze and experience shortness of breath. Sufferers usually experience recurrent attacks.

Asthma can occur at almost any age, with the exception of newborn infants. Most cases develop during childhood. Symptoms your child may have asthma include:

* tightness in the chest
* shortness of breath
* wheezing when exhaling
* coughing, especially at night
* coughing or wheezing after activity
* rapid, shallow breathing

What You Can Do at Home.   As we've stated so many times in this book, breastfeeding can help your child in a variety of ways. Studies have found that breastfeeding a baby can help prevent asthma.

If your child suffers from asthma, *do not* smoke around him! Keep your home dry and well-ventilated. Try to eliminate allergens and irritants in the house.

Research has shown that pets may actually *prevent* asthma in some children. In two studies, it was shown that babies exposed to two or more dogs and/or cats were less likely to develop asthma and allergies by age 6. In fact, early pet exposure may even reduce the risk! How? Certain proteins in dogs and cats seem to help a baby's immune system develop more normally. A pet's germs (most often harmless) may help stimulate baby's body to produce allergy-inhibiting antibodies. Check with your pediatrician if you have questions.

When baby has an asthma attack, hold him upright, in a semisitting position, until he breathes more easily. If it's his first attack, call your pediatrician for advice. If he has had attacks in the past, use whatever methods your doctor has given you.

When to Call the Doctor. Call the doctor if your baby has symptoms of asthma and has not been diagnosed. Call if any of the following develop:

* baby is exhausted
* he has problems with respiration
* he can't cry

After diagnosis, your baby's doctor may prescribe expectorants to loosen sputum, a bronchodilator to open air passages or cortisone medications by nebulizer. Emergency-room care and hospitalization may be necessary for severe attacks.

Studies have shown that babies who receive antibiotics before they are 6 months old are 2½ times more likely to develop asthma than children who do not receive antibiotics. It's another reason not to push your baby's doctor to prescribe antibiotics to cure every ailment.

✴ *Pinworms*

Pinworms, also called *enterobiasis* and *threadworms,* are parasites that cause infection in the intestines and rectum. Infection is transferred by hand-to-hand contact or hand-to-mouth contact with the tiny eggs of the pinworm. Eggs may also be inhaled or swallowed when they float in the air.

> If baby wheezes, it means he's having a hard time breathing—this can be dangerous. If his nostrils flare, he is breathing very rapidly, he sucks his ribs in with each breath or he turns blue, it's very serious. Call 911 immediately!

Pinworms can occur at any age but are most common in school-age children. Symptoms that your child might have pinworms include:

* skin irritation at the anus, especially during sleep
* painful itching around the anus, especially during sleep
* restlessness
* poor appetite

What You Can Do at Home. If you believe your child might have pinworms, wash hands carefully after changing his diapers and using the toilet. Wash hands thoroughly before preparing meals. Keep your infant from playing with his genitals. Don't let him scratch his anal area when he's not diapered.

When to Call the Doctor. Call the doctor if your baby has been exposed to pinworms at day-care or by older siblings. If your baby has pinworms, your doctor will prescribe an antiworm medication. Pinworms are usually curable in one treatment. In addition to treating baby, all family members should be treated. Recurrence is common.

If worms reappear soon after treatment, they usually represent a new infection, not a treatment failure. Call your pediatrician. Retreatment may be necessary.

✎ Tear-Duct Infection

With a tear-duct infection, sometimes called a *tear-duct blockage,* the opening to a tear duct is blocked or infected. Infection can occur at any age but is most common in children. It may be caused by an infection. An *inherited tear-duct blockage* usually appears in infants between 3 and 12 weeks of age. Symptoms that your child has a blocked tear duct include:

- persistent tearing of one or both eyes
- drainage of mucus and pus from the tear duct
- pain, redness and/or swelling beneath the eye
- redness and/or swelling of the tear duct
- redness of the white of the eye surrounding the tear duct

What You Can Do at Home.   Some home treatments include massaging the tear duct twice a day with fingertips to open it. Place warm soaks on the eye to relieve pain and to open an eye that is sticky from discharge.

When to Call the Doctor.   Call the doctor if your baby has symptoms of a tear-duct infection or blockage. If he runs a fever or if symptoms don't improve, let your pediatrician know. If baby's vision seems to be affected, notify your doctor immediately.

Your doctor may prescribe oral or topical antibiotics for the infection. In extreme cases, surgery to dilate and to probe the tear-duct canal may be necessary.

Toys and Play this 44ᵗʰ Week

✎ Scoopy Scoops

Your kitchen drawer and cabinet may provide the best selection for this game. Gather together plastic, metal or wood scoops of various sizes and shapes. You might choose a coffee scoop, various-sized measuring cups, various-sized measuring spoons, plastic teaspoons and some serving spoons.

Place baby on the floor in front of a pan or bowl filled with cotton balls. Place another pan or bowl next to it. Show him how to scoop the cotton balls from the first pan into the second pan with one of the scoops. Encourage him to scoop cotton balls from one pan into the other and to keep repeating his actions.

If you are adventurous, you can use cornmeal, sand, water or beans for scooping. Watch baby carefully so he doesn't put any objects in his mouth.

✴ *Recognizing Voices*
Does baby recognize familiar voices? Test his ability by having different family members record a short message on a tape. Play the tape for baby and watch him closely. He may look up in recognition when he can identify a voice.

Stop the tape after every message. Identify the speaker to baby. Point out anything that's different. For example, you might say, "Uncle John makes funny noises!"

✴ *Hide-and-Seek, Baby Style*
This is a basic version of the more-advanced hide-and-seek baby will play when he gets older. He'll enjoy the fun of finding you. Crouch beside a chair, out of baby's sight. Call his name as you peek around the corner at him. Let him see you.

Duck back so he can't see you, and call to him again. Keep talking and calling to him as he crawls toward you. When he finds you, laugh and say, "Baby found me!" Give him a hug and a kiss, then play the game again.

✴ *The Smelling Game*
Ever wonder what you'll do with all those baby-food jars? Here's an activity you can use them for. Wrap empty jars in foil, and poke some holes in each lid. Put something fragrant in each jar, and put the lid on tightly. Let baby smell the different smells in each jar. After he's smelled what's inside, show him the contents. Some things you might put in a jar include orange rind, banana peel, flower petals, grass clippings and cotton balls soaked in shampoo or eucalyptus oil.

Week 45

Baby's Age as a Monthly Reference—11 months

HOW BIG IS BABY THIS 45TH WEEK?
Baby weighs 21 pounds and is 29¼ inches long this week.

Baby Care and Equipment

✎ *Planning for Baby's 1st Birthday*
Amazing as it seems, your baby's 1st birthday is quickly approaching. You may want to have a celebration with family and friends. It's not too early to start thinking about it. At this time, you might want to consider the following as you begin your party planning.

* How much money do we want to spend?
* Where do we want to have the party? Think about the date, time and place to hold it.
* Whom do we want to invite? How many people will be on the guest list? Should it be "kids only" or do we want to ask adults?
* Do we need to order or to buy invitations? Can we make them? Can we just call the guests?
* What kind of food will we serve—cake and ice cream or more?

By taking the time to plan now, you can make the celebration one that will be enjoyable for everyone! We also cover other aspects of planning baby's 1st birthday celebration in following weekly discussions.

✎ *Cruising Clothes*
No, we're not talking about clothes for baby's first ocean voyage! The cruising we're addressing isn't on the high seas—it's around the furniture in your home.

Baby needs to wear the right clothes for her safety and protection. Now that she's up and moving, some of the clothes she has been wearing probably need to be put away for a while.

Store outfits that have feet in them, except for bedtime or going out (where she won't be cruising anyway). Keep her feet bare, when possible. When her feet need to be covered, such as when it's cold, choose socks that have rubber treads on their soles. Plain socks may be too slippery.

If you can't afford to buy new clothes or to put old ones away, put non-skid socks *over* footed outfits. It's a little bulky, but it'll do the trick.

446

⚜ *Are Public Changing Tables Clean?*

Most of the time, public changing tables are *not* clean. In one study, public restrooms were tested for cleanliness. Researchers found that women's restrooms had *twice as many germs* as men's restrooms! The cleanest restroom areas were found in hospitals and fast-food restaurants. The worst were airport bathrooms.

To protect yourself and baby, always clean a changing surface with wipes that contain disinfectant *before* laying baby on it. Keep a pack in your diaper bag. Changing surfaces are often contaminated with E. coli from previous diaper changes. After you've wiped the surface, put down your own pad or blanket on the changing table (wash it thoroughly after one or two uses). If you don't have one, place several paper towels down on the surface before placing baby on the table.

If there's no changing table, look for a toilet-seat lid that you can close. This is often one of the cleanest places in a public restroom. If baby is small enough, close the lid, clean it with a disinfecting wipe, then cover with your pad or paper towels.

The dirtiest places in a bathroom are the floor and around the sink. *Never* place baby on the floor to change her! You might not want to put your diaper bag down there, either.

When you're finished, wash your hands with soap and water. This helps prevent taking germs with you when you leave.

⚜ *Foods Baby Is Eating Now*

Your baby is eating lots of different things by now. She probably eats infant cereal or other grain foods at all three meals. Portions for each meal are ¼ cup cereal, ¼ slice of bread or ¼ cup of cooked pasta.

She is eating soft fruits at two meals a day and soft veggies at two meals a day. Portions of each at a meal are 2 to 3 tablespoons. Baby isn't eating that much meat, though—about 1 to 2 tablespoons at two meals a day.

A way to provide her with the nutrition she needs in foods she likes is to make combination dishes. Some good choices include macaroni and cheese, a casserole of meat, rice and a vegetable, or jarred combination baby foods. Remember, when you cook, leave out the spices. At this age, baby may not like them.

Milestones this 45ᵗʰ Week

⚜ *Baby's Individuality*

Your baby's personality is evident now. She knows what she does and doesn't like. She even displays a sense of humor. She also has a growing sense of self. She knows she is separate and distinct from those around her. Baby is also aware of her size.

You may notice your baby has better control of her emotions. She may use emotions to persuade those around her to do what she wants. If you take her toy away, she may yell and protest. When you encounter these displays, remain calm. She must learn that she cannot always have her own way.

✑ Her Vocabulary and Understanding of Words

Baby recognizes words as symbols for objects. When you name something, she may point to it. Or she may point to where she expects to find it. For example, if you say juice and she does not see it, she may point to the refrigerator if she knows it is kept there.

She is ready to start learning names for her body parts. When referring to body parts, some people think it's funny to give them "cutesy" names. However, use the correct term for something. It's better to refer to a boy's penis as "penis" instead of "bobo" or some other term.

The more words your baby hears, the better her association with words and objects will be. She needs to hear the terms often. If you say "spoon" every time you feed her with her spoon, she'll make the connection between the spoon and its name.

Your baby continues her patter in baby language. You may be amused by how close it resembles actual speech patterns. She's practicing the rhythm and word intonation of her language.

> Have fun with sound. Put different objects into securely closed containers. Dried beans, uncooked rice or pasta, and small buttons are good choices. Let her shake them as you point out the different sound each makes.

✑ Learning New Tasks Continues

Baby may work very hard to learn a new task. She needs practice to learn to solve a problem on her own. It takes a great deal of repetition, and time, to master a new skill.

She likes to imitate your actions, facial gestures, speech intonations. They all help her process information and continue learning.

Your baby may know the word "No." It's quite common at this age for her to ignore you completely when you say "No" to her.

✑ Separation Anxiety and Stranger Anxiety

Your baby may still want you or her other parent nearby when she's playing. Separation anxiety may continue to be an issue. This is especially true when you are in a strange place. She will want and need you to be close. Baby may also react more strongly to strangers away from home.

At home, she is more relaxed. Even though you may have thought she had outgrown both of these anxieties, they may reappear around this time. It's normal, so don't be too concerned. These, too, will pass.

Note: See also the box *Milestones this 45th Week.*

MILESTONES THIS 45TH WEEK

Changes You May See this Week as Baby Develops Physically
* cruises furniture

Changes You May See this Week in Baby's Developing Senses and Reflexes
* picks up extremely small objects
* holds cup and drinks from it

Changes You May See this Week as Baby's Mind Develops
* recognizes words as symbols for objects—hears "airplane" and points to sky; hears "cow" and moos
* can imitate speech rhythms, inflections and facial expressions

Changes You May See this Week in Baby's Social Development
* does not always cooperate
* withdraws from strangers

Every baby is an individual, and your baby may do some of these things more quickly or more slowly than another baby. If you are concerned about your baby's progress, discuss it with your healthcare provider. Also see page xiii.

What's Happening this 45th Week?

✴ *Baby's Mobility*

Your baby may be an expert cruiser by now. Holding on to furniture for support, she takes little sideways steps to move around. Cruising is a safe way for her to practice her balance and to strengthen the muscles she needs for walking. You may even notice she sometimes forgets to hold on.

When your baby becomes a regular cruiser, be sure the objects she uses for support are stable and not easily pushed or moved. If she's using the furniture for cruising, padding it or using furniture guards helps protect her from the spill she's sure to take.

✴ *When Baby Is Tongue-Tied*

When a baby is born with a very short flap of skin beneath the tongue, she can't move her tongue very well. When the skin flap, called the *frenulum,* is very short, it pulls the tongue toward the floor of the mouth. When a child with this condition sticks out her tongue, the frenulum pulls on the center. Instead of the tongue being rounded, there is a deep "V" in its center. In layman's terms, this condition is called *tongue-tied.*

> While baby is in the cruising mode, keep her play area free of slippery rugs to help prevent accidents and other mishaps.

Usually by the end of the first year, the frenulum will stretch to its normal length and won't interfere with baby talking. However, if it is too short, a child may have trouble making certain sounds. She may also have difficulty swallowing.

Many doctors and speech specialists recommend a minor surgical procedure to release a tight frenulum. If you notice symptoms that your baby is tongue-tied, discuss it with your pediatrician. He or she will evaluate the situation. You may be referred to a pediatric ear, nose and throat specialist for further evaluation.

✴ *Various Developmental Stages*

All babies are individuals. You may notice your baby does something that passes over or skips a step in the "developmental plan" discussed in this book. You may worry that when this happens, baby isn't developing properly. For example, when a child doesn't go through a crawling phase but goes straight to walking, some parents worry.

Put your fears to rest. Occasionally a child with developmental delay won't go through the crawling stage. In these situations, not crawling is an early *symptom* of delays. It is not a *cause* of them. If a baby goes straight to walking at the normal age, without going through a crawling phase, it does *not* indicate any problems.

Babies usually begin walking between 9 months and 15 months of age. When a baby walks without crawling first, she may just be an early walker.

✴ *Prickly Heat*

Prickly heat occurs when sweat pores are blocked and perspiration escapes into the skin because baby is overheated or overdressed. It can occur at any time, not just during the summer months. Tiny blisters can form, which you may not be able to see. But as perspiration goes deeper into the skin, the area becomes painful, accompanied by intense itching.

Prickly heat is common in infants, although it can occur at any age. Symptoms that your baby has prickly heat include:

* itchy rash
* clusters of small, fluid-filled skin blisters, which may come and go within a matter of hours
* a red rash without blisters in areas of heavy perspiration, such as the neck, shoulders, back of the head and in skin folds

What You Can Do at Home.   When you notice these symptoms on your baby's skin, expose the affected area to air as much as possible. Change diapers as soon as they are wet. Dress baby in cotton clothing or other cool, breathable attire. Give baby frequent, cool baths. Apply lubricating ointment or cream to area 4 to 6 times a day.

When to Call the Doctor.   Call the doctor if the rash doesn't improve in 5 to 7 days, despite home care. Your pediatrician may suggest a nonprescription steroid cream to apply 2 to 3 times a day.

✷ *Blood Poisoning*
Blood poisoning, also called *septicemia,* occurs when bacteria enter the bloodstream and cause an infection. It can occur at any age. The occurrence of blood poisoning usually follows a localized infection in some other part of the body, such as the appendix, a tooth, a sinus infection, a urinary-tract infection, ear infections or infected wounds or burns. Symptoms of blood poisoning include:

* high fever, with rapid temperature rise
* rapid, pounding heartbeat
* chills
* warm, flushed skin
* lethargy
* abscesses

What You Can Do at Home.   Treatment you may try at home include acetaminophen or ibuprofen for fever and/or discomfort. Offer lots of fluids. Keep baby as comfortable as possible until you can see your pediatrician.

When to Call the Doctor.   Call the doctor if baby experiences a rapid onset of a high fever or has signs of infection anywhere in the body. Your doctor may prescribe antibiotics to fight infection. Blood cultures are done to identify the bacteria. A child is hospitalized in severe cases for I.V. antibiotic therapy and I.V. hydration.

Toys and Play this 45th Week

When choosing toys for your baby, continue to select ones that are appropriate for her age. Toys for a particular age group suit a child's intellectual capacity. And they're safer for her.

You may also decide to give her objects that are not strictly toys—but she'll love them anyway. Plastic containers that nest inside one another, measuring cups or spoons, an old pan and a wood spoon—all can be great toys for your little one.

✒ *Baby's Own Photo Album*
Put pictures of family members doing something they enjoy in a small photo album. Write a sentence under each photo describing what's happening. Look at the album with baby, and talk about the pictures.

> If you want to buy some baby-sized furniture, now's a good time to consider it. She'll begin using a table and chair more now and in the future. Choose furniture that is durable and painted or finished with lead-free products. Some plastic furniture is very sturdy.

✒ *Playing in the Sand*
Bury your hand in some sand while your baby watches you. Ask her, "Where's my hand?" She may pat the sand on top of your hand or dig down for it. When she finds it, hold your hand up and exclaim, "See, there's my hand!"

Next cover her hand with the sand. Talk about how the sand feels. Ask her where her hand is. To vary the game, together bury a toy or two, then ask her to find it. If she has any difficulty, help her.

✒ *Big, Bigger, Biggest*
To help baby learn the concept of size, gather together some nesting plastic measuring cups and plastic measuring spoons. You can also use aluminum bowls that fit inside one another.

Show baby how to put the next smaller size inside a bowl or spoon. As you nest them, talk about their sizes. When removing the bowls or spoons, you can point out the concepts of big, bigger, biggest and/or small, smaller, smallest.

✎ *Bathtub Basketball*

To help your baby's eye–hand coordination, gather together some plastic balls and a plastic container at bath time. While baby is sitting in the water, show her how to drop a ball into the floating container. Then let her try. This activity helps her develop better coordination.

Week 46

Baby's Age as a Monthly Reference—11 months

HOW BIG IS BABY THIS 46TH WEEK?
Baby weighs 21¼ pounds and is 29¼ inches long this week.

Baby Care and Equipment

✴ *Over-the-Counter Medication Safety*
Most parents use over-the-counter (OTC) medications to help their child feel better when he has a cold, fever or some other minor ailment. There are some things you may not know about OTC medication use. The list below helps you understand how to use these medications wisely.

* Seek the advice of your pediatrician about which medications are OK to use with your baby. You may want to do this at a well-baby checkup.
* Use OTC medications *only* when your baby is sick or needs them.
* Don't use OTCs too much during the day. Many physical symptoms help the body take care of illness. For example, coughing helps clear the lungs.
* Take your baby to the doctor if symptoms don't improve after the recommended time of use found in medication instructions.
* If symptoms worsen while your child is taking a medication, contact your pediatrician.
* If you think your baby needs more than one type of over-the-counter medication (cough syrup and a fever reducer), check with your pharmacist or your pediatrician before giving them to him.
* If your baby is taking a prescription medication, contact your pharmacist or pediatrician before also giving him an OTC medication.
* Follow package directions for how often and how much to give of each medication.
* When giving any medication, use the proper utensil for measuring. Choose a medication syringe, a dropper, a medicine cup or a dosing spoon. An underdose won't help much. An overdose could be serious.
* Don't give your baby a medication longer than the time recommended.
* Don't use multisymptom medications, such as cold remedies, if your baby doesn't have all the symptoms.
* Be alert for any side effects.

✿ *When Baby Is a Picky Eater*

From a very early age, some babies are picky eaters. When a baby is a picky eater, he refuses certain foods, eats only a couple of foods or won't eat at all.

Some foods you offer him supply him with a lot of nutrition. If he doesn't get all of his nutrition in one sitting, eating these foods helps him eat a more-balanced diet. Offer him yogurt, which is rich in calcium, protein and vitamin B_{12}. Egg yolks contain protein, riboflavin and vitamins A, B_{12} and K. Cereals are loaded with vitamins, zinc, iron, magnesium and folate. Beans and lentils are a high-protein source of iron and folate. Tomatoes are rich in vitamin C and lycopene.

Below are some tips that might help you deal more effectively with the situation of picky eating. Use what works best for you and your baby.

* **Give baby enough time to eat**—Some babies need more time to eat. Try setting aside an extra 15 minutes for mealtime.

* **Feed him before offering formula or breast milk**—If he drinks a lot, he may not have room in his tummy for the food. Offer food first, then breastfeed or give him a bottle.

* **Don't let him snack too much during the day**—If you give him snacks whenever he's hungry, he won't want to eat at mealtime. Schedule snacks for certain times. Stick with the schedule.

* **Keep introducing new foods**—Your baby may need time to adjust to a new food, a new taste or a new texture. Wait a few days after he refuses something, then try again. Sometimes you may have to try up to a dozen times before baby will eat a particular food.

* **Give him the same foods, if he'll eat them**—If baby wants to eat only macaroni and cheese for a while, let him. He will eventually tire of it. It's OK to take this approach for a few weeks. It won't hurt him.

* **Set a good example**—When you eat a healthy diet and a good selection of foods, so will your baby.

* **If you don't like it, don't let him know**—We know that certain foods, broccoli for example, may taste great to some and awful to others. Or there may be some foods that you just can't stand. Keep your attitudes to yourself. Let him try different foods and decide on his own.

* **His appetite may be small**—Some babies don't have large appetites. Don't expect him to eat a lot or to eat often. Let him set some of the parameters of his eating. Pushing too much food on him when he can't eat may cause problems. His stomach is only the size of his fist, so it probably doesn't hold as much as you might expect.

❄ **Don't make mealtimes a battle**—These interactions can cause lots of problems, now and later. You may teach him that mealtime battles are a way of gaining your attention. Ignore the situation when you can. Within limits, let baby decide what to eat and how much he wants.

◯ *Drinking "Old Formula"*

Now that baby is moving around and can hold things while he's doing so, different situations may arise. One that may cause a parent some concern is baby drinking formula that is not

> A baby learns respect and various attitudes by watching his parents. Keep this in mind as you go about your daily activities.

fresh. Occasionally baby will find a bottle of formula he left someplace and drink it. Can it hurt him? Probably not, especially if the formula has only been out a short while.

Formula that's been sitting out for a short time doesn't usually cause any problems. However, if you don't know how long it's been unrefrigerated, you might be concerned about salmonella poisoning. Signs that baby is having a problem usually occur between 2 and 72 hours after drinking the formula. Watch for diarrhea or vomiting. If these symptoms occur, contact your pediatrician.

Milestones this 46th Week

◯ *Physical Accomplishments Are Many*

By this time, your baby can do many physical things. He has accomplished quite a lot in these first 10 months. He may stand alone and turn now. He can climb down backward off a chair without falling. When he stands up, he may do it his own way. He may kneel and push up, or he may squat then stand.

He still explores and experiments with everything he can. Nearly every object he comes in contact with (or so it seems!) must be touched, shaken, banged, pulled or pushed. He still likes to put everything in his mouth.

When he masters a task, he may practice it over and over and over again. He loves turning switches off and on. He studies anything that moves with great concentration.

It's amusing to see him imitate household chores and tasks. He may imitate actions that deal with self-care. He may brush his teeth, wash his face or comb his hair.

Your baby still needs at least one good rest a day, even though he might not go to sleep. The best time may be right after lunch, although a little later may make the evening hours more enjoyable for everyone in the family.

✴ His Language Skills Increase

Baby understands many things now about his language. He knows he can make his wants known with language. His vocabulary is growing. He follows verbal directions after a demonstration. He will "give dolly a hug" after he sees you do it.

His babbling is more intelligible. He may use a few meaningful words. Or he may use a few words quite often. You may recognize various words, such as "dada," "kitty," "mama" or "book." Or he may offer substitutes that sound close. For example, he may say "uce" for juice or "gah" for dog. He is becoming more of a participant in his world now.

✴ Baby Play

When baby is playing in the house, but not close to you, you need to keep an ear open to what he may be doing. At this age, a long period of quiet may mean he's into something he shouldn't be. So watch him constantly (or at least know where he is and what he's doing).

A favorite of some babies this age is undressing. He may do it as often as he can. He'll take off his shoes and socks. He'll also take off every stitch of clothes, including his diaper, if he's able. If he revels in this game, put his clothes on backward for a while, until the novelty wears off.

The games he likes to play are more sophisticated now. He may try to sing with you. He may spend more time with books and other things you can study together. He likes to look inside things, so curiosity cubes are good choices.

> When baby takes a tumble, instead of saying "oh no!" say "uh-oh." This helps him take tumbles in stride.

✴ Baby's Cooperation

Baby will cooperate very well sometimes and not so well at other times. One day he may hold out his arms and legs to help get dressed. The next day, he is totally uncooperative. This is normal, so don't get upset when it happens.

Note: See also the box *Milestones this 46th Week*.

What's Happening this 46th Week?

✴ Giving Twins Attention

One of the difficulties of having more than one baby is your ability to tend to each one individually. When both babies want you, what can you do?

MILESTONES THIS 46ᵀᴴ WEEK

Changes You May See this Week as Baby Develops Physically
* may lean over while standing against support
* squats and stoops

Changes You May See this Week in Baby's Developing Senses and Reflexes
* holds out arm or leg to help you dress him
* lifts lid from boxes

Changes You May See this Week as Baby's Mind Develops
* speaks a few intelligible words

Changes You May See this Week in Baby's Social Development
* asserts himself among siblings

Every baby is an individual, and your baby may do some of these things more quickly or more slowly than another baby. If you are concerned about your baby's progress, discuss it with your healthcare provider. Also see page xiii.

Below are a few tips to help you give each baby the time and attention he needs. Over a period of time, each baby will realize you will meet his needs, even if you can't do it immediately.

* **Alternate attention**—One of the best ways to give attention equally is to alternate. Take care of one baby first, then take care of the other one first the next time.
* **One may need you more**—One baby may need you more than the other. When this occurs, it may be for a while. Then the other baby may be more needy for a while. Do the best you can. It usually all works out in the end.
* **Involve them both**—You don't have to ignore one baby to take care of the other one. Include both of them in your conversation while taking care of one baby. As best you can, maintain eye contact with the baby who is not being tended to. Keep him close, if possible.
* **Teach patience**—If one baby is always impatient and wants to be first, be sure you let the other be first sometimes. Tell the impatient one he must wait his turn. This is good for the second baby, too. He won't always feel second best.

⚜ When Baby Is Hot-Blooded

Some babies won't sleep under the covers at night. Some peel off their clothes at every opportunity. Some refuse to wear sweaters or coats. Does this indicate a problem? Not usually.

Some children have a higher body temperature, probably due to a higher metabolism. They burn calories more quickly. Often they are more active than other children. They just feel hotter.

When possible, let your hot-blooded baby set his own comfort level. Don't put too many clothes on him. Layers are better for dressing him. Dress him comfortably for bed. If he's perspiring a lot at night, dress him in lighter pajamas or leave off the blanket sleeper.

If your baby is very overweight, it may cause him to retain heat. He needs to wear cooler clothes and to perspire more to feel comfortable. Overheating may also indicate other problems, such as an overactive thyroid gland. If you are concerned, discuss it with your pediatrician.

⚜ Giardiasis

Giardiasis is an infection that causes inflammation of the bowel. It is caused by a parasite found in contaminated food or contaminated water. It can occur at any age but is most common in older infants and children. Symptoms of giardiasis include:

* diarrhea
* fever
* nausea
* weakness
* flatulence
* belching
* vomiting
* abdominal cramps
* greasy, bad-smelling stools

What You Can Do at Home.   Prevention of this problem is your best bet. Don't let your baby drink water that could be contaminated. Only drink water from normal water supplies. If you don't know if water is safe, boil it for 5 minutes.

Because of nausea, vomiting and diarrhea, give your baby lots of fluids to avoid dehydration. Don't use over-the-counter medications for diarrhea or nausea and vomiting, unless advised by your pediatrician.

When to Call the Doctor.   Call the doctor if your baby has symptoms of giardiasis. It's important to let your pediatrician know if baby has a fever, severe abdominal pain or is dehydrated.

Your doctor may do laboratory stool studies to detect parasites. Usually tests are done three times before being considered negative. An antiparasitic drug, such as metronidazole, furazolidone or quinacrine, may be prescribed. These drugs are very effective. In severe cases, when baby suffers from dehydration or malabsorption, hospitalization may be necessary for I.V. hydration and nutrition supplementation.

✣ *Nose Injury*

A nose injury can occur from a fall, a bump or an accident, such as someone throwing something and hitting baby in the face. It can occur at any age.

Younger children and infants have only cartilage in their noses, which does not break but can be badly bruised. Actual fractures usually occur in older children (over age 8). Injury can also occur in young children and toddlers if they put an object in their nose. Symptoms of a nose injury include:

* pain in the nose
* nosebleed
* swollen, discolored nose
* inability to breathe through the nose
* crooked or misshapen nose

What You Can Do at Home.   Keep small objects away from your baby so he can't put them up his nose. If he does stick something in his nose, remove it if you can reach it. If you can't reach it, take baby to an emergency-care facility to have the object removed.

If injury occurs from a fall or other accident, apply ice packs to the nose immediately to minimize swelling. Control bleeding by pinching the nostrils tightly together. See the discussion of *Nosebleeds* in *Week 48.* Give baby ibuprofen or acetaminophen for discomfort, if he needs it.

When to Call the Doctor.   Call the doctor or take baby to an emergency-care facility if a foreign object is lodged in his nose. It's better for a professional to remove it. If an object cannot be easily removed, removal under anesthesia may be necessary.

If baby has a nosebleed, your doctor will want to know if it is heavy or cannot be stopped. If your baby has difficulty breathing or if there are changes in your baby's level of consciousness, call your pediatrician immediately.

Your doctor may order X-rays of the nose. Minor fractures and injuries usually heal in about 4 weeks. Surgery is sometimes necessary to repair severe fractures.

Toys and Play this 46ᵗʰ Week

Baby is interested in many kinds of toys. If you're thinking about a good birthday present for his 1st birthday, you might want to look for a stable riding toy.

✦ *Repeating Words*

Your baby's vocabulary is increasing. Keep talking to him. To help expand his vocabulary, point out many different things—people, pictures, objects, parts of his body or yours—and repeat the name of each several times.

To make a game of it, ask him, "Where is my eye?" or the cup or the dog or the book or the dolly. If he points to it, praise him. If he doesn't, point it out to him.

✦ *Take Him Dancing*

To help develop baby's sense of anticipation, dance with him. While you're dancing together, have someone else start and stop the music. He'll enjoy this fun interaction.

✦ *"Finger Painting," Baby Style*

Dress baby in a diaper, and put on his bib. Put a drop cloth under his high chair. Place him in his high chair, and put the tray in place. Put a small amount of puréed fruit or some mixed cereal on the tray. Let him finger-paint with it.

✦ *Changes Can Be Fun*

Add some interest to baby's life by making some changes. Put his high chair in a new place. Move his crib to another position in his room. Put on a new crib sheet that has an interesting pattern. A different perspective can be very interesting to him.

✦ *Making Some Noise*

Place a metal pan or bowl on the floor. Place baby next to it, and give him some things to drop in the pan. You can use clothespins, wood blocks, small plastic balls. Show him how to drop the objects in the pan, and listen to the sounds they make. Stay with him while he plays this game. You don't want him putting these objects in his mouth.

Week 47

Baby's Age as a Monthly Reference—11 months

HOW BIG IS BABY THIS 47TH WEEK?
Baby weighs 21¼ pounds and is 29½ inches long this week.

Baby Care and Equipment

✴ *Connect with Baby's Day-Care Provider*

If your baby is in day-care, it may be a good idea to stop a couple of times each week and talk to the person (or people) who take care of her. Don't just drop her off, then pick her up later.

When you build a connection with the person who cares for your baby, it'll be easier to ask questions to find out how baby is doing. It also makes it easier for your day-care provider to talk to you about concerns he or she may have. You both have the same goals—making sure your little one is growing and developing as she should.

✴ *Stools May Indicate What Baby Has Eaten*

Baby is eating many new foods. Until her first molars come in, she can't chew very well. As a result, some of the foods you feed her now may turn up in her stool looking much like they did when she ate them.

When this occurs, don't be alarmed. There's nothing wrong with her digestion. Until her digestive system matures, you'll discover her stools may reflect the various foods she eats. If you feed her carrots, spinach or beets, you may see yellow, green or red stools. When she eats oat-circle cereal pieces, her stools may be a sandy color. Cucumber and tomato seeds and unchewed raisins may show up in her bowel movements.

One way to help deal with the situation is to make sure the foods you give her are easy to digest. Chop, mash, purée, dice and blend foods that she may have difficulty with. These foods will also be safer for her to eat.

✴ *When You Have to Get the Medicine Down*

Medications, especially liquids, may not be pleasant tasting. With an older child, you can usually reason with them (or bribe them) to get them to take something they need that tastes bad. With a baby, reasoning doesn't help.

When this situation arises, you need to know how to get the medicine in her, especially if you're by yourself and don't have an extra pair of hands.

To give liquid medicine to a baby, first fill the dropper or syringe with the correct amount of medicine. Place it next to you on the table. Put baby in your lap, facing you. Her legs should be on either side of your body. Lean her back on your knees so her head is slightly lower than her body.

Insert the medicine holder between her cheek and her gums (or teeth, if she has any). Give her a little of the medication while gently blowing in her face. Blowing results in a reflex that causes her to swallow. Continue blowing gently while you give her the remainder of the medication.

With a very small baby, use a device that has a nipple, like a pacifier. Medicine is put in the dosing reservoir, and the nipple is attached. Baby sucks the medicine as if she were drinking from a bottle.

✒ *Trust Baby to Eat What She Needs*

Unless your baby is sick, trust her to eat what she needs. As long as you offer her a variety of nutritious foods, she'll get the vitamins, minerals and calories she needs to help her grow healthy and strong. The best measure of how she's doing is whether she's growing and thriving. If she's doing well, she's probably getting what she needs from the breast milk or formula you give her and from the food she eats.

Milestones this 47th Week

✒ *Baby May Have Temper Tantrums*

By this age, your baby may have occasional temper tantrums. It's one way she expresses her frustration.

When she has a tantrum, keep your cool. You need to be in control, and your baby needs you to be, too. Walk away from her, or put her in her room when she starts a tantrum. Do it calmly, with no conversation. Without an audience, her tantrum may quickly end.

✒ *She Understands "Acceptable" and "Unacceptable" Behavior*

Your baby is beginning to understand the differences between behavior that is acceptable and that which is unacceptable. It's better to label behavior in this way and not to use "good" and "bad" to describe her actions.

Baby's conscience is beginning to form. She will call attention to her acceptable behavior. She seeks your approval and may repeat an activity if she is praised for it.

When her behavior is unacceptable, she will try to avoid your disapproval. If she feels guilty, she may hide from you.

Try not to be after baby constantly about what she's doing. Let her have some time to play or to explore safely by herself, or she'll stop listening to you. If you must correct her behavior, do so when she does something that really needs correcting. These situations involve her own safety and the safety and rights of others.

> When you need a snack to keep baby occupied while you're doing errands, put some oat-circle cereal pieces in a plastic bag or container. Give her a few pieces at a time, and let her feed herself.

✦ If She's Very Active

If she's very active, your baby may be climbing out of her crib or playpen by now. If she refuses to be confined, there are some things you can do. Leave one side of her crib down so she can climb out more easily (and safely). Or use a mesh cover (made for this purpose) to cover the top of a crib or playpen so she can't get out.

Another tactic is to keep her out of her playpen and crib as much as possible. Set up a safe place that you've babyproofed for her to play by herself.

✦ Baby's Activities

Baby is doing many things now. She can bend halfway over to peer through her spread legs. It's fun viewing the world upside down!

She likes to put small objects into a large container. Stacking blocks is also fun. She may arrange things by color and size. These activities involve problem solving and demonstrate her developing skills.

She may be able to push up from the floor with her hands to stand. She may be taking some tentative steps. She sometimes gets frustrated when she can't do what she sets out to do.

✦ Does She Have a Favorite Stuffed Toy Now?

Around this time, many babies choose one or two stuffed toys as favorites. Experts believe they serve as a comfortable way for baby to transition from waking to sleeping. A stuffed toy could also be a substitute for a parent. You may notice her playing "parent" with her stuffed toys.

✦ Her Physical Growth Slows

Around this time, baby's physical growth slows down. She gains weight at a much slower rate now. One reason for the slower weight gain is her activity level. As her activities increase, she burns more calories.

The range of foods baby eats may be limited. She may be refusing a lot of foods, so she may eat only one good meal a day. However, her digestive system is maturing, so her body is utilizing the food more efficiently. That's a plus.

Note: See also the box *Milestones this 47ᵗʰ Week.*

MILESTONES THIS 47ᵀᴴ WEEK

Changes You May See this Week as Baby Develops Physically
* lowers herself from a standing position without falling

Changes You May See this Week in Baby's Developing Senses and Reflexes
* deliberately places objects
* may untie shoelaces

Changes You May See this Week as Baby's Mind Develops
* may nest objects, such as boxes or cups

Changes You May See this Week in Baby's Social Development
* tries to avoid disapproval
* shows guilt

Every baby is an individual, and your baby may do some of these things more quickly or more slowly than another baby. If you are concerned about your baby's progress, discuss it with your healthcare provider. Also see page xiii.

What's Happening this 47ᵗʰ Week?

✴ *Reasons to Wake the Doctor*
Parents sometimes hesitate to call their pediatrician in the middle of the night. No one wants to bother their doctor. However, there are times your physician will *want* you to call, no matter what time it is! If your baby experiences any of the following signs or symptoms, call your doctor immediately or go to the nearest emergency-medicine facility.

* **Signs of choking**—Difficulty breathing, coughing for no apparent reason and/or turning blue around the lips can be signs of choking on an object. Call 911, and ask for an ambulance. *Never* do the Heimlich maneuver on a baby if she can cough, cry or make noise.
* **Breathing difficulties**—If baby is breathing noisily or rapidly (more than one breath a second), it could be a sign of croup, asthma, bronchiolitis or pneumonia.

* **A change in skin color**—If skin turns blue or gray, it may indicate baby's not getting enough oxygen. Blue skin may also indicate poisoning.
* **Diarrhea in an infant under 3 months old**—In a baby this young, diarrhea can increase the risk of dehydration.
* **Severe vomiting**—In addition to dehydration, severe or persistent vomiting can indicate poisoning. If the vomit contains blood or green bile, a serious problem may be the cause, such as a blocked intestine.
* **A high fever**—Any fever over 103F can mean a serious bacterial infection. Call if your baby has a temperature this high, no matter what her age. If baby is younger than 3 months old, call if her temperature is 100.2F or higher. In a baby between 3 and 6 months of age, call if her temperature is 101F or higher.
* **Signs of dehydration**—If baby is dehydrated, it can be serious. A dry mouth, sunken fontanelle, sunken eyes, little urine production and no tears can mean she needs fluid fast. In serious cases, this must be done by I.V. fluid in the hospital.
* **Tummy pain**—If pain in the tummy seems to worsen when you press on it, especially on the right side, it could mean she has appendicitis. She may cry and put her hands near her tummy, if she can.
* **A purple or deep-red rash**—If baby has a rash like this, press your fingers into it. If it doesn't fade when you press it, it could mean a serious bacterial infection.
* **Sudden groin pain in a boy**—A tender testicle can cause groin pain. This can occur if the testicle is twisted. Surgery must be performed within 8 hours to save the testicle.
* **Signs of bacterial meningitis**—When baby has a fever and a stiff neck, it can be serious. To test for a stiff neck, hold a toy she likes in front of her. While she's looking at it, lower it so she has to look down. If she can't bring her chin to her chest, it may be due to a stiff neck.

Begin Teaching Responsibility

To be successful in life, a person needs to learn how to be responsible. It's something you can begin teaching baby now. By the end of her first year, your baby is beginning to understand cause and effect. She is also beginning to realize there are consequences to her actions.

Based on these understandings, how do you begin teaching responsibility? Try "baby" responsibilities. For example, ask her to give daddy the napkin when you hand it to her. As she grows older, you can suit tasks to her growing capabilities.

✧ Self-Reliance

One of your goals as a parent is to help your child become self-reliant. As with responsibility, you can do this by asking your child to do age-appropriate tasks. At this age, it may be learning to feed herself with a spoon. As she gets older, these tasks will change.

One way to encourage her self-reliance is to make things as easy as you can and to help her when necessary. In this way, she'll learn she can do things for herself. The older she gets, the less help she'll need from you.

At 11 months, baby may be learning to feed herself with a spoon.

✧ Hyperthermia (Overheating)

When a baby experiences hyperthermia, her body creates more heat than she can eliminate. This may result from something happening within her body or from external conditions. It can occur in a baby at any age. It is most common in hot summer months. If your baby becomes hyperthermic, you will notice the following symptoms:

- fever
- crankiness
- bright red cheeks
- loss of consciousness
- seizures
- weakness
- sunken eyes
- dry, hot skin
- rapid heartbeat
- lack of perspiration

What You Can Do at Home. To help avoid the problem, limit outdoor activities in hot weather. Give baby lots of fluids. Dress her in light, loose-fitting clothing. By increasing ventilation, you promote sweat evaporation, which cools her skin. Bring baby's temperature down by wiping her body with a cool, wet sponge or towel.

When to Call the Doctor. Call baby's doctor immediately if you see signs of dehydration or if baby loses consciousness. If your baby has a seizure, is weak and listless, feverish, cranky or doesn't respond to cooling off, contact your pediatrician. The condition can be serious.

Your pediatrician will probably suggest cool applications to the skin to help reduce baby's temperature. A tepid (cool) tub bath may also be suggested. Begin with warm water and gradually add cold water to it. This prevents chilling. The bath should last 20 to 30 minutes. Squeeze water over baby's back and chest. If these measures don't work, hospitalization to lower body temperature and to provide I.V. replacement fluids may be required.

✛ *Hay Fever*

Hay fever occurs when the body has an allergic response to various substances in the air. The throat, mouth, nose, upper air passages and lungs are involved. It can occur at any age. Symptoms that your baby may have hay fever include:

- watery discharge from the eyes
- itchy eyes
- sneezing
- headache
- stuffy nose
- clear nasal discharge
- sneezing
- postnasal drip, which can cause bad breath
- coughing from postnasal drip

What You Can Do at Home.   It's a good idea to eliminate as many allergens (things that cause allergic reactions) as you can from baby's environment. Clean your home thoroughly to remove allergens and to keep dust at a minimum. Do this regularly. Change furnace filters often. Install an air-purification unit in your home. Treat symptoms as your doctor advises. *Don't* give baby any over-the-counter allergy medications without your doctor's advice.

When to Call the Doctor.   Call the doctor if your baby has severe symptoms of hay fever. If she displays any symptoms of infection, such as fever or a thick, discolored nasal discharge, call your pediatrician. It's possible a sinus infection can complicate an allergy.

Your doctor may prescribe medication to treat the problem. He or she may prescribe antihistamines or decongestants to reduce the body's allergic response. Medication can relieve symptoms, but they don't cure the hay fever. If your baby suffers from severe allergies, your pediatrician may refer you to an allergy specialist.

Toys and Play this 47th Week

One reason you keep reading to baby and sharing stories and pictures with her is to help her develop her understanding of two dimensions. When you point to objects, people and animals in books, repeat over and over again what they are. It teaches her to connect the 2-dimensional objects she sees in a book with the 3-dimensional objects she knows in her world.

✎ *Baby's First Puzzle*
To help her eye–hand coordination, make a "puzzle" for baby. Place a muffin tin on the floor in front of her. Put a container with a few tennis balls in it next to her. Show her how the tennis balls fit in the muffin tin. Then let her try.

✎ *S-T-R-E-T-C-H*
This game helps baby exercise her large muscles. Sit on the floor across from her. Gently roll a ball toward her so she has to stretch to get it. Tell her to stretch to get the ball.

If it's nice outside, you can accomplish the same thing by blowing soap bubbles over her head. Encourage her to reach up to grab the bubbles.

✎ *It's a Present!*
Everybody loves a present, even baby! When baby's taking a bath, wrap one of her favorite bath toys in a face cloth. Give her the wrapped toy, and tell her to open the present. It's not the toy that she'll enjoy finding. It's the element of surprise.

✎ *Sprinkle, Sprinkle*
Water play is always fun. You can do this activity in the bathtub or outside in the garden. Fill a small sprinkling can with water. If you don't have a sprinkling can, punch holes in the bottom of a plastic soda-pop bottle, either the 1- or 2-liter size.

Show her how the water sprinkles from the holes into the bathtub or onto the flowers or grass. Sprinkle some water on her. Have fun!

When the can is empty, show her that all the water is gone. Put some more water in the container, and play some more.

> It may be fun to let baby play in mud and water, or with clay. But watch her reactions. Some babies don't like playing in gooey messes. Other babies love it!

Week 48

Baby's Age as a Monthly Reference—11 months

HOW BIG IS BABY THIS 48ᵀᴴ WEEK?
Baby weighs 21½ pounds and is 29½ inches long this week.

Baby Care and Equipment

✎ *Continue Planning for Baby's 1st Birthday*
It's getting closer to baby's 1st birthday. With only a few weeks to go, there are some more decisions to make if you're planning a party.

* Choose a theme or color scheme for the party.
* Start shopping for decorations. The discount party-supply stores are great sources for decorations, paper goods and invitations.
* Make any modifications in your plans.
* Mail or give out invitations. If you're going to invite people by telephone, start calling now.
* If you plan to have anything unusual for food or favors, think about ordering these things now.

Other important points to keep in mind as you make plans include your child's personality. How does he react in various situations? Some babies love lots of stimulation. Others are very shy and don't enjoy a lot of activity. Consider how your baby will react at his party when making plans.

Time the event to occur when baby is rested and alert. A late afternoon or early-evening party may be perfect, if baby has just gotten up from his nap. Keep the length of the party short. One or 2 hours is probably the maximum. It may be a good idea to keep the guest list short if the party will end after a short time.

Are you going to invite other babies and children, in addition to adults? If you do invite children, you'll need activities for them. If there will be other babies there, set up a safe activity area with age-appropriate toys. Don't invite a clown or other dressed-up individual. It may be too frightening for your baby.

✎ *Baby's Food Needs as the End of this 1st Year Draws Near*
Your baby's nutritional needs change somewhat as he nears the end of his 1ˢᵗ year. In a few weeks, he will be drinking whole milk, if your pediatrician says

to offer whole milk. Your baby's nutritional plan at this time may closely resemble the one below.

* Baby is eating yogurt, cheese and cottage cheese. Offer him a little plain vanilla ice cream as a special treat. He should have four servings of dairy foods a day. Serving size varies from ¼ cup to ½ cup.
* Six servings of grain products, including cereal, pasta, rice, bread, muffins, rolls and crackers, should be offered every day. Offer ¼ cup of the cooked grains, ½ bread serving or a couple of crackers.
* Two servings of fruit or fruit juice each day are necessary. Each serving should be about 3 ounces. (Fruit is better than fruit juice.)
* Provide him with three servings of vegetables every day. Each serving should be about 3 ounces.
* Two servings of fish, turkey, chicken, beef, pork, eggs or lentils are adequate. Offer him 1 ounce of meat, 1 egg or ¼ cup of lentils.

Some Useful Feeding Tips

At this age, it's common for baby to eat heartily at one meal, then not want to eat much at the next. Never try to force baby to eat. Offer him small portions. If he doesn't like something, you can always offer it again later.

Vary the tastes and textures of the foods you feed your baby. It makes meals more fun and interesting for him.

Your growing baby *needs* regular meals and snacks. Give him at least three small snacks a day, in addition to his regular meals. He is extremely busy and uses a lot of energy. Snacks provide him the energy he needs to keep going.

When you travel with baby, take foods and snacks that don't need to be kept cold. Crackers, dry-cereal pieces, juices, bread and fruits are good choices. When you eat in a restaurant, share a little of your food with baby. It's a good change for him, and he may be more interested in eating something new and different.

As your baby gets older, he is beginning to distinguish between good smells and bad smells. You may notice more of a reaction from him now when he smells something unpleasant.

Block That Sun!

It may be hard to believe, but even the short, cool days of winter can present sun hazards to baby. By being vigilant about sun protection, you can prevent sun damage to his skin. As we've already discussed, don't use sunscreen on a baby younger than 6 months.

If your baby is going to be outside for longer than 15 minutes, apply sunscreen to any skin that will be exposed. It's best to apply it at least 30 minutes before going outside; this offers the most protection. Choose a sunscreen with a rating of at least 15SPF (sun protection factor). Be sure it also blocks ultraviolet A and B rays.

Your baby's skin is more sensitive than an older child's skin. Chemicals in sunscreen can be harsh. Choose products made for infants and young children.

To keep baby's skin "babylike," use mild, unscented soaps when bathing him. After his bath, put moisturizer on his just-dried skin to keep it hydrated.

In addition to sunscreen as protection, it's a good idea to put a hat on his head. Dress him to protect his skin. Keep him out of the sun as much as you can. Sunscreen offers a degree of protection, but it can't protect a baby completely. Use sunscreen wisely. Always read and follow package directions.

Milestones this 48th Week

✳ *Baby May Be Feeding Himself*
By this time, your baby should be able to feed himself fairly well. He may be able to carry a spoonful of food to his mouth without too much trouble. However, he may spill a lot because his wrist action is not yet fully developed.

If you try to help him eat, he may resist you, even if it's something he likes. He really does want to do it himself! He may be holding a cup quite steadily, and he can drink from it all by himself.

Allow him to practice eating and drinking without much interference from you. He needs to master these important tasks. Stand by with cleaning cloths, and be ready to clean up the mess afterward.

✳ *His Understanding and Curiosity Increase*
Because his memory has improved, your baby remembers many things. He knows where to put certain objects. He can group various items by color, size or shape. He studies how fast an object falls. His attention span is longer, which is the reason he will study something for a fairly long time.

He may love books and has favorites he wants to read many times. He may even want to turn the pages of a book. He can do it if you let him try.

Instead of taking things apart, baby may now try to put them back together. He tries to use an object the way he sees you or others use it. His imitation of your actions provides him with valuable information.

He may be a bit confused with glass and mirrors. He may try to reach through a piece of glass to get something. He may believe he can pick up an object in a mirror. He may even look behind a mirror to see if something is hiding there.

These actions and accomplishments demonstrate how baby is learning to think. He is also learning to solve problems.

⚜ *Baby's Muscle Control*

Your baby is moving toward walking, if he isn't already. When he's cruising the furniture, he may take a step without holding on to anything. He may be taking steps while holding your hands. It may be awhile before he wants to sit down again!

Even if he's cruising and taking a few steps, he will often revert to crawling. For the time being, crawling is a more efficient means of getting somewhere.

⚜ *Offer Him Nongender Toys*

Some parents mistakenly believe that if they offer their son only "boy toys" he won't be interested in anything else. Don't discourage your baby from playing with any type of toy, if it interests him.

Let a boy have a doll and household items. Let a girl have a truck or baby tool kit. Every toy a child plays with offers a new experience. Every new experience contributes to your baby's overall grasp of his world.

⚜ *Coping with Inconsistencies*

A baby needs consistency in his world. It makes him feel secure. However, there are times when his experiences in the "outside" world are not going to be consistent. That's what the real world is like.

Now that he's getting older, it will be easier for your baby to cope with some inconsistency in his world. Relax when it happens. His growing maturity helps him deal with the change.

Note: See also the box *Milestones this 48ᵗʰ Week.*

What's Happening this 48ᵗʰ Week?

⚜ *When Baby Gets Frustrated*

As hard as it might be, your job as a parent is to let baby try to do things for himself. This often results in frustration for him, but it also provides him a feeling of accomplishment when he succeeds.

Don't ignore him when you see he is frustrated. Assess the situation. Is he frustrated because he's too tired to do something? Is the task he's trying to accomplish beyond his abilities? Has he tried too many times without succeeding? If these are some of the reasons he's frustrated, help him out.

However, if you've demonstrated a way to do something, let him try it on his own. He should eventually be able to work it out. These lessons are important now and later. He learns how to do something for himself now. Later, he'll have the confidence to work out a problem without expecting someone else to do it for him.

MILESTONES THIS 48TH WEEK

Changes You May See this Week as Baby Develops Physically
- may take a step without holding onto anything
- may stand on toes
- may carry spoon to mouth

Changes You May See this Week in Baby's Developing Senses and Reflexes
- turns pages of book
- may pull off shoes and socks

Changes You May See this Week as Baby's Mind Develops
- speaks long, babbling sentences with full inflection

Changes You May See this Week in Baby's Social Development
- seeks approval
- engages in parallel play with another child

Every baby is an individual, and your baby may do some of these things more quickly or more slowly than another baby. If you are concerned about your baby's progress, discuss it with your healthcare provider. Also see page xiii.

A Swollen Testicle

A swollen testicle in a baby boy, also called a *hydrocele,* results when fluid collects in one or both scrotal sacs. The condition is painless and harmless. It occurs fairly often–about half of all newborn males have it.

A male's testicles migrate from inside his abdomen into the scrotum, just before or just after birth. See the discussion of *Undescended Testicles* in *Week 42*. Testicles travel down a very small opening in the muscle wall. This opening usually seals up, but occasionally it remains open. When it does, fluid from inside the abdomen accumulates in the scrotal area, causing swelling.

The situation usually goes away on its own by the end of baby's first year when the passage closes up. However, if it doesn't close up and lasts longer than a year, surgery may be necessary to close off the passage. The surgical procedure is safe and is often done on an outpatient basis.

Your Baby's Activities

When you describe your baby's activities for him, you help him focus on what he's doing. When he's doing something, such as playing with blocks, tell him how long the block wall is or how big it is. You can also comment on other aspects of his life, such as talking about the blue shirt he has on or how nicely he's patting the dog.

When you show baby how to do something, you also help him learn. Your baby learns to recall activities by watching you perform a chore. Show him how to wash his hands without any soap and water, or how to comb his hair without a comb or brush. Make a game out of it.

You may also notice your baby's sense of humor and originality are emerging more now. He may make some changes to games you've been playing, making them uniquely his own. His creative side is beginning to appear.

> Baby's sense of humor allows him to appreciate the things you do that seem funny to him. He laughs when you entertain him.

✳ *Head Injury*

When baby falls and hits his head, it can cause you concern. Such accidents are fairly common while baby is learning to walk.

You don't usually need to be very concerned about a tumble, but there are some things you should be aware of that indicate baby has more than a little bump on the head. Symptoms that baby has a head injury that needs to be taken care of include:

- sleepiness
- confusion
- nausea
- vomiting
- pupils are different sizes
- loss of consciousness
- irritability
- head hurts
- bleeding
- an actual lump or bump on his head

What You Can Do at Home. After your baby falls, examine his head. If he has any bumps, apply ice to control swelling. If there is any bleeding, clean off the area the best you can. Examine the wound. If it is deep, it may need stitches. Apply pressure to the wound with a clean cloth, and go to the emergency room.

Call your pediatrician's office and advise them of the situation. Your doctor may want to examine baby or follow up later.

When to Call the Doctor. If you believe your baby has had a serious fall, call your doctor. The seriousness of a head injury is determined by careful evaluation. After your doctor examines baby, he or she will advise you on a course of action. You may have to observe your baby closely for 24 hours. If the situation is serious, your pediatrician may recommend further testing.

⁂ Nosebleeds

When your baby has a nosebleed, it can be unsettling for you. Also called *epistaxis,* it can occur for many reasons. It may occur from dried mucous membranes in the nose, or it may be caused by an accident. Various infections, such as scarlet fever or sinusitis, may also result in nosebleeds. Picking the nose too aggressively or picking it over a prolonged time can cause bleeding. Symptoms of a nosebleed include:

* blood from the nostril
* nausea (from swallowing blood)
* vomiting (might be bright red from swallowed blood)
* dark stools (from swallowed blood)
* blood is bright red in color if the nosebleed is close to the nostril
* blood may be dark in color if the nosebleed is deeper in the nose

What You Can Do at Home. When baby has a nosebleed, sit him upright. Bend his head forward slightly. Clamp his nostrils closed for 5 to 10 minutes. Do not lessen pressure during that time! By holding the nose tightly for this period of time, you allow the blood to clot. This seals the blood vessels.

You may also apply pressure across or under the upper lip to help control bleeding. Applying cold compresses over the nose or to the nape of the neck may help stop bleeding. If bleeding stops, then starts again, repeat the above procedures.

If your baby is getting a lot of nosebleeds, his mucous membranes may be dried out. When he is sleeping, run a cool-mist humidifier in his room. See *Week 13* for information on *Humidifiers.* Apply a small amount of petroleum jelly to a cotton swab, and put some in each nostril to help moisturize the area.

When to Call the Doctor. If bleeding doesn't stop, take baby to the nearest emergency-care facility. Blood vessels may have to be cauterized (sealed shut by applying heat or a chemical to the area).

If your baby has frequent nosebleeds, tell your pediatrician. It's important information to share. Call your doctor if baby has trouble breathing after a nosebleed or a nose injury.

Toys and Play this 48ᵗʰ Week

✃ *What's Making the Noise?*
Help baby make some discoveries. Gather together some objects that make noise, such as keys, some measuring spoons on a ring, a bell, a rattle or some beans in a plastic container. Show them to him, then put the objects in separate small brown paper bags. Shake each bag so he can hear the different sounds. Tell him what is in each bag. Mix up the bags, shake one again, and ask him if it's the keys (or whatever object you have in the bag). He may be able to identify it. If not, let him look inside the bag to see what's there.

✃ *You and Your Shadow*
You can play this game together indoors or outside. With the sun behind you both, sit next to baby in front of a wall. Wave your arm so baby can see it moving on the wall. Tell baby to look at the shadow waving at him.

Next move the shadow so it falls on baby's arm or leg where he can see it. Ask him to catch it or touch it. Show him how to wave his hands and to create a shadow. Holding his hand in yours, talk about what the shadow looks like.

If you're any good at making shadow puppets, entertain him with those. Hold up an object and talk about how its shadow shape compares to what you're holding.

✃ *Puzzle Balls*
A toy you may want to buy for baby is a puzzle ball. These balls separate into different wedges—each wedge has its own sound. These are great tools to help baby learn about the part-to-whole relationship.

✃ *Bubbles in the Bath*
Making bubbles in the bathtub is fun. Using a commercial product or a homemade one, blow bubbles onto baby's skin. Because skin is wet, bubbles may not break. Encourage him to pop them when he can. Aim them for his legs, his arms and his tummy. Name each body part a bubble lands on.

✃ *Blocks Are Fun*
Give your baby a few large plastic blocks to play with. He may stack them or arrange them. If he doesn't stack them, show him how. Help him arrange

the blocks in different ways. Talk about how the arrangement changes by moving one block to another position.

✴ *Get the Photo Album*

Bring out the photo album you made for baby. Let him look at it. He's getting old enough to turn the pages by himself. If he doesn't seem to recognize a familiar face, tell him who it is. Holding the album and turning the pages all by himself is a big accomplishment for him!

Week 49

Baby's Age as a Monthly Reference—12 months

HOW BIG IS BABY THIS 49ᵀᴴ WEEK?

Baby weighs 21½ pounds and is 29¾ inches long this week.

Baby Care and Equipment

❧ Giving Baby Herbal Medications

Some parents use herbal medicine to treat various problems they experience. They want to know if it is OK to give herbs to baby. Before you consider giving *any* herbal substance to your baby, ask yourself the following questions.

Has Baby's Illness or Condition Been Diagnosed? You may be tempted to treat a problem in baby because you believe you know what the problem is and an herb is readily available. *Never* make a diagnosis on your own. You run the risk of ignoring a potentially serious condition.

Have You Checked with Your Pediatrician about Giving Baby Herbal Medication? Before you give your baby anything your doctor hasn't recommended, check with him or her. Never medicate your child without advice from your physician.

What Are the Side Effects of this Herbal Medication? Many people consider herbs as "natural substances," therefore they believe they are harmless. However, even a mild treatment can have side effects in a baby.

Is Baby Taking Any Other Medications? If your child is taking any prescription or over-the-counter medications, think twice about adding an herbal preparation to the mix. Some herbs have an adverse effect when taken with other medicinal substances. Check with your pharmacist or pediatrician before you give baby any herb.

Do I Have Information about the Herb? Do you know what you're giving your baby? Some herbs are made with high concentrations of alcohol. Often the same herb comes in many forms. Some forms are more potent than others. Some herbs made outside the United States can be contaminated with dangerous substances.

What's the Correct Dosage for a Child the Size of My Baby?   The use of herbal medications in children has not been studied to any great extent. The proper dosage for children of various sizes has seldom been established. A smaller amount of an adult dose of an herb *does not* mean it's safe.

⚘ Do You Need Overnight Diapers?

Your baby may need extra protection during the wee hours of the night because she's sleeping for much longer periods now. You may find you need to diaper baby in overnight diapers.

A good choice to help baby get through the night without being soaked in the morning is an extra-absorbent, overnight diaper. These diapers have extra padding to absorb more fluid. If you believe these may offer your baby a drier night, check them out at the store.

If you use cloth diapers and need extra absorbency, check your local stores for pads to add to baby's diapers. These ultra-absorbent pads are laid in the middle of the diaper before baby is diapered; they absorb extra fluid just the way extra-absorbent disposable diapers do. Just throw the pad away in the morning.

⚘ Safety from Glues and Nail Primers

There are some substances you have around the house that baby must *never* be allowed to handle. Two substances to keep out of reach of a curious baby include *super glue* and *nail primers.*

Super glue is dangerous because it can adhere so quickly. If baby gets into it, it can bond her skin together in such a way that you might have to go to the emergency room to get her unstuck.

If you have super glue at your house, keep a can of acetone on hand in case of an accident. (It's also good for you if *you* have an accident.) Acetone helps dissolve the bond, but it may not work in all cases (such as if a lot of glue has been spilled). The best solution is to keep super glue in a locked cabinet or drawer when you're not using it; also keep acetone there.

Nail primers prepare fingernails to bond with acrylic nails. These substances contain methacrylic acid. This acid can cause burns if touched, inhaled or swallowed. Nail primers may not carry warning labels, so you might not be aware of the danger. Keep these locked up.

Milestones this 49th Week

✴ *Baby Displays Many Emotions*
As the end of baby's 1st year draws near, it's an emotional time for her. Her motor skills have improved, so she is more independent physically.

✴ *She Needs Reassurance*
Baby now understands she is a separate entity, so you may find her clinging to you more. Separation anxiety may reappear around this time. Because she understands she can separate from you and others, it unsettles her. She may need more reassurance from you than she has needed.

> Provide your baby with lots of opportunities to make simple choices. She needs to start practicing now so she'll have some experience when choices become more important.

She depends a great deal on you for love and affection. She wants your attention. You may notice her seeking you quite often.

Stranger anxiety may be evident when you're away from home. Reassure her by your presence and attention.

✴ *Crying Is More Predictable*
Now that your baby is approaching "toddlerhood," her crying may become more predictable. There are ways you can deal with her tears and save your sanity.

Determine what is making her cry. If she always cries when you put her in her stroller, distract her with a toy she likes. If she cries when she can't have your car keys, put them away, out of her sight.

A routine may help; she needs one. Knowing what comes next makes her feel secure. When it's necessary to depart from your normal routine, tell her what's going to happen. She understands a lot of what you say to her. She may be less emotional about the change.

Don't let her get too tired. When she's exhausted, she'll go to pieces. Save long outings for times when she's rested and can deal with them.

> By this time, baby cries only about 45 minutes a day.

✴ *She's Mobile and Active*
Baby is crawling, cruising and may be walking. She probably walks holding your hands. She may seem as if she never stops moving.

She is excited by things that move, so she prefers toys that are interactive. If you put her on a baby trike and push her gently, she'll enjoy the ride.

Your baby is demonstrating better eye–hand coordination. She has enough muscle control to put a spoon into her mouth. She may be using her left hand or her right hand more now, but this preference can change. It's not unusual for her to switch back and forth between hands for a few more years.

Note: See also the box *Milestones this 49th Week.*

Baby may be walking with just a little extra support.

What's Happening this 49th Week?

✴ *Staying Connected to Baby When You Work*

Do you work outside your home? If you do, you may feel the need to spend more quality time with your child to feel "connected" to her. Make the most of your time together. Below are some suggestions for doing this.

- **Spend extra time with her.** Get up earlier in the morning so you and baby can cuddle or play. Some quality time together before the day begins can be very beneficial for you both.
- **Learn about baby's routine at day-care.** When you're home together, do some of the same things she does at day-care. This helps make the transition from home to day-care, or day-care to home, go more smoothly.
- **When you get home, focus on baby.** Forget about chores and cooking for a while. Set aside some time to spend with her alone. Even if she can't talk, you can hold her and tell her about your day. Read a story together, or get some toys and play. You'll both have a chance to unwind and to relax.
- **Call her during the day.** If possible (and if it doesn't upset her), call your child during the day to say hi. Even if she can't talk on the phone, she can listen to your voice and will feel connected to you.

MILESTONES THIS 49ᵀᴴ WEEK

Changes You May See this Week as Baby Develops Physically
* may take a step or two without holding onto anything
* may walk with help of wheeled toy

Changes You May See this Week in Baby's Developing Senses and Reflexes
* may prefer to use one hand over the other (be left-handed or right-handed)

Changes You May See this Week as Baby's Mind Develops
* identifies animals in pictures
* remembers events for longer periods

Changes You May See this Week in Baby's Social Development
* gives attention to humans and favored objects
* gives a kiss on request
* reacts sharply to separation from parents
* may resist being fed
* fears strange people and places
* insists on feeding herself

Every baby is an individual, and your baby may do some of these things more quickly or more slowly than another baby. If you are concerned about your baby's progress, discuss it with your healthcare provider. Also see page xiii.

✲ *Baby May Be Walking*

As your baby's confidence in her ability to walk grows, she'll occasionally let go of her support. Then she'll grab it again when she feels herself wobble. Pretty soon she'll venture out on her own.

Usually baby will take only a step or two before sitting down. When you encourage her, she'll try again. Soon she'll be successful in taking quite a few steps.

When your baby starts to walk, her stance is wide legged. She holds her arms out to protect herself. Because she doesn't know how to stop efficiently, she may fall when she does.

> Your baby is a ham. She'll repeat an action if it makes you laugh. She loves it when an audience appreciates her!

When your baby starts walking, you may be concerned about the way she walks. Is she pigeon-toed? Do her legs look bowed? Does she walk on tiptoe?

Your baby's walking style is probably common. You may be concerned that she needs some sort of treatment, but don't worry. These situations usually correct themselves by the time a baby is 5 years old. However, if you are concerned, discuss it with your pediatrician at a well-baby checkup. He or she will advise you.

✴ *Sunburn*

When a person is exposed to the sun or other ultraviolet light source for a prolonged time, a sunburn can occur. It can happen at any age. Symptoms of a sunburn include:

* inflammation of the skin
* redness of the skin
* swelling of sunburned area
* nausea and/or vomiting with serious burns
* skin may blister later
* skin may peel later

What You Can Do at Home. Prevention is the best protection you can offer your baby. Avoid placing her in direct sunlight for any length of time. Overcast clouds do *not* block out harmful ultraviolet rays, which cause the skin to burn. Ultraviolet light also reflects off water, snow and sand.

It doesn't have to be hot outside to get a sunburn. If your baby is over 6 months old, use a sunscreen on her if she will be outdoors for an extended period of time. If she's under 6 months old, keep her out of the direct sunlight and away from reflected sunlight.

If a sunburn does occur, give your baby lots of fluid to prevent dehydration. Cool her off with damp towels on sunburned skin to reduce heat and pain. After swelling decreases, use creams, aloe vera or lotions to keep skin moist. Acetaminophen or ibuprofen may help relieve pain.

Over-the-counter burn remedies that contain local anesthetics may be useful, but check with your pediatrician before using any. Don't pop blisters or peel skin. It could lead to a secondary infection.

When to Call the Doctor. Call your baby's doctor if she has a severe sunburn or if she develops a fever over 101F. If she experiences vomiting or diarrhea, becomes extremely lethargic or irritable, or if pain persists for longer than 48 hours, contact your pediatrician. Your doctor may prescribe pain medication or cortisone drugs to use briefly.

✴ *Hookworm or Roundworm*

A hookworm or roundworm infection can affect the intestines and the rectum. Hookworms and roundworms are commonly found in dogs and cats. An infection can occur at any age. Symptoms of an infection include:

* fine skin rash or very small blisters that progress to a narrow, raised line on the skin
* poor appetite
* weight loss
* fussiness
* abdominal cramps
* diarrhea

The raised line is actually a small tunnel leading from the point of entry of the parasite. Usually several tracks are visible.

What You Can Do at Home. The best course of action is prevention. Keep your baby away from contact with pets, kitty litter, sand or any other area where there is a risk of exposure to an animal's urine or feces. Always wash your hands thoroughly after cleaning the cat's litter box or after contact with pets.

When to Call the Doctor. Call the doctor if your baby has symptoms. Your doctor may prescribe topical creams or ointments. The medication prescribed depends on a child's age. Oral medication is prescribed for serious cases.

◢ *Whooping Cough*
Whooping cough, also called *pertussis,* is a contagious bacterial infection. According to recent studies done by the CDC, it seems to be on the rise in the United States, particularly among babies under 6 months old. The total number of cases of whooping cough rose by 22% in 2002, as compared to figures in the late 1990s. Even adults are now contracting the illness!

Whooping cough in a baby is quite serious. An infant can get a secondary infection or pneumonia when she contracts pertussis. Hospitalization is often necessary in such cases.

Onset of the problem may be a runny or stuffy nose; you might believe it is only a cold. It progresses to vigorous coughing with the whooping sound. With whooping cough, the lungs, bronchial tubes and larynx are involved. Symptoms of whooping cough include:

* dry cough that gradually becomes more severe
* several short coughs, followed by the "whooping" cough
* the whooping sound comes at the end of a coughing spell, as the child gasps for breath
* fever
* runny nose
* loss of appetite
* irritability

What You Can Do at Home.   If you know someone has a cough, keep baby away from him or her. Wash your hands frequently. The best way to avoid the problem is to have your baby immunized! The immunization for whooping cough, diphtheria and tetanus (DTaP) is given in a series of injections. The first one is given around age 2 months. See the *Immunization Schedule* on page 36.

When to Call the Doctor.   Call your doctor immediately if you believe your baby has whooping cough or if she has any trouble breathing. Treatment for the problem includes increased liquids and rest. Antibiotics may be prescribed. Ibuprofen or acetaminophen may be suggested for fever and/or discomfort.

YOUR PREEMIE'S DEVELOPMENT

Your premature baby should be able to do many things now. Remember always to use baby's "due-date age" as your point of reference for the following accomplishments. By this week, she should be doing many things, including:

* crawling
* sitting unassisted
* taking a few steps when you hold her hands
* sitting down from a standing position
* pulling herself up on furniture and other objects (even you!) and cruising

To help her accomplish these tasks, there are many activities you can do with your baby. Try the following:

* keep playing hide and seek
* roll a ball to her, and see if she will roll it back to you
* show her pictures of animals then make animal sounds together
* make a game of picking up her toys together and putting them in a container

---

Toys and Play this 49th Week

Your baby may be walking now. If she is, you may notice she likes to combine her walking with another skill. For example, she might enjoy pulling an object behind her or pushing something ahead of her.

Toys she might have fun with now include a pull-along toy (remember the little dog you pulled behind you?) or a push toy that she can steer. Toys that make noises while she pulls or pushes them are extra fun!

✴ Paint with Water

When you need to work outdoors, let baby "paint." Fill a pail with water. Give baby a few real paintbrushes that aren't too big for her to hold. Sit her down in the grass or on the porch. Place a large piece of construction paper or cardboard in front of her, and show her how to paint it with water.

You can also put her next to a piece of furniture, and let her paint that. Show her how to dip the brush in the water and paint on something. She'll have fun while she keeps cool—the water will go everywhere!

Caution: Never leave baby alone with the water. Always keep an eye on her.

✤ *Walking Barefoot*

To increase your baby's awareness of different textures, let her walk barefoot. She can walk in sand or grass, or on the carpet or bare floor. By experiencing the way things feel on her feet, she will become aware of the various textures around her.

✤ *Let Her Be the "Big Girl"*

When you're out for a walk, take baby out of her stroller, and let her help you push it for a while. She'll enjoy the activity while it helps her improve her stability and balance. Keep one hand on the stroller to keep it from going too fast; keep your other hand near her. When she gets tired, she can ride again.

Week 50

Baby's Age as a Monthly Reference—12 months

HOW BIG IS BABY THIS 50ᵀᴴ WEEK?
Baby weighs 21¾ pounds and is 29¾ inches long this week.

Baby Care and Equipment

⁕ Calorie Check

Do you know how many calories your baby should be eating now to get all the nutrients he needs? According to the American Academy of Pediatrics, there's a formula you can use to figure out how many calories he needs each day.

Multiply his height in inches by the number 40. If he's 31 inches tall, he should consume a total of about 1240 calories every day. See the discussion of foods to offer your baby in *Week 49.*

Normally by this age, a baby is eating between 300 and 500 calories of solids each day. He may be nursing from 10 to 90 minutes a day or taking in 20 to 30 ounces of formula.

⁕ Snacks Can Be Very Important

Your baby may be eating less than he has in the past. He needs snacks to help balance his nutrient intake. They can provide him with the energy he needs to play and to grow.

In addition to his regular meals, give him three snacks a day. Make them nutritious and delicious! Choose from the following:

- yogurt—plain is best
- cheese, thinly sliced
- baby teething crackers
- saltine crackers
- graham crackers
- small pieces of easily chewed fruit, such as bananas
- a half slice of bread
- fruit juice, diluted one to one with water
- pretzels
- frozen juice pops
- pudding
- a small piece of bagel

* a milkshake
* oat-circle cereal pieces
* cut-up raisins

✎ Feeding Baby Food

Some babies love baby food. Parents may wonder if they should stop offering baby food at any particular age and switch to "people food." As long as you've introduced your baby to finger foods by this time (and he's doing all right with them), it's OK for him to still eat some baby food.

At this age, you might want to offer him a grown-up version of his baby food. For example, if he loves baby applesauce, switch to an unsweetened regular one that is fairly smooth.

When you offer him food that is for everyone, choose those that do not have sugar or other additives, when possible. He doesn't need anything extra in his food.

✎ Does It Have to Be Cow's Milk?

In just a few weeks, when he turns 1, baby will probably be ready to stop drinking formula and begin drinking milk. You may be wondering if cow's milk is the only type of milk you can offer him.

There are other kinds of milk you may give him. Check with your pediatrician before you offer him *anything* beyond formula or breast milk. He or she may have specific advice in regards to your baby. In addition to cow's milk, your choices include the following.

* **Goat's milk.** It has a tangy taste. It is deficient in vitamin B_{12} and folacin, so baby must get these nutrients from other sources. It may cause an allergic reaction in a child who is sensitive to cow's milk.
* **Soy milk.** It can be used as an alternative to cow's milk. It should be fortified with vitamin D and calcium.
* **Rice milk.** It can also be used as an alternative to cow's milk. It should also be fortified with vitamin D and calcium.

✎ The Party Approaches

It may not seem like it now, but your baby's 1st birthday is one of the most memorable milestones you will share as a family. As this important day approaches, you've been making plans. It's time to double-check on refreshments and party decorations. If necessary, call people who haven't let you know whether they are coming to the party.

It's important to keep one very significant point in mind. No matter what you've planned or what you anticipate, this is your baby's party. Be prepared to adapt *your* plans to your *baby's* needs.

Dad can get involved in planning baby's party. He can help make up the guest list. He can get out the camera, buy lots of extra film and be cameraman for the day. These memories are ones to cherish for a lifetime.

Milestones this 50th Week

✻ *Playing Together*

Playing with your baby is a lot of fun, especially now that he's getting older. When you play together, let him direct the play. Let him show you what he can do. He's doing a lot of different things with his toys, such as rolling them, spinning them, and pushing and pulling them. You may be surprised by how sophisticated his play may be now.

He still enjoys reading with you. He may want to read books by himself. As long as he is gentle with books (it's better if they're fairly indestructible), let him do this grown-up activity on his own.

Baby will probably enjoy climbing inside a box or cabinet to see if he fits. Provide him the opportunity to make these explorations.

For play activities, talk, sing and read together. Change some of your favorite songs to reflect a particular activity.

✻ *Baby's Sleep Patterns*

By this time, your baby stays up for longer periods. He sleeps less during the day and sleeps longer at night.

He is probably still napping for as long as a couple of hours every afternoon. He may continue to need a nap for quite a while. Some children nap fairly consistently until they are 4 or 5 years old.

✻ *His Efforts to Walk*

Your baby may have already taken his first independent steps. Don't be alarmed by how often he falls while he's mastering this new skill. If he's not walking by himself yet, he's probably still cruising the furniture. But he'll soon be walking on his own!

He may be standing alone. This is a big accomplishment for him. He loves standing, so don't be surprised if he resists sitting down.

✻ *He Imitates Actions*

He is very interested in what you are doing. He will study what you do so he can imitate the way you and other family members use an object.

ↄⸯ *Other Accomplishments*

Baby may be talking and saying various words. Keep talking to him, telling him stories and telling him about what happens each day.

He may be demonstrating other things he has learned. He may use a stick as a tool to get a toy that he can't reach. He may pull a blanket toward him if a book he wants is lying on it. He can reach for an object while looking at something else in another direction.

Note: See also the box *Milestones this 50ᵗʰ Week.*

MILESTONES THIS 50ᵀᴴ WEEK

Changes You May See this Week as Baby Develops Physically
- may walk without help
- lowers himself easily to the floor

Changes You May See this Week in Baby's Developing Senses and Reflexes
- takes covers off containers

Changes You May See this Week as Baby's Mind Develops
- responds to directions
- may speak some words

Changes You May See this Week in Baby's Social Development
- gives and takes a toy
- may refuse to eat new foods

Every baby is an individual, and your baby may do some of these things more quickly or more slowly than another baby. If you are concerned about your baby's progress, discuss it with your healthcare provider. Also see page xiii.

What's Happening this 50ᵗʰ Week?

ↄⸯ *Baby's Curiosity*

Your baby is curious—it's his age. You may not be thrilled when he empties your purse. You may not be happy when he takes your shoes out of the closet or tips the dog's food dish over. To help keep your cool, remember that when he gets into things, he's learning something.

You can encourage baby to explore yet keep the mess to a minimum. The most important thing to remember in all of this is baby's safety. Try the ideas listed on the following page.

Keep Acceptable Alternatives at Hand.   If you have some items that will occupy baby, he may leave other things alone. Provide him with plastic containers, bowls and boxes. Put lots of different objects in them, such as tennis balls, measuring spoons, large empty thread spools, rings from cut-up cardboard paper-towel tubes. (Be sure objects are large enough so he won't choke on them. They should be large enough so they don't fit through a toilet-paper tube.) These fun boxes should keep him entertained for quite a while.

Teach Him to Pick It Up.   Part of the fun of playing is picking up. It's not too early to begin teaching him this important concept. He'll probably enjoy helping you put things back where they belong. Make a game of it when you can.

Eliminate Dangerous Situations, When Possible.   Eliminate situations that can cause harm to baby. For example, you might not realize the garbage can be a very dangerous place for baby. Take care with what you throw away, such as razor blades, broken glass, balloons, eggshells, metal lids from cans, or string and twine. Don't put them in a container that baby might get into. If necessary, put them outside in the garbage can so they are out of his reach.

✸ His Possessions

Before age 1, most babies have not yet developed a sense of ownership. It's easy to share toys between them. However, by this age, your baby may be showing signs of possessiveness.

> If baby doesn't have a full head of hair yet, don't worry. Many babies won't have luxurious locks until they are 2 or 3 years old!

He will begin to feel strongly about what belongs to him. Sharing for him will be more difficult. You may soon start hearing him say, "Mine!"

✸ Is Halloween Close at Hand?

If you're getting ready to celebrate Halloween, you might want to leave baby out of the picture. Around this age, he may be very upset if he sees someone he knows made up as a monster or some other unknown figure. He's not ready to go trick or treating, and he probably won't be until he's about 3. He'll feel safer at home with you.

✸ Roseola Infantum

Roseola infantum, also called *exanthem subitum,* is a skin condition that occurs most often in infants and children up to 3 years old. Symptoms of the problem include:

- ✸ high fever
- ✸ red skin rash that appears as the fever subsides

* fussiness
* irritability
* enlargement of the spleen

What You Can Do at Home.   The problem occurs most often in the spring or autumn. Avoid large crowds during this time. Take measures to reduce baby's fever. Give him cool baths or fever-reducing medications, such as ibuprofen or acetaminophen, as directed by your physician.

When to Call the Doctor.   Call the doctor if baby appears listless, has any seizures, runs a consistently high fever (102F or higher) or if he refuses to eat or drink. Treatment of the problem includes medications to reduce fever and increased fluid intake.

☀ *Cuts and Abrasions*

Cuts and abrasions, also called *lacerations,* can occur because of an accident, a fall, roughhousing or meeting up with an unfriendly cat. As your baby becomes more active and adventurous, he'll experience the normal cuts and scrapes all kids do. Symptoms of a cut, scrape or abrasion include:

* bleeding
* separation of the skin at the site
* swelling
* bruising

What You Can Do at Home.   When baby gets a small cut, gently wash the area with warm water and mild soap. Apply pressure to the area to stop any bleeding. Use ice to help reduce swelling and bruising. Apply triple antibiotic ointment and a bandage.

With a cut, clean it up, then examine it to determine if stitches are required. Larger cuts and scrapes should be examined by a doctor. If there is a lot of bleeding, apply firm, gentle pressure.

Avoid hazardous situations by providing baby a safe environment. Regularly check cups, utensils and toys for any sharp surfaces. Keep stairs and other dangerous areas blocked off.

When to Call the Doctor.   Call the doctor if your baby has a cut that you believe may require stitches. If a cut continues to bleed, does not heal or appears infected (area turns red or leaks yellow or green fluid), contact your pediatrician. He or she can close a cut when necessary with sutures (stitches) or a "butterfly" bandage. Antibiotics or antibiotic gels may be prescribed by baby's doctor.

⋆ *Obesity*

In the past, a fat baby was the picture of "good health." Today, many parents are concerned that their plump baby may have future weight problems. However, research has shown that a chubby baby does not necessarily become an overweight adult.

Although a child of any age can be overweight, the term is rarely used to describe a newborn, infant or young baby. Most babies do not become extremely overweight (obese) in their first year, unless there is a medical reason for it. Obesity is defined as being at least 20% above a person's desirable weight for his or her height.

With babies and young children, there is a range of average weights *and* heights for infants and young children. The key is the height-to-weight comparison. At each office visit with your pediatrician, your baby will be weighed. Your doctor will be able to tell you how your baby's height and weight compare to other children of the same age.

As we've discussed throughout the book, babies develop, grow and gain weight at different rates. Your baby's doctor will help you understand what's normal for your baby.

Do *not* restrict your baby's food and formula or breast milk if you think he's too big. Even if you believe his weight is out of proportion, he needs the vitamins, minerals and other nutrients from the food he eats to develop physically *and* mentally!

Follow the instructions your pediatrician has given you with regards to feeding baby and giving him vitamin supplements. If you are concerned, discuss the situation with your baby's doctor at one of baby's regularly scheduled well-baby visits. Your pediatrician can provide you with specific instructions regarding your child's food intake.

Toys and Play this 50ᵗʰ Week

⋆ *Bath Splash*

Gather together some plastic containers. Poke a small hole in one container and a large hole in the other. Show baby how to pour water into one container. Let it leak into the other container, where it will also leak out. Let him pour the water into the first container while you hold a container in each hand. Adding more holes to one or both containers adds to the fun!

⋆ *Serious Cruising*

Help baby practice his cruising skills. Line up a few chairs against a wall. Do this in a carpeted area so the chairs won't slip. Place him next to the chair at one end of the row. Show him how to propel himself down the row, moving from one chair to the next.

If he holds back, entice him with a favorite toy. Put it on a chair in the middle, then move it to the chair at the end. When he reaches the end, let him have the toy for a while, then put the toy at the other end, and begin again.

✳ *Unwrap the Presents*
For the joy of discovery, wrap a few of baby's favorite toys in newsprint. The colored Sunday comics is a good choice. Don't use tape or string. A small toy can be easily wrapped a couple of times in a large sheet of comics.

Give him the "presents," and let him unwrap them. He'll enjoy discovering what's inside each one. For an added treat, let him play with the paper when he's finished.

✳ *Baby Slam Dunk!*
To help baby develop his coordination, place a laundry basket on the floor near him. Give him a tennis ball or other small object to toss. Show him how to throw the ball into the basket. Begin close to the basket, then move a little farther away. Be prepared to catch some stray balls!

Week 51

Baby's Age as a Monthly Reference—12 months

HOW BIG IS BABY THIS 51ST WEEK?
Baby weighs 21¾ pounds and is 30 inches long this week.

Baby Care and Equipment

Birthday Party Plans

Baby's 1st birthday is fast approaching. By this time, your plans have been made. You're probably looking forward to this big day with anticipation. In this week before her party, the following tasks need to be done.

* Order the cake, if you're not going to bake it.
* Buy the beverages you plan to serve.
* Make out your shopping list for the food.
* Be sure the camera is working—buy enough film. If you have a digital camera, be sure the battery is fully charged.
* If you're going to videotape the birthday celebration, be sure the camcorder is working and the battery (or batteries) is fully charged.
* Plan where decorations are going.
* Order balloons, if you plan to have some filled with helium.

Baby's Interest in Food

Your baby's interest in eating may be almost nonexistent. Don't become anxious about the situation. Spend your energies on other activities, such as playing with her and helping her learn about her world.

> Your baby may have tripled her birth weight by her 1st birthday.

Don't expect her to eat three well-balanced meals every day. If she skips a food group one day, offer her more of that food group the next day. Provide her with nutritious meals and snacks each day.

Over the long run, she'll get the nutrition she needs. And before long, she'll probably begin eating again. If you are concerned, discuss it with your baby's doctor at her next well-baby checkup.

Safety at Mealtimes

You want to protect your baby while she's eating. To protect her from getting hurt, consider the following suggestions.

496

- She's not ready for a fork yet, so don't give her one to feed herself or to play with.
- Don't let her walk or run when she's eating or drinking anything.
- Don't let her walk or run while she's carrying any utensils.
- Use plastic for safety—plastic spoons, plastic dishes, plastic cups.

Milestones this 51st Week

When Baby Repeats Herself

A child's repetitive behavior can be very annoying to an adult. Baby will do something over and over and over again. When she repeats an activity, it reflects her limited experience and understanding of her world.

You may find it difficult to understand, but repetition is her way of exploring her world. Does the ball always roll away from her when she pushes it? Does the spoon drop to the floor every time she drops it? Repeating an action helps develop her motor skills. It also enhances her memory.

Baby's Actions Are Linked to Goals

Your baby's actions are linked to her goals. Carrying the spoon to her mouth allows her to take a bite and feed herself. When she wants a toy, she crawls to get it. Her coordination and dexterity are improving every day.

She'll climb on top of furniture or to the top of the stairs to see what is going on. She uses her improved mobility to explore wherever she can. Watch her closely to keep her safe.

Help her increase her independence by continuing to encourage her to do things for herself. If it takes a little effort to get a toy, tell her she can get it if she wants it. Let her do as much as possible for herself. She'll be very proud when she accomplishes what she set out to do.

Her Perception of Her World

Your baby is very mobile now, which has changed her view of her world. There are many dimensions to this world. The climbing and standing she's engaged in have sharpened her perception. She realizes that an object can be used or played with in many different ways.

She understands that objects exist separately from her. She is beginning to see herself as part of the world around her.

Baby Play

At this age, your baby is very active in her play. She loves to open and to close cabinets. Emptying them is also lots of fun. She likes to pound pegs

Emptying cabinets keeps baby busy.

into a wood holder. Playing with blocks—stacking them or arranging them—entertains her.

When you sing a familiar song, she may supply a word that you leave out (intentionally). She is affectionate with people and favorite toys. She may scribble with crayons.

✵ *Your Baby Is a Social Being*

As she gets older, your baby is becoming more sociable. She's interested in other people. She still speaks in gibberish, but now she speaks a few recognizable words. She may have a conversation with you, although you probably won't know what it's all about.

Note: See also the box *Milestones this 51ˢᵗ Week.*

If baby's birthday falls on or near a major holiday, such as Christmas, Chanukah or New Year's Eve, consider having a "half-birthday" party when she's older. When she can understand the concept, have her party 6 months away from her birthday, when she'll be the center of attention at least one time during the year. For example, if her birthday is on December 28, celebrate her birthday on June 28!

What's Happening this 51ˢᵗ Week?

✵ *Is Baby Stuck in a Rut?*

When your little one repeats negative or unpleasant behavior, there are some things you can do to help her get back on the right track. By following the suggestions below, you can make life happier for her *and* for you!

She Has a Short Attention Span. When she's being unpleasant, distract your little one. If you direct her to some other activity, she may stop her negative behavior. Show her something else she can do that's fun. She may be glad to switch activities.

Keep Your Reactions under Control. When she's being negative, control your response. If you respond strongly, it teaches her that there are things she does that cause you to react. When you don't react, she may lose interest in what she's doing and move on to something else. If you do react, she may repeat a behavior to get a reaction from you.

MILESTONES THIS 51ˢᵀ WEEK

Changes You May See this Week as Baby Develops Physically
- climbs up and down stairs
- may get to standing position by pushing up from a squatting position

Changes You May See this Week in Baby's Developing Senses and Reflexes
- is learning correct use of a toy, such as pegboard and hammer, telephone

Changes You May See this Week as Baby's Mind Develops
- searches for hidden object if she hasn't seen it but remembers last location

Changes You May See this Week in Baby's Social Development
- resists napping
- may demand more help from others than is necessary because it is easier
- gives affection to humans and objects
- may undress herself

Every baby is an individual, and your baby may do some of these things more quickly or more slowly than another baby. If you are concerned about your baby's progress, discuss it with your healthcare provider. Also see page xiii.

Explain to Her What's Coming Next.   When a young child is surprised by an abrupt change in activities, it can be unsettling for her. When you tell her what's going to happen, you prepare her for it. Sometimes her negativity is only a reaction to a change.

Keep Things Calm When Appropriate.   You can't expect your baby to settle down immediately after she's been roughhousing with her siblings or a parent. When you want her to be calm and quiet, such as at bedtime, precede the action with a quiet activity. Reserve stimulating games and activities for appropriate times.

⁂ Baby Is Portable

At this time, your baby is still very portable. You can take her just about anywhere you go. You can buckle her in, and she can't unbuckle herself yet. She's probably very interested in seeing her world.

The drawback is that your baby may not fully understand when you explain things to her. She wants to function at her own comfort level. She may not cooperate when you have errands to run or social gatherings to attend.

But take her with you anyway. She needs to experience different situations to learn how to react properly so you can take her with you again.

↵ *When Baby Feels Pain or Gets Hurt*

A toddler's experiences are based on what she can see and hear. When she gets hurt, she may not be able to express herself to you in words. Ask her where it hurts. She may be able to point to it. Ask her how much it hurts.

Watch for changes; note whether she moves normally. Are there any changes in her eating or sleeping habits? Whining, listlessness or the inability to settle may indicate a problem. If she favors or protects an arm or a leg, it could mean an injury.

Trying to decipher a child's nonverbal clues is sometimes difficult. You have to be a master detective. Stay alert—your baby's health and well-being depend on it!

↵ *Fractures and Broken Bones*

A fracture or broken bone is an unusual injury for a newborn or infant. At birth, a baby's bones are relatively "soft" and more like cartilage than bone. The collarbone (scapula) or bones in the arm (humerus) can be broken during a difficult delivery. When this occurs, usually no treatment is required. Within a few months, a break heals so completely that even an X-ray does not reveal evidence of it.

Broken bones in babies may result from an automobile accident or some other type of major or severe accident. Children crawling or learning to walk occasionally fracture a bone when they take a serious tumble or fall down stairs. Symptoms your child has suffered a broken bone include:

* pain
* tenderness
* redness
* swelling
* bleeding
* bruising

What You Can Do at Home. If you believe your baby has a broken bone, apply ice to the area, then immobilize it. Take your baby to the emergency room.

When to Call the Doctor. If you aren't sure whether baby has suffered a broken bone or if an injury is serious, call your pediatrician. He or she will advise you.

Fractures are usually immobilized with a cast or splint made of plaster or fiberglass. In more serious fractures, surgery may be required. Your doctor can prescribe pain medication if it is needed. Following treatment, call your pediatrician if the dressing or cast appears too tight or if part of the body below the cast is pale or cool to the touch. This may indicate that baby's circulation is restricted.

> If baby has had a bulge or bump in the navel area, where the cord fell off, it should have disappeared by now. If it hasn't, bring it to your pediatrician's attention at baby's 1-year-old well-baby visit.

✴ *Laryngitis*
When laryngitis occurs, your baby may have a very hoarse cry. It may be related to a cold or other upper-respiratory problem and can occur at any age. Symptoms of laryngitis include:
* change in her voice or her cry
* hoarse voice or cry
* fever
* difficulty swallowing
* poor feeding

What You Can Do at Home.   When you hear baby crying hoarsely, use a cool-mist humidifier in her room when she's sleeping. See *Week 13* for information on *Humidifiers.* Increase the amount of liquids you offer her. Give her ibuprofen or acetaminophen to help reduce any fever and to relieve pain.

When to Call the Doctor.   Call the doctor if symptoms don't improve within 1 or 2 days. If baby has difficulty swallowing, shows signs of dehydration, if she's not feeding well or other symptoms worsen, such as her fever rises, contact your pediatrician. Treatment for the problem may include antibiotics, ibuprofen or acetaminophen for relief of pain or fever.

✴ *Sprains and Strains*
We often hear the terms "sprain" and "strain" but may not understand the difference between the two. A *sprain* is a stretched or torn ligament. A *strain* is a stretched muscle.

Sprains and strains aren't common occurrences in young babies. However, they can occur in active infants over 6 months of age and children learning to walk. Symptoms of a sprain or strain include:
* pain
* swelling
* bruising
* tenderness

What You Can Do at Home.   If your baby gets a sprain or a strain, apply a cool compress to the injured area for the first 24 hours. Apply warm compresses after that. When applying a compress, place a washcloth or towel between the baby and the hot or cold compress. Protect the injured part of the body by immobilizing it when necessary.

> In the next few months, your baby will be getting some more teeth. You'll see her first four molars come in, then her four canine teeth.

When to Call the Doctor.   Call the doctor if swelling gets worse after home treatment. If other symptoms worsen, it could be a fracture. Call your pediatrician. Pain medication may be prescribed by baby's doctor. In severe situations, a cast or splint may be necessary.

Toys and Play this 51st Week

Toys your baby will enjoy at this age, which you can suggest as gifts as 1st-birthday presents if she doesn't already have them, include building blocks in wood or plastic, stuffed animals or dolls, riding toys, pounding sets, balls and simple puzzles.

Fun in the Tub
Playing in the tub is always fun. Some activities you can do together when baby's in the tub include the following suggestions.
* Make her hairdo a crazy one when you shampoo it. While it's still soapy, arrange it in funny styles. Hold a hand mirror so she can see how she looks.
* Make washing her hair more fun by using a big soup ladle to wet and to rinse her hair. Let her pour water out of it after you wash her hair.
* Buy a bathtub hand puppet or make one out of a couple of washcloths. The puppet can tickle her while it washes her!

Crawl the Plank!
Baby can improve her balance when she plays this game. Place your ironing board flat on the floor. Stabilize it (it might be wobbly with the stand folded down) with bath towels on both sides. Put a toy at one end of it. Set baby at the other end, and encourage her to crawl to get the toy.

Backward Down the Stairs
It's important to teach baby to climb safely down the stairs. Place her on the stairs on her tummy, with her feet pointing toward the bottom of the stairs.

Gently pull her legs out so she learns how it feels to slide downward on her tummy. This also helps her coordination. Even when she learns to master this "backward slide," don't let her on stairs without your supervision.

✒ *Climb the Mountain*

Baby wants to climb, so let her. Pile pillows and cushions on the floor, then let her climb on them. Put the pillows in the middle of the room. Move any furniture out of the way. Put the biggest pillows from the sofa on the bottom, then add chair pillows and throw pillows. Don't make it too high. Help her climb the mountain to the top. Never leave her alone while she's doing this.

Week 52

Baby's Age as a Monthly Reference –
12 months; 1 year old

HOW BIG IS BABY THIS 52ND WEEK?
Baby weighs 22 pounds and is 30 inches long this week.

Baby Care and Equipment

✴ *Baby's Party*
It's baby's 1st birthday and an exciting day for you! You may be surprised to discover how emotional you are. Your baby has been a central part of your lives for a year. You have seen him grow from a helpless newborn to the toddler he is now.

If you're having a party, there's still work to do. A couple of days before, prepare the area where you'll hold the party. Clean it, and move furniture so it's safe for children. The day before the party, bake the cake or pick it up. The morning of the big day, decorate, prepare any food you will serve, buy ice if you'll need it and get ready for your guests.

✴ *The Car-Safety Vest*
If your child is fairly large at 1 year (between 25 and 40 pounds), you may want to consider buying this piece of equipment. A device for larger babies is the *safety vest*; it can be used instead of a car seat. It is lightweight and has shoulder, hip and crotch straps to secure him in the car. Some vests require an additional tether strap be installed in a vehicle.

A vest is great for travel. You can stick it in your carry-on bag and be ready to buckle baby up when you hail a cab or are picked up by friends or relatives. If you're interested in a safety vest, ask about it at your local baby-products store.

✴ *Raisins and Tooth Decay*
Your baby is just starting to get a mouthful of teeth, and you want to protect them. One way to do that is to brush his teeth every time he eats raisins.

Raisins are chewed longer than most other snacks. They also stick to the teeth. This exposes tooth enamel to mouth acids for long periods, which can lead to tooth decay.

Brushing his teeth after he eats raisins removes the problem. If he can't brush, rinse his mouth out with water to help wash raisin bits out of his teeth.

> At this time, you can begin offering your baby cow's milk. If he hasn't had any problems with egg yolks, you may also want to think about adding egg whites to his diet.

✒ *Nutrients Baby Needs*

Research has shown that during your child's first 2 years, he needs to get about 40% of his daily calories from fat sources. Studies have shown that at 6 months of age, a little over 40% of total calories come from fat. However, by age 1 year, this percentage has dropped to about 30%.

Often a baby eats what his parents eat. If they are eating low-fat foods, parents may believe the same foods are OK to feed baby. These foods are *not* OK to give to a baby. If parents drink low-fat or skim milk, they may give the same product to their baby. This results in less-than-desirable percentages of fat in the diet. A deficit in the amount of fat he eats can be unhealthy.

Don't Limit Fat Intake.   Don't limit your child's fat intake until after he turns 2. At that point, you may begin decreasing it, but it must be done *gradually.* By age 5, he should still be getting about 30% of his calories from fat sources. Until he's quite a bit older, don't feed him fat-reduced foods.

He Needs Certain Nutrients.   Many babies don't get enough vitamin D or zinc in their diets. Some products aren't vitamin-D-fortified, such as cheese and yogurt. Often parents do not realize this, so they feed baby these foods without offering others that do contain vitamin D. Good sources of vitamin D include eggs, fortified milk and butter.

Zinc is found in beef, pork and poultry. Children may resist eating these foods, but encourage your child to eat them. Two or 3 tablespoons a day of beef, pork, poultry or eggs provide him with adequate amounts of zinc.

✒ *Why Have We Waited to Give Him Cow's Milk?*

You have been advised not to give your baby cow's milk until this time. The reason? His digestive system wasn't mature enough to digest it. His kidneys and digestive system could not safely process the proteins and minerals in whole milk. If you had given him milk before this time, you might have caused mild damage to the lining of his intestines. This could have resulted in problems.

Your baby should drink *whole cow's milk* for the next year, until he's 2. As discussed above, he needs the fat and calories to grow and to develop. After he turns 2, until he is 5, you can *gradually* change him from whole cow's milk to low-fat or skim milk. Don't make the transition too abruptly.

> When you introduce your baby to cow's milk, make it *whole milk!* Nearly every child under the age of 2 needs the elements found in whole milk.

Milestones this 52nd Week

✻ *Baby May Express Many Emotions*

By the end of this 1st year, you may see baby begin to express his emotions in many ways. He may be very affectionate with you and other family members. Baby may give a kiss on request. He may hug and kiss a favorite stuffed animal or doll. He outwardly expresses his feelings. These demonstrations indicate his ability to express his affection for you and others.

He has a sense of humor and readily displays it. He laughs and plays "jokes" on you.

Baby has temper tantrums because it is difficult for him to express his frustrations. When he's angry, he'll let you know. He is learning acceptable behavior and may test you quite often. Tell him when you disapprove of his actions.

✻ *Baby's Mobility*

If he's not walking yet, he soon will be. Even if he is toddling around, he may crawl when he wants to get something quickly. He may also crawl when he engages in some activities, such as pushing a truck across the floor. He needs both hands for this task. This type of play helps him learn to coordinate the use of his legs, his arms and his eyes.

He can easily sit in a child-sized chair. He can hold an object in each hand and has figured out how to pick up a third. He'll put an object he was holding in his mouth or under his arm to free up one hand.

He may carry a toy with him when he walks. This provides him with a feeling of support, although it doesn't offer any. He may have trouble going around corners or stopping when he wants to. These are skills he'll perfect in the next few months.

✎ *Changes in Your Baby*

During this first year, your baby has undergone some incredible changes! In this first year, his brain has grown to nearly 60% of its adult size. His vision is nearly mature. Baby's sense of spatial relationships is excellent, but he still has trouble judging distance and speed.

He has matured enough to tell the difference between adults and children. He may now seek out other babies.

Note: See also the box *Milestones this 52nd Week.*

MILESTONES THIS 52ND WEEK

Changes You May See this Week as Baby Develops Physically
- displays some combination of standing, walking and cruising
- may climb out of a crib or playpen

Changes You May See this Week in Baby's Developing Senses and Reflexes
- may put an object in his mouth or under his arm to grasp another

Changes You May See this Week as Baby's Mind Develops
- understands much of what is said to him

Changes You May See this Week in Baby's Social Development
- may have tantrums
- cares for doll or cuddly toy by hugging, cuddling, feeding
- takes only one afternoon nap

Every baby is an individual, and your baby may do some of these things more quickly or more slowly than another baby. If you are concerned about your baby's progress, discuss it with your healthcare provider. Also see page xiii.

What's Happening this 52nd Week?

✎ *Baby's Unpleasant Behavior*

At times, your baby may display behavior that you find unpleasant and unacceptable. He may begin hitting, biting, pinching, pulling hair, throwing food or doing other things you don't want him to do.

When baby misbehaves, it usually isn't an act of defiance. He's just experimenting. If you overreact when he misbehaves, you reinforce his behavior because of your response. The next time your baby is unpleasant, try the following tactics.

- **Ignore him.** Sometimes it's best to ignore his behavior. If he doesn't get any reaction from you or others, he'll soon forget about it and move on to something else.

- **Don't overreact.** When you react strongly to something, you give baby attention for his negative behavior. When you reprimand him, he may see it as a reward because he has your attention. This can reinforce his negative behavior, and he'll do it again.

- **Be consistent.** Always handle the same problem in the same way. Ask others to handle it the way you do. If you tolerate an action sometimes, but not at other times, or if some member of the family thinks it's "cute," it's harder to get baby to stop doing it.

- **Baby *is* curious.** It's his nature to be curious. He wants to explore and to learn more about his environment. When you present him with interesting things to explore, he will explore, with little regard for anyone else. For example, when you have on a brightly colored necklace, he may grab it to learn more about it. If you don't want him pulling it, put it inside your shirt while you're holding him. Help reduce the number of things that are off-limits.

- **React quickly.** When he displays a negative or unacceptable behavior, tell him "No" quickly and firmly. If he repeats an action, distract him or remove him from the situation. The longer you delay, the more likely he is to forget what he did that was unacceptable.

- **Praise him when his behavior is acceptable.** If you always focus on the negative, baby will repeat actions to get your attention. When you ignore the negative and focus on the positive, he'll change his behavior. He wants your attention. If you don't give it to him for being pleasant, he may try to get it by being unpleasant.

> When you turn baby's car seat around to face forward, be sure you install the seat according to the manufacturer's instructions. You may also have to move the harness straps to the top slot.

༈ *Your Conversations with Baby*

When you want your baby to pay attention to you, don't yell at him. Get down to his level or pick him up, and speak quietly to him. Every time a person raises his or her voice to call out, it sounds a bit angry, even when the person isn't angry or upset. Baby may think he's being disciplined for something and may ignore you.

When you talk to baby, use correct words. Save baby talk for occasional interactions. He needs to hear you pronounce words correctly. Use real words for made-up words that you may have used when he was younger.

Speak clearly and use short sentences. Baby doesn't comprehend long explanations or big words. If he doesn't understand you, he may stop listening.

It's common for him to mispronounce words. There are a lot of words for him to learn! Instead of constantly correcting him, use the word correctly. If he says "googie" for "cookie," ask him, "Would you like a cookie?"

It's no fun to be corrected all the time. Let him learn in a positive environment.

♪ Frostbite

Frostbite occurs when a part of the body is exposed to extreme cold and suffers the effect of freezing. Areas usually affected include the nose, cheeks, ears, fingers and toes. It can occur at any age. Symptoms of frostbite include:

* white or pale appearance of affected area
* exposed area is numb or tender to the touch
* tingling in exposed area
* tissue may feel firm
* color may change from pale or white to red, then to purple then black
* exposed area blisters

What You Can Do at Home. If your baby experiences frostbite, give him emergency care until he can be seen by a doctor. Do *not* rub or massage the area. Remove any clothing covering the affected area, then cover the area with loose clothing or gauze. Get medical help as soon as possible.

Baby may need a haircut around this time. You'll know it's trimming time when his bangs hang in his eyes and the hair over his ears is too long.

When to Call the Doctor. Call the doctor if you believe your baby has suffered frostbite. After baby has been treated, call your pediatrician if there is an increase in swelling, tenderness or pain, if there is a discharge of liquid or pus from the area or if other symptoms develop.

Baby's doctor will prescribe pain medication if it is needed. Sometimes the affected body part is placed in warm water (100F), but this should be done *only* by qualified medical personnel.

♪ Lactose Intolerance

When a person suffers from lactose intolerance, also called *lactase deficiency* or *milk intolerance,* he has a problem digesting milk cow's or other milk products. The condition is caused by a deficiency in, or the lack of, the enzyme lactase. Lactase is necessary to digest all milk products other than breast milk.

Lactose intolerance can occur at any age. Some infants are born with this disorder. Symptoms your baby has lactose intolerance include:

- diarrhea
- failure to thrive
- failure to gain weight
- diaper rash
- gas
- stomach pain
- nausea
- vomiting

Lactose intolerance is more common in some races of people than others. Asians, African Americans and Native Americans have a higher incidence of lactose intolerance. It also runs in families. Breastfeed your baby if you and/or the baby's father have a family history of lactose intolerance. If there is no family history, be alert for problems with formula, especially if it is cow-milk based. When baby turns 1 year old, look for signs of lactose intolerance when he switches to regular cow's milk.

What You Can Do at Home.   If lactose intolerance does not run in your family, you may have to become a detective to discover this problem. When baby has symptoms such as those listed above, try to identify what might be causing them.

When to Call the Doctor.   Call your pediatrician if you believe your baby has lactose intolerance, especially after switching to cow's milk from formula or breast milk. If baby suffers from persistent diarrhea or vomiting, or if he doesn't gain weight, let his doctor know.

The best treatment is to change baby's diet. Do not give him any cow's milk or products that contain, or are made from, cow's milk.

If the condition is present at birth, and you choose not to nurse, you may be advised to give baby a soybean-based formula. If the problem appears when baby is older, a supplement (lactase) can be added to milk and milk-containing foods to help deal with the problem. If you want to give him milk, ask your pediatrician about giving him lactose-free milk and milk products. They are available in the supermarket. Your pediatrician will advise you.

Some Warnings Signs

Baby should be doing quite a few things now. If he doesn't do the following activities, discuss it with your pediatrician at baby's next well-baby checkup.

- He doesn't crawl.
- He can't stand, even if you support him or he holds onto something else.
- He always drags one side of his body when he moves around.

With his first efforts at walking, you may be paying more attention to baby's feet. You may notice his legs are slightly bowed. His feet may turn up, and toes may be overlapped. These should all straighten out in the next few months.

Toys and Play this 52ⁿᵈ Week

Most babies of this age love action. When your baby plays with toys that move or ones that he can manipulate, he's learning about make-believe, improving his motor skills and indulging in physical play.

He'll enjoy toys that move, such as toys he can push or pull. He'll have fun with toys he can ride on. Toys he can make into many forms, such as blocks and other shapes, or ones he can pretend with, such as dolls, stuffed animals and hand puppets, are also favorites.

❧ *Learning Teamwork*
It's time to start teaching baby about teamwork. In addition to developing muscle coordination, this game helps baby learn to take turns. Sit facing baby on the floor. Touch your feet to his feet. Roll a ball to him, and tell him to roll it back to you.

❧ *"Loving" His Toys*
Encourage baby to hug and to love his toys and stuffed animals. This helps him learn to express affection. Show baby how to give the toy or doll "a love and a hug." Be sure you give him lots of loves and hugs, too!

❧ *Meeting Strangers*
Make a game out of meeting strangers. Before introducing your little one to someone new, hold him securely in your arms. Shake hands with the new person. Ask the visitor to hand baby one of his toys. Later, ask baby to hand something to the person. Let him move along at his own pace–don't force him into any interactions.

Emergency Situations

This section provides you with information on ways to deal with various emergency situations. We list them alphabetically. We urge you to read it thoroughly and to become knowledgeable about the various responses and treatments to emergencies you might face with a child.

We also suggest you take a CPR course to learn how to perform this life-saving technique correctly. Contact your local hospital or the American Red Cross for information on classes they may offer in your area.

✚ *Anaphylactic Shock*

Anaphylactic shock, also called *allergic shock,* occurs when the body has a severe allergic reaction to something it has become sensitized to, such as a drug or foreign protein. A reaction can occur at any age. Symptoms of anaphylactic shock include:

- loss of consciousness (fainting)
- convulsions
- itching or hives
- sneezing or runny nose
- numbness or tingling around the mouth or on fingers
- itchy or runny eyes
- difficulty breathing
- tightness of chest
- fever
- violent cough
- rapid heartbeat (palpitations)

Anaphylactic shock is a severe reaction. This is an emergency! Get help immediately. Call 911. It may be necessary to perform CPR or mouth-to-mouth resuscitation on your baby until help arrives.

Try to identify a possible cause. It is necessary to identify the cause of this severe reaction for future safety. Your observations will help emergency personnel treat your baby. Medications, such as adrenalin or antihistamines, may be given.

✚ *Bleeding*

How much blood is lost, and how quickly, is a good indicator of how severe bleeding is. Babies have a small volume of blood, so they can't afford to lose as much blood as an older child or an adult. If serious injury results in bleeding from the arteries, a baby can die in minutes, if left untreated.

If your baby has a small cut or abrasion that bleeds slightly, clean the area with mild soap and water. Dry the area, then apply triple antibiotic ointment and a bandage.

If your baby sustains a wound with a lot of bleeding, immediately apply steady, firm pressure to the wound with a clean cloth, clean disposable diaper or your hand until bleeding stops.

Do *not* attempt to clean the wound first or remove any embedded objects. Call 911, or take your child to the nearest emergency-medicine facility.

> When applying a compress to any part of baby's body, place a washcloth or towel between baby's skin and the compress.

✚ *Cardiopulmonary Resuscitation (CPR)*

Parents and others who care for children will benefit from knowing how to administer CPR correctly. You can learn the technique by reading about it, but it's better to take a course. There you can ask questions and learn the right techniques.

Certified courses are held in most communities. Contact the American Red Cross, the American Heart Association or your state or county medical society. It may be necessary to perform CPR if baby:

* is not breathing
* is having difficulty breathing (lips or skin turn blue)
* has no pulse or heartbeat
* is unresponsive

Seven Steps to Perform CPR.   There are seven important steps in performing CPR. Study this section, or review these steps after you take your CPR course. *The first four steps of CPR comprise the four steps of mouth-to-mouth resuscitation.* The steps are as follows.

1. See if baby is responsive or conscious. Nudge, tap or gently shake baby. If he does not respond, call for help. Put your ear next to baby's mouth and nose. Listen for breathing, and watch to see if his chest rises and falls. Don't shake baby hard. It could cause further injury.

2. Place baby on his back on a firm, flat surface. Move baby carefully. Support his head and neck.

3. Open the baby's airway by gently tilting his head back with one hand on his forehead. At the same time, lift his chin up with the fingers of your

other hand. The baby's nose should point toward the ceiling. Again, check to see if he's breathing.

4. If baby is not breathing, make a tight seal with your mouth over baby's mouth and nose. Give him two slow breaths. Watch to see if his chest rises and falls. Don't blow with too much force. If baby's chest does not rise and fall, reposition him. Try again. It may be necessary to check baby's airway again and start over. Also see *Choking,* below.

5. Check baby's pulse. Feel on the inside of his upper arm, between his shoulder and his elbow. Count for 15 seconds, and multiply by 4. If there is a pulse and baby is not breathing, continue breathing for baby at a rate of 1 breath every 3 seconds.

6. If there is no pulse, begin chest compressions. Place two or three of your fingers on the lower portion of baby's breastbone, one finger's width below the nipple line. Gently press down ½ to 1 inch. Give five compressions, at a rate of 100 per minute, then a rescue breath. It helps to count aloud: "one, two, three, four, five, breathe."

7. After 20 cycles (one minute), check for pulse and breathing. If both have returned, place baby on his side and watch him. If he is not breathing but his pulse has returned, give one rescue breath every 3 seconds, and monitor his pulse. If both pulse and breathing are absent, continue CPR. Check for pulse and breathing every few minutes. Continue until help arrives.

+ *Choking*

One of the many things new parents discover is that everything (except maybe the food you feed baby) ends up in his mouth, often with at least one visit to the floor! Any item baby can put in his mouth presents a danger of choking–*anything!* The information in this section may be lifesaving for your baby.

Babies choke on many small objects, such as toy parts, buttons, coins, plastic bags, balloons, and on larger objects, such as pillows and blankets. Toys with removable small parts are dangerous. Food is also a frequent cause of choking. Those that are particularly dangerous include:

* candy
* gum
* nuts
* raisins
* popcorn
* hot dogs
* pieces of hard vegetables
* grapes
* any small food

* any "sticky" or "gooey" food
* peanut butter

When baby chokes, he usually can't make any sound. He will turn blue and appear to stop breathing. Coughing or gasping may come before choking. It may be baby's way of trying not to choke. Do not use the Heimlich Maneuver on an infant; it can injure baby.

If baby's coughing, don't try to stop it. It's a normal reaction and often solves the problem. Use care when trying to remove an object from baby's mouth. You don't want to push it deeper into his throat. It's OK to sweep your finger across or through baby's mouth to remove an obstruction.

If baby is choking, have someone else call 911. Put baby face down on your forearm. Support his head and neck, and hold his jaw. His head should be lower than the rest of his body. Using the heel of your other hand, give him four or five blows between his shoulder blades.

If baby doesn't breathe, keep his head lower than the rest of the body. Using two or three fingers, give four or five chest thrusts on the lower half of baby's breastbone. If baby is still not breathing, it may be necessary to repeat the above steps. Also see *CPR*, above.

> Keep the following numbers close to your phone, or put them on your speed dial:
> * Your pediatrician's office
> * The Poison Control Center
> * The closest hospital
> * The closest emergency-medicine facility
> * 911

+ *Concussion*

A concussion is an injury that results from the body impacting with an object. Most concussions involve the head or the spine. Most often, when we think about concussions, we think about injury to the head. Symptoms of a *head concussion* include:

* drowsiness or confusion
* vomiting
* nausea
* pupils of different sizes
* loss of consciousness
* irritability
* headache
* bleeding of the scalp, if the skin is broken

* bump on the head
* inability to recognize familiar people or objects
* staggering gait or loss of coordination
* weakness, tingling or an uncontrollable twitching of one side of the body, an arm or a leg
* bleeding or drainage of clear fluid from the ears or nose
* seizures

If your baby suffers a head injury, apply pressure to the wound with a clean cloth or clean diaper. If the wound won't stop bleeding, or if it is deep or large, go to the nearest emergency-medicine facility. If the wound is not serious, after bleeding stops, put ice on the spot to reduce swelling. Apply triple antibiotic ointment and a bandage.

After a hard blow to the head, keep the child quiet for the next 12 to 24 hours. Keep him awake for at least an hour, then let him sleep if he wants to. Awaken the child every 2 hours to see if you can awaken him easily and if he recognizes you. Determine if his pupils are of equal size and if they constrict when you shine a light in his eyes.

Notify your pediatrician if your child receives a head injury. Your doctor may want to see him for evaluation. The extent of an injury can be determined only by careful examination and observation. If you suspect your baby has suffered a severe head injury, notify your doctor immediately.

After examination by your doctor, your baby may be sent home with you. He must be carefully observed for the next 24 hours. Report to your doctor immediately if you are unable to awaken or to rouse your baby. You will be given other specifics to watch for. Hospitalization may also occur for studies, such as X-rays, CT scan and MRI, and for observation.

✦ Electric Shock

Electric shock occurs when the human body comes in contact with electricity. Electric-shock injury in babies occurs most often when they put metal objects into electrical outlets or when they put electrical cords in their mouth and bite down.

If your baby sustains an electric shock, immediately shut off the power. Determine if he is touching any wires. Remove the wires with a nonmetal object before giving him aid.

Yell for help if baby is unconscious and not breathing. Begin mouth-to-mouth resuscitation immediately. If there is no pulse, begin CPR. Continue these emergency treatments until baby is revived or until help arrives.

If baby receives an electric shock severe enough to cause injury, such as burns, notify your pediatrician immediately. Or go to the nearest emergency room.

✚ *Mouth-to-Mouth Resuscitation*

Mouth-to-mouth resuscitation is an aspect of CPR. See that entry for detailed information.

> Sometimes in an emergency you forget important information.
> Write down your street address and telephone number.
> Keep it near the phone. It's also handy for babysitters or other care givers.

✚ *Nosebleed*

When baby has a nosebleed, you'll see blood oozing from his nostril. If bleeding is close to the nostril, blood is usually bright red. If it is deeper in the nose, blood may be bright or dark. Nausea from swallowed blood may cause vomit to be bright red. Stools may be black from swallowed blood.

If your baby has a nosebleed, sit him upright in your lap, and bend his head slightly forward. Clamp his nostrils closed with your fingers for 5 to 10 uninterrupted minutes. When you hold the nose tightly closed, it allows the blood to clot and to seal the damaged blood vessels. If bleeding stops then recurs, repeat the above procedures. If bleeding does not stop, take your baby to the nearest emergency-medicine facility.

Repeated nosebleeds may indicate that baby's mucous membranes are dry. Run a cool-mist humidifier to moisten the air when he's sleeping. Apply a small amount of petroleum jelly to a cotton swab, and apply the petroleum jelly inside each nostril.

Call your pediatrician if your baby suffers from frequent nosebleeds. If your baby is having difficulty breathing through his nose after a nosebleed, let your pediatrician know. Go to the nearest emergency-medicine facility for a nosebleed that won't stop after administering home care as described above.

✚ *Poisons*

Poison in the Eye. Poison can get into the eye when liquid splashes into it. Many substances can damage your baby's eyes, but your infant can't tell you about the problem. Potency of a poison, and the length of exposure to it, may determine the severity of damage. Acting quickly may make the difference between a temporary problem and a long-term disability.

If any poison splashes into your baby's eyes, use a large glass or pitcher filled with cool tap water to flood your baby's eye for 10 to 20 minutes. Try to get baby to blink frequently by blinking at him. Keep his hands out of his eyes. You may need to wrap him in a blanket to keep his hands out of the affected eye.

Call the Poison Control Center for advice and information.

WHEN TO CALL 911

Sometimes you know you have to call 911—there's no question in your mind. At other times, you might not be sure whether you should call 911 or your pediatrician. Below is a list of situations that indicate you should call 911 first, then your baby's doctor.

❀ When bleeding is heavy and you can't stop it after 15 minutes or if a cut appears to be large or deep.

❀ If baby is burned, and the burn looks charred (black) or white. If a burn covers at least 5% of his body (5% means the burn is 5 times or more larger than his hand).

❀ When baby is choking. Try to dislodge the object while someone else calls for help.

❀ If baby falls from a high place and/or hits a very hard surface.

❀ If baby has any trouble breathing.

❀ When baby eats or drinks anything you believe might be poisonous. Call the Poison Control Center but also get emergency help.

❀ If baby has been seriously injured in an accident.

❀ When baby has been submerged in water.

❀ Anytime baby loses consciousness.

Inhaled Poison. Many substances are toxic when inhaled. Some toxic substances include carbon monoxide, smoke and fumes from fires, propellants, gasoline, kerosene, turpentine, lighter fluid, glue, paint remover and lamp oil.

A baby's reaction to inhaling a poisonous substance can vary, depending on the amount of substance inhaled and the substance inhaled. Inhaling a poisonous substance can cause various reactions, including:

❀ nausea
❀ vomiting
❀ decreased consciousness
❀ loss of consciousness
❀ headache
❀ breathing difficulties
❀ coughing
❀ lethargy

Call 911 immediately if your baby is in obvious distress, such as having difficulty breathing or showing a decreased level of consciousness, lethargy, convulsions or lack of a heartbeat. Remove your baby from the source of the poison. Take him into the fresh air or to a well-ventilated area. Call the Poison Control Center for specific instructions.

Poison on the Skin.   If you suspect your baby has come in contact with a poison, search for evidence. Spilled household cleaners would probably leave the baby's skin looking red and irritated. Remove contaminated clothes. Call the Poison Control Center for specific treatments.

Swallowed Poison.   The incidence of poisoning in children has been greatly reduced since the passage of the Poison Prevention Packaging Act of 1970. This act provides that certain potentially hazardous drugs and household products be sold in child-resistant containers. However, poisoning remains a significant health concern.

Most cases occur in children under 6 years old. The most frequently ingested poisons are cosmetics, personal-care products, cleaning products and household plants.

If you find your infant with an open or empty container of a toxic substance, you must suspect poisoning. Watch for behavioral differences, burns or redness of the lips, mouth or hands, unexplained vomiting, breath that smells like chemicals, breathing difficulties or convulsions. If poisoning occurs and your child is in obvious distress (unconscious, convulsing, experiencing breathing difficulties), call 911 immediately.

Empty the child's mouth of pills, plant parts or any other material. Identify the poison. Look for clues that may indicate what baby swallowed, if it is unknown. Save all evidence of poison (container, vomit, urine), and take them with you to the nearest emergency-medicine facility.

Do *not* induce vomiting on your own. We once advised parents to use syrup of ipecac to induce vomiting, but this is no longer considered safe.

Call the Poison Control Center for immediate advice about treatment. Be prepared to read the labels on any suspect container and to describe the substance, the amount ingested and any physical changes you detect.

Glossary

Acetaminophen—Nonprescription medicine used to reduce fever and to relieve minor pain. Available in children's strength. *Tylenol* is common brand name.

Acute—Situation that begins suddenly. May also mean severe or intense but of short duration or keen.

Airways—Passageways for air to pass to the lungs. Includes bronchi, bronchioles and windpipe (trachea).

Allergen—Any substance that causes an allergy.

Allergy—Acquired sensitivity to some substance that doesn't usually cause a reaction.

Analgesics—Various medicines used to relieve pain.

Anaphylactic shock—Sudden, severe reaction to allergen; it is so severe that death may result in a short time.

Anaphylaxis—Severe allergic hypersensitivity to a substance. Can result in *anaphylactic shock.*

Anemia—Condition in which the oxygen-carrying substance in blood (red blood cells or hemoglobin) is insufficient.

Antibiotics—Medicine used to attack bacterial germs and to fight bacterial infection; not used against viral infections.

Anticonvulsants—Medications that help control or relieve convulsions (seizures).

Antihistamines—Medication used to relieve allergy symptoms.

B

Bacteria—Germ or microorganism that can cause infection or disease.

Balanitis—Penis inflammation.

Benign—Harmless.

Bilirubin—Waste product of red blood cells found in bile that causes urine to be yellow; can cause jaundice if it builds up in the blood.

Biopsy—Removal of a small amount of tissue or fluid for laboratory study.

Blepharitis—Inflammation of the edges of the eyelid.

Blood cells, red—Cells in the blood that carry oxygen throughout the body.

Blood cells, white—Cells in the blood that fight infection.

Bronchi—Two main passageways from the trachea to the lungs that allow air to enter the lungs.

Bronchial tubes—Same as *bronchi*.

Bronchioles—Smaller air passageways of the bronchi.

Bronchoscope—Tool that passes through the trachea to remove a foreign body or to provide a view of the area.

C

Cardiopulmonary resuscitation (CPR)—Emergency measures for a person who has stopped breathing and whose heart has stopped beating.

Cartilage—Dense connective tissue, with some flexibility, that allows joints to move smoothly.

Cauterization—Destroying tissue by means of heat, chemicals or freezing.

Chronic—Condition that is long-term and continuing.

Circumcision—Surgical removal of the foreskin, or fold of skin, that covers the head of the penis.

Colic—Spasm accompanied by pain. When an infant has colic, he or she suffers from bouts of pain, accompanied by crying and gas.

Compress—Wet or dry cloth applied firmly to skin.

Congenital—Condition or abnormality present at birth.

Conjunctivitis—Inflammation of the mucous membrane that lines eyelids.

Contagious—Disease that is spread from one person to another.

Convulsion—Involuntary muscle contraction and relaxation.

D

Dehydration—Loss of body fluids from the body; occurs when output of body fluids exceeds intake of fluid.

Dermatitis—Inflammation of the skin accompanied by itching, redness and lesions.

Diarrhea—Frequent passing of unformed, watery stools.

Discomfort—Physical problems that cause a person to feel uncomfortable.

Disease—Condition in which a group of signs and/or symptoms are present; usually has an adverse effect on health.

E

Electrolyte—Ionized salts in the body involved in all body functions; may be lost through dehydration, diarrhea, vomiting or other means.

Esophagus—Passageway that extends from the pharynx to the stomach.

Eustachian tubes—Tube that extends from the middle ear to the pharynx.

F

Family history—Information about medical conditions and illnesses that have occurred within a family, including histories of *both* baby's parents.

Fecal—Relating to the waste products the body eliminates; *feces.*

Feces—Undigested food that passes through the gastrointestinal tract to the colon, where it is eliminated as a bowel movement.

Fever—Elevated body temperature, at least 1 degree above normal (98.6F). It is a sign of disease; it is not a disease itself.

Fiber—Ingredient of many carbohydrates that increases bulk in the diet.

Fissure—Break in the skin or the lining of an organ.

Folliculitis—Inflammation of hair follicles.

Fontanelle—Soft spots on baby's head where skull bones have not grown together.

G

Galactosemia—Inherited disease in infants in which milk cannot be digested.

Gastroenteritis—Inflammation of the stomach and intestinal tract.

Germ—Organism that causes infection; can be virus, fungus or bacteria.

Gluten—Protein in wheat that is indigestible by some people; it is an inherited problem.

H

Hernia—Protrusion of part or all of an organ through the wall of the cavity that usually contains it.

Hiccups—Spasm of the diaphragm that causes a short, sharp cough.

Hives—Itchy welts caused by an allergic reaction.

Hyper—Raised or higher; for example, hypertension means "raised blood pressure."

Hyperthermia—Raised body temperature.

Hypersensitivity—Extreme sensitivity to a substance.

Hypo—Lowered or reduced; for example, hypotension means "low blood pressure."

Hypothermia—Lowered body temperature.

I

I.V.–Intravenous; into the vein.

Immunity–Protection against.

Immunization–Vaccine given to produce immunity against a particular germ that causes a disease.

Incubation period–Time between exposure to a germ and the onset of symptoms of the infection caused by the germ.

Infant–Child from birth to 1 year.

Infection–Disease caused by a germ.

Intestinal blockage–Blockage in the intestinal tract.

Intestine, large–Part of the intestinal tract that lies below the small intestine; processes waste products into feces.

Intestine, small–Located just under the stomach, it is the largest part of the intestinal tract.

"Itis"–Inflammation of.

J

Jaundice–Condition of the liver and blood resulting in yellow skin, yellow in the white of the eyes and dark urine.

Joint–Site in body where two or more bones meet.

L

Lactose intolerance–Intolerance to milk and milk products.

Larynx–Enlarged upper end of the trachea below the tongue's base.

Laxative–Medication used to relieve constipation.

Lethargy–Tiredness, fatigue or lack of energy.

M

Malabsorption–Inadequate absorption of nutrients by the body.

Medical history–See *family medical history.*

Mucous membrane–Thin tissue that lines an organ; produces mucus.

Mucus–Fluid produced by the body to protect organs.

N

Nasogastric tube–Tube passed through the nose into the stomach for feeding and draining secretions.

Nausea—Stomach upset that usually occurs before vomiting; a person can experience nausea without vomiting.

Newborn—Baby from birth to 1 month old.

NICU—Neonatal intensive care unit.

Nodule—Lump or swelling beneath the skin.

O–P

Oral—Relates to the mouth.

Pain—Unpleasant feeling in the body associated with tissue damage caused by disease and/or injury.

Palate—Roof of the mouth.

Parasite—Organism that lives within, or feeds upon, another organism.

Pharynx—Passageway for air from the nose to the larynx and for food from the mouth to the esophagus.

Phlegm—Thick mucus, especially from the respiratory areas.

Physical therapy—Rehabilitation to restore function following disease or injury; involves exercise, massage, heat, cold and other treatments.

Preemie—Premature baby; baby born before 37 weeks of gestation.

Pulmonary—Relates to the lungs.

R

Rectum—Lower end of the large intestine.

Regurgitate—To spit up or to vomit.

Relapse—When a person with a disease or illness gets worse after improvement.

Rotavirus—Group of viruses that cause enteritis in babies and children.

Rubella—German measles.

Ruptured eardrum—Break in the eardrum.

S

Scaling—Flakes of dried skin.

Septic—Infected.

Serum—Watery portion of the blood after it coagulates.

Shock—When blood flow is inadequate to return enough blood to the heart for normal functioning of the body.

SIDS—Sudden Infant Death Syndrome.

Soaks—Application of moisture by soaking in water; often used for an inflamed part of the skin.

Spore—Reproductive cell produced by plants and fungi.
Sputum—Matter coughed up or cleared from the throat.
Sterilize—To make completely free of germs; may be done by chemicals, heat and other methods.
Stool—Feces.
Suture—Thin, fibrous material used to hold tissue or skin together.
Symptoms—Change in the body or the body's function; caused by a disease.

T

Tenderness—Soreness or sensitivity.
Testicles—Male reproductive glands; located in the scrotum.
Trachea—Passageway from the larynx to the bronchial tubes.
Trauma—Outside force that injures or damages the body.
Tube feeding—See *nasogastric tube.*

U

Upper-respiratory system—Upper part of the breathing system consisting of nose, throat, larynx, pharynx and bronchial tubes.
Urinary tract—Organs and ducts that produce and eliminate urine; made up of kidneys, ureters, bladder and urethra.

V

Vaccine—Medication that provides protection from (immunity to) a disease.
Virus—Germs responsible for some diseases.
Vitamins—Substances needed for healthy growth and body function.
Vomiting—Ejection of stomach contents through the mouth.

W-X

Wheezing—Whistling sounds produced during periods of difficult breathing.
X-rays—Test that uses high-energy electromagnetic waves to make "pictures" that can be used to diagnose a problem.

Resources

GENERAL INFORMATION FOR PARENTS

For Adoptive Parents
Good resource for adoption information
www.adoption.com

American Academy of Pediatrics (AAP)
P.O. Box 927, Dept. C
Elk Grove Village, IL 60009-0927
www.aap.org

American Academy of Family Physicians (AAFP)
www.aafp.org

American College of Obstetricians and Gynecologists (ACOG)
P.O. Box 4500
Kearneysville, WV 25430
800-762-2264
www.acog.com

American Psychological Association (APA)
202-336-5700
www.apa.org

Car-Seat Installation
877-FIT-4-A-KID

Centers for Disease Control (CDC)
For up-to-date information on many medical issues
www.cdc.gov

Child Care Aware
800-424-2246

Children's Defense Fund
www.childrensdefense.org

COPE
37 Clarendon St.
Boston, MA 02116
617-357-5588

Formulas that contain DHA and ARA
Nestle Good Start
www.verybestbaby.com
Similac Advance
www.similacadvance.com
Enfamil LIPIL
www.enfamil.com

Homemade baby food recipes
www.americanbaby.com/babyfood
www.babytalk.com

Intensive-Care Parenting magazine
ICU Parenting
RD #10, Box 176
Brush Creek Rd.
Irwin, PA 15642

Internal Revenue Service
For information on child-care expenses
800-829-1040
www.irs.ustreas.gov

**Juvenile Products Manufacturers'
Association (JPMA)**
*For information on baby products,
recalls and other pertinent
information*
236 Route 38 West, Suite 100
Moorestown, NJ 08057
www.jpma.org

March of Dimes
*For information on various serious
childhood illnesses and disease*
888-663-4637
www.modimes.org

**National Organization
of Single Mothers**
P.O. Box 68
Midland, NC 28107-0068
704-888-KIDS (704-888-5437)

Neo Gen Screening
*Testing of family history for rare
inherited disorders*
www.pediatrixscreening.com
866-463-6436

Organic Formulas
*For a listing of stores that carry
organic formulas*
www.horizonorganic.com

Parent's Resources
P.O. Box 107, Planetarium Sta.
New York, NY 10024
212-866-4776

**Poison Control Center
(national hotline)**
800-222-1222

Product Recalls
*For the latest baby-product recalls
and warnings*
www.cpsc.gov
www.jpma.org
www.recalls.gov

Social Security Administration
800-772-1213
www.ssa.gov

Tri-Flow Nipple System
From Munchkin
www.munchkininc.com
800-344-2229

Vaccines
*For information on vaccines from the
Children's Hospital of Philadelphia*
www.vaccine.chop.edu

The Women's Bureau Publications
*For summary of state laws on
family leave*
U.S. Department of Labor
Women's Bureau Clearing House
Box EX
200 Constitution Avenue, NW
Washington, DC 20210
800-827-5335

Websites for further information
www.americanbaby.com
www.babycenter.com
www.babyzone.com
www.bellycast.com
www.childmagazine.com

www.family.com
www.ivillage.com
www.parenthoodweb.com
www.rif.org

AT-HOME MOMS

Family and Home Network
866-352-1075
www.familyandhome.org

F.E.M.A.L.E. (Formerly Employed Mothers At The Leading Edge)
P.O. Box 31
Elmhurst, IL 60126
800-223-9399
www.femalehome.org

Miserly Moms
Helps families save money by providing tips for cooking, shopping, decorating and gardening
www.miserlymoms.com

Mothers At Home
800-783-4666
www.mah.org

MOMS (Mothers Offering Mothers Support)
25371 Rye Canyon Rd.
Valencia, CA 91355
805-526-2725

Websites for further information
www.parentsplace.com
www.parentssoup.com

BREASTFEEDING INFORMATION

Avent
800-542-8368
www.aventamerica.com

Beechnut Nutrition Hotline
800-523-6633

Breastfeeding Help
For 24-hour breastfeeding support, referrals to lactation consultants and helpful videos
www.breastfeeding.com

Best Start
3500 E. Fletcher Avenue, Suite 519
Tampa, FL 33613
800-277-4975

FDA Hotline
800-332-4010

FDA Breast Implant Information Line
800-532-4440

International Lactation Consultant Association
www.ilca.org
919-787-5181

La Leche League International
1400 North Meacham Road
Schaumburg, IL 60173-4840
800-LA-LECHE or check local
    telephone directory
www.lalecheleague.org

Medela, Inc.
P.O. Box 660
McHenry, IL 60051
800-TELL-YOU (800-735-5968)

**National Center for
Nutrition and Dietetics**
Consumer Nutrition Hotline
800-366-1655

**National Maternal and
Child Health Clearinghouse**
2070 Chain Bridge Road, Suite 45
Vienna, VA 22182
703-821-8955, ext. 254

Wellstart
4062 First Avenue
San Diego, CA 92103
619-295-5192

Websites for further information
www.breastfeedingbasics.com
www.moms4milk.org
www.breastfeed.com

CHILD CARE

Child Care Aware Hotline
800-424-2246

**Department of Health
and Human Services**
*National Child Care
Information Center*
800-616-2242

International Nanny Association
800-297-1477
www.nanny.org

**National Association of
Child Care Resource and
Referral Agencies**
800-424-2246
202-393-5501
www.childcarerr.org
www.naccrra.net

**National Association for the
Education of Young Children**
www.naeyc.org

**National Resource Center for
Health and Safety in Child Care**
800-598-5437

Working Mother
www.workingmother.com

CHILDREN'S ILLNESSES AND PROBLEMS; CHILDREN WITH SPECIAL NEEDS

Arthritis

**American Juvenile Arthritis
Organization**
1314 Spring St., NW
Atlanta, GA 30309
404-872-7100

Asthma and Allergies

Allergy and Asthma Network
3554 Chain Bridge Road, Suite 200
Fairfax, VA 22030
800-878-4403

American College of Allergy, Asthma and Immunology (ACAAI)
Informative news services for parents and patients; site is maintained by allergists and ACAAI
800-842-7777
http://allergy.mcg.edu

Asthma & Allergy Foundation of America
1835 K St. NW, Suite P-900
Washington, DC 20006
202-293-2950

Autism

National Society for Children and Adults with Autism
1234 Massachusetts Ave., NE, Suite 1017
Washington, DC 20005
202-783-0125

Birth Defects

March of Dimes
1275 Mamaroneck Ave.
White Plains, NY 10605
914-428-7100
www.modimes.com

National Maternal and Child Health Clearinghouse
3520 Prospect St., NW
Washington, DC 20057
202-625-8410

Blindness

American Foundation for the Blind
15 W. 16th St.
New York, NY 10011
212-620-2000

Helen Keller National Center for Deaf-Blind Youths and Adults
111 Middle Neck Rd.
Sands Point, NY 11050
516-944-8900

Cancer

Association for Research of Childhood Cancer
P.O. Box 251
Buffalo, NY 14225
716-681-4433

Candlelighters Childhood Cancer Foundation
1901 Pennsylvania Ave., NW, Suite 1001
Washington, DC 20006
202-659-5136

Cerebral Palsy

National Easter Seal Society
2023 W. Ogden Ave.
Chicago, IL 60612
312-243-8400

United Cerebral Palsy Association
60 E. 34th St.
New York, NY 10016
212-481-2811

Cleft Palate

American Cleft Palate Association
331 Salk Hall
University of Pittsburgh
Pittsburgh, PA 15261
412-681-9620

American Cleft Palate Foundation
1218 Grandview Ave.
Pittsburgh, PA 15211
800-242-5337

Cystic Fibrosis

Cystic Fibrosis Foundation
6000 Executive Blvd., Suite 309
Rockville, MD 20852
301-881-9130

Down Syndrome

**Association for Children
with Down Syndrome**
2616 Martin Ave.
Bellmore, NY 11710
516-221-4700

**National Down Syndrome Society
(NDSS)**
666 Broadway
New York, NY 10012-2317
800-221-4602

Epilepsy

Epilepsy Foundation of America
4351 Garden City, Suite 406
Landover, MD 20785
301-459-3700

Food Allergies

**Food Allergy and
Anaphylaxis Network**
www.foodallergy.org
800-929-4040

Fragile X Syndrome

National Fragile X Foundation
1441 York St., Suite 303
Denver, CO 80206
800-688-8765

Gastrointestinal Disorders

American Digestive Disease Society
7720 Wisconsin Ave.
Bethesda, MD 20014
301-652-9293

General Information

**CARESS (information on services
for parents of children with
disabilities)**
P.O. Box 1492
Washington, DC 20013-1492
800-695-0285

**National Association
for Rare Disorders**
P.O. Box 8923
New Fairfield, CT 06182

Hearing Problems

**American Society for
Deaf Children**
814 Thayer Ave.
Silver Spring, MD 20910
301-585-5400

American Speech-Language-Hearing Association
10801 Rockville Pike
Rockville, MD 20852
301-897-5700

Helen Keller National Center for Deaf-Blind Youths and Adults
111 Middle Neck Rd.
Sands Point, NY 11050
516-944-8900

Heart Problems

American Heart Association
7272 Greenville Ave.
Dallas, TX 75231-4596
800-242-8721

Congenital Heart Anomalies–Support, Education, Resources
2112 North Wilkins Road
Swanton, OH 43558
419-825-5575

Hemophilia

National Hemophilia Foundation
19 W. 34th St., Rm. 1204
New York, NY 10001
212-563-0211

World Federation of Hemophilia
Suite 2902
1155 Dorchester Blvd., W.
Montreal, Quebec H3B 2L3
Canada

Leukemia

Leukemia Society of America, Inc.
800 Second Ave.
New York, NY 10017
212-573-8484

Limb Disorders

Cherub Association of Families of Children with Limb Disorders
936 Delaware Ave.
Buffalo, NY 14209

Liver Disease

Children's Liver Foundation
76 S. Orange Ave., Suite 202
South Orange, NJ 07079
201-761-1111

*Mental Retardation
(also see Down Syndrome)*

Association for Children with Retarded Mental Development, Inc.
817 Broadway
New York, NY 10003
212-470-7200

Phenylketonuria

National PKU Foundation
6301 Tejas Drive
Pasadena, TX 77503
713-487-4802

Psoriasis

National Psoriasis Foundation
6415 SW Canyon Court, Suite 200
Portland, OR 97221
503-297-1545

Reye's Syndrome

**National Reye's Syndrome
Foundation**
426 North Lewis Street
P.O. Box 829
Bryan, OH 43506
800-233-7393

RSV (respiratory syncytial virus)

RSV Information
www.rsvprotection.com
877-819-9851

Sickle-Cell Disease

**National Association
for Sickle-Cell Disease**
3460 Wilshire Blvd., Suite 1012
Los Angeles, CA 90010
213-731-1166

**Sickle-Cell Disease
Association of America, Inc.**
200 Corporate Pt., Suite 495
Culver City, CA 90230
800-421-8453

Spina Bifida

**Spina Bifida Association
of America**
4590 MacArthur Blvd., NW, #250
Washington, DC 20007-4226
800-621-3141

Sudden Infant Death Syndrome

The Guild for Infant Survival
P.O. Box 3841
Davenport, IA 52808

**National Center for the
Prevention of Sudden Infant
Death Syndrome**
330 N. Charles St.
Baltimore, MD 21201
301-547-0300

**National Sudden Infant Death
Syndrome Clearinghouse**
8201 Greensboro Drive, Suite 600
McLean, VA 22102
703-821-8955; 703-625-8410

**National Sudden Infant Death
Syndrome Foundation**
8240 Professional Place, Suite 205
Landover, MD 20785
301-459-3388; 800-221-7437 (SIDS)

Tay-Sachs Disease

**National Tay-Sachs & Allied
Disease Association, Inc.**
92 Washington Ave.
Cedarhurst, NY 11516
516-569-4300

DADS

At-Home Dad Newsletter
61 Brightwood Avenue
North Andover, MA 01845
www.athomedad.com

Dad to Dad Network
Send self-addressed stamped envelope to:
13925 Duluth Court
Apple Valley, MN 55124
612-423-3705

Full-Time Dads
193 Shelley Ave.
Elizabeth, NJ 07208
908-355-9722
FAX 908-355-9723
www.fulltimefather.com

National Center for Fathering
P.O. Box 413888
Kansas City, MO 64141
800-593-DADS

National Fatherhood Initiative
101 Lake Forest Blvd., Suite 360
Gaithersburg, MD 20877
301-948-0599
www.fatherhood.com

Websites for further information
www.babycenter.com/dads
www.daddyshome.com
www.fathersforum.com
www.fathersonline.com
www.newdads.com
www.slowlane.com

FINANCIAL RESOURCES

BankRate
For general financial information
516-627-7330
www.bankrate.com

College Savings Plan Network
For information on saving for college
877-277-6496
www.savingforcollege.com

Consumer Credit Counseling Service
For help with your budget
888-775-0377

Consumer Federation of America
For information on many consumer issues
202-387-6121
www.consumerfed.org

Debtors Anonymous
For debt-management services
781-453-2743
www.debtorsanonymous.com

Easy Saver Plan
For information on government savings bonds and how to buy them
www.publicdebt.treas.gov

Health Insurance Association of America
For information on health and disability insurance
888-869-4078
www.hiaa.org

Insurance Information Institute
For information on various types of insurance
800-331-9146
www.iii.org

IntelliQuote Insurance Services
*For quotes to compare for various
insurance policies*
888-622-0925
www.intelliquote.com

Internal Revenue Service
*For information on child-care
expenses*
800-829-1040
www.irs.ustreas.gov

**National Association
of Personal Planners**
For help with your budget
888-333-6659

**National Foundation
for Credit Counseling**
For debt-management services
800-388-2227
www.nfcc.org

**National Insurance
Consumer Helpline**
*For answers to specific insurance
questions*
800-942-4242

QuickQuote
For a term life insurance quote
800-867-2402
www.insure.com

Quotesmith
For various insurance quotes
800-431-1147
www.quotesmith.com

U.S. Savings Bonds
800-4US-BONDS
www.savingsbonds.gov

Websites for further information
www.financenter.com
www.healthinsurancefinders.com
www.ihatefinancialplanning.com
www.insurance.com
www.localinsurance.com
www.mfea.com
www.morningstar.com
www.myvesta.org
www.naic.org/cis

MULTIPLES

Center for Loss in Multiple Birth
c/o Jean Kollantai
P.O. Box 1064
Palmer, AK 99645
907-746-6123

**Center for Study
of Multiple Births**
333 E. Superior Street, Room 464
Chicago, IL 60611
312-266-9093

Mothers of Supertwins (M.O.S.T.)
(triplets or more)
P.O. Box 951
Brentwood, NY 11717
516-434-MOST
www.mostonline.org

Multiple Birth Resources
70 W. Sylvester Place
Highland Ranch, CO 80126
888-627-9519
www.expectingmultiples.com

Multiple Births Foundation
Queen Charlotte's and
  Chelsea Hospital
Goldhawk Road
London, England W6 OXG
081-748-4666, ext. 5201

**National Organization of
Mothers of Twins Clubs, Inc.**
P.O. Box 438
Thompson Station, TN 37179-0438
505-275-0955

Triplet Connection
P.O. Box 99571
Stockton, CA 95209
209-474-0885
www.tripletconnection.org

**Twin to Twin Transfusion
Syndrome (TTTS) Foundation**
Mary Slaman-Forsythe,
  Executive Director
411 Longbeach Parkway
Bay Village, OH 44140
216-899-8887

Twin Services
P.O. Box 10066
Berkeley, CA 94709
510-524-0863

Twins Foundation
P.O. Box 6043
Providence, RI 02940-6043
401-729-1000

Twins Magazine
5350 S. Roslyn Street, Suite 400
Englewood, CO 80111
800-328-3211

Twins World
*Good resource for couples expecting
multiples*
www.twinsworld.com

PREMATURE INFANTS

Clothing for Preemies
www.preemie.com
www.gap.com
www.babiesrus.com

Cosco Ultradream Ride
Car bed/seat for preemies
www.djgusa.com
800-544-1108

ECMO Moms and Dads
c/o Blair and Gayle Wilson
P.O. Box 53848
Lubbock, TX 79453
806-794-0259

Gerber
Preemie pacifier
www.gerber.com

**Intensive-Care Parenting
magazine**
ICU Parenting
RD #10, Box 176
Brush Creek Road
Irwin, PA 15642

Preemie Diapers
Pampers
www.pampers.com
800-543-3331
Huggies
www.drugstore.com
800-447-9423

Premature Babies
For information on, and products for,
premature infants
www.pediatrics.wisc.edu/
   patientcare/preemies

SAFETY FOR YOUR BABY

Auto Safety Hotline
888-327-4236

Back to Sleep
P.O. Box 29111
Washington, DC 20040
800-505-2742

Car Seats for Pickup Trucks
Pioneered Safety System
from XSCI
800-630-6850

Crib-Sheet Safety
Baby Sleep Safe crib sheet anchor
800-420-1280
Clouds and Stars quick-zip crib
sheets
www.cloudsandstars.com
866-325-6837

The Danny Foundation
For information on crib dangers
3158 Danville Blvd.
P.O. Box 680
Alamo, CA 94507
800-833-2669

General Motors
"Precious Cargo: Protecting the
Children Who Ride with You"
(free booklet)
800-247-9168

**The International Association
of Chiefs of Police**
Operation Kids
800-843-4227

**National Highway Traffic Safety
Administration**
Auto safety hotline
800-424-9393
www.nhtsa.gov

**National Lead Information
Hotline and Clearinghouse**
800-424-LEAD

**The National SAFE KIDS
Campaign**
800-441-1888
www.safekids.org

SafetyBeltUSA
123 Manchester Blvd.
Inglewood, CA 90301
800-745-SAFE
www.carseat.org

**U.S. Consumer Products
Safety Commission**
800-638-2772
www.cpsc.gov

Index

AAP. *See* American Academy of
  Pediatrics
Abrasions/cuts. *See* Cuts/abrasions
A/B spell, 31
Accordion gates, 272
Acetaminophen
  for bronchitis, 284
  definition, 521
  for fever reduction, 113, 174,
    175, 207, 315, 331, 333, 340,
    363, 379, 380, 396, 401, 408,
    416, 425, 435, 441, 451, 486,
    501
  for flu, 331
  for pain/discomfort, 174, 175,
    196, 207, 305, 315, 331, 333,
    340, 379, 380, 396, 401, 408,
    414, 415, 416, 425, 435, 441,
    451, 486, 501
Acetone and super glue, 480
Acid reflux (GERD), 78, 133,
  186–187, 346
Acne, 62–63
Acute condition, 521
Adrenalin, 513
Advice from others, 171
Advil, 421
  See also Ibuprofen
Air bags, 11
Airways, 521
Alimentum formula, 79
Allergen, 521
Allergic rhinitis (hay fever), 253,
  468
Allergic shock, 513, 521

Allergies
  breast milk protection against, 50
  coughing with, 242
  definition, 521
  hay fever, 253, 468
  to insect bites/stings, 371
  to medications, 292–293, 431
  resources for, 530–531
  to rubber, 437
  toxic mold and, 350–351
  See also Food allergies
Amebic dysentery
    (amebiasis/entamebiasis),
    329–330
American Academy of
    Ophthalmology, 91
American Academy of Pediatric
    Dentistry, 306
American Academy of Pediatrics
  breastfeeding, 50, 337, 382
  calories needed, 488
  car seat selection, 9
  checkups, 137
  circumcision, 23
  contact information, 527
  crib safety features, 5
  discipline/spanking, 382
  family bed, 103, 383
  formulas, 70, 71, 268
  immunizations, 142
  iron, 268
  pacifiers, 382
  peanut allergy, 337
  recommendations, 382–383
  SIDS, 132

American Academy of Pediatrics
(*continued*)
solid foods, 154
temper tantrums, 382
vitamins, 201
American Heart Association, 514
American Red Cross, 513, 514
Anal fissure, 108, 166–167
Analgesics, 521. *See also*
Acetaminophen; Advil;
Ibuprofen; Motrin; Nuprin
Anaphylactic shock, 293, 513, 521
Anaphylaxis, 293, 521
Anemia, 267–268
definition, 521
tests for, 21
Animal bites, 377–378
Antianxiety medications (for baby),
394
Antibacterial soap, 241
Antibiotic ointment, 148, 241, 356,
378, 408, 414, 433, 437, 441,
493, 514, 517
Antibiotic-resistant bacteria, 158
Antibiotics
animal bites, 378
asthma, 443
cat scratch disease/fever, 207
definition, 521
eczema, 347
impetigo, 241
infections, 113, 196, 242, 371,
388, 401, 435, 452
I.V. form of, 113
overuse of, 158
puncture wounds, 426
tick bites, 425
Anticipating actions/results, 230,
357, 398
Anticonvulsants, 521
Antidepressants and breastfeeding,
55–56

Antihistamines
anaphylactic shock, 513
definition, 521
eczema, 347
hives, 150
insect bites/stings, 371
Antioxidants, 318
Apgar, Virginia, 20
Apgar score, 20
Apnea
car seats and, 10
description, 64
of premature babies, 31, 64
RSV and, 174
See also A/B spells; Sleep apnea
Arachidonic acid. *See* ARA fatty
acid
ARA fatty acid
benefits of, 29, 50, 51, 71
in breast milk, 30, 50, 51
formulas and, 71
Arthritis resources, 530
Aspirin use, 380, 388, 415
Asthma, 442–443
bathing frequency and, 58
BPD and, 32
breast milk protection against,
50, 442
coughing with, 242
resources for, 530–531
sleeping and, 32
Athlete's foot, 395
Atopic dermatitis. *See* Eczema
Autism
resources for, 531
vaccines and, 143
Axillary thermometers, 94–95, 363

Baby acne, 62–63
Baby-care mistakes, 237–238
Babyproofing
away from home, 256–257

of home, 174, 231, 237, 248, 271–272, 290, 355, 368, 386, 492
Baby wearing, 75, 112
Back to sleep, 132, 133
Backpack carriers, 1, 85, 211, 271, 302
Bacteria, 521
Bacterial meningitis, 466
Bactrim (sulfamethoxazole), 421
Balancing
    maintaining, 376
    standing and, 361–362, 376
Balanitis, 79–80, 521
Bassinets, 5
Bathing, 58, 73–74
    bathtub seats, 279–280
    in family tub, 98
    frequency of, 58, 74, 414
    kitchen sink for, 112
    method for, 74
    play with, 300, 309, 325, 372, 373, 409, 453, 469, 477, 494, 502
    sponge baths, 58
    temperature of water, 98, 333, 395
Behavior, 222
    acceptable/unacceptable behavior, 463–464, 506
    temper tantrums, 382, 463, 506
    unpleasant behavior/parental reactions, 498–499, 506, 507–508
Belly button, 37, 58, 83. *See also* Umbilical-cord stump care
Benadryl, 150, 253, 261, 421
Benign condition, 521
Bilirubin, 47, 48, 521
Bilirubin lights, 28, 48
Biopsy, 521
Biotinidase deficiency, 21

Birth. *See* 1st 48 hours
Birthday on major holiday, 498
Birthday party (1 year)
    planning, 446, 470, 489–490, 496, 504
    toys for, 461, 502
Birth defects, resources, 531
Birthmarks, 16–17
Birth weight, 9, 13, 56, 64, 82, 93, 126, 129
Bisphenol-A (BPA), 131
Bleeding
    being alert for, 268
    dealing with emergency of, 513–514
Blepharitis, 521
Blindness resources, 531
Blisters, 433
Blood cells (red), 521
Blood cells (white), 522
Blood-glucose levels test, 21
Blood poisoning (septicemia), 451
Blood-pressure monitors, 28
Blood tests of newborns, 21
Body language, 251–252, 266
Body lice, 347–348
Bonding, 64–65
    baby wearing and, 75
    bottlefeeding and, 69–70
    breastfeeding and, 51, 52, 65
    description, 64, 237, 430
    family bed and, 102
    methods for, 65
    parent working outside home and, 482
    physical bonding, 64–65
    playing and, 141
    with premature babies, 25, 26–27
    See also Trust
Bottlefeeding, 38, 68–73
    advantages of, 68–69
    baby's stool and, 73

Bottlefeeding (*continued*)
  bonding and, 69–70
  breastfeeding vs., 38, 68
  burping and, 73
  declining interest in, 273, 296,
    375
  equipment for, 71–72
  method for, 70
  switching to, 110–111, 264
  tips for, 72–73
  travel and, 161
  weaning from, 375
  See also Formula
Bottles
  plastic-bottle safety, 131, 359
  slanted type of, 71, 160
Botulism, 319, 323
  from honey, 319, 323
Bouncers
  description/use, 4, 161–162, 205
  safety and, 162
Bowed legs, 17, 215
Bowels, 93, 107–108
  changes with new foods, 198, 400
  constipation, 198
  during first 48 hours, 17–18
  intussusception, 364
  normal vs. problems, 82
  See also Diarrhea; Giardiasis;
    Intestinal blockage; Stool
BPA (bisphenol-A), 131
BPD (broncho-pulmonary
  dysplasia), 32
Bradycardia, 31
Brain development
  DHA/ARA and, 50–51, 71, 107
  overview, 42, 506
  REM sleep and, 91
  skull growth and, 181–182
  stimulation and, 60
  See also Intellectual development

BRATT diet, 434
Brazelton Neonatal Behavioral
  Assessment Scale, 21
Breastfeeding, 49–57
  AAP recommendations on, 50,
    337, 382
  antidepressants and, 55
  antimicrobial properties in breast
    milk, 50
  baby's declining interest in, 228,
    273, 353
  baby's sense of smell and, 18
  baby's stool and, 18, 107
  benefits of, 38, 49–51, 158, 224,
    338–339, 442
  bonding and, 51, 52, 65
  bottlefeeding vs., 38, 68
  burping and, 53, 57
  diet of mother and, 52, 56, 339
  disadvantages of, 51–52
  during first year, 221, 228
  food allergies and, 224, 338–339
  help with, 52
  increasing milk supply, 56
  insufficient milk syndrome and,
    57
  jaundice and, 15
  lactose intolerance and, 68, 510
  laws regarding, 49, 106–108
  medications (mother) and,
    55–56
  multiple babies, 54, 183–185
  at night, 102, 375
  positions for, 53
  premature babies and, 28, 29–30
  in public, 106–107
  pump use and, 29, 161, 184
  resources/contact information,
    529–530
  safe medications (mother) and,
    55–56

smoking of mother and, 51
sufficient milk and, 56
switching to bottlefeeding,
    110–111, 264
tips for, 52–53
travel and, 161
weaning from, 369
Broken bones. *See* Fractures/
    broken bones
Bronchi, 522
Bronchial tubes, 522
Bronchioles, 522
Bronchiolitis. *See* RSV (respiratory
    syncytial virus/bronchiolitis)
Bronchitis, 284–285
Bronchodilator, 443
Broncho-pulmonary dysplasia
    (BPD), 32
Bronchoscope, 522
Bruises, 298–299, 387
Burns
    avoiding, 119, 394–395
    bathing water and, 98, 333, 411
    care of, 394
    description/types, 394
Burping
    bottlefeeding and, 73
    breastfeeding and, 53, 57
    crying and, 66
    gas and, 160
    spitting up/vomiting and, 63
    techniques for, 38

Café au lait spots, 16
CAH (congenital adrenal
    hyperplasia), 21
Calming baby, 43, 92–93, 112,
    121–122, 203
    familiar scents and, 76
    fussy baby, 92–93
    soothing himself, 315, 360

teaching baby to be calm, 377
    when excited, 179
Calories needed, 488
Cancer
    prevention of, 318
    resources for, 531
Caput, 14
Car
    boredom and, 206
    car bed, 10, 34
    car seats and small babies, 9–10
    car-seat safety, 9, 10–11, 12, 108,
        230, 422, 441, 508, 538
    car-seat selection, 9–10
    combination car seat/stroller, 152
    entertainment for, 165
    essentials for, 144–145
    for plane travel, 195, 197–198
    for pick-up trucks, 12, 538
    mistakes in car-seat use, 10
    multiple-use car seats, 11
    safety and, 344
    saving money on car seats, 11
    travel by, 164–166
Cardiopulmonary resuscitation.
    See CPR
Cardiorespiratory monitors, 28
Care giver numbers, 213–214
Carriers
    baby wearing, 75, 112
    backpack carriers, 1, 85, 211, 271,
        302
    framed carriers, 271
    front carriers, 1, 69, 84–85, 143,
        211
    infant carriers, 203–204
    overview, 84–85
    safety tips, 84–85, 108, 211
    selection of, 1
    sling-like carrier, 69, 78, 79, 81,
        84–85

Car-safety vest, 504
Car seats
  boredom and, 206
  car bed, 10, 34
  combination stroller type, 152
  mistakes in use, 10
  multiple use type of, 11
  for pick-up trucks, 12, 538
  for plane travel, 195, 197–198
  safety and, 9, 10–11, 12, 108,
    230, 422, 441, 508, 538
  saving money on, 11
  selection of, 9–10
  small babies and, 9–10
Cartilage, 522
Cats, diseases and, 207. *See also* Pets
    and baby
Cat scratch disease, 207–208
Cat scratch fever, 207–208
Cauterization, 522
CDC. *See* Centers for Disease
    Control
Celiac disease, 224–225
Centers for Disease Control
  contact information, 527
  vaccines, 143, 431
Cereal, 219, 228–229, 346
Cerebral palsy resources, 531
Changing table/area
  in nursery, 4, 7–8
  public changing tables, 447
  supplies for, 7–8
Chapped skin, 188
Checkups
  first checkup, 61–62
  first year schedule, 137
  getting the most from, 191–192,
    202–203
  parent activities during, 139–140
  well-baby checkups, 137–139,
    191–192, 202–203
See also Immunizations

Chicken pox (varicella), 142, 307–308
Child care
  connecting with day-care
    provider, 462
  costs, 90
  options for, 87–90
  public funding for, 90
  references and, 87, 88
  resources/contact information,
    530
  for sick children, 90
  special-care needs, 90
  staying connected to baby and,
    482
Child Care Aware, 87, 527
Childproofing. *See* Babyproofing
Chloramphenicol, 425
Choking
  handling of, 73, 465, 516
  prevention of, 210, 220, 326, 327,
    328, 343, 411, 416, 428–429,
    515–516
Christmas/tree safety, 366–367
Chronic condition, 522
Cipro (ciprofloxin), 421
Circulation, cut off, 210, 501
Circumcision
  care following, 37–38, 58
  definition, 522
  overview, 22–23
Citrus juices, 339, 397
Classical music, 171, 203
Cleft palate resources, 532
Climbing, 361, 439, 503
Clinging babies, 286, 297
Cloth diapers, 6–7, 8
Clothes, 40–41
  baby's removal of, 457
  basic needs, 6–7
  for breastfeeding (mother), 52
  for cold weather/keeping warm,
    86, 107, 191, 410

cruising clothes, 446
first 48 hours, 6–7
first shoes, 419–420, 433
for going out (week 3), 75
for hot-blooded baby, 459
keeping head covered, 107, 301
for snowy weather, 410
for travel, 134, 135, 136
in warm weather, 136
when baby has a cold, 301–302
See also Temperature (of baby)
regulation
Clubfoot (talipes), 175
Coal tar, 347
Cochlear implants, 143
Colds
coughing with, 242
first aid for, 301–302
flu vs., 331, 417
heated air and, 144
overview, 157–158
passing on to baby, 157
plane travel with, 196
prevention of, 113, 158
Cold sores (fever blisters), 413–414
Colic, 70, 78–79, 109, 522
"Colic curl," 79
Colormate TLc BiliTest, 47
Colostrum, 49, 50
Comforting baby. *See* Calming
baby
Communication
baby talking on toy phone, 411,
426
crying and, 46, 66, 100–101,
146
talking to baby, 47, 48, 60, 80,
96, 105, 167–168, 361,
508–509
tiredness of baby, 192–193
warning signs about, 385
See also Language development

Comprehensive newborn screening
test, 20
Compress
definition, 522
use of, 355, 433, 502, 514
Concussions, 516–517. *See also*
Head injuries
Confidence/self-esteem (of baby),
46, 101, 233, 396
Congenital adrenal hyperplasia
(CAH), 21
Congenital condition, 522
Congenital hypothyroidism tests,
21
Conjunctivitis (pinkeye), 148, 522
Constipation, 198, 331
Consumer Product Safety
Commission
carriers, 204, 211
car seat selection, 9
contact information, 528, 538
crib safety features, 5
DINP, 131, 359
playpen/portacrib, 311
recalls, 403, 528
walkers, 390
Contact information. *See*
Resources/contact information
Contagious disease, 522
Continuous positive airway
pressure (CPAP) device, 25, 31
Convulsions, 233–234, 522
Coombs test, 20
Cooperation of baby, 457
Cords from drapery/blinds, 6, 7,
248
Cortisone (steroids), 347, 443
Cosco's Ultra Dream Ride, 34
Coughing, 83, 241–242
Cow's milk, 489, 505–506, 509–510
CPAP (continuous positive airway
pressure) device, 25, 31

CPR
  definition, 522
  as important skill, 120, 210, 513
  steps in performing, 514–515
  when to use, 514, 516, 517
CPSC. *See* Consumer Product
  Safety Commission
Crabs (lice), 347–348
Cradle cap, 46
Cradles, 5
Crawling, 344, 383
  beginnings of, 312, 335, 337
  expected timing of, 408
  help with, 254, 337, 349
  practice and, 346
Crawling reflex, 22
Creeping, 266, 290, 297, 312, 322
Cribs
  placement of, 6, 144
  safety and, 5, 432, 538
  use of, 4, 5
Crib sheets, 6
Crohn's disease, 51
Crossed eyes, 19, 76, 93, 215–216.
  See also Strabismus
Croup (laryngo-tracheo-bronchitis),
  193, 242, 276–277
Cruising, 376, 403, 439, 446, 449,
  450, 473, 481, 490, 494–495
Crying, 43, 44, 46, 66, 146, 241,
  286, 348, 481
  amount of, 46, 66, 241, 348,
  481
  communication and, 46, 66,
  100–101, 146
  pacifiers and, 59
  parental response/baby's trust,
  46, 101
  parental understanding of, 82,
  92, 162, 216
  responding to, 100–101

Cup use, 259–260, 264, 295, 296,
  375
Curiosity, 311, 346–347, 385, 438,
  472, 491–492. *See also*
  Exploration
Cuts/abrasions
  keeping moist, 437
  overview, 493
Cystic fibrosis resources, 532

Dancing, 461
Day/night mixup, 59–60
Decosahexaenoic acid. *See* DHA
DEET, 371
Dehydration, 103–104
  as emergency, 466
  giardiasis, 459, 460
  overview, 103–104
  plane travel and, 196
  with upper-respiratory infections,
  416–417
Delivery marks, 15–16
Depression in babies, 214
Dermatitis, 112, 522. *See also*
  Rashes
Development. *See* Growth/
  development
DHA fatty acid
  benefits of, 29, 50–51, 71
  in breast milk, 30, 50–51
  in formulas, 71
Diabetes
  juvenile diabetes, 51
  Type-1 diabetes, 268
Diaper bags, 8, 120–121, 244
Diapering baby, 39–40
Diaper pails, 4
Diaper rash, 39, 124–125
Diapers
  cloth, 6–7, 8, 35
  diaper rash and, 39–40, 125

disposable, 6–7, 8, 34–35
free diapers for multiples, 8
number needed, 6
number of daily changes, 39
overnight diapers, 480
for premature babies, 34
super-absorbent type of, 125,
238, 480
for travel, 134–135
types of, 6–7, 8, 125
Diaper service, 6, 8
Diaper splint, 24
Diarrhea, 136–137, 522
breastfeeding and, 50
as emergency, 466
formulas and, 70
yogurt and, 410
DINP (phthalate), 131, 359
Diphtheria, 142
Discipline, 222–223
parental firmness, 386
restrictions on baby, 265, 392,
393–394
spanking, 382
See also "No"
Discomfort (definition), 522
Disease (definition), 522
Dislikes of baby, 180
Dislocated hips, 17–18, 138
Disposable diapers, 6–7, 8
Doctor. *See* Pediatrician
Dogs. *See* Pets and baby
Down syndrome resources, 532
DPT vaccine, 142
Dressing baby. *See* Clothes
Drinking
from a cup, 259–260, 264, 295,
296, 375
juices, 128, 198, 258, 288, 289,
295, 320, 334, 358, 397, 415,
421, 429, 471, 488

milk (non-breast milk), 489,
505–506, 509–510
thirst quenchers, 429–430
water, 86, 126–127
See also Bottlefeeding;
Breastfeeding; Water
Drooling, 192, 193
Drug allergy/hypersensitivity,
292–293, 431
Dysentery (amebiasis/
entamebiasis), 329–330

Ear-check monitor (home
otoscope), 310
Ear infections
breastfeeding and, 50, 314
drinking position and, 71
ear-check monitor and, 310
ear pulling and, 441
flying with cold and, 196
prevention of, 314
secondhand smoke and, 312
Ear piercing, 143–144
Ears
cleaning of, 74
cochlear implants (tubes), 143
piercing of, 143–144
pulling of, 441
ruptured eardrum, 401, 525
wax blockage of, 339–340
See also Hearing
Ear thermometers, 8, 9, 94, 95–96,
363
Ear wax, 74, 138
Ear-wax blockage, 339–340
Easter, 368
Echinacea, 157–158
E. coli, 343, 447
Eczema, 347
bathing frequency and, 58
breast milk protection against, 50

Elavil, 55
Electric shock, 517
Electrolytes
 definition, 522
 dehydration and, 104, 172, 286, 434
Emergencies
 baby turning blue, 443, 466
 burns, 394
 croup, 277
 heat stroke, 400
 medication poisoning, 315–316
 numbers/addresses to keep by phone, 516, 518
 reasons to wake the doctor, 465–466
Emergencies (how to deal with)
 anaphylactic shock, 513
 bleeding, 513–514
 choking, 515–516
 concussion, 516–517
 CPR (cardiopulmonary resuscitation), 514–515
 electric shock, 517
 mouth-to-mouth resuscitation, 514–515, 518
 nosebleed, 518
 poisons, 518–520
 when to call 911 (summary), 519
Emotions, 212, 258, 352, 398–399, 411–412, 481
 laughing, 200, 205, 222, 273
 smiling, 109, 111, 145, 147, 155, 212, 232, 273
Endo-tracheal (ET) tube, 25
ENT (ear, nose, throat specialist), 19
Entamebiasis (amebic dysentery), 329–330
Enterobiasis (pinworms/ threadworms), 443–444

Epiglottitis, 193
Epilepsy
 resources/contacts for, 532
 symptoms of, 234
Epinephrine, 150
Epistaxis (nosebleeds), 460, 476–477, 518
Esophagus, 523
Eustachian tubes, 523
Excitement
 calming down from, 179
 expression of, 110, 111
Exploration, 320, 369, 386, 412, 491–492
 by mouth, 123, 163, 238, 296, 456
 See also Curiosity
Eye-hand coordination, 212
Eyes
 color change in, 14, 206
 conjunctivitis (pinkeye), 148, 522
 crossed eyes, 19, 76, 93
 injury/contusion, 355
 poison in, 518
 tear ducts, 44, 444
 wandering eye (lazy eye/ strabismus), 215–216
 See also Vision

Face at birth, 14, 15
Failure to thrive, 93–94
Falls
 description/reactions to, 362, 387, 430, 457
 head injuries, 475–477
Family bed, 31, 102–103, 133, 161, 383
Family medical history (definition), 523
Family pictures, 199, 452, 478

Fathers
  involvement with newborn, 39,
    77–78, 143, 146, 490
  resources for, 534–535
Fat requirements, 219, 505
Favoritism
  baby's preference, 312, 352
  multiple babies and, 185–186
FDA. *See* Food and Drug
  Administration
Fears
  week 37, 384
  week 40, 405
  See also Separation anxiety;
    Stranger anxiety
Febrile convulsions/seizures, 113,
  233, 363
Fecal impaction, 331
Fecal products (definition), 523
Feces (definition), 523
Federal Aviation Administration
  (FAA), 197
Feeding tube, 28. *See also*
  Nasogastric tube
Feet
  at birth, 17
  flat feet, 123
Ferber basics, 274–276
Fetal position, 17
Fever
  acetaminophen for, 113, 174,
    175, 207, 315, 331, 333, 340,
    363, 379, 380, 396, 401, 408,
    416, 425, 435, 441, 451, 486,
    501
  with cat scratch disease/fever, 207
  definition, 112, 362, 523
  febrile convulsions/seizures, 113,
    233, 363
  ibuprofen for, 315, 331, 333,
    340, 363, 379, 380, 396, 401,
    408, 416, 425, 435, 441, 451,
    486, 501
  neurological damage and, 363
  See also specific health problems
Fever blisters (cold sores), 413–414
Fiber (definition), 523
Financial resources contact
  information, 535–536
1st 48 hours after birth
  birth weight, 13
  functions during, 21–22
  hospital care, 22–24
  physical traits, 14–18
  premature babies and, 24–35
  reflexes and, 21–22
  senses, 18–19
  tests during, 19–21
First aid
  for colds, 301–302
  kit, 119–120, 135
  skills, 120
Fissure (definition), 523
Floxin (ofloxin), 421
Flu, 330–331
  cold vs., 331, 417
  vaccine for, 142, 143, 158, 331
FluMist, 142
Fluoride supplementation, 69, 159
Folliculitis, 340, 523
Fontanelle (soft spots)
  closing of, 173
  definition/description, 14, 523
Food allergies
  breastfeeding and, 224, 338–339
  celiac disease, 224–225
  common foods causing, 320, 337
  identifying cause, 220, 289, 338,
    339
  immunizations and, 338, 431
  overview, 337–339
  peanuts and, 337, 339, 383–384

Food allergies (*continued*)
  resources for, 532
  symptoms of, 273
Food and Drug Administration
  formulas, 70
  safety of plastic bottles, 131
Food/feeding, 38, 99, 128–130,
      211, 244–245, 295–296, 302,
      310–311, 358, 397, 421, 447,
      465, 470–471, 472, 488–489,
      496–497
  amount summary, 127, 128
  avoiding battles, 264–265, 302,
      346, 456
  BRATT diet, 434
  calories needed, 488
  during plane travel, 197
  eating off floor, 368
  fat and, 219, 505
  favorite foods, 257
  feeding himself, 351, 391,
      403–404, 472
  finger foods, 295, 351, 391
  foods to avoid, 237, 257–258,
      319, 320, 326, 327, 334
  fruits/vegetables, 288–289,
      318–319, 320, 411
  gagging on, 429
  grain-based finger foods, 351
  introducing new foods, 320
  lumpier foods, 403–404, 429
  making baby food, 350
  mealtime fun, 422–423
  middle-of-the-night feedings, 375
  nourishment needed, 280, 463,
      488
  nutrients needed, 505
  organic food/formula, 71, 343
  picky eaters, 455–456
  playing with food, 256, 259, 328,
      423

premature babies, 28–30
puréed foods, 318–319, 326, 350,
      403
puréed protein foods, 128, 375
raisins and tooth decay, 504–505
refusing, 310, 343
seeds in fruits, 411
snacks, 471, 488–489
social interaction and, 334, 404
supplemental feedings, 86–87
sweets, 319
vegetarian diet, 438
yogurt benefits, 410
See also Bottlefeeding;
      Breastfeeding; Choking;
      Minerals; Solid food; Vitamins
Food poisoning, 424, 456
Foreign language development,
      155, 232–233, 292
Formulas
  colic and, 70, 79
  containing DHA/ARA, 527
  drinking "old" formula, 456
  during first year, 221, 228
  free formula for multiples, 71
  iron-fortified type, 68, 69, 70
  losing interest in, 228
  organic formulas, 71, 528
  for premature babies, 185
  sufficient amount of, 73
  types of, 70–71
  See also Bottlefeeding
4TH of July, 368
Fractures/broken bones, 500–501
  during delivery, 17
  nose injuries, 460
Fragile X syndrome resources, 532
Framed carriers, 271
Free supplies for multiples
  diapers, 8
  formula, 71

Front carriers, 1, 69, 84–85, 143, 211

Front sling
colic and, 79
family interactions and, 81

Frostbite, 509

Frustration (of baby), 473

Furniture for baby, 451

Fussy baby, 92–93. *See also* Calming baby

Galactosemia
definition, 523
tests for, 21

Gas
formulas and, 70
massage and, 102, 131–132
ways to relieve, 102, 131–132, 160

Gassiness, 167

Gastrocolic reflex, 73

Gastroenteritis, 433–434, 523

Gastroesophageal reflux disease (GERD/acid reflux), 78, 133, 186–187, 346

Gastrointestinal disorders
resources, 532

Gates (safety gates), 272, 352

Gavage feeding, 29

Gender
nongender toys, 473
stereotyping and, 353–354

Genitals
baby discovering, 239
at birth, 17

GERD (acid reflux), 78, 133, 186–187, 346

Germ (definition), 523

Giardiasis, 459–460

Gluten (definition), 523

Goat's milk, 71, 489

Grasp, 139, 150, 192, 199, 209, 212, 232, 240, 250, 282, 296, 321, 329, 334–335, 343, 352, 354, 376, 404, 406, 412. *See also* Hands

Grasping reflex, 21, 67, 92, 94, 100, 156, 163

Groin pain in boys, 466

Growth/development, 42–43
areas of, 114
individual variation in, 391–392, 450
iron and, 70
of premature babies, 114–118
skull growth, 181–182
sleep and, 172, 173, 211–212
sleeping on back and, 211–212
walkers and, 390–391
warning signs, 181, 329, 385, 510
See also Brain development;
Intellectual development;
Language development; Motor skills development; Physical development; Reflexes development; Senses development; Size by week; Social development

Gums
bumps on, 179
care of, 102, 179, 333
stimulating, 102
See also Teeth; Teething

Hair
care of, 428–429
changes in, 14, 111, 199, 492
loss of, 111, 234, 428

Hair facts, 111

Halloween, 368, 492

Hand-foot-and-mouth disease, 408

Handling of baby, 39

Hands
  control of, 352, 404
  fascination with, 134
  right/left preference, 482
  use of, 123, 163, 181, 199, 250,
    296, 328, 344
  See also Grasp
Hay fever (allergic rhinitis), 253, 468
Head at birth, 14–15
Head injuries, 475–476, 516–517
Head lice, 348
Hearing, 43, 60, 250
  enjoying sounds, 99, 114, 124,
    145, 282, 294, 309, 345, 352,
    448, 461, 477
  "finding" sounds, 317, 320
  following birth, 18
  interpretation of, 376–377
  of premature babies, 116
  sounds babies dislike, 180
  testing of, 19, 250
  See also Ears
Hearing problems
  identifying, 308
  resources for, 532–533
Heart problems resources, 533
Heat exhaustion, 400
Heat prostration, 400
Heat stroke, 400
Heimlich maneuver, 120, 210, 465,
    516
Hemangiomas, 16
Hemophilia resources, 533
Hepatitis B, 142
Herbal medications, 157–158,
    479–480
Hernias, 125, 523
Herpes simplex virus Type 1, 413
Hiccups, 104, 523
Hide-and-seek games, 325, 445
High chairs, 220, 236, 255–256,
    302, 404, 423, 437, 461

High-maintenance baby, 246–247
Hips, dislocated, 17–18, 138
Hives
  definition, 149, 523
  overview, 149
Hives, 149, 523
Holiday safety, 366–368
Home otoscope (ear-check
    monitor), 310
Homocystinuria, 21
Honey warning, 237, 319, 334
Hookworms/roundworms,
    484–485
"Horse" riding, 200
Hospital care
  first 48 hours, 22–24
  See also NICU
Hot-blooded baby, 459
Houseplants and poisoning, 249,
    332, 367, 520
Human growth hormone, 173
Humidifier
  types, 171, 178
  use, 4, 157, 175, 178, 188, 242,
    276, 277, 331, 350, 379, 395,
    416, 435, 476, 501, 518
Hyaline-membrane disease, 31
Hydrocele, 474
"Hyper" (definition), 523
Hyperbilirubinemia, 47. *See also*
    Jaundice
Hypersensitivity, 523
Hyperthermia (overheating), 467,
    523
"Hypo" (definition), 523
Hypoallergenic protein formula,
    70, 73
Hypothermia (definition), 523

Ibuprofen
  for fever reduction, 315, 331,
    333, 340, 363, 379, 380, 396,

401, 408, 416, 425, 435, 441, 451, 486, 501
for pain/discomfort, 305, 315, 331, 333, 340, 379, 380, 396, 401, 408, 414, 415, 416, 425, 435, 441, 451, 486, 501
pediatrician and, 157
See also Advil; Motrin; Nuprin
Ichthyosis, 216
Identity theft, 191
Immunity
breast milk and, 38, 50
definition, 524
Immunizations
babies at risk with, 431–432
chicken pox, 308
definition, 524
ear infections and, 314
egg allergies and, 338, 431
importance of, 142–143
measles, 142, 143, 199
as nasal spray, 142
rubella, 379
tetanus shot, 378
whooping cough, 486
Immunization schedule
birth through year 6, 36, 140
for premature babies, 62
Impetigo, 241
Incubation period, 524
Independence, 101, 322, 344, 405, 422, 435, 439, 467, 497
Individuality of baby, 447–448
Infant (definition), 524
Infant car bed, 10, 34
Infant carriers, 203–204
Infections
definition, 524
of kidneys, 208
playing in sand and, 441
salmonella from reptiles, 359
See also specific types

Influenza. *See* Flu
Insect bites/stings, 370–371
Insufficient milk syndrome, 57
Intellectual development, 42
babywearing and, 112
breast milk (DHA/ARA) and, 50–51, 107
talking to baby and, 47
See also Brain development; Language development
Intellectual development milestones. *See each weekly discussion*
Interaction. *See* Social interaction
Intestinal blockage, 252–253, 522
following delivery, 17–18
Intestine (large), 524
Intestine (small), 524
Intracranial hemorrhage (ICH), 32–33
Intraventricular hemorrhage (IVH), 32–33
Intussusception, 364
Iron
deficiency in, 267–268, 319–320
food/vitamin supplements containing, 228, 267–268, 319–320, 351
in fortified formulas, 68, 69, 70
See also Anemia
Iron deficiency anemia (IDA). *See* Anemia
Itching, 260–261, 374–375
"Itis" (definition), 524
I.V.
definition, 524
dehydration and, 104
for premature babies, 25, 29

Jaundice
definition, 524
of newborns, 15, 47–48

Jaundice (*continued*)
  in premature babies, 30–31
  testing for, 47–48
Jogger stroller, 152
Joint (definition), 524
JPMA. *See* Juvenile Product
    Manufacturers' Association
Juice, 128, 198, 258, 288, 289, 295,
    320, 334, 358, 397, 415, 421,
    429, 471, 488
Jumpers, 279
Juvenile diabetes, 51
Juvenile Product Manufacturers'
    Association (JPMA)
  carriers, 85
  car seats, 9
  contact information, 528, 538
  cribs, 5
  strollers, 152–153

Kangaroo care/carry, 27, 121
Kidney infections/problems, 208
Kisses
  to baby, 180
  from baby, 393, 506
  cold sores and, 414

Lacerations. *See* Cuts/abrasions
Lactase deficiency. *See* Lactose
    intolerance
Lactase enzyme, 509
Lactose-free formula, 70
Lactose intolerance, 509–510,
    524
  breastfeeding and, 68, 510
  formulas and, 70
Lacto vegetarian diet, 438
La Leche League, 52, 529
Language development, 127,
    154–155, 181, 205, 212, 222,
    231, 232, 258–259, 274, 282,

    296, 320, 328, 329, 345, 365,
    368–369, 375–377, 378, 385,
    392, 398, 405, 406, 430, 439,
    448, 449, 457, 461, 491, 498,
    508–509
  baby talk, 439
  bilingual/multilingual babies,
    155, 232–233, 292
  imitating baby's sounds, 243
  labeling things for baby, 239
  overview, 42, 291
  reading to baby, 214–215, 226,
    234, 361, 384
  word recognition, 80, 322,
    368–369
  See also Communication
Large intestine, 524
Laryngitis, 501
Laryngo-tracheo-bronchitis (croup),
    193, 242, 276–277
Larynx (definition), 524
Laughing, 200, 205, 222, 273
Laundry detergents/softeners and
    rashes, 272
Laxative (definition), 524
Lazy eye (wandering eye/
    strabismus), 215–216
Legs at birth, 17
Length
  at birth, 13, 14
  changes during first year, 13
Lethargy
  definition, 524
  as trouble sign, 47
Leukemia resources, 533
Lice, 348
Limb disorders resources, 533
Lindane, 348
Liver disease resources, 533
Lyme disease, 425
Lymphoma, 51

Malabsorption syndrome, 136, 524

Maple-syrup urine disease, 21

Massage, 66, 75, 101, 102, 108–109, 122, 131–132

  for a fussy baby, 92–93

  benefits of, 26, 75

  bonding and, 65–66

  colic and, 78, 79

  gas and, 102, 131–132

  importance of, 19

  method for, 66, 75

  for premature babies, 26–27

  sleeping and, 19, 405

  of tear ducts, 44

  tension from sucking and, 86

  tummy upset, 122

MCAD (medium chain acyl-CoA dehydrogenase deficiency), 21

Measles (rubeola), 142, 199

Meconium, 17–18

Medical care

  notarized medical permission slip, 324

  See also Checkups; Immunizations; Pediatrician; *specific health problems*

Medical history. *See* Family medical history

Medical supplies, 171–172

Medications

  allergic reactions to, 292–293, 431

  for allergies, 253

  anaphylactic shock, 513

  animal bites, 378

  bronchitis and, 284

  for burns, 394

  for celiac disease, 225

  colds and, 157–158, 242

  cold sores, 414

  colic and, 78, 79

  constipation and, 198

  for dermatitis, 112

  during breastfeeding, 55–56

  for ear infections, 315

  for ear-wax blockage, 340

  eczema, 347

  for fever, 113, 363

  fever reduction (acetaminophen), 113, 175, 207, 315, 331, 333, 340, 363, 379, 380, 396, 401, 408, 416, 425, 435, 441, 451, 486, 501

  fever reduction (ibuprofen), 315, 331, 333, 340, 363, 379, 380, 396, 401, 408, 416, 425, 435, 441, 451, 486, 501

  for flu, 331

  folliculitis, 340

  getting baby to take, 269, 462–463

  guidelines for, 201–202, 237

  herbal medications, 157–158, 479–480

  for infants under 2 months, 157

  for insect bites/stings, 371

  itching and, 261

  lice, 348

  measuring of, 172, 201–202, 207, 237, 269

  mumps, 415

  over-the-counter, 374, 348, 157–158, 187, 454

  for pain/discomfort (acetaminophen), 175, 196, 207, 305, 315, 331, 333, 340, 379, 380, 396, 401, 408, 414, 415, 416, 425, 435, 441, 451, 486, 501

  for pain/discomfort (ibuprofen), 305, 315, 331, 333, 340, 379, 380, 396, 401, 408, 414, 415, 416, 425, 435, 441, 451, 486, 501

Medications (*continued*)
  poisoning from, 315–316
  for RSV, 175
  sunlight reactions with, 421
  for teething symptoms, 305, 333
  See also specific medications
Medications (over-the-counter
    medications)
  anti-itching, 374
  for lice, 348
  safety, 157–158, 187, 454
Medication syringes, 269
Medium chain acyl-CoA
    dehydrogenase deficiency
    (MCAD), 21
Memory, 133, 281, 393
Mental retardation resources, 533
Metabolic disorder detection, 20
Middle-ear infection (otitis media),
    314, 401
Milia, 62–63
Milk (*nonbreast* milk), 489,
    505–506, 509–510
Milk allergies, 50
Milk intolerance. *See* Lactose
    intolerance
Milk-protein sensitivity, 73
Mind development. *See* Intellectual
    development
Minerals
  in fruits/vegetables, 318
  picky eaters and, 455
  supplements and, 323
  yogurt and, 410, 455
Mirrors and baby, 81, 117, 134,
    141, 206, 234, 267, 285,
    308–309, 312, 313, 388–389
Misconceptions about babies,
    213–214
Mistakes in baby-care, 237–238
MMR vaccine, 142, 143
MMRV vaccine, 142

Mobiles, 4, 7, 67, 141, 216
Mobility. *See* Crawling; Creeping;
    Motor skills development;
    Walking
Mold (toxic mold), 350–351
Moles (pigmented nevi), 16, 17, 293
Mongolian spots, 16
Monitors, 4
Mood changes, 282
Moro reflex, 21
Motor skills development, 42, 223,
    291
  encouragement of, 276, 401–402
  variations in, 391–392
  See also specific skills
Motrin, 421. *See also* Ibuprofen
Mouth exploration, 123, 163, 238,
    296, 456
Mouth-to-mouth resuscitation
  steps in, 514–515
  when to use, 514, 517
  See also CPR
Mucous membrane (definition), 524
Mucus (definition), 524
Multiple babies
  favoritism and, 185–186
  feeding of, 183–185
  free diapers for, 8
  free formula for, 71
  giving attention to, 457–458
  playing with, 185
  premature babies as, 184, 185
  preparation/adjustment to,
    182–183, 186
  resources for, 536–537
Mumps, 142, 414–415
Muscular development, 81, 92,
    109, 150, 215, 360–361
  See also Physical development
Music
  baby's sense of rhythm and, 353
  for calming baby, 203

classical music, 171, 203
playing with baby and, 96–97,
    215, 262, 325, 381
week 5, 105

Nail care, 85–86, 420
Nail-primer warning, 480
Name recognition, 80–81, 167, 209,
    296
Nasal bulb syringe, 301, 416
Nasal congestion, 277–278, 301,
    416
Nasogastric tube/feeding, 187, 524
Nausea (definition), 525
Neonatal intensive care unit. *See*
    NICU
Neonatal maturity assessment,
    20–21
Neonatal nurses, 25–26, 27
Neonatologist, 25, 27
Nestle's Good Start formula, 79
Newborns, 525. *See also* First 48
    hours
NICU
    definition, 525
    description, 25–30
    equipment in, 26, 27–28
Night/day mixup, 59–60
911
    when to call summary, 519
    See also Emergencies
Nits, 348
"No"
    alternatives to, 406–407
    babyproofing your home and,
        174
    baby's reaction to, 327, 398–400,
        448
    baby's understanding of, 327
    use of, 376, 392, 407
    See also Discipline
Nodule, 525

Nose
    injuries to, 460
    nasal congestion, 277–278
Nosebleeds (epistaxis), 460,
    476–477, 518
Nuprin, 421. *See also* Ibuprofen
Nursery preparation, 3–9
Nursing. *See* Breastfeeding
Nursing tubercle, 15
Nutramigen formula, 79

Obesity, 494
Ophthalmologist, 19
Oral (definition), 525
Organic food/formula, 71, 343
Otitis externa (outer-ear infection),
    314
Otitis media (middle-ear infection),
    314, 401
Otoscope, home use, 310
Outer-ear infection (otitis
    externa/swimmer's ear), 314
Overhead warmer, 28
Overheating (hyperthermia), 467,
    523
Ovo-lacto vegetarian diet, 438
Oximeters, 28, 31
Oxygen saturation monitor, 28, 31
Oxytocin, 64–65

Pacifiers, 58–59, 76, 123–124
    DINP and, 131, 359
    teething and, 331
    thumb vs., 59, 123
Pain/discomfort
    acetaminophen for, 174, 175,
        196, 207, 305, 315, 331, 333,
        340, 379, 380, 396, 401, 408,
        414, 415, 416, 425, 435, 441,
        451, 486, 501
    with circumcision, 23
    definition, 525

Pain/discomfort (*continued*)
  expression of, 252
  groin pain in boy, 466
  ibuprofen for, 305, 315, 331,
    333, 340, 379, 380, 396, 401,
    408, 414, 415, 416, 425, 435,
    441, 451, 486, 501
  See also specific health problems
Paint, 4, 5
Palate, 525
Palmar grasp, 21
Parachute reflex, 22
Parasites
  amebic dysentery, 329–330
  definition, 525
  giardiasis, 459–460
  See also Worms/parasites
"Parentese" voice, 80, 96
Parents
  baby's attracting attention of, 327
  baby's preference in, 312, 352
  as examples, 354–355, 377, 456
  trusting instincts of, 82, 110, 171,
    191, 214
Parents' kit, 171–172
Pat-a-cake, 188–189, 380
Patent ductus arteriosus, 32
Patience
  of baby, 353, 458
  of parent, 386
Peanut allergies, 337, 339, 383–384
Pedialyte electrolyte solution, 434
Pediarix vaccine, 142
Pediatrician
  common issues and, 82–83
  hospital visits by, 22
  insurance/HMO and, 2
  selection of, 1–3
  solid food readiness and, 211,
    218
  See also Checkups

Pediatrician (when to call)
  acid reflux/GERD, 187
  allergies to medications, 293
  amebic dysentery, 330
  anal fissure, 166–167
  asthma, 442–443
  bacterial meningitis, 466
  balanitis, 80
  blisters, 433
  blood poisoning, 451
  botulism, 323
  bowel movements, 83
  breathing difficulties, 465
  bronchitis, 284
  bruises, 299, 387
  burns, 394
  cat scratch disease/fever, 207
  celiac disease, 224–225
  chapped skin, 188
  chicken pox, 307–308
  choking, 465
  colds, 158
  cold sores, 414
  colic, 78, 79
  conjunctivitis, 148
  constipation, 198
  convulsions/seizures, 233
  coughs/sneezes, 83, 242
  cradle cap, 46
  cuts/abrasions, 493
  dehydration, 104, 466
  diaper rash, 125
  diarrhea, 137, 179, 466
  during day, 278
  ear-wax blockage, 340
  eczema, 347
  emergencies (reasons to wake
    doctor), 465–466
  eye injury, 355
  failure to thrive, 94
  fecal impaction, 331

feeding refusals, 73
fever, 113, 179, 363, 466
food allergies, 339
food poisoning, 424
fractures, 500–501
frostbite, 509
gas, 160, 167
gastroenteritis, 434
giardiasis, 459–460
groin pain (boy), 466
hand-foot-and-mouth disease, 408
hay fever, 468
head injuries, 476
hiccups, 104
hives, 149
hookworm/roundworm, 485
hyperthermia, 467
ichthyosis, 216
impetigo, 241
insect bites/stings, 371
intestinal blockage, 253
intussusception, 364
itching, 261
jaundice, 48
kidney infection, 208
lacerations, 387
lactose intolerance, 510
laryngitis, 501
malabsorption syndrome, 136
measles, 199
medication poisoning, 316
milia/baby acne, 63, 83
mumps, 415
nasal congestion, 278
nosebleeds, 476–477
nose injuries, 460
parasites, 300
pinworms, 443
pneumonia, 435
prickly heat, 451

puncture wounds, 426
pyloric stenosis, 208
rashes, 83, 112, 466
ringworm, 395
roseola infantum, 493
RSV, 175
scabies, 365
shaken baby syndrome, 226
sleep apnea, 64
splinters/slivers, 356
sprains/strains, 502
strep throat, 395–396
styes, 408
sunburn, 484
tear-duct infection, 444
teething, 291
thrush, 262
tick bites, 425
tonsillitis, 379
trouble signs/symptoms, 47, 179
tummy pain, 466
unusual swellings, 210
upper-respiratory infection, 416–417
vaginal discharge, 48
vomiting/spitting up, 63, 80, 179, 285–286, 466
wandering eye (lazy eye/strabismus), 216
whooping cough, 486
yeast infection, 372
Peek-a-boo, 286, 293, 300, 325
Penis
care of, 37–38
inflammation of, 79–80
Periodic breathing, 31
Personality, 100, 250–251, 447–448
temperament assessment, 245–246
Petechiae, 299
Pets and baby, 59, 169–171, 377

Pharyngitis (tonsillitis), 378–379
Pharynx, 525
Phenylketonuria (PKU), 20, 533
Phlegm, 525
Phototherapy, 31, 47–48
Phthalate (DINP), 131, 359
Physical development
  help with, 176
  muscular development, 81, 92,
    109, 150, 215, 360–361
Physical therapy, 525
Pigmented nevi (moles), 16, 17,
  293
Pillow splint, 24
Pinkeye (conjunctivitis), 148, 522
Pinworms
    (threadworms/enterobiasis),
    443–444
PKU (phenylketonuria), 20, 533
Plane travel, 193–198
  carry-on bags, 195
  ear-popping advice, 196
  preparation for, 194–195
  seating, 195–196
Plastic and safety, 131, 359
Playing/toys
  baby's photo album, 452, 478
  baby's self-esteem and, 396
  best time for, 162–163, 380
  bonding and, 141
  games, 325, 392, 440, 445, 457,
    475
  mirrors, 81, 117, 134, 141, 206,
    234, 267, 285, 308–309, 312,
    313, 388–389
  multiple babies, 185
  in sand, 427, 441
  by self, 238, 258, 259, 351, 376,
    432, 440
  See also each weekly discussion
Playpens, 311

Pneumonia
  overview, 434–435
  whooping cough and, 485
  x-rays for identifying, 242, 435
Pointing, 441–442
Poison Control Center, 518, 519,
  520
  phone number of, 528
Poisoning
  blood poisoning, 451
  food poisoning, 424, 456
  houseplants and, 249, 332, 367,
    520
  inhaled poisons, 519
  poison in eye, 518–519
  poison on skin, 520
  protection from, 249
  swallowed poison, 520
Poison ivy/poison oak, 374–375
Polio, 142
"Portable" baby, 499–500
Portable seating, 437
Portacribs, 311
Port-wine stains, 16
Possessions (week 50), 492
Postpartum distress, 65
Preemie 24–25, 525. *See also*
    Premature babies
Premature babies, 35, 114–118,
    149, 209, 269, 285
  being involved with, 25, 26
  breathing help for, 25, 31–32
  car seats/beds and, 9–10, 34
  circumcision and, 23
  description, 26
  DHA/ARA and, 71
  "due-date age," 114, 117, 118,
    149, 209, 269, 285
  feeding of, 28–30
  first 48 hours, 24–35
  helping development, 117

immunization schedule, 62
iron and, 267
kangaroo care for, 27
massage for, 26–27
as multiples, 184, 185
NICU for, 25–30
problems of, 30–33
reaching milestones, 116
reasons for, 24
reasons for concern, 118
resources for, 537–538
sleeping position, 45
sleep/wake states of, 116
statistics on, 24
supplements for, 29–30
taking home, 33–34
vision problems of, 33
Preparation
  car seats, 9–12
  comparison shopping, 1
  nursery preparation, 3–9
  pediatrician selection, 1–3
Prevacid, 187
Prevnar, 143
Prickly heat, 451–452
Prilosec, 187
Product recalls, 403
Projectile vomiting, 47, 48, 80
Prolactin, 64–65
Prostaglandin E, 32
Proton pump inhibitors, 187
Prozac, 55
Psoriasis resources, 534
Pulmonary (definition), 525
Pulmonary hemorrhage, 351
Pulse oximeters, 28, 31
Puncture wounds, 425–426
Pyloric stenosis, 208

Quiet time, 156, 238–239, 259,
  266, 351

Raisins and tooth decay, 504–505
Rashes
  with drooling, 193
  echinacea and, 157–158
  laundry detergents/softeners and,
    272
  with measles, 199
  normal vs. problem, 83
  prickly heat, 450–451
  with sunblocks/sunscreens, 229
  See also Dermatitis
Rattles, 97, 105, 188, 200, 232,
  262–263
RDS (respiratory distress
  syndrome), 31–32
Reading to baby
  baby's hearing and, 250
  baby's love of books, 439
  importance of, 283–284, 361
  language development and,
    214–215, 226, 234, 361, 384
  website ideas for, 215
Recalls, 403
Rectal thermometers, 8, 94–95, 363
Rectum (definition), 525
Referrals for pediatrician, 2
Reflex assessment, 20
Reflexes, 21–22, 44, 61
  fading of, 145, 147, 156, 180
  See also Senses/reflexes
    development milestones;
    specific reflexes
Reglan, 79
Regurgitate (definition), 525
Relapse (definition), 525
Relaxing baby. *See* Calming baby
REM (light) sleep, 91, 116
Repetitive behavior, 412–413, 497
Reptile warning, 359
Resources/contact information
  at-home moms, 529

Resources/contact information
    (*continued*)
  breastfeeding, 529–530
  child care, 530
  for fathers, 534–535
  financial resources, 535–536
  general information, 527–529
  illnesses/special needs, 530–534
  multiples, 536–537
  premature babies, 537–538
  safety, 538
Respirator, 31–32. *See also*
    Ventilator
Respiratory distress syndrome
    (RDS), 31–32
Respiratory syncytial virus. *See* RSV
Responsibility, teaching, 466
Restrictions on baby, 38, 265, 392,
    393–394. *See also* Discipline;
    "No"
Retinopathy of prematurity (ROP),
    33
Retrolental fibroplasia, 33
Reye's syndrome
  aspirin and, 380, 388, 415
  resources for, 534
Rh-antibodies, 20
Rice milk, 489
Ringworm, 395
Rocky Mountain spotted fever,
    425
Rolling over, 205, 209, 213, 217,
    231, 254, 282
Rooting reflex, 21
ROP (retinopathy of prematurity),
    33
Roseola infantum (exanthem
    subitum), 492–493
Rotavirus, 142, 525
Roundworms/hookworms,
    484–485

Routines
  at bedtime, 126, 164, 213
  consistency/inconsistency and,
    473
  high-maintenance babies and,
    247
  importance of, 192
RSV (respiratory syncytial
    virus/bronchiolitis), 33, 142,
    174–175, 534
Rubber allergies, 437
Rubella (German measles), 142,
    379–380, 525
Rubeola (measles), 142, 199
Ruptured eardrum, 401, 525

Safety gates, 272, 352
Safety guidelines
  avoiding burns, 98, 119, 333,
    394–395, 411
  bouncers, 162
  carriers, 84–85, 108, 211
  car seats, 9, 10–11, 12, 108, 230,
    422, 441, 508, 538
  of cribs/crib sheets, 5–6, 432,
    538
  holidays, 366–368
  paint and, 4, 5
  playpens/portacribs, 311
  resources/contact information,
    538
  secondhand items, 4, 5, 11
  shopping-carts and, 281
  sleeping, 45, 110, 132, 133, 161,
    211–212
  stair safety, 352, 385, 493,
    502–503
  strollers, 153–154
  summary guidelines for, 226,
    333–334
  toys, 159, 208, 216, 317, 322

walkers, 390–391
water and, 98, 333, 411
Saline nose drops, 157, 301, 416
Salmonella from reptiles, 359
Salmon patches, 16
Scabies, 364–365
Scaling (definition), 525
Sears, William, 102
Seborrheic dermatitis of the scalp, 46
Secondhand items
  carriers, 211
  car seats, 11
  safety standards, 4, 5, 11
  saving money and, 4
Secondhand smoke and baby's
  exposure, 39, 103, 132,
  156–157, 174, 175, 312, 442
Seizures. *See* Convulsions
Self-esteem/confidence (of baby),
  46, 101, 233, 396
Self-reliance. *See* Independence
Sense of humor (baby's), 447, 475,
  506. *See also* Laughing
Sense of self, 351
Senses
  during first 48 hours, 18–19
  See also specific senses
Separation anxiety
  description, 297, 311, 321, 376,
  448–449, 481
  help with, 341
  parent return and, 336
  saying "good-bye" to baby,
  306–307
"Septic" (definition), 525
Septicemia (blood poisoning), 451
Serious baby, 407
Serotonin reuptake inhibitors
  (SSRIs), 55
Serum, 525

Shaken baby syndrome, 39, 225–226
Shampooing, 7, 46, 58, 74, 98, 112,
  428
Shock, 525
Shoes, 419–420, 433
Shopping-cart safety, 281
Shyness, 386
Sibling rivalry, 335
Sickle-cell disease resources, 534
SIDS
  decreasing risk of, 45, 103, 126,
  132–133
  definition, 526
  facts on, 132
  family bed and, 103
  overheating and, 191
  resources for, 534
  sleeping on back and, 45, 132,
  133, 161, 211–212
  smoking and, 103, 132, 156–157
Singing to baby, 215, 262–263, 427
Sitting down, 344, 376
Sitting up, 205, 221, 231, 297, 327,
  384–385
Skin
  baby acne, 62–63
  at birth, 15–16
  care for sensitive skin, 272
  chapped skin, 188
  cold and, 74
  lying on side/redness and, 62
  milia, 62–63
  poisoning on, 520
  See also Rashes
Skull growth, 181–182
Sleep apnea, 31, 63–64, 346
Sleeping, 45, 76–77, 90–91, 145,
  147, 164, 172–173, 181, 191,
  239–240, 281, 291, 304, 328,
  344, 386, 405, 421–422, 456,
  490

Sleeping (*continued*)
activities effects on, 223–224
alternative (to back) position, 133
amount of, 45, 76, 90–91, 145, 147, 172, 191, 239–240, 291, 405, 421–422, 490
apnea and, 31, 346
on back, 45, 110, 132, 133, 161, 211–212
bedtime routines, 126, 164, 213
family bed, 31, 102–103, 133, 161, 383
Ferber basics, 274–276
furniture for, 4–6
massage and, 19, 405
premature babies and, 116
safety tips, 45, 110, 132, 133, 161, 211–212
solid food and, 154, 220
stress and, 336–337
through night, 155, 240–241, 296, 304, 321, 369–370
trouble with, 181, 344, 345–346
See also SIDS
Sling-like carrier, 69, 78, 79, 81, 84–85
Small intestine, 524
Smell (sense)
familiar scents and, 76
following birth, 18
week 48, 471
Smelling game, 445
Smiling, 109, 111, 145, 147, 155, 212, 232, 273
Smoking
breastfeeding and, 51
secondhand smoke and baby, 39, 103, 132, 156–157, 174, 175, 312, 442
Snacks, 471, 488–489

Snugglies, 28
Soaks, 526
Social development
baby's reactions to strangers, 258, 307, 407
overview, 42
parental help with, 354–355, 377
See also Social interaction; Stranger anxiety
Social development milestones. *See each weekly discussion*
Social interaction, 154–155, 212
games and, 325, 392, 440, 445, 457, 475
laughing, 200, 205, 222, 273
mealtimes and, 334, 404
with other children, 88, 206, 325, 440
readiness signs, 243
shyness and, 386
smiling, 109, 111, 145, 147, 155, 212, 232, 273
Social Security Administration
contact information, 190, 528
Social Security number, 190–191
Soft spots. *See* Fontanelle
Solid food, 231, 244–245, 264–265
beginning timing, 154, 236, 268
caution on, 221
cereal, 219, 228–229, 346
cereal guidelines, 228–229
changes with, 228
definition, 127
determining readiness for, 129, 211, 218–219
early choices, 219
first year summary, 127–128
logistics of feeding, 220, 236–237
meal timing/amounts, 244–245
sleeping and, 154, 220
starting on, 219–221

Solitude for baby, 156, 238–239, 259, 266, 351

Soothing baby. *See* Calming baby

Sound enjoyment, 99, 114, 124, 145, 282, 294, 309, 345, 352, 448, 461, 477

Soy-based formula, 70–71, 510

Soy milk, 489

Spider nevi, 16

Spina bifida resources, 534

Spitting up, 63, 80. *See also* Vomiting

Splinter/slivers, 356

Splints for dislocated hips, 24

Spoiling baby, 101, 171, 376

Spore, 526

Spotted fever, 425

Sprains/strains, 501–502

Sputum, 435, 526

SSRIs (serotonin reuptake inhibitors), 55

Stair safety, 352, 385, 493, 502–503

Standing
  balancing and, 361–362, 376
  beginnings of, 298, 304, 321, 327, 412, 430
  help with, 298, 321, 352, 365, 412
  on his own, 404, 432, 456, 490

Startle reflex, 22

Stepping reflex, 22

Stereotyping and gender, 353–354, 473

Sterilize (definition), 526

Steroids (cortisone), 347, 443

Stimulation for babies, 214

Stool, 462, 526
  blood in, 73, 108, 137, 166, 167, 198, 237
  bottlefeeding and, 73
  breastfeeding and, 18, 107
  See also Bowels

Stork bites, 16

Storytelling, 141, 234–235

Strabismus (wandering eye/lazy eye), 215–216

Strains/sprains, 501–502

Stranger anxiety
  description, 265, 273, 297, 312, 321, 430, 448–449, 481
  overcoming, 327–328, 370, 384, 511

Strawberry marks, 16

Strep throat, 395–396

Stress (baby's), 336–337, 405

Strings, 210

Strollers
  backpack combination, 302
  checking of, 327
  safety and, 153–154
  selection of, 151–153
  types of, 151–152

Styes, 408

Sucking, 76, 122, 123–124, 235

Sucking reflex, 21

Sudden Infant Death Syndrome. *See* SIDS

Sugar water, 78–79, 86

Sulfamethoxazole (Bactrim), 421

Sunblock advisory, 249

Sunblocks/sunscreens, 201, 229–230, 249, 471–472, 484

Sunburn, 104, 249, 484

Sun exposure
  avoiding, 153, 201, 229–230, 249, 471–472, 484
  medications and, 421
  strollers and, 153
  vitamin D and, 201

Sunscreen. *See* Sunblocks/sunscreens

Sunstroke, 400

Super-glue warning, 480

Suture, 526
Swaddling, 41–42
Sweat glands, 125–126
Sweets, 319
Swimmer's ear (outer-ear infection), 314
Swimming and *E. coli*, 343
Swimming reflex, 22
Swings, 4, 98–99
Symptoms (definition), 526

Taking baby out (week 2), 58
Talipes (clubfoot), 175
Talking to baby, 48, 60, 80, 96, 105, 167–168, 361, 508–509
Tapeworms, 299–300
Taste
  bitter/sour tastes, 180
  following birth, 18
  salt, 231
Taste bud development, 180, 231, 281
Tay-Sachs disease resources, 534
Tear-duct infection/blockage, 444
Tear ducts, 44, 444
Teeth
  breast milk and, 51
  brushing of, 306, 397–398, 505
  caring for, 306, 358, 374, 397–398, 504–505
  decay from raisins, 504–505
  functions of, 358
  gum care, 102, 179, 333
  thumb sucking/pacifiers and, 59
Teething, 304–306
  beginning of, 222, 266, 291
  care for, 398
  myths on, 305–306
  symptoms of, 266, 333, 441
Temperament. *See* Personality
Temperature (of baby)
  normal ranges, 96

taking of, 94–95, 363
  See also Fever
Temperature (of baby) regulation
  avoiding overheating, 107, 191, 237
  of hot-blooded baby, 459
  keeping head covered, 107
  keeping warm, 86, 107, 191
  See also Clothes
Temperature monitor, 28
Temperature of bathing water, 98, 333, 395
Temper tantrums, 382, 463, 506
Tenderness (definition), 526
Testicles
  definition, 526
  swelling of, 415, 474
  twisted testicle, 466
  undescended testicles, 32, 423–424
Tests during first 48 hours, 19–21
Tetanus, 142
Tetanus shot, 378
Tetracycline, 425
Texture exploration, 97, 163, 188
Thermometers
  types of, 8, 94–95, 363
  use methods, 94–95
  See also specific types
Threadworms
  (pinworms/enterobiasis), 443–444
Thrush (*Candida albicans*), 179, 261–262
Thumb sucking, 59, 123–124
Tick bites, 425
Tick fever, 425
Tickling, 208–209, 235, 243, 286, 380, 389, 398, 426
Tick typhus, 425
Toiletries, 7
Toilets, 405, 411

Tongue-thrust reflex, 219, 220
Tongue-tied condition, 450
Tonic neck reflex, 22, 107, 180
Tonsillitis (pharyngitis), 378–379
Touch (sense), 19, 163. *See also*
    Massage
Toxic mold, 350–351
Toys
    for first birthday, 461, 502
    introduction to balls, 278
    nongender toys, 473
    safety and, 159, 208, 216, 317,
        322
    selecting, 96, 217, 452
    stuffed toys, 464
    for travel, 135, 136, 165
    See also Playing/toys
Trachea (definition), 526
Trauma (definition), 526
Travel
    by car, 164–166
    by plane, 193–198
Trust
    establishment of, 283
    parental response to crying, 46,
        101
    self-esteem and, 233
Tube feeding
    of premature babies, 28–29
    See also Nasogastric tube
Tubes in ears, 143
Tucker sling, 78
Tummy
    making movements while on,
        145–146
    time on, 110, 118, 140–141
Tummy pain, 466
Twins
    giving attention to, 457–458
    See also Multiple babies
Tylenol. *See* Acetaminophen
Type 1 diabetes, 268

Umbilical artery catheter (UAC),
    25, 28
Umbilical-cord stump care, 37, 58,
    83
Umbilical hernia, 125
Undescended testicles, 32, 423–424
Upper-respiratory infection,
    415–417. *See also* Colds
Upper-respiratory system
    (definition), 526
Urinary tract, 526
Urinary-tract infections (UTIs)
    breastfeeding and, 50
    circumcision and, 23
UTIs. *See* Urinary-tract infections

Vaccinations. *See* Immunizations
Vaccine (definition), 526
Vaccine Information Statements
    (CDC), 431
Vaginal discharge, 17
Valentine's Day, 368
Vaporizer, 4
Varicella (chicken pox), 142,
    307–308
Vegan vegetarian diet, 438
Vegetarian diet, 438
Ventilator, 28, 31
Vernix, 15
Virus, 33, 526
Vision, 42–43, 48, 60, 76, 77, 81,
    91, 100, 110, 111, 122–123,
    126, 155, 156, 163, 172, 173,
    180, 182, 189, 192, 194, 212,
    213, 214, 231, 258, 260, 290,
    291, 292, 296, 304, 308, 392,
    52, 506–507
    colors, 155, 205, 262
    following birth, 19
    of premature babies, 116
    problems in, 33, 91, 312–313
    stimulation of, 48

Vision (*continued*)
  tests for, 19
  See also Eyes
Vitamin B, 351
Vitamin D, 201, 505
Vitamins
  definition, 526
  in fruits/vegetables, 318
  multivitamin, 201
  picky eaters and, 455
  for premature babies, 30, 93
  supplements and, 93, 201,
    323–324
  yogurt and, 410, 455
Voice recognition, 18, 26, 43, 92,
    99, 445
Vomiting, 285–286, 526
  of newborns, 38
  projectile vomiting, 47, 48, 80
  when to call the doctor, 63, 80,
    179, 286, 466

Walkers, 390–391
Walking
  barefoot walking, 419, 487
  beginnings of, 385, 393, 412
  cruising, 376, 403, 439, 446, 449,
    450, 473, 481, 490, 494–495
  description of legs/feet during,
    510
  helping with, 393
  on his own, 481, 483–484, 490
  shoes and, 419–420
Wandering eye (lazy eye/
    strabismus), 215–216
Water
  drinking of, 86, 126–127
  play and, 278, 300, 309, 325, 372,
    373, 409, 453, 469, 477,
    486–487, 494, 502
  safety and, 98, 333, 411

  swimming and *E. coli*, 343
  See also Dehydration
Weaning, 369
Websites. *See* Resources/contact
    information
Weight
  at birth, 13, 14
  changes during first year, 13
  chubbiness, 77
  failure to thrive and, 93–94
  newborn loss of, 82
  See also Size by week in each
    weekly discussion
Well-baby checkups, 137–139,
    191–192, 202–203
Wheezing, 32, 174, 443, 526
Whooping cough (pertussis), 142,
    485–486
Word recognition, 322, 368–369
  "parentese" voice and, 80
Worms/parasites
  diarrhea and, 137
  hookworms/roundworms,
    484–485
  pinworms
    (threadworms/enerobiasis),
    400, 443–444
  tapeworms, 299–300

Xiphoid process, 17
X-rays, 526

Yeast infections
  description, 124, 186, 261–262
  thrush, 179, 261–262
  of vaginal area (*monilia*), 371–372
Yogurt, 410

Zantac, 79
Zinc, 505
Zinc oxide, 261, 414